UNDERSTANDING THE LAW OF ZONING AND LAND USE CONTROLS

By

Barlow Burke
Professor of Law
American University

LexisNexis™

PREFACE

Zoning, land use, and environmental regulation was one of my first professional interests. My students in any course I taught in the early 1970s, can attest to this. Trained as a city planner, I have long been familiar with the literature and discipline of land use planning. Yet, I came to know that the field is a crowded one. A brief survey of the legal periodicals will confirm that land use and takings law is a tough area in which to write and not be preempted by the annual out-pouring of writing, both from law professors and students. Aside from a law review article published to gain myself a promotion, I went elsewhere to find subjects for my writing, all the while teaching and thinking about this subject. I am happy now to return to it in print.

Not only is the field a crowded one, but it is also jurisdiction-specific. The practice of land use law does not travel well across state lines, and few practices are even state wide in scope. The opinions of state Supreme Courts reflect this. It takes time to learn what does travel and what is worth learning in law school about this subject. I'm glad I waited.

This book is the result of that wait. It is written for two types of readers. First, there is the first-year law student whose professor presents the law of zoning, land use controls, and regulations, in the context of the required course on real property. It is also rich enough in detail to appeal to a more advanced student in an upper-level elective course or seminar on the same subject, although this reader can be selective because she will have less difficulty understanding the constitutional and administrative framework for land use controls. For neither type of reader is this book intended as a treatise. I have always tried to include and discuss leading cases, but otherwise citations are kept to a representative-case minimum.

First, I set out the constitutional framework for land use regulation in a discussion of the takings clause, with a summary of the salient constitutional rules as the discussion proceeds and at the end of this part of the book. The United States Supreme Court opinions on the takings clause present a jurisprudence that will provoke useful and lively discussion in class about the make-up of the Court, and its short and long range purposes in deciding these cases. They provide fascinating material for Court watchers. The land use bar provides experts more sensitive to the nuances of these opinions than your constitutional law professor is likely to be. The discussions of these opinions here are intended to give you a background to participate in further analysis of these cases and a context in which to set the Supreme Court's future land use opinions.

Next appears a discussion of the basic form of land use controls — Euclidian zoning. Once the basic form of a zoning ordinance is summarized and presented, the text discusses more complex forms of land use regulation — so-called non-Euclidian regulations; these require an attorney to exercise increasing amounts of administrative and professional discretion and involve negotiation with municipal officials. Along the way, these chapters present and discuss basic problems, as well as problems based on the United States Supreme Court opinions that relate to these types of land use regulations.

Administrative and legislative relief from land use controls is the bread and butter of a land use practice. This discussion proceeds in that way, and from the straight-forward to the discretionary. Distinguishing a client's need for a variance, special exception, rezoning, or other administrative actions, is often the first task of an attorney presented with a land use problem. It is basic and imperative that an attorney understand the uses to which each can be put, separately and in combination, and not waste a client's time and money pursuing the wrong one.

Finally, halting further regulation of a client's property by pursuing vested rights and estoppel is the last task of the attorney discussed in the body of the book. A short glossary of terms used in the practice are presented at the end.

In writing this book, I owe three debts. First, I owe much to the students and research assistants who have read it over the years. They are Esten Goldsmith, Patricia Hammes, Sean Fleming, Julie Richmond, and Stephanie Quaranta.

Second, as my friend and co-teacher for more than two decades, John J. Delaney, of the Maryland firm of Linowes & Blocher, has unstintingly provided me with a wealth of knowledge of, enthusiasm for, and professionalism of the highest caliber in land use practice as he has seen it evolve during the four decades of his own law practice. This book, *donum indignum*, is dedicated to John.

Third, and more recently, Phil J. Tierney has added to it with the insights of a state administrative law judge and hearing examiner with a special interest, enthusiasm, and expertise in land use.

To John and Phil, both distinguished attorneys, I, my students, and this book owe much.

Barlow Burke
Washington, D.C.
February 28, 2002

TABLE OF CONTENTS

Page

Page

Page

Part 1

Fundamental Concepts: The Police Power, Takings, and Zoning

Chapter 1

The Police Power

The practice of land use attorneys depends on their ability to investigate the regulations applicable to a client's land[1] and on their knowledge of a blend of constitutional, administrative, and local government law, with two basic concepts — the police power and the takings clause — underlying most that they do. Land use attorneys constantly refer to both when either challenging, defending, interpreting, or drafting, any regulation, and so an understanding of both is basic to a grasp of the basics in this field of law. Among the best and the brightest of them, a knowledge of the takings cases is, for example, a precondition for discussing almost any type of land use control— and a knowledge of the facts of these cases is equally important. They usually ask something like the following: "If the Supreme Court said . . ., what's the effect on . . .type of control." This Chapter and the next discuss these basic concepts, and later Chapters will review various effects.

The **police power** is the power of the states and their legislatures to enact regulations over persons and property to prohibit all things inimical to their citizens' health, safety, morals, and general welfare. It protects the welfare of the citizenry and has at least three attributes:

(1) It is an **inherent** power of a state legislature, meaning that it is within the legislative function.

(2) It is a **plenary** power — a complete and unqualified legislative power, empowering the legislature to do whatever is necessary to ascertain what it needs to know and to enact legislation to implement it. Whatever affects the general welfare comes within its scope and may be used in so far as it is necessarily exercised to secure its ends. It is broad.[2] It is also plenary in a second sense, in that it is a legislative power reserved for use by the legislature itself and so that body need not articulate the standards that will guide or limit the exercise of the power.[3]

(3) It is a **reserved** power in another sense under our constitutional system; that is, it is reserved, under the Tenth Amendment to the federal constitution, to the states — and often by the states delegated to local governments or municipalities. Recent United States Supreme Court cases

---

[1] *See Atkin v. Tittle & Tittle*, 730 So. 2d 376, 378 (Fla. App. Ct. 1999) (affirming a legal malpractice award against an attorney not sufficiently investigating land use regulations applicable to a client's land).

[2] However, the breadth of the power is limited by the ends for which it works, even if those ends need not be articulated when the legislature acts; within it is a concept of substantive due process. *See* Lawrence Friedman, *Government and Slum Housing* 7 (1968) (making this connection).

[3] *See, e.g., Tiber Petroleum v. The Parish of Jefferson*, 391 So. 2d 1178, 1180 (La. 1980) (Dennis, J., dissenting) (involving the location of unsafe oil refineries).

restricting (say) commerce clause powers of the federal government and Congress to enact laws regulating the use of guns around schools, highlights the fact that, in our system, there is no equivalent plenary federal police power.[4]

The police power is not the power of eminent domain.[5] Eminent domain takes private property for governmental use, while the police power only denies some use or uses of private property to its owner. Eminent domain is exercised because property is useful to the public; the police power is exercised because some use of private property is harmful to the public.[6]

The limits of the power were once more apparent than they are today. Earlier statements of the scope of the power covered only the protection of the health, safety, or morals of a state's citizenry. Courts early in our legal history upheld ordinances that prohibited certain uses considered noxious from certain areas — laundries,[7] taverns,[8] and most commonly, slaughter houses, among them. Affirmatively protecting the general welfare was not then the business of the state. For example, the enactment of laws requiring landlords to provide tenants with hot water were beyond its scope; they were said to be *ultra vires* the police power. The states were able to prevent the citizenry's health or safety from deteriorating, but were not able to promote these things.

Today the police power "is not confined to a narrow category; it extends . . .to all great public needs."[9] For example, after 12% of Chicago's population died in a cholera epidemic in 1885, the city regulated the provision of water to enhance the health, safety, and welfare of its citizens.[10] The police power became "a concept of social cost; it validates legislation designed to limit or alleviate the burden of social costs."[11] Thus, even though authorizing a government to legislate for the health, safety, and morals of the community might not seem limiting, to this triad a fourth category was added by the 1930's, the decade of the New Deal. This was a reference to "the general welfare" of the community. Now the community's health was regarded as being protected and enhanced when apartment house owners were required by statute or ordinance to provide tenants with hot water and heat. Likewise, tenants' safety is enhanced when buildings are limited to a height reachable safely by then-existing fire apparatus;

---

[4] *See, e.g., United States v. Lopez*, 514 U.S. 549 (1995), as interpreted in *United States v. Wilson*, 133 F. 3d 251 (4th Cir. 1997). *Wilson* is noted in James Bryant, *United States v. Wilson: A Change in Wetlands and Clean Water Act Jurisprudence*, 28 Real Est. L. J. 37, 45–50 (1999).

[5] *See, e.g.,* Ernst Freund, *The Police Power* § 511, at 546–557 (1904).

[6] *See Lemp v. Town Board of Islip*, 394 N.Y.S.2d 517, 521 (N.Y. Sup. Ct. 1977) (involving the prohibition of construction of a house on a sand dune on the beach at Fire Island and invalidating an ordinance prohibiting such construction).

[7] *In re Hang Kie*, 10 P. 327 (Cal. 1886).

[8] *Shea v. City of Muncie*, 46 N.E. 138 (Ind. 1897).

[9] *Day-Brite Lighting Inc. v. Missouri*, 342 U.S. 421, 424 (1952).

[10] Anne Spirn, *The Granite Garden* 148–149 (1984); *see also* J. R. McNeill, *Something New under the Sun* 126–127 (2000).

[11] Friedman, op. cit n. 1, at 7.

indeed, the whole neighborhood is protected against fire.[12] Legislation could, in other words, be justified by its limiting of the "neighborhood or external effects" of an owner's behavior.

Consider, as an exercise of the police power, the traffic ticket you get for running a light at midnight with no other traffic in sight? A law which requires riders of motorcycles to wear a helmet or prohibits building on a flood plain or in a wetland or marsh? That regulates the aesthetics of a building, down to the type of material and facade? Down to the door handle? All of these are valid exercises of the police power. Even the building of large public parks — Central Park in New York City, Fairmont Park in Philadelphia, or the Fens in Boston — have been conceived as public health measures.[13] Today farmland preservation is viewed as a matter of police power matter of creating "food security," environmental benefits, and the control of urban sprawl.[14]

§ 1.01 Dillon's Rule.

Federal and state governments each operate under their own constitutions. Municipal government is constitutionally weak when compared with them.[15] It obtains all of its power and authority from the state.[16] It is the creature of that state government.[17] Any activity that municipal government undertakes: (1) must be expressly authorized by the state legislature — it must be authorized in express words in a state statute; or (2) it must be reasonably necessary to the achievement of an activity that is expressly authorized — it must be incidental to an express authorization; or (3) it must be essential to the declared objects and purposes of the municipality.[18] This is a rule of delegation of authority as well as a canon of construction for municipalities. It is often called Dillon's Rule. It is named after a nineteenth century Iowa judge who was one of the first to use this formulation.[19] John F. Dillon was also the author of an early, influential treatise on local government law.[20] He wrote in defense of state power. One of his

---

[12] *Welch v. Swasey*, 214 U.S. 91 (1919) (validating height restrictions on buildings in Boston's Back Bay neighborhood).

[13] Mel Scott, *American City Planning* 11 (1971).

[14] Mark Cordes, *Takings, Fairness, and Farmland Preservation*, 60 Ohio St. L. J. 1033, 1041–1050 (1999).

[15] *Capalbo v. Planning & Zoning Bd. of Appeal of the Town of Greenwich*, 547 A.2d 528, 533 (Conn. 1988) ("Under our law, a municipality, as a creation of the state, has no inherent powers of its own.").

[16] *Id.* at 534 (holding that a town could not regulate the color of billboards when the enabling statute permits regulation of their "height, size, and location.").

[17] *See Trustees of Dartmouth College v. Woodward*, 17 U.S. 250 (1819) (Chief Justice John Marshall's conclusion when distinguishing a private college from a municipal corporation).

[18] *Smith v. City of New Bern*, 70 N.C. 14, 18–19 (1874) (using this canon of construction); *City of Philadelphia v. Fox*, 64 Pa. 169 (1870) (same). *See* David Barron, *The Promise of Cooley's City: Traces of Local Constitutionalism*, 147 U. Pa. L. Rev. 487, 506–509 (1999) (tracing the history of Dillon's Rule).

[19] *City of Clinton v. Cedar Rapids & Mo. River R.R.*, 24 Iowa 455, 475 (1868) (Dillon, C.J.).

[20] *See* John F. Dillon, *The Law of Municipal Corporations* (2d rev. ed., 1873).

opinions struck down a state statute that authorized municipalities to levy taxes to aid railroads coming to the municipality.[21] Two related things are wrong with such statute, he wrote: first, it lacked a "public" purpose, and second, it intruded into the realm of the private markets and corporations that worked best if left unregulated.[22] In the area of land use regulation, the analogous debate is between municipalities and private property. Using Dillon's Rule, the municipality is restrained by the very creature that created it — a state's government.

The United States Supreme Court later restated Dillon's Rule. It stated: "Municipal corporations owe their origin to, and derive their powers and rights wholly from, the legislature. It breathes into them the breath of life, without which they cannot exist. As it creates, so may it destroy. If it may destroy, it may abridge and control.* * * [Municipal corporations] are, so to phrase it, the mere tenants at will of the legislature."[23]

The lesson of the Rule is always to check the statutory authority of a municipality to act or enact its ordinances because any reasonable doubt as to the power or authority of a municipality is to be resolved against it. The Rule is a canon of strict construction. As one court said, it "controls our determination of the powers of local governing bodies. The rule provides that municipal corporations have only those powers that are expressly granted, those necessarily or fairly implied from expressly granted powers, and those that are essential and indispensable."[24] Thus, the Rule is a judicial gloss on the judiciary's relationship with its state legislature, and provides a standard of judicial review for municipal actions. It is also a preference for judicial dispassion over the passions of local politics.

Dillon's Rule has been used both to invalidate ordinances and well as to uphold them. It has a benefit for municipal governments. Judge Thomas Cooley of the Michigan Supreme Court provided it. As a justice on the Michigan Supreme Court, he held unconstitutional a state law that permitted a pledge of municipal credit to aid the construction of a private railroad running from Detroit to the municipality.[25] A municipality, he wrote, could not be compelled by the state to issue bonds for the benefit of a private corporation — the deal struck between the railroad and the state legislature was beyond the legislature's authority.[26] This asserted a municipality's right to be free of the bankruptcies that followed such pledges.[27] Municipalities cannot be forced to use their delegatee powers.[28] More generally,

---

[21] *Hanson v. Vernon*, 27 Iowa. 28 (1869).

[22] *Id.* at 31.

[23] *Hunter v. City of Pittsburgh*, 207 U.S. 161, 178 (1907).

[24] *City of Chesapeake v. Gardner Enterprises, Inc.*, 482 S.E.2d 812, 814 (Va. 1997), used and quoted in *City Council of Alexandria v. The Lindsay Trusts*, 520 S.E.2d 181, 182 (Va. 1999).

[25] *People ex rel. Detroit & Howell RR v. Twp. Bd. of Salem*, 20 Mich. 452, 1870 Mich. 4149 (Mich. 1870).

[26] *Id.* at 20-21.

[27] *See* Thomas M. Cooley, *A Treatise on the Constitutional Limitations Which Rest upon the Legislative Power of the States of the American Union* 459 (1874).

[28] *People ex rel. Le Roy v. Hurlbut*, 24 Mich. 44, 107–108 (Mich. 1871) (Cooley, J., concurring).

Dillon's Rule has been most actively used to strike down municipal ordinances imposing taxes not clearly authorized by the state.

The Rule was present at the inception of municipal land use and zoning regulation,[29] and has informed its progress. For example, the Rule's third element, operating without an inquiry into statutory authority common in its first two elements and concerning powers "essential to the objects and purposes" of the municipality, has often been used to justify regulations enacted in the name of safety and health problems.[30]

The breadth of the police power and the limitations in Dillon's Rule combined to bring about a era of conflicting cases regarding the constitutionality of local land use regulation in the first three decades of the twentieth century. There is no inherent municipal power to zone.[31] Neither does such a power spring from the creation of a municipal corporation or local government. Absent home rule powers, some specific state enabling act or statutory authority is required. Such authority in fact exists today in every state. Even a general delegation of police power would probably be insufficient.[32] It would at best only provoke litigation.

Once enabling statutes were in place, some state courts upheld the constitutionality of zoning as an exercise of the police power,[33] but others did not. The Maryland Court of Appeals did not, finding that the zoning ordinance under review replaced the forces of the private market with a segregation of land uses.[34] A few municipalities saw the advantages of zoning, but used their eminent domain powers to effectuate it.

In 1926, zoning was held to be a facially[35] valid exercise of the police power.[36] The United States Supreme Court held that there was no violation of due process in a municipality's enactment of a zoning ordinance that was: (1) comprehensive in scope — that is, covered all of the municipality's land area; (2) classified various land uses of property (residential, commercial, etc.), all the land being placed in one classification or another; and (3) created geographic and geometric use districts where each land use was permitted. What the court did not validate was (say) the placement of the

---

[29] *See, e.g., State v. Whitlock*, 63 N.C. 123, 124 (N.C. 1908) (finding municipality with power to regulate billboards, but invalidating the instant ordinance doing so).

[30] *See* Chapter 9, *infra* (a discussion of moratoria).

[31] *Detroit Osteopathic Hosp. v. Southfield*, 139 N.W.2d 728 (Mich. 1966).

[32] *See, e.g., Tiber Petroleum v. The Parish of Jefferson*, 391 So. 2d 1178 (La. 1980).

[33] *Lincoln Tr. Co. v. Williams Bldg. Corp.*, 128 N.E. 209 (N.Y. 1920).

[34] *Goldman v. Crowther*, 128 A.2d 50 (Md. 1925) (invalidating a Baltimore Cty., Md., ordinance).

[35] "Facially" is a word often used in land use practice. It means "on its face." Thus to say that a zoning ordinance is facially valid means that there is nothing in the text of the ordinance to invalidate it upon its enactment, before it is applied to particular facts and circumstances. This is to say that it is not overbroad or written in vague language, and so is valid as enacted. By the same token, to find an ordinance facially valid is not to say that later it might be found invalid "as applied" in particular situations. Land use attorneys thus speak of challenging an ordinance either "facially" or "as applied."

[36] *Village of Euclid v. Ambler Realty Co.*, 272 U.S. 365 (1926), noted at 40 Harv. L. Rev. 644 (1927) and 36 Yale L. J. 427 (1927), and discussed infra, Chapter 5.

land owner's land in a residential instead of an industrial land use district. So the court was able to avoid more than passing consideration of the fact that the owner thought that the fair market value of its land was drastically affected, and reduced, by the ordinance. If the court had decided that case as an "as applied"[37] challenge to the ordinance, it may well have been decided in favor of the owner.

Two years later, in another case, the Supreme Court used the police power and the due process clause again, this time to invalidate a zoning ordinance that, although facially valid, was applied to a particular parcel in a way that made the parcel of little value.[38] The land in question was restricted to residential uses; was bisected by the boundary between residential and industrial land use districts; and was adjacent to parcels actually used for industrial purposes. Moreover, the landowner had lost a contract of sale because of the ordinance's regulation. This invalidation too was grounded in the police power, the opinion was written by the same justice, and seemed to indicate that the Supreme Court would review zoning ordinances with care. Two lessons of *Nectow* were clear: municipalities should place the boundaries of use districts in the middle of their streets, and pay more attention to surrounding uses. However, the Supreme Court's close supervision of the exercise of the police power in zoning matters was not to be. The events of the next decade intervened, producing the Depression, the New Deal, and judicial restraint in many areas of constitutional law, and that court's next zoning case would be decided in 1974.[39] This hiatus came about despite attempts to appeal zoning decisions to the court. Between 1949 and 1955, for example, writs of certiorari were denied 21 times.[40]

In the meanwhile, the same court did decide some cases that had implications for the use of the police power as a basis for zoning. In *Berman v. Parker*,[41] the court upheld the use of the power of eminent domain to uphold an urban renewal program. The court upheld a municipal land use decision to condemn a neighborhood it found blighted and riddled with substandard housing, even though the property of the plaintiff was well maintained and not sub-standard. The *Berman* opinion spoke of the legitimate concern of a municipality to become "beautiful as well as healthy," "spacious as well as clean," and "well-balanced as well as carefully patrolled."[42] All these quotations became famous phrases in the history of zoning and land use controls. In another phrase with implications for the police power, the court said that the "concept of the general welfare is broad and inclusive."[43] An area approach, rather than a structure-by-structure

---

[37] *See* op. cit, n. 35, for a definition of this term.

[38] *Nectow v. City of Cambridge*, 277 U.S. 183 (1928).

[39] *Village of Belle Terre v. Boraas*, 416 U.S. 1 (1974).

[40] John Johnson, *Constitutional Law and Community Planning*, 20 L. & Contemp. Prob. 199, 208 (1955).

[41] 348 U.S. 26 (1954).

[42] *Id.* at 33.

[43] *Id.*

approach, was justified, wrote the court, adding: "Miserable and disreputable housing conditions may do more than spread disease and crime and immorality. They may also suffocate the spirit . . . . *** [and also] may despoil a community as an open sewer may ruin a river."[44] Once the purpose of the legislation was found to be within the police power's general welfare rubric, the use of eminent domain was justified as well. The breadth of the police power licensed the use of eminent domain. All this was good news for attorneys working for municipalities.

In another case in the 1960s, the court upheld an ordinance that prohibited rock quarrying below the water table and required that the quarry below the water table be filled unless there was a showing that the land lacked other, reasonably profitable uses.[45] This case in effect prohibited quarrying in the area. A later case involving another quarry, whose appeal to the Supreme Court was dismissed, was even more drastic.[46] These cases confirm the authority of a municipality to exclude nuisance-like uses. Not only does an owner have no right to zoning that permits the extraction of minerals from a parcel of land, but the total exclusion of mining may be upheld as a valid exercise of the police power. Extraction of a piece of land's natural products may be regulated by a municipality in a way no different from other commercial uses of its undisturbed land surface.

The urban renewal and quarry cases thus confirm the ability of a municipality to impose reasonable regulations on the conduct of a business when delegated the authority to do so and when the regulation is rationally related to some legitimate police power objective. For example, the municipality's total prohibition on curb service street vending by ice cream trucks may be invalid, but an ordinance prohibiting them from conducting their business along heavily traveled streets may be reasonable as a method of regulating the flow of traffic while providing such street vendors with a means of doing business elsewhere. Likewise, prohibiting billboards along residential streets may be valid, while no such prohibition along commercial streets would likely be sustained. And prohibiting so called "adult" entertainment or bookstores from locating near churches may be reasonable, but broader bans on such uses may not.

What may be prohibited may also be regulated. Thus, prohibiting door to door solicitation may be too severe, but requiring that such solicitors be licensed is not. Likewise, junkyards and car lots may be required to be surrounded by fences, and businesses such as laundromats or gas stations may be required to have an attendant on the premises when open for business. Thus, police power regulations of street vending, billboards, obscenity, and even a reasonable regulation of a municipality's aesthetics are today all valid exercises of the police power.

---

[44] *Id.*

[45] *Goldblatt v. Town of Hempstead,* 369 U.S. 590 (1962).

[46] *See Consolidated Rock Products Co. v. City of Los Angeles,* 370 P.2d 342 (Cal. 1962), *appeal dismissed,* 371 U.S. 36 (1962) (a case in which there was evidence that there is no other profitable use for a quarry zoned residential).

Chapter 2

The Takings Clause and Its Public Use Requirement

§ 2.01 The Takings Clause.

". . .nor shall private property be taken for public use, without just compensation."

So reads part of the Fifth Amendment to the United States Constitution. It is known as the takings clause.[1] It serves as a limitation on the exercise of the police power. Its antecedents go back as far as the Magna Carta.[2]

The clause may not be read literally: it does not mean that if property is taken for a *private* use, no compensation need be paid. That reading would, if adopted, stand the clause on its head, so ignore such constitutional literalism. The clause assumes the exercise of a governmental function in taking private property, but puts a limitation on that use — to the effect that it can only be exercised after just compensation is paid.

The clause is read backwards. It means that "[w]hen private property is to be used by the public and until just compensation is paid, no such property shall be taken by the government."[3] James Madison initially proposed a draft of this clause that read this way. His version stated: "No person shall be . . .obliged to relinquish his property, where it may be necessary for public use, without a just compensation."[4] Read this way, the clause is not a prohibition on government's taking private property; instead,

---

[1] This clause is also sometimes known as the just compensation clause.

[2] *See* Magna Carta, Ch. 39 (1215): "No free man shall be . . .disseised . . .except by lawful judgment of his peers or by the law of the land." Similar language was incorporated in Parliament's Petition of Right, signed by King Charles I of England in 1628. *See generally* Richard Pipes, *Property and Freedom* 120–158 (1999) (and summarizing the Petition at 142).

[3] *See* 1 William Blackstone, *Commentaries on the Laws of England* 139 (1776) (stating that compensation had to accompany any exercise of the government's power to take private property).

[4] *Speech Proposing the Bill of Rights* (June 8, 1789), 1 Annals of Cong. 451–452 (J. Gales, ed., 1834). Madison intended that his draft limit only the acquisition of property and prohibited only direct, physical takings, and even then only by the federal government, not the states. His focus was on a near total diminution of the value of the property taken. In practice, it is difficult to focus on diminished value and on the thing taken without also focusing on the actions of the government doing the taking — hard to focus on just compensation without also focusing on the government's fairness or arbitrariness in the taking. So the use of the takings clause today overlaps with that of the due process clause immediately preceding it in the text of the Fifth Amendment — reading "nor [shall any person] be deprived of . . .property, without due process of law." *See also* Andrew Gold, *Regulatory Takings and Original Intent: The Direct, Physical Takings Thesis "Goes Too Far,"* 49 Am. U. L. Rev. 181, 184, 186 and notes 27 & 28 (1999) (arguing that Madison's post-ratification writings support a broader view).

it requires that what is taken be property[5] and then only imposes a condition on the taking of such property — that is, the government's taking is conditioned by its first paying just compensation for its actions. This reading does not validate the citizenry's right to acquire, hold and sell property. The drafters of the federal Constitution intended that the recognition and protection of such a right be in the states' constitutions then in force; some of them then recognized that there was a "natural right" to property.[6] No one argued against recognizing a right to property during the debates over ratification of either the federal Constitution or its Bill of Rights. In addition, because the drafters of the Bill of Rights recognized the law of eminent domain, it made no sense to word this clause like the First Amendment — i.e., "Congress shall make no law concerning [property]." Eminent domain certainly did affect property and, after all, the enactment of practically any law or legislation affects some form of property. If the clause read this way, the scope of the eminent domain power would arguably be narrower than it is. As it is, this is not the way the clause reads and the power of eminent domain is broadly used. For example, in over thirty states, easements of necessity may be condemned by a land-locked private landowner. In many states, the power is available to and frequently used by public utilities and mining companies, in addition to governmental entities.

All but one of our state constitutions today contain a similar clause. North Carolina's constitution is the sole exception.[7] That the Fifth Amendment's clause protecting property is located in a Bill of Rights Amendment that also restrained the federal government's criminal procedures, shows that property and personal liberty were closely associated in the drafters' minds. Many of them were content to permit institutional and political arrangements to become the chief protector of property rights. Some doubted that property was a "natural right." Instead, they preferred to think of it as one that would be utilitarian — that is, instrumental in developing the nation's economy.

This clause is not an express grant of authority to use the power of eminent domain. Eminent domain is sometimes referred to as the power to condemn land or property. It is the power to acquire and take possession of property in order to promote the health, safety, and welfare of the citizenry.[8] The takings clause does not grant this power; it is rather a power inherent in sovereignty. The clause only imposes a governmental responsibility for using it. It long predates our Constitution, being recognized by law treatise writers in the 16th and 17th centuries, and as previously

---

[5] See Eastern Enterprises v. Apfel, 524 U.S. 498, 540 (1998) (Kennedy, J., concurring and providing a fifth vote, finding a statute unconstitutional but not a taking, there being no infringement of a specific property interest).

[6] John Ely, "That due satisfaction may be made:" The Fifth Amendment and the Origins of the Compensation Principle, 36 Am.J. Leg.Hist. 1 (1992) (arguing that colonial governments pre-1789 often paid compensation).

[7] In North Carolina, the courts have read similar protections into that state's constitution by implication.

[8] See, e.g., Bd. of Health v. Van Hoesen, 49 N.W. 894 (Mich. 1891).

mentioned by Blackstone in his famous and widely read commentaries. In our federal Constitution, the government's duty to pay just compensation is made express. That was, at the time, a unique requirement when made a precondition to the power's exercise.

Moreover, the takings clause makes plain that a "taking" includes a condemnation under the power of eminent domain, but that it is more: it includes condemnation, but extends also to state actions that result from police power regulations such as zoning and other types of land use controls. In this respect, the protection of property in our federal and state constitutions is broader than is provided in other countries.[9]

The clause is self-executing: that is, it provides a direct remedy for a taking and its consequential damages without requiring the government to waive its sovereign immunity. There is no sovereign immunity for an action for which the sovereign, in its authorizing document, is responsible.[10] This direct remedy is known as a cause of action for inverse condemnation — a claim that the government committed an action that required the use of eminent domain, but did not use this power, and should be forced to.

The United States Supreme Court reaffirmed Madison's reading of the takings clause and his view that it was a restriction on the federal government, but not on the states.[11] That was the way things stood up to the passage of the Fourteenth Amendment; then, in 1866, one of the leading drafters[12] of the Fourteenth Amendment proposed to include within that Amendment a clause to protect the property of loyal Southern unionists from confiscation by rebels in control of state governments after the Civil War. This clause became the clause that reads "nor shall any State deprive any person of life, liberty, and property, without due process of law" — including the law that had developed around the takings clause of the Fifth Amendment. This latter clause implicitly authorizes the regulation of property, short of its being taken. Soon after the debate and passage of the Fourteenth Amendment, the takings clause was applied to the actions of a state government and the definition of a taking was expanded to include a diminution in the usefulness of land, even though the title to the land was not taken from the owner.[13] So, by the end of the 19th century, both the takings and the due process clause of the Fifth Amendment applied to the states.[14]

---

[9] See A. J. van der Walt, *Constitutional Property Clauses* 423 (1999).

[10] See, e.g., *Colman v. Utah State Land Bd.*, 795 P.2d 622, 630–635 (Utah 1990) (discussing self-executing nature of federal and state provisions).

[11] See *Barron v. Baltimore*, 32 U.S. 243 (1833).

[12] This person was John Bingham, a Republican Congressman from Ohio.

[13] *Pumpelly v. Green Bay Company*, 80 U.S. 166, 181 (1871) (finding a taking in the construction of a dam, authorized by state statute, backing water up on plaintiff's land). *See generally* Kris Kobach, *The Origins of Regulatory Takings: Setting the Record Straight*, 1996 Utah L. Rev. 1211 (1996) (arguing that both federal and state cases leading to *Pumpelly* recognized not-trespassory, non-destructive, incremental takings all during the 19th century). *See, e.g., Gardner v. Trustees of Newburgh*, 2 Johns Ch. 162 (N.Y. Ch. 1816).

[14] *Chicago, Burlington and Quincy RR Co. v. Chicago*, 166 U.S. 226, 235–241 (1897).

Once the Fourteenth Amendment made the Bill of Rights (including the takings clause in the Fifth Amendment) applicable to the states, there was a need to consider the extent of the clause's protection of private property. Thus began the development of federal takings jurisprudence that would guide and control state court interpretation of similar clauses in all state constitutions and that today limits the regulation of land under the police power.

§ 2.02   The Public Use Requirement.

". . .nor shall private property be taken **for public use** . . . ." The traditional view of this requirement is that it is a threshold test for the proper use of the power of eminent domain.[15] The issue is whether the purpose or objective of the government in taking private property is a legitimate one. "It is just as important that the proposed use . . .be limited to what the court decides is a 'really public' use as it is that the property owner be given just compensation."[16]

An early test read the requirement as a "use by the public."[17] Early on, condemnation for roads and mill-dams were the uses permitted — in the latter instance, the mills for grinding corn and grain were open to the public, but not operated by the government. There are also fairly recent examples of this view.[18] The use of condemnation powers for the development of a casino has been held to lack a sufficient public use.[19] Similarly, condemning land for parking garages around shopping and retail centers has also been found to fail this test. Turning property over after condemnation to private parties was forbidden; such was not a use by the public.[20] It was on this ground that some state courts struck down state cartway statutes, permitting a landlocked owner to condemn and take a private roadway off property to obtain access to the nearest public road. Such statutes in part codified the law of easements by necessity,[21] but were essentially for the benefit of a private, landlocked, landowner as a condemnor.

A second test was devised for urban renewal and redevelopment programs. The statutes on which these programs were based were enacted after World War II. Their purpose was to redevelop blighted urban areas,

---

[15] *See* Matthew Zinn, Note, *Ultra Vires Takings*, 97 Mich. L. Rev. 245, 260–269 (1998). *See also* Joseph Lazzarotti, *Public Use or Public Abuse*, 68 UMKC L. Rev. 49 (1999).

[16] *Hogue v. Port of Seattle*, 341 P.2d 171, 193 (Wash. 1959).

[17] *See Cole v. City of LaGrange*, 113 U.S. 1, 6 (1885).

[18] *Riden v. Philadelphia B.& W. RR Co.*, 35 A.2d 99, 102 (Md. 1943).

[19] *Mayor of Vicksburg v. Thomas*, 645 So. 2d 940, 941 (Miss. 1994) (so holding and requiring that the public purpose for the condemnation be direct, not indirect or speculative).

[20] *Karesh v. City Council*, 247 S.E. 2d 342, 344 (S.C.1978) (holding that the city could not condemn land for a parking garage and convention center).

[21] *See* Joseph Kalo & Monica Kalo, *Putting the Cartway Before the House: Statutory Easements by Necessity, or Cartways, in North Carolina*, 75 N.C. L. Rev. 1943, 1946, n.14 (1997) (reviewing state court results).

replacing sub-standard structures with new ones. The renewed area typically comprised new housing. In these programs, the land condemned was held only briefly by the public condemnor. The condemnor was usually a special purpose housing or redevelopment authority with the power to issue local revenue bonds to finance its program. Once it acquired the blighted area, it re-subdivided the area and transferred the titles to the parcels in it to previously unidentified private parties.[22] The parties were typically, though not necessarily, low-income persons or households. In cases reviewing these programs, public use was held to mean "public benefit." Eminent domain here created a public benefit through better land planning and the elimination of blighted housing so the requirement was met.[23]

Under this second test, it is not essential that a majority of the public benefit from the governmental action or program.[24] Thus, the condemnation of hunting rights in order to establish a migratory bird preserve was found a "public use" in *Swan Lake Hunting Club v. United States*,[25] even though only limited public hunting would be permitted in the future by the government.

In the process of expanding the definition of what was a public use by incorporating public benefit or purpose analysis, the definition of public use became a legislative function. Thus, an action of a state administrative agency requires the authorization by the state legislature in order to further a public use.

[A]   The *Berman* Case.

In *Berman v. Parker*,[26] an urban redevelopment authority in Washington, D.C., sought to condemn the plaintiff's property. That property was not itself run down or blighted, but it was located within a neighborhood that was. That neighborhood was an extensive one, comprising most of the Southwest quadrant of the District of Columbia. The United States Supreme Court held that the takings clause's public use requirement was satisfied when the urban redevelopment had a "public purpose." In this third reading of the requirement, a legislative finding of a public purpose in the statute authorizing the use of eminent domain was "well-nigh conclusive"[27] that the public use requirement was met. Defining whether a public use was present, the court said, was "essentially the product of legislative

---

[22] *See, e.g., New York City Hous. Auth. v. Muller*, 1 N.E. 2d 153 (N.Y. 1936).

[23] *See Berman v. Parker*, 348 U.S. 26 (1954) (upholding an urban redevelopment program for the District of Columbia, and discussed in more detail in the next section).

[24] *Rindge Company v. County of Los Angeles*, 262 U.S. 700, 707 (1923) (involving the condemnation of coastal land for a county highway, and stating: "It is not essential that the entire community, nor even any considerable portion, . . . directly enjoy or participate in any improvement in order [that the improvement] constitute a public use. . . . Public uses . . .extend to matters of public health, recreation and enjoyment.").

[25] 381 F.2d 238, 245 (1967).

[26] *Berman v. Parker*, 348 U.S. 26, 32 (1954).

[27] *Id.*

determinations addressed to the purposes of government."[28] In this case, Justice Douglas wrote for the court:

> The concept of the public welfare is broad and inclusive. The values it represents are spiritual as well as physical, aesthetic as well as monetary. It is within the power of legislature to determine that the community should be beautiful as well as healthy, spacious as well as clean, well-balanced as well as carefully patrolled. . . .[29]

In *Berman*, the public use requirement was measured on an area, rather than a structure by structure, basis. The court rejected the argument that the public use requirement must be satisfied structure by structure. Not every property for which condemnation was sought, need be blighted or substandard under applicable housing codes. It was enough that its surroundings were blighted in some measurable way. After all, urban planning, not just architecture, was the governmental function involved. Moreover, the reuse of the land for a factory was also valid when the public purpose was to create jobs for the community. That the property is to be passed to a corporation identified at the time of condemnation, does not lessen its public purpose. That purpose need not involve the property directly, but could be tied instead to the effects of the end-use of the property.

Berman's holding was later to extend beyond urban planning. Economic development legislation was later validated, particularly in "rustbelt" states in which the industrial economy was then sagging.[30]

[B]   The *Midkiff* Case.

The title to large portions of land on the Hawaiian Islands is held by only a few large holdings. Traditionally used for agriculture, some of these holdings have over the years been split into smaller residential leaseholds. Hawaii's state legislature enacted a statute permitting the holders of these long term leases to buy the underlying fee simple. In *Hawaii Housing Authority v. Midkiff*,[31] the court held that this state statute, technically authorizing the condemnation of lessors' ground lease reversions that were, it said, held by a "landed oligopoly," was a use of eminent domain for a public use. The system of land tenure at issue here was relatively specialized and not found everywhere, but the court did not focus on the needs of the state in dealing with its tenure system. While not passing on the merits of the condemnation program, the court found that the legislative finding of a widespread problem with land tenures was conclusive.[32] "Where the exercise of the eminent domain power is rationally related to

---

[28] *Id.*

[29] *Id.* at 33.

[30] *See New Jersey Housing & Mortgage Fin. Agency v. Moses*, 521 A.2d 1307 (N.J. Super. Ct., App. Div., 1987) (condemning land for private shopping center proper, but condemnation action dismissed for failure to bargain with landowners in good faith).

[31] 467 U.S. 229, 240 (1984).

[32] *Id.*; *See also Kansas ex rel. Tomasic v. The Unified Government of Wyandotte Cty. / Kansas City, Kansas*, 962 P.2d 543, 553 (Kan. 1998) (using language similar to *Berman's*).

a conceivable public purpose, the [C]ourt has never held a compensated taking to be proscribed by the Public Use Clause. . . ."[33]

The court made three doctrinal points about its holding. First, the court said that state legislatures are better able to assess the need for condemnation than the courts are. Judicial deference and the resulting breadth of the public use requirement is in turn the result of a prudential concern of the court for the relative competencies and fact-finding abilities of the legislature and the judiciary.[34] This deference is also rooted in separation of power concerns. Second, the court said that only if the definition of a public use results in an impossibility or is without palpable reasonable foundation, will a legislative determination in this area be invalidated.[35] Third, the court stated that the public use requirement of the takings clause "is thus coterminous with the scope of the sovereign's police power."[36]

One further point might be made — if only to show how far beyond the plausible one might go in analyzing a holding. The court stated that the public purpose need only be "conceivable." This word might suggest to some that it need not be articulated — meaning that it need not be articulated during the legislative process and prior to being challenged. The writer meant no such thing. "Conceivable" means conceivable in a rationale mind and is another way of saying that the public purpose must be conceived by the legislature in such a way that it is supported by substantial evidence — that is, by that amount of evidence that a reasonable mind would require when choosing one of several options — even if it must be "conceived" from the text of the statute itself, or from the facts and circumstances surrounding its enactment.[37]

Two more basic points need to be made about the holding as well. First, as to the Court's language about the takings clause being "conterminous" with the police power, the important point is that the power of eminent domain is regarded as a corollary or implementing power of government, not a plenary or primary one. If the police power could properly be used, then so could the eminent domain power. The former licenses the latter.[38] This works both ways. Because the eminent domain power is coterminous with the police power, anything permissibly done by condemnation can also be achieved by regulation. Thus Hawaii might have regulated the ground lease reversion out of existence by limiting the landlord's right of reentry or his ability to sue in trespass to enforce the reversion. Second, it converts the public use requirement into a descriptive term, rather than a limitation on government. It requires only that the legislature articulate a "clear and significant" public purpose. This articulation must both precede the condemnation and provide a "rationale basis" for it, and must also relate the

---

[33] *Midkiff*, 467 U.S. at 245.

[34] *Id.* at 244.

[35] *Id.* at 240–241.

[36] *Id.* at 244.

[37] *Id.* at 245.

[38] This is thinking suitable for government in which economic regulation is far-reaching and in which uncompensated regulation is more far-reaching than the use of eminent domain.

purpose of the condemnation and the program used to implement that purpose. (Respectively, these are, in constitutional law terms, the "rational basis" standard for judicial review, and the "reasonable nexus" required of any police power regulation.)

The holding in *Midkiff* is not limited to residential land reform. Consider some applications. If the land reform effort of Hawaii is valid, then the condemnation of scattered residential lots for public housing is valid too. Its public purpose is that it avoids the problems associated with large hi-rise public housing. Condemnation of scattered site shopping center leases may also be expected to expand low income businesses.[39] Housing is just as important as jobs.[40] After all, using *Midkiff*, a reviewing court asks, not whether the legislation will in fact achieve its goals, but whether the legislature "rationally could have believed" that the legislation "would promote its objective."[41]

Lawrence Tribe, a Harvard law professor and author of a prominent constitutional law treatise, was the attorney for the State of Hawaii in *Midkiff*. Apparently seeing his work in the broadest terms, he reportedly told a reporter that states had acquired authority to "rearrange property interests" in this opinion.[42] However, the *Midkiff* opinion states that the Housing Authority could begin condemnation proceedings when requested to do so by twenty five or more lessees or lessees of more than fifty percent of the leased lots, whichever is less, in a residential subdivision with an area not less than five contiguous acres. Analogous groups may be hard to find, and this feature of Hawaii's program significantly narrows the holding of the case.

After *Midkiff*, a municipality might condemn a scheme of restrictive, residential only covenants in a subdivision which has been zoned commercial as a means of encouraging the expansion of its downtown.[43] The argument against such a purchase is that downtown building developers could negotiate as easily as the municipality,[44] but another "rational belief" for validating such a purchase is that the condemnation will reduce transaction costs that "conceivably" no developer would bear. Residential land has been subdivided in parcels too small for downtown development; condemning the covenants "clearly and significantly" makes redoing this pattern of parcelization easier. *Berman* first requires that the subdivision be blighted and its housing a threat to public health or safety, but that was

---

[39] However, some state statutes prohibit the condemnation of an on-going enterprise.

[40] *See* David Callies, *Requiem for Public Purpose*, 36 Zoning Dig. 194 (1984) (who suggests these hypos). What about a middle western state's legislature deciding to condemn all farmland held by corporate interests in a program to reestablish family farming? Or, to condemn farmland held by absentee owners, or foreign investors? Such programs seem no less permissible.

[41] *Midkiff*, 467 U.S. at 242–243.

[42] Note, *Hawaii Housing Authority v. Midkiff: A Wolf in Sheeps' Clothing?*, 12 Cal. West. L. Rev. 325, 341, n. 118 (1984) (reporting Tribe's remarks).

[43] *See* Stephen Jones, op. cit., 50 Syra. L. Rev. at 303 (citing several instances reported in newspapers).

[44] *In re City of Seattle*, 638 P.2d 549 (Wash. 1981) (suggesting not).

not true in *Midkiff*. So when the holdings in *Midkiff* and *Berman* are combined, a municipality might condemn a general scheme of private, residential only, restrictive covenants in a subdivision in order to permit its downtown area to expand more easily.

[1] Later Developments.

Some state courts have refused to go along with the holdings in *Berman*[45] and *Midkiff*.[46] Some of these cases have involved parking lots and facilities adjacent to private commercial uses — and operating such facilities is a matter of competing with private activities of a similar nature. Thus, a municipality could not condemn land for a convention center containing rental commercial space and a parking garage that the public had "no fixed and enforceable right to use" and so the condemnation lacked a public purpose.[47] In some of these cases, the private benefit is too widely regarded as a private activity, and in others, the persons benefitted are too prominent to clothe themselves in the mantle of a public purpose. The condemnation of land adjacent to a privately run riverboat casino has also been found to lack a public purpose.[48] And a credit agreement with a private developer that does not guarantee that the public use will be maintained is insufficient justification for a finding of a public purpose for a condemnation.[49] Many of these cases are typically litigated when the municipality proposes to issue municipal bonds whose proceeds will be used to acquire the condemned land, but one recent case held that a statutory right of first refusal given to tenants in a mobile home park to purchase the pad on which their mobile home sat, was an exercise of eminent domain for a private instead of a public purpose.[50]

[C] The *Poletown* Case.

Another important state court opinion on "public use" is *Poletown Neighborhood Council v. City of Detroit*.[51] There, the city[52] proposed to

---

[45] *See Karesh v. City Council of Charleston*, 247 S.E.2d 343 (S.C. 1978) (decided before *Midkiff*); *Baycol, Inc. v. Downtown Dev. Authority*, 315 So. 2d 451 (Fla. 1975) (refusing to authorize condemnation of land for a parking facility).

[46] *See, e.g., Casino Reinvestment Dev. Authority v. Banin*, 727 A.2d 102 (N.J. Super. Ct., Law Div., 1998) (refusing to authorize condemnation of a house owned by an elderly widow for a parking lot adjacent to the Trump Plaza casino), *noted in*, Stephen Jones, *Trumping Eminent Domain Law: An Argument for Strict Scrutiny Analysis under the Public Use Requirement of the Fifth Amendment*, 50 Syra. L. Rev. 285 (2000).

[47] *See Karesh v. City Council of Charleston*, 247 S.E.2d 343 (S.C. 1978).

[48] *See Mayor of Vicksburg v. Thomas*, 645 So. 2d 940 (Miss. 1994).

[49] *See Casino Reinvestment Dev. Authority v. Banin*, 727 A.2d 102 (N.J. Super. Ct., Law Div., 1998).

[50] *See Manufactured Hsg. Communities of Washington v. State of Washington*, 13 P.3d 183 (Wash., *en banc*, 2000).

[51] 304 N.W.2d 455 (Mich. 1981).

[52] In *Poletown*, the Detroit city council, not the state legislature, articulated the public purpose. A local legislative judgment is "conceivably" entitled to less weight than a state legislature's. Even if the city has plenary, home rule powers, it does not have jurisdiction over

condemn what amounted to a whole neighborhood for a new General Motors plant, to be located just inside the city's limits: 465 acres, 3,000 residents' homes, and sixteen churches. The condemning authority was the state Industrial Development Corporation. Reviewing this condemnation, the Michigan Supreme Court held that (1) this condemnation has a public purpose with "clear and significant" public benefits, and (2) because of the presence of clear private benefits as well, it was applying "heightened scrutiny" to identify those benefits to make certain that the public benefit is the predominant one.

The Michigan court acknowledged that the case involved the transfer of property from one private party to another. For many state courts, this alone makes the case problematic.[53] It suggests that the takings clause is not a requirement that property taken be for a public use, but only that when the taking is for a public use, just compensation must be paid. This narrower interpretation of the clause leaves open the possibility that takings for what is ultimately a *private* use, are valid.[54]

The Chrysler Corporation got the same treatment as GM in *City of Detroit v. Vavro*,[55] in which the court again upheld the condemnation of land for an auto plant. This time the opinion was written by Michigan's intermediate appellate court, which expressed its reluctance and distaste for the condemnation: "While we agree with defendants that the use of the power of eminent domain . . . is unconscionable, the doctrine of *stare decisis* constrains us to affirm the trial court."[56] The court also called on its Supreme Court to overrule *Poletown*.[57] Later, the heightened scrutiny announced

a large enough sector of the economy for its council to be representative of its needs. So when legislative authority is not as clear as in *Poletown*, the judicially permissive attitude in this opinion might disappear: the less clear the articulation of the public purpose is, and the less comprehensive and more localized the legislative mandate is, the greater the possibility of heightened scrutiny and a different result.

[53] Two "slippery slope" hypotheticals show some of those problems. (1) Suppose, with the plant established, General Motors receives complaints from neighbors about pollution from it. In response, what about condemning pollution easements over neighboring land in order to immunize the plant from nuisance suits? If the initial condemnation has a public purpose, shouldn't this one be valid too? Granted that, anytime it wants, the legislature can restrict condemnation powers by statute, this condemnation still intrudes on the judicial function in nuisance cases and interference with judicial remedies doesn't come close to involving a public use. (2) Suppose further, once the plant is old and out-dated, it is condemned anew when General Motors proposes to move its operations out of town. This condemnation doesn't develop the local economy, it preserves it, but what's wrong with that? The state's being in the auto manufacturing business is one answer. *See infra*, this Chapter, for a discussion of the *Oakland Raiders* case.

[54] *See* Nathan Sales, *Classical Republicanism and the Fifth Amendment's "Public Use" Requirement*, 49 Duke L. J. 339, 344–349 (1999).

[55] 442 N.W. 2d 730 (Mich. App. Ct. 1989) (in which Chrysler had not entered into a binding agreement with the city ensuring the public purposes' achievement).

[56] *Id.* at 731 (subject to a strong dissent, *id.* at 644–645, noting that: "Any business enterprise produces benefits to society at large. Now that we have authorized local legislative bodies to decide that a different commercial use or industrial use of property will produce greater benefits than its present use, no . . .property is immune from condemnation for the benefit of other private interests that put it to a 'higher' use.").

[57] *Id.* at 732.

in *Poletown*, was used in *City of Center Line v. Chmelko*,[58] to prohibit the condemnation of several small businesses to permit a Japanese auto dealership to expand its operation.[59]

[1] Industrial Parks.

The condemnation of land for municipal industrial parks has been a controversial topic in the law of public use.[60] When the statutory authority for such activity was clear, this alone persuaded many courts. For some not persuaded, express statutory authority to issue municipal bonds to finance such projects, made plain that the legislature considered luring industry to a jurisdiction to be a public purpose. Similarly controversial are state statutes that today authorize a power of condemnation for mining and natural resource extraction companies — on the theory that the development of such resources is a public benefit.[61]

[D] The *Oakland Raiders* Case.

City of Oakland v. Oakland Raiders[62] held that the defendant, attempting to move its football franchise to Southern California, was not entitled to summary judgment on the question of a public purpose for the franchise's proposed condemnation by the city. If the city could condemn park-land, own and operate the stadium in which the Raiders played their games, it could condemn the team's franchise as well. The team was first franchised in Oakland and played there for 20 years before moving out. Isn't it possible to say that the franchise is what it is and owes its value to the city and to its fans?[63] Tempting as it is to answer the question affirmatively, the court's substantive holding was limited. There is nothing, it said, in the takings clause that would prevent its application to intangible personal property such as a franchise; the clause does not distinguish between real and personal, or tangible and intangible property — and all of these categories of property are subject to being taken by the exercise of eminent domain.[64]

---

[58] 416 N.W. 2d 401 (Mich. App. Ct. 1987).

[59] *See also Wilmington Parking Auth. v. Land with Improvements, Situated in Wilmington, New Castle County*, 521 A.2d 227, 231 (Del. 1986) (citing and quoting *Poletown* and finding no public use in a city condemnation proceeding for land for a parking garage, part of which would be used to permit an adjoining newspaper plant to expand, because the condemnation would not have proceeded without the newspaper company involvement).

[60] *See Hogue v. Port of Seattle*, 341 P.2d 171 (Wash. 1959) (finding no public use).

[61] *See* Nathan Sales, *Classical Republicanism and the Fifth Amendment's "Public Use" Requirement*, 49 Duke L. J. 339, 376–377 (1999) (reviewing the genesis of such statutes).

[62] 646 P.2d 835, 840 (Cal. App. Ct. 1982).

[63] The trial was held, not in Oakland, but in rural Salinas, California, when the team had been the Los Angeles Raiders for two seasons.

[64] The football team's league's charter prohibited the long-term ownership of a franchise by the city, so the court envisioned that upon retransfer to private owners, the public purpose of the condemnation would have to be suitably protected, probably by a covenant in the franchise prohibiting its relocation out of town.

After *Midkiff, Poletown,* and *Oakland Raiders*, there are few limitations left on a legislature's reach under the takings clause. Thus, when a municipal government imposes a rent control ordinance on mobile home parks and a provision of the ordinance requires the owners of such parks to offer tenants of space in a park assignable leases of unlimited duration, such a provision does not lack a public purpose and is not a taking.[65]

Three limiting lines of attack, however, may still be possible in the future: (1) state legislatures may enact legislation limiting the reach of its state constitution's clause; or (2) the courts will narrowly interpret that clause or statutes enacted under it; or (3) they will impose a heightened scrutiny (a higher burden of proof) to show a public use or benefit than is present.

---

[65] *See Yee v. City of Escondido*, 274 Cal. Rptr. 551 (Cal. App. Ct. 1990), *affirmed*, 503 U.S. 519 (1992).

Chapter 3

Types of Takings — Physical and Regulatory Takings

§ 3.01   Physical Takings.

A physical taking is an eminent domain type of taking. It involves the trespass on, invasion of, or occupation by a governmental entity of an owner's private property. Such a taking is referred to as a *per se* or categorical taking.[1] An example occurred in *Loretto v. Teleprompter Manhattan CATV Corp.*[2] There, an apartment house owner in New York City challenged a state statute which permitted a cable television company to place cable television boxes and cables on her property. The boxes took up one and one half cubic feet. The United States Supreme Court held, 6-3, that any governmentally authorized, permanent, and physical occupation or invasion of private property, no matter the governmental benefit and no matter how minor the invasion, requires just compensation — no matter the amount.[3] The holding in *Loretto* shows that, with physical takings, the damage done by the invasive action may be close to nil. For example, the building of a road through vacant land is likely to create more value in the remaining land than is destroyed in the land taken. This does not mean that there is no taking — there is; it just means that the resulting just compensation will be nominal.

"Physical invasion cases are special," and the "holding today is very narrow," Justice Thurgood Marshall wrote for the majority in *Loretto*.[4] He meant what he said: the Supreme Court left the amount of compensation to state courts to determine. Likewise, the court did not decide whether the nominal damages provided satisfied the compensation requirement: the challenged statute permitted "reasonable compensation" and the regulatory agency in charge of cable-television in New York City had concluded that: (1) compensation would in most cases be nominal, one dollar damages; and (2) the landlord benefitted from being able to offer apartments for rent with access to cable.

Justice Marshall justified the majority's holding in four ways. First, it invoked the "historical rule."[5] Historically, he wrote, "our cases uniformly

---

[1] In Chapter 12, *infra*, another type of categorical taking, involving the destruction of all economically beneficial use, will be discussed. In reviewing U. S. Supreme Court takings cases, see Robert Hopperton, *Litigating Regulatory Takings and Other Land Use Cases: An Analytical Framework for Standards of Judicial Review*, available at <www.law.utoledo.edu/faculty/hopperton/lrt/> (visited July 2, 2001).

[2] 458 U.S. 419 (1982).

[3] *Loretto*, 458 U.S. at 441.

[4] *Id.*

[5] The physical invasion rule traces its jurisprudential roots back to *Pumpelly v. Green Bay*

23

have found a taking to the extent of the occupation, without regard to whether the action achieves an important public benefit or has only minimal economic impact on the owner."[6] Two fundamental rules can be drawn from this statement: (1) the magnitude of, or the necessity for, the public use is not to be balanced against the "extent of the occupation" or taking; (2) that little or no just compensation is due, cannot justify not finding a physical taking. Second, this historical rule "has more than tradition to commend it": a physical invasion is "the most serious form of a taking."[7] This is so because the government does not merely take one right out of the bundle of rights held by the owner; rather, "it chops through the bundle, taking a slice of every strand." The government denies *pro tanto* the right of possession, the power to use, and decreases the right to sell that portion of the property occupied.[8] Third, the rule avoids "otherwise difficult line-drawing problems." Its alternative lacks crispness and presents proof and evidentiary problems. And, fourth, it is crisp and simple, and "presents relatively few problems of proof." Thus *Loretto's* rule that "a permanent physical occupation of property is a taking"[9] is justified by (1) the seriousness, permanence, and exclusivity of any physical occupation or invasion, as well as (2) every owner's "historically rooted expectation of compensation," and (3) some notions of judicial economy.

Loretto's three dissenting Justices (Blackmun, writing the dissent, for himself, Brennan and White) thought that the distinction between permanent and temporary occupations will be difficult to draw in practice, and opted instead for a balancing test, weighing the interference with the owner's post-regulation uses against the public benefits flowing from the

---

Company, 80 U.S. 166 (1872) (framing the cause of action as trespass on the case), in which the court found a taking by inverse condemnation when the government built a dam which backed the water of a river up further than expected, so flooding the land of the plaintiff.

[6] *Loretto*, 458 U.S. at 434–435.

[7] Physical invasions are taken so seriously that, even though Mrs. Loretto stipulated that she did not have a use for the space the cable occupied, this stipulation did not effect her case. The regulatory impact of installing the cable along the baseboard on a wall would not affect Mrs. Loretto's claim of physical invasion.

[8] Marshall concludes that all three rights were taken here. This discussion of "rights" is inconsistent with a test used in the Supreme Court's regulatory taking cases — notably in *Penn Central Transportation Company v. City of New York*, 438 U.S. 104 (1978) (upholding historic landmark regulation and so denying an owner the right to lease air rights in which would be built a 55 story office building over Grand Central Terminal, thus denying the owner $1 million a year during construction and $3 million thereafter as the landlord). But Marshall is building a majority of his Court by emphasizing (for those justices who thought *Loretto* should be seen as a regulatory takings case) part of the *Penn Central* rule that finding a taking requires in part a consideration of the "character of the governmental action." Such emphasis in *Penn Central* was intended to get away from an examination of particular "strands" in the "bundle" of property rights.

[9] Definitional questions might be: what is "physical", what is "permanent", and what is an "occupation"? If any one of these is not present, there may be no physical taking. The *Loretto* opinion sets up a word play between a temporary intrusion, resulting in no taking, and a permanent physical occupation, which results in a taking. A "permanent physical invasion" is, for Marshall, an example of a situation in which the "character of the governmental action" (one of the three parts of the *Penn Central* test) proves dispositive and requires a finding of a taking.

regulation.[10] Their focus is on the post regulation, reasonable return available to the owner. The lesson of the dissent is that, for physical takings, the resulting benefit available to the owner is irrelevant.

[A] Criticism and Response.

The *Loretto* majority's holding has been criticized in the following way: other governmental actions, involving million of dollars,[11] but classified as regulatory takings, go uncompensated, while the actions in *Loretto*, involving much less money, require compensation. A starting point in formulating a response to this criticism and to justifying this seemingly unfair comparison, is the idea that the finding of a physical taking does not depend on the degree of invasion,[12] or extent of the injury to private property, or to the percentage decrease in the fair market value. The takings clause is self-executing and does not depend on balancing tests because in that way, the property of the citizenry is best protected from governmental intrusion.[13]

Another way to formulate a response is to put the unflattering comparison in terms of a physical invasion: why is requiring a landlord to install mailboxes in the foyer of an apartment house not a physical taking, while the installation of the cable-TV wires and boxes is a physical taking? The *Loretto* majority's opinion is clear that mailboxes must be provided and other building code requirements met, without having to pay any compensation. This is: (1) because the landlord is there dealing directly with the government, whereas in *Loretto* the government was authorizing occupation by a third party — the cable company, over whom the government does not exercise everyday supervision; and (2) because the mailboxes and building code requirements are to be met before the apartment house gets its occupancy permits — before, in other words, the right to possession arises.

[B] Citations to Other Cases in *Loretto*.

Justice Marshall uses two World War II cases, both finding a taking, but their special wartime situation militates against giving them great weight. Two other cases are more interesting. The *Loretto* opinion distinguished *PruneYard Shopping Center v. Robins*,[14] as involving only a temporary

---

[10] *Loretto*, 458 U.S. at 442–456.

[11] *See, e.g., Penn Central Transportation Company v. City of New York*, 438 U.S. 104 (1978) (discussed, *infra*, in Chapter 4) and *Keystone Bituminous Coal Association v. DeBenedictis*, 480 U.S. 470 (1987) (upholding a state underground mining regulation controlling surface subsidence and so denying affected miners the right to extract 27 million tons of coal).

[12] As we will see in Chapter 4, *infra, Loretto's* holding is a decision to confine Justice Brennan's "whole parcel analysis" in *Penn Central* to regulatory takings, so Justice Marshall does not explain why the whole parcel is the focus of the analysis in *Penn Central*, with another (regulatory) type of taking, while here the occupation of merely a portion of the apartment house results in a taking.

[13] As we will see in Chapter 4, *infra, Loretto's* holding is also a decision to confine Justice Holmes' diminution in value test in *Mahon* to regulatory takings.

[14] 447 U.S. 74 (1980).

intrusion on an owner's property. There, the intrusion was for the purpose of soliciting signatures for a petition to the government in the owner's shopping center. The right to petition the government is protected by the First Amendment to the U.S. Constitution.[15]

The opinion also relies on *Kaiser Aetna v. United States*.[16] This case involved a Hawaii marina development. The developer asked the Army Corps of Engineers if a navigational servitude[17] would be imposed once a non-navigable lagoon was dredged, connected to navigable water, and improved with boat slips. The Corps said no. Once the development was completed, the Corps changed its mind and imposed the servitude. The Supreme Court found that the Corps had extracted a right for which compensation should have been paid and its belated assertion of the servitude was a *de facto* taking, taking advantage of the marina owner's improvements to the waterway and defeating his investment-backed expectations.[18] Marshall characterizes the servitude as "not being a permanent occupation of land," but, even though the public's right was only one of passage, it was permanent from the time it was asserted by the Corps. While Marshall, as previously discussed, recognizes the right to possess, use, and dispose of property, and finds each affected, his discussion of *Kaiser Aetna* reveals that he sees *Loretto* as involving the right to exclude in particular. He calls this right "one of the most essential sticks on the bundle of rights that are commonly characterized as property" and "one of the most treasured strands in an owner's bundle of property rights."[19] Its deprivation denies an owner control over the property's use, and even though legal title is retained, is likely to "empty" the legal title of value.

[C] Personal Property and the *Loretto* Rule.

As is true in state takings law, the *per se* rule of *Loretto* extends to personal property. Personalty is in some ways more easily subject to a permanent physical seizure than is land, is more easily concealed from its owner after the fact, and so is deserving of protection on these accounts.[20] Moreover, in the context of a permanent physical occupation of land, seizing items within the improvements on the land, although these items are not technically fixtures and so remain personal property, should also be compensable. However, prior to *Loretto*, another case held that the right

---

[15] *But see Judlo, Inc. v. Vons Companies, Inc.*, 259 Cal. Rptr. 624, 626 (Cal. App. Ct. 1989), *rev. denied*, 1989 Cal. LEXIS 2820 (Cal., Sept. 6, 1989) (holding that a shopping center tenant did not create a public forum by permitting news-racks in the front of its grocery store within the center; that the store owner had no constitutional duty to permit publisher to place rack there; and that the issuance of an injunction requiring it to do so was a taking, citing *Loretto*.)

[16] 444 U.S. 164 (1979).

[17] This is an easement of passage for the public over navigable waters, even though the bed of the waterway is owned by private persons.

[18] *Loretto*, 458 U.S. at 393.

[19] *Id.* at 635.

[20] *See Nixon v. United States*, 978 F. 2d 1269 (D.C. Cir. 1992) (applying the *Loretto* doctrine to a federal statute asserting governmental control over President Nixon's presidential papers).

to alienate or sell personal property is not equally protected.[21] Thus, the right to protect possession and to exclude appear essential rights of property, with specially high protections. It is an open, much debated, question whether *Loretto* overrules or weakens the precedential value of *Allard*.

Governmental regulations protecting wildlife roaming from public wildlife refuges onto private lands where they kill domestic animals like sheep and cattle, do not work a physical taking.[22] In general, physically invasive actions of government are not limited to its employees and agents, but may also extend to those acting under the authority of its regulations.[23] The protected wildlife are not acting in any such capacity. Moreover, the statutes in *Loretto* involved governmental monopolies and so placed special responsibilities on the cable operators. Even if the governmentally protected wild horses and burros ate the grass on a rancher's pastures, so that a rancher's sheep had little to eat, forcing the rancher to provide forage for them, there would, even then, be no physical invasion.[24]

[D]   The Aftermath of the Case.

In 1988, rejecting Mrs. Loretto's application for attorneys' fees, a New York court called the finding of a taking "of purely academic interest" because the just compensation requirement of the U.S. Constitution would provide little more than the statutory requirement in place for reasonable compensation. The judge suggested that one dollar would suffice in most cases.[25]

In response to *Loretto*, several state statutes provide for provision of reasonable compensation for cable access to multi-unit apartment houses.[26] Another statute provides the cable company with access for a nominal sum, but permit the apartment house owner to sue for additional compensation

---

[21] *See Andrus v. Allard*, 444 U.S. 51, 65–66 (1979) (holding that there is no taking in this situation because the right to possess, transport, devise, and donate the artifacts is unaffected and there is "no physical property restriction" and involving, in order to protect endangered and migrating wildlife, a prohibition on the sale of bird artifacts, such as feathers, and a trader in such artifacts protesting that his feathers were acquired before the prohibition, claiming that the prohibition is a taking).

[22] *See Christy v. Hodel*, 857 F.2d 1324 (9th Cir. 1988).

[23] *State of Ohio ex rel Jenkins v. Division of Wildlife, Dept. of Natural Resources*, slip opinion (Ohio App., Franklin County, Oct. 10, 1978) (involving an owner that has land adjacent to a state forest, in which the wildlife is protected from trapping and hunting and in which beavers built a dam along a stream, the dam causing the stream's water to back up onto the owner's land, flooding a large portion of it; owner sued the state, claiming a taking of his property). A *Loretto*, permanent physical invasion is not present: the beavers are not the agents of the state.

[24] *See Clajon Production Corp. v. Petera*, 854 F. Supp. 843, 852–853 (D. Wyo. 1994); *Mountain States Legal Foundation v. Hodel*, 799 F.2d 1423 (10th Cir. 1986).

[25] *Loretto v. Group W. Cable,* 522 N.Y.S.2d 543, 545–546 (N.Y. App. Div. 1987), *cert. denied,* 488 U.S. 827 (1988).

[26] *See, e.g.,* Nev. Rev. Stat. Ann. § 711.255 (Michie Supp. 1989) (providing for a rebuttable presumption that access is worth $1 a unit, or $1,000, whichever is greater).

and if successful, to collect costs and attorneys' fees as well.[27] Another permits a local government to authorize a cable company to exercise the power of eminent domain.[28] In Michigan, the courts have held that a cable company is a public utility and therefore entitled to exercise the eminent domain power on that account.

Also in response to *Loretto*, the Congress deleted a mandatory access provision to a federal communications statute and an accompanying compensation requirement — indicating that Congress did not intend to confer condemnation powers on cable companies.[29]

[E]   Utility Easements.

If within a residential subdivision or a condominium regime, a developer dedicates a utility easement and subsequently a cable company attempts to route its wires along the easement, courts have divided on the issue of whether *Loretto* compensation is paid to the developer or the utility.[30] On the one hand, the landowner may be seen as giving up the right of way, but, on the other hand, the physical occupation of the easement's space is for a purpose unintended at the time of the dedication and arguably a per se physical invasion. If the utility easement uses poles owned by a utility, *Loretto* requires compensation to the owner of the pole for its use, although rent for attaching the cable to the pole can be set by regulation at considerably less than market rates.[31]

§ 3.02   *Yee* Limits on *Loretto's* Categorical Rules.

Yee v. City of Escondido,[32] decided a decade later in 1992, indicated that *Loretto's* holding was not as elastic as some had thought. The petitioner, John Yee, was the owner of a mobile home park and the landlord of the "pad" on which the homes sat. In 1988, the City of Escondido enacted a rental control ordinance limiting the amount by which a mobile home park landlord could raise the rents, even upon the transfer of the mobile home on the pad. Park owners were required to accept their new tenants at controlled rents. In addition, a state statute required that the park owner could not require the removal of a mobile home from the pad upon its sale or transfer. Yee sued the city.

Yee alleged that the combined effect of this ordinance and statute was to increase the amount for which mobile homes sold (reflecting the lower

---

[27] *E.g.,* Me. Rev. Stat. Ann., tit. 14, § 6041 (Supp. 1988).

[28] Ill. Ann. Stat. ch. 24, para. 11-42-11(c) (Smith-Hurd 1988).

[29] *See Cable Associates v. Town & Country Management Corporation,* 709 F. Supp. 582, 585–586 (E.D.Pa. 1989).

[30] J. G. Howard, *Real Property Issues in CATV Use of Public Rights-of-Way and Easements Dedicated for Compatible Use,* 23 Real Prop. Prob.& Tr. J. 413, 423–427 (1991) (collecting the cases).

[31] *Federal Communications Commission v. Florida Power Corporation,* 480 U.S. 245, 253–254 (1987).

[32] 503 U.S. 519 (1992) (O'Connor, J., writing for the majority).

rent on the pad), thus enabling the tenants to capture the value of living in a rent-controlled park. This premium price showed that the purpose of rent control, to supply affordable housing, was not being accomplished by the ordinance. What was accomplished, he said, was a transfer of a benefit from the landlord to the tenant, while the ordinance was not, under *Nollan v. California Coastal Comm'n*,[33] "substantially advancing a legitimate state interest." At the time, between 1987 and 1992, some suspected *Nollan* was a physical invasion case,[34] so it is easy to see why, in a further pleading, Yee alleged that the effect of the regulation amounted to a physical taking of his property. The United States Supreme Court held that the effect was not a physical taking. The park owner voluntarily invited the original mobile home owner onto the pad, so the right to exclude was not affected. No physical, categorical, *Loretto*-like taking was involved.

The Court recognized that neither the issue of a regulatory taking, nor the issue of a physical taking, is subsidiary to the other: "they exist side by side, neither encompassing the other."[35] Petitioner had asked whether the state courts below erred in ignoring the applicability of cases, from two federal circuits, involving physical takings and holding that a physical taking was involved in similar settings.[36]

The Court's answer was that California's state courts had not erred. The "government effects a physical taking only when it requires the landowner to submit to the physical occupation of his land."[37] The Yees voluntarily opened a mobile home park on their land, and voluntarily stayed in business, and the rent-control ordinance and the state statute did not require that they stay in business, "no government has required any physical invasion of petitioners' property." End of case.[38] In the final analysis,

---

[33] 483 U.S. 825 (1987), discussed *infra*, Chapter 14.

[34] *Nollan v. California Coastal Commission*, 483 U.S. 825 (1987). In the process of garnering a majority of the court, Justice Scalia in *Lucas v. South Carolina Coastal Council*, 505 U.S. 1003 (1992), had to explain that *Nollan* was not a physical invasion case; instead, it was the deprivation of a well-recognized right, an easement of access, over a beachfront parcel. This uncertainty was prolonged by *Hall v. City of Santa Barbara*, 813 F.2d 198 (9th Cir. 1986), *modified*, 833 F.2d 1270 (9th Cir. 1987) (suggesting that a mobile home ordinance might be a physical occupation), *cert denied*, 485 U.S. 940 (1988). *See also Seawall Associates v. City of New York*, 542 N.E. 2d 1059 (N.Y. 1989) (holding that a five-year moratorium on the conversion, alteration, or demolition of single-room occupancy housing and that a statute requiring that the owner restore all such housing to habitable condition and lease it at controlled rents for an indefinite period, resulted in a physical, per se, taking of property and was compensable).

[35] *Yee*, 503 U.S. at 537 (language following Justice Scalia's logic in *Lucas*, discussed *infra*, Chapter 12).

[36] This lesson in Supreme Court pleading leaves the regulatory taking issue open, perhaps as a warning to government attorneys that someday the Court might consider benefit-shifting regulations to be a regulatory taking under a *Penn Central* analysis.

[37] *Yee*, 503 at 527.

[38] On occasion, a state court decides differently. *See Lee Cty. v. Kiesel*, 705 So. 2d 1013 (Fla. App. Ct. 1998) (recognizing a physical invasion of a riparian right to view a river, the view being blocked by the construction of a state bridge), *noted at* 109 Yale L. J. 849 (2000).

the Court used the final section of *Yee* to emphasize the separateness of the type of (physical) taking found in *Loretto*.[39]

[A] *Loretto* and *Yee* Combined.

Conflicts between the results in *Loretto* and *Yee* are often found in the context of the reform of the telecommunications industry currently underway. In one case, a state public utility commission required that a telephone company install the electronic data transmission equipment — software and data — used by another phone company. Authorized by statute, the commission's joint location requirement is a legislative judgment entitled to judicial deference, is reasonable, and substantially advances the state's interests. However beneficial to consumers it might be, *Loretto* still suggests that there has been a physical taking. However, the holding in *Yee v. City of Escondido* that a regulation giving mobile home park residents a right to transfer their occupancy of the mobile home pad at a controlled rent was not a physical invasion of the park owner's property, suggests also that the utility commission will argue that it minimized and limited *Loretto's* focus on physical occupancy.

Limitations on *Loretto* do not overrule it, so its core concern with physical invasion, present here, disposes of this case. The invasion here has the same permanence that appeared important in *Loretto*. Likewise, *Yee* is distinguishable: the mobile home park ordinance in *Yee* was a regulation, not a direct invasion of the property — city officials did not appropriate the mobile home pad. So the presence of the electronic data transmission company's equipment on the telephone company's premises looks more like the intrusion of the cable lines in *Loretto* than a regulatory exaction.[40] Similarly, the company's property might be seen as their operating certificate; once granted by the state, the state commission does not have the right to add a condition to it.

§ 3.03 Regulatory Takings.

A physical taking occurs when the government takes and occupies property. A regulatory taking is the result of the government regulating a property's use in a way that unreasonably diminishes its value without physically occupying it. Neither type of taking is derivative of the other — each is a separate and distinct type of taking.

---

[39] Rejecting any review of *Yee* as a regulatory takings case, the Court cited its own rule of procedure: Rule 14.1(a) states that "only the questions set forth in the opinion [appealed], or fairly included therein, will be considered by the Court." The physical taking issue was both included in the opinion below and presented in the petition for review. The regulatory taking issue was not in the opinion below and was not, the Court held, "fairly included" within it. The theory of notice pleading, as well as the Court's reluctance to rule on a matter not fully briefed and litigated below, also counseled against ruling on a regulatory takings issue. "In fact, were we to address the issue here, we would apparently be the first court in the Nation to determine whether an ordinance like this one effects a regulatory taking." No thanks, said the Court.

[40] *See GTE Northwest, Inc. v. Public Utility Comm'n of Oregon*, 900 P. 2d 495 (Or. App. Ct. 1994).

[A]   Early Nuisance Abatement Cases.

In English law, since at least the 12ᵗʰ century, no landowner has had the right to operate or conduct a public nuisance on his or her land and the legislature has had the right to abate such a nuisance. When it did so, American case law on takings in the 19ᵗʰ and early 20ᵗʰ centuries show landowners seeking compensation for the results of governmental abatement actions, losing their cases. In *Mugler v. Kansas*,[41] a brewer contested the validity, under the takings clause, of a statute prohibiting the manufacture of alcoholic beverages to be sold within the State of Kansas. The statute was upheld and the brewer was held not to have suffered a compensable taking of his property, even though his brewery was essentially worthless because of the statutory prohibition.

Again, in *Hadacheck v. Sebastian*,[42] the City of Los Angeles enacted an ordinance prohibiting the manufacture of bricks within its city limits. The Court upheld the ordinance just because it was within the city's legislative authority; it abated a public nuisance and this purpose was held to render the ordinance valid, even if it at the same time had a severe impact on the fair market value of the owner's property.[43] The severity of that impact did not matter. So long as the legislature stayed within the bounds of the police power, compensation was not due because the diminution in fair market value was the result of a proper regulation.

Both of these two cases have precedential value only when the legislature declares that a particular use of property is a public nuisance, but once this occurs, the judicial finding of legislative authority for the regulation immunizes it from being a taking. The legislation was absolutely bullet-proofed against a regulatory taking claim, at least until Justice Holmes reformulated the law of takings in his 1922 majority opinion in *Pennsylvania Coal Co. v. Mahon*.[44] However, it took time, a great deal of time, to recognize the implications of what Holmes had done, so the nuisance abatement line of case survived *Pennsylvania Coal*.[45] By the 1920s, when a legislature was not abating a nuisance, it was instead regulating uses and activities that did not amount to a nuisance. Regulation could nonetheless be heavy-handed and substantially affect property values, as Congress and state legislatures had sought to regulate many land uses. In the face of this activism, Justice Holmes thought that a new approach to takings law was necessary.

There are several tests for determining when a regulatory taking has occurred. Two of the most frequently used are (1) the diminution in value

---

[41] 123 U.S. 623 (1887).

[42] 239 U.S. 394 (1915).

[43] The record had evidence that the fair market value of the property was reduced by 93%.

[44] 260 U.S. 393 (1922).

[45] *See Miller v. Schoene*, 276 U.S. 272, 279–280 (1928) (finding no taking when a state regulation required owners to cut down red cedar trees harboring a virus killing local apple trees and noting that the legislative judgment, here preferring ownership of apples over cedars, is one of the "distinguishing characteristics of every exercise of the police power," Justice Holmes voting with the court's majority).

test, and (2) the public benefits/private injury test. Both are discussed in the following, 1922 opinion by Justice Holmes.

§ 3.04 *Pennsylvania Coal Co. v. Mahon.*

This case held that a state statute requiring a coal mining company to support the surface above its mines is unconstitutional when the company holds a pre-existing waiver of a right to such support from the surface owner; it is a violation of the Fifth Amendment's taking clause.

[A] The Facts.

This case is set in Pennsylvania's anthracite coal fields. In 1878, 43 years before the case reached the United States Supreme Court, Mr. and Mrs. Mahon[46] first held a surface estate to land which they long thereafter used for a residence. What they did not purchase was the coal company's subsurface mineral estate. It had earlier been severed from their surface estate; neither did they purchase the right to have their surface supported from below. This right to support was also held by the company. In Pennsylvania this right is known as the third estate — the right to the surface, and the right to mine, being the first two. Once notified that the company was about to start mining under their surface, the Mahons sued to enjoin the company from mining their subsurface.[47]

At the time the surface was sold, the risk of the surface caving in or subsiding was low. Coal companies then removed about two-thirds of the subsurface coal and left pillars of coal to support the surface, using the "room and pillar" method of mining. Later however, the original mining companies sold their holdings to scavenger companies. Technology also improved, so a larger percentage of the coal could safely be mined. Meanwhile, the surface population increased in the Mahons' neighborhood and a large portion of the surface verged on collapse.

"Government could hardly go on," Holmes wrote in introducing his two takings tests in this opinion, "if to some extent values incident to property could not be diminished without paying for every such change in the general law."[48] These are famous words.[49] They require both a presumption of validity for land use regulations as well as a first tier rational basis

---

[46] Mr. Mahon was an attorney.

[47] This made for an unusual takings case. The usual plaintiff in such cases is the owner whose property is harmed by the government. Here the state (Pennsylvania) is attempting to protect the plaintiff's surface rights and it is the defendant company whose property was harmed, allegedly to the point of a taking. Moreover, the company was seeking neither compensation nor any other affirmative relief. It just wanted the regulations to go away.

[48] *Mahon*, 260 U.S. at 413.

[49] Holmes was past 80 when he wrote them, eager to do the work assigned by the new Chief Justice, William Howard Taft, and at the same time was picking up the threads of a long-term friendship with Justice Brandeis, recently appointed to the Supreme Court and the dissenting Justice in the case. *See* Shelton Novick, *Honorable Justice: The Life of Oliver Wendell Holmes* 343–345 (1989).

standard of judicial review, applied occasionally (as here) with a rigor sufficient to overturn legislation.

[B] Diminution in Value.

"In the field of land use regulation, the emphasis which Justice Holmes placed on the degree of value diminution suffered by the property owner has continued to be the central focus of modern case law on the subject."[50] This "diminution in value" test is measured by the value of the plaintiff's property.[51] Recent cases have used this test.[52] However, figuring out which unit of property to measure is another question.

[C] Balancing Public Benefits against Private Injuries.

In the very next paragraph of his opinion, Holmes presents a second, very different test. This is the public benefit/private injury balance. This is the test which he intends to be dispositive — it has certainly proven to be the most influential over the long term.[53]

It is not always easy to apply. Public benefits are often held very diffusely. In this test, however, they must be weighed against private injury that is often severe and specific. The resulting comparison is like weighing apples and oranges. Moreover, a very great private injury may be outweighed by a greater public benefit, but the test makes no provision for defining a point at which the absolute enormity of the private injury controls. This can result in unfairness.

If *Mahon's* legal backdrop is *Mugler* or *Hadacheck*, then *Mahon* is a departure from precedent.[54] Holmes' opinion for the majority said that the Kohler Act is not a safety measure: notice to the Mahons to get out in advance of mining would, Holmes said, protect their safety. Nor was the safety of the miners the state's concern: restrictions on mining methods could accomplish that end, he said. The surface itself was not protected:

---

[50] *Skaw v. United States*, 740 F.2d 932, 939 (Ct.Cl. 1984) (citing *Mahon*).

[51] Holmes had no definite idea of what degree of diminution was necessary; he only felt that when "positive law" (his era's term for a statute) upset an owner's expectations as to what he owns too violently, it went "too far" and required compensation. *See Commonwealth v. Parks*, 30 N. E. 174 (Mass.1892) (Holmes, J.) (a Holmes opinion structured much like *Mahon*); Robert Brauneis, *The Foundation of our "Regulatory Takings" Jurisprudence: the Myth and Meaning of Justice Holmes's Opinion in Pennsylvania Coal Co. v. Mahon*, 106 Yale L. J. 613 (1996).

[52] *See Ruckelshaus v. Monsanto Company*, 467 U.S. 986, 1003–1004 (1984) (holding that public disclosure of business data by the EPA under assurance of confidentiality constitutes a taking).

[53] Its effects can be seen in the majority opinion in *Penn Central Transportation Co. v. City of New York*, 438 U.S. 104 (1978), and again in the majority opinion in *Keystone Bituminous Coal Ass'n v. DeBenedictis*, 480 U.S. 470 (1987), discussed *infra*, this Chapter.

[54] Holmes later wrote a friend: "I have always thought that old Harlan's decision in *Mugler* was pretty fishy. Letter of O.W. Holmes, Jr. to H. Laski, 1 *Holmes-Laski Letters* 346 (Mark deW. Howe, ed., 1963). What's "pretty fishy" about *Mugler* is either that it is hard to believe that the brewery in that case is worth nothing after Kansas went dry, or that the legislature thought in terms of Mr. Mugler's brewery being a public nuisance.

when the surface and the mineral estate were in the same hands, the Act did not apply. The company could destroy, for example, any surface farmlands which it owned. Thus, Holmes found no public purpose or benefit of the type that the state was entitled to seek.

That said, Holmes turned to the specifics of the case: "This is the case of a single private house."[55] This is akin to saying that the Mahons knew what rights and estates they were buying and, more importantly, what they weren't buying. They purchased their home with eyes wide open, but were now receiving an additional right via the Act, thus redoing their original deal. No right that they possessed was interfered with, because they only held the thin crust of the earth's surface. The government was not intruding on that, and the taking was not a physical one, vis a vis the Mahons. Instead, the intrusion was on the coal company's rights. It had purchased the right of support and the Act prevented them from exercising it.

So Holmes thought that the state was not just choosing to elevate one person's property right over another's. If that were all it was doing, then the "government could hardly go on" language would resolve the case in the Mahons' favor.[56] No, Holmes thought instead that the Act had permitted the Mahons and others to redo their bargain in purchasing the surface, by successfully lobbying the legislature, and he saw no "public benefit" (as previously discussed) in the legislative response to that lobbying. The Coal Company simply was not treated fairly and equally by the Act.

Justice Brandeis' dissenting opinion[57] viewed the Kohler Act as a public safety measure.[58] He said that the purpose of the Act does not cease to be public because some private citizens benefit thereby. If it were otherwise, much legislation would be stymied as a result. In addition, Brandeis said, the coal regulated by the Kohler Act "may be negligible as compared with the value of the whole property." (That is, the private injury may be

---

[55] Holmes was exaggerating. The paragraph for which this statement is the topic sentence was originally the whole of a first draft for this opinion. Chief Justice Taft read the draft and wrote Holmes a letter expressing the opinion that the Kohler Act was unconstitutional. After receipt of the letter, Holmes added the rest of the opinion (presumably to gather a majority). J. Dimento, *Mining the Archives of Pennsylvania Coal: Heaps of Constitutional Mischief*, 11 J. Leg. Hist. 396, 407 (1990).

[56] Holmes' attitude toward legislatures was often one of judicial restraint. If the dispute in *Mahon* had been between a farmer using the surface profitably and a miner causing sinkholes on otherwise good agricultural land, Holmes may have conceded that the legislature could decide that some of the coal needs to be left in place in order to save the farmland above. If in a Western state the legislature decided to save farmland or pasturage from surface mining, Holmes would probably not have stood in its way. This deference to legislatures stemmed not from a belief that they were wise, or always right, but from his realization that, as a practical matter, every decision they make, gives a benefit or an advantage to some portion of society, and by the same token, disadvantages another portion. Hence the "government could hardly go on" language.

[57] Because Holmes and Brandeis have been famously paired in their dissents in the Contract Clause cases early in the twentieth century, you might wonder about their disagreement in *Mahon*. As to Holmes, it might be said that he saw a textual warrant in the Constitution for what he wrote here, but saw nothing similar in the Contract Clause cases.

[58] Brandeis privately attributed Holmes' decision to old age and class bias. Philippa Strumm, *Louis D. Brandeis* 313 (1984).

negligible in comparison with the public benefit achieved, or the diminution in value a relative matter.)

Holmes resolved the case in a single paragraph, but his opinion did not stop there. Holmes had circulated the first draft of the opinion, containing its single paragraph of analysis. Chief Justice Taft objected, not to the draft so far, but saying that more was needed in view of the *amicus* briefs filed and the interests of the state involved, not directly through the two private parties litigating, but indirectly. So Holmes wrote the remainder of the opinion as it was handed down, and continues in the manner of an "advisory opinion."[59] This portion of the opinion may technically be *dicta*, but it contains the opinion's most quotable material. Three aspects of this second portion of Holmes' opinion are worth high-lighting.

[1] The Property.

Holmes first recognizes that the takings clause may be violated, not just by a taking of a person's title to property, but also by a taking of the value in using it, here by mining the coal in it. He is not concerned just with the "thing-ness" of property, but with the value in its use, that it may be "exercised with profit" and in a "commercially practical" manner. Underlying this idea of property is the "bundle of sticks" view of property — the support estate being one of the sticks missing from the Mahons' bundle originally, but impermissibly restored by the legislation under review.

An up-to-date example of a *Mahon* type taking involves information rights. The common law says that the holder of mineral rights has the exclusive power to explore and develop them (known as the exploration right). The state's Geological Survey, a state agency, conducts a seismic survey of a region including an owner's mineral properties and releases geologic data showing that there are no minerals within the owner's boundaries. If the third estate is a recognized property right in *Mahon*, then the exploration right should have the same status — Holmes' definition of property can dis-aggregate the property into various sticks in the bundle of property rights, and when a stick is deprived of all its value, then there is a taking. Clearly, the state has an interest in knowing what minerals lie within its jurisdiction, but that only means that the seismic survey was a valid exercise of state power. The interest at issue is an informational one, and information has value when released to the public. Release prevents the owner from capitalizing on the information, even information about the absence of minerals. The state has made exploring for minerals "commercially impractical" in Holmes' words so a taking has arguably occurred.[60]

---

[59] The phrase is Justice Steven's in *Keystone*, discussed in this Chapter, *infra*.

[60] For another discussion of this problem, in light of a later Supreme Court opinion, *see infra*, Chapter 12, discussing *Lucas v. South Carolina Coastal Commission*, 505 U.S. 1003 (1992).

[2] Reciprocity of Advantage.

A good way to distinguish Holmes' and Brandeis' approaches to analyzing the case is to look at Holmes' discussion of the idea that a statute regulating the mines might be justified by its "reciprocity of advantage" — that is, by the idea that the mining company whose workplace was regulated by health and safety measures got healthy employees in return. Holmes dealt with this idea in the second, or advisory portion of his majority opinion. He thought that every statute was to be examined separately to determine whether regulations were reciprocated by conferring some benefit on the employer. On the other hand, Brandeis thought that a regulation might be justified when it provided "the advantage of living and doing business in a civilized community" — by, in other words, a very generalized idea of reciprocity.[61] His idea of a proper reciprocity of advantage goes beyond each statute evaluated by the courts.[62] There was no room, thought Brandeis, for considering Holmes' narrow version of reciprocity of advantage, except that of acceptance of the regulation in exchange for "the advantage of living and doing business in a civilized community."

Holmes next paragraph, starting with "the rights of the public in a street" hypothesized that if the legislature "have been so short sighted as to acquire only the surface rights without the right of support" for the street, the legislature should not thereafter, once the street is recognized as a public use, be able to acquire the support right by regulation when the takings clause required compensation.[63] This would be a bad faith attempt by the legislature to do "on the cheap" what it should pay for. Since there is, however, no evidence in the case of legislative bad faith, this paragraph presents a weak argument.

[3] A Regulation that "Goes Too Far."

The closest that Holmes comes to stating a general rule for the *Mahon* case appears (like the discussion of reciprocity of advantage) in the second portion of his opinion. There he states: "The general rule is that, while property may be regulated to a certain extent, if regulation goes too far it will be recognized as a taking." Too far beyond what? We are not told: the line between regulation and taking is not defined, nor are criteria for identifying that line given. In another context, a person might say that "citizens are supposed to be good, but when they are not good enough, they are bad — and the worst of the bad people are criminals." Any criminal defense lawyer might object to this as a rule of law. However, Holmes is not proposing the same type of rule for takings cases. What he means is

---

[61] *Mahon*, 260 U.S. at 422.

[62] Brandeis' general reciprocity is a theme taken up by Justice Stevens 65 years later, writing for the majority of the United States Supreme Court in the *Keystone Bituminous Coal Ass'n v. DeBenedictis*, 480 U.S. 470, 491–492, discussed in the next Chapter: "one of the state's primary ways of preserving the public weal is restricting the uses individuals can make of their property. While each of us is burdened by such restrictions, we, in turn, benefit greatly from the restrictions that are placed on others."

[63] *Mahon*, 260 U.S. at 415.

that the Pennsylvania legislature moved too fast or abruptly, unsettling the Coal Company's (and the Mahons') expectations about the deal they had struck when the Mahons took the deed to the surface without either the coal or the support right. You might think of this deal as the Mahons' agreement not to sue the company in either nuisance or trespass for unsettling the surface of the land on which their house stood. Holmes' talk of a taking at the end of this sentence may likewise be taken in the context of the case — that is, a case in which the Fifth Amendment takings clause and its due process clause is made applicable to the states through the due process clause of the Fourteenth Amendment. Thus, there is reason to see *Mahon* as both a takings and a due process case. In the first portion of the opinion, the "this is the case of a single private house" paragraph, Holmes finds a violation of the due process clause, and in the latter portion of the opinion, he finds a violation of the takings clause.

[D] Takings Jurisprudence.

The second, advisory portion of Holmes' opinion contains the "too far" language previously quoted. This language is often taken to mean that the two clauses of the Fifth Amendment — the due process and the takings clause — are co-equal and on a continuum. A regulation which goes too far also offends the takings clause. So the reach and scope of the police power in the due process clause is limited by the clause following.

Another view is that Holmes synthesizes the two clauses in the Fifth Amendment: the due process clause is the place to which the courts look to determine whether a regulation works a taking; if so, then the takings clause is remedial: it provides the remedy of just compensation, as determined by the courts.

The relationship between the two clauses is crucial. If a regulation does provide due process and satisfies the tests for constitutionality under that clause, a litigant after *Mahon* remains free to challenge it again, under the takings clause. Concurrently, evidence of a denial of due process, becomes evidence of a taking.

[E] The Natural State Exception.

One of the most interesting ancillary rules to develop from *Mahon's* discussion of a taking is the holding of *Just v. Marinette County*.[64] There a shorelands zoning ordinance prevented the filling of wetlands without a permit. Because the county ordinance, enacted under a state-wide program of shoreline protection, was in furtherance of a pre-existing public right — the state's public trust doctrine — and preserved the property zoned in its natural state, its enactment is not a taking. The ordinance did not create a public benefit (that would require just compensation) where none had existed previously, it preserved a public right and protected the resource held in that trust. This distinction owes much to a formulation first made

---

[64] 201 N.W. 2d 761 (Wis. 1972), *noted at* 86 Harv. L. Rev. 1582 (1973).

at the turn of the 20th century, between a prevention of a harm to the public (no compensation required), as opposed to the extraction of a public benefit (just compensation required).[65]

In *Just*, the preservation of a natural use was held not to be a taking. Like the Mahons, the Justs purchased their land subject to a preexisting right, although here the burden on their fee was not in their deed. For Holmes, that might have made a difference: Holmes' distaste with attempting to redo a private bargain in the legislature may have motivated his opinion and his disagreement with Justice Brandeis. As to defining the "natural use," the court in *Just* regards forestry as a natural use of land.[66] Today it is best to regard the land protected in *Just* as riparian or littoral forest land, protecting wetlands.[67] Preserving this land in its natural state may be a governmental purpose satisfying the public use requirement of the takings clause,[68] but such preservation may still require that compensation be paid in some circumstances.[69]

[F]   The Police Power, Nuisances, and *Mahon*.

The *Mugler-Hadacheck* line of cases, discussed earlier in this Chapter, continues well past *Mahon*. Its first use after 1922 is found in *Miller v. Schoene*[70] in 1928. The *Miller* opinion said: "When forced to such a choice (choosing between ordering the destruction of cedar trees harboring a pest that also liked to kill apple trees, in a region of the state full of apple orchards), the state does not exceed its constitutional powers by deciding upon the destruction of one class of property in order to save another which, in the judgment of the legislature, is of greater value to the public."[71] This is a statement applying Holmes' "government could hardly go on" language. Holmes joined the majority opinion in *Miller*,[72] so Holmes didn't view his opinion in *Mahon* as establishing the exclusive method of analysis for takings cases. For him it remained more obnoxious to run a brickyard in a city (as in *Hadacheck*) than to attempt to undermine that city, as the coal company was about to do in *Mahon*.

---

[65] *But see Lemp v. Town Bd. of the Town of Islip*, 394 N.Y. S. 2d 517, 521 (N.Y. Sup. Ct., Special Term, 1977) (rejecting *Just* and invalidating a ordinance prohibiting the construction on a dune on the beach as applied to petitioner's land).

[66] For a case with a similar theory, see *Potomac Sand and Gravel Co. v. Maryland*, 293 A.2d 241 (Md. 1972) (finding that the preservation of natural resources is a valid public purpose under the police power).

[67] *See, e.g.*, Alan Flenner, *Municipal Riparian Buffer Regulations in Pennsylvania — Confronting the Regulatory Takings Doctrine*, 7 Dick. J. Env. L. Pol. 207 (1998) (discussing the protection of riparian forest land by excluding development thereon).

[68] *See* Scott Wilder, *Tree Preservation Methods: Zoning Regulation vs. Conservation Servitude*, 14 J. Nat. Res. & Envir. L. 253, 254–259 (1998).

[69] *Id.* (suggesting that preservation at the time of subdivision, or reforestation using impact fees are constitutional).

[70] 276 U.S. 272 (1928) (finding no taking in order of state entomologist to cut down ornamental red cedar trees with cedar rust disease fatal to apple trees cultivated in large quantities nearby).

[71] *Id.* at 279.

[72] *Id.* at 279–280.

A second use was in *Goldblatt v. Town of Hempstead*.[73] In this case, the facts established that a sand and gravel pit, into which water was drawn, was amid an otherwise residential community. Here safety concerns seem paramount. The *Goldblatt* opinion assumes that an ordinance must deprive the owner of all reasonable use of a property before a taking will be found. It also holds that the landowner has the burden of proof to establish a taking.

As later chapters will show, this post-1922 line of nuisance cases engendered considerable controversy, and were eventually re-positioned (but not abolished) within the whole of the United States Supreme Court's takings jurisprudence. This re-positioning took place in later cases, particularly *Lucas v. South Carolina Coastal Council*.[74]

[G] Holmes and the *Euclid* Case.

Holmes also signed the majority opinion in*Village of Euclid v. Ambler Realty Co.*[75] There, the court upheld a zoning ordinance when the record showed that the fair market value of the applicant's land was reduced in value between 66% and 75%. In this opinion, the purpose of the zoning ordinance was portrayed as the prevention of development in the village that would locate nuisances side-by-side. The ordinance was held to be a valid exercise of the police power given to the Village by the State of Ohio and as such is not a violation of the Due Process Clause of the Fourteenth Amendment because the ordinance bears a reasonable relationship to the police power — protecting the health, safety, morals, and general welfare of its community. *Euclid*, the court found, was more like *Hadacheck* than *Mahon*. The Village's ordinance was not a regulation going "too far," so no taking.

§ 3.05   *Keystone Bituminous Coal Association v. DeBenedictis*.[76]

This later United States Supreme Court case extensively discussed and re-considered the majority opinion in *Mahon*. Without overruling Holmes' opinion, it undercut *Mahon* and some of the advisory language in the opinion's second part;[77] respect for Justice Holmes and the number of times

---

[73] 369 U.S. 590 (1962) (ordinance requiring a permit to mine sand and gravel below water table had the purpose of protecting health and safety and was not a taking absent evidence that the prohibition of further mining would reduce the value of the property).

[74] 505 U.S. 1003 (1992).

[75] 272 U.S. 365 (1926).

[76] 480 U.S. 470 (1987) (John Paul Stevens, J., writing for the majority). *Keystone* was a 5-4 decision. Two members of the majority (and one dissenter) retired within five years of the decision.

[77] The majority's purpose was to incorporate new jurisprudence into the facts of *Mahon*, without repudiating Holmes' jurisprudence of the Fifth Amendment, and to embrace the ideas of Brandeis' dissenting opinion in *Mahon*.

his opinion had been cited preclude overruling it.[78] It is hardly necessary to state the facts of this case because they are so similar to those in *Mahon*.[79] The statute in *Keystone* required that 50% of the coal be left in place under certain types of buildings in order to prevent surface subsidence. This Subsidence Act was upheld. The buildings protected included public buildings and dwellings not repaired by the mining company causing subsidence.

Keystone's majority opinion provided a three pronged analysis of the Act.[80] First, the court considered the nature of the governmental intrusion. Second, it considered the diminution of value. Third, it considered the degree of interference with the owner's investment-backed expectations.

[A] Distinguishing *Mahon.*

The court distinguishes *Mahon* in four ways. First, it emphasizes the *ad hoc* nature of the tests for a taking — in particular, it states that, in the field of regulatory takings, the balancing of private injury with public benefit is dependent on the circumstances of each case.

Second, the court finds that there is a public benefit associated with the Pennsylvania Subsidence Act that distinguishes it from the Kohler Act. The recent statute applied to all the state's land area, not just the anthracite fields, and not just lands where the title to the coal was severed from the title to the surface. Its concern was with conserving the land surface of the state, in its own right, whether in public or private hands, and whether or not the minerals have been previously severed from the surface of the land. The public benefit thus found is a general one and involves many factors, not just health and safety, but also the conservation of land and the environmental protection of the state's land surface; it is not merely a re-doing of a private transaction, meant to protect private parties. Evaluating this case, Justice Stevens assigned to greater value to environmental protection in the 1980s as opposed to the 1920s. Then, the economic development of the region depended on the continuation of the coal companies ability to mine — while the region was not so dependent on this one industry in the 1980s; many of the mines were by then exhausted and abandoned. This abandonment creates, in turn, problems of locating the parties responsible for mine subsidence.

Third, Holmes' opinion is called "uncharacteristically advisory": Holmes found that the Act was invalid as applied to a particular transaction and particular parties, but went on to invalidate it generally when he did not have to.

---

[78] Carlisle, *The Section 1983 Land Use Case: Justice Stevens and the Hunt for the Taking Quark*, 16 Stet. L. Rev. 565, n. 1 (1987) (reporting that, between 1922 and 1986, *Mahon* was cited 99,732 times).

[79] *Mahon* arose in the anthracite fields of Eastern Pennsylvania and *Keystone* concerned bituminous coal in the Western part of that state.

[80] This analysis was derived from Justice Brennan's test for a taking in *Penn Central Transportation Co. v. City of New York*, 438 U.S. 104 (1978).

Fourth, the court refers to the *Mugler*, *Hadacheck*, and *Goldblatt* line of authority for precedent in abating "nuisance-like activity." The majority cites this line of cases when discussing the takings claim; they are here understood, in the footnotes to the opinion, has representing an instance when the "character of the governmental action" is the predominant consideration in deciding that no taking has occurred.

After defining the public benefit, the court went on to find a minimal impact on private parties — only minimal adverse effect on "investment-backed expectations" in the profitable mining of coal. Thus, the Act's public benefits outweighed the private injury it inflicted.

[B]   Narrowing *Mahon.*

Mahon concerned opening of new portions of an existing mine; here the impact surveyed was on to total amount of coal in existing mines, the coal in place, and the support estate (the coal in the pillars of an existing deep mine). In *Mahon*, Holmes focused exclusively on the coal pillar necessary to prevent subsidence of the surface; here the focus is on the whole coal mine.[81] Justice Stevens said that when a property interest was as a business matter inseparable from other unregulated interests, the regulated interest may not be the sole subject of a takings claim.[82]

Thus, the *Keystone* majority opinion first rejected the definition of property in Holmes' opinion in favor of a review of the profitability of the industry as a whole. Holmes only in passing and in *dicta* assayed the statute in *Mahon* for its effect on the profits of the Pennsylvania Coal Company. There was no showing that the right to mine was made "commercially impractical." Holmes only suggested that it was. Stevens rejected Holmes' narrow analysis of the property taken.[83] Holmes focused on the support estate; Stevens on the profitability of the industry and on the expectation of investment profit.[84] Stevens found that in the western Pennsylvania coal fields, a very small percentage of the coal in the ground would have to stay there because of the regulation — this percentage being between one and nine percent, depending on the mine surveyed. One reason for explaining the difference between Holmes' and Stevens' approach was that *Keystone* was treated as a matter of the facial validity of the Pennsylvania Act, and not as an "as applied" case.[85]

Second, the majority opinion used the "reciprocity of advantage" test used by Holmes in *Mahon*, but in a way that Brandeis would agree with, and

---

[81] This again is the "economic impact on the claimant" prong of the *Penn Central* analysis.

[82] This accords with *Penn Central's* view of the matter.

[83] The sharpest differences between the majority and the dissent have to do with the definition of the parcel at issue, what is called the third or the support estate.

[84] This focus was from *Penn Central*, not *Mahon*.

[85] Like Holmes in *Mahon*, the *Keystone* majority indicated that a facial challenge to a regulatory taking was an up-hill battle at best and so difficult as to be not worth bringing when administrative remedies remain. The Court seemed only to want to see "as applied" cases before it — a point borne out in later cases, e.g., Justice Scalia's opinions in *Nollan* (1987) and *Lucas* (1992).

Holmes would not.[86] Justice Stevens wrote: "While each of us is burdened somewhat by such restrictions, we, in turn, benefit greatly from the restrictions that are placed on others." Note 21, following this statement, states that:

> [t]he takings clause has never been read to require the States or the courts to calculate whether a specific individual has suffered burdens under this generic rule in excess of the benefits received. Not every individual gets a full dollar return in benefits for the taxes he or she pays; yet, no one suggests that an individual has a right to compensation for the difference between taxes paid and the dollar value of benefits received.

Regulation, Stevens said by way of quotation, was the "burden of our common citizenship." This was a broad validation of governmental regulation.

§ 3.06 Conclusion.

Although Justice Stevens does not embrace Holmes' "too far" language in *Mahon*, noting that it was found in that part of the *Mahon* opinion which he labeled "advisory" or *dicta*,[87] it and the "reciprocity of advantage" language was one part of the *Mahon* majority opinion to survive.[88] The second part left was Holmes' two tests for a taking. Justice Stevens used both of them in *Keystone*: the diminution in value test was applied in light of the plaintiffs' investment-backed expectations, and, using a narrow definition of the affected property, the public benefit of the statute was weighed against the private injury it works.[89] The *Keystone* majority thus kept *Mahon* in touch with changing times.

---

[86] *Keystone*, 480 U.S. 492, n. 21.

[87] The dissent made a point of keeping that language alive, reading the due process and the takings clauses together, as Holmes had implied should be done, federalizing the state law used to review the exercise of the police power, and limiting both federal-state comity in our federal system and Brandeis' notion that states should be a place of experimentation in exercising the police power.

[88] Stevens rejected both Holmes' definition of the property involved and his discussion of the public benefit of the Act.

[89] *See Bernardsville Quarry, Inc. v. Borough of Bernardsville*, 608 A.2d 1377 (N.J. 1992) (involving a quarry and decided with heavy reliance on *Keystone* by a state supreme court). *See also Karam v. State of New Jersey, Dept. of Envir. Protection*, 705 A. 2d 1221, 1226 (N.J. Super. Ct., App. Div., 1998) (involving riparian land and again decided using *Keystone*).

Chapter 4

The Evolution of Regulatory Takings

Justice William Brennan wrote a 1978 opinion containing his restatement of the law of takings. His restatement is still influential — although it was modified two years later by another Justice's (Justice Powell's) attempted restatement of the same law, this time in *Agins v. City of Tiburon* (1980). To understand *Agins*, it is necessary to understand Brennan's opinion in *Penn Central Transportation Company v. City of New York*,[1] to which we will now turn. Understanding both cases is necessary to understanding the permissible scope of land use controls.

§ 4.01   The Facts in *Penn Central*.

In 1965, New York City adopted a landmarks preservation ordinance designed to protect and preserve historic buildings, including Grand Central Terminal, from decisions to alter and destroy them without public review and permission.[2]

The city agency established in the ordinance to oversee its provisions refused to permit Penn Central to construct a fifty-five story building on the air rights over the terminal. This proposed building was to be cantilevered above the existing facade, resting on the roof of the Terminal, and stripping away some of its facade. The agency justified its decision on aesthetic grounds: it labeled Penn Central's development plans "an aesthetic joke." Penn Central then brought suit in state court, alleging both a due process and a takings claim. The trial court granted Penn Central relief, but the New York Court of Appeals reversed. Amid much publicity, the litigation reached the Supreme Court, which reversed the New York Court of Appeals and upheld the ordinance.

Justice Brennan wrote the Supreme Court's majority opinion. He found: (1) that the ordinance did not interfere with the present use of the building as a terminal; (2) that the ordinance allowed Penn Central to make a reasonable return on its investment; and (3) the transferable development rights (TDRs) helped mitigate the severity of the economic impact of the ordinance.

---

[1] 438 U.S. 104 (1978).

[2] The Landmark Preservation Law enacted by the city was itself a response to the mid-1960s demolition of Pennsylvania Station, a structure equally grand and architecturally significant, but lost forever.

[A] The *Penn Central* Test.

This opinion is often cited for its new, so-called three prong test for a taking. That is, three factors have particular significance in determining whether or not a governmental action is a taking: (1) the **economic impact** of the regulation on the owner; (2) the **character** of the governmental action; and (3) the extent to which the regulation interferes with the owner's **investment-backed expectations**. This test for a taking is still good law and in use today, although its impact is limited by the later establishment of two types of *per se*, categorical taking doctrines for total[3] and physical takings.[4]

The **first factor**, the economic impact, is close to the older statements in the case law that state that a regulation must leave an owner with economically viable uses for his property or with a reasonable number of uses.[5] Thus, its focus is on that portion of the property that is left to an owner after the imposition of a regulation.[6] In discussing this factor, defining the unit of property to be considered in assessing a takings claim is crucial to its consideration, and is sometimes dispositive of the claim.

The **second factor**, the character of the governmental action, is probably the hardest to classify. First, if this phrase refers to a physical invasion or occupation of property by the government, its focus would then be directed to the intrusiveness of the action. Justice Brennan states that a "taking can more readily be found when the interference with property can be characterized as a physical invasion . . . ."[7] Second, the phrase might refer to the extraction of a public benefit from a private party who is uniquely affected by the regulation. Third, the phrase might be applied and the character of the governmental action dispositive when the ordinance or regulation aims at abating a public nuisance, as in *Mugler, Hadacheck*, or *Goldblatt*.

The first meaning seems to have been in Brennan's mind (the next sentence, quoted in the last paragraph, refers to the physical invasion situation), but each of the three is possible. When a physical invasion is not involved, the focus is on whether the regulation confers a broadly held

---

[3] *Lucas v. South Carolina Coastal Council*, 505 U.S. 1003 (1992).

[4] *See Loretto v. Teleprompter Manhattan CATV Corp.*, 458 U.S. 419 (1982) (finding a physical taking when a cable wire and box were installed in a N.Y.C. apartment house under statutory authority). However, a partial loss of access due to the construction of a median barrier on a highway is often still viewed as a regulatory taking, rather than a physical taking. *See, e.g., County of Anoka v. Blaine Bldg. Corp.*, 566 N.W. 2d 331 (Minn. 1997).

[5] *See, e.g., Karam v. State of New Jersey, Dept. of Envir. Protection*, 705 A. 2d 1221, 1226-1227 (N.J. Super. Ct., App. Div., 1998) (involving riparian land).

[6] *Id.* (including upland and riparian land in the unit of property considered with regard to a regulatory takings claim).

[7] *Penn Central*, 438 U.S. at 124. This seems tentative, but recall that Justice Brennan earlier dissented in the case of *Loretto v. Teleprompter Manhattan CATV Corp.*, 458 U.S. 419 (1982) (holding that, when there is even a slight physical invasion, the "character of the governmental action" overrides the other two factors and requires a finding of a taking) discussed in Chapter 3, *supra*.

public benefit and thus on, more generally, the justification for the regulation. In *Penn Central*, the finding was that the designation of a property as historic, even without the consent of its owner, is for the benefit of the public at large.

The first two factors resemble, when taken together, the test applied when the facial validity of a police power ordinance is challenged: does the owner have a reasonable return, or economically viable uses, and does the ordinance advance a substantial government interest? If the answers are yes both times, a facial challenge is turned away.[8]

The *Penn Central* opinion discussed all three factors and treated the situation before it as an "as applied" case, rather than one presenting a facial challenge to the landmark law. Its precedential value in the area of traditional zoning was limited on that account because, although the court asserted that this was a zoning case, it was a very special one.

The **third factor** opens the way to a holding that, even if the regulation is within the police power, it might still be a taking when it violates an owner's reasonable, investment backed expectations. Justice Brennan gathered many friends for this notion among the more conservative Justices. He thought that the investment backed expectations of the railroad were met so long as the property remained useful as a terminal — because that was its intended use when it was built. Generally, an investment backed expectation means a reasonable return on the privately contributed ingredient of the terminal's value, and not the ingredient added by the presence of surrounding properties and facilities. The idea of investment backed expectations appealed to a broad spectrum of the Justices — liberals and conservatives alike — on the court.

[1] Investment-Backed Expectations.

The idea of investment-backed expectations (IBEs) has only been part of takings jurisprudence since *Penn Central*. Its meaning is still evolving. These expectations might either be formed when the investment is made or the initial expectation might be subject to change thereafter. Moreover, this aspect of the test might be differently used once the initial investment is recouped along with a reasonable profit. This term suggests that an investor, just by making an investment, has a vested right to pursue his investment, regardless of the regulation; this might explain its appeal to some of the Justices, but is arguably overbroad. The expectations of a person who inherits property might be different from a purchaser, but it is also hard to suggest that an heir can be more strictly regulated than an investor/purchaser. Thus, a legal preference for an investor over other types of owners is difficult to rationalize. The appeal of this term may also lie in its restatement of Holmes' "diminution in value" test stated in *Mahon*; it had become a dead letter and this term revives it in an updated, modified form. Further, an IBE might vary according to the governmental interest advanced in the regulation, for surely the expectation of the investor would

---

[8] *See Keystone Bituminous Coal Association v. DeBenedictus, discussed in* Chapter 2.

lessen in the face of prior regulation, and the purchase of regulated property would naturally diminish the IBEs of an owner.

[2]   Two Applications of IBEs.

First, if we reached back in time and applied the IBEs of *Penn Central* to *Mahon*, the Mahons' investment-backed expectations seem slight. The mineral estate had been severed from the surface in 1878, so that the holders of the Mahons' chain of title had been in possession of the surface since that time. If their surface interest were regarded as a lease of the surface, then the elapsed time was sufficient to amortize a considerable investment in the site. It is thus arguable that their IBEs had been fulfilled by the time of the Kohler Act. On the other hand, as to the Pennsylvania Coal Company, its investment in the right of support was not recouped yet. Indeed, it had not started to mine under the Mahons' land. Thus, compared with the Mahons, there is still no recoupment of its investment. This is particularly so if the company was a secondary recovery miner — a company that purchased a coal property already mined once by the room and pillar method, and that proceeds to remove the pillars, relying on the waiver of damages provision in the Mahons' deed to the surface. Yet IBEs should be held in good faith: an investment in a secondary recovery of coal that started up in the face of the Kohler Act, can hardly have been conducted in good faith, so what is protected in *Mahon* must have been the primary recovery miner's expectation of the right to sell the pillars.

Second, suppose a developer purchased a site with an old office building on it, paying more for the land than for the building, and thereafter a historic landmark law is enacted, the building is designated a landmark — designated because it is an example of the free-standing masonry building techniques pre-dating the introduction of structural steel. The old building's facade is neither historic nor attractive. The developer alleges that the rental income from a new building would be 10 times greater than the old one, and his building lacks outward aesthetic appeal and historic value but any takings challenge will fail.[9] The building's structural components still give it cultural value. There is no reason why paying more for the land under his building should be relevant to the takings issue; were it otherwise, his accountant could create a violation of his IBEs by allocating more of the purchase price to the land. The expectation of higher profits from the new building does not qualify as a "property" interest protected by the takings clause so long as the developer has the ability to make a reasonable return on the whole of what he purchased: the developer must prove an unreasonably low income for the old building, instead of projecting higher income from the new one.

---

[9] This developer's position is stronger than Penn Central's: his investment has not yet been recouped, while Penn Central had 60 years to recoup its investment in the terminal.

[3] *Palazzolo v. Rhode Island*[10] **and IBEs.**

The Supreme Court decided that a purchaser or successive title holder, even though on notice of earlier-enacted regulations, is not barred from claiming interference with IBEs and a taking based on the earlier restriction. The purchaser's IBEs may, but need not be, affected by the earlier restriction. Post-enactment purchasers, it said, should be protected in this way because: (1) otherwise unreasonably burdensome enactments would become less so only because of the passage of time; (2) the state would only have to justify unreasonable enactments before either a later transfer of title or the (early) death of the person holding title at the time of enactment; (3) the enactment would otherwise strip an owner of the right to transfer what he purchased — "a critical alteration in the nature of property"; (4) vendors of property would be in different positions depending on their age and whether they are rich or poor; (5) takings law should be harmonized with eminent domain law, where the owner at the time of the condemnation is always entitled to just compensation[11] ; and (6) a prior Supreme Court takings case[12] rejected the idea that post-enactment purchasers had no claim. Thus "a regulation that otherwise would be unconstitutional absent compensation is not transformed into [a defense for the regulatory agency] by the mere passage of title."[13] IBEs are not diminished by inaction either.[14]

§ 4.02 Justice Brennan's Majority Opinion.

[A] The Restatement Section.

Justice Brennan began his discussion of the Supreme Court's takings cases by invoking the *Mahon* opinion. He quoted the proposition that "government could hardly go on" if some property value decreases were not tolerated as a consequence of governmental regulation. Brennan then discussed the cases most tolerant of governmental regulation: the so-called "nuisance abatement" line of cases—*Mugler, Hadacheck,* and *Goldblatt.* In a footnote in a later section of the opinion, when refuting Penn Central's arguments, he went further and attempted to give these cases the widest possible use, saying that they were best understood not as "noxious" use or nuisance abatement cases, but as instances of governmental action where "the restrictions were reasonably related to the implementation of a policy — not unlike historic preservation — expected to produce a widespread

---

[10] 533 U.S. 606 (2001).

[11] *Id.* at **38–43 (stating the foregoing rationales).

[12] *Nollan v. California Coastal Comm'n*, 483 U.S. 825, 834, n.2 (1987) (Justice Scalia, responding to Justice Brennan's dissent, *id.* at 860).

[13] *Palazzolo*, 533 U.S. at 43-44.

[14] *See McQueen v. South Carolina Coastal Council*, 530 S.E.2d 628 (S.C. 2000) (finding that an owner who did not seek development permits "in the face of ever more stringent regulations" demonstrated a "distinct lack" of IBEs), cert. granted, vacated, and remanded for consideration in light of *Palazzolo*, 533 U.S. at 606.

public benefit and applicable to all similarly situated property." Thus were the nuisance exception cases made into cases in which the "character of the governmental action" controlled.

Brennan concluded this section of the opinion with a restatement of *Mahon*'s holding in terms of his own test, one that would have startled Justice Holmes: "a state statute that substantially furthers important public policies may so frustrate distinct investment-backed expectations as to amount to a 'taking'."[15] Brennan's first use of *Mahon* in this section, and his conclusion to the section, thus bracketed the nuisance abatement cases, making those cases an instance of the type of taking (a regulatory one) involved in *Mahon*.

[B]   The Refutation Section.

Justice Brennan then set out to refute four arguments made by Penn Central. First, that the ordinance had deprived the company of the gainful use of the air rights. In reply, Brennan stated that simply because the company had been denied the ability to exploit the air space above the terminal, space the company previously had expected to exploit, does not convert the city's action into a taking. The terminal property was not, for takings purposes, to be divided into discrete units, for which the denial of development became a taking. Instead, the terminal's parcel as a whole provided the relevant field of inquiry.

Second, the company argued that the only means of protecting landmark owners from being singled out to provide a public benefit is to find the preservation of individual landmarks a taking. No merit in this argument, thought Brennan, because the ordinance was the subject of a city-wide comprehensive plan for preservation, and subjected each of over four hundred landmarks designated in the city to the same review procedure — of which the company has not fully availed itself.

Third, the company argued that the ordinance has a disparate, non-uniform impact on each landmark owner, according to the needs of the landmark. Any zoning ordinance impacts more severely on some landowners than it does on others. The ordinance here is no different, states Brennan.

Fourth, Brennan turned aside an argument that the air space had been appropriated for a city enterprise (providing cultural amenities) through the use of a governmental procedure. Not so, said Brennan: neither exploitation of the company's parcel for city purposes nor appropriation of it, arises here.

[C]   The "As Applied" Section.

In this next section of the opinion, Justice Brennan set out to determine whether Penn Central was permitted under the ordinance to make a reasonable return on its investment backed expectations — whether the

---

[15] *Penn Central*, 438 U.S. at 127.

regulation had interfered with those expectations. This issue, Brennan said, "may be narrowed to the question of the severity of the impact of the law on the appellant's parcel." There was no intent by the city to prohibit the occupation of any of the company's air space, nor was there an intent to prohibit any and all construction within that space. The company could have sought permission to build a smaller, less overwhelming structure — and did not do so. Neither was there any intent to interfere, or interference, with any of the present uses of the terminal and this, Brennan said, "must be regarded as Penn Central's primary expectation concerning the use of the parcel."

At this point Justice Brennan switched back to refuting and narrowing the appellant's arguments. The use of *some* of the remaining unused airspace had not been denied them. In addition, the presence of the transferable development rights, or TDRs, meant that Penn Central had not been denied all use of its parcel. TDRs are the rights otherwise available under the city's zoning regulations, not used because of the landmark ordinance, but transferable to other parcels.

The court here measured a taking by what was left the owner, rather than by what was taken from him. The constitutional requirement is for just compensation for what is taken, but Justice Brennan here seemed to turn this requirement into an inquiry into whether the railroad had been given — or denied — a reasonable return on its property, meaning the terminal parcel. What constituted a reasonable return was either a return on the property in its restricted use, or on its present or future uses.

Those rights (under the TDR scheme) could be used only on properties that the railroad company already owned. Fortunately for the city, the company already owned eight or so properties further up on Park Avenue, north of the terminal.[16] (It actually owned more than that, but the opinion mentions only eight.) Those properties were available to receive the TDRs unused on the company's terminal site.

The TDRs were relevant, Brennan stated, to the issue of whether or not there was a taking: they may be considered as mitigating the severity of the economic impact (his first factor for assessing) a regulation. The traditional approach was first to address whether there was a taking, and then, if there was a taking, to confront the compensation issue. Brennan's opinion, in this last section, seemed to some critics to meld these two issues into a very untraditional whole. Critics have pointed out that the TDRs were certainly relevant to the issue of whether just compensation had been paid, but they were less clearly relevant to the first issue of whether a taking had occurred.

---

[16] It would have been difficult for the company to add onto its other properties. Imagine 20 more stories added on top of the Waldorf-Astoria Hotel, one of the other nearby properties owned by the company.

[D] TDRs.

TDRs separate the right to possess from the right to develop a parcel. Development rights are severed from the sending parcel and transferred to a receiving one. They have been used, not only around New York City's Grand Central Terminal, but around its South Street Seaport as well.[17] Justice Brennan regarded the city's program as less than ideal, but by the time he wrote the opinion, it was clear from state court opinions on the subject that at a minimum, a transferable developments rights program needed a transfer right (1) whose existence was not dependent on further administrative rulings or appeals, (2) whose use was available in pre-determined, clearly mapped, and reasonable large receiving zones,[18] and (3) with the government bearing the risk that the right will prove valueless and be without a market of potential purchasers.[19] The last requirement may have meant the creation by regulators of a "TDR bank" for holding unused and unsold rights — the bank itself "making a market" in the rights, giving their holder immediate money for them. In 1997, the Supreme Court declined to review another TDR scheme.[20] In a concurring opinion signed by three Justices, however, Justice Scalia said that their view — not taken in *Penn Central* — was that TDRs were appropriate for determining the amount of compensation due, but not in determining whether or not there had been a taking.

§ 4.03 The Holdings.

There are five of them. Most narrowly, and first, the Supreme Court majority held that the Company has not met its burden of proof or that it stipulated away its case. Second, using the reciprocity of advantage formula, it held that the benefits to the affected owners of historic land-marks and to the municipality made the injury to the owners non-compensable.[21]

Third, it broadly held that aesthetic and historic landmark regulations are justified under the police power, notwithstanding their substantial economic impact on the owner of an affected landmark and, unless the owner's investment backed expectations are taken away, no compensation need be paid for such an impact.

---

[17] They have also been used in downtown Chicago and Seattle, as well as for open space protection in New Jersey's Pinelands and for agricultural preservation in Montgomery County, Maryland.

[18] *See, e.g., Fred F. French Inv. Co. v. City of New York*, 350 N.E.2d 381 (N.Y. 1976) (invalidating an early scheme for its failure to meet either of the first two requirements).

[19] *See* Note, *Past, Present, and Future Constitutional Challenges to Transferable Development Rights*, 74 Wash. L. Rev. 825 (1999); Andrew Miller, *Transferable Development Rights in the Constitutional Landscape: Has Penn Central Failed to Weather the Storm?*, 39 Nat. Res. J. 459 (1999); R. S. Radford, *Takings and Transferable Development Rights in the Supreme Court: the Constitutional Status of TDRs in the Aftermath of Suitum*, 28 Stetson L. Rev. 685 (1999).

[20] *Suitum v. Lake Tahoe Regional Planning Agency*, 520 U.S. 725 (1997).

[21] Only 0.1% of the property in the city was landmarked.

Fourth, the majority held that, in assessing whether there was a taking, the TDRs were properly considered in assessing the economic impact of the regulation.[22] Thus, *Penn Central* is some evidence that non-monetary compensation is constitutional, since the TDRs provide substitute property instead of cash.[23] The *Penn Central* court considered the value of the TDRs in determining the economic impact of the landmark regulation — that is, a regulation does not "go too far" if it either (1) gives some proportionate benefit back to the landowner[24] or (2) even if it goes too far, it can be pushed back by giving TDRs as just compensation.[25]

The definition of the property at issue was the subject of a fifth holding, as it had been in other takings cases so far reviewed. In *Mahon*, Holmes talked about profit and "commercially practical" mining. He was talking about the removal of the coal pillars from a mine. *Penn Central's* majority talked of the "whole parcel" that Grand Central Terminal occupied, not just the portion then used, and not just the air rights over the terminal: "'Taking' jurisprudence does not divide a single parcel into discrete segments and attempt to determine whether rights in a particular segment have been entirely abrogated." Later, the *Keystone* court would talk broadly about the holdings of the mining companies in Western Pennsylvania: there Justice Stevens looked at the mine as a whole, not just at the coal pillars in it.

§ 4.04   The Dissenting Opinion.

As to the dissent, written by Justice Rehnquist, its starting point was that analysis should begin with an expansion of the "physical invasion" cases. The regulation substantially destroyed the value of the railroad's property, and also destroyed the air rights, viewed as a separate commodity. Further, the use of these rights was neither a nuisance nor prohibited under a comprehensive zoning scheme. For the dissent, this was not a zoning case, and an office building in mid-town Manhattan was not out of place and a nuisance on that account. The dissenters thought that the landmark ordinance imposed an affirmative preservation covenant on the company. This servitude imposed on the property is the equivalent of a physical invasion of the property.

Two things distinguish the majority and dissent. First, they disagree about the proper role of both the physical invasion and nuisance abatement cases. Second, the dissent subdivides and disaggregates the railroad's property interests in order to find a taking — and the majority, in contrast,

---

[22] Assessing other landmark programs, the TDRs will likely become a limiting aspect of the case.

[23] If the Constitution means otherwise, its drafters could have used the word "cash" or "money," not just compensation.

[24] D. Kendall & J. Ryan, *"Paying" for the Change: Using Eminent Domain to Secure Exactions and Sidestep Nollan and Dolan*, 81 Va. L. Rev. 1801, 1827-1828 (1995) (suggesting that a general right to develop be substituted for the TDRs).

[25] By analogy, under eminent domain law, the amount of just compensation due is reduced by the value of the benefit to the non-condemned portion of the parcel that the landowner receives from the condemnation of a part of it.

aggregates the use of the terminal with the use of all the railroad's other properties in the area.[26]

§ 4.05 The Aftermath.

At the time of this litigation, the terminal had a maximum floor area ratio of 18, but was using about 1.5. The railroad owned 23 properties in the area, mostly north of the terminal on Park Avenue. It has leased the air rights on some, and improved some itself. In addition, the railroad owned over forty acres under the Avenue. The terminal site is approximately 130,000 square feet. Under the ordinance, such an area permits a building with about two million square feet. Only about 300,000 were used in the terminal. Thus the TDRs available for transfer represented about 1.7 million square feet. At the beginning of 1989, none of these TDRs had in fact been transferred.[27]

§ 4.06 The *Agins* Test.

Penn Central has provided one of two principal tests for a regulatory taking. *Agins v. City of Tiburon*[28] has provided another. *Agins* was a facial challenge to an open space regulation. The landowners purchased five acres ridgeland property for residential development in the City of Tiburon, California. Their ridgeland overlooked both San Francisco Bay and the Pacific Ocean. It had, in other words, tremendous potential for residential building lots because of its spectacular views. The state of California, some six years after their purchase, required the City to prepare a comprehensive plan governing both land use and the preservation of open space. The plan was implemented by two ordinances that downzoned the land and when applied, permitted the owners to build between one and five residences on the land. After the rezoning, dwellings were limited to one per acre. The owners had no particular plans for building, and submitted no development proposals to the City, so their later attack on the regulation was a facial one.

The Supreme Court upheld the open space regulation.[29] Its test for doing so had two prongs. It asked: (1) whether the regulation advanced a substantial state interest and/or (2) whether the landowner was left with an economically viable use of his land once the regulation was imposed. The two prongs were, in the original opinion, connected by the disjunctive conjunction.

---

[26] A good guide to the dialogue between majority and dissent can be found in M. Davis & R. Glickman, *To the Promised Land: A Century of Wandering and a Final Homeland for the Due Process and Taking Clauses*, 68 Or. L.Rev. 393, 446–453 (1989).

[27] S. Kowaloff, *Grand Central Zoning Game*, N.Y. L. J. (Sept. 20, 1989), at 33, col.3 (reporting that the Planning Commission denied the transfer of 800,000 square feet from the terminal site 1,000 feet away to a receiving parcel on Madison Avenue).

[28] 447 U.S. 255 (1980).

[29] The Court had also been asked to review the issues of the property remedies for a taking, but since it found no taking, it declined to do so in this case.

The application of a general zoning law to particular property effects a taking if the ordinance does not substantially advance legitimate state interests . . . or denies an owner economically viable use of his land.[30]

Applying this test and writing for the majority, Justice Powell cited California statutes mandating the development of open space plans to discourage premature and unnecessary conversion of open space land to urban uses. He found that there was a substantial state interest in the preservation of open space and avoidance of the harmful effects of premature urbanization, which the regulation (he said) helps to forestall. Justice Powell's opinion did not discuss the ridgeland characteristic of the Agins' parcel, but subsequent state cases have upheld ordinances restricting the height of buildings to protect existing views[31] and one state, North Carolina, has enacted state-wide legislation to protect the view of mountain ridges from lower elevations.[32] Powell also found that the ordinance was of general applicability (in the language of *Euclid* and zoning attorneys, it was found to be comprehensive, although Powell did not use that word). All this is due process analysis, applied through a takings test.

Justice Powell found that, because, the owner had not submitted a development plan or application, it was premature to ask, on the record in front of the court, whether the second prong of *Agins* was involved. He said: "the appellants are free to pursue their reasonable investment expectations by submitting a development plan to local officials." After they did so, the ordinance could be evaluated "as applied." Powell's language on this aspect of the case was later used to formulate a ripeness rule, requiring first a "meaningful application" to develop a property.[33]

A negative conclusion on either prong of the *Agins* test will provoke a close look at the regulation. That is, it will shift the burden of proof to the municipality or other governmental agency, to justify it.

[A] The Uses of *Agins*.

The two-pronged *Agins* test provided an influential, but malleable rule for later United States Supreme Court opinions. More specifically, it has been involved in three United States Supreme Court opinions on exactions

---

[30] *Agins*, 447 U.S. at 260.

[31] *See Ross v. City of Rolling Hills Estates*, 238 Cal. Rptr. 2d 562 (Cal. App. Ct. 1987) (upholding denial of permits for addition to house under ordinance restricting blockage of existing views as a stated objective of ordinance and as needed to protect scenic character of area), review denied, July 29, 1987; *Landmark Land v. City of Denver*, 728 P.2d 1281 (Colo. 1986) (upholding ordinance restricting height of building in office part to protect Rocky Mountain views); *In re Interim Bylaw, Waitsfield, Vermount*, 742 A.2d 742 (Vt. 1999) (upholding interim ordinance for forest land above 1700 feet elevation in town). *See generally* Lisa Healy, *Trophy Homes and Other Alpine Predators: The Protection of Mountain Views through Ridge Line Zoning*, 25 B.C. Envtl. Aff. L. Rev. 913 (1998).

[32] N.C. Gen. Stat. § 113A-205 to -214 (enacted 1983) (ridgelands include all lands up to 100 feet below the crest of the ridge. *Id.* at §§ 206). *See generally* Robert Kessler, *North Carolina's Ridge Law: No View from the Top*, 63 N.C. L. Rev. 197 (1984).

[33] *See, e.g., MacDonald, Sommer, & Frates v. Yolo County*, 477 U.S. 340 (1986).

and regulatory takings. First, in *Nollan v. California Coastal Commission*,[34] the Court used the first prong of *Agins* to invalidate a regulation of the commission. *Nollan* was the first time that the Court had done this. In the majority opinion in *Nollan*, Justice Scalia re-phrased the *Agins* rule, using a negative and conjunctive version of it, stating:

> We have long recognized that land use regulation does not effect a taking if it substantially advances legitimate state interests and does not deny an owner economically viable use of his land. (Internal quotation marks omitted.)[35]

Second, in *Lucas v. South Carolina Coastal Council*,[36] the court used the second prong to invalidate a council prohibition on building a beach house. Thus by 1992 both prongs of the *Agins* test had been used once. Both times Justice Scalia wrote the majority opinion.

Third, in 1994, the *Agins* test was elaborated in *Dolan v. City of Tigard*,[37] in order to invalidate yet another exaction that had conditioned the granting of a development permit.

[B]   The Aftermath of *Agins*.

Donald and Bonnie Agins had purchased their ridgeland acreage in 1968, for a price of $50,000. Their plans were to build a residence for themselves on one of the five acres, and subdivide the parcel so that they could finance their home from the proceeds of the other (they hoped) four lots. After their case was decided by the United States Supreme Court, they submitted a development proposal and were permitted (about two years after the 1980 opinion) to subdivide their property into three lots, but this approval was a conditional one. A road to the cite, and a hiking trail would have to be designed to pass through their three parcels. After the decision in *First English Evangelical Lutheran Church of Glendale v. City of Los Angeles*,[38] recognizing a damages remedy for temporary takings of property, their threat of a law suit altered their bargaining power. Four lots were approved for development in 1988. Four years later, however, the plans for one of the homes, containing some 14,000 square feet of space, was disapproved. Homes now occupy the ridgelands, but the Agins don't live there. They were divorced in the late 1980s.

[C]   Using *Penn Central* and *Agins*.

What if an owner purchases a tract on which he plans to operate a quarry, but shortly thereafter a zoning ordinance designates the surrounding district as a conservation district from which quarries are excluded? When the owner brings suit, alleging a taking under *Agins* because the use for

---

[34] 483 U.S. 825 (1987).

[35] *Id.* at 834.

[36] 505 U.S. 1003 (1992).

[37] 512 U.S. 374 (1994).

[38] 482 U.S. 304 (1987).

which it purchased is no longer "economically viable," the claim will fail. *Mahon* makes this result difficult to accept: the regulation has made it "commercially impractical" to operate the quarry and so, as to the quarry, this regulation seems to "go too far." However, first, the "too far" language was in the "advisory portion" (Justice Steven's term) of Holmes' opinion. Second, later cases suggest that *Mahon* is not controlling. Economic viability, one test for avoiding a takings under *Agins*, is defined as the equivalent of making a "reasonable return" as in *Penn Central*. What controls is the ability to develop or sell the property for its remaining uses, rather than its profitability for the owner's intended use; if the owner can sell and make a return on the investment of its purchase price, he has been given a reasonable return on its investment and there is no taking. If the *Penn Central* majority had intended the focus to be on the profits to be reaped solely from an owner's intended use, then the Court would have focused on the owner's investment, rather than its "investment backed expectations." Instead, the opinion focused on the uses remaining to the owner of the regulated property and the return possible for the property once regulated. It focused, in short, not on what's taken, but on what's left. When considered along with the economic impact and the character of the governmental action, there is no taking under either *Penn Central* or *Agins*. This owner's claim exposes the tension between focusing either on the owner's "investment backed expectations" or on making a reasonable return from the property. The former focused on the pre-regulation expectations and uses, while the latter focus was on post-regulation uses.

More generally, many commentators have suggested that the more elaborate, three prong test from *Penn Central* is to be used with the "as applied" challenge to a regulation.[39] Commentaries on *Agins* have suggested that its two prong test is most useful in "facial" challenges to regulations.

§ 4.07   The Just Compensation Requirement.

Just compensation requires the equivalent of the computation of damages in a civil suit. This computation is made after there has been a finding that a taking for a public purpose has indeed occurred. The compensation is that which is also available in an eminent domain action. It is to this body of law that the regulatory land use bar looks to when they seek analogies for the types of compensation available in their regulatory takings claims.

The compensation required in eminent domain actions, then, is the fair market value of the property taken, as well as severance damages for the remaining property abutting that taken, but off-set by any benefit accruing to the owner by having the condemned property nearby in the government's hands.[40]

---

[39] The *Penn Central* opinion itself does not completely bear this out, because there the railroad company did not seek all of the administrative relief available to it.

[40] *Cf. United States v. Fuller*, 409 U.S. 488 (1973) [holding that the presence of nearby, leased (from the government) grazing lands not be considered in determining compensation].

When tangible property is taken, intangible property, such as the good-will of a business, is also condemnable and compensable when present and diminished by the taking of the tangible property.[41] On the other hand, if a property owner has had the site of his business condemned, but can conduct it elsewhere, intangible property losses are not recoverable.[42]

[A] Computation Methods.

The methods used to compute the compensation do not differ appreciably from those used to appraise real property in other settings. First, a capitalization rate (or cap rate) may be used: this method establishes a fair market value by evaluating the income received from the property (its rental value), assuming that that income represents a percentage of the fair market value (often determined by a comparison of various rates of return offered by alternative investments for a potential purchaser consid-ering buying the property), and computing the ratios involved. That is, if the rental value is 8% of the fair market value, then x is 100%, when x is the fair market value. Second, a fair market value can be established from data collected from the sales of similar properties and adjusted to reflect a sale of the appraised property. A third method is to figure the replacement cost of the property from data collected from construction agreements for similar properties, adjusted for the appraised property, adding a value for the land, established by another method, but subtracting the depreciated value of the property. Often, as the third method indicates, a combination of methods is used. This is so because condemnation trials can be before a jury and it is proper for the jury, or other fact-finder, to consider several methods in reaching a determination of just compensation. Finally, it is well to remember that compensation can be in kind, as well as in money. In *Penn Central*, for example, the majority opinion suggested that the transferable development rights offered by the city might in fact be found to constitute an element of just compensation.[43]

§ 4.08 Summary of the Law of Takings.

The law of takings discussed thus far has five rules: First, without a public purpose, neither regulation nor condemnation is permitted the government. Second, even when the government has a public purpose for what it does, only implementing action reasonably related to that purpose is justified and will satisfy the due process clause. Third, no regulation which destroys all use, or an essential right (to exclude, for example), is justified, no matter the purpose. Fourth, any permanent physical occupa-tion of property authorized by the government, is a *per se* taking, no matter how beneficial to the public and no matter the extent of the occupation. Fifth, a regulation is valid when it substantially advances a legitimate

---

[41] *Kimball Laundry Company v. United States*, 338 U.S. 1 (1949) (laundry forced to suspend service, lost goodwill as well).

[42] *Cf. West River Bridge Company v. Dix*, 47 U.S. (6 How.) 507 (1848).

[43] *Penn Central Transportation Co. v. City of New York*, 438 U.S. 104, 136–137 (1978).

public purpose or when it does not deny an owner all reasonable economic use of the property.[44] When a regulation fails to do either, it is a taking. When considering the validity of the regulation, *Penn Central* teaches that the character of the governmental action, particularly its nuisance-abating character, and the severity of the economic impact on the owner, particularly on his or her investment-backed expectations, are all considered as part of a balancing analysis.[45]

Throughout these United States Supreme Court cases, a majority of its Justices have indicated an increasing impatience with *ad hoc* tests. In order to provide more certainty and black-letter law to this area, the court has created two more types of takings: first, for governmental exactions and conditions imposed on the granting of various types of development permits, and second, for another type of categorical or *per se* taking — a total taking.[46]

---

[44] *See infra*, Chapter 12 [discussing *Lucas v. South Carolina Coastal Council*, 505 U.S. 1003 (1992)].

[45] *See also* Norman Williams, *Planning Law in the 1990's*, 31 Ariz. L.Rev. 471, 484 (1989) (providing another summary and a statement useful for the municipal attorney); *Sintra, Inc. v. City of Seattle*, 829 P.2d 765 (Wash. 1992) (a state court opinion attempting to cover all these bases).

[46] *See* Chapters 12 and 14, *infra*.

Chapter 5

Temporary Regulatory Takings

§ 5.01 Background.

In addition to *Keystone Bituminous Coal Association,* [1] the United States Supreme Court decided one other significant takings case in 1987. The subject of this case was a temporary regulatory taking, defined as a freeze on (all) uses of real property for the period of time that a regulation going too far is in effect, thus denying development permits for the property. The time involved must be unreasonably long, but otherwise a temporary taking is a type of regulatory taking.

San Diego Gas & Electric Company v. City of San Diego [2] involved the company's claim that the municipality's open space program had deprived it of the "entire beneficial use of the property" when the municipality denied the company a development permit for any uses inconsistent with its program. The company asked for a ruling that the program was an inverse condemnation of its property and requested money damages. The court's majority found no finding of a taking in the record before the lower courts, and so felt constrained not to rule on this takings issue.

In dissent, however, Justice Brennan, along with three colleagues, felt that because a final decision had been rendered below, the court had appellate jurisdiction to rule on the takings issue. Thus freed to address the merits, Brennan reached the question "whether a government entity must pay just compensation when a police power regulation has effected a "taking" of "private property" for "public use" within the meaning of that constitutional provision." [3] Quoting the "too far" language of Holmes in *Mahon,* Justice Brennan saw little distinction between physical invasions (requiring compensation) and land use regulations that go too far (that he saw as requiring compensation too). [4] He also suggested several factors to consider in measuring whether the regulation goes too far; factors drawn from his majority opinion in *Penn Central.* [5]

While recognizing that the traditional remedy for a regulation going too far was merely invalidation of the regulation, Justice Brennan thought that the money damages that the company sought were also an appropriate remedy; even though the government repealed the invalid regulation, the owner was entitled to damages for the time before repeal. Brennan wrote in dissent, but his views on the merits of the case as well as the damages

---

[1] Discussed *supra,* Chapter 4.

[2] 450 U.S. 621, 633 (1981).

[3] *Id.* at 646.

[4] *Id.* at 649, 652–653.

[5] *Id.* at 648.

remedy, were approvingly echoed by Chief Justice Rehnquist in his concurrence with the majority opinion. Thus, a five-member majority of the court thought that a temporary regulatory taking was possible and would give rise to money damages in a case on which a final judgment had been reached below.

While similar cases were granted certiorari during the next six years,[6] it was not until *First English Evan. Lutheran Church of Glendale v. Los Angeles County*[7] that the court was presented with the issue of whether a compensable regulatory taking occurred.

§ 5.02   *First English Evan. Lutheran Church of Glendale v. Los Angeles County*

[A]   The Facts.

In *First English Evan. Lutheran Church of Glendale v. Los Angeles County*,[8] a church owned 21 acres in a remote part of Los Angeles County — up a creek, in a canyon. It used 12 acres of flat land along the creek as a camp for the handicapped, named Lutherglen. A fire destroyed the forest up-stream from the camp in 1977. This reduced the water-retention capacity of the soils, resulting the next year in a flood which destroyed all of the camp's buildings and in which several lives were lost.

Some facts in this case must be seen in their local context. A creek in the context of Los Angeles means, for most of the year, a dry creek-bed. A flood in this context means a combination of flood and mudslide.[9] The "flood" came in 1978. In early 1979, after the flood, the county enacted an interim, emergency ordinance which denied the church the right to rebuild on the flood plain on which the camp's buildings had been located. The ordinance provided in part that "(a) person shall not construct, reconstruct, place or enlarge any building or structure, any portion of which is, or will be, located with the outer boundary lines of the interim flood protection area." The ordinance was effective immediately because the county viewed the situation as a health and safety matter. In quick response, the church sued, but only for damages, alleging a regulatory taking. The interim ordinance was made permanent in 1983. It was enacted in response to a tragedy in which lives were lost. For police power purposes, it was a safety measure, not a general welfare one; so the county thought that the traditional heart of the police power (protecting health, safety, etc.) was involved, strengthening its case.

---

[6] *See, e.g., Williamson County Regional Planning Commission v. Hamilton Bank*, 473 U.S. 172 (1985) (claim not ripe for judicial determination because state administrative remedies were not yet exhausted); *MacDonald, Sommer, & Frates v. Yolo County*, 477 U.S. 340 (1986).

[7] 482 U.S. 304 (1987).

[8] *Id.*

[9] John McPhee, *The Control of Nature*, The New Yorker (Sept. 26, 1988), at 45, 67–72, gives some background on the area.

The trial court granted the county's motion to strike the church's allegation that the church was denied all use of the property and so, before the United States Supreme Court granted certiorari in this litigation, no trial on the merits had been held on the takings issue.

[B] The Holding.

The Supreme Court held that temporary takings, accomplished through regulatory measures rather than a physical occupation, entitle the property owner to damages. When "a burden results from governmental action that amounted to a taking, the Just Compensation Clause of the Fifth Amendment requires that the government pay the landowner for the value of the use of the land during this period."[10] This holding, narrowly read, is that there is a cause of action for a temporary taking as well as a permanent one. "[W]here the government's activities have already worked a taking of all use of property, no subsequent action by the government can relieve it of the duty to provide compensation for the period during which the taking was effective."[11] The holding did not authorize the plaintiff's recovery of damages — that recovery still depends on a trial on the merits and a finding that there was a taking in this case. However, the court further held that "invalidation of the ordinance without payment of fair value for the use of the property during the [pendency of the ordinance] would be a constitutionally insufficient remedy."[12]

To reach these holdings, the court proceeded in several steps. First, it found that the issue not presented in *San Diego Gas* and subsequent cases, was "squarely presented here." Second, the opinion noted that the Just Compensation Clause is "self-executing" and that any inverse condemnation action recognizes as much. Third, a regulation that goes too far is a taking and that temporary and permanent takings are different only in degree. Finally, once the government has already taken "all use" of a property, it must pay compensation; the injunctive remedy is inadequate.

A temporary regulatory taking has three elements: it (1) is temporary (lasting only so long as the invalid regulation is enforced or is effective); (2) denies the owner "all use"[13] of the property; and (3) exceeds the police power. This court also says what it is not deciding, i.e., it is not deciding that there is a taking, but rather assuming that the state court below found

---

[10] *First English*, 482 U.S. at 320.

[11] *Id.* at 305.

[12] *Id.*

[13] The opinion repeatedly states that "all use" was denied. This phrase provides a bright line test because the opinion does not use the phrase "all reasonable use." It is intended to be a part of the holding and to make clear the court's assumption about the finality of the decision below. The regulatory taking found here applied from the time of the enactment of the interim ordinance to the time it was made permanent. After being made permanent, if "all use" is still denied, a "total taking" under *Lucas v. South Carolina Coastal Comm'n*, 505 U.S. 1003 (1992) (discussed in Chapter 17, *infra*), occurs.

a taking here. The court's failure to find a taking here opens up the possibility of inconsistent state and federal court results on this issue.[14]

Chief Justice Rehnquist wrote the majority opinion, joined by Justices White, Marshall, Brennan, Powell and Scalia. The three elements of this type of a regulatory taking, recited previously, were not all incorporated into the holding: the third element, the requirement that the regulation be an invalid exercise of the police power, was omitted. Its omission means to indicate that this element is irrelevant in situations in which damages are given, that even if the regulation is found to have a public purpose, that finding is irrelevant. This is all consistent with Holmes' "too far" language in *Mahon*.[15] In any event, the majority assumes that an award of damages makes such findings irrelevant.

The temporary taking, once found, is effective when the last required administrative form of relief, such as a variance, is denied by the administrative agency authorized to grant it (and does not include, then, any period of judicial review of the denial). It continues until the regulation going "too far" is withdrawn or repealed, and if no express withdrawal or repeal is forthcoming, it continues as a temporary taking until a decision on repeal or withdrawal is reached; it was, in other words, on-going until some decision otherwise is communicated to the complaining landowner.[16]

Citing *Mahon*, the majority emphasizes that policy arguments such as the prediction of "a flood" of litigation coming in the wake of this opinion, the risk of draining the public fisc, as well as the chilling effect of the opinion on land use planners devising regulations, must give way to the taking clause's requirement of just compensation. The majority expected better planning studies and less resort to *ad hoc* exactions and remedies to be the result of *First English*.

[C]   The Dissent.

Justices Stevens, Blackmun, and O'Connor dissented, urging four points. First, that the case was not ripe for decision. Second, that the ordinance was a health and safety measure (so like *Hadacheck*, in terms of U.S. Supreme Court precedent). Third, that the majority relied on physical invasion cases (like *Loretto*) to find a taking and those cases were inopposite (here the dissent strikes a raw nerve because it is precisely those physical

---

[14] *See Sea Cabins on the Ocean IV Homeowners' Ass'n v. City of North Myrtle Beach*, 523 S.E.2d 193 (S.C.App. 1999) (holding that no taking occurred under *First English* because there was no deprivation of "all economically viable use" when city required a 4-year license agreement for public use of an association pier and using a property-as-a-whole analysis from *Penn Central* and *Keystone*), affirmed in result, 2001 S.C. LEXIS 106 (S.C., June 11, 2001) (using *Nollan/Dolan*, physical exaction analysis).

[15] *First English* should be seen as a remedies case. Even so, its constitutional basis in either the due process or the takings clause is still worth considering: the opinion does not expressly address whether the two clauses should be read as one, as Holmes' "too far" language in *Mahon* suggests. If the clauses are read together, in *First English*, the takings clause provides a remedy for substantive due process violations.

[16] *See* Gregory Stein, *Pinpointing the Beginning and Ending of a Temporary Regulatory Taking*, 70 Wash. L. Rev. 953, 961, 979 (1995).

invasion cases that several in the majority would like to expand). Fourth, that the due process clause, not the takings clause, was involved. Writing the dissent, Justice Stevens stated that the majority opinion would likely have a chilling effect on land use and urban planning, although such effects have proven difficult to measure.[17]

[D] Effects on Other Supreme Court Cases.

While *First English* did not overrule public nuisance abatement/character of the governmental action cases, its facts made it look like such a case: the Los Angeles County legislature had visions of handicapped children being sweep away by a flood. (As the dissent points out, lives were lost in the flood that provoked the ordinance.) The court overlooked this aspect of the case and that indicates that, in any event, substantive due process nexus requirements will continue to be imposed in these types of cases, notwithstanding the seriousness of the health and safety addressed by an ordinance.

[E] The Exception for Normal Administrative Delay.

One exception to this holding is that there is no compensation for normal administrative delays. The rationale for this exception is that expectations of unregulated use are not reasonable investment backed expectations under *Penn Central* when a regulatory scheme or program is in effect at the time of a developer's purchase. *First English* sanctions normal administrative delays inherent in the regulatory process for the development of property.

Distinguishing normal delay from an excessive delay is difficult. Many state zoning enabling acts contain a provision requiring an administrative decision be made with 90 days of the hearing. Arguably a decision that is not made until the 91st day is the product of excessive delay, although the excessive delay might be measured either from day one or starting from the 90th day. Moreover, the good faith of an agency is relevant to the question of delay. If a land use agency is given an advisory opinion to the effect that a regulation is constitutional, then great weight should be given to the opinion if and when the regulation is later held unconstitutional. However, such an opinion would not insulate the agency from the payment of regulatory damages: assuming *arguendo* that the agency acts in good faith reliance on the opinion, there is as yet no judicially-created good faith exception to the holding of *First English*.

Normal delay can also result from litigation. The mere assertion of regulatory jurisdiction is not the start of a temporary taking when the

---

[17] After *First English*, some state regulators explored insurance policies, issued to pay litigation costs and compensation awards and spreading the risk of being found to have taken property across a metropolitan area or region. States with aggressive urban planning programs found such insurance policies more difficult to acquire than other states; this was one chilling effect on land use planning, of which Justice Stevens warned in his dissent.

agency is later found to be in error.[18] So the mistaken denial of a permit that an owner must litigate to correct is not a temporary taking so long as the regulator intended to advance a substantial state interest and the administrative mistake was not unreasonable.[19] The time consumed in a judicial appeal, to either the trial court or the appellate level, is not compensable: there may be harm suffered by an owner as the result of the time consumed, but no matter that the result of the trial and appeal is favorable to an owner, that harm does not rise to the level of a temporary taking.[20] Normal regulatory delays do not give rise to a temporary taking.

§ 5.03 *First English* and Moratoria.

In general, legislative or administrative motives and objectives may be scrutinized in setting damages. For example, when a permit moratoria is enacted and extends for 18 months in order to write and implement an open space preservation plan by the planning board, the moratoria is not a health and safety matter. Therefore, the urgency of the problem should figure in the length of the administrative delay considered reasonable. Here, however, environments once developed, is in a sense and absent expensive public programs, lost forever. So there is every reason to continue evaluating moratoria according to the rules in effect preceding *First English*. One example, *Zilber v. Town of Moraga*,[21] indicates that the 18 month moratoria is not an excessive delay — and that the importance of the objective may indeed argue for lengthening the period countenanced as a normal administrative delay. Similar considerations will probably apply to a phased-growth plan, as in *Ramapo*, or to a rate of growth plan, as in *Petaluma*, or to an up-dating of the comprehensive plan.[22]

A developer seeking a judgment of a temporary taking must be an owner. A developer with an option to buy land does not qualify as such, even in a municipality enacting an invalid moratorium on new developments; a developer with an option does not have a claim for compensation for a temporary taking. Although the period of time that the invalid moratorium was in effect might well not be a normal administrative delay, the developer had an option, not an equitable or contract right to the land, so the municipality can argue that there is no "property" right that can be taken in this instance.[23] An option works no equitable conversion of the title, and so does not give rise to an action for specific performance by the developer. The

---

[18] See *Landgate, Inc. v. California Coastal Comm'n*, 953 P.2d 1188 (Cal.), *cert. denied*, 119 Sup. Ct. 179 (1998).

[19] *Id.* (involving the commission's assertion of jurisdiction over a lot boundary adjustment as involving the "density or intensity" of land use and finding the assertion not unreasonable), *noted at* 7 Hastings W.-N.W. J. Envtl. L. & Policy 55 (2000).

[20] See *Sea Cabins on the Ocean IV Homeowners Ass'n, Inc. v. City of North Myrtle Beach*, 345 S.C. 418, 436 (S.C., June 11, 2001).

[21] 692 F.Supp. 1195, 1206 (N.D.Cal. 1988) (holding such a moratoria valid).

[22] See *infra*, Chapter 9.

[23] *Bd. of Education, Gadsden Indep. School Dist. No 16 v. James Hamilton Const. Co.*, 891 P. 2d 556 (N.M. App. Ct. 1994).

developer/optionor has no interest in the property compensable under the takings clause.[24] Even if the developer had exercised the option during the moratorium, the takings claim would still fail. The investment backed expectations of the developer in exercising the option cannot include the costs of waiting out even an invalid moratorium.

§ 5.04   Determining the Time of the Temporary Taking.

The *First English* majority stated that the temporary taking occurred when the regulation takes effect and ends when a court finds the regulation invalid. That will present a question of fact to the courts. Some commentators on *First English* think that the taking was effective when the invalid regulation first is enacted or becomes effective by its terms. When the Supreme Court's decisions on the doctrine of ripeness are considered alongside *First English*, however, this conclusion may be applicable to a facial challenge to a regulation, but it becomes tenuous for an as applied challenge. When the challenge is as applied, the time of the taking is when (1) the claim to compensation arises and (2) when the statute of limitations begins to run on it. This is so, first, because property owners cannot discover whether they have a claim until the regulators have denied their application to develop; only a punitive notion of compensation favors awarding it from the date of enactment. And, second, because owners have no vested rights in any jurisdiction until much later in the development process.

A better rule is: after the municipality has considered a reasonable application — along with its attendant applications for administrative relief — for a reasonable amount of time, and finally denied it, does a temporary regulatory taking occur.[25] By then, the identity of the administrative or legislative body in the role of the taker is apparent and the extent of the taking is clearer. Such a rule melds the law of ripeness[26] with *First English*. First, such a "final decision" rule will encourage owners wishing to develop to work with regulators. Certainly filing an application is not an indication of an owner's final position on what development is economically feasible, and similarly, the regulators' first or preliminary decision may be ill-considered — both sides in the development process should have a reasonable amount of time to consider and re-consider their positions; regulators should not have to pay for their preliminary decisions.. Second, this rule recognizes that regulation is a process, requiring a "normal" time to implement. Third, the rule does not reward owners who file development plans prematurely, in an attempt to "vest" a takings claim. Fourth, having a rule such as this avoids an *ad hoc* approach to determining the time of the taking.

---

[24] *Eco v. Board of Comm'nrs of Jay County, Indiana*, 57 F. 3d 505 (7th Cir. 1995).

[25] *See City of Pompano Beach v. Yardarm Restaurant, Inc.*, 641 So. 2d 1377, 1384-89 (Fla. Dist. App. Ct., 1994) (a two decade dispute over converting a restaurant into a marina and hotel), *rev. denied*, 651 So. 2d 1197, *cert. denied*, 115 Sup.Ct. 2583 (1995) (adopting a similar rule), *discussed in* Gregory Stein, *Pinpointing the Beginning and Ending of a Temporary Regulatory Taking*, 70 Wash. L. Rev. 953 (1995).

[26] Discussed *infra*, Chapter 19.

In reacting to a finding of a temporary regulatory taking, a municipality is permitted to do one of three things: first, it may repeal the regulation; second, it may move to take the affected property in eminent domain; and, third, it may amend the regulation, eliminating its over-inclusive aspects but achieving as much of its original purposes as are consistent with the requirements of the takings clause.

However, a judicial finding of a temporary regulatory taking may sometimes be greeted by municipal regulatory inaction or silence.[27] Such inaction may thereafter be found to be a permanent taking. Because *First English* recognizes that the exercise of eminent domain is a legislative function, such a finding will be subject to a high burden of proof. Inaction may be found just as easily to be an abandonment of the municipality's regulatory authority, even though this finding intrudes on municipal authority over its own programs. The path of judicial restraint is to treat municipal inaction as a continuing temporary taking, recognizing that the inaction is most likely the result of indecisiveness, not malice. The need is for minimal intrusion into municipal autonomy while still providing an incentive to repeal, amend, or pay for the regulation.

§ 5.05   Measuring Regulatory Damages.

The plaintiffs in *First English* wanted millions of dollars in interim damages. They asked for so much because the owner's intent was to force the lifting of the regulation. The church did not really want to force the county to buy their acreage. Indeed, most developers want to develop, not litigate with the government. Filing for damages is the lever with which to lift the regulation. Perhaps a money damages claim against a local government is only for the developer fed up with the regulators (and who doesn't care if he or she does business in that municipality again).

When damages are awarded, what is the measure of damages? Early in the development process, a developer is likely to spend lots of money on engineering, planning, and market studies of the property proposed for subdivision or development. Such expenses are not recoverable in a temporary takings claim: just compensation for a regulatory taking is measured by the fair market value of the property subject to the taking, not by studies related to the use to which the developer wishes to put it. One proper measure might be the rate of return available on the difference in fair market value with and without the invalid regulation. There are better measures. Consider the following four alternatives:

First, damages may be measured by the **value of the public benefits** achieved. In *San Diego Gas*, Justice Brennan first suggested that if the public gained something by the temporary regulation, it should pay for it. However, this measure is flawed by the poor fit between the public benefit and the private injury worked by the regulation. The two will seldom be equal. The majority opinion in *First English* did not discuss this issue. The

---

[27] Gregory Stein, *Pinpointing the Beginning and Ending of a Temporary Regulatory Taking*, op. cit., 70 Wash. L. Rev. at 1005–09.

court might have done better to adopt Brennan's dissent in *San Diego Gas* verbatim. More generally, in eminent domain cases, measuring damages by the benefit to the government, rather than the loss to the landowner, is unusual. The fair market value of what is taken is the normal measure in eminent domain.

Second, the **fair rental value** of the property during the time of the taking could be used. Such rent might either be computed on the basis of the highest and best use of the property, or the use of the property as regulated, but without the confiscatory regulation. However computed, this measure assumes a hypothetical negotiation over rent, but because the government does not have possession during the time of the taking, the rent which becomes the measure of damages will be very low, and is likely to be speculative too. Moreover, there being little market for rentals of non-possessory rights, there are no experts to appraise such things and testify in court on such a measure.

Third, the **price of an option to purchase** the real property, effective for the period of the taking, could also be used to measure regulatory taking damages. This would be an amount necessary to keep the land off the market for the period of the regulatory taking. Will most developers want to sell? No. And do most municipalities want to buy? Again, no. So this measure is based on a fiction — untruthful answers to unrealistic questions. Moreover, the lack of a market in options might again make appraisal of such damages more than usually difficult — and the results of such appraisals suspect — and increase the litigation costs involved.

Fourth, a **contractual difference money** measure of damages could be used. This could mean two things. It could mean the difference in the value of the property just before and just after, the invalid regulation is imposed. Or, it could mean the difference between the value before the regulation is imposed, and the value after the regulation is removed. The first meaning is usual and workable, but the second meaning seems unfair to the government — unfair to make it pay for fluctuations in value during the period of the taking. That is a risk of ownership, unless it is shown to be a reflection of the lost value of the development rights.

The latter measure could also include consequential damages, e.g., lost profits. Courts often say that lost profits in a new business are too speculative. This means that, if this measure is used, the effect of strikes, cost overruns, construction delays, and the unavailability of financing will somehow have to be factored into the award. This however may only be an example of a rule stating that an owner should receive his or her actual loss or damage, including but not limited to, any lost profits, carrying costs, any lost option opportunities, or any rent lost — in other words, any measure reasonably susceptible of proof.

In part because all of these measures have some drawbacks, traditionally remedies other than damages have been used for a regulatory taking. One example is affirmative injunctive relief, such as judicial rezoning and a decree ordering the granting of permits. Anything less faces the prospect that a municipality will rezone the affected property again and again, always to an unreasonable use, unless the damage claim is permitted to proceed. If the court allows the damage action to proceed, but only awards enough damages to make the owner think twice about further appeals, he will just sell to a speculator at a modest profit and quit the field.

In *First English*, the time period for which damages can be awarded, is the time from the effective date of the ordinance to the time of its invalidation by the courts. This fits the facts of the case: the owner had, since 1957, continuously used the property as a campground and retreat center.

§ 5.06   Off-setting the Takings Award.

Another source of law for fleshing out the dimensions of *First English* lies in the eminent domain codes of the state. Once an owner brings a regulatory takings claim and is awarded damages, statutory provisions governing eminent domain actions may permit the condemnor to off-set the condemnation award by an amount equal to the value of having the public improvement for which the condemnation is made, nearby or adjacent to the condemnee's remaining property. So a municipality confronted with paying for a temporary taking might claim that it is entitled to set-off the award in this way. To what extent the law of eminent domain will provide a guide to *First English* takings is an open question, but the off-set defense is worth asserting.

§ 5.07   The Effects of *First English* on Zoning Administration.[28]

Problems in awarding damages for the enforcement of invalid regulations which go "too far," are likely to arise in one of three situations: (1) a municipality's refusal to rezone; (2) a downzoning; and (3) a situation in which there are damages, undertaken in reliance on the existing zoning in which the owner has a vested right.

As to a rezoning into (say) a duplex residential zone, in a district in which apartment houses are the surrounding and prevailing use (so prevalent that duplexes would not be marketable on this parcel), the owner applying for a rezoning of his parcel into a commercial use district could have the application denied and then bring both a takings claim and a damage claim to court. However, there is probably no taking, and so no damages are available here. A landowner is not entitled to the highest and best use of his or her property. There is no regulatory taking here because some use is still available. The issue is whether *First English* damages may be limited to situations in which the loss of fair market value is near total.

As to a downzoning, suppose that it is applied to a parcel previously zoned for apartments and occurs after an owner's purchase in which a premium price is paid for the parcel. The downzoning permits only single-family housing. The parcel is in the midst of other apartments and the property

---

[28] First-time readers may wish to skip this section and refer back to it, as needed, with reference to Chapters 16–19.

is unmarketable for single-family uses. A rezoning application to permit the use of the parcel for commercial uses is denied. On appeal, this would be seen as a case much like *Lucas v. South Carolina Coastal Council.*[29] It is a categorical total taking of all economically viable uses and value of the parcel.

As to the vested rights, suppose an owner with a parcel zoned for apartments, secured all necessary permits, and commences construction of an apartment house on a parcel. During construction, the property is rezoned for duplexes, to a use district which excludes apartments. In a suit for an injunction against enforcement of the new ordinance and damages, the injunction will issue. Here the rezoning interferes with the owner's development in progress and in almost every jurisdiction, he has acquired a vested right to proceed with his apartments.[30] An even clearer case would be one in which the regulators obtain a stop order against the owner's proceeding with further work or the denial of an occupancy permit; at both of these points, a regulatory taking would be found. Even here, however, the issue arises whether an injunction isn't still a completely satisfactory remedy. Assuming that it is not, an actual loss measure of damages is appropriate because the owner's situation is closely analogous to a tort claim, and so consequential damages for his loss of opportunities should be compensated as well.

§ 5.08 Ripeness and Regulatory Takings.

A state agency or municipality can defer a temporary taking damage award by requiring that it first be presented to a court or an administrative agency of state or municipal government.[31] In earlier cases not resolving the question of interim regulatory damages, the Court had invoked the doctrine of ripeness — finding those cases not ripe for decision, either because there was no final decision or the plaintiff had not sought a compensation remedy as previously discussed.[32] *First English* is then an exception to the usual standards for ripeness in Supreme Court jurisprudence: first, California courts had determined that "all use" was denied, but the administrative process had not yet run its course — the county had

---

[29] 505 U.S. 1003 (1992), discussed *infra*, Chapter 12.

[30] *See infra*, Chapter 21.

[31] Not every municipality has the expertise to handle such claims and such a constitutionally-based right cannot be denied judicial review.

[32] While the United States was looking for the right case to decide the question of regulatory takings, the state courts were busy deciding the same issue in favor of the developer. *See, e.g., Scherr v. Township of Evesham*, 445 A.2d 46 (N.J. Super. Ct., L.Div., 1982). Many state cases involve facts in which the state first attempted to condemn the land, but then pulled back and regulated it for the same purpose as would have been served by the condemnation. *See City of Austin v. Teague*, 570 S.W.2d 839 (Tex. 1978) (involving the denial of development permits for vacant land); G. Rankin, *The First Bite at the Apple: State Supreme Court Takings Jurisprudence Antedating First English*, 22 Urban Law. 417 (1990) (finding that N. J. and Tex. courts found regulatory takings compensable before Justice Brennan's dissent in *San Diego*, Oregon and Rhode Island courts did so afterwards on state constitutional grounds, and Arizona, New Hampshire, North Dakota, and Wisconsin courts did so citing his dissent).

not determined with finality the effect of the regulation on the property; second, another earlier opinion of the court (*Hamilton Bank*) required that a plaintiff seek a variance, a requirement not met in *First English*.

§ 5.09 Section 1983 Actions.

As an alternative to a *First English*, a regulatory takings cause of action, brought under 42 U.S.C.A. § 1983, has some tactical appeal. A § 1983 action is a damages claim against "any person who, under color of any statute, ordinance, regulation, custom, or usage, of any State, subjects or causes to be subjected, any citizen . . . to the deprivation of any rights . . . secured by the Constitution and laws [of the United States]."[33] If a developer wins a due process and takings case, without including a regulatory damages claim, a state court might be quicker to give him or her judgment; a judge who sees the possibility of draining the public treasury will look hard at the case. With the judgment in hand, however, filing a § 1983 claim later provides a forum in which such reluctance will not affect the merits of the prior, regulatory case.

An owner/developer might, however, layer causes of action in federal court after a finding of a taking is made. That is, in addition to the statutory and inverse condemnation claims made in *First English*, he or she might include § 1983 action as well as a takings claim.[34] Any judgment or monetary award under this federal statute is likely to track the takings claim, but under § 1983, awards may be for actual damages, emotional distress, and punitive damages, although not consequential damages. Also recoverable in a successful § 1983 action are attorneys fees. Recovering the latter is another tactical reason to use this section.

In 1999, the United State Supreme Court decided that there was a right to a jury trial in an inverse condemnation action brought under § 1983, but the Court declined "to define with precision the elements of a temporary regulatory takings claim."[35] For example, as a tort claim, consequential damages should be available, but in condemnation cases, only actual or direct damages have typically been given.

Another federal statute, 28 U.S.C.A. § 1331, provides: "The district courts shall have original jurisdiction of all civil actions arising under the Constitution, laws, or treaties of the United States." The law under this section is also likely to track § 1983. But nothing in the statute suggests such a tracking, so that a plea for consequential damages is appropriate here.

---

[33] 42 U.S.C.A. § 1983 (1994).

[34] *See generally Sintra, Inc. v. City of Seattle*, 829 P. 2d 765, 770–771 (Wash. 1992) (containing a general discussion of § 1983 actions).

[35] *City of Monterey v. Del Monte Dunes at Monterey, Ltd.*, 1999 U.S. LEXIS 3631 (U.S. Sup. Ct., May 24, 1999).

§ 5.10   *First English* on Remand.

On remand, the California courts found that "all use" of the plaintiff's property had not been denied in this case and so no damages were payable. [36] The California appeals court also found the ordinance justified as a health and safety measure. [37] It cited *Mugler* and said: "We recognize a brewery is a far cry from a Bible camp. But here the threat to public health and safety emanates not from what is produced on the property but from the presence of any substantial structures on that property." [38] Moreover, the ordinance was not a taking under *Mahon*: "Justice Holmes did not contest the main legal premise of Justice Brandeis' dissent — government has an absolute right to prohibit land uses which constitute a public nuisance." [39] Indeed, the opinion found Holmes' *Mahon* opinion attacking only the minor premise of Brandeis — to the effect that the Kohler Act was not a "private benefit" statute as applied to the facts. The court found that the public safety concerns were more dominant than they were in *Mahon* and *Keystone*:

> It would not be remarkable at all to allow government to deny a private owner "all uses" of his property where there is no use of that property which does not threaten lives and health. So it makes perfect sense to deny compensation for the denial of "all uses" where health and safety are at stake but require compensation for the denial of "all uses" where the land use regulation advances lesser public purposes. [40]

The "lesser" purposes are not enumerated, but they might include moratoria and growth controls. Further, "all use" of the property was not prohibited by the ordinance. Tenting and campfires were still possible: "Meals could be cooked, games played, lessons given, tents pitched." [41] Finally, the later opinion found that, as a moratorium, the ordinance was reasonably drafted to accomplish its purpose.

Shortly after the *First English* case was decided, the United States Supreme Court refused to hear and decide a case that some thought would have expanded its holding, reviewing the constitutionality of a Denver ordinance which was broadly aimed at protecting the view of the Rockies from downtown. [42]

---

[36] *First English Evan. Lutheran Church of Glendale v. County of Los Angeles*, 258 Cal. Rptr. 893, 894, 899–900, n. 9, 901–902, 906–907 (Cal. App. Ct., 2d Dist., 1989).

[37] Did you expect a remand to a *trial* court to consider what uses remained to the owner of the camp? The state appeals court, without taking further testimony or evidence, decided the matter remanded here.

[38] *First English*, 258 Cal. Rptr. at 899.

[39] *Id.* at 900, n. 9.

[40] *Id.* at 901.

[41] *Id.* at 902.

[42] *Harsh v. City and County of Denver*, 728 P.2d 1281 (Colo. 1987), *cert. denied,* 483 U.S. 1001 (1987).

§ 5.11 Governmental Confusion and Bad Faith.

As previously indicated, a line of cases predating and surviving *First English* involves governmental bad faith. An example is *Arastra Limited Partnership v. City of Palo Alto*.[43] There, the locale was the Palo Alto foothills; the city sits in a bowl in their midst and had annexed the foothills in the 1950s in order to gain control over their development.[44]

In *Arastra*, a partnership owned 515 acres in the foothills. In 1967, the city built an overlook on land above the partners'. During the years 1967-1972, the city took steps to acquire the land by eminent domain; it explored financing the acquisition by using federal grants, the proceeds of municipal bonds, and other monies; it searched the title and appraised the land; finally, it enacted a resolution declaring its intent to acquire the land by eminent domain. But it never did; it walked up to the point of acquisition, but never crossed over. Instead, it enacted an "open space regulation", permitting three houses per acre, reducing the fair market value (in the partners' appraiser's opinion) by about two million dollars.

The partners sued in inverse condemnation, claiming that a *de facto* taking had occurred and measuring the damages from the date the open space ordinance was enacted.

Judgment was for the partnership. There was a taking and the just compensation was measured on the date of the ordinance. The city's reversal of policies after so much preparation for eminent domain showed that its true intent was to accomplish by regulation what it could not afford by eminent domain. Thus, the regulation was not aimed at preventing over-development of the foothills, but at extracting a public benefit — open space — from the plaintiffs.

The city argued that there was no physical invasion and so no taking. The district court responded that this argument took a lot of nerve, because physical invasion was precisely the thing the city meant to avoid with its ordinance.

Government ineptitude and an inability to decide on a policy, not amounting to bad faith, has also been found to be a taking.[45] The *Benenson* opinion harks back to earlier cases of planning blight, occurring when an urban renewal or redevelopment agency makes plans to condemn an area, which is denied public services in anticipation of the condemnation, with the result that property values fall prior to the date that the condemnation is legally effective. In this situation, the condemnees are compensated for the fair market value of their property before the planning blight occurred.

---

[43] 401 F. Supp. 962 (N.D. Cal. 1975, *vacated by agreement of the parties*, 417 F. Supp. 1125 (N.D. Cal. 1976).

[44] For background on the foothills controversy, see *Eldridge v. City of Palo Alto*, 129 Cal. Rptr. 575 (Cal. App. Ct. 1976).

[45] *See, e.g., Benenson v. United States*, 548 F.2d 939 (Ct. Cl. 1977) (a decade of uncoordinated agency efforts and policy uncertainty, including a reversal of policy on historic preservation of the Willard Hotel on Washington D.C.'s Pennsylvania Avenue, causing the Court of Claims to find a taking as of the date the building had to be preserved).

§ 5.12   States Takings Legislation.

Many states have considered, and several have enacted, controversial legislation defining (more broadly than does *First English*) situations in which property owners are entitled to compensation when their property is diminished in value by regulation.[46] Twenty five states enacted such legislation between 1991 and 1996. The legislative objective is to provide a bright line to the diminution in value test for a taking used since the *Mahon* case. Two states (Arizona and Washington) enacted such legislation, only to have the enactments repealed by the voters. The scope of this type of legislation varies from state to state. Louisiana and Mississippi have enacted statutes providing for compensation for owners when a regulation produced a diminution in value amounting to a specific percentage of the pre-regulation fair market value — 40% in Mississippi, 20% in Louisiana — but applies it only to timber or agricultural land. Texas uses a 25% decrease, but broadly applies its statute to any regulated real property. Finally, Florida has a statute compensating generally any "inordinate burden" on the use of real property, leaving it to the courts to define such a burden.[47]

---

[46] *See* Harvey Jacobs, *The Impact of State Property Rights Laws: Those Laws and My Land*, Land Use Law and Zoning Digest (March, 1998), available on the web at <www.planning.org/pubs/zdmar98.htm/> (visited June 3, 2000).

[47] *See* and *compare* Frank Michelman, *Testimony before the Senate Committee on Environment and Public Works, June 27, 1995,* 49 J. Urban & Contemp. L. 1, 13–15 (1996) (reviewing similar federal legislation) *with* Richard Epstein, *Whose Democratic Vision of the Takings Clause? A Comment on Frank Michelman's Testimony on Senate Bill 605, ibid.* at 17.

Chapter 6

The Structure of Zoning: The *Euclid* Case

§ 6.01 Introduction.

All land is held subject to the regulation of its use by government at many levels.[1] As we have seen in previous Chapters, such regulation is authorized by and derived from the police power as well as limited by the due process and takings clauses of the federal and state constitutions.[2] Today, along with education and the real property tax, land-use regulation is one of three activities on which municipal officials spend the bulk of their time and effort.[3]

With regard to land use regulation, it was not always so. Until the late 19th century, the law of nuisance and private restrictive covenants were the principal means of controlling land use. Absent those means, the size of a lot or parcel and adjustment of the placement and location of improvements on realty were the principal means of avoiding the effects of nearby intrusive or undesirable uses.

The use of zoning became common in the early decades of the 20th century and spread with particular rapidity in the post-World War I era of the 1920s. Zoning is the product of the exercise by state and local governments of the police power. Dillon's Rule[4] applies. Thus, a municipality's planning and zoning activity must be conferred by the state's planning and zoning enabling act or be reasonably necessary to achieve a power expressly delegated by the state in that act. Only so much of the police power as is necessary to achieve a scheme of land use regulation is conferred. In many states, planning and zoning powers are often delegated in separate statutes.

Every state has enacted a separate, state-wide, zoning enabling act. The purpose of such acts is to delegate authority to municipal governments to formulate and conduct a scheme of land use regulation.[5] The prototype for

---

[1] In their first year of law school, students learn that a person holding a freehold title to land has *"seisin"* as one component of that title. Seisin is possession that is responsive to governmental authority — what we mean when attorneys say that all titles are "subject to" regulation by the government.

[2] Although federal environmental regulations everywhere have an indirect impact on land use, the federal government seldom directly regulates land use and, except for a few states (e.g., Florida, Hawaii, and Vermont), neither do the states. Regional agencies do sometimes regulate land with special environmental problems (e.g., wetlands).

[3] In this and succeeding Chapters, "municipal" means either the city, county, town, or township level of government.

[4] As discussed *supra,* Chapter 1.

[5] All of these delegations of authority are in the first instance to municipal legislative bodies — such as city or town councils, county or township commissioners, or boards of selectmen — who are therein authorized to enact zoning codes and ordinances. Some states delegate the

these acts is the Standard Zoning Enabling Act ("SZEA"), drafted originally by the United States Department of Commerce and ready for adoption in 1924.[6] It is still the model for state enabling acts today. It authorizes the municipal legislative body to enact a zoning scheme (an ordinance[7] containing the text for the regulatory scheme, and a zoning map). It then establishes two administrative bodies to consider matters of zoning administration: first, a **zoning commission** to handle requests to change the zoning designation of a property ("rezoning"); and second, a **board of zoning adjustment or appeals**, to hear requests for variances, special exceptions, and appeals from administrators interpreting the ordinance. This two-body administrative structure still prevails in most municipalities today.

The Standard Planning Enabling Act followed in 1928. It establishes a **planning commission** as a quasi-independent agency of local government, presumably to keep it non-political. To this agency was committed the formulation of land use plans. Although many states have since enacted more comprehensive statutes to authorize these activities, many still use the basic provisions of these two early acts.

The subdivision of land is also typically enabled by a separate state statute, and delegations of the police power may be made as well — typically through the enactment of home rule charters for some municipalities. The subdivision review process is often conducted by the municipality's planning commission.

The activities of planning and zoning, undertaken by municipal governments, must be grounded in these enabling acts. A first question in any controversial action is whether the activity is *ultra vires* — that is, beyond the authority conferred on a municipality by the act.

The further, constitutional constraint on the planning and zoning powers of municipalities are found in due process clause of the Fifth Amendment, made applicable to the states through the Fourteenth Amendment, and on comparable constitutional provisions in state constitutions. Due process not only has a procedural meaning — a course of proceedings according to rules and procedures established for the protection of private rights — but it also has a substantive meaning, to the effect that the burdens imposed by government, by regulation or otherwise, should be roughly off-set by the benefit engendered by it. This idea of rough equality between the benefits and burdens of a regulation is known as economic, or substantive, due process. A regulation should not be so onerous that there is no benefit back to the regulated person, considered either directly or as a member of the

---

power to enact land use ordinances to two municipal entities at once — say, to counties and towns. *See, e.g., Quinn v. Town of Dodgeville*, 364 P.2d 149 (Colo. 1985) (upholding such dual authority). Some states also permit zoning ordinance to be established by voter initiatives and some (but fewer) states permit enacted ordinances to be reviewed in voter referenda.

[6] Standard State Zoning Enabling Act, *reprinted in* A.L.I., *Model Land Development Code*, Tent. Draft No. 1, at 210 (1968).

[7] Zoning ordinance refers to legislation enacted by a municipality of some type. In this sense, an ordinance is an enactment made with the consent of the state and authorized by it, valid until the enabling act requires that something else be done. In this sense, an ordinance refers back to its English origins, as an edict of the King valid until Parliament began its next session.

public. In this connection, Holmes' "reciprocity of advantage" phrase in *Mahon* was his attempt to use this type of analysis without identifying it as such — in part because he objected to its use in *Lochner v. People of the State of New York*.[8] Another alternative statement of economic due process is that particular persons not be singled out and forced to bear unfair burdens. A regulation that does not have this reciprocity, is labeled "arbitrary and capricious." This phrase is also commonly used by courts when referring to a standard of judicial review for legislative zoning matters.

However, there is traditionally no taking issue raised by economic losses caused by health and safety regulations. The evaluation of such regulations is a matter reviewed under the due process clause of the Fourteenth Amendment or its state constitutional counterpart. There, the judiciary's concern is for the economic burden imposed by a regulation, as well as legislative arbitrariness. Thus the clause has both substantive and procedural concerns.

§ 6.02 *Village of Euclid v. Ambler Realty Company.*

While zoning became very popular, planning did not. Even zoning had an uncertain constitutional status until 1926, when the United States Supreme Court handed down its opinion in the case of *Euclid v. Ambler Realty Co.*[9] The petitioner, the Ambler Realty Company, owned a 68 acre tract, shaped roughly like a parallelogram, in the Village of Euclid. Euclid was a suburb of the City of Cleveland. Ambler's tract was bordered on two sides — to the east and west — by residential land uses. On its southern boundary, it abutted Euclid Avenue. At the time, the avenue was a major thorough-fare in the Cleveland area. It was lined with substantial residences, mostly facing north toward Lake Erie and including the mansion of John D. Rockefeller.

In *Euclid*, the United States Supreme Court upheld the zoning ordinance of an Ohio municipality that divided its land area in use, height, and area districts. The owner was made to look like a land speculator, not a housing developer; it had, at the time of the litigation, no definite plans for the development of their property.

The percentages of fair market value lost by Ambler Realty to regulation were alleged to be severe. Unzoned, the fair market value per acre was allegedly four times what it was zoned. Along Euclid Avenue, the front foot value was supposed to be three times greater unzoned than it was zoned.

Ambler Realty's tract was zoned into three use districts — for two-family dwellings abutting the Avenue, for apartments and hotels in the center of the property, and, on the northerly portion of the property, abutting railroad tracks, for industrial uses.[10] These use districts were "cumulative"

---

[8] 198 U.S. 45 (1905).

[9] 272 U.S. 365 (1926) (hereafter *Euclid*).

[10] *Euclid*, 272 U.S. at 379–383 (describing the village ordinance).

— that is, any use permitted in a higher or less dense district were also permitted in lower, more dense districts. Perhaps the most profitable resale of Ambler Realty's property would have been for industrial uses, but while the ordinance permitted industrial uses along the northern edge of the tract, along a railroad, such uses were prohibited in the southern portion of the property which had roadway access along the avenue.[11]

The Village's initial ordinance had placed the Ambler tract into two zones — U-6 and U-2 — but Ambler protested and a strip of U-3 district was added along the middle of the tract. Today Ambler Realty would probably have pursued further legislative and administrative remedies before bringing suit to invalidate the ordinance. Indeed, today it would probably be required to do so, unless the further request would be a futile act.

The *Euclid* opinion spent little time disputing Ambler Realty's allegations of loss. Its analysis started by applying a presumption of validity to the legislative acts of the Village and continued with a search for some rational basis for the ordinance — and so did not require a close look. Rather, it looked at the purpose and character of the regulation and the nexus or connection between that purpose and the ordinance's provisions. This type of analysis involved was what, and is, called substantive due process analysis.

In *Euclid*, the financial impact of the regulation on Ambler Realty's tract, while recognized, seemed to play little role in the Supreme Court's analysis. At the time that the regulations were imposed, there were no industrial uses in the Village. Yet part of Ambler's property was zoned for industrial uses, and other parts were zoned more restrictively, for multi-unit residential structures.

Ambler was buying in advance of development. It had in fact (though a fact not cited in the opinion) developed some property along Euclid Avenue further in, toward the city, but had imposed covenants which restricted the uses in its development to non-industrial uses.

Sutherland's holding was a broad-brush validation of the Village ordinance, and of zoning ordinances in general, not a look at their details. Its generality is one of its important features. His opinion represents a "facial" analysis instead of an "as applied" analysis of the ordinance. It contains, for example, a discussion of the exclusion of apartments from a single-family residential use district, although this was a matter not raised by the facts of Ambler Realty's ownership. Sutherland's opinion emphasizes the segregation of potentially conflicting land uses. A nuisance, he says, "may be merely a right thing in the wrong place — like a pig in the parlor instead of the barnyard."[12]

---

[11] *See* Richard Epstein, *The Conceptual Approach to Zoning: What's Wrong with Euclid*, 5 N.Y. U. Envir. L. J. 277, 286–287 (1996) (suggesting this).

[12] *Euclid*, 272 U.S. at 388 (suggesting that Sutherland had private, not public, nuisance in mind and recalling *Alred's Case*, 77 Eng. Rep. 816 (King's Bench 1611) (involving a pig sty interfering with the use of a house)). A comparable issue today might be the problems posed by livestock feedlots. *See* John Hartzell, *Agricultural and Rural Zoning in Pennsylvania: Can You Get There From Here?*, 10 Vill. Envir. L. J. 245, 271–274 (1999).

It is important that the zoning ordinance laid down a general scheme of land uses rather than permitting the Village officials to permit development of its land area only on a case-by-case basis or by meeting special conditions. At the time, this would have made the Village's case a weaker one, for then it could be said that the legislature had not enacted a general scheme which the jurisdiction's administrators could implement. The *Euclid* opinion was a pre-New Deal one, and the product of an era when only the narrowest delegations of authority to administrative bodies were likely to survive judicial review. For instance, to secure a special permit, a developer would have to show that its plans were in accordance with the general welfare of the community and would not have any adverse impact on adjacent land. In such a situation, administrative standards would be more suitably implemented by legislative decisions. As a general rule, the exercise of the police power could not then be delegated once the state legislature had provided that a particular municipal body shall exercise it.

In subsequent years, *Euclid's* general finding of validity accomplished three things.[13] First, the Supreme Court said that it would use a flexible and case-by-case approach to zoning issues. Second, its lengthy discussion of the background of zoning laws endorsed the use of urban planning as a pre-condition for a zoning ordinance; the court endorsed its use, but did not hold that such planning was a necessary precondition to enacting a zoning ordinance. Third and finally, the court found that the validity of an ordinance was measured by the extent to which it sought to prevent a land use pattern or situation that would require nuisance litigation to resolve. In contested and doubtful situations, Justice Sutherland said, "the maxim *sic utere tuo ut alienum non laedas*, which lies at the foundation of the law of nuisances, ordinarily will furnish a fairly helpful clue as to the resolution."[14] The court also said that so long as the owners of the regulated property were still permitted a "reasonable return" on their investments regulation was valid.

Because of the general nature of the discussion, it is difficult to determine what portions of the Village ordinance are upheld. The ordinance was upheld generally, but the impact of its separate provisions was not assessed, and the applicability of those provisions was not discussed in the context of a specific piece of property like Ambler Realty's. Two years later, the court did as promised, use a case-by-case approach, and invalidated an ordinance "as applied" to particular property.[15] *Nectow v. City of Cambridge* seemed to presage Supreme Court involvement in the zoning field, but thereafter the court did not consider any zoning cases until the 1970s. So much, then, for the court's promise in *Euclid* of close review of such ordinances in the future. Its next zoning opinion was in 1974, in *Village of Belle Terre v. Boraas.*[16]

---

[13] *See* Michael Allan Wolf, *Euclid at Threescore Years and Ten: Is This the Twilight of Environmental and Land-Use Regulation*, 30 U. Rich. L. Rev. 961, 963–964 (1996).

[14] *Euclid*, 272 U.S. at 387.

[15] *Nectow v. City of Cambridge*, 277 U.S. 183, 188–189 (1928).

[16] 416 U.S. 1 (1974), discussed *infra*, Chapter 14.

Thus the questions raised, but left unanswered by *Euclid* involve the day to day administration of a zoning ordinance. Would the court uphold any or all of the following: a prohibition on motels from a commercial district where hotels are permitted? A prohibition on bed-and-breakfast businesses from a commercial district in which motels are permitted? A prohibition of fast food restaurants from an area permitting sit-down restaurants? A prohibition on residential development on a flood plain? All of these involve close distinctions. All mimic the prohibition of apartment houses from single-family residential use districts upheld in *Euclid*.

All of the forgoing distinctions might plausibly be made today and, using the presumption of validity and the narrow standard of review used in this opinion, upheld by the courts. While they all present interesting questions, there really is no answer to be found in Sutherland's opinion; rather, he says that the law of nuisance will often "furnish a helpful clew" as to whether an ordinance's validity. Nuisance law was the one guidepost the law had in his day. However, Justice Sutherland did not say it was the only, or exclusive guide.[17] He cited it "not for the purpose of controlling, but for the helpful aid of its analogies in the process of ascertaining the scope of"[18] the police power. It also provided him with a way of avoiding directly endorsing zoning as an expansion of the police power. The validity of the zoning ordinance here was a signal to municipalities that in the future they need not rely on nuisance litigation to sort out their land use conflicts; they also need not wait for matters to get so bad that private plaintiffs come forward to seek resolution of such conflicts. A zoning ordinance is presumed valid and the presumption remains intact until the ordinance is shown to be arbitrary or capricious. (Of this presumption, more *infra*.)

The *Euclid* opinion dealt specifically with only one such distinction — whether apartment houses could be excluded from a residential district. Justice Sutherland called this the "serious question" of the case.[19] Apartments had long been a subject of controversy.[20] With such a history, it is little wonder that apartment buildings appear in the *Euclid* opinion as a form of urban blight.[21] The apartment house is a "parasite" taking "advantage of open spaces and attractive surroundings created by the residential character of the district,"[22] blocking light and air, bringing noise and traffic, depriving children of a place to play, and finally destroying the character of the neighborhood. Justice Sutherland saw zoning controlling apartments not as a deprivation of property rights, but as a method of conserving residential property values. He also seemed to see overcrowding of uses as one of the problems that zoning might permissibly address, along with

---

[17] *Euclid*, 272 U.S. at 387–388. The extent to which land use controls must rest on a local legislature's authority to control or abate nuisances is today a matter of renewed debate. *See Lucas v. South Carolina Coastal Council*, 505 U.S. 1003 (1992).

[18] *Euclid*, 272 U.S. at 387–388.

[19] *Id.* at 390.

[20] *See* Kenneth Jackson, *Crabgrass Frontier* 89–92 (1985).

[21] *Id.*

[22] *Euclid*, 272 U.S. at 390.

safety problems like the danger of fires.[23] Sutherland's emphasis is on the validity of separating and segregating land uses.

Because of this emphasis, under *Euclid*, the Village probably could not have zoned its land area into one district, in which only residential uses were permitted. That would have been an admission by the Village that land uses were not a problem, and not in need of separation, one from another. If nuisance was a guideline for permissible zoning, the separation of otherwise incompatible land use was a precondition to the exercise of the police power via zoning.[24]

Today, a court might evaluate a prohibition on apartments in one of two ways. First, the court can look at what other uses, besides apartments, are excluded. Are they uses of similar intensity? If the answer is yes, the ordinance is under-inclusive. However, if the court finds that there are no other similar uses excluded, then the court can broaden its inquiry: the question then becomes, are there uses of similar intensity, which are included? If the answer is yes, then the ordinance is over-inclusive (except of course, as to the protesting landowner).

In the present, the issue of the need to exclude apartments might be rephrased as an issue of whether apartments cannot be zoned into a residential district, but without the side effects Sutherland saw. When Sutherland discussed the impact of apartment houses in single-family residential use districts, he dealt only with the external effects of the apartments.[25] There was no discussion demonstrating that their effects can be dealt with a zoning ordinance. For instance, if automobiles are a problem, the apartment house owners can be compelled to provide on-site parking. If they block light and air, set-back regulations can be imposed. And so on. Sutherland did not deal with the fact that real people live in apartment houses because he is concerned primarily with the nuisance-abating provisions of the Village's ordinance. On the other hand, to be fair to Justice Sutherland, it should be said that techniques for including apartment uses in otherwise single-family districts rely on post-1930 views of what it is permissible to delegate to an administrative agency, the later-invented techniques of city planners, and twenty-twenty hindsight. Sutherland endorsed the separation of land uses, rather than validating an attempt to combine or mix them.[26] In particular, the *Euclid* opinion endorsed the separation

---

[23] *Id.*

[24] *See, e.g., Rockhill v. Chesterfield Twp.,* 128 A.2d 473 (N.J. 1956).

[25] Apartments were considered mildly shady until the end of the 1800s: entrances did not front the street and busybodies could not monitor comings and goings; in New York City until the Stuyvesant Apartments (built in 1870) "overcame the risque image of the French flat," respectable Americans who could afford a private dwelling were not attracted to them. Kenneth Jackson, *Crabgrass Frontier* 90 (1985). Only in the 1880s did multi-unit buildings become good downtown development: the Dakota Apartments were built on Central Park West at 79th St. — so far uptown that they might as well have been in the Dakota Territory, with its liberal divorce laws.

[26] For example, if livestock feedlots need to be abated as nuisances, then ordinances regulating them ought to think in terms of "odor zones" and buffers, holding lagoons for waste, restrictions on size, and impact fees for local roads transporting the animals. Illinois and North Carolina have enacted special regulations for feedlots.

of homes from more intensive commercial and industrial uses.[27]

§ 6.03   A Post-*Euclid* Presumption of Validity.

As in *Euclid*, the usual rule is that a zoning ordinance enjoys a presumption of validity. Yet this presumption does not apply when the exclusion of a particular land use is total, unless this total exclusion is necessary to preserve the overall character of the zoning jurisdiction.[28]

In land use opinions, the presumption is not an evidentiary one, allocating the burden of producing evidence; here the "evidence" (if one can call it that) is a mixture of social science data and legislative judgments. So instead, the presumption of validity typically refers to a standard of judicial review — a statement of the relationship between courts and local legislatures — to the effect that once an ordinance is shown to be fairly debatable, the presumption of constitutional validity attaches to it. If there is a plausible rationale for the ordinance, a court will sustain it. (By the way, if it truly were an evidentiary presumption, a court would sustain it, a prima facie case having been made out, unless the facts that are developed later overcome it.)

The necessity for an exclusion is judged by one of two ways; first, the need for the use within the use district, and second, the need for the use within the municipality. Incompatibility with the surrounding and permitted uses provides a third way. Similarly, where a use is totally excluded from a zoning jurisdiction, the necessity for the exclusion is judged either by the need for the use within the jurisdiction or within the surrounding metropolitan region.

§ 6.04   Some Background on *Euclid*.

The advocates of zoning were, at the time of the *Euclid* litigation, unhappy that this case went to the United States Supreme Court. Alfred Bettman, one of these advocates, and the writer of the most influential of the *Amicus Curiae* briefs before the court, thought the ordinance ill-considered.[29] The Village had done little in the way of studies to support its ordinance and Bettman considered that its industrial zone, along the railroad tracks running through the Village, was too narrow to be of much use to industry. Bettman's brief thus made little of the ordinance as it applied to the plaintiff's land and defined (or redefined) the issue so that

---

[27] *Euclid*, 272 U.S. at 388 (citing its own cases restricting a brick yard and a stable from a residential area, and permitting height limits on building in Boston's residential Back Bay neighborhood). *See Hadacheck v. Sebastian*, 239 U.S. 394 (1915) (as to the brick yard); *Reiman v. Little Rock*, 237 U.S. 171 (1915) (as to the stable); and *Welch v. Swasey*, 214 U.S. 91 (as to the height limits).

[28] *McNeill v. Twp. of Plumsted*, 522 A.2d 469, 471 (N.J. Super. Ct., App. Div., 1987) (remanding case to consider conditions requiring ordinance excluding removal of topsoil from township parcels).

[29] Alfred Bettman, *Village of Euclid v. Ambler Realty Co. Brief, Amicus Curiae*, in Arthur Comey, ed., *City and Regional Planning Papers* 157, 172 (1946).

only the general validity of the ordinance was at issue. The Sutherland opinion accepted this premise.[30]

Justice Sutherland was in the process of writing an opinion striking down the Village's ordinance as applied when he changed his mind, had the case reargued, and then wrote the opinion handed down.[31] What had been going to be a loss for zoning advocates, was ripped from the jaws of defeat at the last minute; and zoners won the day — gaining general approval for zoning.

The Supreme Court probably knew of the widespread adoption in the states of the Standard Zoning Enabling Act — over one half of the states had adopted it by the end of 1925.[32] Indeed, in a general way, the opinion seemed to take judicial notice of such a fact. Moreover, the Act was promulgated by the successive Republican administrations of the 1920s. Finally, Ambler Realty made it easy for the court to uphold the ordinance by bringing what could be characterized as a facial challenge to the ordinance. It had no definite plans for the development of its sixty-eight acres. It probably should have developed a plan before bringing suit. Perhaps it did not because its capital gains would look disproportionate to their initial investment, and so the claim to have suffered a "diminution in value" would have a hollow ring.

§ 6.05   A Presumption + A Rational Basis = Deference.

Judicial deference is the dispositive principle of the *Euclid* opinion. It leads to a presumption of legislative validity, which leads in turns to a rule that if the matter before the legislature is fairly debatable, the presumption applies: the legislature need only muster "substantial evidence" or have a "rational basis" for its decision. Often this standard of review is phrased negatively, and means only that the legislature shall not act in an arbitrary or capricious manner. There is no requirement that the legislature pick the best solution to a matter it considers; there is no requirement of legislative efficiency in this sense; on the contrary, the legislature can pick one of several, equally well justified solutions, so long as it is supported by substantial evidence.

---

[30] *Id.*

[31] Mel Scott, *American City Planning* 240 (1971) (reviewing the background of the *Euclid* case, *id.* at 238–240).

[32] Early zoning was used differently in different locations. In the central cities of our metropolitan areas, it was used to separate commercial uses. New York City's first zoning ordinance, enacted in 1916, was used to separate department stores from the sewing lofts that produced the goods sold in the stores — particularly women's dresses. (Residential uses were not protected as well because absentee landlords owned much of the residential property.) Cities as large as Chicago were over-zoned for commercial uses, and cities in California, which saw themselves becoming the Chicagos of the future, were overzoning vacant land as well. In the suburbs, in contrast, zoning was used to segregate residential land-uses from other uses. In any event, zoning proved a popular device in many locations. By 1926, seventy six cities has enacted ordinances. By 1936, more than 1,300 cities — 85% of American cities — had ordinances.

§ 6.06   The Remedy.

In *Euclid*, as in *Hadacheck v. Sebastion*[33] and *Mahon*, the remedy asked was an injunction against the enforcement of an ordinance. The earlier majority opinion in *Mahon* is not cited or discussed. Would the result in *Euclid* have been different if damages had been sought? The answer is probably not. Arguably then the issue would not have involved the Fifth Amendment's due process clause, but the takings clause of that Amendment. Citing these different constitutional clauses could have become a wedge driving the *Mahon* and *Euclid* cases apart, into separate lines of authority; the first involving the takings clause, the second involving the due process clause. As it was, in both of these cases, what was sought was the traditional remedy in a nuisance suit.

§ 6.07   The District Court Opinion in *Euclid*.

The federal district judge in *Euclid* invalidated the Village's ordinance.[34] The judge said: "The purpose to be accomplished is really to regulate the mode of living of persons who hereafter inhabit" the village. [T]he result . . . is to classify the population and segregate them according to their income or situation in life."[35]

His authority for this included Holmes's opinion in *Mahon*. That opinion provided a reasonable basis for striking down the ordinance. It was also accompanied in that era by a series of state supreme court decisions which perceived zoning ordinances as aimed at separating the rich from the poor and from "undesirable" commercial activities.[36]

The Supreme Court's *Euclid* opinion ignored these cases and *Mahon* because the due process and takings clauses for most of the Justices (Holmes excepted) presented distinct inquiries and separate issues.

In the process of invalidating the Village ordinance, the federal district judge also had harsh things to say about the discriminatory effects he expected to flow from the ordinance. He saw the zoning ordinance as a method of economic exclusion and class separation.

In order to set the scene as the district judge saw it, you need to know that, generally, there are two strains of opinions with regard to the intersection of zoning and civil rights. One is represented by the *Euclid* opinion, in which the rights of persons excluded from the two are not closely examined. Another is represented by the opinion in *Buchanan v. Warley*,[37] in which the United States Supreme Court held invalid an ordinance of

---

[33] 239 U.S. 394 (1915) (upholding zoning out petitioner's brickyard), discussed *supra*, Chapter 2.

[34] *Ambler Realty Co. v. Village of Euclid*, 297 F. 307, 309 (N.D. Ohio 1924), *reversed*, 272 U.S. 365 (1926).

[35] *Id.* at 316.

[36] *See, e.g., Spann v. City of Dallas*, 235 S.W.2d 513, 516 (Tex. 1921) ("the true reason why some persons live in a mansion and others in a shack . . . is primarily economic").

[37] 245 U.S. 60 (1917).

the City of Louisville, Kentucky, which prevented blacks or whites from moving into blocks on which resided persons of the other race.[38]

In *Buchanan*, the plaintiff was a white property owner, whose right to alienate his property was impaired by the ordinance, which limited the class of purchasers to whom he could sell. He was injured in fact for purposes of the requirements of standing, but the Court's substantive holding was premised on a due process concern with an African-American's right to purchase the white person's property. The *Buchanan* opinion reached those in the African-American community (or other protected minority) who could afford to purchase property. Renters could take little comfort from it.

More recently, such a creative joinder of the interests of both races led to cases like *United States v. City of Black Jack, Missouri*,[39] holding a zoning ordinance invalid because of its violation of the Fair Housing Act of 1968, and *United States v. City of Parma*,[40] another suit brought, this time by the Department of Justice, under the Act. Both of the last two cases are decided on statutory, and not constitutional, grounds.

Later chapters on exclusionary zoning will return to the civil rights implications of the *Euclid* opinion. Justice Sutherland did not, in *Euclid*, deal with the broader context of the region in which the Village of Euclid enacted its ordinance. Later cases have done so.

---

[38] *See also Yick Ho v. Hopkins*, 118 U.S. 356, 374 (1886) (invalidating ordinance requiring permit to operate a laundry that, the Court found, was motivated by a desire to exclude Chinese laundries).

[39] 508 F.2d 1179, 1188 (8th Cir. 1974), *cert. denied*, 422 U.S. 1042 (1974).

[40] 661 F.2d 562 (6th Cir. 1982) (a "pattern or practice suit" bought under the Act).

Chapter 7

Euclidian Land-Use Controls and Non-Conforming Uses

§ 7.01 Zoning and Planning.

Zoning is the regulation and restriction of land uses according to a pre-determined plan. Under many state zoning enabling acts, zoning ordinances are required to be "in accordance with a comprehensive plan."[1] This means one of three things: either that (1) some type of urban planning is a precondition to their enactment,[2] or (2) the zoning must initially be enacted on a comprehensive basis, considering whatever planning had been done,[3] or (3) the decisions made in drafting the ordinance must be internally consistent and the ordinance itself implemented and interpreted in a consistent manner. The third and last approach is the majority rule. The first is generally the result of the legislature's making urban planning a mandatory activity of municipalities by statute. California and Oregon are examples of this first approach.

If and when this precondition is met, in any of its three forms, comprehensive land use ordinances are entitled to twin presumptions of constitutionality and validity. They are then upheld when they are fairly debatable and for purposes of judicial review, have a rational basis, having a nexus between the statutory authority and the ordinance under review.

The presumption of validity is not always accorded. It is not accorded a later piece-meal rezoning of land in several situations: (1) when it is spot zoning[4] (affecting a small parcel in a non-uniform manner), or (2) when there is no showing of either a public need for the rezoning or a substantial change in the neighborhood of the change requested,[5] or (3) when its application is exclusionary.[6] These exceptions will be discussed in later Chapters.

Enactment of a zoning or land use ordinance is typically subject to procedural requirements: notice,[7] hearings,[8] and comment periods are

---

[1] Standard Zoning Enabling Act § 3.

[2] *Town of Jonesville v. Powell Valley Ltd. Partnership*, 487 S.E.2d 207 (Va. 1997) (ordering a building permit issued when the zoning ordinance of the town was not based on a comprehensive plan mandated by statute).

[3] *See, e.g., Udall v. Haas*, 235 N.E.2d 897, 900–901 (N.Y. 1968).

[4] Discussed *infra,* Chapter 12.

[5] Discussed *infra,* Chapter 12.

[6] Discussed *infra,* Chapter 15.

[7] *See Golden Gate Corp. v. Town of Naragansett*, 359 A.2d 321, 324 (R.I. 1976).

[8] *See F. P. Plaza, Inc. v. Waite*, 196 S.E.2d 141, 144 (Ga. 1973).

typical.[9] At legislative hearings, the rules of evidence do not apply and there is no right to cross examine witnesses. There is, however, a requirement that such hearings be conducted with basic fairness.[10] Sometimes an administrative body will first hold a hearing and study the ordinance, and sometimes the ordinance is even prepared by an administrative body, such as the planning commission, and then the ordinance is referred to the municipal legislature for hearings and adoption. Amendments to the ordinance are also likely to be reviewed by the planning commission.[11]

After *Village of Euclid v. Ambler Realty Company*,[12] zoning assumed its current form: that is, as with the process involved in and approved in *Euclid*, local land use control ordinances mapped the municipality, dividing it into different use districts. The "highest" (or one use) district was reserved for residential uses;[13] typically, one residential district was reserved for single-family, detached residences. In another residential district, town-houses, or duplexes might be added to the list of permitted residences.[14] And so on: types of multi-family structures were added, either as uses permitted "as of right" — that is, without further administrative action or without an application for a special exception.[15] "Highest" in this context does not refer to the most profitable use, or the "highest and best use" of property when it is appraised, but rather to a less dense use. A rezoning from a commercial to a residential zoning use district is sometimes referred to as a "down-zoning" because less density of development is allowed and its market value has been decreased.

All permitted uses assigned to residential zones were also permitted in commercial use districts as well. And all permitted types of commercial uses enumerated as of right in commercial districts are also permitted in manufacturing, or industrial districts. This pattern of cumulative permissiveness marked most zoning ordinances until well after World War II.

Use districts, when they are not cumulative, are said to be exclusive:[16] that is, the highest use district is exclusive by definition,[17] but districts "lower" in the hierarchy of uses may be exclusive as well when designated

---

[9] *See, e.g., Bisson v. Town of Milford*, 249 A.2d 688 (N.H. 1969).

[10] *See Alger v. City of Mukilteo*, 730 P.2d 1333, 1336–1337 (Wash. 1987); *Smith v. Skaget Cty.*, 453 P.2d 832, 847–848 (Wash. 1969).

[11] *See, e.g., Wilgus v. City of Murfeesboro*, 532 S.W.2d 50 (Tenn. 1975).

[12] 272 U.S. 365 (1926), the police power aspects of which are discussed in Chapter 1, and discussed generally in Chapter 6, *supra.*

[13] *See* Roy Lubove, *The Urban Community: Housing and Planning in the Progressive Era* 1–22 (1967) (reviewing why this is so and suggesting why the *Euclid* opinion reflects such a hierarchy of uses).

[14] *See Pierro v. Baxendale*, 118 A.2d 401 (1955) (finding the exclusion of motels from a residential district permitting rooming and boarding houses, to be reasonable).

[15] The latter are discussed *infra*, Chapter 10.

[16] *See People ex rel. Skokie Town House Builders v. Village of Morton Grove*, 157 N.E.2d 33, 36 (Ill. 1959) (holding an exclusive residential use district valid).

[17] *See Brett v. Building Comm'nr*, 145 N.E. 269, 271 (Mass. 1924) (viewing the exclusive residential single family district as justified as a means of preventing the spread of fires and as a health matter).

as such by the express provisions of the ordinance. Thus a commercial use district may be designated as exclusively commercial in the ordinance and all residential uses are prohibited unless grandfathered by the ordinance. There is no reason or policy limiting the designation of exclusive use districts to residential uses, and no enabling act has ever been found to preclude expanding these designations to other uses.[18] Exclusive use districts are most often used for manufacturing and industrial uses.[19]

Each use district is defined two ways. First, the zoning map locates the use within the municipality's land area.[20] The totality of a municipality's land area is thus mapped, and the map shows the area divided into territorial districts. With the passage of time, zoning maps have become more detailed, in the sense that the number of districts have increased, even as they (mostly) confirm existing patterns of land use. Second, each district is the subject of part of the text of the ordinance — where the (number of) permitted uses is listed (in an all-inclusive list) as well as any uses that are prohibited. With time, the texts of ordinances have become more restrictive and their definitions have become tighter. Also listed are height and area restrictions. Height is limited to a maximum number of feet. Area restrictions include maximum square footage[21] and coverage restrictions, and (in the case of residential uses) minimum dimensions for front, side, and rear yards. Thus the text of an ordinance actually has many different uses, height, and area restrictions for each type of district.

Cumulative, map and text, ordinances are at the heart of zoning in the post-*Euclid* zoning schemes. It is no wonder that such zoning was often referred to as *Euclidian* zoning, so called because of the geometric dimensions of its regulations and its genesis in the *Euclid* case.

Into the 1950s, the hierarchy of land uses continued apace — ordinances would contain several types of cumulative residential use districts — single family detached, duplexes, town houses, and garden apartments, for example — as well as several types of commercial use districts — convenience store retail, light retail, multi-purpose retail, department stores and big box stores, etc. In this decade also, some ordinances first contained not only exclusively residential use districts, but also permitted exclusively commercial use districts as well[22] — that is, permitted districts from which all residential and industrial uses were excluded. Such districts readily found enabling act authority. Often they were used for the light industry emerging during the post-World War II era.

Euclid thus authorized single use zoning and land use regulation has used that as its pattern for the past eight decades. Euclidian ordinances

---

[18] *See* Note, 32 N.Y. U. L. Rev. 1261 (1957).

[19] *See Katobimar Realty Co. v. Webster*, 118 A.2d 824 (N.J. 1955) (an opinion laden with the language of Euclidian zoning and upholding an exclusive industrial use district).

[20] *See Wheaton Moose Lodge N. 1775 v. Montgomery Cty.*, 397 A.2d 250, 252 (Md. App. Ct. 1979).

[21] Sometimes the maximum square footage is expressed as a floor area ratio — that is, a ratio of so many square feet in a building for every square foot of land on the underlying tract.

[22] *See, e.g., Kozesnik v. Twp. of Montgomery*, 131 A.2d 1, 9 (N.J. 1957).

provide that regulations shall be uniform within use districts, and effectively mandate that by providing that all parcels conform to the same requirements for a minimum lot size, front and side yard size, and setback distances from neighbors' parcels. Intruding uses for industry and even apartments are zoned out. All in all, these provisions have enabled many municipalities to insulate single family suburbs from their central cities.

Euclid and Euclidian zoning are often blamed for encouraging suburban sprawl, traffic congestion, too expensive housing, social isolation, and racial segregation.[23] Residential, single family uses screened out those who, for reasons of lack of income, cannot afford to live in a house. Some have claimed that Euclidian zoning has failed to protect low-income neighborhoods with the same rigor afforded middle and upper income neighborhoods. During the decade of the 1990s, New Urbanism architects and planners strove to create communities with a central commercial district, housing grouped together to create a sense of community, narrower streets to encourage pedestrian use, and parks and public buildings used to provide visual focal points.[24]

Euclid's progeny are numerous and make fine distinctions between uses.[25] For example, when an ordinance in its text for a residential use district, defines a residence as a non-business use, and further defines a nursing home, permitted as of right in such a district, as a "convalescent or rest home for the chronically ill, infirm, or aged, but not including hospitals, clinics, or similar institution devoted to the diagnosis or treatment of injury, disease or mental illness," it has been held to permit an owner, formerly using a parcel as a nursing home, to use it as a home for the mentally retarded.[26]

Several canons of ordinance construction control such decisions. First, the particular definition controls the general one; thus the exclusion of businesses from the residential district is not construed as all-inclusive when a more particular definition was also used in the ordinance. Evidence that most nursing or rest homes were in fact located in residential districts may provide support for the use of this canon. Second, a permissive provision controls an exclusionary one. The right to possess and alienate one's property provides a rationale for this canon. Third, a component of a definition may be read permissively. Thus here the proposed home for the retarded fits within the "home for chronically ill" language of the nursing home definition. Fourth, absent evidence that a proposed use is more

---

[23] *See, e.g.,* James Kunstler, *Home from Nowhere*, The Atlantic Monthly (Sept., 1996), at 43–66.

[24] *See, e.g.,* M. Southworth, *Walkable Suburbs? An Evaluation of Nontraditional Communities at the Urban Edge*, 63 J. Am. Inst. Planners (No. 1, Winter, 1997), at 1, 28–44.

[25] *See, e.g., Borough of Demarest v. Heck*, 201 A.2d 75 (N.J. Super. Ct., App. Div., 1964) (whether a riding academy is a agricultural use); *Sioux Falls v. Cleveland*, 70 N.W.2d 62 (S. Dak. 1955) (addressing whether a "dwelling house, double house, or duplex" includes a trailer); *In re Application of LaPorte*, 152 N.Y. S.2d 916 (N.Y. App. Div. 1956) (whether a dorm is a single-family dwelling).

[26] *Cf. Kastendike v. Baltimore Association for Retarded Children, Inc.*, 297 A.2d 745 (Md. 1972).

intensive than the past one, an existing definition should be liberally construed.

When a use is permitted, but defined in only one word, say "gas station," its ordinary and customary meaning must be sought. For example, a gas station owner may wish to open a convenience store in the cashier's area, or, as in one case, a gas station owner wished to sell to a fast food restaurant chain. The regulations for a commercial use district permitted as of right, but without further definition, a "restaurant." A restaurant is a commercial use in which food is prepared only after it is ordered from a menu and served by the restaurant's staff. If this customary definition is used, pre-prepared food served from behind a counter or on a drive thru basis may not fit the definition. Moreover, the hours of operation and the seating capacity might exceed those of any existing restaurant currently located in the district. If however the existing use was a business with an even more rapid rate of customer turn-over than a fast food restaurant, this fact provides an argument in favor of a liberal interpretation of the word "restaurant." The suitability of the property for the new use is relevant as well: here curb cuts were already in existence. An owner's efforts to contain the external impacts and effects on the fast food business also support a liberal reading: screening for light, automobile fumes, fences, and shrub-bery buffers, might be provided.[27] Close cases like this one produce amendments to municipal regulations, defining fast food restaurants and then specially regulating them.

"In construing a zoning ordinance, the permissive widest use of land is the rule and not the exception, unless specifically restrained in the valid and reasonable exercise of the police power."[28] As previously discussed, this canon of construction is justified because of the primacy of owners to use their property as they choose. Using it, a big box retailer was found to be a "retail" commercial use,[29] even though such super-stores were not the norm when an ordinance was enacted.[30]

The burden of proof to bring a requested use within the uses expressly permitted in an ordinance is on the applicant.[31] Thus a nudist colony has been found not to be a "recreational facility" permitted in a residential district[32] when the ordinance contained a statement that "uses not specifi-cally permitted are prohibited." The fact that a nudist facility would not seem to support the principal use permitted in a district, is another rationale for the result. To paraphrase Mark Twain, naked people have little or no influence in most use districts. So a lack of inconsistency with the principal use may be insufficient to meet the applicant's burden of proof; the burden is an affirmative one.

---

[27] *Taco Bell, Inc. v. City of Mission*, 678 P.2d 133 (Kan. 1984).

[28] *Amcare 2 Partners v. Zoning Hearing Bd.*, 609 A.2d 887, 891 (Pa. Commwlth. Ct. 1992).

[29] *Beale*, 671 N.E.2d 1233 (Mass. 1996); *Indian Trail Property Owner's Ass'n v. City of Spo-kane*, 886 P.2d 209 (Wash. App. Ct. 1994).

[30] *See Great Atlantic & Pacific Tea Co. v. Town of East Hampton*, 997 F. Supp. 340 (E.D. N.Y. 1998) (reviewing a big box ordinance).

[31] *See Cty. of Fairfax v. Parker*, 44 S. E.2d 9, 13 (Va. 1947).

[32] *Bd. of Supervisors of Madison Cty. v. Gaffney*, 422 S.E.2d 760 (Va. 1992).

Euclidian definitions are applied with reference to the parcel employing the use. Thus the use of a residentially zoned parcel to gain access to a nearby commercially zoned use, is itself a commercial use, and may be prohibited in a residential zone.[33] The access is considered to be in the same use as the parcel to which the access leads.[34] Similarly, a pig, pictured at home in his sty in the *Euclid* case only in an agricultural use district, might be considered a "household pet" permitted in a residential use district — in Hawaii,[35] but not in Illinois.[36]

Zoning maps must confirm existing use patterns. When they do not, the ordinance has moved too far in advance of the market and the regulation (say, a restriction to a residential use) has been found to be a taking — the ordinance restriction being as a result invalid and unenforceable.[37] Comprehensive planning for the ordinance may be too far-sighted. The ordinance must be justified by organizing an existing market for (say) undeveloped land, rather than attempting to make a market that has not previously existed. Often this can be accomplished by placing land in a so-called holding zone or a use district that is only slightly more restrictive than persons in the present market would have liked.

§ 7.02 Accessory Uses.

An accessory use is permitted when it is clearly, customarily, and incidentally subordinate to the a principal, permitted use of a parcel.[38] For example, millinery work is a permitted "home occupation" because it is an outgrowth of a home-centered activity such as sewing.[39] So might the work of a laundress qualify as a home occupation. Hour by hour evidence might support these results.

No similar support is possible for a stained glass window business operated from a residence in a residential use district that defines a residence as a "non-business, residential use, including customary home occupations." When the owner's business is the principal use of the parcel and not an accessory one, the ordinance is violated. Several types of evidence show such a violation: advertising in the telephone book, the incorporation of the business, its taking federal and state income tax deductions designed for businesses, and signs along the nearby roads directing customers to the parcel. All will provide evidence that the owner is not conducting an accessory use or where permitted, a "home occupation." Because stained

---

[33] See *City of Providence v. First Nat'l Stores, Inc.*, 210 A.2d 656, 659 (R.I. 1965).

[34] *Beale v. Planning Bd. of Rockland*, 671 N.E.2d 1233, 1236 (Mass. 1996) (hereafter *Beale*).

[35] See *Foster Village Community Ass'n v. Hess*, 667 P.2d 850 (Haw. App. Ct. 1983).

[36] *Village of Glenview v. Ramaker*, 668 N.E.2d 106 (Ill. App. Ct. 1996).

[37] See, e.g., *Averne Bay Const. Co. v. Thatcher*, 15 N.E.2d 587, 590–591 (N.Y. 1938).

[38] See *Cty. Comm'nrs of Carroll Cty. v. Zent*, 587 A.2d 1205, 1213-1216 (Md. App. Ct. 1991) (thoroughly reviewing the law of accessory uses); *In the Matter of N.Y. Botanical Garden v. Bd. of Stds. and Appeals of the City of New York*, 694 N.E.2d 424 (N.Y. 1998).

[39] See, e.g., *People v. Kelly*, 175 N.E. 108 (N.Y. 1931).

glass is not customarily found in homes, its creation on a residential parcel arguably violates the ordinance. [40]

An accessory use is one that is clearly and customarily incidental to a principal use. [41] Tool-sheds, a garage, patios, and small decks might be typical examples of an accessory use. When a zoning ordinance does not expressly provide for accessory uses, they may be implied by the courts. [42] Even when carrying penal sanctions, accessory uses, defined as customary and incidental to a principal use, have been upheld against a charge of unconstitutional vagueness. [43] Determining what constitutes a use as an accessory one is normally a question of fact and to be determined by the zoning administrator reading the ordinance liberally but reasonably. [44]

Accessory uses are typically expressly defined in terms of smaller, ancillary structures on a parcel, [45] but their definition need not be limited to structures. They must usually be located on the same parcel as the principal use is. They must be so necessary to the principal permitted use, and thus expected to be present, that it cannot be inferred that the regulation was intended to prevent their presence. [46] Thus parking a commercial vehicle on the street abutting a residential use is not an accessory use of a parcel. [47]

The storage of general contracting equipment on a parcel legally used for conducting this business, is an accessory use. [48] Thus an accessory use must be defined in light of the principal use. An use accessory to a residential use must not be a commercial use. A large chicken coop in a residential use district is not an accessory use. [49] A child care operation might be an accessory to a religious use, [50] but a storage shed might not. [51]

---

[40] *Narbonne v. Town of Rye*, 534 A.2d 388 (N.H. 1987) (finding a stained glass business a violation of regulations for a residential district).

[41] *Whaley v. Dorchester Cty. Zoning Bd. of Appeals*, 524 S.E.2d 404, 410 (Va. 1999) (hereafter *Whaley*); *Platts v. Zoning Hearing Bd. of the Borough of Bradford Woods*, 654 A.2d 149, 152–153 (Pa. Commwlth. Ct. 1994).

[42] *Treisman v. Town of Bedford*, 563 A.2d 786 (1989) (so holding).

[43] *See State of Arizona v. Trachman*, 947 P.2d 905, 908–909 (Ariz. App. Ct. 1997) (involving the storage of autos for repair and restoration); *Bitts v. City of Littleton*, 765 P.2d 1077 (Colo. 1988).

[44] *The UpJohn Co. v. Planning and Zoning Comm'n of the Town of North Haven*, 616 A.2d 786, 789 (Conn. 1992).

[45] *Whaley*, op. cit, 524 S.E.2d at 411 (quoting, in the dissenting opinion, the definition of "a detached building or structure which is detached from and subordinate to a principal building/facility or use on a lot and used for [a] purpose customarily incidental to the principal use, including, but not limited to, garages, greenhouses, guest homes, servants' quarters, custodial or security quarters, swimming pools and tennis courts, cable satellite antenna or other radio transmitting/receiving antenna.").

[46] *Borough of Northvale v. Blundo*, 203 A.2d 721, 723 (N.J. Super. Ct., App. Div., 1964).

[47] *Id.*

[48] *Greenfield v. Bd. of City Planning Comm'rs of the City of Los Angeles*, 45 P.2d 219 (Cal. 1935).

[49] *Chudonov v. Bd. of Appeals of Bloomfield*, 154 A.2d 161 (Conn. 1931).

[50] *Shim v. Washington Twp. Planning Bd.*, 689 A.2d 804, 807 (N.J. Super. Ct., App. Div., 1997); *City of Richmond Heights v. Richmond Heights Presbyterian Church*, 764 S.W.2d 647 (Mo. 1989).

A sign is an accessory use for an office building.[52] Likewise, a gas fuel pump might be accessory to a convenience store.[53]

An accessory use definition must be formulated in light of the changing land use pattern of the district. When a parcel is rezoned from agricultural to residential, a riding facility might be grandfathered into the new district, but might nonetheless be considered a specially permitted use requiring that a special exception be applied for and granted before the owners' private rodeo is permitted to continue.[54] Changing environmental sensibilities may be considered as well.[55]

Accessory uses must be both customary and incidental to a principal use. "Customary" has most often been taken to mean common.[56] As such, landing and parking a helicopter in a residential use district might be prohibited as not customarily done.[57] The prohibition might also be justified on the ground that, if every user in the district were allowed to do this, the resulting noise, dust, and disruption would be out of proportion to anything resembling a reasonable use of the parcels in the district.[58] Most people don't commute or travel by helicopter.

A customary accessory use must further habitual and long established practice.[59] Thus what is customary need not always be common in the neighborhood, or considered unobjectionable by most, but should instead be evaluated by means of a "community sensitive" but state wide standard.[60] Testimony about whether a use is customary must go beyond whether any two uses are found together on one parcel, but must also indicate that one use is principal, and one accessory, as well.[61]

"Incidental to a principal use" means subordinate to a use, not necessarily the predominant use, but a dominant one nonetheless. Thus, an accessory use might be attached to a home occupation conducted on a residentially zoned parcel.[62] The word means that the use requested must not be the

---

[51] *Grandview Baptist Church v. Zoning Bd. of Adjustment of the City of Davenport*, 301 N.W.2d 704 (Iowa 1981).

[52] *Towers Management Co. v. Thacher*, 2 N.E.2d 273 (N.Y. App. Div. 1936).

[53] *Borough of Fleetwood v. Zoning Hearing Bd. of Borough of Fleetwood*, 649 A.2d 651 (Pa. 1994). *But see Singal v. City of Bangor*, 440 A.2d 1048 (Me. 1982).

[54] *Murphy v. Town of Chino Valley*, 789 P.2d 1072 (Ariz. App. Ct. 1989). *See also Cty. Comm'nrs of Carroll Cty. v. Zent*, 587 A.2d 1205, 1213–1216 (Md. App. Ct. 1991).

[55] *See The UpJohn Co. v. Planning and Zoning Comm'n of the Town of North Haven*, 616 A.2d 786 (Conn. 1992) (holding that the storage of waste was not an accessory use).

[56] The word might also mean "customarily incidental."

[57] *See Redington Ranch Assoc. v. Redman*, 737 P.2d 808 (Ariz. App. Ct. 1987).

[58] *Id.* at 809.

[59] *See McKinnney v. The Kent Cty. Bd. of Adjustment*, 1995 Del. Super. LEXIS 83, *10 (Del. Super. Ct., Feb. 13, 1995).

[60] *"The Comm'nrs of Bellefonte" v. Coppola*, 453 A.2d 457, 461 (Del. 1982) (citing Lewis J. Smith, *Zoning: Accessory Uses and the Meaning of the "Customary" Requirement*, 56 B.U. L. Rev. 542, 549).

[61] *Kobyluck v. Zoning Bd. of Appeals, Town of Montville*, 1998 Conn. Super. LEXIS 454, *8 (Conn. Super. Ct., Feb. 18, 1998).

[62] *Cf. Dupont Circle Citizens Ass'n v. District of Columbia Bd. of Zoning Adjustment*, 749 A.2d 1258, 1262 and n.11 (D.C. App., Apr. 27, 2000) (finding catered events for guest in a bed and breakfast house permitted).

primary one, but minor in significance or importance in comparison to the primary use.[63] An hour by hour comparison might be used to show an incidental use.[64]

Finally, accessory uses may be restricted to side or rear yards in residential districts, or confined to the rear portion of a parcel, or made subject to set-back restrictions.[65]

§ 7.03 Non-Conforming Uses.

A land use which precedes the zoning regulation, but which becomes illegal under the subsequently effective ordinance, is called non-conforming.[66] "The primary purpose behind zoning is to bring about the orderly physical development of a community by confining particular uses to defined areas. A goal of zoning is to gradually eliminate nonconforming uses because they are inconsistent with the purpose of development use-consistent areas in communities."[67]

Such a use could be "taken" through the use of eminent domain procedures, but this is costly and as early advocates of zoning thought, unnecessary because such uses would, like the Marxist state, just wither away. They seldom do. Indeed, sometimes their non-conforming nature makes them more valuable and gives them, as in the instance of a grocery store in a residential district, a monopoly value. They are recognized and permitted to continue, simply because they existed prior to the enactment of the zoning ordinance, but their extension and expansion is limited because of the overall goal of zoning. For example, barns built in a formerly agricultural area become non-conforming uses as the farms are given over to residences and are zoned into residential use districts.

Municipal ordinances usually restrict the use's enlargement and prohibit both rebuilding it after destruction and its reuse after abandonment. Typically, sixty to seventy five percent of the value of the improvements must be destroyed before reconstruction can be enjoined.[68] Lapse of time showing an abandonment may also justify a use's discontinuation.[69] Thereafter, subsequent owners of the parcel may be bound by the prior owner's abandonment of the use.

---

[63] *See Henry v. Bd. of Appeals of Dunstable*, 641 N.E.2d 1334 (Mass. 1994).

[64] *Id.* at 389.

[65] *Sundeen v. Rodgers*, 141 A. 142 (N.H. 1928).

[66] *Odegard Outdoor Advertising, LLC v. Bd. of Zoning Adjustment of Jackson Cty.*, 6 S.W.3d 148, 150, n.1 (Mo. 1999).

[67] *In re Gregoire*, 742 A.2d 1232, 1235 (Vt. 1999) (citations omitted).

[68] *See Mayberry v. Town of Old Orchard Beach*, 599 A. 2d 1153, 1154–1155 (Me. 1991) (nonconforming use for house unoccupied for two years, lapses).

[69] *See generally* Annot., *Right to resume nonconforming use of premises after voluntary or unexplained break in the continuity of nonconforming use*, 57 A.L.R.3d 279 (1974); Annot., *Right to resume nonconforming use of premises after involuntary break in the continuity of nonconforming use unrelated to governmental activity*, 56 A.L.R.3d 14 (1974).

A single parcel may be the source of multiple non-conforming uses. Thus, a hotel can be both a hotel and an entertainment complex,[70] and a gas station can be both a gas station and a convenience store.[71]

The legal doctrines protecting non-conforming uses are a particular instance of the use of estoppel and of the problem of vested rights we will discuss later in this book. The owner is claiming that the right to the use vested before the ordinance was enacted.[72] Indeed, to establish a non-conforming use, an owner must prove that the use existed before the ordinance.[73]

State zoning statutes may show a protectiveness toward such uses. Their policy is to prevent zoning ordinances from having retroactive application merely because of deterioration and wear and tear. Permitting non-conforming structures to be "reasonably repaired" or rebuilt when "partially destroyed" are typical statutory phrases used to protect them.[74] Without enabling act guidance, however, courts may resist rigid rules about continuing a use.[75] Statutes and ordinances also typically provide that an abandoned non-conforming use is terminated.[76] In this, the common law meaning of an abandonment typically provides the standard for fleshing out the meaning of such a provision.[77] At common law, abandonment is a voluntary, affirmative act, coupled with a clear intent to repudiate the use; non-use is insufficient, even if long continued.[78] A less frequently encountered approach is an ordinance provision that states that a non-conforming use discontinued for (say) six months, is terminated or presumed to be abandoned, but no finding of a common law abandonment is necessary.[79]

The change of a non-conforming use is often an occasion for obtaining a legal opinion from land use counsel. Suppose, for example, that a Civil War era mansion was first used as a residence, then from 1915 on, as a funeral home, and, with the advent of the municipality's first zoning ordinance in 1922, it remained a funeral home as a non-conforming use located

---

[70] *Cape Resort Hotels, Inc. v. Alcoholic Licensing Bd. of Falmouth*, 431 N.E.2d 213, 215–216 (Mass. 1982).

[71] *In re Newton Enterprises*, 708 A.2d 914, 915 (Vt. 1998).

[72] *See Cosseboom v. Town of Epsom*, 771 A.2d 565 (N.H. 2001) (lot found non-conforming as to acreage requirement of zoning ordinance).

[73] *Comforti v. City of Manchester*, 677 A.2d 147 (N.H. 1996); *Hitz v. Zoning Hearing Bd. of South Annville Twp.*, 734 A.2d 60, 68 (Pa. Commw. Ct. 1999).

[74] *Avalon Home & Land Owner's Ass'n v. Avalon*, 543 A.2d 950 (N.J. 1988) (striking down an ordinance permitting non-conforming structure to be rebuilt when the footprint and volume did not exceed the pre-existing structure was ultra vires the state enabling act authorizing rebuilding only upon partial destruction).

[75] *Ruby v. Carlisle Zoning Hearing Bd.*, 488 A.2d 655 (Pa. Commw. Ct. 1985) (ordinance found invalid when terminating use if 50% of bulk or value was destroyed)..

[76] *Washington Arcade Assoc. v. Zoning Board of Review*, 587 A.2d 736 (R.I. 1987).

[77] *Id. See also Lewis v. Maine Coast Artists*, 770 A.2d 644, 650 (Me. 2001).

[78] *Id.* (involving a renovation permit for a non-conforming art gallery).

[79] *Toys "R" Us v. Silva*, 676 N.E.2d 862 (N.Y. 1996); *Hartley v. City of Colorado Springs*, 764 P.2d 1216 (Colo. 1988).

in a residential district. Its owners then proposed to sell the mansion and relocate their business elsewhere; they contracted to sell the property to new owners who propose to use the mansion as is for a bed and breakfast establishment.

Although restoration, resumption, reconstruction, or substantial expansion of a non-conforming use is subject to reasonable regulation, the substitution of one non-conforming use for another raises the issues of (1) whether the substituted use is more or less appropriate than the pre-existing on,[80] and (2) whether there is a substantial similarity between the use as it was at the time it became non-conforming and the changed use. With a more appropriate use or substantial similarity established, the right to the use continues.[81] Because any ordinance should be read so as to uphold its constitutionality, when the substituted use is "determined to be closer to the desired residential use, then it is a move 'up the use chain' and would satisfy the ordinance."[82] When a substituted use is closer to permitted uses than the pre-existing one, the transfer is permitted to protect the alienability of the non-conforming parcel.[83] When both the quantity and the quality of the use changes, however, the change will not be permitted.[84] Even if the new use is a more intensive one, that alone is not a sufficient basis to refuse to continue a structure's status as a non-conforming use.[85] For example, a non-conforming deck might be permitted to expand into an existing garage, so that the overall land use is no more intense than it was before the expansion.[86] Non-conforming uses are permitted to continue, even though their survival is not encouraged. Non-conforming uses that do not amount to a nuisance, are not to be treated differently from other land uses.[87]

Ordinances typically provide that no non-conforming use may be "enlarged, increased, expanded, or moved." Interpreting these words is a question of law, and courts will not strain them beyond their ordinary meaning; thus increasing the height of a communications tower is not to "move" it.[88] On the other hand, even leasing a tower might signal an expansion under appropriate circumstances.[89]

---

[80] *Shire Inn, Inc. v. Borough of Avon-By-The-Sea*, 729 A.2d 473 (N.J. Super. Ct., App. Div., 1999) (refusing to permit inn to become a rooming house, even when it would be arguably an affordable housing project).

[81] *See Town of Salem v. Wickson*, 770 A.2d 1120, 1123 (N.H. 2001) (involving a pig farm's stockpiling treated manure).

[82] *Kopietz v. Zoning Bd. of Appeals for the City of the Village of Clarkston*, 535 N.W. 2d 910, 912 (Mich. App. 1995) (permitting such a change).

[83] *Adolphson v. Zoning Bd. of Appeals*, 535 A.2d 799 (Conn. 1988).

[84] *See Turbat Creek Preservation, LLC v. Town of Kennebunkport*, 753 A.2d 489, 493 (Me. 2000) (boathouse converted for overnight stays).

[85] *See In re Miserocchi*, 749 A.2d 607, 612 (Vt. 2000).

[86] *See Sproul v. Town of Boothbay Harbor*, 746 A.2d 368, 371–372 (Vt. 2000) (reviewing legislation for junkyards).

[87] *Cf. Husti v. Zuckerman Property Enterprises, Ltd.*, 508 A.2d 735 (Conn. 1986) (prohibiting the use of country club as a concert and theater venue)

[88] *See Kelsea v. Town of Pembroke*, 771 A.2d 587, 590 (N.H. 2001).

[89] *Cf.* Zachs v. Zoning Bd. of Appeals, 589 A.2d 351, 355 (Conn. 1991).

The expansion of a non-conforming use is, in some municipalities, regulated by requiring the owner to apply for a special exception of some type.[90] Junkyards and auto graveyards are particularly apt subjects for such regulation.[91] The administrative proceeding reviewing such an application is to assess whether the expansion will have a substantially different effect or impact on the surrounding parcels or neighborhood than the non-conforming use had previously.

[A] Amortization.

Sometimes ordinances also adopt a more aggressive policy toward non-conforming uses. This policy is pursued in so-called amortization ordinance provisions. These permit the continuance of the use for a time certain — say, five years, during which time the property is to be brought into compliance — and its termination thereafter. A reasonably long period of time must be provided. The amortization is a reference to the time period necessary for an owner to recoup his investment in the non-conforming structure on the site, but legislatures and courts are not very specific about what exactly is being amortized. Thus, an amortization period of five years, applied to a structure with a remaining economic life of twenty years, is void.[92] Besides a structure's life expectancy, an owner's initial investment, the amount of an investment realized up to the date the amortization period starts to run, or leasehold income derived from the use, are all relevant to setting the amortization period.

In general, amortization periods must take account of their rationale. A billboard that is found to create a traffic safety problem may be subject to a shorter amortization period on that account. Likewise, a manufacturing plant creating a nuisance or an environmental hazard may be amortized in a shorter time. On the other hand, a non-conforming use that does not fit the aesthetic pattern of its neighborhood may take longer to amortize on that account.[93]

Amortization provisions run into trouble when applied to structures tailored to the use because often the period is then too short.[94] Structures are amortized through depreciation, but land does not depreciate. If a non-conforming use exists in an untailored structure, the amortization period may be short — say three to five years.[95] Long amortization periods present

---

[90] See Hurley v. Town of Hollis, 729 A.2d 998, 1000 (N.H. 1999).

[91] See Balough v. Fairbanks North Star Borough, 995 P.2d 245 (Alaska 2000).

[92] City of La Mesa v. Tweed and Gambrell Planing Mill, 304 P.2d 803 (Cal. App. Ct. 1956) (so holding).

[93] Modjeska Sign Studios v. Berle, 373 N.E.2d 255 (N.Y. 1977).

[94] See Jones v. City of Los Angeles, 295 P. 14 (Cal. 1930) (involving a sanatorium, against which a twenty year amortization period was invalidated), discussed in City of Los Angeles v. Gage, 274 P. 2d 34 (Cal. App. Ct. 1954) (upholding a five year amortization period for a plumbing business, the moving costs of which were 1% of its yearly gross revenue).

[95] Cf. Lone v. Montgomery County, 584 A.2d 142, 153–154 (Md. App. 1991) (involving a ten year amortization period for converting single family structures with accessory apartments from a multi-family use to single family use and holding that this was not a taking without compensation).

zoning officials with record-keeping problems.[96]

Non-conforming uses like junkyards, gasoline stations, and animal facilities, like dog kennels, have been subjected to the amortization process. Billboards have been a frequent subject of amortization ordinances.[97] In fact, the majority of courts dealing with amortization provisions have upheld them, if only generally.[98]

Amortization is rationalized in one of two ways. Prior to the era of zoning, a use could be terminated only by a cause of action in nuisance, so that, first, amortization is upheld as providing for the abatement of a nuisance, probably a public nuisance. Second, it is upheld under a multi-factor rule of reason. The factors weighed are: the character of the structure, its location, its cost, its depreciated value (sometimes using IRS guidelines), its salvage value, and remaining useful life, the legal arrangements under which the use is maintained (e.g., a short or long term lease, or absolute ownership), its monopoly value, and the injury to the public in maintaining the use. Under this second test, the validity or invalidity of the provision becomes a matter of degree and non-nuisance uses can be abated.[99] In some jurisdictions, however, express enabling act authority for an amortization scheme has been required.[100]

In *Pennsylvania Northwestern Distributors, Inc. v. Zoning Hearing Bd. of Moon Twp.*,[101] the Pennsylvania Supreme Court joined a minority of state courts holding a ninety day amortization provision invalid as a taking of property under the state constitution. The court found the amortization provision facially invalid and a per se taking of an adult bookstore. In response to an opinion like that of *Pennsylvania Northwestern Distributors*, a municipality might provide for amortization of adult bookstores operating within 100 feet of a school, after one year, and provide further for a transferable development right (TDR), alienable to third parties, for operation of the store elsewhere. Such an amortization procedure is probably valid. TDRs have been broadly upheld as a means of compensating owners for regulation of their uses, otherwise prohibited and even though an adult bookstore might be the highest and best use of the parcel.[102]

Other responses to *Pennsylvania Northwestern Distributors* might be a statute providing that a short period of dormancy or non-use terminates a non-conforming use. Such statutes have, in other areas such a mineral

---

[96] *See Lone*, op.cit., 584 A.2d at 153, n. 18 (collecting amortization cases).

[97] *See, e.g., Art Neon Co. v. City & Cty. of Denver*, 488 F.2d 118 (10th Cir. 1973). Billboard companies have raised First and Fifth Amendment claims as well. *See, e.g., Naegele Outdoor Adv. Co. v. City of Durham*, 803 F. Supp. 1068 (M.D. N. C. 1992).

[98] *National Adv. Co. v. City of Raleigh*, 947 F.2d 1158, 1164, n.6 (4th Cir. 1991) (collecting cases); *LaChappelle v. Town of Goffstown*, 225 A.2d 624 (N.H. 1967).

[99] *Northend Cinema, Inc. v. City of Seattle*, 585 P.2d 1153 (Wash. 1978) (en banc), *cert. denied, Apple Theatre, Inc. v. City of Seattle*, 441 U.S. 946 (1979) (upholding ninety day amortization period for adult theater operating under lease terminable on short notice).

[100] *State v. Bates*, 305 N.W.2d 426 (Iowa 1981).

[101] 584 A.2d 1372 (Pa. 1991), *noted at* 37 Vill. L.Rev. 161, 181–192 (1992)

[102] *See Penn Central Transp. Co. v. City of New York*, 438 U.S. 104, 114 (1978).

interests, been held constitutional against attacks on both due process and takings grounds.[103]

Finally, the distinctiveness of a structure for a non-conforming use may enhance its legal durability: i.e., a hot dog stand located in the middle of a residential area before the neighborhood was zoned residential. If the stand is shaped like a huge hot dog and roll and the municipality enacted a three year amortization period for all non-conforming uses in the district, the architectural uniqueness of the improvement on this site gives its status as a non-conforming use a strength that use non-conformance alone does not possess. Amortization statutes are most effective when other parcels in the jurisdiction are available to receive the use. The uniqueness of this improvement makes that unlikely: compliance with building codes at any new site makes substantial alteration of the improvement the likely consequence of moving it. Portable uses can be amortized much more easily.

[B]   The Natural Expansion Doctrine.

Regulations typically restrict the extension, repair, alteration, or reconstruction (when destroyed or otherwise demolished) of non-conforming structures. However, in some states, particularly those with a heavy industrial base when zoning was in its formative stage, non-conforming uses do not by any means wither away.[104]

Instead, these uses are permitted to expand under what is called the "natural expansion" doctrine.[105] There, they are not limited to their size in existence at the time of enactment of the zoning ordinance — not limited, that is, to a plant capacity unused at the effective date of the ordinance, to the machinery in use then if more modern methods are now available, or to the out-put produced as of the ordinance's effective date. Rather, they may be increased in size to the extent required by natural expansion and growth in the use and the trade for which they are used, provided that the expansion has no adverse impact on the general welfare. However, that caveat imposed on the naturally-expanding non-conforming use is usually taken care of by applying the ordinance's usual set-back, height, bulk, density, and other restrictions to the use.

The rationale for this doctrine has been explained as follows: "An ordinance which would allow the housing of a baby elephant cannot evict the animal when it has grown up, since it is generally known that a baby elephant eventually becomes a big elephant."[106] Denying the natural expansion of a non-conforming use is thought to deny its owners the use as effectively as would its out-right prohibition. This doctrine is said to "run

[103] See Texaco, Inc. v. Short, 454 U.S. 516 (1982) (involving a state statute on the lapsing of titles to unused mineral estates).

[104] See In re Gilfillan's Permit, 140 A. 136 (Pa. 1927) (a leading case).

[105] Hitz v. Zoning Hearing Bd. of South Annville Twp., 734 A.2d 60, 67–68 (Pa. Commnw. Ct. 1999) (restating the doctrine and collecting the cases).

[106] Upper Darby Twp. Appeal, 138 A. 2d 99, 102 (Pa. 1958).

with the title," rather than to benefit the owner at the time of the enactment of the ordinance.[107]

In a jurisdiction adopting the natural expansion doctrine, a municipality might impose a 50% limitation on the expansion of non-conforming uses — that is, provide that the footprint of any non-conforming use may increase not more than 50% after the enactment of the ordinance. Such a provision has been upheld.[108] In implementing such a limitation, however, the issue of whether a percentage restriction is related to the adverse impact on surrounding uses, will have to be considered. For example, the size of a parcel may make the relationship tenuous. Moreover, imposing such a limitation is problematical in the case of a quarry, for what would be its footprint?

Most jurisdictions do not follow this doctrine.[109] They limit non-conforming uses more strictly than it does.[110] Neither the use or the structure may be expanded or enlarged.[111] Municipalities may in general impose reasonable conditions on the expansion of a non-conforming use.[112] Most would also refuse to permit a non-conforming owner to demolish an existing structure in order to replace it with a newer one.[113]

[C] Changes in Use.

A non-conforming use need not stay exactly as it was at the time of enactment of the ordinance. However, a change in the methods or the quantity of production can be so great as to constitute a new use.[114] If a changed use will have a lesser impact on its surroundings, it is permissible; if the impact is greater, then the user runs the risk that it will be found to be a new use and the change will be subject to injunction. A quarry and stone-crushing business cannot build a cement plant. However, a change in the intensity of the present, non-conforming use does not amount to a change or expansion of that use.[115] For example, if the owner of a non-conforming used car lot wishes to change the parcel's use and open a gas station, the likely response of zoning officials will be negative and to the effect that this is a new use and a permit should be denied.[116] Because

---

[107] *Eitnier v. Kreitz Corporation*, 172 A.2d 320, 323 (Pa. 1961).

[108] *See Schiller-Pfeiffer v. Upper Southampton Twp.*, 276 A.2d 334 (Pa. Commw. Ct. 1971) (holding, 5-2, that such a restriction is reasonable).

[109] *But see Hurley v. Town of Hollis*, 729 A.2d 998, 1002 (N.H. 1999) (indicating that New Hampshire follows it); *Town of Salem v. Wickson*, 770 A.2d 1120, 1125 (N.H. 2001) (holding that a pig farm's stockpiling treated manure is not a natural expansion).

[110] *State ex. rel. Dierberg v. St. Charles Cty. Bd. of Zoning Adjustment*, 869 S.W.2d 865 (Mo. App. Ct. 1994).

[111] *Id.*

[112] *See Peabody v. Town of Windham*, 703 A.2d 886 (N.H. 1997).

[113] *In Re Stowe Club Highlands*, 668 A.2d 1271 (Vt. 1995).

[114] *Bd. of Zoning Appeals of Spotsylvania Cty. v. McCalley*, 300 S.E.2d 790 (Va. 1983).

[115] *Town of Wolfeboro v. Smith*, 556 A.2d 755, 759 (N.H. 1989).

[116] *Hanna v. Bd. of Adjustment*, 183 A.2d 539 (Pa. 1962) (so holding).

the methods of operation and the environmental risks and regulation, are significantly different when comparing the present and the proposed use, the change is all the more likely to be found illegal. In a further example, suppose that a non-conforming landfill, operates in a residential district under a state permit allowing receipt of many cubic yards of waste per day. When its owner applies for a new permit to take in six times the number of cubic yards, the new permit application is evidence that the use is being illegally expanded.[117]

---

[117] See Twp. of Chartiers v. William H. Martin, Inc., 542 A.2d 985, 987–988 (Pa. 1988) (reviewing the Pa. cases on the natural expansion doctrine), noted in 27 Duq. U. L. Rev. 391 (1989).

Chapter 8

Aesthetics and Zoning

§ 8.01 The Police Power and Aesthetics

The broadest scope is given the police power when zoning is enacted to protect the aesthetics of the community. This protection is typically needed for the preservation of compatibility amid various architectural styles for housing in a residential use district. Compatibility of uses is a traditional objective for zoning. However, sometimes an ordinance is drafted to create visual beauty — an affirmative and much less traditional objective. The courts have taken three views of aesthetic regulation. Each view represents a stage in the development of a state's zoning law for this area.

The **first stage** is a judicial refusal to validate regulations based on aesthetic considerations. Every state has passed through this stage, thus today it is an historic relic.

In a **second stage**, aesthetics might be considered a legitimate purpose of zoning if it has a substantial relationship to other, more traditional purposes (other than aesthetics), such as the preservation of property values or the local economy. However, the relationship need not be a direct one. For example, aesthetics can protect property values, which affects the tax base, which in turn affects the amount of money in the treasury, which affects the general welfare. This type of analysis looks very much like substantive due process, so often used in zoning opinions.

Most states are currently categorized as passing through this second stage. Administration of such ordinances are generally left to persons, such as architects, with professional training in the fine arts. Often these ordinances delegate decision-making powers to an administrative board (often called an architectural review board) and contain one of two types of standards. First, architectural details may be provided, down to the type of door-knob or the color of paint which is permitted. (The most detail is provided in historic district ordinances, less detail in the residential subdivision setting.) Merely stating that the style must be "early American" will not suffice: that phrase justifies adobe, log cabin, or Cape Cod styles, or even a tepee. Second, the architectural principles which constitute a particular style may be defined: the relationship of windows to walls, roof lines, voids and solids on the facade, etc. The administrative decision then is whether a proposed development or renovation "looks like" or "does not look like" the prescribed style. The decision is yes or no, and the courts seldom second-guess it.[1]

---

[1] *See, e.g., State ex rel Stoyanoff v. Berkeley*, 458 S.W.2d 305, 311–312 (Mo. 1970), *discussed in* Peter Salsich, *Land Use Regulation* 165 (1991).

In order for the ordinance to avoid the charge that it impermissibly delegates the local police power, adequate criteria for decisions are necessary and should be spelled out in the ordinance's provisions. The less professional the board, the more detailed the standards must be. Moreover, aesthetics may be a stand-in for other concerns; compatibility with surrounding uses and buildings is one acceptable concern.[2] So architectural review boards are typically authorized to decide that a structure has no adverse impact on surrounding uses, or represents no incompatibility of architectural style.

Deciding what does harm to the existing visual beauty of a neighborhood is easier than deciding, *a priori*, what beauty is. For example, justifying an ordinance requiring screening and land buffers around a junkyard, is a matter of preventing visual blight or harm, rather than conferring a benefit on neighbors of the junkyard by improving their view — thus regulation is appropriate. However, because both the harm and the benefit are visual, some courts may find the traditional police power rubrics translated into this arena hard to accept; that is, preventing the harm and conferring the benefit may seem inseparable.[3] Which is why some courts do not accept aesthetics as the sole justification for an ordinance.

Finding itself in this second stage, a municipality might ban all types of billboards from residential use districts and permit them as of right only in manufacturing and industrial districts. Such a regulation is valid. Traffic safety and visual blight would bring this ordinance well within the police power, without regulating the content of the speech on the billboards. Should First Amendment, free speech based, constitutional challenges arise, the counter argument would be that there are many alternative channels of communication available — newspapers, magazines, circulars, mailings, e-mail and the internet, tele-marketing, television, cable TV, and radio. Such arguments would be persuasive.

In this second stage, the disapproval on architectural grounds of a design for an ultra-modern house to be located in a (say) Georgian colonial residential use district has been justified when there is an established pattern of development in the neighborhood. Thus screening out incompatible styles may be seen as akin to preventing a (cultural or aesthetic) nuisance.[4] Compatibility standards are often seen by the courts as a shorthand for promoting aesthetic values.

A **third stage** permits the consideration of aesthetics alone when drafting a regulation.[5] As of 1988, about 21 states are in the third

---

[2] *See Rolling Pines Limited Partnership v. City of Little Rock*, 40 A.W.2d 828 (Ark. App. 2000) (upholding compatibility standards for manufactured housing units involving the pitch of their roofs, the removal of mobile features, permanent foundations, finished exterior walls, as well as off-street parking).

[3] *See Nollan v. California Coastal Comm'n*, Chapter 14, *infra*.

[4] *See Reid v. Architectural Bd. of Review*, 119 Ohio App. 67, 192 N.E.2d 74 (1963); *State ex rel. Saveland Park Holding Corp. v. Wieland*, 269 Wis. 262, 69 N.W.2d 217, *cert. denied*, 350 U.S. 841 (1955) (both cases upheld architectural design ordinances with compatibility standards).

[5] *See generally* Jeffrey Strouse, *Redefining Trademark Alteration Within the Context of Aesthetic-Based Zoning Laws: A Blockbuster Dilemna*, 53 Vand. L. Rev. 717, 720–725 (2000).

category.[6] In effect, they now invite some affirmative definition. Here too, however, ordinances are seldom divorced from architectural details or compatibility standards.

The opinions of the United States Supreme Court can be categorized as being in this third stage. *Penn Central Transportation Company v. City of New York*[7] is an example. In *Penn Central*, the United States Supreme Court sustained the validity of New York City's Landmarks Preservation Law. Justice Brennan, writing for the majority, said: "[T]his Court has recognized, in a number of settings, that States and municipalities may enact land use restrictions or controls to enhance the quality of life by preserving the character and desirable aesthetic features of a city."[8] This sounds broadly permissive as far as municipalities are concerned, but Justice Brennan went on to say, in characterizing what was not in dispute in that case, that Penn Central had not contested either the legitimacy of the city's objective or public purpose, the nexus between that purpose and the regulations at issue, or the fact that the railroad could still earn a reasonable return from the property with the regulations in place. Clearly the attorneys for Penn Central conceded too much in this case.

That a substantial number of states (21), though still a minority, endorse this third stage's "aesthetics alone" rule, is explained by the possibility of misuse of aesthetics in decision-making. Aesthetics may be a mask for more sinister factors — just as economic and class prejudice, racial intolerance, etc. What is not tolerated openly, should not be tolerated indirectly.

Another reason for judicial reluctance is that beauty, to paraphrase Hume, is in the eye of the beholder and thus aesthetic decisions must either be based on a trust of the beholder or criteria to guide his sensibilities; most courts still trust criteria and judicial review more than the beholding board member. Is not judicial review really the answer to the criticism that the aesthetics alone rule is an invitation to subjective decisions? If the decision is subjective, it can be invalidated.

So aesthetic regulation is valid when it has a substantial relationship to a public purpose other than aesthetics and even solely aesthetic regulation is valid when harm to the surroundings is clear and not merely a matter of taste. Thus, for example, a rural mountainous municipality in a scenic region might prohibit the night-time use of "internally lighted signs." In a stage three jurisdiction, the standard of review is a rational relationship review. "It is reasonable to infer that the scenic vistas sought to be preserved by the town include the splendor of mountains at twilight and the brilliance of stars at night;"[9] thus the restriction on internally lighted signs is reasonably related to the aesthetic goal of "discouraging development that competes with the natural environment."[10]

---

[6] *See, e.g., Asselin v. Town of Conway*, 628 A.2d 247, 249-250 (N.H. 1993) (shifting from second to third stage rule); *City of Fayetteville v. McIlroy Bank & Trust*, 647 S.W.2d 439, 441 (Ark. 1983).

[7] 438 U.S. 104 (1978).

[8] *Id.* at 129 (1978).

[9] *Asselin v. Town of Conway*, 628 A.2d 247 (N.H. 1993).

[10] *Id.*

With the advent of this third stage, aesthetics became too general a subject for treatment; instead, the use of aesthetics should be put in a more specific regulatory context. For example, when an ordinance prevents the removal of topsoil without a permit, it has been argued that it can be justified solely on aesthetic grounds. However, the preservation of the natural environment is arguably easier to justify solely on aesthetic grounds if public need for an ordinance can be shown.[11] A similar issue might arise in a use district aimed at preserving farmland. Farmland provides aesthetic relief from urbanization, serving as a buffer between urban development and wetlands and riparian lands, as well as serving as a reminder of a region's agricultural heritage.

The use of aesthetics by a municipal architectural review board has provided most of the law detailed thus far; an historic district, landmark preservation, incentive zoning, and the regulation of billboards, provide other contexts for discussing the law in this area.

§ 8.02 Historic Districts.

State and federal courts have upheld aesthetic considerations as a proper basis for imposing architectural controls on buildings within an historic use district. Such districts preserve the visual quality of an historic neighborhood. Such districts are typically authorized expressly by state enabling statutes.

In a historic district, more regulation might be justified because of the setting: the neighborhood's character is dependent on maintaining the historic appearance of each property. Conversely, a property of little or no historic value can be brought into conformance with the neighborhood's character because of the same inter-dependency. This is the "tout ensemble" doctrine.[12]

Often aesthetics is not a stand-alone justification for the regulations imposing a certain architectural style. Tourism and economic development are also used to justify regulating such districts as the Vieux Carre in New Orleans, Santa Fe in New Mexico, old Charleston in South Carolina, or Nantucket Island in Massachusetts. These areas provided first-generation, multi-purpose historic districts. Every town or city has, in some sense of the term, a historic district: whether it be the home of its first settlers, or merely somewhat older and quainter areas of town, there is some historic value there. Giving the citizens a sense of what the place was, has some value. The issue is whether this is sufficient to justify freeze-framing the district as it is now, or forcing it to become what it was. For some advocates of historic preservation, the answer is a definite yes.

---

11 Cf. McNeill v. Township of Plumsted, 522 A.2d 469, 472–473 (N.J. Super. Ct., App. Div., 1987) (remanding case for consideration of need for ordinance prohibiting topsoil removal).

12 Figarsky v. Historic District Comm'n, 368 A.2d 163, 172 (Conn. 1976) (upholding a regulation for a property located on the edge of the district); Lafayette Park Baptist Church v. Scott, 553 S.W.2d 856. 861 (Mo. App. Ct. 1977) (finding that a historic district with architectural controls "is essentially a zoning ordinance").

The justifications for a historic district ordinance prevail even when the market for renovated houses in the historic style is weak. Aesthetics regulation has often been justified as a matter of preserving property values; here, that protection is afforded and indeed expected by the market — herein of *Penn Central's* "investment-backed expectations." Protecting existing investments, rather than encouraging new investments, is the rationale here; thus the strength of the market is irrelevant.

Even a one-house historic district has been validated. In an Illinois opinion involving the establishment of a four block district planned around one house, the home in Springfield (Illinois) of Abraham Lincoln, such a district was upheld.[13] Several types of uses were permitted in the district, but retail sales were excluded and the plaintiff had sought a permit to operate a restaurant there. The opinion upheld the state legislation creating the district, not only as a matter of a presumption of validity for legislation, but also with the observation that the plaintiff's property values were enhanced by the proximity of the Lincoln home. This opinion stressed the historical and cultural values justifying the district, not the economic benefits of creating it; the court does this because the plaintiff's building fronted on a downtown commercial street.

Historic district regulations must, however, have limits. In one case, applying to code officials for a building permit for an approved 15 lot subdivision near a district with registered landmark buildings in it, residents in the district noted that when a development permit "involves a building, structure, or site on the landmark registry, the plan shall be referred to the planning board."[14] Residents sued the officials and the subdivider, claiming that the permit "involves" the landmarks and so should be reviewed by the planning board. Their claim was non-suited, the court holding that a landmark existing nearby is not a sufficient reason to refer the permitting to the board. Absent a more explicit regulation, the involvement of the permit with the district should entail more than proximity.[15]

§ 8.03 Preservation of Historic Landmarks.

Early landmark preservation efforts involved Independence Hall in Philadelphia, Mount Vernon, and the Gettysburg battlefield.[16] Landmarks preservation, when not coupled with a historic district, prevents more difficult problems of justifying architectural regulation. There are initially problems of whether the enabling act authorizes a preservation as a category of aesthetic regulation; its purpose is usually to regulate development and so does not clearly bring a preservation regulation within it. This

---

[13] *Rebman v. City of Springfield*, 250 N.E.2d 282 (Ill. App. Ct. 1969).

[14] *Monkton Preservation Society v. Gaylord Brooks Realty Corp.*, 669 A. 2d 195 (Md. App. Ct. 1996).

[15] *Monkton Preservation Society*, 669 A. 2d at 199..

[16] *See United States v. Gettysburg Electric Railway Co.*, 160 U.S. 668 (1896) (recognizing that historical preservation is within the powers of the federal government).

is so because there is no reciprocity of advantage for the owner of an isolated landmark; in economic terms, it could have become a landmark just because it is the single building remaining after similar structures have been demolished or renovated. Its owner gains no benefit from being included in a historic district. Instead, the owner seems singled out and the landmark regulation takes on a the look of "spot zoning."

In *Penn Central*, the United States Supreme Court gave a tepid endorsement to landmark preservation and regulation. The court found that New York City had a comprehensive plan for the preservation of more than four hundred isolated landmarks. The presence of the plan itself seemed conclusive on the issue of whether there was reciprocity of advantage. However, less than .10% of the property in the city was affected, so that the landmark owners had (in the view of the dissenting opinion by Chief Justice Rehnquist) a good argument that they were being singled out in order to provide a public benefit at their expense.

A landmark may be a complex of buildings, having something in common with a historic district. For instance, a municipality with a rule that any structure more than 50 years old was eligible for designation as a landmark and seeking to designate an amusement park built in 1945 as a landmark, was met with the argument that all of the park's structures had been renovated, modernized, and reconstructed over time, so that the park was not eligible as a whole.[17] However, if the park gained historic significance over 50 years, it should not lose its significance because it has been renovated, modernized, or reconstructed. The issue was the significance of the park as a whole. The "tout ensemble" doctrine applies to the park built all at once, just as it would to a historic district built over time, but not all at once.[18]

The planning for landmark preservation becomes all the more important when the statutory authority for regulation is weak. An owner was held entitled to a demolition permit for a historic building when it was eligible for listing on the National Register of Historic Places, but was not listed there. Without specific authority in the state zoning enabling act for historic zoning, the act nonetheless did permit planning for cultural and aesthetic purposes. So after denying the permit, the municipality then enacted a floating zone for historic buildings and rezoned the building for the use already announced to replace it on its site. This rezoning was found to be *ultra vires* the enabling act, was found not to be comprehensive rezoning, was not entitled to the presumption of validity, and was spot zoning.[19]

Churches and non-profit institutions in a historic district or when subject to a landmark preservation law, rarely make a reasonable return on the property, if that is defined to mean a market rate return.[20] Because they

---

[17] *Metropolitan Dade County v. P. J. Birds*, 654 So. 2d 170, 173 (Fla. App. 1995).

[18] *Id.*

[19] *See Donovan v. City of Deadwood*, 538 N.W. 2d 790 (S.Dak. 1995).

[20] *See, e.g., Society of Jesus in New England v. Boston Landmarks Comm'n*, 564 N.E.2d 571 (Mass. 1990) (interior regulation of church violated First Amendment's Religion Clause).

may not have an expectation that they will use the return on their properties to carry out their non-profit purpose, their taking arguments have not been any easier than that of other landmark owners." Such owners have been assigned the burden of showing that the demolition of the protected features of the structure or landmark, such as the facade, is the only way that the owner can realize a reasonable return or is the only solution to the structure's inadequacy for the intended use.[21] That the non-profit user intends to construct a large replacement building is irrelevant to such a showing.

Some municipalities compound the legal problems of such ordinances by permitting either its legislature or the administrative body designating such landmarks as historic to go as far as the law of takings will permit.[22] This permits the implementation of landmark regulations to adjust to changes in the law of takings, but such permissiveness leaves landmark ordinances open to charges of being without sufficiently definite standards.[23] About 1,500–2,000 municipalities around the country have landmark preservation regulations; some apply to the interior as well as the exterior of a landmark.[24]

[A]   Landmark Interior Regulation.

When interior as well as exterior control of a landmark is involved, the non-uniformity of the treatment is all the more exaggerated.[25] No two interiors are exactly alike and so the impact of the landmark designation is unique. Moreover, any regulation of the landmark owner's interior is non-uniform vis-a-vis surrounding properties.

An ordinance authorizing a municipal landmark commission to designate "those buildings, structures, sites, and objects which the commission determines are significant to the municipality, exemplifies its cultural heritage, or contains elements of innovative design, detail, materials, or craftsmanship,"[26] did not clearly authorize the commission to regulate and

---

[21] *Society for Ethical Culture v. Spatt*, 415 N.E.2d 922 (N.Y. 1980) (reflecting the decision in *Penn Central*).

[22] *See, e.g., 900 G Street Assocs. v. Department of Housing and Community Dev.*, 430 A.2d 1387, 1389 (D.C. App. 1981) (where a regulation permitted demolition of a historic landmark when not to do so will result in an unreasonable economic hardship for the owner and defining such a hardship as a taking).

[23] *See Donnelly Assocs. v. District of Columbia Historic Preservation Review Bd.*, 520 A.2d 270, 279–281 (D.C. App. 1987) (discussing *900 G St.* and temporary, regulatory takings).

[24] *See Weinberg v. Barry*, 634 F.Supp. 86 (D.D.C. 1986) (upholding interior regulation); *United Artists Theater Circuit, Inc. v. City of Philadelphia*, 595 A.2d 6 (Pa. 1991) (finding interior regulation a taking), *reversed*, 635 A. 2d 612 (Pa. 1993), *noted in* 22 B. C. Envtl. L. Rev. 593 (1995) (reviewing the two opinions in the *United Artists* case).

[25] *See, e.g., United Artists Theater Circuit, Inc. v. City of Philadelphia*, 595 A.2d 6 (Pa. 1991) (holding Philadelphia's landmark preservation ordinance a taking under the state constitution), *on rehearing*, 635 A.2d 612, 622 (Pa. 1993) (finding no taking under the state constitution but holding that the Philadelphia ordinance did not authorize designation of an interior as historic landmark).

[26] *United Artists Theater Circuit, Inc. v. City of Philadelphia*, 595 A.2d 6, 10 (Pa. 1991).

preserve the interior of what would otherwise (considering its facade or exterior) be a landmark. The phrases most favorable to interior regulation depend upon the "building or structure" language preceding them.[27] Reviewing this language, the Pennsylvania Commonwealth Court found both that it was adequate authorization for the regulation of historic interiors and that the language was within the police power. An art deco, 1928 movie theater was the locus of the controversy in this case. However, at the Pennsylvania Supreme Court level, the case became a takings case.

The Pennsylvania Supreme Court issued two opinions. Its first opinion took Pennsylvania out of the mainstream, denying judicial approval of the landmark preservation ordinance, while its second opinion returned it to the mainstream. The cases were decided under the Pennsylvania Constitution provision[28] analogous to the federal Takings Clause. The holding of the United States Supreme Court in the *Penn Central* opinion, upholding New York City's landmark preservation law, has quieted any number of challenges to similar laws. It helped in this case. The second *United Artists* opinion used a test much like *Penn Central's*: (1) an examination of the need for the governmental regulation; (2) the necessity of the means chosen to alleviate the need; and (3) the economic impact of the regulation.

The interior of a restaurant from the 1950s has also been regulated and preserved.[29] The opinion doing so found that a designation of the Four Seasons Restaurant's interior, to which the public is customarily invited, is subject to regulation, regardless of the purpose for which it was built. Public access to the space justified the regulation. The court found that, even though an interior currently open to the public might be converted to a private space in the future, this should not shield it from regulation.

An ancillary problem involves the law of fixtures. A fixture is any thing that is intended to be, and is, permanently annexed or attached to the real property in which it is located. Should the regulation include items not fixtures? One opinion found that the law of fixtures was irrelevant to its decision, and so hanging sculptures, a walnut bar, metal drapes, railings, and ceiling panels created and installed at the architect's direction, were subject to regulation as integral elements of the interior design.[30] This rationale can get out of hand: is the glassware integral to the design too?

---

[27] This is a paraphrase of the language in the Philadelphia preservation ordinance under review in *Sameric Corp. of Chestnut St. v. City of Philadelphia*, 558 A.2d 155 (Pa. Commw. Ct. 1989), *rev'd sub nom.*, *United Artists Theater Circuit, Inc. v. City of Philadelphia*, 595 A.2d 6 (Pa. 1991) (finding a taking).

[28] "Nor shall private property be taken or applied to public use, without authority of law and without just compensation being first paid or secured." Pa. Const., Art. I, § 10, interpreted in *Commonwealth v. Edmunds*, 586 A. 2d 887 (Pa. 1991) (presenting the four prong test used in the first opinion in *United Artists*, examining the text of the state Constitution, its historic evolution, case law including federal cases, and policy considerations).

[29] *Teachers Insur. & Annuity Ass'n v. New York City*, 623 N.E.2d 526 (N.Y. 1993) (hereafter *TIAA*) (holding, under the N.Y.C. ordinance involved in *Penn Central*, that such a designation was not arbitrary and capricious), *noted at* 26 Conn. L. Rev. 1105 (1994).

[30] *Teachers Insur.*, 623 N.E. 2d at 530 (noting that the noted architect Philip Johnson directed installation).

When a municipality seeks to regulate historic interiors that are private and not accessible to the public, such regulation presents additional problems. The issue is whether there is a public benefit in regulating a space to which the public does not have access. Regulation in this instance is akin to the creation of sound that no one hears. Only with express authority should such a regulation be valid. The lower court *TIAA* opinion expressly states: "this restaurant is not a private club."[31] The New York Court of Appeals, however, did not include such language in its opinion affirming the lower court. So this silence leaves the issue an open one.

[B] Landmark Designation Procedures.

Most landmark designations can be accomplished without the consent of the owner. Many provide for a petition procedure. Neighbors, local preservation groups, and an administrative preservation agency may use it. Filing a petition for landmark designation typically starts a process of expert study and hearings on the structure. In all but a few ordinances, a legislative finding is necessary before a landmark is designated.

Once a structure is designated a landmark, any proposal for repair, renovation, or demolition, will require a permit — often called a certificate of appropriateness. In these proceedings, a showing of economic hardship or an insufficient return on investment will result in the issuance of a certificate, although sometimes a hardship showing is the subject of special proceedings for an exemption from the regulation.[32]

Significantly, the New York City landmark ordinance guaranteed an owner of a landmark a reasonable return on his or her property. Recall from the discussion of the *Penn Central* opinion that counsel for the company unwisely stipulated that its client could earn a reasonable return on the Terminal. The District of Columbia regulation in *900 G Street* did not contain a similar guarantee: it merely said that if the owner was permitted a reasonable use, as an alternative to the property's historic use, the regulation was not a taking. The *900 G Street* court's acceptance of that regulation is a broadening of the holding in *Penn Central* and broadens the legal basis for historic preservation.

Some commentators have suggested that a facade easement program, encouraged by provisions of the Internal Revenue Code concerning charitable deductions for the fair market value of such easements, would work as well as regulation for preserving a landmark. The same argument might be made more forcefully with regard to historic interiors. The preservation of interiors prevents owners from modifying the use of the building (otherwise in accord with the zoning regulations) to update and renovate it. Not being able to renovate the interior may make the preservation of the exterior less economically viable.

---

[31] *Ibid.*, 586 N. E. 2d 262, 263 (1992).

[32] *Second Baptist Church v. Little Rock Historic Dist. Comm'n*, 732 S.W.2d 483, 487 (Ark. 1987) (construing Ark. Stat. Ann. § 19-5001 and upholding denial of permit for church to construct parking lot within district). *See* Peter Salsich, *Land Use Regulation* 163–164 (1991).

§ 8.04   Aesthetics and Incentive Zoning.

In the central business districts of many cities, planners have found incentive zoning useful. With the advent of the skyscrapers, many city ordinances abandoned height limits in their downtown core. Instead, the regulations used Floor Area Ratios (FARs). The FAR is a multiplier for the area of the lot used to determine the permitted square footage of the improvement. The sky's the limit, so long as the FAR is not exceeded. Originally intended as a maximum (an "envelope" for development), in some cities bonus FARs are awarded to buildings with features considered aesthetic. In New York City, the first such feature was a street-front plaza. Such plazas appeared on many plans. Then came atriums, gallerias, roof-top gardens, and pedestrian walkways through the building — all justified by the better aesthetics achieved.

Added to these bonuses were tax abatements for aesthetic features — the original thought was don't penalize good aesthetics with a higher assessment. The controversy in the 1960s over the tax assessments for the Seagram Building in New York City was one focus for this controversy. However, this rationale was expanded into an affirmative effort to encourage certain architectural features.

§ 8.05   Aesthetics and Billboards.

Billboards typically display "commercial speech," defined as an "expression related solely to the economic interests of the speakers and its audience."[33] Until 1976, the United States Supreme Court left it largely unprotected, along with obscenity and defamatory speech. In that year, however, the Court found that the First Amendment protects commercial speech because its auditors have an interest in the free flow of information.[34] Free speech and free enterprise go hand in hand. Regulation of such speech is constitutional when: (1) it is justifiable without reference to its content; (2) advances a significant governmental interest; and (3) provides ample alternative channels of communication for the regulated information. This is the so-called *Virginia Pharmacy* test.

When the first prong of this test is not met — that is, when the content of commercial speech is limited — a different, four prong test is applied. The limitation must first confine itself to misleading speech or speech involving unlawful activity; thus, when speech is inaccurate or unlawful, the First Amendment provides no protection. Second, the government must have a substantial interest in the regulation. Third, the regulation must directly advance that interest. And fourth, the regulation must be no broader than necessary to accomplish its purpose.[35] Together these four

---

[33] *Va. State Bd. of Pharmacy v. Virginia Citizens Consumer Council*, 425 U.S. 748, 762 (1976).

[34] *Id.* at 763.

[35] *Central Hudson Gas and Electric Co. v. Public Service Comm'n of New York*, 447 U.S. 557 (1980). This is *Lochnerian*, economic, or substantive due process in a First Amendment context.

prongs are known as the *Central Hudson* test. A later case discussed the fourth prong, holding that the regulation need not be the least restrictive, but need only be reasonably tailored to accomplish its purpose. [36]

The United States Supreme Court, in *Metromedia, Inc. v. City of San Diego*, [37] invalidated parts of a city ordinance which prohibited outdoor, off-premises advertising from most of the city, along with on-site noncommercial advertisements. The ordinance contained some exceptions, for example in the case of political campaign signs. The court had no majority opinion and showed itself in disarray over the reason for the invalidation. The result was achieved by a 6-3 vote.

In *Metromedia*, the plurality opinion (Justice White writing) said that the first, second, and fourth prong of *Central Hudson* was met, although it discussed the fourth prong briefly. Whether the San Diego ordinance directly advanced governmental interests was an issue left to local officials in the absence of evidence that the city's traffic safety and aesthetic purposes were unreasonable. Likewise, the ordinance's favoring on-site over off-site signs, and so favoring one type of commercial speech over another, was a permissible local judgment: municipalities are free to decide that one type of commercial speech is more important to the flow of information and the functioning of business.

As to the *Virginia Pharmacy* test, Justice White concluded that the ordinance was not neutral because it was not limited to a time/place/manner regulation. It offended the first and third prongs of the *Virginia Pharmacy* test. It could not be justified without reference to the content of the speech and did not provide ample alternative channels of communication.

In a second line of *Central Hudson* analysis, the plurality opinion struck down part of the ordinance. Construing the ordinance as exempting on-site commercial advertisements, Justice White found it failed to exempt non-commercial speech — a category of speech more protected than commercial speech — barring such speech unless it fell within some narrow exceptions listed in the ordinance.

This said, Justice White found that the ordinance was over-inclusive by limiting non-commercial as well as commercial speech. (Non-commercial in this context means political or highly protected speech.) Thus the restrictions on off-site commercial advertising were valid, but the restrictions on on-site non-commercial advertisements were invalid. The former restrictions were justified on safety and aesthetic grounds. So for instance, if a municipality were to ban all commercial billboards, but allow all non-commercial ones, the problem with regard to *Metromedia* would be that, in administering the ordinance, local officials will run afoul of Justice White's concern that they will be making content-oriented judgments to distinguish commercial or non-commercial speech. In addition, using a partial ban, the municipality may encourage an Equal Protection Clause challenge to the ordinance.

---

[36] *Bd. of Trustees v. Fox*, 492 U.S. 469 (1989).
[37] 453 U.S. 490 (1981).

Because six of the Justices focus on *Virginia Pharmacy* and the first and third prongs of its test, content neutrality and the alternative channels of communication have become the focus of later cases. The majority of six, although not writing jointly, suggested that billboard restrictions on commercial speech were not a violation of the First Amendment. Indeed, the Justices said enough to indicate that a majority of them thought that aesthetics alone could be sufficient justification for an ordinance. That majority is drawn from those in the plurality and the dissenters; a concurring opinion thought that the City did not justify the ordinance sufficiently. What was wrong with San Diego's ordinance was that it threw a protected class of speech into a catch-all category of non-commercial speech by not defining the type of restricted speech narrowly enough.

[A] How Should Cities Like San Diego Respond to *Metromedia*?

Four responses are possible:

(1) In view of the numerous (twelve) exceptions for both commercial and non-commercial speech that seemed based on content, Justice White concluded that the ordinance valued some types of protected speech over others but found that the city could remedy this defect by banning all commercial billboards while permitting all non-commercial billboards;

(2) The city should define commercial speech in greater detail, so that political speech does not inadvertently come within the prohibitions of an ordinance. Defining the commercial speech to be regulated first, and providing that non-commercial speech is not regulated, would do the trick;

(3) Probably also, the city should respond by eliminating the series of exceptions, which in effect forced on the administrators an interpretive effort to categorize speech; such an effort, the court felt, verged on prior restraint of otherwise protected speech; and

(4) The city should allow any sign to go up, but require that it be dismantled by the advertiser or the city (at the advertiser's expense) if it falls within the restrictions. This eliminates a claim that the ordinance is a prior restraint on free speech. "In *Metromedia* . . ., a plurality of the court recognized that an ordinance prohibiting off-premise commercial billboard advertising would not have offended the first amendment if it had not preferred commercial over noncommercial advertising."[38] The *Naegele* opinion continues: "Contrary to Naegele's contention, the location of the billboard in commercial and industrial areas does not preclude the city from relying on aesthetics to justify its exercise of police power. The San Diego ordinance banned billboards in similar areas."[39] Apparently "once ugly, always ugly" is *not* the law.

Six years later, the Supreme Court in *Members of the City Council of the City of Los Angeles v. Taxpayers for Vincent,*[40] upheld an ordinance

---

[38] *Naegele Outdoor Advertising, Inc. v. City of Durham*, 844 F.2d 172, 173 (4th Cir. 1988).

[39] *Id.* at 174.

[40] 466 U.S. 789 (1984).

prohibiting posting of an local political candidate's signs on utility poles.[41] The Court, however, went out of its way to endorse the aesthetic purpose of the ordinance, which was to eliminate "visual assault on the citizens of Los Angeles presented by an accumulation of signs posted on public property."[42] The *Vincent* opinion makes plain that a prohibition on signs justified by aesthetics is valid, just as it was clear after *Metromedia* that a prohibition of commercial advertising is valid.

The *Vincent* opinion clarifies several points unclear after *Metromedia*. The opinion should be read, as an aesthetics case, by looking for all of the *Metromedia* citations and reading around them. In addition, the poles were found not to be a public forum necessary to the dissemination of political ideas — there was plenty of private property around on which Vincent could have his signs placed. As one state court said later, "the *Vincent* opinion makes it clear that a content-neutral regulation limiting expressive activity on non-forum public property is tailored narrowly enough if it is not "substantially broader than necessary" to protect the interest. . . ."[43] In the same vein, the *Vincent* opinion states: "By banning these signs, the City did no more than eliminate the exact source of the evil it sought to remedy."[44] What is required here is not legislative efficiency, but rather only a reasonable nexus between the public purposes sought to be advanced and the regulations in the ordinance.

The distinction between on-site and off-site advertisements is not acceptable in all jurisdictions today. In jurisdictions which have endorsed aesthetics alone as a valid reason for an exercise of the police power, the difference between on-premises and off-premises signs and billboards should logically disappear.[45]

There is a large amount of case law in the area of billboard regulation. This is so because, first, the outdoor advertisers are tenacious litigators and the urge to "beautify" is strong at the local level. In *National Advertising Co. v. City and County of Denver*,[46] the court upheld an ordinance banning all off-site commercial signs within 600 feet of a freeway, but permitting non-commercial and on-site signs in the same proximity to a freeway. In *National Advertising Co. v. Town of Babylon*,[47] the court held that a town's billboard ordinance was unconstitutional for its failure to state the substantial governmental interest advanced by it, or because the town in the alternative failed to offer extrinsic evidence of that interest.[48]

Second, basic definitions for a sign are likely to provoke disputes. One ordinance usefully defined a sign as "any structure, part thereof or device

[41] *Id.* at 814–815.

[42] *Id.* at 827.

[43] *State v. Hodgkiss*, 565 A.2d 1059, 1064 (N.H. 1989).

[44] *Vincent*, 466 U.S. at 808.

[45] *See generally Bell v. Township of Stafford*, 541 A.2d 692, 696–699 (N.J. 1988) (reviewing U.S. Supreme Court cases).

[46] 912 F.2d 405 (10th Cir. 1990).

[47] 900 F.2d 551, 555 (2d Cir. 1990).

[48] *See generally* Peter Salsich, *Land Use Regulation* 445–449 (1991).

attached thereto, or painted or represented thereon, which displays or includes any messages or representations used as an announcement, advertisement, direction, or designation of any goods or services located on any land or any building in such a manner as to draw attention from beyond the land or building." Likewise, a message was "any number, word, symbol, emblem, insignia, trademark,[49] model, banner more than four inches high." Before regarding this definition as too vague, consider the variety of sizes and shapes for signs that any definition must cover: there are standard roadside billboards, but there are also corporate logos atop buildings, signs painted on the side of a building, and signs declared historic landmarks. Signs can be neon, flashing, or fiber optic — and regulated as traffic safety matters. Signs can be permanent or portable.[50]

Third, many types of signs have some protected, political content — for example, a garrison flag flown by a car dealership. Some make use of public space either (1) directly — for example, a billboard hung on a elevated light-rail track over a public street — or (2) indirectly — for example, a sign for a local political candidate suspended between a utility pole and a tree. Consider the free speech implications of prohibiting the latter sign, situated between the pole and tree, as before, but while a candidate for public office stands under it on the sidewalk distributing leaflets to passers-by.[51] Thus regulation of signs by physical type easily runs afoul of the free speech clause of the First Amendment. Thus, many definitions are likely to be challenged "as applied."

§ 8.06   Low-Income Neighborhoods and Billboards.

Some local problems with billboards will require less than jurisdiction-wide regulation. For instance, nation-wide surveys show that over one half of the revenue from billboard companies comes from tobacco and liquor companies advertising their products to low-income persons. Local groups have whitewashed the billboards advertising such products; they also have engaged in civil disobedience when billboard owners attempt to have the police stop them. Faced with such a situation, a municipal legislature might permissibly ban such advertising from low-income neighborhoods. A local municipality need not do its own studies on this matter.[52] If national studies show that tobacco and liquor has adverse effects on health, the municipality may regulate this advertising on that account. This will not likely be found to be content neutral regulation, but the adverse health effects of such

---

[49] *See Blockbuster Video, Inc. v. City of Tempe*, 141 F.3d 1295 (9th Cir. 1998), *noted in* Jeffrey Strouse, *Redefining Trademark Alteration Within the Context of Aesthetic-Based Zoning Laws: A Blockbuster Dilemna*, 53 Vand. L. Rev. 717 (2000).

[50] *Harnish v. Manatee County*, 783 F.2d 1535 (11th Cir. 1986) (upholding a prohibition of portable signs). The ordinance also provided: "No sign shall have more than eight messages, although a premium of one message is permitted if the sign is lower than ten feet in height."

[51] *See State v. Hodgkiss*, 565 A.2d 1059 (N.H. 1989).

[52] *City of Renton v. Playtime Theatres, Inc.*, 475 U.S. 41 (1986) (finding that no independent localized study is required before regulating adult movie theaters), discussed *infra*, in Chapter 16.

billboards are arguably included within a regulation of offending billboards' "secondary effects."[53] Those effects bring the matter within the police power, and arguably provide a rational basis for a municipality to enact a neighborhood ban on such billboards, or else to require placing tobacco or liquor advertising alongside public service announcements with an anti-smoking or sobriety theme.

§ 8.07   A Ban on Billboards.

Faced with the complexity of the law in this area, a municipality might be tempted to ban all types of billboards. Courts have said in dicta that a municipality might limit the number of billboards to a certain, maximum number or prohibit them altogether.[54] In *Lucas v. South Carolina Coastal Council*,[55] the United State Supreme Court held that "when an owner of real property has been called upon to sacrifice *all* economically beneficial uses in the name of the common good, that is, to leave his property economically idle, he has suffered a taking."[56] Reading this, a municipal attorney might suspect that a total ban raises the possibility that *Metromedia* and *Lucas* may intersect for the benefit of the billboard industry. What *Metromedia* seems to permit — a total prohibition on billboards — may deprive the billboard company of "*all* economically beneficial uses" of its property in the municipality. In this instance, the company's property will be a collection of billboard leases, licenses, and easements, as opposed to the fee simple underlying the billboard or the land improved with a billboard and incapable of another use. Imagining an alternative use for a billboard is difficult. So the "total takings" analysis of *Lucas* might apply, unless the state's background common law of nuisance and property permit the ban. As background law, numerous state cases upholding billboard regulations should suffice to show that they are a visual blight and a nuisance. Therefore, a ban on billboards, when content-neutral and when other means of advertising are available, makes, in the words of *Lucas*, "what was previously permissible no longer so."[57] The widespread judicial approval of aesthetic regulation should trump *Lucas*.

---

[53] *Young v. Am. Mini-Theatres, Inc.*, 427 U.S. 50 (1976) (Powell, J., writing a plurality opinion, finding that regulation of adult movie houses might be justified by the secondary effects occurring around them — e.g., incidental criminal conduct).

[54] *See, e.g., Bell v. Township of Stafford*, 541 A.2d 692 (N.J. 1988) (holding that the township failed to justify a total ban, but admitted the possibility on aesthetic grounds).

[55] 505 U.S. 1003 (1992).

[56] *Id.* at 1019.

[57] *Id.* at 1031.

Chapter 9

Moratoria and Growth Controls

§ 9.01 Moratoria.

In order to meet some emergency, municipal legislatures sometimes enact moratoria on building permits, sewer hook-ups, or other permits and approvals. These are stop gap, time buying measures. Often moratoria are enacted in order to prevent the overloading of public facilities such a schools, sewer systems, or water supply facilities. Sometimes they are enacted to prevent a permitting rush in the face of proposed new regulations or to keep the status quo in place while decisions are made on capital improvements. However, a long-continued problem to which the legislature suddenly responds with a moratoria, when unaccompanied by a simultaneous increase in the seriousness of the problem or emergency, does not lay the basis for a valid moratoria.[1]

Authority for enacting moratoria is often found as an implied power in a state's zoning enabling act to exercise the police power to protect a municipality's zoning and planning authority, and by liberally construing the act.[2] When a statute authorizes zoning for a particular purpose, there is implied authority to adopt a moratoria for that same purpose. Likewise, if a municipality has authority to operate sewer and water facilities, implied authority for a moratoria on providing them may be readily implied.

If such a moratoria is enacted (1) in good faith, (2) on a temporary basis, (3) is non-discriminatory, (4) is an interim step while a comprehensive plan is worked out to deal with the emergency, and (5) a prompt adoption of the plan follows, then the moratoria is a valid exercise of the police power and by the same token it is not a taking. While the moratoria is in force, a municipality must continue to conduct its administrative business as usual while the moratoria on other types of permissions is in place. The permits denied must be linked to the problem addressed in the moratoria and may not be denied on an arbitrary or case-by-case basis.[3] However, if valid, a moratoria can reach even vested rights, permitting a municipality to revoke prior approvals.[4]

---

[1] *See Westwood Forest Estates Inc. v. Village of South Nyack*, 244 N.E.2d 700 (N.Y. 1969) (involving a rezoning prohibiting multiple dwellings throughout the town); *see also Q.C. Construction Company v. Gallo*, 649 F.Supp. 1331 (D. R.I. 1986) (due process violation found, with injunctive remedy given).

[2] *See Brazos Land, Inc. v. Bd. of Cty. Comm'nrs*, 848 P.2d 1095 (N. M. App. Ct. 1993) (moratoria to protect groundwater from pollution). *But see Bd. of Supervisors v. Horne*, 215 S.E.2d 453 (Va. 1975) (finding moratoria *ultra vires* a county's express and implied authority).

[3] *See Pritchett v. Nathan Rogers Const. & Realty Co.*, 379 So. 2d 545 (Ala. 1979).

[4] *See Almquist v. Town of Marshan*, 245 N.W.2d 819 (Minn. 1976) (applying moratoria on permits to partially completed development); *Belle Harbor Realty Corporation v. Kerr*, 323 N.E. 2d 697 (N.Y. 1974) (problem with the whole sewer system, not just the capacity of a treatment plant involved).

The seriousness of the problem to which the moratoria responds is more easily justified when the health of the population is at stake (as with sewers).[5] On the other hand, moratoria on the provision of public facilities are harder to justify, in large part because the municipality's problem is then general in nature, and in this situation its forcing particular property owners to bear the consequences of its failure to solve a municipal problem violates the "reciprocity of advantage" required in substantive due process cases.

Factors indicating the seriousness of a problem are: (1) inter-governmental disputes over how to solve it (a longer moratoria is justified here); (2) the protection of natural resources (a river, into which sewage might overflow from an inadequate sewage treatment plant); and (3) the presence of state or regional effects wider than the jurisdictional writ of the moratoria (e.g., state administrative actions producing a ban at the local or regional level — in effect saying, "we did not create this problem, we're under orders."[6]

Often moratoria are the herald of the imposition of growth controls — when there is no health and safety problem, but instead there is an on-going planning process, the effectiveness of which the local legislature wishes to preserve. A quick spike in development permits provides the precipitating emergency. Similarly, moratoria may be used particularly in rural, agricultural jurisdictions containing second home communities for which there are no public sewer lines and treatment facilities;[7] a three-year moratoria on the installation of new septic systems in order to protect the groundwater supplies in the jurisdiction tests the scope of the good faith element for a moratoria. The time period during which criteria for adequate septic systems may be devised is unreasonably long when lasting more than 2 or 3 years; such a lengthy ban is neither "temporary" nor does it allow a solution to be put in place within a reasonable time, so it also violates both the second and the fifth criteria for a valid moratorium. On the other hand, a moratoria lasting as long as the process needed to respond to the emergency, is valid and not a taking.[8] A second, similar example involved a moratoria on mobile home sales stores. It was enacted to prevent a municipality from having "an unwanted reputation" the mobile home sales capital of its region, but was struck down.[9] Its good faith was suspect.

---

[5] See Kaplan v. Clear Lake Water Authority, 794 F.2d 1059 (5th Cir. 1986).

[6] See Smoke Rise, Inc. v. Washington Suburban Sanitary Commission, 400 F.Supp. 1369 (D.Md. 1975) (upholding five year sewer hook-up moratoria against due process and taking claims); see also Unity Ventures v. County of Lake, 631 F.Supp. 181, 197-199 (N.D. Ill. 1986) (a civil rights case discussing Smoke Rise).

[7] See, e.g., Kaplan v. Clear Lake Water Authority, 794 F.2d 1059 (5th Cir. 1986) (upholding such a moratoria against due process and equal protection challenges).

[8] See Tahoe-Sierra Preservation Council, Inc. v. Tahoe Regional Planning Agency, 216 F.3d 764 (9th Cir. 2000) (finding no categorical, total taking under the Lucas v. South Carolina Coastal Council opinion), cert. granted, 2001 WL 69237 (June 29, 2001).

[9] Herrington v. City of Pearl, 908 F. Supp. 418 (S.D. Miss. 1995). See also Begin v. Inhabitants of the Town of Sabbatus, 409 A.2d 1269 (Me. 1979) (invalidating moratoria applicable only to mobile homes as a violation of the equal protection clause).

On occasion, moratoria have even reached matters that might be regarded as a title matter, such as the creation of time shares in apartments in a destination resort municipality.[10]

Property owners affected by a moratorium followed by a valid downzoning might wish to consider further steps, one of which might be to appeal their next property tax assessment.[11] If a client's parcel is worth less than before the moratoria, then the assessment, premised on the "full value" of the parcel, should logically be reduced. Such a reduction will not result automatically and must be applied for, but is more easily achieved than would be a judgment in a takings claim brought as a result of the moratoria and downzoning.

[A]   Statutory Prohibitions on Moratoria.

Several states — e.g., New Jersey[12] and New Mexico — have enacted statutes prohibiting certain types of moratoria. New Jersey prohibits them when used in order to prepare a comprehensive plan. New Mexico prohibits them when they are used to buy study time to impose impact fees. Arizona, Montana, and Washington also have some type of statutory restrictions on the use of moratoria, requiring specific legislative findings, limiting its duration, or imposing hearing requirements, respectively.

§ 9.02   Interim Zoning Controls.

Municipalities sometimes experience a problem with a land use for which its land use regulations are unprepared. Fast food restaurants in commercial use districts, bed and breakfasts in residential land use districts, and adult entertainment uses in commercial districts,[13] provide examples. An interim regulation may restrict the rezoning of sites for such purposes, or the subdivision of such sites, or the issuance of special exceptions for them. A moratoria on applications for such uses may then provide a bridge between the planning necessary to deal with such uses and the implementation of that planning by preserving the status quo in the affected use districts while the planning takes place.[14] It may even be used in part to

---

[10] *Jackson Court Condominiums, Inc. v. City of New Orleans*, 665 F. Supp. 1235 (E.D. La. 1987) (upholding the interim regulation as preserving the residential integrity of the use district by discouraging transiency and promoting a sense of belonging, and by preserving the aesthetics of the district, citing *Penn Central Transp. Co.*).

[11] *See State Department of Assessments and Taxation v. Clark*, 380 A.2d 28 (Md. 1977).

[12] N. J. Stat. Ann. § 40:55D-90 (1997), *used in N. J. Shore Builders Ass'n v. Mayor and Twp. of Middletown*, 561 A.2d 319 (N.J. Super. Ct., L. Div., 1989) *and Toll Bros., Inc. v. Mayor and Council of the Twp. of West Windsor*, 712 A.2d 266 (N.J. Super. Ct., App. Div., 1998) (invalidating a timed, sequential growth control and distinguishing *Golden v. Planning Bd.*, discussed in this Chapter, *infra*).

[13] *CR of Rialto, Inc. v. City of Rialto*, 975 F. Supp. 1254 (C.D. Cal. 1997) (striking down an interim ordinance and enjoining its enforcement on First Amendment grounds).

[14] *See State ex rel. SCA Chemical Waste Services, Inc. v. Konigsberg*, 636 S.E.2d 430, 435 (Tenn. 1982).

provoke public debate about such uses. Reasonably prompt planning and implementation of the plan is all that is required.

This use of interim regulations with a moratoria on applications has a public purpose.[15] It prevents a plan's defeat before it is implemented.[16] However, the duration of the moratoria is crucial: its duration should not be so long as to provide the affected property owner with a cause of action for a temporary taking.[17] Two to three years provide the outside limits on the duration of interim ordinances.[18] Some states limit such moratoria by statute, but about ten states authorize some use of interim and restrictive regulations so long as the municipality diligently pursues the enactment of new or amended regulations.[19]

Express statutory authority exists for interim zoning in several states. At least eighteen state courts in different jurisdictions have held that interim zoning is within the general police power delegation inherent in zoning enabling acts.[20] An electoral initiative or referendum may attempt to take such pressing matter out of hands of the local authorities, but such a preemption has been held invalid when the state legislature has enacted an express authority to enact interim land use regulations.[21]

§ 9.03 Growth Controls.

In the landmark case of *Village of Euclid v. Ambler Realty Co.*,[22] land use regulation that permits a landowner the reasonable use of his land was authorized; there reasonable use was measured once, at the moment of the regulation's enactment. Later cases recognized that what is a reasonable use may change with the approach of urbanization. Moreover, it was recognized that such uses needed to be measured differently as urbanization approached — that what was reasonable without urbanization was not

---

[15] *See Schafer v. City of New Orleans*, 743 F. 2d 1086 (5th Cir. 1984) (rejecting a substantive due process claim involving fast food restaurants and upholding an interim ordinance applying to five city blocks and whose duration was 10.5 months long).

[16] Robert Frielich, *Interim Development Controls: Essential Tools for Implementing Flexible Planning and Zoning*, 49 J. Urban L. 65, 66–67 (1971).

[17] *See First English Evan. Lutheran Church v. City of Los Angeles*, 482 U.S. 304 (1987) (finding that an action for a temporary regulatory taking occurs when the time passing is more than a "normal administrative delay").

[18] *Zilber v. Town of Moraga*, 692 F. Supp. 1195, 1207 (N.D. Cal. 1988) (upholding a 1.5 year development moratoria while open space preservation regulations were developed); *see also Kawaoka v. City of Arroyo Grande*, 796 F. Supp. 1320 (C. D. Cal. 1992).

[19] *See, e.g.*, Minn. Stat. Ann. § 394.34 (1998).

[20] *Sprint Spectrum L.P. v. Jefferson Cty.*, 968 F. Supp. 1457, 1464–65 (N.D. Ala. 1997) (finding no Alabama statutes or decisions on the matter, but listing, *id.* at n. 9, California, Colorado, Kentucky, Michigan, Minnesota, Montana, New Jersey, Oregon, Washington, and Wisconsin, as providing express statutory authority for interim land use regulations; and also listing Arkansas, Connecticut, Florida, Georgia, Hawaii, Illinois, Maryland, Massachusetts, New York, Ohio, Oklahoma, Pennsylvania, South Carolina, Tennessee, Texas, Utah, and Wyoming as having judicial decisions on this matter).

[21] *See Bank of the Orient v. Tiburon*, 269 Cal. Rptr. 690 (Cal. App. Ct. 1990) (so holding in a situation in which the municipal legislature already enacted a similar interim regulation).

[22] 272 U.S. 365 (1926), discussed *supra*, Chapter 6.

the same as what was required when it came. Thus was born the idea of regulating a reasonable uses of land over a reasonable length of time — in short, growth controls. Growth controls require land developers to wait a reasonable period of time until public services and facilities catch up with their projects. They involve planning in and over time, rather than spacial planning.[23]

The need for such controls may be seen, in relief and in the alternative, in the phrase "urban sprawl."[24] It is costly in many ways to society as a whole — for example, in the uneconomical provision of urban facilities and services over long distances, when it often refers to a spreading and low density of population and land use affecting the rate at which land is urbanized and denied to other uses, such as agriculture.[25] It is also seen in the lack of control over the quality of public services and facilities, as when a dependence on the automobile defeats the purposes of public transportation. It is sometimes further described as a lack of balance among various land uses, or in the lack of control over the specifics and eventual development of a municipality. In contrast, the alternative to urban sprawl is seen by urban planners as the use of compact, high-density urban designs of mixed land use — an updated version of a traditional town, with a town center.[26] There is considerable debate in economic circles over the costs of sprawl as opposed to un-sprawled, compact dense development. Some urban costs, e.g., schools, are less related to sprawl than to a concern with quality.[27]

Thus, after a jurisdiction enacts a moratoria on permits, its officials generally start a planning process resulting in the enactment of some type of growth controls ordinance, involving the timing and sequence of development. These controls are an overlay on already existing zoning and subdivision regulations and so require a developer to obtain special permits certifying that the development is served by certain public facilities. Only essential facilities are involved: waste water sewers, drainage facilities, roads with a capacity to handle subdivision traffic, parks, and fire protection.

Growth controls must not be just a moratoria in disguise. They are aimed at preventing the imposition of moratoria in the future by dealing with the

---

[23] In this regard, see *Marx v. Zoning Board of Appeal of the Village of Mill Neck*, 529 N.Y.S.2d 330 (N.Y. App. Div. 1988) (denying a BZA the right to alter a subdivision approval of the village planning board in an attempt to maintain the distinct jurisdiction of each agency).

[24] The effects of sprawl are hotly debated. *Compare* Timothy Dowling, *Reflections on Urban Sprawl, Smart Growth, and the Fifth Amendment*, 148 U.Pa. L. Rev. 873 (2000) *with* Clint Bolick, *Subverting the American Dream: Government Dictated "Smart Growth" is Unwise and Unconstitutional*, 148 U. Pa. L. Rev. 858 (2000).

[25] *See generally Mayhew v. Town of Sunnyvale*, 964 S.W.2d 922 (Tex. 1998) (finding that the denial of a development application is not a regulatory taking when designed to steady a municipality's rate of growth and remedy the "ill effects of urbanization" with the expansion of the urban areas within the municipality).

[26] This is sometimes called "New Urbanism," discussed *supra*, Chapter 8.

[27] *See generally Points of View: Paying for Sprawl*, at <www.planning.org/info/pointsof view/ sprawl.htm/> (visited July 5, 2001).

provision of essential services. One case, however, concluded that a mandatory phasing ordinance for a large development otherwise permitted as of right, was an invalid moratoria.[28]

Thus growth controls impose additional requirements on the platting of subdivisions, requirements that channel subdivisions into areas of the jurisdiction for which public facilities are available. The purpose is to coordinate the subdivision of land with the provision and availability of such facilities.

Availability means one of two things. It can mean proximity. This is the simple definition: the public facilities must be within a certain distance of the proposed subdivision or development. Somewhat more difficult to apply is a definition in which available means adequacy — with this definition in place, the discretion of the administrators of the system becomes much greater.

If the services involved, and required to be available, are in fact available, then the subdivision application receives so many points. A minimum number of points must be assembled by the application and its proposed plat before a subdivision permit is issued. This is the system of the Town of Ramapo, validated by the New York Court of Appeals in *Golden v. Planning Board of Ramapo*.[29] The United States Supreme Court's dismissal of the appeal in *Ramapo* should not be interpreted as its validation of the town's ordinance. Caution is warranted after the Supreme Court's opinion in *First English*.[30]

§ 9.04 The Ramapo Plan.

With growth controls imposed, land which is zoned residential cannot be used that way. In *Ramapo*, the landowner, Mrs. Golden, wanted to develop at a density below the level permitted in the zoning ordinance, but without meeting the extra requirements of the growth control system. The planning board would not permit her to do so.

Mrs. Golden had contracted to sell her land for development purposes to a commercial builder. The planning board denied approval on the ground that she had failed to obtain the special permit required by the town's growth controls ordinance. (Such a system had better apply to a wide spectrum of owners, as here, or else equal protection clause concerns are raised.) Golden sued the planning board, seeking to annul its denial of her purchaser's subdivision plan.

Ramapo is one of five towns in Rockland County, a suburban and rural municipality twenty-five miles north of New York City. Between 1960 and

---

[28] *Toll Bros., Inc. v. West Windsor Twp.*, 712 A.2d 266 (N.J. Super. Ct., App. Div., 1998).

[29] 285 N.E.2d 291 (N.Y.), *appeal dismissed sub nom.*, *Rockland County Builders Ass'n v. McAlevey*, 409 U.S. 1003 (1972), *noted at* 47 N.Y.U. L.Rev. 723 (1972), 26 Stan. L.Rev. 585 (1974), 58 Minn. L.Rev. 1009, 1054–1058 (1974) (a comment co-authored by the principal drafter of the Ramapo ordinance law, Professor Robert Freilich).

[30] Involving temporary takings, discussed *supra*, Chapter 5.

1970, its population more than doubled and its county's population increased 68%. The town adopted its growth control plan in 1969.

Behind the Ramapo plan and ordinance lay eight years of planning studies, sewage and drainage studies, adoption of an official map, master planning, and capital budgeting. Moreover, the town's ordinance was not an exclusionary device. Its plan and ordinance also provided for some, not a lot, of low and moderate income housing.

In addition, the town had, as noted, grown rapidly during the 1960s and had grown nearly 300% in population during the years 1940-1968. Moreover, its planning board had the authority under the ordinance to issue permits granting the right to proceed with development in future years, once capital improvements called for in the town's capital budget were constructed.

In Ramapo's ordinance (the ground for denying Mrs. Golden's subdivision plan), the eligibility of each project for a special permit was based on the availability of five essential services:

1. sewers or an approved substitute,

2. drainage facilities,

3. parks or recreational facilities,

4. public roads improved with curbs and sidewalks, and

5. firehouses.

A variable number of points was given, the greater number given for proximity of the proposed subdivision to these five types of facilities. A score of fifteen was the minimum required, and no more than five points could be awarded in any one of the five categories. An applicant had to obtain the fifteen points and with them a special permit before beginning the subdivision process.

Ramapo's controls applied to all residential districts, to single family as well as multi-family development districts. This aspect of the controls is reminiscent of the "reciprocity of advantage" discussed by Justice Holmes in *Mahon*. Underlying the plan was the fiscal assumption that it would lower municipal bond financing costs for the town. (However, the town's growth controls plan would have been in a still stronger position — and probably further lowered financing costs too — if commercial and industrial uses had been included as well.)

The court found this scheme "an over-all program of orderly growth" and "a sequential development policy commensurate with progressing availability and capacity of public facilities."[31] Moreover, it found authority for the growth controls in the language of the enabling act "to restrict and regulate" land use; that included by implication the authority to direct the growth of population within the confines of the jurisdiction. New York State's enabling statute governing the town's authority was based on the Standard Zoning Enabling Act — enhancing the persuasive value of this opinion for other states.

---

[31] *Ramapo*, 285 N.E.2d at 144.

Finally, it is important to note that any developer whose property was prohibited from development by the controls until some future year might provide the facilities himself and so accumulate enough development points to gain the right to subdivide. Thus, the developer willing to pay the price of his development in municipal facilities was not precluded from going ahead. It is likely though that only well-financed developers could do so, and would choose the facilities that they could build most cheaply.

Ramapo's sequence of development proceeded in three six-year phases. This phasing was necessary because the enabling statute for capital budgets provided for six-year plans. For holding some property from development for eighteen years, the town gave decreased real property tax assessments. Such decreases were reminiscent of contractual consideration and of an agreement between the developer and the town — based again on a reciprocity of advantage.

[A] Summary.

Ramapo's growth control plan was approved because it:

1. was supported, before-the-fact, by a comprehensive planning process,

2. involved no permanent land use restrictions (although 12-18 years — the program's life — does stretch the meaning of the word "temporary,"

3. admitted of exceptions, variances, and some tax relief for burdened landowners, and

4. found authority in the state's enabling statute.

Ramapo establishes the rule that a comprehensive planning process, resulting in a plan neither designed to exclude population growth nor involving permanent restrictions on land, justifies both (1) a refusal to rezone, and (2) if no rezoning is needed, a denial of an overlay development permit required pre-subdivision when available public facilities are inadequate and the subdivision is "premature."[32] In contrast, a finding that a municipality's road system is inadequate, and the consequent enactment of a capital improvement program for it, envisioning its completion in fifty years' time, but in the meanwhile imposing a point system delaying development from one to fifteen years, are neither temporary nor reasonable because the completion of the system and the delay in development were not in sync.[33]

---

[32] For another discussion of the control of premature subdivision, see *supra*, Chapter 14.

[33] *Toll Bros., Inc. v. West Windsor Twp.*, 712 A.2d 266, 271 (N.J. Super. Ct., App. Div., 1998) (distinguishing *Ramapo* because N.J. Stat. Ann. 40:55D-90 limited moratoria to situations certified as a "clear imminent danger" to health by a qualified public health professional and also stating that otherwise no moratoria on development applications or interim zoning shall be permitted).

[B]   Future Issues.

Several issues are left open by this opinion. Initially, the court noted that the underlying mix of land uses and their exclusionary impact were not before the court. Because of this, the opinion might be viewed as a planning response to early exclusionary zoning opinions, like that of the Pennsylvania Supreme Court in *National Land and Investment Company v. Kohn*.[34] Exclusionary zoning cases present separate and open questions, for this court. Additionally, the court also left open the issue of the actual effect or impact of the Town's plan.

Interesting issues also arose once the town's growth controls ordinance was approved. Whether the town was "committed to the construction and installation of capital improvements" in the sense that a waiting developer could, in the year named in the capital budget, sue for specific performance of the commitment, was an open issue. The court suggested that the town was committed. Later, however, the town might find that when it spent the money committed in its budget, the money bought less facilities than the town had expected. The town's commitment to developers like Mrs. Golden probably does not rise to the level of a development contract when unforeseen events intervene.[35] What looks like contractual consideration — postponed development followed by an decrease in the real property tax assessment — should not be confused with the reciprocity required to sustain the ordinance as a development agreement. The town's failure to meet its capital budget obligations may well be excusable.

The validity of the town's growth controls resulted in a holding involving their facial validity — rather than an "as applied" holding. There was no discussion of whether a few or many parcels could gain subdivision approval, of the precise need for the controls, or of the exclusionary effects of those controls. They too are all open questions. On the last unaddressed question, critics have noted that 65% of the town was zoned into districts with large lots.

[C]   Creating Sounder *Ramapo* Plans.

The Ramapo ordinance singles out residential subdivisions, but would be more comprehensive and uniform in its treatment of owners if it encompassed other land uses as well. So, first, municipalities like Ramapo will achieve sounder planning if all types of developments — residential, commercial, and industrial — were included in the future. This comprehensiveness for municipal planning is particularly important when (as here) the town does not control all of the facilities whose availability gave developers points towards its permits.

Second, a further method of testing a municipality's comprehensive plan lies in its conformance to, and consistency with, regional plans; that consistency provides an assurance that no exclusionary requirements were

---

[34] 215 A. 2d 597 (Pa. 1970), discussed *infra,* Chapter 10.

[35] *See infra*, Chapter 21, discussing development agreements.

involved. For example, when another municipality used a state projection of population growth, coupled with a questionnaire distributed to municipal residents asking for their opinion of what the ideal municipal growth rate should be, the municipality's land use plan was found not to be a sound statistical basis for a recommended 3% growth rate."[36] As another growth controls opinion stated, growth controls "should be the product of careful study."[37]

Third, a municipality's capital budgets must be more definitive than they were in this case, with regard (for example) to the types of municipal bonds to be used. A shorter period than eighteen years would make budgetary planning projections more secure as well.[38] So further changes in budgeting might (1) shorten the eighteen year restrictive period to (say) a decade, or (2) be more specific in tying the capital budget to the capital program and to the official map of the municipality. The Ramapo ordinance envisioned a complete build-out of the town during the eighteen year financial plan underlying the restrictions; this seemed reasonable because Ramapo was a relatively small town. When in contrast the municipality seeking to control growth was larger and would not be built out during such a period, then shortening of the period for using the restrictions was warranted.

A fourth change for the better involves the *Ramapo* criteria. The proximity criteria in the Ramapo ordinance were tied to services which invoke heath and safety considerations: water, sewer, and fire services. These provided the safest of criteria. Thus, for instance, an ordinance using the presence of nearby schools instead, suggests a concern to exclude people in families with school age children. According to *Ramapo*, "[t]here is something inherently suspect in a scheme that . . . effects a restriction upon the free mobility of people . . . ." The opinion also suggested that it was on watch for "an array of exclusionary devices" in the guise of growth controls. The presence of a police station, or a water treatment plant, or a trunk line sewer, should be used instead of schools. Moreover, a developer's attorney might point out that a school can be made to appear adequate or inadequate to serve more students by changes in school service-area boundaries.

Ramapo's ordinance required that five essential services be "available" as the precondition to subdivision approval. "Adequate" public facilities is a less discretionary and so more desirable term than availability. Adequacy can be measured more objectively, in terms of, to mention a few, calls to the fire house, response times for the fire truck, etc. Availability however might mean proximity, but also might have other meanings as well. For example, public facilities might be found unavailable when the market for municipal bonds needed to finance the facilities turns sour, marked by

---

[36] *Rancourt v. Town of Barnstead*, 523 A.2d 55 (N.H. 1986).

[37] *Beck v. Town of Raymond*, 394 A.2d 847, 852 (Me. 1978) (also requiring constant reexamination with a view to ending the controls).

[38] For an opinion in which a town singled out sewer hook-up permits and allocated its remaining sewer capacity over twenty years in equal numbers annually, see *Bryant v. Town of Essex*, 564 A.2d 1052 (Vt. 1989) (validating the town policy).

rising interest rates or by a reduction in capital available to purchase such bonds.

The *Ramapo* opinion sought to avoid giving too much discretion to municipal officials: for example, a municipality could not merely require that a developer show that tax revenue generated by a project would exceed its costs in public services. *Ramapo* suggested that a developer does not have the right to insist that a municipality engage in deficit financing to provide public services, but this need not mean that because no deficit financing is involved, the municipality must approve a project.

Fifth, the geographic reach of the growth control ordinance should be considered. The Ramapo ordinance was applicable in all of the town's residence districts and the ordinance looked like the product of comprehensive planning and zoning on that account. Thus, a growth control ordinance only applicable to the urbanizing edge of its jurisdiction, but not applicable throughout the jurisdiction, would be viewed with suspicion by the courts — as reverse spot zoning, as exclusionary zoning, and as a regulatory wall at the municipality's boundary. A narrow reach also runs afoul of the language in the *Ramapo* opinion quoting from Pennsylvania exclusionary zoning cases: "[T]hough the issues are framed in terms of the developer's due process rights, those rights cannot, realistically, be viewed separately and apart from the rights of others 'in search of a [more] comfortable place to live.'" The ordinance must be seen as a method of assimilating new residents, not denying them a place to live.

Sixth, and finally, a Ramapo-like ordinance should provide that the decisions of the planning board on growth control permits are reviewable by the municipal legislature. This review feature tends to make the decisions legislative in nature and so entitled, like rezoning decisions, to the presumption of validity and the fairly debatable/arbitrary and capricious standard of judicial review.

A town on the cusp of urbanization, that has not yet experienced population growth while nearby towns have, may also seek to respond with a growth control ordinance in advance of urbanization. In this regard, the planning and growth factors that *Ramapo* recited, seem like a factual precondition to the court's finding the town ordinance valid. So a review of the planning that has been done should be conducted to derive the terms of the ordinance. If studies detailing these factors have not been done, they should be done and a temporary moratoria imposed while they are being done. However, a moratoria will only be upheld under stringent conditions[39] — one of which is the town's undertaking planning to solve the problem to which the moratoria is addressed. Data on the number of applications for rezonings, variances, special exceptions, or subdivisions pending, and being at historic highs, is one set of statistics justifying both the moratoria or the ordinance. Overall, a growth controls ordinance not preceded and justified by dramatic and objective comprehensive planning

---

[39] *See* this Chapter, *supra. See also Toll Bros., Inc. v. Mayor and Council of the Twp. of West Windsor*, 712 A.2d 266 (N.J. Super. Ct., App. Div., 1998) (invalidating a timed, sequential growth control as a moratoria prohibited by state statute and distinguishing *Ramapo*).

estimates on population growth is not entitled to the presumption of validity and may be subject to attack as exclusionary, even if its terms mimic those of the Ramapo ordinance. [40]

Finally, consider whether the holding in *Ramapo* is suspect after the United States Supreme Court opinions in *First English* and *Lucas*. [41] If the municipality has done comprehensive planning in advance of the effective date of its growth controls ordinance, then the compensation remedy for the temporary taking discussed in *First English* is inapplicable because the reasonableness of the period during which the growth controls are imposed has already been addressed in the plan. In addition, if the plan considers the magnitude of the growth as a justification for the ordinance, it imposes no more than normal administrative delays justified by the problem of growth. By the same token, if the ordinance permits very low-intensity development of the affected properties as an interim measure, it cannot be said that the ordinance offends the concern of the *Lucas* court with a total deprivation of all economically viable uses. Thus *Lucas* is distinguishable.

[D] Development Options.

Developers finding themselves subject to *Ramapo*-like growth controls have three options: (1) to wait for the municipality to provide the improvements necessary for a parcel to amass the required points; (2) to wait for the period scheduled for the necessary facilities' installation to run and then apply for a permit again; or (3) to install the improvements themselves. In Ramapo, during the period 1969-1983, developers owning tracts large enough to enable them to provide off-site drainage and other improvements achieved the required number of points. Meanwhile, the town provided real property tax reductions for owners waiting out the capital budget period and so lessened the financial impact of the permit program. The reductions lasted only until the improvements were provided or the relevant period in the capital budget lapsed without provision of the improvements. This lower tax burden, once extended to some, required that the assessment and taxes on other properties and their owners be increased.

Two unexpected events also played a part in the use of the town's controls. First, a hurricane (named Agnes) hit the town in 1972, changing its fiscal priorities from support of the Ramapo plan to the rebuilding of existing services and facilities. Second, the 1973 oil embargo made commuting by automobile between Ramapo and New York City more expensive. Soon afterwards, the rate of growth in the town slowed. The plan and the permit system ordinance were repealed in March, 1983 — 14 years into the 18 year plan, on the ground that it was discouraging needed growth. It took a newly elected, legislative majority to enact the repeal.

---

[40] In this regard, see the cases litigating population projections for the State of Washington's growth controls; *see, e.g., King Cty. v. Central Puget Sound Growth Mgmt. Hearings*, 951 P.2d 1151, 1158 (Wash. 1998) (litigation over allocating county population growth estimates among county's municipalities); *Clark Cty. Citizens v. Resource Council*, 972 P.2d 941 (Wash. App. Ct. 1999) (involving population growth allocations between county's urban and rural areas).

[41] *See supra* Chapter 5 (as to *First English*) and, *infra*, Chapter 12 (as to *Lucas*).

§ 9.05 Concurrency.

Statutory regulation of growth has only come to a few states. These statutes, applicable state-wide, require in some jurisdictions that some infrastructure and public facilities be available concurrently with development.[42] They link development approval with the provision of public facilities. "Public facilities and services needed to support development shall be concurrent with the impacts of such development."[43] The objective of such statutes is to provide for the sequencing of public and private development in a municipality, although a concurrency requirement is not in itself a growth control. However, the failure of a state legislature to authorize funds for the facilities that are required to be in place preceding any development, is likely to limit growth — and may be seen as a *de facto* moratoria.

Florida has a broad concurrency requirement,[44] while Washington state has provided for concurrency with regard to roads and transportation.[45] The latter statute makes the provision of a minimum level of service ("LOS") for transportation a concurrent requirement of development.[46] An LOS service is a ratio of (say) road's use to its capacity, taking account of all demand for the road.

§ 9.06 Large Lots and Growth Controls.

A municipality in the path of urban growth may not zone its land area into large lot use districts so as to zone out all but the most expensive residential housing. Nonetheless, a system of growth controls may in some instances still use large lot zoning. In a state in which the zoning enabling act to authorize ordinances that "regulate and control the timing of development," an amendment of the land use regulations to establish a forestry use district with a 50 acre minimum lot size, locating this district in the rural sector of the municipality, is not a growth control ordinance. It has no time-related or phasing controls; that it has the effect of steering development to other sectors of the municipality, does not make it so. Were it otherwise, most zoning would be considered growth controls. Whether the large minimum size of the lots in the district is rationally related to the legitimate goals of encouraging forestry is another, separate issue: large lots may be necessary to encourage efficient timber harvests and to give the logger access to the forest under production. The objective of the amendment must be assessed in light of the municipality's zoning goals.[47] There may be other methods of preserving forestry, less restrictive in their

---

[42] *See generally* Boggs & Apgar, *Concurrency and Growth Management: A Lawyer's Primer*, 7 J. Land Use & Env. L. 1 (1991).

[43] Fla. Stat. Ann. § 163.3177(10)(h) (enacted 1985).

[44] *Id.* at § 163.3202(2)(g) (1998).

[45] Wash. Rev. Stat. Ann. § 36.70(6)(e) (1998).

[46] *Id.*

[47] *See Caspersen v. Town of Lyme*, 661 A.2d 759 (N.H. 1995) (upholding such a fifty acre minimum lot size in a forestry district).

impact on landowners, but such an inquiry does not figure in a rational basis, due process analysis of the amendment. Second-guessing the town's legislature is not usually part of a court's function here. The same device might be used in an active agricultural area.[48]

§ 9.07 The Petaluma Plan.

A second generation growth controls opinion is *Construction Industry Association of Sonoma County v. City of Petaluma*,[49] which validated a five year plan to limit building permits to 500 per year within the city. The quota on permits was enacted to control the imbalance between types of housing being constructed by the market, to curb urban sprawl, and to slow the city's accelerating growth rates. The quota was set at a level well below what had been demanded by the market. The allocation of permits was distributed both geographically around the city, and divided equally between multi-family and single family developments — whereas 88% of pre-control permits were issued for single family developments. A point system was devised and points were assigned to a development on the basis of conformance with the city's comprehensive plan. Other points were assigned for environmental controls, architectural and urban design, and recreation facilities, as well as the inclusionary provision for low and moderate income housing.

The overall purpose of the Petaluma Plan was to develop "in-fill land" (near the core of the city and surrounded by already developed land) before expanding the urban area of the city. The federal circuit court of appeals held that this purpose was carried out in the Plan without any substantial impact or effect on the mobility of residents of the San Francisco Bay region. But whether the appeals court began its analysis by assaying the purpose of the plan or its impacts, was unclear. If this case were an out-and-out civil rights case, this would be important, but here the effect on the right of persons to travel interstate was being balanced against the right of the municipality to enact this plan.

The Petaluma Plan had two interesting features not a part of the Ramapo controls. First, a greenbelt or urban boundary was drawn around the center of the existing city. Second, the allocation of the 500 permits was in effect a design competition between developers — and their architects and planners. The point system gave a great degree of credit to developers who presented interesting, innovative architecture, landscaping, and urban designs. These two features (the greenbelt boundary and the design competition) incorporated, respectively, more urban design and more administrative discretion into Petaluma's plan than Ramapo's plan contained.

The federal district court and the appeals court disagreed about nearly everything regarding the case. Their constitutional analyses appear

---

[48] *See Oregonians in Action v. LCDC*, 854 P.2d 1010, 1014–1015 (Or. App. Ct. 1993) (an 80 acre farming district upheld).

[49] 522 F.2d 897 (9th Cir.), *cert. denied*, 424 U.S. 934 (1975).

somewhat dated — the right to travel, for example, was touted in the late 1960s and early seventies as a vehicle for gaining federal review of municipal decisions. It never served that purpose.

This right proved to be an inflexible analytical tool — what about intrastate travel? It is no control over it. Notice too that the standing requirements of *Warth v. Seldin*[50] tossed a lot of the industry's arguments out of federal court. (State courts have not been kind to *Warth*'s tough standing requirements, but state courts are used to zoning and subdivision issues!) *Warth* was concerned with a specific housing project — this plan applied city-wide — so shouldn't the standing requirements have been loosened a bit? Federal abstention may be the ultimate ground for this holding.

The Petaluma Plan too was backed by extensive planning studies, so the resulting planning documents were comprehensive. It was limited in time (more so than Ramapo's) to five years. And it was more inclusive of low and moderate income housing than the private market had been in pre-control years. Such features made its validation reasonable. Courts measure the validity of similar growth controls by their

— comprehensiveness

— limited duration, and

— inclusiveness.

The court of appeals held this plan valid against both due process and interstate commerce challenges. Its interstate commerce analysis asked first, whether the state agent (the city, in this case) had a legitimate public purpose in enacting the plan (the court decided it did). If a legitimate public purpose was found, it then asked whether the plan reasonably carried out its purpose (again, it did), and if so, whether its impact or effect unreasonably impedes the flow of interstate commerce. To the last issue, the appeals court responded in the negative.

Its due process analysis relied on an analysis of three cases: (1) *Berman v. Parker*,[51] (2) *Boraas v. Village of Belle Terre*,[52] and (3) *Ybarra v. City of Los Altos Hills*.[53] It was Justice Douglas who wrote the opinion in both *Berman* and *Boraas*; he was also, at the time, the Supreme Court Justice overseeing the 9th Circuit. It was also he who stayed the district court opinion invalidating the city's plan. Much of the opinion in *Petaluma* seems written with him in mind.

In both *Ramapo* and *Petaluma*, the population growth rate that spurred the planning behind the growth controls was substantially above that of other jurisdictions in the surrounding metropolitan area. The rate in Petaluma was ten times the metro-rate and Ramapo was the fastest

---

[50] 422 U.S. 490 (1975)

[51] 348 U.S. 26, 33 (1954) (opinion written by Justice Douglas, involving the validity of an urban renewal program, that established, in 1954, a broad reach for the police power).

[52] 416 U.S. 1 (1974) (an opinion, again written by Justice Douglas, that upheld a more restrictive ordinance), discussed *infra*, Chapter 18.

[53] 503 F.2d 250 (9th Cir. 1974) (which upheld a less inclusive one).

growing unincorporated area in New York State at the time controls were imposed.

Nonetheless, should timing controls turn out to have exclusionary effects, the holdings in each opinion should be narrowly construed for the future.[54] Otherwise, the growth control and the exclusionary zoning case law are on a collision course. This is particularly true in the case of the Petaluma Plan, which might be re-characterized by some developer's attorney as a cap on growth, rather than merely as a regulation of it.

[A] Challenging a Petaluma-Like Ordinance.

A developer seeking to challenge a timing of growth control might wish to bring a **facial challenge** to the control. However, unless the challenged control is a *de facto* moratoria on growth, effective indefinitely and with no accompanying attempt to provide the infrastructure necessary to accommodate a reasonable amount of growth, a facial challenge is unlikely to succeed. Most important here is the fact that growth controls do not deny existing land uses and typically do no prohibit less intensive land uses. Because facial takings claims will likely be judged under the *Agins* two-prong test, it is likely to fail.[55] Additionally, because a growth control ordinance generally allows some growth every year, a *Hamilton Bank* ripeness requirement is likely to prevent a facial takings challenge until the applicant has been denied development permission for several cycles of permit allocations.

A further, **"as applied" challenge** might be brought in state court under either a substantive due process or a takings theory. Several variables might affect the decision about which theory to use. The due process claim examines the validity of the government's actions, while the takings claim looks primarily at their impact.

The test for a substantive due process claim is the same test as is used in the first prong of the *Agins* test. Given the presumption of validity that attaches to municipal controls, they will not violate the due process clause unless they are arbitrary and have no substantial relationship to the police power. A plaintiff has the burden of proving their arbitrariness, showing that the goals of the police power are not even "fairly debatably" related to them. *Petaluma* is the leading case on this claim, and shows how difficult it is to win a case based on this claim. There, when no link between the infrastructure resources of the city and the controls was apparent on the face of the regulations, the city's interests were balanced against the restrictive and even exclusionary effects of the controls. Indeed, in *Petaluma*, the vague "quality of life" purposes of the controls (taken particularly from *Euclid* and *Belle Terre*) sufficed to sustain them.

---

[54] *See Bryant v. Town of Essex*, 564 A.2d 1052, 1056 (Vt. 1989) (noting that the exclusionary effects were not pleaded).

[55] *See Agins v. City of Tiburon*, 447 U.S. 255, 260 (1980) (requiring that the regulation (1) not substantially advance a legitimate state interest and (2) effectively prevent all reasonable land uses, before it will be declared a taking).

The test for an "as applied" takings is taken from the *Penn Central* opinion: while it is admittedly ad hoc, it has three prongs — the action's economic impact, its interference with the owner's investment-backed expectations, and the character of the governmental action. They are the primary considerations. The first prong might be addressed in several ways: for instance whether the owner is deprived of much of the fair market value of the property during the period development is delayed; whether the before and after regulation values of the property are substantially different; and whether the owner receives reciprocal benefits back in exchange for the regulation. As for the second prong, a developer's investment-backed expectations are unlikely to contribute to a finding that a taking has occurred. Because growth controls are so common, the fact that one owns the land before the controls were imposed is unlikely to carry much weight. She will be expected to know that such controls are a common regulatory device. Finally, so long as the growth controls are widely applicable and do not single out a few owners for this layer of regulation, the third prong is met.

Three other variables will affect counsel's decision making process. First, the **measure of damages** for a due process violation may be broader than it is for a taking; in the latter instance, the claimant is limited to the value of the property taken, while a due process claim encompasses damages falling outside the realm of property value — encompassing consequential damages, for example. (This limitation on takings claims may change when the state constitution provides a remedy for property "taken or damaged.") Likewise, the **statute of limitations** for a taking will be that applying to property interests generally, while the statute applicable to a due process claim will be shorter: limited either to the very short period of time permitted for an appeal from an administrative action, or to the period provided for torts when the claim is plead as a § 1983 or negligence cause of action. [56] Third, **ripeness** requirements apply to a takings claim (*Hamilton Bank*), but not to a due process claim.

Consider whether the ordinance in *Petaluma* is suspect after the later United States Supreme Court opinion in *First English*. The rate of growth ordinance first imposing a limit on the number of development permits and then applying two sets of criteria for allocating those limited permits, imposes time delays only on those developers not assigned a permit over the period they seek an approval. This is harder to justify than a *Ramapo* ordinance, but whether *First English* is offended is an open question, in part because of the urban design concerns shown by the municipality in *Petaluma*. It might be advisable for a state wishing to permit its municipalities to enact rate of growth ordinances to enact them only for a limited number of years.

---

[56] *Cf. Charles v. Diamond*, 360 N.E. 1295 (N.Y. 1977) (discussing the availability of damages in instances of governmental bad faith and physical invasion cases).

§ 9.08   Growth Controls and Utilities.

In some jurisdictions, courts have held that municipalities may use their ownership of water and sewer utilities for planning purposes and may therefore deny permits to hook up to the utilities' lines as a means of growth control. There is no public policy that would prevent municipalities from using their utilities in this way. Normally a public utility (of whatever type) receives a certificate of authority with a duty to serve all citizens requesting service in a definite geographic area, in exchange for being granted a monopoly for that service in the same area. For a municipal utility, even when a proposed subdivision abuts an existing line with the capacity to serve it, a hook-up denial is proper when the subdivision is on an out-lying parcel in an area unserviced in other ways. [57]

Reaching this point has been difficult in some jurisdictions. In *Robinson v. City of Boulder*, [58] the Colorado Supreme Court held that a municipality could only refuse to serve new development outside its municipal boundaries for reasons relating to its ownership of the utility; it could not there justify its refusal with reasons related to implementing its planning and land use regulations. This result may have rested more on a judicial suspicion of an extra-territorial assertion of legislative power than anything else. Presumably however, a refusal within its boundaries would be permissible, since utility services and regulatory powers could be used concurrently.

When a municipal utility "may" provide service outside its boundaries, the power to do so is discretionary and may not be mandated by injunction. This "no duty" rule has an exception when the municipality holds itself out as willing to supply services or where it is the exclusive provider of services. [59] Thus a duty to provide services may be found by implication. Even then, however, future annexation of the parcel provided with service may be made a condition of its provision. [60] Because annexation is a discretionary act and may not be compelled, [61] enacting conditions on it is permissible. [62]

In the same manner, charging higher utility fees to non-residents than are charged to those within the municipal boundary, is justified on the ground that residents have been paying the property taxes used to fund

---

[57] *Dateline Builders v. City of Santa Rosa*, 194 Cal. Rptr. 258 (Cal. App. Ct. 1983) (involving a joint agreement between a city and county to share subdivision powers under the city's statutory right to prezone county land within a certain number of miles from the city boundary).

[58] 547 P.2d 288 (Colo. 1976), *overruled in, Bd. of Cty. Comm'nrs. v. Denver Bd. of Water Comm'nrs*, 718 P.2d 235, 244 (Colo. 1986).

[59] *Yakima Cty. (West Valley) Fire Protection District No. 12 v. City of Yakima*, 858 P.2d 245 (Wash. 1993).

[60] *Id.*

[61] *Mayor and Council of Rockville v. Brookville Turnpike Const.* Co., 228 A.2d 263 (Md. 1967); *Wilkerson v. City of Coralville*, 478 F.2d 709 (8th Cir. 1973).

[62] *Mayor and Council of Rockville v. Brookville Turnpike Const.* Co., 228 A.2d 263 (Md. 1967).

the utility, while non-residents do not. The latter have the burden of proof that the higher fee is unreasonable or discriminatory and, considering that attacking the higher fee as unreasonable is just as complex a piece of litigation as a utility rate regulation case, the case is seldom proven.

There is some question whether the imposition of growth controls is justified only in fast growing municipalities.[63] Infrastructure problems and an urban core surrounded by sensitive or scenic land areas might justify the use of both growth controls, either in their *Ramapo* or *Petaluma* versions, and concurrency requirements without preconditioning their use on there first being a fast growing population.[64]

§ 9.09   Inter-Governmental Growth Control Cooperation.

For reasons of economy, and to take advantage of the expertise of particular municipal staffs, planning and zoning are often conducted on a cooperative basis among municipalities. This is sometimes expressly authorized by statute. However, absent such statutory authority, a municipal government cannot generally contract away or delegate its police powers and, in jurisdictions in which the sum of all zoning and piece-meal rezonings constitute the general plan of the area, it has arguably delegated its power to plan as well. The argument against any delegation is particularly strong in states in which urban and regional planning is a mandatory activity of municipalities. Sharing administrative powers over subdivision[65] is one thing, but it is quite different when planning and rezoning powers are shared without express statutory authority.[66] Thus, when a city and its surrounding county both have zoning authority under the state's zoning enabling act, and both share a concern to preserve a large tract of open pasture lands in both the county's unincorporated areas and the city, their memorandum of understanding that before any rezoning of the tract in the county takes effect, the city must consent to it — and vice versa — is an important delegation when the county approves a pasture land rezoning suitable for development, but the city disapproves. The city may not become the delegate of the county, because the police power, with mandatory planning duties attached to it, is non-delegable.

§ 9.10   Growth Caps.

Growth caps have had a checkered history when facing judicial review.[67] In *Boca Raton*, the court reviewed a cap on the maximum number of

---

[63] See Amy Brandt, *Sedona's Sustainable Growth Ordinance: Testing The Parameters of Dolan v. City of Tigard*, 28 Ariz. St. L. J. 1297, 1302–1304 (1996) (reviewing both *Ramapo* and *Petaluma*).

[64] *Id.* (arguing this).

[65] See *Dateline Builders*, op. cit.

[66] *Alameda County Land Use Ass'n v. City of Hayward*, 45 Cal. Rptr. 2d 752 (Cal. App. Ct. 1995) (so holding).

[67] See, e.g., *City of Boca Raton v. Boca Villas Corporation*, 371 So.2d 154 (Fla. App. Ct. 1979), *cert. denied*, 449 U.S. 824, *noted in* 16 Stet. L.Rev. 617, 619–624 (1987).

dwelling units permitted in the city. After the city council failed to enact an ordinance to put the question of adopting the cap as a city charter amendment to a popular vote, a citizens group brought the question to the voters.[68] The group's proposed amendment to the charter passed with 57% of the votes cast. To this charter amendment, now adopted by popular vote, the city council responded first with moratoria, and then with zoning amendments cutting in half the permitted densities in all multi-family use districts.

The city's planners were not consulted beforehand; planning studies about the cap were only done *post hoc* and to implement the charter amendment under pressure. As a result, the testimony of the planning director at trial did not confirm the need for the cap. The court found that the planning department of the local government wasn't even consulted before the cap was imposed. The Florida court in this case held that the cap was an absolute limit on population and was invalid.

It may be difficult to distinguish an annual quota on permits — as in *Ramapo* or *Petaluma* — from a cap on growth — as was involved in *Boca Raton*. Unlike the Petaluma Plan, Boca Raton's growth cap was a permanent one, fixing an upper ceiling on the number of dwelling units in the city, justified only by after-the-fact planning studies, and based on estimates of future growth, rather than a response to historical growth rates. There really is not much good that can be said for what the city did, but by negative implication, a temporary, flexible quota of permits, enacted after study, and applying to a comprehensive set of land uses, would survive judicial review.

The *Boca Raton* opinion contained greater scrutiny of the city's actions than would normally be found using due process analysis. For instance, the city made much of its "water crop" — the amount of rainwater falling within the city limits and available for its water supply. The trial court found that such considerations, while possibly relevant on a regional basis, were not a proper concern of the city when there was no creditable evidence that the regional water authorities would fail to carry out their responsibilities in this area. The city must study factors within its own control to justify the cap, because once the court finds that the presumption of validity is rebutted, the court reassigns the burden of proof to the city to justify the cap. The city might have considered the following three types of caps.

First, consider an ordinance limiting the number of building permits issued annually for new residential subdivision lots to ten percent of the number of similar permits issued over the past decade. Here, the purpose of the ordinance might be seen as leveling out past growth, avoiding swings

---

[68] The question to the voters of Boca Raton was: "Shall the charter of the City of Boca Raton be amended by the addition of the following provisions: 'The total number of dwelling units within the existing boundaries of the city is hereby limited to 40,000. No building permit shall be issued for the construction of any dwelling unit within the city which permit the total number of dwelling units with the city to exceed 40,000.'"

in the annual number of permits issued, and there is thus a nexus between growth and the number of permits.[69]

Second, consider an ordinance limiting the number of new building permits to a number corresponding to a population growth rate of not more than two percent annually. This ordinance has a nexus between growth and permits that the *Boca Raton* growth caps lacked and would probably survive judicial review on that account.[70]

Third, consider a limitation on the number of dwelling units, whether single or multi-family, up to a number increasing the jurisdiction's housing stock by three percent a year, for the next five years, or by five percent a year if federal regional air quality, water quality, and waste disposal standards are met for the jurisdiction. The nexus between the allocation scheme for permits and the region's environmental health is an important connection to draw if the controls are to be found non-exclusionary. Although flexible, the increase in the overall numbers of dwelling units built in the municipality would help sustain the controls. More dwelling units for low and moderate income housing would add strength too. Moreover, the time period involved in these controls permits revisiting the matter within a reasonable time, and so might be seen as "temporary."

§ 9.11 Urban Boundaries.

The state of Oregon is the primary example of a jurisdiction that has a statute, enacted in 1973, authorizing the establishment of a boundary providing a separation between urban and urbanizable lands on one side, and rural lands on the other. Outside the boundary, development is discouraged.[71] These boundaries are set based on seven factors measuring the projected need for urban land over the up-coming twenty years for the city or cities within the boundary. Consistency with each factor is necessary for setting the boundary, but even more crucial has been the designation of the county or city agency to make the population projections for the region.[72]

Maryland has a more modest program of "smart growth," enacted in 1997, and prohibiting the development of new, state-funded, water, sewer, and transportation projects outside of "priority funding areas."[73] Such areas are

---

[69] This type of growth control was upheld in *Sturges v. Town of Chilmark*, 402 N.E.2d 1346 (Mass. 1980). Chilmark is a town on Martha's Vineyard, where land is a scarce resource indeed (which might well make some difference to the outcome of the litigation).

[70] *See Boulder Builders Group v. City of Boulder*, 759 P.2d 752 (Colo. App. Ct. 1988) (upholding such a limitation).

[71] *1000 Friends of Oregon v. Land Conservation and Dev. Comm'n (Curry Cty.)*, 787 P.2d 498 (Or. App. Ct. 1998). *See also* Or. Rev. Stat. § 197.296 (2) (1997).

[72] *See* Edward Sullivan, *Remarks to University of Oregon Symposium Marking the Twenty-fifth Anniversary of S.B. 100*, 77 Ore. L. Rev. 813, 834–836 (1998). *See also* James Bross, *Smart Growth in Georgia*, 35 Wake Forest L. Rev. 609. 610–611, 615, 616 (2000) (reviewing the Oregon history and contrasting it with more recent Georgia efforts).

[73] *See Smart Growth in Maryland*, <www.op.state.md.us/smartgrowth/index.html>.

either municipal corporations, designated neighborhoods, enterprise zones, or are areas designated around existing interstate highways. The legislature has authorized and reserved to itself, the authority to designate such areas, consistent with local comprehensive plans.

Part 2

The Zoning Forms of Action

Chapter 10

Administrative Relief from Zoning Ordinances

§ 10.01 Definitions and Introduction.

There are four forms of action which a landowner has to deal with unfavorable zoning. Distinguishing between them is necessary, in the same way that recognizing the common law writs was once necessary, to the practice of land use law. They are the variance, the special exception, the administrative appeal, and the rezoning. Typically, the attorney will combine them to achieve a client's objectives, but knowing each one will in turn enable the attorney to blend them in a creative whole for a client's project.

A variance is a waiver of the application of the terms of an ordinance and is authorized in an ordinance for undue hardship (a Standard Zoning Enabling Act phrase[1]) or practical difficulty or unnecessary hardship (a phrase from the *Euclid* opinion). Criteria for granting a variance are not usually specified in the ordinance. It provides elasticity in applying the literal terms of the regulations.

Second, a special exception (sometimes called a conditional use permit) can be sought. The uses authorized by such permits are not ones permitted as of right by the ordinance. Rather, they are only permitted on condition that certain criteria are met. Such criteria are specified in the text of the ordinance. Group houses of various types, home offices, and accessory commercial uses are often the subject of special exception provisions in ordinances.

Both variances and special exceptions are issued initially by a local administrative board, often called the Board of Zoning Adjustment or Appeals (hereafter the board). These boards typically function without much in the way of staff, so that it typically falls to the winning attorney to write or draft the board's order. In a minority of jurisdictions, these forms of action are heard by the local legislatures — the village board of trustees, the town or city council, the township commissioners, or the county council or board of supervisors. Performing this function, these bodies may act in either a legislative or an administrative capacity.

Third, an attorney might seek clarification or definition of the local ordinance from a zoning enforcement official or administrator. Such definitions may be sought either in the text of the ordinance, or in the definitions already provided for it. Appeals from these decisions typically are taken to the board, which in such matters sits in an appellate capacity.

---

[1] *See Stop & Shop Supermarket Co. v. Bd. of Adjustment of Twp. of Springfield*, 744 A.2d 1169, 1175 (N.J. 2000) (stating that N.J.'s first enabling act authorizing variances was based on the Standard Zoning Enabling Act).

Fourth, one can seek to rezone the land, either by amending the text of the ordinance, or by amending the zoning map (without a text amendment). Rezonings are done by the local legislature or by a Zoning Commission. This and the next several chapters discuss these four forms of action.

§ 10.02   The Variance.

A variance is a waiver of the zoning regulations when they work a hardship on a particular parcel of real property. It takes the form of a request to the Board of Zoning Adjustment or Appeals (hereafter board or BZA). If granted, it results in an order of the board granting a waiver of, or relief from, the literal enforcement of the regulations,[2] specifying which regulations will not be enforced. When a direct attack upon the ordinance, as applied to the parcel would in a court's view succeed, a variance should be granted.[3] The variance is typically granted when the applicant can show that an "undue or unnecessary hardship" is visited upon him as a result of the application of the ordinance to his property.[4]

An "unnecessary hardship" variance in use requires proof of three elements. First, the applicant must show that she is uniquely affected by the literal terms or the implementation of the ordinance.[5] Second, the owner must show that he or she cannot realize a reasonable return or is not left a reasonable number of uses by the terms or implementation of the ordinance.[6] Third, the applicant must show that the use authorized by the variance if granted will not adversely affect the surrounding neighborhood.[7]

An owner's parcel being irregular in shape, on a very steep slope, or rough terrain, may well be "uniquely affected" (as required by the first element). The unusual geography tends to show the uniqueness of the owner's situation. However, if other owners have similar conditions, no uniqueness is shown,[8] unless the enabling statute for the BZA expressly makes this

---

[2] See Simplex Technologies v. Town of Newington, 766 A.2d 713, 715 (N.H. 2001) (waiver without sacrifice of the spirit and purpose of the ordinance).

[3] Thus, a request for a variance is often a replay of takings jurisprudence, this time set in an administrative forum. Id.

[4] OK Properties v. Zoning Board of Review of City of Warwick, 601 A.2d 953, 954–955 (R.I. 1992) (stating that the Rhode Island equivalent phrase is "special condition").

[5] Otto v. Steinhilber, 24 N.E.2d 851, 853 (N.Y. 1939). See also Victor Recchia Residential Const., Inc. v. Zoning Bd. of Adjustment of Cedar Grove, 768 A.2d 803, 810 (N.J. Super. Ct., App. Div., 2001).

[6] Puritan-Greenfield Improvement Ass'n v. Leo, 153 N.W.2d 162 (Mich. App. Ct. 1967); Grey Rocks Land Trust v. Town of Hebron, 614 A.2d 1048, 1049 (N.H. 1992).

[7] These tests have often been combined differently, into one long statement of the elements necessary to obtain a variance. Thus, a variance requires a showing that (1) strict application of the ordinance would produce an unnecessary hardship, meaning that it cannot yield a reasonable return, (2) hardship is not shared generally by the other properties in the use district, but is attributable to unique character of the applicant's property, and (3) granting the application will not be a substantial detriment to adjacent property and will not change the essential character of the district. See Pepperman v. Town of Rangeley, 659 A.2d 280, 283 (Me. 1995); Prince William County Bd. of Zoning Appeals v. Bond, 300 S.E.2d 781, 782–783 (Va. 1983).

[8] See Nance v. Town of Indialantic, 419 So. 2d 1041 (Fla. 1982).

an element of the applicant's proof.[9] An applicant's land is not "uniquely affected" when the application is based on a situation common to other parcels in the neighborhood or use district.[10] An application must point to a specific application of the ordinance not suffered by other owners in the district — and for some land uses, even that is insufficient. Thus, an owner of a wetland must show that, considering all other owners of wetlands in the municipality, not just neighboring owners of dry land in the same use district, she is uniquely affected; if all owners of wetlands are affected in the same way, uniqueness is not shown.[11]

Much variance litigation revolves around the second "no reasonable return" element. The applicant must show that a literal or strict enforcement of the ordinance would result in a substantial loss or an unreasonably low return, resulting in the practical loss of all beneficial use of the parcel for which a variance is sought.[12] In this regard, reasonable return does not mean maximum return. The applicant is often said not to be entitled to the maximum return that might yield, and the fact that an applicant might increase the yield on the parcel is insufficient to support a showing of no reasonable return.[13] Other jurisdictions use this element to track takings jurisprudence more closely, emphasizing that the applicant for a variance must show "interference with a reasonable use."[14] Then the applicant must show that there is no other reasonable alternative (to granting the variance) in order to enjoy an otherwise legal use.[15]

The third element — that there be "no adverse impact" on the surrounding neighborhood — is sometimes restated as a requirement that the variance not alter the essential character of the neighborhood[16] and if granted would not be contrary to the public interest.[17] This element is generally stated in the negative to avoid granting the board too much discretion and authority. In this regard, it is often interpreted to require the board when granting a variance in the use of a parcel to reconcile its decision with continuance of the legislative prohibition on and exclusion of that use from the list of uses permitted as of right.[18] In some jurisdictions, this element is measured, in a looser fashion, by the otherwise

---

[9] *See, e.g.,* Cal. Gov't Code § 65906 (West 1983), which makes "size, shape, topography, location or surroundings" a "special circumstance" and authorizes area variances only.

[10] *See Victor Recchia Residential Const., Inc. v. Zoning Bd. of Adjustment of Cedar Grove,* 768 A.2d 803, 810 (N.J. Super. Ct., App. Div., 2001).

[11] *Chester Haven Beach Partnership v. Bd. of App. for Queen Anne's Cty.,* 653 A.2d 532 (Md. App. Ct. 1995) (holding that an owner's offer to build cluster housing on wetland at lower density than permitted by regulation does not satisfy the uniqueness element necessary for a variance).

[12] *Goldstein v. City of South Portland,* 728 A.2d 164, 165 (Me. 1999).

[13] *Id. See also Rowe v. City of South Portland,* 730 A.2d 673 (Me. 1999).

[14] *See Simplex Technologies v. Town of Newington,* 766 A.2d 713, 715 (N.H. 2001); *Hill v. Town of Chester,* 771 A.2d 559, 560 (N.H. 2001).

[15] *See Sciacca v. Caruso,* 769 A.2d 578, 583 (R.I. 2001).

[16] *See Commons v. Westwood Zoning Bd. of Adjustment,* 410 N.J. 1138 (N.J. 1980).

[17] *See Gray v. Seidel,* 726 A.2d 1283 (N.H. 1999).

[18] *See Medici v. BPR Co.,* 526 A.2d 109 (N.J. 1987) (explaining *Commons,* op. cit.).

applicable terms of the ordinance: that is, the applicant must demonstrate that "no fair and substantial relationship exists between the general purposes of the zoning ordinance and the specific restriction on the property,"[19] thus requiring the no adverse impact on the effectiveness of the ordinance as a whole.

Sometimes a fourth element is added, to the effect that the hardship is not the result of action taken by the applicant or a prior owner of the property.[20]

[A]   Two Types of Variances.

Variances are of two types: area and use variances. The classification of variances into two types is a judicial gloss on enabling acts, which often do not mention the distinction. The standards of review vary depending on which type is at issue. **Area variances** are applications to lift or modify minimum acreage, height, area, set-back, side or back yard, or other dimensional requirements imposed by the ordinance; there is no prohibition on the petitioner's use of his property. They are sometimes called a "deviation."[21]

[1]   Use Variances.

Use variances are applications to permit an otherwise unpermitted land use. They require proof of unnecessary hardship.

They are more difficult to obtain because the list of permitted uses is, in effect, expanded, for this one parcel. The effect on the ordinance is more drastic, the standard is consequently higher, and they are sometimes called "true variances."[22] Such a variance is generally not viewed as a delegation by the municipal legislature to the board of the power to rezone; as such the delegation would be unconstitutional. Most courts uphold the use variance, but only because a variance usually involves a small, irregularly shaped parcel with atypical geography, not because of the type of decision required to grant the petition.

[a]   Differences in Analysis between Use and Area Variance.

An area variance requires proof of practical difficulties. An area variance requires that the board look at the impact of the regulation on the owner/applicant, the extent of the variance, its impact on neighboring parcels, and whether the owner has less onerous, alternative means. In some jurisdictions, there is no difference between the applicant's showing of unnecessary

---

[19] See *Simplex Technologies v. Town of Newington*, 766 A.2d 713, 717 (N.H. 2001) (the court recognizing that it was adopting a less restrictive approach to the granting of variance, an approach justified in order to keep pace with constitutional law and takings jurisprudence). See also *Hill v. Town of Chester*, 771 A.2d 559, 560 (N.H. 2001).

[20] Of this fourth element, see this Chapter, *infra*.

[21] See *Sciacca v. Caruso*, 769 A.2d 578, 582 (R.I. 2001).

[22] *Id.*, and n. 5 (collecting R.I. cases).

hardship (for a use variance) and the lesser showing of practical difficulties (for an area variance), but this is a minority view.[23]

Any financial impact on, or improved, profitability of the parcel alone is insufficient to establish unnecessary hardship necessary for a use variance. So is the fact that the applicant is operating the current use on the parcel at a deficit; such an applicant will still have to meet each element of the test for a use variance.[24] With an area variance, however, there is a tendency to balance the applicant's need for the variance (and/or the public purposes and benefits of the varied use) against the impact on the surrounding uses.[25] Thus, the financial burden of the applicant might (as to, say, a set-back or parking requirement) be balanced against the impact on neighboring parcels, particularly when a requirement was devised with another land use in mind. An area variance application might be supported by an existing site plan, showing the placement of mature trees and screening landscaping, or the use of walkways of brick and sand that decrease water run-off onto surrounding parcels.[26] The approval of an area variance to prevent the destruction of such trees might even prevent an adverse impact on neighboring parcels.[27] The applicant might then argue that alternative but permitted development plans, will be more onerous than the one proposed utilizing the variance, with regard to their impact on the neighbors.[28]

The enlargement of a non-conforming use (one pre-existing a use regulation) is generally treated as a use variance rather than as an area variance.[29]

[2] Hybrid Variances.

Gathering evidence for a variance from a parking requirement will be harder than for a strictly dimensional variance. The applicant might show that the parking for the proposed use is needed at different times of the day or week, so that the applicant might get by with less parking than otherwise, without adversely impacting his neighbors.[30] It is for this reason that a variance from parking requirements is often seen as a hybrid between the use and area variance, so that the standard of proof is somewhat lower than "unnecessary hardship" and somewhat higher than "practical difficulties."

---

[23] For an expression of this minority view, see *Snyder v. Waukesha Cty. Zoning Bd. of Adjustment*, 247 N.W.2d 98, 102–104 (Wis. 1976).

[24] See *Otto v. Steinhilber*, 24 N.E.2d 851, 853 (N.Y. 1939).

[25] *Kali Bari Temple v. Bd. of Adjustment of Twp. of Readington*, 638 A.2d 839 (N.J. Super. Ct., App. Div., 1994).

[26] *Mastandrea v. North*, 760 A.2d 677, 696 (Md. 2000).

[27] *Holmes v. Zoning Hearing Board of Kennett Twp.*, 396 A.2d 859, 861 (Pa. Commwlth. Ct. 1978).

[28] *Gilmartin v. District of Columbia Bd. of Zoning Adjustment*, 579 A.2d 1164, 1172 (D.C. 1990) (rejecting variance from parking requirements when alternative means are available).

[29] *NYNEX Mobile Communications Co. v. Hazlet Twp. Bd. of Adjustment*, 648 A. 2d 724, 729-730 (N.J. Super. Ct., App. Div., 1994).

[30] *Id.*

In one famous case, a restaurateur sought a variance from the ordinance's parking requirements for his type of business. The ordinance required that 25 spaces be provided within 500 feet of the front door of his business, which was otherwise (aside from this parking requirement) permitted in the commercial zone in which the restaurant was located. Instead of classifying this application as either an area or a use variance, the reviewing court called this a hybrid variance and applied an intermediate standard of proof, mid-way between unnecessary hardship (which can often mean that no reasonable use or return is left to the property owner) and practical difficulties (which balances the adverse impact on the neighborhood with the injury suffered by the applicant). Thus, the hybrid variance used both tests and with such a multi-faceted test, the range of evidence available to the applicant expanded to the point at which the variance was likely to be granted. [31]

If the application could reasonably be construed either way, then which way should the board go? [32] In *Taylor*, the applicant overreached; he piled requests for bulk, height, and acreage variance on top of each other, until taken together, all the requests looked like a use variance and caught the applicant in its higher standard of proof.

[B] Variances and Takings Law.

The *Puritan-Greenfield* test, used previously to state the elements of a use variance, has the sound of takings law. [33] This is no more than an analogy. Variance applications are handled by an administrative agency — the board — not a court. Although variance law does track the constitutional analysis of the ordinance itself, this means that the variance is a buffer, saving the ordinance from an attack on its constitutionality when some property owners are severely affected. [34] Courts recognize an inevitable tension between zoning ordinances and property rights and attempt to respect those rights and protect them from unreasonable regulation.

One municipality enacted an amendment to its zoning ordinance providing that the board may grant use variances "upon the applicant's showing that he or she cannot reasonably use the subject property for any of the uses permitted under this ordinance and that the denial of the application would constitute an unconstitutional taking of property without compensation as defined by the laws of the state and of the United States." This

---

[31] *See Palmer v. District of Columbia Bd. of Zoning Adjustment*, 287 A.2d 535 (D.C. App. 1972).

[32] *Taylor v. District of Columbia Board of Zoning Adjustment*, 308 A.2d 230 (D.C. App. 1973) (toward a use variance, with its higher standard of proof, says the court in an opinion rejecting an area variance for 27 townhouses on land zoned for ten single family residences).

[33] *See Puritan-Greenfield Improvement Ass'n v. Leo*, 153 N.W.2d 162 (Mich. App. Ct. 1967).

[34] *See Simplex Technologies v. Town of Newington*, 766 A.2d 713, 717 (N.H. 2001) (remanding after board denial of a variance and citing the state constitution's guarantee of the right to acquire, possess, and protect property as limiting a delegation of zoning authority to municipalities and so informing the state's variance rules); *Stop & Shop Supermarket Co. v. Bd. of Adjustment of Twp. of Springfield*, 744 A.2d 1177, 1175 (N.J. 2000).

amendment was improper and *ultra vires* the enabling act. An agency like the board may not act like a court finding an unconstitutional taking without usurping the judicial function.[35] Any direct consideration of a constitutional right is beyond the board's statutory scope of authority in every jurisdiction.

Likewise, an ordinance requiring that the board not grant variances for outdoor decks unless the applicant "shall respect the privacy of adjacent properties" is a delegation of authority on a constitutional issue — that of a right to privacy. As such, it is again improper; however, it also may be interpreted only amount as a first-in-time rule of (temporal) priority for improvements or it may also permit the board to condition the grant of a variance by the planting of screening and/or landscaping without enumerating the criteria for doing so.[36] When the delegation to the board has been consistently and narrowly interpreted, a reviewing court may sustain the board's action.

Parcels that are ecologically-sensitive, such as a wetland, may well be so restricted by a regulation that virtually no development is permitted. Such regulation may give rise to a claim that the property has been the subject of a regulatory taking of "all viable economic or beneficial use" and so the landowner should be given just compensation under the Fifth Amendment's takings clause. When there is an allegation of such a total taking (under rules laid down in *Lucas v. South Carolina Coastal Commission*[37]), such an allegation also entitles the owner to a variance. The related showing for a variance is that the property is not capable of yielding a reasonable return or being used reasonably and that showing can be made by an owner showing a total taking.[38]

[C]   Proof of a Hardship.

A showing of hardship is easiest when it is created by the zoning or subdivision regulations themselves. When a tract of land is subdivided into lots by the planning commission, using dimensions called for by the zoning and subdivision ordinances, but there is left over a substandard or remnant lot — a too small lot, not conforming to the minimum acreage requirements — a hardship has been created by the general provisions of the ordinances and the left-over, remnant lot qualifies for an area variance. The law

---

[35] See *Zoning Bd. of Appeals v. Planning and Zoning Comm'n of the Town of Wallingford*, 605 A.2d 885, 889 (Conn. App. Ct. 1992) (holding that the BZA is an aggrieved party with standing to appeal the enactment and further invalidating the amendment because the BZA is deprived of its authority to grant variance under statutory criteria).

[36] See *Briggs v. City of Rolling Hills Estates*, 47 Cal. Rptr.2d 29 (Cal. App. Ct. 1995) (holding such language not unconstitutionally void for vagueness).

[37] 505 U.S. 1003 (1992), discussed *infra*, Chapter 17.

[38] *Greenberg v. DiBiase*, 637 A.2d 1177, 1179 (Me. 1994) (involving, but without mentioning *Lucas*, a residential-only, shoreland zoning regulation to a lot in which regulations setting permitted residential improvement back from lake shore would preclude the construction of any residence on applicant's parcel).

created this problem and the law should solve it.[39] So too, where a parcel is divided into two use districts by an ordinance and is a sub-standard parcel in both, a hardship is shown.[40] In contrast, an applicant's need for a larger living area for her family does not warrant a variance.[41] A variance is not justified by the personal or life-style needs of the user, zoning dealing with land uses, not users. In addition, a need for a satellite dish in the backyard, or for a garden shed, is unlikely to establish an unnecessary hardship. An inconvenience is insufficient to support a board's granting a variance.

A hardship must be an undue restriction on the use of the applicant's land and a deprivation of value "so great as to effectively prevent the owner from making any reasonable use of the land."[42] Operating a reasonable use before the application is conclusive proof that no hardship is present. Likewise, a hardship may not arise from a structure located on the parcel for which a variance is sought — as when an application is predicated on extra construction costs incurred because of a lot's terrain. The purpose of such a rule is to discourage investment in sub-standard lots; only when the extra expenditure results in no greater intensity of use than permitted other owners in the district, should the variance be granted.

[D]   The Burden of Proof and Substantial Evidence.

In any variance proceeding, the applicant has the burden of proof. The applicant must present substantial evidence in support of the request.[43] Substantial evidence is that quantum of evidence as a reasonable mind will accept as adequate to support a finding or conclusion;[44] or, that evidence with which "a reasoning mind reasonably could have reached the same conclusion that the agency reached."[45] It requires a reviewing court to draw inferences from the evidence as the agency or board did in order to make its decision, rather than the court's substituting its judgment for the board's.[46] It affords a substantial basis of fact from which an issue or

---

[39] See Eagan v. Zoning Bd. of Appeals of Old Lyme, 568 A.2d 811, 813 (Conn. App. 1990) (when locating a house of any size on a residential lot is impossible within the required setbacks, applicant has shown an undue hardship).

[40] See Lewis v. New Castle County Bd. of Adjustment, 601 A.2d 1048, 1050 (Del. Super. Ct. 1989). Cf. Victor Recchia Residential Const., Inc. v. Zoning Bd. of Adjustment of Cedar Grove, 768 A.2d 803, 810 (N.J. Super. Ct., App. Div., 2001) (upholding board decision that a split-zoned parcel could be used in complying manner in two districts upheld and affirming a denial of a use variance).

[41] See, e.g., Larsen v. Zoning Board of Adjustment of the City of Pittsburgh, 672 A.2d 286 (Pa. 1996) (finding that an applicant's need for a larger play area for a child did not warrant a variance to build a 400 square foot deck).

[42] See Governor's Island Club v. Gilford, 467 A.2d 246, 248 (N.H. 1983).

[43] When a use variance is involved, substantial evidence is also said to be evidence sufficient to make the matter "fairly debatable." See White v. North, 736 A.2d 1072, 1079–1080 (Md. 1999).

[44] See Mastandrea v. North, 760 A.2d 677, 691 (Md. 2000).

[45] Id.

[46] Several empirical studies have shown that zoning boards tend to issue variances as an

conclusion might be inferred. The test is the reasonableness, not the rightness, of the decision. In the course of judicial review of an administrative proceeding, it is also enough evidence to avoid the charge that the board acted in an arbitrary and capricious manner. In a trial, it is enough evidence to avoid a directed verdict.

[E]   Two Statutes Compared.

Often, zoning ordinances and regulations concerning variances do little more than mimic the undue hardship language of the enabling act authorizing the granting of variances. However, some statutes and ordinances attempt to narrow the grounds for a variance in an attempt to prevent them from being granted too freely. Consider the impact of the following typical statute on variances:

> If there are practical difficulties or unnecessary hardships in the way of carrying out the strict letter of the ordinance, the board of appeals may in passing upon appeals vary or modify any of its rules or provisions relating to the construction, or structural changes in, equipment, or alteration of buildings or structures, or the use of land, buildings, or structures, so that the spirit of the ordinance shall be observed, public safety secured, and substantial justice done. [47]

Consider also the following, somewhat more complicated statute:

> Where, by reason of exceptional narrowness, shallowness, or shape of a specific piece of property at the time of the original adoption of the regulations or by reason of exceptional topographical conditions or other extraordinary or exceptional situation or condition of a specific piece of property, the strict application of any regulation adopted under [the zoning enabling act] would result in peculiar and exceptional practical difficulties to or exceptional and undue hardship upon the owner of such property, a variance from such strict application so as to relieve such difficulties or hardship, provided such relief can be granted without substantial detriment to the public good and without substantially impairing the intent, purpose, and integrity of the zone plan as embodied in the zoning regulations and map. [48]

In both of these statutes, variances are authorized for either practical difficulties or undue hardships experienced by landowning developers. In interpreting them, courts have held that a showing of practical difficulties is necessary when the applicant for a variance seeks an **area variance**.

---

accommodation for the applicant, and that appellate courts serve a disciplinary function for boards, forcing them to consider only the criteria relevant for variances. Nonetheless, there is a great volume of appellate litigation and reported opinions involving variances.

[47] Mich. Comp. Laws Ann. § 125.585(9) (West 1988). *See also* N.Y. Gen. City Law § 81(4) (McKinney 1988) and Standard State Zoning Enabling Act, § 7 (1923).

[48] D.C. Code Ann. § 5-424(g)(3) (1988).

An area variance may properly be granted when (1) the regulation unreasonably prevents the owner from using the property for a permitted use or conformity with the regulation is unreasonably burdensome, (2) granting the variance does substantial justice between the owner and his neighbors, and (3) the variance observes the spirit if not the letter of the regulation. [49]

These three criteria for an area variance present an applicant with a substantial burden of proof. However, in interpreting the undue hardship language, courts have held that the *Otto* test for a **use variance** is applicable, and the burden even heavier.

Often two standards are not set out in an enabling act. When this is the situation, the default rule is that the undue hardship standard is used for both types of variances. However, labeling a variance as one or the other, might make a difference. [50] Good pleading is necessary to exploit that difference. For example, where owners have a 1.9 acre tract zoned for one house and single-family residential use with a minimum lot size of 1 acre and two houses are located on the tract, the board granted them a variance in order that they might rent the houses to two families — a single family in each house. When their neighbors challenged the granting of the variance in court, the issue turned on identifying the requirement from which a variance was requested: was it the single family residence requirement, or in the alternative, was it the minimum acreage requirement? The former would be a use variance, the latter an area variance. [51] The latter is much more common and easier to obtain because less of the zoning scheme is upset by granting it, and so it has a lower standard of proof.

If the structures on the 1.9 acres were unequal in size, with one an accessory to the other, the board should refer this matter to the planning commission; it may not condition its granting of the variance on the subdivision of the property into two lots, each with a house, or on the accessory structure's not being used as a dwelling. Such a condition is a matter for the planning commission or whatever board is responsible for the subdivision of land in the municipality. [52] The existence of subject-matter authority elsewhere, in another board or agency, is grounds for finding that the board has no authority to impose a restriction with the same subject matter.

[F] Variances as an Administrative Remedy.

The granting of one or more variances to nearby landowners is irrelevant to the consideration of a variance. Each variance is granted — or denied

---

[49] *North v. St. Mary's Cty.*, 638 A. 2d 1175, 1179 (Md. App. Ct.1994); *Red Roof Inns, Inc. v. People's Counsel for Baltimore County*, 624 A.2d 1281, 1284 (Md. App. Ct. 1993).

[50] *See, e.g., Matthew v. Smith*, 707 S.W.2d 411 (Mo. 1986), *noted in*, 52 Mo. L. Rev. 537 (1987).

[51] As a lesson in how important it is to understand terms, consider *Bamber v. Zoning Bd. of Review of the Town of Foster*, 591 A.2d 1220, 1223 (1991). In Rhode Island, an area variance is "a deviation." This is a term of long standing in that state. *See Viti v. Zoning Bd. of Review of Providence*, 166 A.2d 211 (R.I. 1960) (term deviation defined).

[52] *Marx v. Zoning Bd. of Appeals*, 529 N.Y.S. 2d 330 (N.Y. App. Div. 1988).

— on the basis of facts peculiar to the property of the applicant.[53] In part, this is so because a request for a variance is an administrative, rather than a legislative, procedure.[54] If a general policy lying behind a regulation is not working well, it is the function of the legislature in a zoning jurisdiction to change it — such changes are beyond both the competence and the jurisdiction of the board of zoning appeals.

A zoning ordinance that provides "the board may, with appropriate conditions and safeguards, vary the application of this ordinance in accord with its general intent, if not its literal terms," would be upheld by most courts against a charge that is void for vagueness, the board having to act like a municipal legislature in order to implement it. A court would either interpret this provision as authority to decide that a variance if granted is "not inconsistent with the general welfare" or have "no adverse impact on adjacent parcels" or else find that a hardship standard was implied from the word "vary"; the rest of the language about "appropriate conditions and safeguards" would then be authority for the board to impose reasonable restrictive covenants when granting an application for a variance.[55] Some state enabling statutes have made this authority express.

Sometimes privately imposed restrictive covenants applicable to a subdivision may arguably require that an owner undertaking a renovation obtain permission of the subdivision owners' architectural review committee or property owners association before seeking any necessary variances to carry out the renovation. Covenants on which such arguments are based, must be clear in limiting the right of access to a public forum, else they will be interpreted as permitting an owner to choose whether to apply for a variance before or after obtaining a variance.[56]

When an ordinance does not use its enabling act's hardship standard, but instead substitutes other standards, the board is nonetheless authorized either to imply the hardship standard from the standards that are expressly authorized, or else use the hardship standard in any event.[57] Thus, the enabling act standard is incorporated by reference into the ordinance's standards. The inference that, the ordinance's drafters may

---

[53] *Haines*, 599 A.2d at 401.

[54] *See Victor Recchia Residential Const., Inc. v. Zoning Bd. of Adjustment of Cedar Grove*, 768 (A.2d 803, 809 (N.J. Super. Ct., App. Div., 2001) (stating that a board may not usurp the legislative function when granting variances).

[55] *See Driesbaugh v. Gagnon*, 522 N.E.2d 1019 (N.Y. 1988) (restrictions imposed shall relate to the use, not the user of the property, and not to other property not subject to the application).

[56] *Little Whale Cove Homeowners Ass'n, Inc. v. Harmon*, 986 P.2d 616, 620 (Or. App. Ct. 1999).

[57] *See Green v. Bair*, 549 A.2d 762, 764–765 (Md. App. Ct. 1988) (holding that the board should use a hardship standard when the word appears in the enabling statute but not in the ordinance, involving an enabling statute defining a variance as "a relaxation in the terms of the ordinance, not contrary to the public interest and owing to unique conditions, not self-created, on the land or intended use, but resulting in undue hardship" and an ordinance authorizing the board to grant variances upon finding that: (1) there are unique circumstances applying to the applicant's parcel; (2) the variance is necessary for the applicant to enjoy the same rights as his neighbors; and (3) granting of the variance will have no adverse impact on neighbors).

have intended the board to exercise less authority than the enabling act permits, should not be made without support on the face of the ordinance.

[G] The Board and Legislative Judgments.

In considering an application for a use variance, it is improper and *ultra vires* the board's authority to conclude that "the neighborhood is changing and becoming a center for [whatever use the applicant proposes]," even though several similar non-conforming uses and variances are present in proximity to the proposed use. This rationale would be appropriate when used by the municipality's legislature to justify a rezoning, but it is inappropriate when used by the board. A variance may not be used to confirm an emerging land-use pattern.[58] An owner need not present evidence of attempting (and failing) to sell the parcel for a conforming use in order to show an undue hardship; although such evidence is helpful, it is not dispositive. Likewise, a board may not, after many applications for use variances for (say) two family occupancy in a single family district, announce that hereafter all such requests will be granted, that announcement involving again a legislative judgment, and not one for the board.[59]

In the same vein, if an owner seeks a variance for a "wholesale" business in a commercial use district in which the ordinance permits only "retail" businesses, no variance may be issued because the classification of uses into districts is a legislative function, not an administrative matter delegated to the board; granting such a variance would again be akin to a rezoning. It is for this reason that the zoning enabling statutes of some jurisdictions deny boards the authority to grant "use variances."[60]

On the other hand, if in a deteriorating neighborhood, a corner movie theater is losing money, is out of step with the prevailing market for theaters and unsaleable for use as a cineplex, its owner will obtain a variance to change the use on the parcel to use the parcel for other uses permitted uses under the zoning ordinance and utilized by nearby owners. Standing alone, evidence of financial loss is insufficient to grant a use variance.[61] Likewise, the deterioration of the neighborhood puts every owner at the same disadvantage, meaning that every owner is affected the same way and there is no "unique" hardship. This is particularly so when the applicant's problem is created by enforcing the regulations — for example, by the presence of the use district boundary line. This, when coupled with (1) a land use pattern to which the owner's use does not conform and (2) evidence of failed attempts to sell the parcel, makes the

---

[58] In many older residential neighborhoods owners want to expand the square footage or add a deck, porch, or other modernizing features to keep their residences up to date, but a variance is not the proper remedy for such improvements, a rezoning being the correct one.

[59] *Feiler v. Fort Lee Bd. of Adjustment*, 573 A.2d 175, 178 (N. J. Super. Ct. 1990) (reversing BZA grant of variance for mixed commercial and high rise residential project).

[60] *See* Cal. Gov't Code § 65906 (West 1983).

[61] *City of Pittsburgh v. Zoning Bd. of Adjustment of City of Pittsburgh*, 559 A.2d 896, 903 (Pa. 1989) ("Mere economic hardship will not of itself justify a grant of variance."); *see, e.g.,* Mass. Gen. Laws Ann. ch. 40A, § 10 (West 1988) (where the authority is express).

owner's evidence sufficient for a variance. His is uniquely affected land (a proper basis for a variance) as opposed to his having just an affected improvement (an improper basis).[62]

[H]   Variances and Social Benefits.

Sometimes an owner wishes a variance for a use which might be regarded as socially beneficial, as when wanting an area variance in order to install solar collectors in his front yard, or a use variance for low income housing. Sometimes the enabling act for the ordinance is specific on this point, providing that the social purpose of the project for which a variance is sought may be considered. If it is not, then the "no adverse impact" branch of variance law controls, and might also support the variance: that is, the board might offset the impacts of the proposed use against the benefits obtained from it. This finds, in the "no adverse impact" requirement, the authority to balance the impacts from any off-setting benefits.[63] Some courts, however, reject such balancing, as being without statutory authority. They give each element for a variance equal weight, implying that each is necessary and is to be considered independently of the others.

[I]   Variance Conditions and Remedies.

When a parcel for which a variance is sought is unimproved, it is often difficult for neighbors to determine if the "no adverse impact" element for a variance will be met without seeing the improvement proposed. However, the variance for an unimproved lot may not be granted upon the condition that the applicant show his development plans to neighbors and obtain their consent to an improvement built according to those plans. Such a condition would be an improper delegation of the authority given the board to the neighbors.[64] There is no provision for it in the Standard Zoning Enabling Act or other enabling statutes. Similarly, no condition can be imposed on granting a variance that prohibits the rental of the property; such a condition is an unreasonable restraint on alienation and violates the policy against creating economic waste of property.[65] Likewise, if an applicant had no specific plans to develop the lot, neither could the variance be granted unless the neighbors wished to buy the sub-standard lot, there being no express authority for this either. That condition would offend the owner's right of alienation.

---

[62] See this Chapter, *infra*, discussing a self-created hardship.

[63] *See, e.g., Kaufmann v. Planning Bd.*, 542 A.2d 457 (N.J. 1988) (deciding that granting a variance to permit two non-conforming residences on a parcel would promote the general welfare and that the benefits out-weighed the detriment to the neighborhood; decided under a statute presented as an alternative to a hardship variance); *see* N.J. Stat. Ann. § 40:55D-70(c)(2) (West 1991); *Burbridge v. Governing Body of the Twp. of Mine Hill*, 568 A.2d 527 (N.J. 1990) (holding that aesthetic benefits justified variance to expand a non-conforming auto body shop use).

[64] See the discussion of contract and conditional zoning, discussed *infra*, Chapter 12.

[65] *See Gangemi v. Zoning Bd. of Appeals of the Town of Fairfield*, 763 A.2d 101, 1015–1016 (Conn. 2001).

A condition forcing the applicant to sell would be invalid and surely be something the owner probably did not expect to happen when filing his application. Moreover, the neighbors might be wary of buying. They would not as purchasers have the same right to apply for a variance thereafter, because then the hardship would be found to be a self-created one, so the sale could only be the limited purpose of buying protection from abutting development. This possibility would decrease what they would pay, unless a merger of non-conforming lot with the purchasers' gave a right to greater development on the purchasers' side of the boundary. With all of these problems, it is probably safe to conclude that such a condition will not be found to be authorized.

When a tract can be subdivided into conforming, but odd-shaped lots, the subdivider should do so; failing to do so, a developer will not thereafter have grounds for a variance.[66] Thus, when possible, the subdivider must use the subdivision regulations in such a way as to avoid the necessity for a variance; otherwise, the need for the variance would be self-created, and no variance may be granted when the hardship is self-created.[67] This leads to the question, why isn't the desire to subdivide a self-created hardship to begin with, no matter what number or shaped lots result from the process?[68] It is not because there should be no penalty for using a public regulation available to all.

[J] The Self-Created Hardship.

A self-created hardship is on occasion both an element of the proof of a variance, as well as a defense to the granting of an application for it. A variance may not be granted when the hardship, even when proven by the applicant, is self-inflicted. This is often called a "self-created" hardship. It arises typically when an owner purchases property with the knowledge that the use he proposes for it will require a variance from existing regulations applicable to the property. It can also arise when the improvements made on the property, for a specific purpose, become out-moded but might be renovated for another use if a variance is granted. It applies to both use and area variances.[69]

In some jurisdictions, the self-created hardship rule is made an element of the proof that the applicant must offer the board.[70] In others, it is an affirmative defense — not necessarily part of the applicant's proof — but need only be negated when raised by others, such as neighbors or the board's attorney on appeal.

A purchaser's knowledge of zoning restrictions from which her development plan requires a variance traditionally creates a self-inflicted hardship

---

[66] *Gottlieb v. Bd. of Appeals*, 527 N.Y.S.2d 258 (N.Y. App. Div. 1988) (finding and imposing a statutory standard of "minimum adjustment" when granting a variance).

[67] *City of Pittsburgh v. Zoning Bd. of Adjustment of City of Pittsburgh*, 559 A.2d 896, 903 (Pa. 1989).

[68] *Aitken v. Zoning Bd. of Appeals*, 557 A.2d 1265 (Conn. 1988) (holding that it is).

[69] *See Sciacca v. Caruso*, 769 A.2d 578, 583 (R.I. 2001).

[70] *See Otto*, op. cit., n.5.

barring variance relief. The knowledge can be actual or constructive, because a purchaser is deemed to know the provisions of the zoning regulations and to have figured out how they will affect the purchaser's property. This traditional rule has in many jurisdictions been modified so that purchase with the knowledge of the need for a variance does not preclude its granting, but is one factor in the consideration of the application for a variance.[71] For example, a purchaser may have purchased the property with the knowledge that the prior owner obtained variances, but that further variances may be necessary. In such a situation, using the traditional rule might seem to some unfair. Other jurisdictions go further and hold that the right to a variance runs with the land and is available to an applicant's successors in title.[72] By the same token, the specific explanations and representations of an applicant should not be taken to bind the successor in title when the application process is incomplete when taken over.[73] In addition, an owner seeking a variance in order to legitimate improvements to the parcel done in violation of the ordinance, will be granted a variance when that owner did not install the violating improvement — but not if he did.[74]

[1] More Executory Period Problems.

Self-created hardship issues also often arise during an executory period when an applicant for a variance sells a parcel during the application process, and the board, seeing the sale as an opportunity to enforce the ordinance, denies the variance, arguing that by buying the purchaser has a self-created hardship. On an appeal by a purchaser denied a variance in this situation, the board's argument will likely fail. A variance may not properly be denied here, for to deny the variance is to deny the initial applicant the power to alienate the parcel during the application process. If the vendor is entitled to a variance, the purchaser should be too, even if the purchaser takes the title with knowledge of the restriction from which a variance is sought. The right to a variance in this situation "runs" with the land. Otherwise, the right to alienate is needlessly impaired.[75]

Another executory period problem concerns a purchaser who buys more than one parcel, purchasing (say) two contiguous, vacant parcels, in order to construct a building on one, hoping to apply for a variance from front

---

[71] *Twigg v. Town of Kennebunk*, 662 A.2d 914, 916 (Me. 1995). *See also Hill v. Town of Chester*, 771 A.2d 559, 560–561 (N.H. 2001).

[72] *See Stop & Shop Supermarket Co. v. Bd. of Adjustment of Twp. of Springfield*, 744 A.2d 1169, 1177 (N.J. 2000) (so stating and collecting the cases).

[73] *Id.* at 1178. *See also Dexter v. Town Bd. of Gates*, 324 N.E.2d 870, 871 (N.Y. 1975).

[74] *See generally City of Pittsburgh v. Zoning Bd. of Adjustment of City of Pittsburgh*, 559 A.2d 896, 903–904 (Pa. 1989) ("Self-inflicted economic hardship is not justification for grant of variance."); *Appeal of Gro*, 269 A.2d 876 (Pa. 1970) (hardship is self-created only where an increment of the purchase price anticipates the granting of the variance).

[75] *But see Tharp v. Zoning Bd. of Appeals*, 526 N.Y.S. 2d 646, 648 (N. Y. App. Div. 1988) (holding that a purchaser without actual knowledge of the provisions of the applicable zoning regulations, is nonetheless bound by them and by what he or she could learn of them using reasonable diligence).

and rear setback requirements on the other in order to meet off-street parking regulations to serve the building. This application (for an area variance) should be denied, unless the owner can prove that if the owner had constructed the building over the boundary between the two parcels, the parking regulations could have been met; in his present posture, the applicant's hardship is self-created. Even if the parcelization needs reconfiguring in market terms, and even if the parcel for which the variance is sought is an undersized lot, not meeting minimum lot area requirements is determinative of the application. The application should be considered from the standpoint of the present owner and applicant — and the existing parcel's dimensions. [76]

[2] Construction Mistake Problems.

In another scenario that is a builder's nightmare, a structure may be half-built when an owner discovers that the set-back or other area or bulk requirement of the ordinance is not met. The cases are split when addressing this situation, but "after the fact" area variances have been granted. Surveying and construction errors are sometimes a basis for a variance, but implicitly courts granting the variance are engaging in a type of balancing — balancing the costs of correction versus the impact on the neighbors. This type of case is best regarded as an equitable exception to the rules on variance — not a rule in itself, for then the good faith of the applicant would become an element of the variance. [77]

[K] Variances from Special Exceptions.

Finally, an applicant requesting a variance from the requirements for a use controlled by a special exception in an ordinance, is regarded as seeking a variance from a permitted use, from which a variance might be requested. Special exceptions are the subject of the following section.

§ 10.03 Seeking a Special Exception.

While a variance is a waiver of the provisions of the zoning regulations, a special exception or special use is something very different. It is a use which, upon request to the board, will be permitted in a use district if certain criteria, already set out in the regulations, are met. "The fundamental distinction between [a special exception and a variance] is that [a special

---

[76] *Blow v. Town of Berlin Zoning Administrator*, 560 A.2d 378, 379 (Vt. 1989).

[77] *See Devaney v. Town of Windham*, 564 A.2d 454, 457 (N.H. 1989); *In re Cumberland Farms, Inc.*, 557 A.2d 486, 488–489 (Vt. 1989) (both cases requiring correction of non-complying structures); *but see Almeida v. Zoning Bd. of Review of the Town of Tiverton*, 606 A.2d 1318 (R.I. 1992) (holding that denial of a variance to permit the conversion of a basement to a separate dwelling unit in a single family residence district was not a hardship and ordering owner to comply with an administrative order halting a partly completed conversion under an illegally issued permit).

exception] is legislatively permitted in a zone subject to controls whereas the latter is legislatively prohibited."[78]

The special exception is expressly set out in the ordinance, but rather than being incorporated into the litany of uses permitted in a district as of right, its uses are permitted only conditionally. There is no requirement that a zoning ordinance contain provisions for special exceptions.[79]

Permitting a use conditionally often sets the stage for a semantic battle between applicants and any opposition. The former argue the requested use is permitted by the ordinance, and subsequent arguments seek to minimize the discretion of the board in hearing the application. The opponents stress the conditions and the discretion given the board. Generally, a special exception is considered to be a permitted use,[80] and so is entitled to a presumption that granting it is consistent with the general welfare of the jurisdiction and its comprehensive plan, and is therefore valid.

A hearing on the application for a special exception is, in almost all states, an administrative procedure. The applicant has the burden of proof and the state's administrative procedure act controls the proceedings. This burden is to present substantial evidence of compliance with the criteria which condition the use. Allocating the burden this way is not always fair, particularly when one of the criteria for the special exception is a finding of "no adverse impact." As with a variance, this requires the petitioner to prove a negative — that there is no adverse impact on the adjacent parcels or (worse yet, from petitioner's standpoint) the public interest. In a majority of jurisdictions, courts require that the municipal legislature adopt standards or criteria for granting or denying an application for a special exception.[81] Express criteria protect an application from arbitrary decisions, prevent discrimination, and facilitate judicial review, particularly when the board must make written findings of fact when deciding to grant or deny the application.

Under a rule followed in a small minority of jurisdictions, the hearing on a special exception is held by the municipal legislature and is classified as legislative in nature; thus, a presumption of validity attaches to the regulation and, so long as the board's decision is fairly debatable — that is, so long as reasonable minds could read the record and reach opposite conclusions — it will be upheld.[82] Even in this minority, the courts require a written record containing findings of fact pertinent to the ordinance's or any statutory criteria imposed on the board.[83] In another minority rule

---

[78] *Value Oil Co. v. Town of Irvington*, 377 A.2d 1225 (1977). *See also Citizens Coalition v. District of Columbia Bd. of Zoning Adjustment*, 619 A. 2d 940, 948 (D.C. 1993) (stressing that a use is permitted by a special exception when in harmony with its neighborhood, whereas a variance would be prohibited but for the hardship resulting from the prohibition).

[79] *Piscioneri v. Zoning Hearing Bd. of the Borough of Munhall*, 568 A.2d 610, 611 (Pa. 1990) (holding that special exceptions in residential districts are not required).

[80] *See, e.g., Light of Life Ministries, Inc. v. Cross Creek Twp.*, 746 A.2d 571, 573 (Pa. 2000).

[81] *See, e.g., Ackman v. Bd. of Adjustment for Black Hawk Cty.*, 596 N.W.2d 96, 104 (Iowa 1999).

[82] *Bd. of Supervisors of Fairfax County v. Southland Corp.*, 297 S.E.2d 718 (Va. 1982).

[83] *Ames v. Town of Painter*, 389 A.2d 702, 704 (Va. 1990).

jurisdiction, where express criteria are not required, the decision is adjudicatory in nature and is not entitled to a presumption of validity, so the burden is on the decision-maker to justify it.[84]

A better term for a special exception is a conditional use.[85] It is intended to deal with predictable problems of land-use compatibility and anticipate (and keep to a minimum) requests for rezonings. It is the product of an order issued by the administrative board, setting out the pre-conditions for that use.[86]

A zoning may permit churches in a residential use district as a special exception. This is a way of balancing First Amendment, Free Exercise of Religion clause, concerns with police power concerns — churches may well create spin-off or external effects on neighboring parcels, but there are reasons to tolerate them. Other uses that are often the subject of special exceptions in residential neighborhoods, such as funeral homes, nursing homes, home offices, and half-way houses for drug addicts and parolees, are less popular. Sand, gravel, and stone quarries have also provided a good deal of the appellate case law on the subject.[87] They require proximity to the final use of the material excavated, but generate noise and dust. All these uses require lawyering in the face of local opposition and that is one reason why the criteria are pre-set. The attorney for the applicant can insist that the board follow the criteria provided in the ordinance, even in a hearing room packed with opponents. For example, a special exception for group housing or mobile homes in a single family residential zone, may be included not because the legislature wanted to include such uses, but because if it excluded them totally, the exclusion would not promote the general welfare under the police power.

The procedural effect of making the use a special exception is to shift the burden of proof to the applicant. The applicant's burden is to present substantial evidence that he qualifies for the exception.

A special exception's criteria, set out in the regulations, will have as their subject matter minimum standards for set-backs, side-yards, screening, parking, bulk, density of use — all designed to prevent the conditionally permitted use from exerting external effects on neighboring parcels. Such criteria are meant only in a limited sense to insure the compatibility of the special exception with its surroundings. Under the most commonly used

---

[84] *Sunderland Family Treatment Services v. City of Pasco*, 903 P. 2d 986, 994 (Wash. 1995).

[85] Judges sometimes confuse terms which zoning attorneys routinely use, even to the point of calling a variance a special exception. Such confusion can be traced to inattentive drafting in § 7 of the SZEA. The most famous example of such confusion is Chief Justice Burger's doing just this in his opinion in *City of Eastlake v. Forest City Enterprises*, 426 U.S. 668 (1976), discussed *infra*, Chapter 20.

[86] *Steen v. County Council of Sussex County*, 576 A.2d 642, 646 (Del. 1989) ["A conditional use (sometimes called a special exception) is not truly an exception to a zoning ordinance, but is a use in compliance with, rather than in variance of, the ordinance and is allowable when the prerequisite facts and conditions specified in the ordinance are found to exist."].

[87] *See, e.g., Ackman v. Bd. of Adjustment for Black Hawk Cty.*, 596 N.W.2d 96, 103–104 (Iowa 1999); *Quality Sand and Gravel, Inc. v. Planning and Zoning Comm'n of the City of Torrington*, 738 A.2d 1157 (Conn. App. Ct. 1999).

standard, once the applicant has carried his burden of proof as to all of the enumerated and specific criteria, an applicant has carried his burden of proof as to the "adverse impacts" of the proposed use when showing that it is no more burdensome on surrounding parcels than uses permitted as of right are. A more specific standard requires the applicant to show that the use, at the proposed location, would not have adverse impacts *above and beyond* those impacts inherently associated with that use in the district for which it is proposed. For example, with a special exception for a waste disposal site, the board need not consider all adverse impacts of the applicant's use; the municipal legislature has found them tolerable when providing for a special exception. As an administrative body, the board may not, and need not, re-consider this legislative decision. Neighbors might allege that the proposed waste disposal use will cause run-off into a stream and that trash trucks entering and leaving will create noise on abutting streets. If the owner then introduces evidence that the run-off will be no heavier than that which occurs at other disposal sites and that the trucks will be no noisier at this site than anywhere else, the owner has met his burden. The issue is whether the adverse effects are greater here than they would be elsewhere: is the drainage pattern unique on this site? Do the trucks using the abutting roads shift gears, or stop and start, more than usually? Those are the appropriate types of questions of fact for the board. [88]

What uses may be classified as a special exception has also received judicial attention. [89] Certain uses, considered essential to the zoning jurisdiction's welfare when not incompatible with uses permitted as of right in a use district, but not compatible at each and every location within the district, may be treated as within the text of a special exception. [90] In an agricultural use district, it is permissible to classify a junkyard or a machine repair shop as a special exception, but not a landfill. [91] The two former uses are frequently found in agricultural districts and are ancillary to an agricultural use, even though they may have adverse impacts on neighboring uses. Likewise, a special exception for water well drilling, but not oil, may be permissible in an agricultural district because irrigation is necessary for agriculture. Whether a proposed use falls within those allowed by special exception is a question of law. [92] The language is construed reasonably and with regard to the ordinance's general purpose and structure, and in order to avoid illogical or inconsistent results. [93]

---

[88] See *Schultz v. Pritts*, 432 A.2d 1319, 1325 (Md. 1981) (the leading case for this proposition); *Mossburg v. Montgomery County*, 666 A.2d 1253 (Md. App. Ct. 1995) (reviewing Maryland cases to this effect).

[89] But see *Ackman v. Bd. of Adjustment for Black Hawk Cty.*, 596 N.W.2d 96, 103–104 (Iowa 1999) (considering whether a quarry is appropriate in an agricultural use district).

[90] See *Tullo v. Millburn Twp.*, 149 A.2d 620, 624–625 (N.J. Super. Ct., App. Div., 1959)

[91] *Bierman v. Twp. of Taymouth*, 383 N.W.2d 235 (Mich. App. Ct. 1985) (upholding this distinction).

[92] See *Wells v. Portland Yacht Club*, 771 A.2d 371, 374 (Me. 2001) (whether a yacht club is a "private club" and permitting a conditional use for a junior sailing program open for a fee to non-club members).

[93] *Id.*

Generalized use of the special exception is invalid.[94] When a small jurisdiction's zoning ordinance contained no residential uses permitted as of right, except for single family housing, but instead required that special exception permits be obtained for any other residential development, the resulting regulatory scheme can be found invalid on at least three grounds. First, the purpose of zoning is both to integrate compatible uses and separate those which need protection from each other, while this scheme carries out only the last purpose. Second, this scheme has by definition no uniformity and no preexisting comprehensive plan here; instead, every issue is left to the discretion of the local administrative board. Third, viewed as a delegation of power, this scheme is too broad; the local legislature cannot delegate its zoning powers to such a degree.[95] Wait-and-see zoning may not be the primary method of a jurisdiction's land use regulation without stepping outside the bounds of many zoning enabling acts.

[A] Generalized Mop-Up Criteria for Special Exceptions.

One of the oft-used express criterion for a special exception is a "public need" for its use. This, too, has been attacked as too broad a delegation of legislative power to an administrative board: zoning boards have no authority to regulate competition — for example, to decide how many gas stations should be located at an intersection.[96] A "public need" criterion is too vague because it can be related to matters of competition, a concern beyond land-use compatibility and the authority and competence of the board administering a special exception. In addition, making findings of public need or public welfare might be seen as non-delegable duties of the municipal legislature.

The best evidence, but not the only evidence permitted, of a "public need" is in the municipality's comprehensive plan. The granting of a special exception may also be challenged on the ground that it is not in accord with the comprehensive plan. A special exception is subject to the comprehensive plan, while a variance (being a waiver of zoning regulations) is not.[97] So an application for a special exception is best challenged by a showing of non-conformance with that plan.

---

[94] See Massey v. City of Charlotte, 2000 N.C. Bus. Ct. 4 (Apr. 17, 2000) (invalidating a conditional use district as ultra vires the enabling act).

[95] Compare Rockhill v. Twp. of Chesterfield, 128 A.2d 473 (N.J. 1956) (criteria for duplexes, quads, townhouses, and multiple family structures were enumerated in the ordinance, in terms of: (1) minimum acreages, (2) set-backs, (3) height restrictions, (4) side and back yard restrictions, and (5) the ordinance provided that no special exception shall issue when to do so would have an adverse impact on adjacent parcels or the public interest) with Klem v. Zoning Hearing Bd., 387 A. 2d 667 (Pa. Commw. Ct. 1978) (where only two percent of the township was zoned and ninety percent was left to the special exception procedure, the court held that the zoning was comprehensively planned).

[96] Wesco, Inc. v. City of Montpelier, 739 A.2d 1241 (Vt. 1999).

[97] Anderson v. Zoning Bd. of Review, 219 A.2d 484 (R.I. 1966).

[1] "No Adverse Impact" Criteria.

Another mop-up criterion for a special exception will be to the effect that "there is no adverse impact on neighboring parcels." Although, for many legislatures, a "no adverse impact" criterion is the next best thing to a public need criteria, its focus is clearly land-use compatibility and so it will survive legislative/administrative line-drawing, and is generally found to be a proper consideration for a board conducting an administrative hearing.

"No adverse impact" criteria may mean that, as a practical matter, the applicant has to deal with whatever concerns the opposition raises. Viewed in this light, the burden is less onerous and the criteria is a reflection on the fact that an application for a special exception is heard in a quasi-judicial proceeding — one often designed to settle a dispute between the applicant and his neighbors. In this context, the applicant's attorney should encourage the applicant to discuss the application with neighbors and gain their approval for it.[98] But the hearing record and the board's order should not slip from a discussion of potential adverse impact to a consideration of the general welfare; the board should hear, and rule on an application on the basis of land-use compatibility criteria. The extent of the adverse impacts considered, however, increases with the extent of the special exception proposed; thus for a big-box discount store, the adverse impacts of a municipality's entire "viewshed" might be considered.[99]

[2] Specialized and General Criteria.

A frequently litigated issue with special exceptions is whether, when all the enumerated, specific criteria for a special exception are met by the applicant, the board must then issue an order granting the application. The better view of this matter is that it must.[100] The inclusion of the special exception in a district is a legislative finding that this use, with the conditions met, is in harmony with those uses permitted as of right in the district. In this instance, the criteria define the parameters of the police power, and unpublished conditions would be ultra vires. This result also follows from the local legislature's duty to provide notice to the applicant of the criteria which it is necessary to satisfy before a special exception shall be granted.

Another view is of this issue is that, when the applicant meets the enumerated, specific criteria, a rebuttable presumption generally arises in favor of issuance.[101] This is consistent, courts say, with the presumption of validity accorded a special exception in most states.

---

[98] See, e.g., Nat'l Cathedral Neighbors Ass'n v. District of Columbia Bd. of Zoning Adjustment, 753 A.2d 984, 987 (D.C. 2000).

[99] See Wal-Mart Stores, Inc. v. Planning Bd. of the Town of North Elba, 668 N.Y.S.2d 774, 776–777 (N.Y. App. Div. 1998) (calling the viewshed integral to a town at the "western gateway" to Lake Placid in a tourism-dependent region).

[100] See Value Oil Co. v. Town of Irvington 377 A.2d 1225, 1232 (N.J. Super. Ct., Law Div., 1977) ("Once an applicant has demonstrated compliance with the provisions of the zoning ordinance, a duty is imposed upon the board to grant the permit."), affirmed, 396 A.2d 1149 (N.J. Super. Ct., App. Div., 1978).

[101] Steen v. County Council of Sussex County, 576 A.2d 642, 646 (Del. 1989) (citing cases from Maryland and Pennsylvania).

Still another view of this issue arises when the regulation for the exception, after setting out the criteria for a group home as a special exception, provides that "when all such criteria are met, the board may by order issue the permit." Here, the discretionary verb "may issue" means that the board has the authority to deny the permit, but need not. When it does not, however, the board needs to make a special showing of its findings and conclusions. The municipal legislature may have only intended to shift the burden of proof to the board to justify its denial or its imposition of additional conditions once all published criteria are met. This is sometimes known as the Pennsylvania rule on this issue.

[B] Legislative Review of Special Exceptions.

Sometimes a municipal legislature will delegate to itself the authority to hear special exception applications. This is a reservation of authority and is generally regarded as within the legislature's power to delegate.[102] Sometimes too, zoning regulations authorize the board to hear special exception cases, but provide for review by the legislature thereafter. This review provides for a reading of the board order (and discussion of it) in the midst of a legislative session. It may further justify the board's decision and provides insulation from judicial attack on the grounds of an impermissible delegation of a legislative function, but the legislature must still have a written decision to review because during its review it is functioning in an administrative, rather than a legislative capacity. As such, it is subject to the standard of substantial evidence and the state's administrative procedure act.

[C] Special Exceptions with Variances Attached.

Another category of problems with special exceptions arises when both a special exception and a variance are applied for. When an owner is granted a special exception with the proviso that the development proposed must be built within two years from the date of the grant, such a proviso is valid,[103] having been upheld in other contexts, particularly rezonings. Later delays in obtaining financing will find the applicant seeking to stay the effect of the "use it or lose it" provision in the grant by petitioning for a variance from its requirement. Such an application is in effect asking relief from inaction. Inaction is a self-created hardship.[104] Only if the delay in financing is caused by a lack of capital in financial markets beyond the control of the owner is this question in doubt.

---

[102] *Harford Cty. v. Earl Preston, Jr., Inc.*, 588 A.2d 772 (Md. 1991).

[103] *See Nat'l Waste Managers v. Anne Arundel Cty.*, 763 A.2d 264, 267 (Md. App. Ct. 2000).

[104] *See Farrington v. Zoning Bd. of Appeals*, 413 A.2d 817 (Conn. 1979) (holding that inaction is a self-created hardship).

[D]   Special Exceptions and Non-Conforming Uses.[105]

A special exception may not be used to expand an adjacent non-conforming use. Suppose a municipality permitted waste disposal sites by special exception and the board granted a special exception application to the owner of both a non-conforming sand and gravel pit and an abutting, proposed disposal site. The owner's proposal, calling for trucks bringing construction refuse to the site from a nearby city to return there, loaded with sand and gravel, might easily be seen as promoting efficiency. Nonetheless, this is an improper use of the special exception. Non-conforming uses (because they are also protected by some enabling statutes and the takings clause) may be expanded, but not substantially changed or increased.[106] Permitting an expansion of the scope of a non-conforming business is more that a mere increase in the rate of quarrying the sand and gravel. Expanding its owner's business off-site is an unreasonable expansion, giving neighbors a case for denying the permit; what results is not substantially the same as what was on site when the use became non-conforming.[107] The board's decision would likely be struck down as *ultra vires* the protection given non-conforming uses in the enabling act.[108] The municipality might amend its ordinance in order to authorize the quarry as a special exception, so that authorization for two businesses could proceed either in tandem or separately.

[E]   Procedural Due Process.

Both the variance and the special exception are the product of an administrative hearing. Conducting such a hearing, the board accords rights of procedural due process: the right to notice, the right to cross-examine the witnesses in some way, and a prohibition of *ex parte* communications with board members. These processes govern the conduct of the hearing and assure the adequacy of the record for judicial review.

§ 10.04   Administrative Appeals.

The board (Board of Zoning Adjustment or Appeals) also hears one other type of administrative matter — that is, appeals from administrative determinations and interpretations of the zoning ordinance and regulations. In this capacity, it sits as an appellate agency to review the work of land use administrators. Often the opinion of an administrative agency is entitled to a presumption of correctness because harmonizing and defining the terms of the ordinance is often a difficult matter. Administrative appeals may be subject to the doctrine of exhaustion of remedies in

---

[105] Discussed in Chapter 7, *supra.*

[106] *Ray's Stateline Market, Inc. v. Town of Pelham*, 665 A.2d 1068 (N.H. 1995) (changed signage and plumbing for convenience store are not an improper expansion of a non-conforming use).

[107] *Cf. Lazy Mtn. Land Club v. Matanuska-Susitna Borough Board of Adjustment and Appeals*, 904 P. 2d 373 (Alaska 1995).

[108] *Nickels v. City of Wildwood*, 658 A.2d 291 (N.J. 1995).

some jurisdictions.[109] After all, when a dispute may be resolved by clarifying a definition, rather than litigating the effect of a whole ordinance, judicial efficiency dictates that the parties do the former. Once in the hands of a reviewing court, however, questions involving the interpretation of an ordinance are matters of law, reviewed narrowly to determine whether the board abused its discretion.[110] Terms are interpreted either to assign them a plain and sensible meaning (when clear), or to give them (if unclear) their usual meaning in the context of the ordinance.[111] So a street looping around to end on the same street it began, is not a "dead-end" street.[112]

In a more broadly applicable example, when a building is to be constructed on a slope and recessed into the ground, it will matter whether the building's height, for purposes of compliance with a zoning regulation, is measured from the grade of the lot or from the base of the building because a building may be in compliance on its up-hill side, but not on its down-hill side. Where the architect puts its front door may be determinative if the height is measured only on its front side.[113]

Similarly, when an ordinance permits a two-story building, sinking the building into the earth, with one grade below ground level and two above, creates a non-complying structure. A "story" is generally defined as an interior measurement. It is "the portion of a building from the upper surface of a floor to the upper surface of the floor next above."[114] On the other hand, a "cellar" or basement may be defined as "being no more than four feet above ground level," but such a definition will not stop the developer of an in-fill residential project in a use district permitting houses that are no more than three stories tall, from building a fourth floor on a house by excavating and making the "cellar" deep enough to stand in.[115]

An administrator must exercise common sense. When a building's maximum length is prescribed by a regulation and an administrator is presented with a building plan that puts a "jog" or break in the building's facade, such that the length on either side of the break does not exceed the maximum, the plan fails to comply with the regulation when its two segments have common hallways, elevators, and other facilities.[116]

A administrator's exercise of interpretative authority should be done so that the administrative decision is in accord with the opinions of the

---

[109] *Josephson v. City of Annapolis*, 728 A.2d 690 (Md. 1999).

[110] *See Marzullo v. Kahl*, 783 A.2d 169 (Md. 2001) (holding that a facility for breeding snakes is not a "farm").

[111] *Id.* at 1121–1122.

[112] *See Springborn v. Town of Falmouth*, 769 A.2d 852, 856 (Me. 2001) (an ordinance limiting dead-end streets to a 1500 foot length).

[113] *Laforce v. Bucklin*, 373 A.2d 144 (Md. 1971).

[114] Bdlg. Officials Conf. of America (BOCA), Basic Building Code (an excellent source of many definitions for zoning enforcement officers), *quoted in Nether Providence Twp. v. R.L. Fatscher Assoc.*, 674 A.2d 748, 751 (Pa. Commw. Ct. 1996).

[115] *See* Sandra Fleishman, *When is a Floor a Floor? Therein Lies a Story*, Wash. Post (Apr. 29, 2000), at G1, col. 2.

[116] *Bd. of Comm'rs of Township of O'Hara v. Kakim*, 339 A.2d 905 (Pa. Commw. Ct. 1975).

municipality's attorney.[117] As a general rule, an administrator may not do more than interpret the regulation; decisions on constitutional or vested rights issues, although not expressly denied him, are nonetheless reserved for the courts.[118] Some examples show the difficulties that administrators face. For example, "residents" of a parcel might be specially permitted to engage in various "home occupations" such as renting rooms to boarders. Under this rule, an administrator might rule that residents may not be tenants, or are not summer residents, or even nine months a year residents.[119]

In a further example, suppose that an owner had a parcel located in an exclusively agricultural use district: that is, only agricultural uses were permitted as of right. Agriculture was defined as "the growing or harvesting of crops and other farm commodities, including the processing or storage of products harvested on the premises." The owner's parcel had a natural spring that the owner proposed to tap and sell its water in bottled form. Applying to the administrative official to certify that her proposed use of the spring was an agricultural use, she argued: that water was raised from the ground, just as was any crop; that it was a renewable resource, just as wheat or corn; and that water is involved in agriculture, even though not traditionally thought of as a crop, not sold as a farm commodity, nor an agricultural "product" or the subject of a harvest, as the ordinance seemed to require.[120] The plain meaning of the phrase prevailed, and the owner failed to convince the administrator.[121]

In a final example, an owner obtained approval for a shopping center. The applicable ordinance provided that "in all non-residential use districts in which shopping centers are permitted, no primary entrances or exits shall direct traffic into adjacent residential districts."[122] Neighbors in adjacent residential district appealed the approval, alleging that, while customers of the center would not be directed into their residential district, delivery vehicles would be. The neighbors won the appeal. The neighbors' appeal raised issues regarding the meaning of "primary" access as meaning both customer and service access. So the affidavits of engineers and planners to the effect that delivery trucks, including large eighteen-wheelers, would be necessary to service the center and that "primary" access must account for both vehicle trips and the type of traffic generated

---

[117] *Houston v. Town of Waitsfield*, 648 A.2d 864, 865 (Vt. 1994) (where the administrator said that the extraction of spring water for bottling required a variance in an agricultural zone, while legal counsel opined that it was an as-of-right use; the BZA rejected both interpretations, denying the application for an extraction permit).

[118] *Holland v. Johnson, Zoning Administrator*, 403 S.E. 2d 356 (Va. 1991).

[119] *Richert v. City of South Portland*, 740 A.2d 1000, 1002–1003 (Me. 1999).

[120] *See* Annot., *Construction and application of terms "agricultural," "farm," "farming," or the like*, 97 A.L. R. 2d 702, 706 (1964).

[121] *See Houston v. Town of Waitsfield*, 648 A. 2d 864 (Vt. 1994) (considering also the effect of the state legislature's recently enacted statutory program for certifying the quality of spring water and run by the state agriculture department).

[122] *See Ryan v. City of Bay Minette*, 1995 Ala. LEXIS 260 (Ala. Sup. Ct., June 9, 1995) (reversing a summary judgment for the owner).

by the use. Separating customer and delivery traffic would be overly formalistic: the customer's use of the center during its peak hours might have been just as noisy as one eighteen-wheeler arriving at midnight.[123]

Conclusion. In the following chapter, we turn our attention to the last of the zoning forms of action — a rezoning. It is not an administrative matter. It is presented, not to the BZA, but to a zoning commission or municipal legislature. It requests a use change. As with the initial zoning of land in the municipality, it is a matter that is legislative in nature.

---

[123] *See id.*

Chapter 11

Seeking a Rezoning

§ 11.01 Introduction.

There are two types of rezonings. First, an owner asking to have his parcel taken out of one use district and placed in another, is seeking to have the zoning map for the jurisdiction redrawn. Redrawing the map is called a **map amendment** rezoning. Second, an application may, in addition or solely, request that the text of the ordinance be modified, usually expanding the list of uses permitted as of right in a district. This second type of rezoning is an application for a **text amendment**. Thus, a rezoning application, once granted, results in either a map or a text amendment.

Both types of rezoning amendments are typically regarded as legislative actions. Such applications are heard by the local legislative body of the jurisdiction — or, in the alternative, heard by a zoning commission or a hearing examiner, whose decision is subject to legislative review.

In enacting any amendment, municipal legislatures must follow the procedures set out in their own enabling statutes.[1] Typically, these procedures require a notice and a hearing, and usually also, several readings of the amendment before it may be enacted and become effective. No formal written record of the debate, or the finding underlying the action, is required, again because the action is a legislative one, and it speaks for itself. Its action must, however, be codified (that is, incorporated into the zoning code or ordinance) and made available to the public.

§ 11.02 Twin Presumptions.

A comprehensive zoning scheme is entitled to twin presumptions of constitutionality and validity. After such a scheme is enacted, if the local legislature changes its mind and rezones an owner's property, is its action entitled to the same presumptions? What was reasonable at the time of the original zoning may become proof of the unreasonableness of the rezoning.

The answer, as a matter of logic, is that, if the original zoning was justified only by its having a rational basis, then it is possible that the rezoning may have the same basis — and that both actions can fit within the range of all reasonable options open to the local legislature. This is what is meant when a court, reviewing the rezoning decision, states that if the action of the local legislature is fairly or reasonably debatable, then a court will not overturn it.[2]

---

[1] See Riggs v. Twp. of Long Beach, 538 A.2d 808, 812–813 (N.J. 1988).

[2] Prete v. City of Morgantown, 456 S. E.2d 498 (W. Va. 1995) (finding that a rezoning is fairly debatable when the totality of the evidence when viewed "both quantitatively and qualitatively, . . . would lead objective and reasonable persons to reach different conclusions").

Any rezoning must be based on evidence making it fairly debatable, meaning that it bears a substantial relation to the general welfare. Merely because the amendment was initially proposed by private parties (say a land developer) is no reason to overturn it. If the rule were otherwise, few amendments would survive judicial review. Moreover, courts do not generally inquire into or consider the legislative motives for a zoning amendment, unless the reasonableness of the amendment is not facially apparent.[3] Even though a particular amendment can serve two purposes, one of them illegal or invalid, the remaining other one, being legal or valid, will be sufficient to sustain it.[4]

§ 11.03   Tests for the Validity of a Rezoning.

The tests which are used to evaluate a non-comprehensive or piece-meal rezoning application are three in number and focus on:

(1) Whether there is a public need for the rezoning amendment, and whether that need is met by the rezoning amendment. This test requires the identification of the public need, and then the establishment of a rational nexus, or substantive due process connection, between the need and the amendment. It may be seen used in the opening portion of Justice Holmes' majority opinion in *Mahon.*

(2) A balancing of the public need for the rezoning against the injury worked on neighbors. For example, if an applicant seeks an amendment making airstrips an accessory use in a use district and seeks to install an airstrip on a parcel rezoned in this way, the issue is whether this type of use will impact in a confiscatory way on the applicant's neighbors, not whether it will reduce the value of their property.[5] Some "diminution in value" is to be expected from any zoning or rezoning. If this were not the rule, only up-rezones, to a more intensive use, would be valid, while down-zoning, to a less intense use, would always be invalid; such a result would be an impermissible restriction on the legislative function in rezoning matters. Sometimes this test amounts to an uniformity test that tracks either equal protection clause analysis[6] or Holmes' "reciprocity of advantage" test in *Pennsylvania Coal Co. v. Mahon*[7] : may many landowners, or just the applicant, benefit from the change in the zoning? If the former, then the rezone will be upheld. Tested this way, the rezoning must typically involve many owners or a large area.

---

[3] *See Clary v. Borough of Eatontown,* 124 A.2d 54 (N. J. Super. Ct., App. Div., 1956), and *see infra,* this Chapter, at n. 17.

[4] *Gallo v. Mayor and Twp. Council of Lawrence Twp.,* 744 A.2d 1219, 1225 (N. J. Super. Ct., App. Div., 2000).

[5] *Norbeck Village Joint Venture v. Montgomery County Council,* 254 A.2d 700 (Md. 1969) (stating that cutting the neighbors' property values by two-thirds did not invalidate the rezoning as a taking).

[6] *See, e.g., Thomas v. City of West Haven,* 734 A.2d 535 (Conn. 1999) (holding that requiring a site plan of a rezoning applicant when not all such applicants were required to present such a plan, gives rise to a prima facie violation of the equal protection clause, using federal cases as precedent).

[7] 260 U.S. 438 (1922).

(3) Whether the rezoning is "in accord with the comprehensive plan." This is a statutory test, based on a phrase taken from the Standard Zoning Enabling Act, § 3. In using this test, the comprehensive plan is generally taken as a general guide. It is advisory rather than binding, and need not be a separate and discrete document, being regarded instead as a comprehensive approach or scheme. "It is only a series of statement and precepts, representing community choice and decision as to the space needs of various activities and the interrelationships of land uses, that the master plan can effectively fulfill its role as a guide to regulatory action."[8] Nonetheless, a well conceived and implemented master plan for a particular neighborhood or use district, when tied into a larger, comprehensive plan for the region, will strongly influence the outcome of a rezoning case. For example, suppose that an amendment directs urban growth away from a sensitive watershed on which the jurisdiction's water supply depends, or that the watershed itself is down-zoned for large lot zoning to protect the water supply. In each instance, the identification in the plan of the public resource to be protected is an indication to any reviewing court that the rezoning was done in good faith and is not directed at benefitting a small group of owners.

Down-zoning is a type of rezoning amendment that results in lower densities or less intense land uses being permitted than were formerly. It is often introduced by the planning staff of the municipality or a legislator. In order to survive judicial scrutiny, they should be: (1) comprehensive in nature; (2) not solely for the benefit of special interests or existing landowners, but rather directed toward a public need; and finally (3), not directed against any particular person or not acquisitory or confiscatory in nature, but rather conforming to the site and to the uses presently surrounding the downzoned area.

§ 11.04   Spot Zoning.

The converse of an amendment's meeting the three tests for a rezoning is often labeled "spot zoning." That is a rezoning locating a parcel in a district out of character with the neighborhood which surrounds the rezoned parcel. It is "an attempt to wrench a single small lot from its environment and give it a new rating which disturbs the tenor of the neighborhood."[9] Thus spot zoning implicates all the foregoing tests — the public need, the uniformity, and (perhaps) the comprehensive planning tests.[10]

Spot zoning has two elements: treatment of a (1) parcel with a small area — a "spot" of land — in a way (2) not in accord with a comprehensive zoning scheme or plan.[11] Sometimes there is a third element, or perhaps an

---

[8] Charles Haar, *In Accordance with a Comprehensive Plan*, 68 Harv. L. Rev. 1154, 1174 (1955), *quoted with approval in Holmgren v. City of Lincoln*, 256 N.W. 2d 686, 690 (Neb. 1977).

[9] *Magnin v. Zoning Comm'n*, 138 A.2d 522, 523 (Conn. 1958).

[10] *See Green v. County Council of Sussex County*, 508 A.2d 882, 889 (Del. Ch. 1986) (linking the doctrine of spot zoning with a finding that a rezoning fails to meet the equal protection clause requirement of uniform treatment for otherwise similar owners).

[11] *Blaker v. Planning and Zoning Comm'n of the Town of Fairfield*, 562 A.2d 1093, 1099 (Conn. 1989).

alternative to the second — viz., (3) a treatment of a parcel benefitting private interests.[12] It is the antithesis, then, of zoning "in accord with the comprehensive plan," as required by the SZEA. As one court put it, spot zoning "refers to the situation where a small area or 'spot' of land is zoned differently than the surrounding area for the benefit of the owner of such property and to the detriment of others."[13] The detriment can either be shown by the rezoning's being a nuisance, by its having adverse effects on neighbors, or by non-conformance with a comprehensive plan for the neighborhood.

As a substantive doctrine, it is judge-made and a product of the common law, rather than a statute. It purpose is often (not always) to enable judges to invalidate rezoning decisions which treat landowners in a non-uniform way, even to the point sometimes of bestowing political favors.

Sometimes the term is used to refer to a reverse proposition — namely, a small parcel being restricted more severely than neighboring parcels. Generally, the geography, location, and characteristics of the rezoned parcel are considered before a rezoning is found to be a spot zoning.[14]

Although spot zoning cases are likely to be site-specific and have limited value as precedent, two alternative rules have emerged in the case law: first, spot zoning is illegal *per se*; or, second, spot zoning is a descriptive, not a legal, term and the real question is the reasonableness of the action. The second rule considers numerous factors, but particularly stresses the size of the parcel; its compatibility when rezoned with surrounding parcels, its neighborhood, and the community as a whole; and the benefits and injuries conferred and worked by the rezoning on owners of surrounding parcels, in the neighborhood, and within the community.

The general issue raised in spot zoning cases is whether the doctrine is a substantive rule of law or represents a shift in the presumption of validity usually accorded rezoning when the court identifies facts (smallness of the parcel, etc.) that are not in accord with surrounding uses or preexisting policies or plans. Because rezoning is a legislative act, the latter is most likely, for so long as the legislature rebuts the factors indicating a spot zoning with evidence making the matter a fairly debatable one, the courts will sustain a rezoning.[15]

---

[12] *See, e.g., Kuehne v. Town of East Hartford*, 72 A.2d 474 (Conn. 1950).

[13] *Gallo v. Mayor and Twp. Council of Lawrence Twp.*, 744 A.2d 1219, 1225 (N. J. Super. Ct., App. Div., 2000) (rejecting neighbor's allegation of spot zoning, alleging only that the rezoning request was for a higher density); *Riggs v. Twp. of Long Beach*, 514 A.2d 45, 52 (N.J. Super. Ct., App. Div., 1986), *reversed on other grounds*, 538 A.2d 808 (N.J. 1988) (rezoning to lower density invalid); *Eden v. Town Planning & Zoning Committee*, 89 A.2d 746 (Conn. 1952).

[14] *Knight v. Lynn Twp. Zoning Hearing Bd.*, 568 A. 2d 1372, 1375 (Pa. Commwlth. Ct. 1990) (extending a residential zone into an agricultural use district in such a way as to establish an "island or peninsula" of residential land within another type of district, is spot zoning and reviewing Pennsylvania opinions on this subject).

[15] *Bd. of Supervisors of Fairfax County v. Snell Const. Corp.*, 202 S.E. 2d 889, 893 (Va. 1974).

§ 11.05   Rezoning or Special Exception?

With rezonings, how the application is styled matters. When the use that an applicant seeks is only one of several uses permitted if a map amendment rezoning is approved, seeking a text amendment or even special exception might be preferable. For example, an applicant might want to sell only a few of many items permitted for sale in a commercial use district. The municipal legislature might more readily approve the rezoning application if it sought to permit only the commercial sale of a few items, not all the other commercial items or uses available in the district to which rezoning is sought. Such limited approval may also be more readily supported by local consumers and might reduce the opposition by residential neighbors. So the application might be styled either as a rezoning or treated as an occasion to establish a special exception (and referred to the Board of Zoning Appeals or Adjustment). As a rezoning, it may be spot zoning. As such, it is either illegal *per se* or the finding of spot zoning will require that the legislature provide additional support in the record when granting it. Moreover, any conditional approval of the rezoning application might be illegal contract rezoning.[16] So drafting a special exception, having it approved, and then applying to the Board might be the preferable tactic.

§ 11.06   General Considerations.

(1) The variation in the standard of proof and of review evident in rezoning cases reflects the nature of the rezoning action itself. If broad in scope and affecting a large geographic area, the action looks comprehensive and akin to rule-making under the state's Administrative Procedure Act; but when narrower in scope, the action of the legislature has the appearance of a dispute between neighbors. Of this type of rezoning, piece-meal rezoning, more later.[17]

(2) The extent of the change will also be considered. A rezoning from residential to commercial, or from commercial to industrial, is more likely to be invalidated than a change which permits garden apartments in a residential zone. Likewise, a rezoning which redraws a boundary line between use districts, rather than places a new use in the middle of otherwise harmonious uses, will likely be upheld.

(3) Judicial review of rezonings tests a reviewing court's attitude about the municipality's legislative body; if it is broadly representative of the body politic, its actions will be given more deference than if it represents a narrow slice of society. So a completely residential suburb's municipal council gets less deference than a large city's council.[18]

---

[16] *See supra* Chapter 12 (discussing contract zoning). *See also Chrismon v. Guilford County*, 370 S.E.2d 579 (N.C. 1988).

[17] *See* this Chapter, *infra*.

[18] Municipal legislative bias, financial and associational conflicts of interest, ex parte contacts, and out-right graft need continuous attention. *See, e.g.,* Conn. Gen. Stat. Ann. § 8-11 (West 1989) (conflict of interest statute for zoning commissions and other local government agencies); Mark Cordes, *Policing Bias and Conflicts of Interest in Zoning Decisionmaking*,

§ 11.07   Evidence Needed for a Rezoning.

Once a rezoning application's denial is appealed and under review in court, counsel for the applicant must ask a basic question: what types of evidence must be produced in support of a petition to rezone? Here we are discussing a piece-meal application for a rezoning by a landowner, rather than a comprehensive rezoning initiated by the government. In many cases, the hearing on the application to convert a parcel to a commercial use often becomes a battle of traffic experts: trip generation and traffic counts become the focus of the hearing. Other land use changes in the vicinity become of secondary interest.

Two other questions often arise. First, must there be changes in actual uses in the neighborhood since the last comprehensive rezoning and replanning of the area? In many states, the answer is, not necessarily. And, second, what is the evidentiary value of comprehensive and master plans applicable to the neighborhood? In many states, the evidentiary value is considerable. These two questions are addressed in the next section.

§ 11.08   The Change/Mistake Rule.

In Maryland, there must first be substantial changes in the neighborhood before the rezoning can be justified on any other ground.[19] A showing of changes made "on the ground" is a threshold requirement of a rezoning. Population increases, standing alone, will not justify a rezone. This is one portion of Maryland's "change-mistake" rule for rezonings.

Maryland requires planning as a precondition to zoning an area, but for a piece-meal rezoning thereafter, requires a showing of substantial change in the actual land uses in the neighborhood. It is not enough that a new plan has been formulated.[20] Neither is it sufficient than rezonings similar to the applicant's have been approved, if they have not been acted upon — that is, if no construction followed the approval. Similarly, evidence of an increased flow of traffic past the parcel for which rezoning is sought, widening of nearby streets, the improvement of water and sewer facilities serving the parcel, or a gradual increase in the residential density of the neighborhood, will not show a substantial change. Likewise, changes outside the "neighborhood" are irrelevant to a showing of substantial change. In a rural area, the neighborhood may be a large one, and in an urban area,

---

N.Dak. L.Rev. 161 (1989). Perhaps because of a need to distinguish between legitimate interest group election politics and improper conduct, courts tread lightly in this area. *See Woodland Hills Residents Ass'n v. City Council*, 609 P.2d 1029 (Cal. 1980) (political campaign contributions to a majority of local legislature hearing plat application not improper).

[19] *See The Bowman Group v. Moser*, 686 A.2d 643 (Md. App. Ct. 1996) (also holding that a trial court merely finding that the substantial change "amounted to nothing," would be reversed).

[20] *Chapman v. Montgomery County Council*, 271 A.2d 156, 159 (Md. 1971) (finding that a change in density prescribed in master plan, without substantial change, does not justify rezoning).

small.[21] Once substantial change is shown, the general need for the use and its suitability for the parcel can buttress a decision to rezone.

The second aspect of Maryland's rule concerns legislative mistakes in the initial zoning. "It is well settled that in zoning an original error or mistake may be established by showing that the assumption, upon which a particular use was predicated, proves with the passage of time to have been erroneous."[22]

Applicants for a rezoning will seldom be able to show such a mistake, but they occasionally do, finding a glaring, legislative error. If at the time of a legislative comprehensive rezoning, the legislators failed to take account of existing land use facts, projects, or trends reasonably foreseeable; or if events subsequent to the rezoning have shown that the legislators' policy assumptions turned out to be incorrect, then the presumption of validity accorded a comprehensive rezoning is overcome.[23]

§ 11.09   Planning Studies and Documents as Justifying a Rezoning.

In most other states, it is sufficient that such changes be planned — that is, recommended in the applicable master or comprehensive plan. Then the adopted plan becomes a finding of the public's need for the use subject to the rezoning and becomes evidence of the validity of the rezoning decision.[24]

The SZEA requires that zoning be "consistent with the comprehensive plan." This statutory requirement has (as discussed previously) become the basis for one of the three tests of validity for a rezoning; it has sometimes been taken by courts reviewing rezoning decisions to mean that the rezoning decisions of the jurisdiction, taken as a whole, have to have an internal consistency. If it is what the statutory requirement means, then a changed condition — the advent of new demographic groups, with new housing needs — might justify a rezoning. These conditions can be reflected in planning documents.

Where changes proposed in planning documents are evidence of validity for a rezoning, some states go further and require that the plan be adopted by the local legislature. For the legislature acting on the changed conditions, it is better to have adopted the plan rather than left it in an administrative limbo. Thus, plans devised by planning staffs of a municipality are often thought to be of less evidentiary weight that those adopted by a municipality's legislature.

---

[21] *Buckel v. Board of County Comm'nrs of Frederick County,* 562 A.2d 1297 (Md. App. Ct. 1989) (summarizing the cases).

[22] *Anne Arundel County v. A-PAC, Ltd.,* 506 A.2d 671 (Md. App. Ct. 1986) (down-zoning based on assumption property would be taken in eminent domain for highway, was mistake warranting rezone).

[23] *Howard County v. Dorsey,* 438 A.2d 1339, 1343 (Md. 1982).

[24] *Pierrepont v. Zoning Comm'n of the Town of Ridgefield,* 226 A.2d 659, 662 (Conn. 1967).

§ 11.10 Individual vs. Cumulative Change.

When an owner applies to have a parcel rezoned from residential to commercial use and the municipal legislature grants the application, there will be a finding that there was a substantial change in the neighborhood and a public need for the rezoning. The basis for such finding might be that the up-grading of neighborhood intersections, the extension of sewer and water lines to the property, and nearby rezonings not yet built — all show a substantial change in the neighborhood. Neighbors might still argue that each change (the highway up-grading, the new lines, and the rezonings) in and of itself, does not show substantial change. Such an argument will be unavailing because each change would, in most jurisdictions, be considered cumulatively, rather than separately. A legislature may consider changes separately only when the mix of uses in the neighborhood is substantially the same as they were when the last comprehensive zoning took place. In a piece-meal, non-comprehensive rezoning, the issue of whether to consider neighborhood changes separately or cumulatively in a rezoning is a legislative matter. A reviewing court will not substitute its judgment for the legislature's once the latter finds a matter fairly debatable.[25]

§ 11.11 Invalid Reasons for a Rezoning.

Much in the same way courts speak of the presence of spot zoning as a reason why the rezoning is invalid, there are several invalid rationales for a rezoning action or decision often black-lettered. Invalid rationales include, first, the regulation or prevention of competition, or the increase in market demand for a particular use.[26] A second invalid rationale is the denial of prior applications, unless the application is made within an ordinance's period of repose after the prior request has been denied. A third invalid rationale is the applicant's purchase of the property for which application is made with knowledge of the need to rezone; for rezonings, there is no self-created hardship rule, as exists for variances. Fourth, the decision-maker cannot cite the length of time the zoning of surrounding parcels has been in effect. Zoning does not get stale, even presumptively. Fifth, and finally, the decision-maker may not cite the lack of changed conditions surrounding the parcel — unless the application is made in Maryland, as previously discussed — because the zoning may originally have been unreasonable.

§ 11.12 Drafting a Complaint to Challenge a Rezoning Amendment.

A complaint seeking judicial review of a rezoning should first describe the action taken by the municipal legislature, with particularity as to the time, resolution or ordinance number, and enacting body. It should detail the chronology of the application leading up to the action, and the request

---

[25] *The Bowman Group v. Moser*, 686 A.2d 643 (Md. App. Ct. 1996).

[26] *Aspen Hill Venture v. Montgomery County Council*, 289 A.2d 303 (Md. 1972).

made in the application, naming both the prior and the requested use of the parcel for which the application was filed; the date and time of any hearing held on the application, as well as who conducted the hearing; any municipal staff reports, recommendations, or actions taken before the hearing and considered at it, and any findings, report, or description of the action taken. The plaintiffs should be named, the statutory basis for the appeal cited, and the plaintiff's standing as aggrieved and injured parties and/or persons who appeared at the hearing established. Finally, in a final series of paragraphs, the basis for the appeal — the invalidity or arbitrariness of the action, and/or the lack of substantial evidence for it — should be pled. For example, the inappropriateness of the proposed use at the requested location, or the lack of a need for a medium density buffer between lower and higher density of uses, might be pled.

§ 11.13   Rezoning "in Accord with the Comprehensive Plan" and Environmental Law.

A rezoning generally may not be denied because of other applications filed or under review, at whatever stage. This is another way of stating that the cumulative effect of the application case load is not a proper subject for consideration; each application is entitled to be considered on its own merits. This rule was formulated well in advance of the environmental movement, one of the lessons of which has been that governmental actions have impacts and effects that should be considered with regard other actions because the over-all impact may be a cumulative one. Thus, no single action may have a significant impact on the environment, but when taken together, several actions may indeed be significant.

During the 1970s, some states enacted Environmental Policy Acts, modeled the National Environmental Policy Act, or NEPA, the 1970 federal Act of the same name.[27] Like NEPA, their federal counterpart, SEPA's require that an Environmental Impact Statement be prepared by a lead agency whenever a government-sponsored project will have a "significant effect" on the environment.[28] Significant effect is typically defined as resulting from "the existence of two or more *related* actions, none of which has significance, but when considered together would have a significant effect on the environment." An EIS is an evaluation of the short and long-term environmental effects of a proposed action, including its associated and cumulative effects, as well as a recitation of the facts relied on in making its evaluation.[29] It has to contain enough analysis of data to allow an informed consideration of its methodology and the issues it raises.[30] A

---

[27] *See* 42 U.S.C.A. § 4321-437(a) (1988).

[28] *See, e.g.,* N.Y. Envir. Conser. L., § 8-0101–0117 (1992).

[29] Cal. Pub. Resources Code, §§ 21167, 21168 (1995).

[30] *Akpan v. Koch*, 554 N.E. 2d 53 (N.Y. 1990). It is normally also subject to the notice, public comment, and hearing requirements. *See, e.g.,* Cal. Pub. Resources Code, § 21167(b)–(c).

reasoned elaboration of its conclusions is sufficient.[31] An EIS might also consider hypothetical projects and developments.[32]

Viewed in this light, an EIS can be a substitute for a comprehensive plan in states that do not require one before comprehensive rezonings. An EIS is an attempt to think about the consequences of a governmental action — to foresee them, and if appropriate take steps to avoid or mitigate them, much as a plan does. A rezoning decision, like an EIS, also considers the cumulative impact of land use changes, so a municipality containing state-protected, ecologically sensitive lands, that rezoned these lands to permit improvements, may have to write an EIS during the rezoning process, even though no specific land uses are changed until subsequent piece-meal rezoning applications are approved. The fact that the lands have been zoned all at once or comprehensively gives later rezoning decisions a "relatedness" that calls for an EIS.[33] The EIS provides an early-warning consideration of cumulative impacts, complementing what will later take place in the piece-meal rezoning process.

However, governmental activity by itself does not amount to a plan or policy triggering an EIS when a rezoning is sought. Consider a municipality has a very sensitive aquifer underlying it and regulated by federal drinking water standards, state public health laws, a regional planning agency, and municipal ordinances (prohibiting land fills and solid waste disposal there). When an owner applies for a rezoning for land above the aquifer, the application need not be held in abeyance until an EIS is written. Three rationales explain this result. First, there is no comprehensive plan or rezoning effort for the area — merely a host of uncoordinated federal, state, and local efforts, sharing only a common focus on the aquifer.[34] Second, if an EIS were to be written, it is not clear what agency a court should designate to write it. Third, the courts' role is not to piece together various statutes and regulations in order to fill the gap left by the legislature; a judicial call for legislative action is the best course here.[35]

---

[31] *Sutton Area Community v. Board of Estimate of City of New York*, 568 N.Y.S.2d 35 (N.Y. App. Div. 1991) (noting also that any shift in the basis for collecting the data — say, from one sewage plant to another — may require that the EIS be rewritten and offered again for public review and comment).

[32] *Neville v. Koch*, 593 N.E.2d 256 (N.Y. 1992). Conversely, a finding that no EIS is required is called a negative declaration. *See Har Enterprises v. Town of Brookhaven*, 548 N.E.2d 1289 (N.Y. 1989). It is issued by the state environmental protection department.

[33] *Save the Pine Bush, Inc. v. City of Albany*, 512 N.E.2d 526 (N.Y. 1987).

[34] *North Fork Environmental Council, Inc. v. Janoski*, 601 N.Y. S. 2d 178 (N. Y. App.Div., 2d Dept., 1993).

[35] *Long Island Pine Barrens Society, Inc. v. Planning Board of the Town of Brookhaven*, 606 N.E. 1373 (N.Y. 1992) (involving the Long Island Pine Barrens and distinguishing the *Save the Bush* opinion), *noted at* 3 Buff. Envir. L. J. 37 (1995) (noting that, in response to the *Pine Barrens Society* opinion, the N.Y. state legislature enacted the Long Island Pine Barrens Protection Act).

§ 11.14   The *Fasano* Doctrine.

Both spot zoning and the change-mistake rule for rezoning are judicial doctrines for heightening the standard of review for some rezonings. Over the history of zoning, there has been a tendency to zone vacant or developable land for uses that do not reflect its development potential. These zones may permit only agricultural uses and become "holding zones" reflecting a "wait and see" attitude by the municipal legislature. It is one way to ensure control over the future development of the municipality, putting the regulatory and development processes in sync, permitting correction of mistakes or omissions in the original zoning, and perhaps allowing the municipality to coerce developers into concessions the municipality does not otherwise have the authority to obtain.

Calling a decision legislative in nature implies that a clash of opposing views prevents hasty, ill-considered actions, and that shifting coalitions of legislators can be trusted to air all views and arrive at a consensus decision reflecting the public welfare, knowing that logrolling and vote trading is the stuff of legislative life. Applying this label to a municipal legislative body, however, may result in a fiction: the small homogenous nature of a municipality may mean that there is no clash of interests, and that there is rather more of special interest than consensus in its decisions.

Fasano v. Bd. of County Comm'nrs of Washington County,[36] further heightened the standard of review for rezonings. Its holding is that a rezoning action (to a floating zone via a map amendment) by the municipal legislature was not entitled to a presumption of validity and, when neighbors challenge a rezoning, it becomes a quasi-judicial action, to which requirements of notice and a properly conducted hearing, with the right to cross examine witnesses, applies. Here an applicant for a rezoning of a 32 acre parcel requested a map change from a residential, single family, use district to a planned unit development zone, in order to permit the development of the parcel as a mobile home park. He was challenged by neighboring owners.

The *Fasano* court found that, when the land use issues involve an owner or applicant and his neighbors, the action is a request not for legislative action, but instead seeks a hybrid of judicial and administrative action. It is not judicial action, in part because the decision makers lack the security in office characterizing judges. In addition, it is not administrative action, in part because the decision makers lack the expertise and technical background found in administrators and administrative agencies. Finally, a rezoning is neither purely administrative nor purely legislative because the doctrine of separation of powers does not typically apply to municipalities.[37] Rather, in rezoning proceedings, the *Fansano* court stressed the hybrid nature of the decision. The issues before the municipality involve, not the policies of the legislature nor the community as a whole, but the application of those policies to a specific parcel. With regard to a rezoning,

---

[36] 507 P.2d 23 (Or. 1973).

[37] *See, e.g., Building Authority v. State,* 321 S.E.2d 97, 102 (Ga. 1984) (so finding).

the *Fasano* court held that an applicant has the burden of proving four things:

(1) the requested change conforms to the comprehensive plan of the jurisdiction (this opinion was decided in a state making planning a mandatory activity of local governments),

(2) there is a public need for the requested use,

(3) his request best meets the need he shows, and

(4) the request conforms to the general welfare (a mop-up standard).

Each of these four elements of the applicant's burden must be shown by substantial evidence.

The Oregon Supreme Court later modified the *Fasano* doctrine in two respects. First, it dropped the third element in *Neuberger v. City of Portland*.[38] Second, it narrowed the reach of the doctrine to apply it only to piece-meal rezonings. It thus excluded from the doctrine's reach a comprehensive rezoning — which the *Fasano* opinion characterized as rule making, rather than the application of a rule to specific individuals or properties, the situation which it sought to control in its original opinion. Still, most map amendments are likely to be regarded as piece-meal, and quasi-judicial and adjudicative, in nature. Urban renewal agencies, boards of zoning appeals, fine arts and architectural review boards also may be subject to the *Fasano* doctrine.[39] However, just because a decision concerns infrastructure and the provision of governmental services, does not make it legislative in nature; if such were the case, there would be nothing left of *Fasano*.[40]

Taken as a whole, the doctrine's original elements require a showing that there is a nexus between the plan and the request, and between the public's need and the requested use, that the fit between these two is the "best" one, and that the need and the request fit into the general welfare. Viewed this way, these elements amount to a new elaboration of a substantive due process test wrapped around the public need test for a rezoning. Its use is only possible in a state that requires comprehensive planning.

In its opinion, the *Fasano* court also makes "some brief remarks" on procedural due process for future zoning decisions taken under the aegis of this decision. "Parties at the hearing . . . are entitled to an opportunity to be heard, to an opportunity to present and rebut evidence (but not a right to cross examination? -Ed.), to a tribunal which is impartial in the matter — i.e., having had no pre-hearing or ex parte contacts . . . — and to a record made and adequate finding executed."

---

[38] 607 P.2d 722 (Or. 1980) (hereafter *Neuberger*) (deciding that the rezoning of a 601 acre parcel was quasi-judicial because, notwithstanding the large parcel, the rezoning affected relatively few owners, required the application of pre-established criteria and a decision choosing among a set number of options).

[39] *Gold v. City of Portland*, 740 P.2d 812 (Or. App. Ct. 1987).

[40] *Neuberger*, op. cit.

[A] The *Fasano* Doctrine in Other States.

Kansas, Idaho, and Washington have also adopted the *Fasano* standard. Michigan and South Carolina have rejected it. "To regard the act of adopting an ordinance rezoning a single tract as anything other than a legislative act would be to sanction an impermissible encroachment upon the presumption of legislative validity." It would also encourage, argues South Carolina's opinion, "countless" challenges to such actions, "debase the local legislature challenged, and increase the burdens on zoning commissions and the courts."[41] Moreover, the doctrine makes rezoning procedures more costly and cumbersome for all persons involved in it. Its judicialization requires the employment of attorneys, and thus lessens the effective participation of lay citizens; it also strains the resources of some municipalities.

Florida has found a comprehensive rezoning to be legislative and a piece-meal rezoning to be quasi-judicial, and adopted a modified *Fasano* doctrine, requiring that when an applicant shows that the application is consistent with the comprehensive plan, the burden shifts to the government to show that maintaining the existing zoning accomplishes a legitimate public purpose and that the refusal to rezone is not an arbitrary one.[42] Florida has limited this doctrine to neighbors' challenges to a piece-meal rezoning, however, on the theory that there is a constitutional right to deal with one's land as one wishes. Florida's leading case on this subject has not been extended to amendments to a municipal comprehensive plan, even when the amendment was sought in conjunction with an application for a rezoning of a 54 acre parcel.[43] Although the leading case suggested an order of presentation for rezoning proceedings, later cases have detailed the procedural due process requirements of the Florida rule: subpoenaes may be issued to witnesses, who may be sworn and cross-examined, although here as elsewhere no prior discovery is generally available.[44]

The Oregon distinction between legislative and quasi-judicial actions has held up well in that state over the years. The *Fasano* opinion is singular because it makes the municipal exercise of the police power depend on following and according procedural due process rights.[45] Participating

---

[41] *Hampton v. Richland County*, 357 S.E.2d 463, 467 (S.C. App. Ct. 1987), cert. dismissed, 370 S.E.2d 714 (S.C. 1988):

[42] *Bd. of County Comm'rs of Brevard County, Florida v. Snyder*, 595 So. 2d 65 (Fla. App. Ct. 1991) (arguing that vacant land is typically "short zoned," or underzoned, so that rezoning becomes and rule not the exception), opinion quashed, 627 So. 2d 469 (Fla. 1993) (also finding that judicial review "is subject to strict scrutiny" meaning that a court should require strict compliance with the plan, and defining the plan as only a guide to maximum future development in the jurisdiction and not setting minimal intensity of land uses), *discussed in* Joni Coffey, *Practical Aspects of Quasi-Judicial Hearings: Basic Tools and Recent Fine-Tuning*, 30 Stetson l. Rev. 931, 937 (2001).

[43] *Martin Cty. v. Yusem*, 690 So.2d 1288 (Fla. 1997).

[44] *See* Coffey, op. cit, 30 Stetson l. Rev. at 947–954 (2001) (collecting the cases).

[45] *Eastlake v. Forrest City Enterprises*, 426 U.S. 668 (1976), classifies matters subject to a referendum as "legislative" in nature. *See supra* Chapter 20. The word is not used in the same sense there as it is in the *Fasano* opinion, so beware of cross-citation and confusion of the issues involved in each case.

citizens need a stable and well thought out procedure at any rezoning hearing; *Fasano* wisely provides that stability. In the last analysis, the distinction between what actions are legislative and which quasi-judicial or adjudicative, is for a municipal legislature to make and depends on the decision itself and the findings leading to it, not whether its effects are felt only by one parcel or just by a small group of owners.[46] Thus the imposition of an impact fee is a legislative action because the legislature has reserved little discretion in the matter.[47] However, the imposition of a special assessment may be quasi-judicial or adjudicative because whether to impose it, as well as the method of assessment, is open.[48]

Some legislative decisions need not involve comprehensive city planning for the municipality. For example, suppose a municipality prohibited the erection of any fences in the town because an endangered species of deer need to roam freely over its habitat. An owner with a 100 acre parcel within this habitat, applies for a permit to erect a 400 foot fence over it. This ordinance is a legislative act, is entitled to the usual deference, and should be regarded as a general policy decision, even though the application affects neighborly relations. It is within the police power of a municipality to protect its environment, including the flora and fauna in it; such a land use regulation will be upheld, unless it bears no substantial relationship to the police power, and a critically low population count for the deer should be sufficient to show such a nexus. That the regulation is consistent with federal and state environmental policy, is additional evidence of its rational basis as well.[49] An owner wanting to fence his garden, might have a stronger argument — for while the deer have a right to their habitat, even though it encompasses private property, they do not have a right to take the food off the owner's table.

[B] Some Open Issues.

While both *Fasano* or its progeny raise the prospect of local legislators being subpoenaed to testify as to the motives and reasons for their actions, it is more likely that the *Fasano* standards are intended (as the procedural due process quotation indicates) more narrowly to make and protect a record for further judicial review.[50] A legislator who campaigns on a platform generally opposed to urban growth and is elected, is surely not disqualified from voting on all zoning matters, whether or not they are major rezonings. "The quasi-judicial decisions of local general-purpose governing bodies resemble, or should resemble, adjudications in important respects that bear

---

[46] *See Bucktail v. Talbot Cty.*, Md., 723 A.2d 440 (Md. 1999).

[47] *Home Builders Ass'n v. City of Beavercreek*, 1996 WL 812607 (Ohio App. Ct., Feb. 12, 1996) (so holding).

[48] *City of Rockville v. Woodmont Country Club*, 705 A. 2d 301, 306 (Md. 1998).

[49] *Dept. of Community Affairs v. Moorman*, 664 So. 2d 930 (Fla. 1995).

[50] *Cf. New Castle County Council v. BC Dev. Assocs.*, 567 A.2d 1271, 1275–1276, n. 4 (Del. 1989) (citing *Fasano* in an opinion that rejects the labels as determinative, but requires the council to make an adequate explanation of its rejection of a rezoning application beyond inconsistency with the comprehensive plan).

on the procedural fairness and substantive correctness of the decision, but in other respects these bodies remain more 'quasi' than 'judicial.'"[51] Once elected, they have many functions, executive, legislative, and quasi-judicial, and exercise them in overlapping and simultaneous ways. "The combination leaves little room to demand that an elected board member who actively pursues a particular view of the community's interest in his policy making role must maintain an appearance of having no such view when the decision is to be made by an adjudicatory procedure."[52] Even restrictions on the business activities of judges should not apply to local unpaid or low-pay officials.[53]

§ 11.15   Distinguishing Municipal Legislative from Administrative Actions.

This distinction matters to zoning litigation in several contexts. The application of the ripeness doctrine,[54] whether or not to apply the takings' rules governing development exactions,[55] the issue of a municipal official's immunity from § 1983 or damage suits,[56] issues of procedural due process,[57] the application of referendum and initiative procedures[58] — all depend on the distinction. So as one might expect, calling an action legislative in the rezoning context is no guarantee that the label will stick in another context.[59] Moreover, even when a jurisdiction has not adopted the rules in either *Fasano* or *Snyder*, referenda or initiative procedures still may not be available, even though the legislative label remains broadly applicable.[60]

§ 11.16   Remedies for a Denial of Rezoning.

Upon a denial of a rezoning, The issue before the reviewing court is whether a continuation of the existing zoning is unreasonable (and amounts to a taking). That would be the narrowest way to put the question. More

---

[51] *1000 Friends of Oregon v. Wasco County Court*, 742 P.2d 39, 43 (Or. 1987).

[52] *Id.*

[53] *Id.*

[54] *See infra* Chapter 13.

[55] *See Dolan v. City of Tigard*, 512 U.S. 374, 379 (1994) (distinguishing between legislative and adjudicative actions and applying exactions rules only to the latter), discussed *infra*, Chapter 14..

[56] *Maynard v. Beck*, 741 A.2d 866, 872 (R.I. 1999) (immunizing planning commission members when performing a component of a legislative rezoning).

[57] *Hyson v. Montgomery Cty. Council*, 217 A.2d 578, 584 (Md. 1966) (finding a piece-meal rezoning quasi-judicial in nature and requiring a right of cross examination in a rezoning proceeding).

[58] *Arnel Dev. Co. v. City of Costa Mesa*, 620 P.2d 565 (Cal. 1980), discussed *infra*, Chapter 20.

[59] *See, e.g., Margolis v. District Ct.*, 638 P.2d 297 (Colo. 1981) (rezoning is a legislative action in the context of a referendum, but quasi-judicial when being judicially reviewed).

[60] *See, e.g., Citizen's Awareness v. Marakis*, 873 P.2d 1117 (Utah 1994) (discussing special criteria to be met before subjecting a rezoning to a referendum vote).

broadly put, a court might decide whether the proposed use is a reasonable one.

When a court is willing to consider the remedy issue in its broadest sense, the remedial options would include at least three remedies: first, declaring the existing zoning unreasonable and invalid and enjoining the zoning officials from enforcement of the present regulation, as to that land, leaving no zoning in effect. This will encourage the municipality to act promptly to respond to the applicant, and encourage all applicants to challenge unreasonable regulations.

Second, the court might order the officials to rezone to the applicant's proposed (or another, similar, and reasonable) use. This will require that the court exercise continuing jurisdiction in the case — something it may be reluctant to do.

Third, the court might order the officials to rezone to any reasonable use. Missouri case law, for example, provides good examples of each of these three options.[61]

Faced with the possibility of a judicial order of the types just discussed, an applicant's counsel along with the municipality's counsel, might enter into a consent decree involving a rezoning. In entering into the agreement to the decree, the municipality will not be deemed to have bargained away the exercise of its regulatory powers. No statute like the Standard Zoning Enabling Act or similar statute, should be presumed to deny judicial review and all of its remedial consequences.[62]

§ 11.17   The Need for Uniformity in the Standard of Review.

In any judicial review of a variance or special exception granted or denied by a zoning board, or other administrative order or action taken by zoning officials, substantial evidence for the action must typically be shown. In contrast, in an appeal of a comprehensive rezoning matter, the action taken by the local legislature must only be shown to be fairly debatable — that is, a rational basis for the action must be present. It is typically the case that several rational bases could fit comfortably within the preponderance of the evidence before the legislature, so that this latter standard is the lowest one available to a court and accords great deference to the legislative judgment. If, however, the rezoning is a piecemeal one, then courts often regard the matter as a quasi-judicial one and substantive evidence is required.

This contrast is illogical: why should some types of (piece-meal, non-comprehensive) rezonings be treated differently from variances, special

---

[61] See Ohmes v. Lanzarini, 720 S.W.2d 425 (Mo. App. Ct. 1986) (permitting the parcel to remain unzoned); Despotis v. City of Sunset Hills, 619 S.W.2d 814 (Mo. App. Ct. 1981) (ordering officials to rezone); Home Bldg. Co. v. City of Kansas City, 666 S.W.2d 816 (Mo. App. Ct. 1984) (ordering any reasonable use, leaving the property zoned in the meanwhile).

[62] But see Warner Co. v. Sutton, 644 A. 2d 656, 661–662 (N.J. Super. Ct., App. Div., 1994) (reporting a split in state court decisions and deciding it did not).

exceptions, and administrative appeals. Logic and uniformity require one standard of review and one evidentiary standard on all these occasions.

Chapter 12

Non-Euclidean Rezoning: Administrative Flexibility in Zoning

Euclidian zoning is defined as the division of a municipality into districts, classified by height limitations, use limitations, and other regulations regulating the bulk, density, and minimum acreage of a parcel.[1] It is also an alliterative illusion to the *Euclid* case, the leading case, approving this type of land use regulation.[2] Non-Euclidian zoning is taken to include everything else — that is, those regulatory patterns varying the traditional pattern of parcel-by-parcel, district-by-district zoning. It comes in several varieties, with and without standards that are expressly pre-set in the applicable zoning ordinance.

§ 12.01 Contract Zoning.

An amendment to a zoning ordinance changing either its text or the zoning map to permit a change of use is called a rezoning amendment. A rezoning that is approved so long as a particular use is maintained on a parcel, embodies a reciprocity of rights and obligations between a user and the local legislature. This is contract zoning and is invalid.[3] It involves a bargaining away or a delegation of the police power to the user or owner by the municipal legislature. A prohibition on such bargaining rests on three premises. First, the exercise of the police power is a non-delegable duty of the municipal legislature. The state zoning enabling act does not authorize any body or persons but those constituting that legislature, to enact zoning regulations, and this lack of authority supports the further idea that the legislature may not further delegate such enactment to others. It must exercise the authorized powers itself, and sub-delegations are prohibited. Thus contract zoning is ultra vires the enabling act. Second, one session of a municipal legislature cannot bind future sessions — the general welfare cannot be bargained away; every future session must be free to respond to the problems of its day and time, unhindered by its predecessors' decisions. Moreover, in the context of one legislative session, contract zoning may introduce a bias into the hearing and deliberative process. Third, there is the possibility of legislative abuse in contract zoning: legislators might be tempted to demand through agreements what they do not have authority to accomplish by regulation. Keeping legislatures honest is more important

---

[1] Standard State Zoning Enabling Act, §§ 1, 3, discussed *supra*, Chapter 6, and *reprinted in* Am. L. Inst., *Model Land Development Code*, Tent. Draft No. 1, at 210 (1968).

[2] *See supra* Chapter 6.

[3] *See Chung v. Sarasota Cty.*, 686 So. 2d 1358, 1359 (Fla. App. Ct. 1996); *Hale v. Osborn Coal Co.*, 729 So. 2d 853 (Ala. Civ. App. 1997).

than achieving the flexibility in regulation which the agreements might promote. So bilateral contracts or agreements between a developer and the legislature are invalid.

§ 12.02 Conditional Zoning.

A variation avoiding this prohibition occurs when the rezoning is sought during an executory period for the purchase and sale of the land subject to rezoning. Here the vendor and/or the purchaser (usually a developer) apply for the rezoning either while the land is under an option to purchase or to fulfill a contingency clause in the contract of sale.[4] Bargains with the legislature are still prohibited, but if the applicant appears before the legislature with a contract or an option to purchase, makes representations to the legislators, and then embodies them in the form of covenants, the presence of the covenants should not invalidate the rezoning. In one state, this process is called "concomitant agreement zoning." It permits courts to analyze, on a case-by-case basis, whether the agreement minimizes the negative externalities caused by the new development for which the rezoning, is sought.[5] More commonly, this variation on the rezoning process is known as conditional zoning. It takes the form of an agreement made between a developer and neighbors, executed in advance of the legislative hearing on a rezoning application filed by the developer, and restricting the use of the developer's property. This agreement is (again) in the form of a set of real covenants, running with the land attaching to the developer's title) and enforceable by neighbors; the agreement is then recorded and thus provides notice to subsequent purchasers of the land that the covenants burden or restrict what they bought. The covenants may last longer than the zoning which gave birth to them.[6] They terminate in the same ways that real covenants do. Courts have, in most jurisdictions, validated this process and the agreements that come with it.[7]

There are at least five reasons why conditional zoning approvals are, by the weight of the case law today, deemed valid. First, the legislature is not a party to the agreement.[8] Instead, the neighbors or a home owners or civic association, is made a party to it.[9] Second, the promise of the developer

---

[4] See Bucholz v. City of Omaha, 120 N.W.2d 270, 278 (Neb. 1963) (protective covenants executed by vendor seeking rezoning for the holder of an option to purchase his land did not invalidate the rezoning amendment), discussed in Comment, Variances and Parcel Rezoning: Relief from Restrictive Zoning in Nebraska, 60 Neb. L. Rev. 81, 111–112 (1981).

[5] See State ex rel. Myhre v. City of Spokane, 422 P.2d 790 (Wash. 1969).

[6] See, e.g., Equitable Trust Company v. Towson Manor Associations, Inc., 340 A.2d 759 (Md. App. 1975).

[7] See Dacy v. Village of Ruidoso, 845 P.2d 793 (N.M. 1992).

[8] See State ex rel. Zupancic v. Schimenz, 174 N.W.2d 533 (Wisc. 1970) ("We hold that when a city itself makes an agreement with a landowner to rezone the contract is invalid; this is contract zoning. However, when the agreement is made by others . . . and the city is not committed to rezone, it is not a contract in the true sense and does not vitiate the zoning if it is otherwise valid.").

[9] Occasionally the agreement is made between the neighbors, the planning commission, and

is unilateral, executed prior to the legislative action. In this regard, a developer will promise (through the covenants) to take protective measures to eliminate adverse effects of the development on neighboring or adjacent properties; to control the sequence of development; to assure proper maintenance of the development; or to designate the location or nature of the development. Third, it avoids the appearance of an impermissible exercise of power and displays the agreement resulting from the bargaining in the sunshine of the legislative chamber.[10] Fourth, it avoids reliance on developer representations at a legislative hearing. Fifth, conditional zoning separates rezoning issues from those concerning neighbors not resolvable in the rezoning process and permits mediation involving city and regional planners working as the staff of the commission and attorneys for the parties.

Because the agreement is not tied to the continuance of the new zoning and may outlast it, the future effectiveness of future land-use regulations may be curtailed by it. Sometimes the municipality will have standing to enforce the covenants underlying conditional zoning, even though these agreements were executed by others. The municipal legislature might enforce them, for example, as a third-party beneficiary. For this purpose, the municipality may be required, absent a statute on the subject, to own some land in the neighborhood to which the benefit of the covenant can attach.[11] Thereafter, a purchaser has to check the local zoning records as well as do a title search in order to find these agreements.

[A]   Testing Conditional Zoning.

In reviewing conditional zoning situations, the courts have not only uniformly required that the negotiations for and the formalities of the agreement not involve the legislature, but also have assumed that the rezoning and the agreement are interrelated, being part and parcel of the same process. With this assumption in mind, the courts have devised three tests for the validity of the conditional (re)zoning.[12] One test focuses on the subject matter and scope of the agreement, no matter who the parties to it are. Thus when it is reasonably related to the land-use regulation under which the municipal legislature or planning commission acts, it is valid.

---

a developer. Tripartite agreement is not with the legislature either, although at this point, the avoidance of a contractual relationship with the legislature begins to look like a dry exercise or dodge. *Compare Pressman v. City of Baltimore*, 160 A.2d 379 (Md. 1960) *with City of Greenbelt v. Bresler*, 236 A.2d 1 (Md. 1967). Both the commission and the legislature are, after all, agents of the same municipal government.

[10] *See Prock v. Town of Danville*, 655 N.E.2d 553 (Ind. App. Ct. 1995).

[11] *See London County Council v. Allen*, L.R. [1914] 3 K.B. 642, Ann.Cas. 1916C 932.

[12] A now generally discredited theory for conditional zoning is that the agreement between the developer and the neighbors is "induced voluntary action" on the developer's part. *See Sylvania Electric Products, Inc. v. City of Newton*, 183 N.E.2d 118 (Mass. 1962). Drawing the line between voluntary and involuntary action, proved too difficult a task. *See Meredith v. Talbot County*, 560 A.2d 599 (Md. App. 1989) (upholding an agreement, by which developer agreed to set aside a wildlife preserve in exchange for a plat approval and describing the agreement as voluntary and not executed under duress.)

The agreement's subject matter is tested according to the standard tests for the validity of a regulation. The underlying rationale for this test is that, what the commission could do by regulation, it may also do by agreement.

If the agreement flunks this test, a second alternative test, asks whether its subject is any broader than that any regulation that the legislature could have enacted, judged by the scope of the enabling act, rather than the regulation enacted in fact under it. [13] The underlying rationale for this test is that if the legislature could have incorporated the subject of the agreement into its regulation, the agreement is an exercise of the authority that the legislature had, but did not use. The agreement in this sense embodies a power that the legislature reserved to itself. Refining this "reserved power" test, one court has said the legislature is exercising a power often delegated to an administrative board, like a board of zoning appeals, authorized to hear applications for a special exception, but here it has reserved that power to itself. [14] That is, the legislature could have responded to a rezoning application by (in part) amending the ordinance with a special exception for the requested land use. The underlying rationale of this test is that the agreement accompanying the rezoning has to eliminate the adverse off-site externalities or impacts of a development just as a special exception might. In *Chrismon v. Guilford County*, [15] the opinion approves conditional zoning with such a rationale. [16]

In a third test, the agreement is be judged more broadly by the scope of the police power: if the neighbors are benefitted in proportion to the restrictions imposed on the developer, the substantive due process clause is satisfied. When, for example, a municipal legislature agrees to approve a rezoning on the condition that the developer execute a recorded covenant that the planning commission may disapprove an enlargement or expansion in the approved use "in its sole discretion, without giving any reason therefor." What if the developer agrees, executes the covenant in advance of the rezoning's approval, and later asks for permission to expand? When permission is refused without comment or explanation by the municipality, the leading case in this area upheld the refusal as valid conditional zoning. The agreement pertained to the land use for which the developer sought the rezoning and was regarded as a restrictive covenant, the effect of which is to restrain future development of the permitted use, except when the

---

[13] See *Giger v. City of Omaha*, 442 N.W.2d 182 (Neb. 1989) (approving a conditional rezoning in which four separate development agreements between a downtown developer and city agencies; requiring that conditions imposed in the rezoning ordinance or by development agreement, must be reasonably related to the purposes of the zoning enabling statute, although not expressly authorized there), *discussed in* J. Patrick Green, *Giger v. City of Omaha: Of Contracts, Comprehensive Plans, and Master Plans in Nebraska Zoning, Questions With and Without Answers*, 23 Creighton L.Rev. 289 (1990).

[14] See *Collard v. Incorporated Village of Flower Hill*, 421 N.E.2d 818 (N.Y. 1981) (conditional zoning is not spot zoning, nor an illegal delegation of the legislature's police power, and is implicitly enabled by state statute).

[15] 370 S.E.2d 579 (N.C. 1988).

[16] *Chrismon*, 370 S.E.2d at 585, note 2, 586–587 (conflating conditional zoning and special exception procedures and involving an agricultural supply storekeeper's application to rezone land in an agricultural use district for some uses permitted in a commercial district).

commission finds that some aspect of the general welfare requires its expansion.[17]

A fourth, and broadest, multi-factor test has been adopted in Mississippi.[18] There, so long as during the legislative process, (1) all parties are given an opportunity to speak, (2) the record contains no indication that the process is a sham or is not conducted in good faith, (3) the legislators reveal a familiarity with the facts and issues relating to the specific rezoning and (4) support it as in the best interests of the municipality, (5) the conditions imposed are those inherent in the type of rezoning sought, and (6) the type of rezoning used is useful in addressing neighbors' land use compatibility concerns — then the rezoning is valid as conditional and not contract zoning. Using such a test, the conditions were said to last only so long as the rezoning does; any further rezoning of the property annuls them.[19]

[B] The U. S. Supreme Court and Conditional Zoning.

A Supreme Court opinion, *Nollan v. California Coastal Commission*,[20] held invalid a condition imposed on a development permit for rebuilding a house along the California coast line. The condition required that the applicants (the Nollans) dedicate a portion of their property, located on the dry sand area of a beach in front of their house, for the public's use. *Nollan* thus calls the right of a body like a planning commission to contract with applicant like the Nollans into question, as if the Nollans had signed an agreement promising to dedicate the easement over their beach and then breached it by suing the promisee. This is what they in fact did. Conditional zoning, whose subject is an allegedly unconstitutional exaction, singles persons like the Nollans out for unduly burdensome conditions on their permit. If the condition were the subject of a conditional zoning agreement, it would flunk the third test previously discussed.[21] The court protects the reasonable expectations of private landowners; because the Nollans had actual notice of the development restrictions at the time they purchased their property, it is the singling the Nollans out for the exaction that is improper. By the same token, a conditional zoning agreement that does that is improper and violates the takings clause.

Negative or restrictive covenants have fared better than affirmative ones as the proper subject for conditional zoning agreements.[22] So landscaping

---

[17] *See Collard v. Incorporated Village of Flower Hill*, 421 N.E.2d 818 (N.Y. 1981). Another view is that the commission's refusal is a denial of a rezoning request that is not subject to judicial review, but this would be a delegation of the rezoning power to the commission, and so contract, not conditional, zoning.

[18] *See Old Canton Hills Homeowners Ass'n v. Mayor and City Council of the City of Jackson*, 749 So. 2d 54 (Miss. 1999) (upholding 23 conditions).

[19] *Id.* at 58–59.

[20] 483 U.S. 825 (1987) (this opinion is the source of the law of development exactions, discussed *infra*, Chapter 14).

[21] The Commission would have been wise to ask for an in-lieu-of payment of money from every permit applicant.

[22] *See Scrutton v. County of Sacramento*, 79 Cal.Rptr. 872 (Cal. App. Ct. 1969) (here the developer was being required to pave a street to which her development had no access).

and design restrictions are more easily approved than obligations to provide public service funds or land. Automatic reversions, effective upon a breach of the agreement and restoring the pre-agreement zoning, have not fared well either.[23] They are viewed as, in effect, a second rezoning, adopted without compliance with procedural and substantive safeguards. However, a "use it or lose it" provision of the rezoning amendment, requiring application for a building permit within one year or else the prior zoning classification is reinstated, has been upheld if limited and reasonable in time.[24] And similarly, when the developer "loses it" by failing to develop within a set time, the homeowners who meanwhile purchase in reliance on now-void plat, can take rights in open space reserved on it.[25] Conditional zoning has thus proceeded, even more than other areas of zoning law, on a case-by-case basis. Good politics gets the nod, but a corrupt deal does not.[26]

[C]　Enabling Act Authority.

Some states have express statutory authority for conditional zoning. California, Hawaii, Nevada, and Florida are examples. Often hearing requirements are imposed before an agreement is executed. Rhode Island[27] has a narrower statute authorizes rezonings for a limited time, and if the development is not built within that time, the rezoning may be revoked. Arizona has a similar statute. Other states, such as Maryland, continue to strike down this type of zoning, no matter how labeled.[28] However, a Maryland statute[29] permits continuing design review of a development after a rezoning, but that state's courts have refused to use the statute to authorize conditional zoning.[30]

§ 12.03　Floating Zones.

A Euclidian use district is a geographic area specified on the zoning map, with boundaries previously determined by the municipal legislature. A floating zone has no such pre-designated boundaries.[31] Rather, it is a use

---

[23] *Id. at 878.*

[24] *See Colwell v. Howard County*, 354 A.2d 210, 213–214 (Md. App. Ct. 1976).

[25] *Hickory Point Partnership v. Anne Arundel County*, 557 A.2d 626 (Md. 1989).

[26] *See* Judith Wegner, *Moving Toward the Bargaining Table: Contract Zoning, Development Agreements, and the Theoretical Foundations of Government Land Use Deals*, 65 N.C. L.Rev. 957, 978–995 (1987) (providing a summary of the law on conditional zoning).

[27] *See Sweetman v. Town of Cumberland*, 364 A.2d 1277 (R.I. 1976) (citing such a statute).

[28] *See Rodriguez v. Prince George's County*, 558 A.2d 742 (Md. App. Ct. 1989) (holding that the exclusion of permitted uses from site plan which forms the basis of rezoning review is an illegal conditional rezoning); *People's Counsel for Baltimore County v. Mockard*, 533 A. 2d 1345, 1346 (Md. App. Ct. 1987) ("This Court continues to reaffirm the invalidity of conditional zoning.").

[29] Md. Code Ann., art. 66B, § 4.01.

[30] *See, e.g., Bd. of Cty. Comm'rs v. H. Manny Holtz, Inc.*, 501 A.2d 489 (Md. App. 1985).

[31] *See, e.g, Treme v. St. Louis Cty.*, 609 S.W.2d 706, 710 (Mo. App. Ct. 1980) (collecting the cases and holding valid a commercial use district floating zone).

district whose permitted uses are spelled out in the ordinance, but is of undetermined size, form, and location. As to its undetermined location, it can be said to float above those Euclidian use districts with which its own permitted uses might potentially be compatible. So it is known as a "floating zone." It rests on a finding that the state enabling act does not mandate the mapping of every land use permitted in an ordinance.[32] Thus may a municipal legislature determine such a zone's general location, but its precise location on the zoning map awaits some landowner's application for a rezoning to a use permitted only in the floating zone. An application is then a request for a precise mapping of the boundaries of the zone.[33]

A floating zone is a useful zoning tool when the need for the presence of a particular land use is hard to predict.[34] Thus, such zones are used to locate quarries, or oil wells; or on a more prosaic level, to locate garden apartments or a bed-and-breakfast in a single-family residential zone.[35]

Sometimes the reviewer of the application to locate the zone is the municipal legislature.[36] Sometimes the reviewer is an administrative agency, the planning commission or the board of zoning appeals.[37] Where an administrative agency hears the application, the floating zone is likely to be treated like a special exception and justified in the same way. The legislature has determined the potential compatibility of the use in the zone with the other uses permitted as of right, and the agency's task is to apply the standards (set out in the floating zone ordinance) which assure that compatibility.[38]

For a legislative mapping, locating the zone on the ground, the standard of review is more relaxed than it is in an administrative setting. The leading case treats the location amendment to the zoning map as a rezoning and tests it accordingly.[39]

Three justifications for floating zones emerge from the case law. First, the courts say, what the legislature is authorized to do by way of a zoning amendment, it may also do by way of a floating zone.[40] This is a both a

---

[32] Pennsylvania early determined that a floating zone required express enabling authority in the statute. *See Eves v. Zoning Board of Adjustment*, 164 A.2d 7 (Pa. 1960). New York and Maryland, decided *contra*.

[33] There is no limit on the number of landowners who may apply; the only precondition is ownership within a use district above which the floating zone hovers.

[34] *See generally* Philip Tierney, *Bold Promises by Basic Steps: Maryland's Growth Policy in the Year 2020*, 23 U. Balt. L. Rev. 461 (1994).

[35] *Rodgers v. Village of Tarrytown*, 96 N.E.2d 731 (N.Y. 1951) (the leading case, where the village's planning board conducted a site plan review before the legislature passed on it, and involving the location of garden apartments in various types of residential use districts, subject to mapping of the floating zone).

[36] *Id.*

[37] *Huff v. Board of Zoning Appeals*, 133 A.2d 83 (Md. 1957) (another leading case, where manufacturing facilities were the subject).

[38] *Rodgers v. Village of Tarrytown*, 96 N.E.2d 731 (N.Y. 1951), *followed in Bellemeade v. Priddle*, 503 S.W.2d 734 (Ky. 1974) *and Sheridan v. Planning Bd.*, 266 A.2d 396 (Conn. 1969).

[39] *Rodgers v. Village of Tarrytown*, 96 N.E.2d 731 (N.Y. 1951) (rejecting the charge that this is spot zoning).

[40] In Maryland, for example, the rezoning rule involving "change or mistake" does not apply to a floating zone determination. *See supra* Chapter 11.

justification and a test of validity. Second, the zone's consistency with the comprehensive plan provides courts with another test of a zone's validity; the floating zone is thus a rezoning in accordance with a pre-conceived plan, not an exercise of unbridled legislative discretion. Third, some courts have treated the floating zone as a large special exception and if the legislature could have provided for the zoned-in uses by way of special exception, the floating zone too is valid and within the enabling act.[41] However justified, once a floating zone is located, the regulations for the use district in which the parcel was formerly located no longer apply.

§ 12.04 Planned Unit Developments.

Another non-Euclidian zoning device involving pre-set standards but allowing negotiations with a developer is a planned unit development (PUD). Like a floating zone, it permits the introduction of flexibility into the rezoning process, particularly when compared to the relatively rigid requirements of Euclidian zoning.[42] A PUD ordinance lifts the lot-by-lot requirements of Euclidian zoning and substitutes instead a site plan review process, under which the overall density of the pre-existing Euclidian zoning remains in place, but the placement of individual improvements may be clustered.[43] A land parcel is developed as a single large unit, rather than on lot-by-lot basis, allowing better urban design than is possible in cookie-cutter subdivisions, allowing regulators a more detailed review, and giving PUD applicants a reciprocal advantage because of the efficiencies of clustering and the greater profits permitted by mixing land uses. PUDs became a much-used method of land development after World War II: in PUD ordinances, zoning and subdivision approvals are merged; both types of approvals are typically given by the planning commission.[44]

Permitted uses within the PUD are usually both greater in number and more diverse than is found in a Euclidian use district.[45] The developments permitted are mixed-use ones, integrating residential and commercial uses. Thus, a commercial PUD ordinance authorizing "multi-use developments" may not be used for a PUD applicant who wants to locate various types of warehouse and retail uses within it.[46] Used for such a project, the land

---

[41] See Carron v. Bd. of Cty. Conn'rs, 976 P.2d 359 (Colo. App. 1998).

[42] See Jan Krasonowieki, Planning Unit Development: A Challenge to Established Theory and Practice of Land Use Control, 114 U. Pa. L. Rev. 47 (1965).

[43] See Peters v. Spearfish ETJ Planning Commission, 567 N.W.2d 880, 885 (S. Dak. 1997).

[44] The planning board or commission is probably the agency best prepared for PUD reviews because its traditional workload includes the review of applications to subdivide land. In some states, the Board of Zoning Adjustment or Appeals may perform this site review. The commission, however, is an administrative body, and where rezonings are an exclusively legislative function, a challenge to the PUD procedure is warranted. See Lutz v.City of Longview, 520 P.2d 1374 (Wash. 1974). But see Cheney v. Village 2 at New Hope, Inc., 241 A.2d 81 (Pa. 1968) (the leading case, deciding that the planning commission is best suited for PUD reviews), discussed infra, this Chapter.

[45] See, e.g., Wooland Manor Assoc. v. Keeney, 713 A.2d 806 (R.I. 1998) (describing a multi-use, phased apartment, condominium, elderly housing, and nursing home, development).

[46] See City of Little Rock v. Pfeifer, 887 S. W. 2d 296, 298 (Ark. 1994) (affirming the trial

abutting the highway could easily resemble strip commercial uses — the very pattern that many PUD ordinances are intended to avoid. However, a mixed group of business, or of various types of residential development, would have sufficient diversity of uses to warrant the use of a PUD.[47]

A PUD applicant need not apply for a variance from Euclidian zoning regulations, as the PUD review process itself is intended to contain both variance and special exception processes and procedures within it.[48] When developer/regulator negotiations precede the approval of a PUD, those negotiations are not evidence of contract zoning.[49]

The use of a PUD procedure depends on private initiative. A municipal legislature may not, *sua sponte*, rezone property into a PUD district. Only a voluntary application by a landowner precipitates the rezoning into a PUD district.[50] Thus a developer seeking a Euclidian rezoning cannot be forced to purchase additional adjacent land to meet a minimum acreage requirement in an ordinance.[51]

General, pre-set standards, set out in the ordinance, define who may apply for PUD review. It is these standards that save a PUD ordinance from the charge that the municipal legislature has improperly delegated its power to rezone to an administrative body such as the planning commission, to review PUD applications. A PUD application is typically only available to land owners holding a minimum contiguous acreage, say, ten or more acres, located in pre-determined use districts.[52] Thus the development will be large enough that adverse, off-site impacts can be limited (as would be the case with a special exception). The increased density of the developed portion of the PUD is considered a fair trade for the preservation of other portions as undeveloped or as a buffer against adverse impacts on other parcels.[53] When this is so, then the density can be greater than that

court's finding PUD ordinance invalidly used when applied to such a development when ordinance authorized PUD use "to encourage orderly, clustered, multi-use development," and the planning board approved a PUD for a store with large showroom, a wholesale warehouse, and a retail area, all on 15 acres along a main highway, and holding that this use of the ordinance was improper because the project did not cluster a mix of land uses and that a store will serve both wholesale and retail markets was an insufficient reason to use a PUD).

[47] *See Frankland v. City of Lake Oswego*, 517 P.2d 1042 (Or. 1973).

[48] *See, e.g., Chandler v. Kroiss*, 190 N.W.2d 472 (Minn. 1972) (making this point).

[49] *Rutland Envir. Protection Ass'n v. Kane Cty.*, 334 N.E.2d 215 (Ill. App. 1975).

[50] *Porpoise Point Partnership v. St. John's County*, 532 So.2d 727 (Fla. App. Ct. 1988) (invalidating a PUD rezoning initiated by a municipality).

[51] *Id.*

[52] The characteristics of a typical PUD have changed over time. The minimum acreage requirement is a good example. Today, more than 30 years after *Cheney*, Pennsylvania does not require either a minimum acreage or a minimum number of dwelling units in its enabling act for PUDs, but the act authorizes a locality to set a minimum number of dwelling units. 53 Pa. Cons. Stat. Ann. § 10705(g) (Purdon 1972). Idaho permits a locality to establish a minimum acreage without prescribing one. Idaho Code § 67-6515 (1980). New Jersey requires a 10 acre minimum. N.J. Stat. Ann. § 40:55D-6 (West 1988). Massachusetts, perhaps looking to PUDs as a good vehicle for urban in-fill, requires 60,000 sq. ft. or five times the underlying district's minimum lot size. Mass. Gen.L. ch. 40A, § 9 (1987).

[53] *Friends of Shawangunks, Inc. v. Knowlton*, 476 N.E.2d 988, 992 (N.Y. 1985).

permitted under pre-existing zoning, so long as the planning commission has power to insure that the development is self-contained.[54] Uses may also be restricted to a percentage of the land area; that is, a maximum of eighty percent may be devoted to residential uses and twenty to commercial uses, etc. Proposed commercial uses may be limited to types that will serve only PUD residents.[55] A maximum number of dwelling units may be permitted within any one structure, and there may have to be a minimum number of feet between structures. A minimum percentage must be devoted to open space. PUD review must available only in certain pre-designated Euclidian use districts[56] — available, but unmapped precisely — requiring that an rezoning application for a map amendment be made.[57] Only one use district need be named.[58] The application maps the PUD, previously a floating zone — planned for, located generally within specific use districts, but unmapped precisely within those districts beforehand. Thus, with the approval of an application, the proposed development will become a permitted use in a way thought out in advance, being thus also "in accord with the comprehensive plan" advanced by the zoning ordinance[59] ; this prevents the development from appearing to be a private deal cut for a particular "aspiring developer."[60]

The foregoing standards are those found in the ordinance validated in *Cheney v. Village 2 at New Hope, Inc.*[61] Decided in 1968, *Cheney* is the first state supreme court case to have validated a PUD ordinance in a jurisdiction without express statutory authority for one in the zoning enabling act.[62] In Pennsylvania, post-*Cheney* legislation required that a PUD comply with the elements of a municipality's comprehensive plan.[63]

[A]   The Standard of Review for PUD Approvals.

The PUD is sometimes likened to a large special exception. It is analogous to a special exception[64] ; it is not the same thing.[65] A PUD is also like a

---

[54] *See, e.g.,* N.Y. Town Law § 281(b) (1987 and Supp. 1989).

[55] *See, e.g.,* N.J. Stat.Ann. § 40:55-57(a) (West 1967) (repealed 1976).

[56] *See City of Waukesha v. Town Bd.*, 543 N.W.2d 515 (Wis. App. 1995) (invalidating a PUD ordinance that did not name the use districts into which a PUD might be located).

[57] *See Town of North Hempstead v. Village of North Hills*, 342 N.E.2d 566 (N.Y. 1975).

[58] *Id.*

[59] *See Amcon Corp. v. City of Eagan*, 348 N.W.2d 66 (Minn. 1984) (remanding matter to planning commission that had refused PUD rezoning when the commission's denial was not in accord with the comprehensive plan, citing the plan as "strong evidence" of arbitrary action).

[60] This term is from *Cheney,* op. cit.

[61] 241 A.2d 81 (Pa. 1968).

[62] *See also Chrinko v. South Brunswick Township Planning Board*, 187 A.2d 221 (N. J. Super. Ct., L. Div., 1963) (also finding authority for a PUD district in an enabling act based on the Standard Zoning Enabling Act).

[63] 53 Pa. Cons. Stat. Ann. § 10702 (Purdon Supp. 1989).

[64] *See, e.g., Hotel Tabard Inn v. District of Columbia Dept. of Consumer & Regulatory Affairs*, 747 A.2d 1168 (D.C. App. 2000); *Cathedral Park Condominium Committee v. District of Columbia Zoning Comm'n*, 743 A.2d 1231 (D.C. App. 2000) (both cases showing how a PUD can be used for in-fill developments in highly urban settings).

floating zone. Like the floating zone for garden apartments in *Rodgers*, it is the legislative response to a felt need, offered in accord with pre-set criteria.

These two analogies make the standard of review difficult to determine. The special exception is the product of an administrative act. The floating zone is the product of a legislative action. Thus a standard of review based on either substantial evidence or a fairly debatable standard, is appropriate. Assuming *arguendo* that PUDs are the product of a hybrid process, mixing both legislative and administrative actions, the standards used for reviewing a floating zone and a special exception not only provide substantive rationales for these ordinances, but also standards for the judicial review of actions taken under them.

When a heightened evidentiary standard is required for a rezoning, as in Maryland, the analogy of the special exception has meant that a rezoning to a PUD district does not have to comply with the heightened standard — in Maryland's case, the substantial change rule [66] — and only substantial evidence need be shown.

Heightened judicial scrutiny may sometimes be warranted on other grounds as well. When the Pennsylvania court validated the ordinance in *Cheney*, it overlooked some of its salient features. The ordinance restricted the development to structures with two bedrooms. This restriction seems "exclusionary" in the sense that it only provided for low-density, upper income zoning. The high costs of the site plan review, as well as some of requirements of PUD ordinances, such as a minimum acreage, indicate that only the best capitalized developers will be able to afford the use of this zoning technique and buttress the conclusion that the ordinance is exclusionary. Thus the better view is that the *Cheney* opinion is a general validation, rather than as an "as applied" review of the PUD. In jurisdictions with exclusionary zoning rules, residential PUD ordinances typically include a low income, or affordable housing component.

The PUD device is a reaction by government against self-executing Euclidian ordinances that leave too many of the details of development in private hands. Rezoning land without seeing the site development plans for it, often seems irresponsible to municipal legislators. PUD ordinances provide developers and the municipality's planning staff and commission with an opportunity to sit down together and discuss the elements of a development, in the hope that better planning should result from such discussions. These discussions, however, are screened from public view, and so subject to a charge of being arbitrary in nature. When this is so, further procedural reforms in the rezoning process may be necessary — either that,

---

[65] *See Todd Mart, Inc. v. Town Board of Town of Webster*, 370 N.Y.S. 2d 683 (N.Y. App. Div. 1975) (involving a large commercial PUD and stating: "The distinguishing factor between special use permits and planned unit developments is the size and significance of the proposed development. Whereas special use permits usually seek approval for a specified single use on a small parcel, such as service stations or swimming pools, the PUD is by its very nature a multi-use proposal for large scale developments . . . .").

[66] *See Beall v. Montgomery County Council*, 212 A.2d 751 (Md. 1965).

or stricter standards of judicial review.[67] The administrative record within the planning commission may make that review easier.

[B] The *Fasano* Rule.

A judicial concern with review of PUD approvals lacking a public record has resulted in stricter standards of judicial review in some jurisdictions. A good example, discussed in the previous Chapter, is *Fasano v. Board of County Commissioners of Washington County*,[68] There the court found that the resolution of a rezoning dispute was a quasi-judicial action (as opposed to a legislative one), and required not only substantial evidence but also procedural safeguards. *Fasano* involved a PUD for a mobile home park, but the type of development involved got lost in the opinion's concern for the general standard of judicial review for rezonings.

[C] Challenges to PUD Ordinances.

PUD enabling acts or ordinances are very occasionally invalidated on constitutional grounds. The usual ground is that the act or ordinance lacks adequately detailed standards for municipalities to enact ordinances or to decide whether to grant or deny applications brought under their aegis.[69] Most ordinances have been upheld when attacked on constitutional grounds. A home rule municipality might in addition argue it needs no enabling statute to enact a PUD ordinance.

Other challenges to PUDs have been made on several statutory or common law grounds. First, that such ordinances violate the uniformity requirement of the SZEA; that is, that the enabling act requires that the use districts enabled by the Act be "uniform" in nature. So long as the PUD technique is available to all landowners, provided the threshold requirements are met, this argument has been rejected by the courts.[70] Second, that the ordinances violate the "in accord with a comprehensive plan" language of the Act. Again, this is not so: they embody a plan, but one with performance standards, rather than more fixed criteria for development. Third, that a PUD might be "spot zoning." However, such a charge takes account only of the fact that it may be mapped at many locations on the zoning map, not of the conditions placed on their mapping. The large acreage requirement also tends to refute this charge. Fourth, that they are tantamount to letting the planning commission rezone property. This charge is harder to dismiss, particularly when the legislature approves a PUD site plan generally, but the commission later substantially changes it.[71]

---

[67] *See, e.g., Kenart & Assoc. v. Skagit Cty.*, 680 P.2d 439 (Wash. App. Ct. 1984) (remanding for findings to guide further review).

[68] 507 P.2d 23 (Or. 1973), discussed *supra*, Chapter 11.

[69] *Tri-State Generation and Transmission Co. v. City of Thornton*, 647 P.2d 670 (Colo. 1982).

[70] *Orrinda Homeowners Committee v. Bd. of Supervisors*, 90 Cal. Rptr. 88 (Cal. App. Ct. 1970).

[71] *See Lutz v. City of Longview*, 520 P.2d 1374, 1376 (Wash. 1974).

This fourth charge has lead to reform in the PUD procedures. Typically today, the site planning process requires that the rezoning application be accompanied by a general schematic plan for the site. The municipal legislature initially approves this, but then, getting down to details, the commission amends it, and then finally the whole plan goes back to the legislature for re-approval. [72] Thus, many ordinances require a general plan approval, followed by site plan review by the planning commission, followed by review of the commission's actions by the legislature. With this sequence of legislative-administrative-legislative action established, any judicial review proceeds only after the legislature has had the last word, and proceeds under the "fairly debatable" standard. [73] By the same token, material changes in the site plan either at the administrative level or in the latter stages of legislative review will require that the general plan be re-approved by the municipal legislature. [74] Such procedures address the concern that the process of rezoning needs to be thoroughly considered, and when it is, the results of the process are unlikely to present opportunities for fraud or the exercise of undue influence wielded by developers when dealing with the public officials.

When a PUD ordinance provides that the municipal legislature "shall give its a final approval" to the site plan after the map amendment is enacted and the administrative review by the planning commission is complete, the local legislature need not approve the plan when, although all the express requirements of the ordinance are met, it finds that the development is worse than would be achieved by Euclidian zoning or does not conform to the public needs or the general welfare. [75] In *Todd Mart*, the legislative-administrative-legislative action sequence requires, the court held, a standard of review for a legislative action: unless the final legislative action is arbitrary and if it is fairly debatable, it will be affirmed on review. Thus proceedings to rezone after the administrative site plan review are legislative in nature. Unless expressly negated, the local legislature has reserved to itself a general welfare or mop-up review of the development plan, even after its approval by the planning commission.

The review process for PUD applications often results in the imposition of easements and covenants applicable to the parcels under review. The enforcement of such less-than-fee interests is often given to owners' non-profit associations established during the course of development, but which the developer initially controls. To avoid disputes about the scope and applicability of such interests, their terms and documents should be clear and

---

[72] *Cf. Bartlett v. Cinemark USA, Inc.*, 908 S.W.2d 229 (Tex. App. Ct. 1995) (finding that municipal legislators who reject a PUD may not have immunity from suit when acting on a final development plan).

[73] *Todd Mart, Inc. v. Town Board of Town of Webster*, 370 N.Y.S. 2d 683 (N.Y. App. Div. 1975). *Cf. Millbrae Association for Residential Survival v. City of Millbrae*, 69 Cal. Rptr. 251 (Cal App. 1968) (invalidating a rezoning when the commission substantially changed the general plan by changing the location of high rise buildings, parking lots, and open space areas in the course of reviewing a developer's site plan).

[74] *Malowski v. City of Naperville*, 617 N.E.2d 1251 (Ill. App. Ct. 1993).

[75] *See Todd Mart Inc. v. Town Board of Town of Webster*, 370 N.Y.S. 2d 683 (N.Y. App. Div. 1975).

express.[76] Likewise, it should be clear who has the right to participate in the later modification of any PUD plan.[77] Otherwise the planning commission may have to decide which owners are affected by the modification, and so have the right to participate. This is an area of law (the law of real covenants) traditionally reserved to the courts, and so beyond the competence of the commission.

[D]   Staged PUDs.

Planned unit developments often involve large enough parcels of land that they are approved in stages. From the developer's standpoint, the staging is useful because it permits him to build to a market which he can foresee at the time of construction.

Many times, restrictions on the use of the land in the PUD are written on the plat. While they do not create real covenants and easements encumbering the title to the land and are not recordable in the land records as such, the enactment of the plat and plan in the ordinance rezoning the land as a PUD is sufficient to put future purchasers on constructive notice of the restriction.[78] Such plat restrictions are in effect implied easements.

A PUD applicant, staging a development in three parts and obtaining separate approvals, may make legal mischief when parcel owners in the earlier stage one wish to assert "residential only" use restrictions, noted on the stage one plat and referenced in their deeds, on residential parcels in stage three. When no such restrictions are noted either on the plat or in the deeds for stage three parcels, perhaps the stage one owners might assert that later owners hold their titles restricted by an implied reciprocal negative easement. But not all jurisdictions recognize such an easement. Another theory might be the developer, in restricting stage one, implicitly promised to restrict later stages in the same way and in fact had no power to create an unrestricted plat in the future. Staged approvals for a PUD require the planning commission to coordinate the restrictions imposed in each stage and, when it does not do so expressly, create legal issues that plague the law of real covenants.

§ 12.05   Transferable Development Rights.

Some zoning ordinances recognize that a parcel's development rights are a severable estate in land — and are alienable as such. Thus all or a part of the development rights (measured by what the zoning ordinance would normally permit) to a parcel are severed from the "sending parcel," much as the mineral or air rights might be, and transferred to the "receiving

---

[76] See Glenbrook Homeowners Association v. Glenbrook Company, 901 P.2d 132 (Nev. 1995) (a dispute over the amount of land to be conveyed to a PUD homeowners' association).

[77] 1330 Conn. Ave. v. District of Columbia Zoning Commission, 669 A.2d 708 (D.C. App. 1995).

[78] South Creek Associates v. Bixby & Associates, Inc., 781 P. 2d 1027 (Colo. 1989) (holding a parking agreement with an adjacent school, noted in the PUD plan, was effective against subsequent purchasers of the PUD).

parcel" where a developer receives the right to use them to create a project of greater density than would otherwise be permitted under the zoning ordinance.

Once the development rights are recognized as severable from a "sending parcel" to which they would otherwise attach, their owners can either be given a right to develop elsewhere at a receiving parcel, or else they can be paid for the right, in which case thereafter the purchaser (a governmental entity) holds their rights to develop until they can be sold to someone with a "receiving parcel" on which they can be used. The later alternative involves holding the rights purchased in a "development bank."[79]

Transferable development rights (TDRs) are most often they are used in conjunction with a land use scheme that has become, due to market forces, highly restrictive. They are meant to offset the burden of preserving a landmark or a land use, such as farming or forestry. They shift the costs of preservation to the public, making such programs appear fairer to owners denied capital gains from converting lands away from the preserved use. They thus both compensate owners for lost development opportunities and provide funds for reinvestment in the preserved use. Once sold, TDRs may not be bought back for use on the sending parcel.

TDRs have been used since the 1960s — for example, in New York City for the preservation of historic landmarks; in Collier County, Florida, for the preservation of wetlands; in Calvert and Montgomery Counties in Maryland, to preserve farmland against urbanization; and in New Jersey to protect the Pinelands.[80] Municipalities in New York, New Jersey, and Pennsylvania have also attempted to preserve farmland this way.

The United States Supreme Court recognized TDRs as a valid planning device in its *Penn Central* opinion.[81] TDR programs are easily within the police power when they deal with the carrying capacity of a parcel or land area and recognize that the reasonable use of a parcel with development potential should reflect that potential. In addition, because they preserve and protect existing, and admittedly beneficial, uses of property, the character of the governmental action in running even a mandatory TDR program is not one that triggers a finding of a taking. Likewise, because of the pre-existing uses of the property, there is unlikely to be any undue economic impact on the owner or an interference with an owner's investment-backed expectations. Thus a regulatory takings claim will not succeed.[82] Moreover, once in place, TDR programs are less susceptible than Euclidian zoning is to shifts in the political climate with regard to land development.

---

[79] *See Matlock v. Bd. of Chosen Freeholders*, 466 A.2d 83 (N. J. 1983) (validating county development bank as purchaser of last resort and prices set for TDRs)

[80] *See Gardner v. New Jersey Pinelands Comm'n*, 593 A.2d 251 (N.J. 1991) (as to the Pinelands program).

[81] *See Penn Central Transportation Company v. City of New York*, 438 U.S. 104 (1978), discussed in Chapter 4, *supra; see also Appeal of Buckingham Developers, Inc.*, 433 A.2d 931 (Pa. Commwlth. Ct. 1981) (noting their use without reaching their merits).

[82] *See Gardner v. New Jersey Pinelands Comm'n*, 593 A.2d 251 (N.J. 1991).

However, a less than fully developed TDR program may result in a taking. An owner of a TDR sending parcel, learning that all receiving parcels are currently developed to the extent permitted by the ordinance, may be offered a very low purchase price for the TDR, one discounted because it cannot be presently used on a receiving parcel. Unless compensation is offered at this point in the program (by a development bank or other device), a taking has occurred. This is so because the "whole parcel" definition of the sending parcel, sanctioned by the United States Supreme Court in *Penn Central*, otherwise results in unfairness "as applied"; that is, when the municipality itself segments the parcel into its existing use and TDR value, the municipality should be estopped from using the "whole parcel" doctrine. It should instead recognize that the segmented property interest in the TDR that it has created. In this instance, the takings claim should be measured by either the amount of the discount or the fair market value of the TDR. On the other side of town, once the purchaser owns both a parcel in the designated, but fully developed, receiving district and a TDR, that purchaser has a right to a variance — and a variance denied should result in a takings claim as well. His is, after all, a problem created by the literal implementation of a governmental program, and so the purchaser would both be a strong position to negotiate with the municipality for a variance. The constitutionality of the TDR program depends on there being active and valuable sending and receiving parcels, otherwise the owner has a takings claim.

Thus the foundation for a TDR program must be laid in the comprehensive plan for a municipality and in a comprehensive set of land use regulations. This is particularly so when TDRs are transferred over long distances, as when they are used to shift development between agricultural and urban areas. A less than comprehensive program will result in (say) fragmented agricultural holdings that cannot sustain farming as a way of life, and the neighbors adjacent to the receiving parcel will see "spot zoning" when the developer applies for his development permissions. A TDR program established in conjunction with a downzoning of either the sending or the receiving parcels will be particularly suspect.

Another foundation stone in a TDR program is the designation of the receiving use districts. They must be designated in advance and contain a number of receiving parcels sufficiently great to accommodate the market for such rights.[83] A TDR program aimed as preserving open space was invalidated because the TDRs could not be used on the sending parcels and yet lacked any receiving parcels.[84]

---

[83] *West Montgomery County Citizens Association v. Maryland-National Capital Park & Planning Commission*, 522 A.2d 1328 (Md. 1987) (failing to designate receiving parcels invalidated a TDR program for farmland).

[84] *Fred F. French Investing Company v. City of New York*, 350 N.E.2d 381 (N.Y. 1976), appeal dismissed 429 U.S. 990 (1976) (". . . it is a tolerable abstraction to consider development rights apart from the solid land from which as a matter of zoning law they derive. But severed, the development rights are a double abstraction until they are actually attached to a receiving parcel, yet to be identified, acquired, and subject to the contingent future approvals of administrative agencies . . . ."), *noted at* 90 Harv. L. Rev. 637 (1977).

[A]   TDR Documents.

A TDR program requires that participants use three basic documents. All should be recorded on the public real property records after they are executed. They are: first, an easement, from the owner of the sending parcel, restricting the development by however many development rights were transferred to the local government or other holder, such as a private land trust; second, a deed transferring the rights to their purchaser — whether that person be a speculator or a developer; and third, a plat map for the development of the receiving parcel, on which map is noted the use of the rights, referring back to the easement and deed. The easements are by their terms perpetual. Thus one advantage of a TDR program is that it relies on the development of a private market to set the prices paid and does not require continuing regulatory supervision.

Chapter 13

Judicial Review of Zoning Actions

§ 13.01 Some Procedural Problems.

[A] Standing.

Generally, standing is a matter of limiting litigation to issues that are justiciable, conducted by capable parties sufficiently interested in the outcome to give them an incentive to do it well.[1]

Standing in land use regulation and zoning matters is always given to landowners of the parcel at issue. Only a minor, adverse consequence is typically required to confer standing on owners.[2] All others have standing when they show special injuries or interests; standing is premised on the principle that the persons who should litigate a dispute are those either injured or about to be injured. A citizen's status as a taxpayer in a municipality is generally insufficient to confer standing.[3] As a restriction on persons entering into litigation, standing seeks to limit litigated issues to those that are justiciable, i.e., based on the constitutional limits on land use regulations. Typically, standing is not merely a matter of constitutional law, but rather is a combination of statutory law, ordinances, and judicial administration.

Adjacent property owners usually have standing to seek judicial review. Adjacency[4] is also usually defined by statute or ordinance as holding property with a certain distance of the parcel affected by the application.[5] Any adjacency is, however, a stand-in for the idea that adjacent owners will likely have a property interest injured by the decision on the application.

Adjacency has in some cases been taken to include owners nearby the property at issue, but not within the boundaries of the municipality acting as the zoning authority, e.g., to parcel owners in a neighboring town or village.

---

[1] See *Citizens for the Protection of the North Kohala Coustline v. Cty. of Hawaii*, 979 P.2d 1120, 1126 (Haw. 1999); *Richards v. Planning & Zoning Comm'n*, 365 A.2d 1130 (Conn. 1976).

[2] See *Sproul v. Town of Boothbay*, 746 A.2d 368, 371–372 (Vt. 2000).

[3] See *Committee for the Responsible Development on 25th Street v. Mayor and City Council of Baltimore*, 767 A.2d 906, 913 (Md. App. Ct. 2001) (finding state law controlling a home rule county ordinance on standing and finding that a taxpayer is not "aggrieved"under state law).

[4] Adjacency is defined for this purpose as abutting, confronting, or nearby.

[5] The American Law Institute's Model Land Development Code, § 9-401(2) (1976), suggests that 500 feet of the applicant's parcel is the right measure.

Sometimes, notwithstanding adjacency, a showing of injury is made a threshold test for standing.[6] The *222 East Chestnut* opinion makes sense in the locale of its decision — downtown Chicago, Illinois.

More typically, participation in administrative proceedings raising issues relevant to the issues before the agency is sufficient to give adjacent owners standing for purposes of judicial review. Sometimes it is said that an adjacent owner has *prima facie* standing if he or she participated in the administrative proceedings giving rise to the review and is adversely affected by the decision therein.[7]

Participation in the hearing can take several forms: filing a letter with the Board, submitting a written petition with the board, even identifying oneself in the record as a party — any action which puts one name into the record of the proceedings.[8] Generally, the issue of standing must be raised at trial, not on appeal for the first time.[9]

When a state imposes, by statute or judicial decision, an obligation to provide affordable housing on a municipality, only those persons of low or moderate income who would benefit from such housing, have standing to contest the methods the jurisdiction uses to meet its obligation.[10] As we shall see, ruling that those who might benefit but are not yet residents of the municipality have standing is more generous a rule than federal courts provide.[11]

[B] "Aggrieved Party" Status.

Standing is typically a matter controlled by statute or ordinance: a party given a right to appeal a zoning regulation decision must show that he or she is "a person aggrieved by" the decision of the administrator or BZA. This is the language of Section 7 of the Standard State Zoning Enabling Act. The courts have generally found that this statute requires two things: (1) that the party appealing have a legal interest in adjacent property and

---

[6] *222 East Chestnut St. Corp. v. Bd. of Appeals*, 152 N.E.2d 465 (Ill. 1956) (showing that parking lots usually affect the fair market value of neighboring residential use does not relieve that neighbor of the burden of making an affirmative showing of injury to his parcel).

[7] *Bryniarski v. Montgomery County Bd. of Appeals*, 230 A.2d 289, 292–293 (Md. 1967); *but see Boulden v. Mayor and Comm'nrs of the Town of Elkton*, 535 A.2d 477 (Md. 1988) (when an ordinance granted a right of appeal to a "taxpayer," *Bryniarski* is distinguishable); *see generally Dyer v. Zoning Bd. of Appeals of Arlington Heights*, 534 N. E.2d 506 (Ill. App. Ct. 1989) (holding that adjoining landowners who participates in variance proceeding, lacked standing when failing to prove special injury).

[8] *Cf. Morris v. Howard Research and Development Corp.*, 365 A.2d 34 (Md. 1976) (involving a statute requiring that any party to the administrative proceeding be given notice of a judicial appeal).

[9] *Baker v. Montgomery County Council*, 215 A.2d 831 (Md. 1966).

[10] *Alexander's Dept. Stores of New Jersey v. Borough of Paramus*, 578 A.2d 1241, 1245 (N.J. Super.Ct., App. Div., 1990); *see generally* J.D. Ayer, *The Primitive Law of Standing in Land Use Disputes: Some Notes from a Dark Continent*, 55 Iowa L.Rev. 344 (1967).

[11] *See infra* this Chapter.

(2) that he or she show special damages, as opposed to an injury suffered by the public at large. [12]

The first prong of this requirement makes standing an issue for a purchaser under an executory contract of sale, a lessee, or the holder of an option to purchase. [13]

Although the cases may split on specific results, there is a tendency to extend standing to all the classes of persons listed previously. As to the contract purchaser, courts look at the contingencies in the contract; as to the lessee, courts look at the length of the term, the protections which a lessee has against termination, and whether the lease is oral or written; likewise, the courts look for a contract right of the optionee to participate in or appeal the decision. In each case, the security of the holder's interest in the affected property is the subject of the inquiry.

The second prong of this requirement is taken to mean that there must be an affirmative showing of damage, not just judicial notice taken of the probability of damage. [14] The showing of special damages is not made with a showing of increased competition for a person's adjacent business. Nor is it made when the complaint is on the basis of considerations addressed in the zoning ordinance itself. [15] However, the presence of noise, odor, and traffic problems, as well as diminished value, have been found to be the basis of a claim of special damages.

Although the status of an adjacent competitor with the prospective business seeking a rezoning is insufficient to confer standing in a rezoning decision, [16] neither does competitive status *per se* bar standing. The potential competitor might show increased traffic flow, or new demands on public facilities in the area. Such a showing is not of an economic interest, but is well within the ambit of the type of land use conflicts which can properly be presented to a board or legislature.

Participation in the disputed matter is a pre-condition to gaining standing. An expression of concern about a pending variance application to a member of the local zoning appeals board is insufficient to confer standing, even when the member of the board in response states that he will relay his concerns to the board. This is so even when the member does in fact relay such concerns, which thus appear as a part of the record. A municipal ordinance typically requires that in order to appeal, the appellant "shall

---

[12] The two prongs of this test are intended to make plain that the doctrine of standing is not a surrogate for a test of the merits or the legal theory of the plaintiff's or petitioner's case;, even though judges may be tempted to deny standing to a petitioner with a weak case, they are in error when doing so. That case can be tested, in a procedurally distinct manner, as early as a demurrer can be filed. *See Miller v. Fulton County*, 375 S.E. 2d 864, 884 (Ga. 1989).

[13] *See generally* Note, *The "Aggrieved Person" Requirement in Zoning*, 8 Wm.& Mary L. Rev. 294 (1967).

[14] *See 222 East Chestnut Street Corporation*, 152 N.E.2d at 467.

[15] *Columbus, Georgia, v. Diaz-Verson*, 373 S.E.2d 208, 210 (Ga. 1988) (addressing protection of residents on a flood plain from flooding).

[16] *See Hendel's Investors Co. v. Zoning Bd. of Appeals of the Town of Montville*, 771 A.2d 182, 188–189 (Conn. App. Ct. 2001) (involving competing gas station owners).

have participated in the proceeding." Attending the hearing is necessary to establish the necessary participation when the board grants the application. The municipality's later objection that the person expressing concern has no standing to appeal is well taken. A person seeking judicial review of an adverse zoning decision "shall have been a participant in the proceeding" before the administrative board.[17] Whatever interest is found sufficient for standing, it must be maintained throughout the appeal.[18]

Land use regulation and zoning matters often arise when the title to property is changing hands and the new owner wishes to change the use of the property. Typically, both the old and the new owners (i.e., both vendors and purchasers) have standing once a contract of sale is executed. Even a sale-leaseback, taking place while a rezoning is pending, will not change this; both the applicant and the purchaser will still have standing, the purchaser as the title holder and/or mortgagor, and the applicant as a lessee (if the lease is more than a tenancy at will). That the lease is on terms making the landlord's termination rights non-automatic, and that the lessee has guaranteed the rents, makes a lessee's standing all the stronger.[19]

[C]   Standing in Neighborhood Citizens' Associations.

Neighborhood and civic groups generally have standing, although the recent cases on the issue are split. They are the municipal equivalent of the Sierra Club or the Audubon Society, given standing in federal court on questions of environmental concern when their members are injured. Thus, pleading prudence dictates that one of the members satisfy the test for adjacency, legal interest, or injury or aggrievement and thus be the nominal plaintiff.[20] Granting standing might, however, depend on whether a variance, special exception or rezoning is at issue. The capacity of the association to take a adversary role, the extent that it can represent the whole interest of the neighborhood, and its ability to spread attorneys' fees, are some of the considerations that courts use to weigh their standing. By the same token, all the owners of land affected by an ordinance affecting a limited amount of a municipality's acreage, have been given standing to contest it.[21]

Standing has also been given to native peoples through their tribal organizations. Standing here involves the interests of native peoples and

---

[17] See *Jaeger v. Sheehy*, 551 A.2d 841, 842 (Me. 1988) (holding that, because the citizen did not appear at the hearing in person or through counsel, she lacks standing to prosecute an appeal).

[18] *Primerica v. Planning and Zoning Commission of Town of Greenwich*, 558 A.2d 646, 650–651 (Conn. 1989).

[19] *Primerica*, 558 A.2d at 650.

[20] Annot., *Standing of civic or property owners' association to challenge zoning board decision (as aggrieved party)*, 8 A.L.R. 4th 1087 (1981).

[21] See *Lewis v. Planning and Zoning Comm'n of the Town of Ridgefield*, 771 A.2d 167, 172–174 (Conn. App. Ct. 2001) (involving an increase in minimum acreage requirements for new subdivision lots and stressing that "a very limited amount of property" in the municipality was affected).

is based on their customary and cultural rights to hunt and fish, aggrievement of those rights being shown in the use of the land affected by an application. Participation in the hearing, by itself, typically gives the natives a right to appeal the granting of the application. [22]

Standing rules in state exclusionary zoning cases are more lenient in state, as opposed to federal courts. [23] This leniency has more to do with the familiarity of state courts with the problems of establishing standing in such cases and with the fact that the cases themselves are intended to establish residency within a jurisdiction, so it is antithetical to the very nature of the cause of action to enforce standing rules in the traditional way.

[D]   A BZA's Standing to Appeal.

Once a board is reversed by a trial court in an appeal taken by a citizens' association from its grant of a variance, the board itself may wish to appeal the trial court's decision. When it has been given notice of appeal to the trial court, and has had to certify the record to the reviewing court, perhaps a right to appeal and appear itself can be implied. The cases, however, are split on this issue. [24] The better view is that the board may represent interests greater than those of the parties to the application, and, because municipal governments are granted standing to appeal board decisions with which some other branch of its government disagrees, the right of the board to defend itself on appeal has been recognized, and granting it standing has become the general rule. Likewise, the municipal legislature might obtain standing once concluding that an appeal involves a matter of legislative policy and the board overstepped its authority. [25]

[E]   Standing in Federal Civil Rights/Zoning Litigation.

The issue of standing in federal court depends on whether there is a case or controversy in the constitutional sense. In the 1970s, civil rights attorneys hoped that federal courts would review the exclusionary effects of municipal zoning on patterns of housing segregation along racial lines. It was not to be.

---

[22] *See Public Access Shoreline Hawaii v. Hawaii County Planning Comm'n*, 903 P.2d 1246 (Haw. 1995) (considering standing for native Hawaiians in a hearing on an application for a special exception for a hotel on a lake front long used by natives to hunt and fish while denying standing to a civic, non-profit ecology group).

[23] *See infra* this Chapter.

[24] *See Simko v. Zoning Bd. of Appeals of the Town of Fairfield*, 538 A.2d 202, 205 (Conn. 1988) (where the enabling statute required that the BZA be given notice of an appeal from its order, but said nothing more); Annot., *Standing of zoning board of appeals or similar body to appeal reversal of its decision*, 13 A.L.R. 4th 1130 (1982) (indicating a split of authority). *See also Valley & Siletz R.R. v. Laudahl*, 681 P.2d 109, 110 (Or. 1984) (reviewing this split).

[25] Countervailing considerations are that allowing the board standing to appeal casts doubt on the impartiality of the application process, and just as judges do not appeal their own decisions, so in a variance proceeding or quasi-judicial proceedings for a rezoning — often pitting neighbor against neighbor — granting standing may be unseemly.

[1] Round One.

In *Warth v. Seldin*,[26] the United States Supreme Court dashed such hopes with standing rules which in practical effect precluded such a review. Not that it slammed the doors to federal court; rather, it refused to widen them. In *Warth*, the plaintiffs were residents in the Rochester, N.Y., metropolitan area, home builders, and representatives of fair housing organizations. They sued a suburban town (Penfield) in the same area. None of the individual plaintiffs were themselves residents of Penfield, nor did they own any legal or equitable interest in property there. They did attempt to show that the efforts of a third party to build low income housing, which efforts proved (they alleged) impossible under the town's current zoning ordinance; 98% of Penfield's land was zoned for single family detached housing.

Not enough, said the United State Supreme Court. The individual plaintiffs' inability to find housing in the town was not caused by the zoning, nor did they show that they could have afforded to live in projects rejected by the town's officials. Neither did the taxpayers of the central city have standing to challenge the Town's zoning. Moreover, the claims of the builders was not couched in terms of the rejection of a specific project. All this meant that if the court were to accept the standing of the plaintiffs, it would be unable to frame appropriate relief.

Thus in federal court there must be a claim that the plaintiff would benefit in some specific way from the judicial relief requested. The facts must concern a specific project. *Warth* gives new meaning to the "injury in fact" test for standing. Its requirements for standing in federal court is the equivalent of the federal courts' declining to take up municipal zoning as a law reform project.

While this case may have been intended to have a chilling effect on federal court review of zoning decisions, there are still several categories of plaintiffs who would indeed have standing after *Warth*. Persons who own parcels in town, a housing authority, a potential purchaser prevented from closing, and residents of the town — any of whom are denied development approvals — would still have standing.

[2] Round Two.

In *Village of Arlington Heights v. Metropolitan Hous. Dev. Corp.*,[27] the United States Supreme Court again considered the standing question. *Arlington Heights* was a suit brought on both constitutional and statutory grounds. As to standing, it clarifies *Warth*. The case presented one plaintiff who worked in a village, this time a suburb of Chicago. However, that individual plaintiff lived in Evanston, some twenty miles away, commuting to work in Arlington Heights. Moreover, he testified that he would move into the plaintiff's non-profit, subsidized housing development should it be built.

---

[26] 422 U.S. 490 (1975).

[27] 429 U.S. 252 (1977),

Arlington Heights was a suburb that had less than one thousand minority residents, out of a population over 70,000. Here, unlike *Warth*, a specific project on a specific site was rejected by the village zoning officials, after the corporate developer had expended several thousand dollars for planning and market studies for its project. The petitioner held a 99 year lease (granted perhaps for purposes of establishing standing) and a agreement to buy a fifteen acre site within the village. The legal title to the site — and that of a larger, surrounding parcel — was held by a religious order, which had given the plaintiff developer a bargain basement price for the fifteen acres so that it could qualify for federal housing subsidies.

The court held that the petitioner's expenditure of planning funds was sufficient to satisfy the injury in fact test for standing in *Warth*. (In *Arlington Heights*, the Supreme Court went on to provide a test for evaluating the village's zoning which held that exclusionary effect alone was not the standard against which the ordinance was to be tested; rather that effect was only one factor among six to be used to determine the intent or purpose of the ordinance. The six factors, however, had more to do with a showing of intent than the impact of the ordinance — the latter being only one of the six factors.)

Moreover, on the standing question, *Warth* and *Arlington Heights* seem to be marching in different directions. Why is that? The former seems to shut the door to the federal courthouse, but the latter leaves it ajar for the egregiously injured plaintiff.

§ 13.02   Exhaustion of Remedies.

Plaintiffs may not sue to challenge the validity of an administrative decision until the agency has made a final decision. Nor may they sue to challenge an ordinance or regulation until they have exhausted their administrative remedies, unless (1) the attack is on the general or facial validity of the ordinance, (2) seeking the remedy would be futile, or (3) the remedy is inadequate.[28] The inadequacy of the remedy might be shown by the protracted or onerous nature of the remedy, or its expense. The futility might be shown by repeated and unsuccessful applications.[29]

This doctrine represents deference to the expertise of administrative agencies to gather information pertinent to their decisions as well as to the legislative judgment that the decision is best made by the agency. Even if the decisions required of the agency are one traditionally thought of as judicial, the agency can marshall and sift through the evidence before a court hears the case. Conversely, pursuit of an administrative remedy is no waiver of the right to attack an ordinance generally — otherwise the doctrine of exhaustion would be a Catch-22.

Three exceptions to the exhaustion requirement are typically recognized. First, when the constitutional invalidity of a statute or ordinance is put

---

[28] *Poe v. City of Baltimore*, 216 A.2d 707 (Md. 1966).

[29] *Karches v. City of Cincinnati*, 526 N.E.2d 1350, 1355–1356 (Ohio 1988).

in question by a facial challenge (as opposed to an "as applied" one), some courts have found that there is no need to exhaust administrative remedies beforehand. One rationale for this is that an agency cannot adequately weigh questions about its own authority, particularly when its very jurisdiction is questioned. This is an argument premised on agency bias. Second, a person will not be forced to use an administrative remedy, when to do so would be futile — when the result is known in advance. Third and finally, when the remedy that the agency has authority to give is inadequate, the plaintiff need not seek it, but may instead seek a judicial remedy.

The doctrine in many states is codified as a provision of the Uniform Declaratory Judgment Act, which requires that when a statute dictates a particular form of administrative remedy, that this remedy must be pursued before an action under the Act is brought.

The United States Supreme Court turned aside several takings cases in the early 1980s on grounds that appear to be related to the doctrine. In addition, the imposition of a procedure for issuance of permits to fill or dredge wetlands by the Army Corp of Engineers, makes a taking claim premature. [30]

More recent holdings of the Supreme Court may affect this doctrine in the future. For example, the *Keystone* holding [31] may mean that the doctrine will be more rigorously enforced against developers. A further example lies in the holding of *First English*. [32] It may mean that as municipalities risk interim damages when an ordinance is found to be a temporary taking, this increased risk may give municipalities a right either to seek earlier review on the validity of an ordinance, or in states where it is possible, to receive an advisory opinion.

§ 13.03   Ripeness.

A issue arising in an administrative agency must be ripe for judicial review. Ripeness is intended to avoid premature adjudication or review of administrative action. Until the agency has made a final decision and its economic impact is felt in a concrete way, courts are presented with abstract or hypothetical issues. They wish to avoid that situation. They do not wish to decide what that impact is until the full extent of the ordinance or regulation has been fixed and the amount of damage caused by it is measurable. Ripeness is thus a doctrine seeking to protect a court from having to decide an issue with less than a fully developed record. For example, when a developer proposes that a municipal legislature adopt and enact an amendment to the municipality's comprehensive plan permitting the project, any judicial challenge by opponents to this amendment, once it is enacted, is subject to a defense on the grounds of ripeness. There has as yet been no application to rezone on the basis of the amendment, and only

---

[30] *United States v. Riverside Bayview Homes, Inc.*, 474 U. S. 121, 127 (1985) ("the very existence of a permit system implies that permission may be granted").

[31] *See* Chapter 3, *supra.*

[32] *See* Chapter 5, *supra.*

if the amendment was proposed and adopted in furtherance of a pending application would this challenge be ripe.[33]

A further example of the application of a ripeness defense would be encountered when early purchasers of lots in a subdivision bring a declaratory judgment action ripe for decision when a developer loses his subdivision permit mid-project by not proceeding with a development within a period of time during which his permit must be used — by a so-called "use it or loose it" provision. The developer must first resubmit plans for a plat approval. However, a developer's loss of platting status did not operate to extinguish the existing homeowners' rights in the open spaces described on the plat on file when they purchased.[34] The early lot purchasers would still have standing before the planning commission to contest the subdivision plat plan as proposed by the subdivider and that is the forum in which their remedy lies.

Ripeness is thus generally related to a court's ability to distinguish and define the claim before it and in that sense, it goes to the court's subject matter jurisdiction. This is an issue that a court may consider *sua sponte*.[35]

[A] United States Supreme Court Opinions on Ripeness.

In the early 1980s, the United States Supreme Court granted the writ of certiorari in several cases which, it apparently thought at the time of the vote on the writ, would resolve the issue of whether or not damages were an available remedy for a regulatory taking. In each, up to the time the *First English* opinion was issued in 1987, the court found that the case was not ripe for review. Little was learned in these 1981-1987 opinions about the remedy of damages, but much was learned about the issues of ripeness and exhaustion.

First, in *Agins v. City of Tiburon*,[36] Justice Powell held for a unanimous court that because the appellants "have not submitted a plan for development of their property as the ordinances permit, there is as yet no concrete controversy regarding the application of the specific [down]zoning provisions." The court dismissed an as-applied challenge to the provisions and proceeded to uphold the ordinance on the remaining facial challenge. Thus the threshold test of ripeness is the submission of a development plan by the applicant.[37]

In *Williamson County Planning Commission v. Hamilton Bank*,[38] the petitioner had passed the *Agins* threshold. It had submitted a "plan for

---

[33] *Boyds Civic Ass'n v. Montgomery County Council*, 526 A.2d 598, 601 (Md. 1987).

[34] *See Hickory Point Partnership v. Anne Arundel County*, 557 A.2d 626, 631 (Md. 1989) (suggesting that the point at which the subdivider acquires a vested right to proceed is the point at which a declaratory judgment will lie).

[35] *Villas of Lake Jackson, Ltd. v. Leon County*, 906 F. Supp. 1509 (N. D. Fla. 1995).

[36] 447 U.S. 255, 260 (1980).

[37] In *Christiansen v. Yolo County*, 995 F. 2d 161, 164 (9th Cir. 1993), the circuit court held that the development plan element requires "at least one 'meaningful application'" and that the variance element encompasses the applicant's seeking "compensation through the procedures the state has provided for doing so."

[38] 473 U.S. 172 (1985).

development." Nonetheless, the Supreme Court held that a taking claim was not ripe for judicial review because there had been no "final decision" on the plan. No such decision is present until the county agencies authorized to administer the development regulations had not only reached a final decision on the plan, but also on any variance available to the applicant. In this case, the developer had also not shown that he had sought a remedy available under a state inverse condemnation statute — and the court required that this remedy be sought and refused as well. The court also held that a due process violation was also premature because whether the regulation has proceeded "too far" (Holmes' words in *Mahon*) cannot be determined until the impact of the regulations on the plaintiff is known and that impact also cannot be measured until there is a final decision on variances and other available remedies.[39]

In the wake of *Hamilton Bank*, many zoning agencies have instituted administrative appeals in order to forestall takings and inverse condemnation claims, to encourage judicial economy, and to save the municipality's attorney time and public money. So a likely response to *Hamilton Bank* is for a board to enact procedural regulations that state that "no appeal from any order or decision of the board shall be taken unless the applicant has first made an application for a rehearing." If at the re-hearing, there are new issues considered, and new grounds are used for a further decision, then there must a rehearing on the rehearing.[40] On the other hand, if the board in its rehearing decision were to invoke new law from the state highest court, a second rehearing would not be required; the new case law raises a matter with which a court is better equipped to deal than is the board — and the applicant's appeal should proceed.

[B] Premature Takings Claims.

With regard to a takings claim, the claim remains premature until the impact of the ordinance is known.[41] After *Hamilton Bank* then, the court seems to be requiring the developer do three things:

(1)   prepare and submit a development plan,

(2)   obtain a final decision on the plan, and

(3)   seek and be refused any available variances or other remedies mitigating the impact of the alleged taking,

before seeking federal court review.[42]

---

[39] In contrast, in *United States v. Riverside Bayview Homes Inc.*, 106 Sup. Ct. 455 (1985), a wetlands case, the Supreme Court said that as to a wetlands fill permit, the availability of a judicial action for inverse condemnation after a denial of a permit, is sufficient to deny an injunction (issued on the grounds of a taking) against the wetlands administrator.

[40] *See Dziama v. City of Portsmouth*, 669 A.2d 217, 219 (N.H. 1995) (requiring a second application for a rehearing on new issues).

[41] *See Smithfield Concerned Citizens v. Town of Smithfield*, 907 F.2d 239 (1st Cir. 1990).

[42] One pleading tactic for owners seeking is to bring a facial challenge to the ordinance, claiming it invalid upon enactment, alleging arbitrary and capricious action in enacting it, challenging its terms before they are applied to any particular development, and invoking the

A year later, the court found another applicant's takings claim not ripe.[43] This case further defined a "final decision" as a "final and authoritative of the type and intensity of development legally permitted on the subject property." It also noted that "valuable use" might still be made of the land from continuing its prior, agricultural use (the trial court's conclusion) and that "valuable residential development was open" to it (a state appellate court conclusion).[44] Thus revision of the development plan, after the refusal of all variances, seems to be yet a fourth requirement of a showing of ripeness. At the same time, however, the court said that the final decision requirement does not force an owner to "pursue a development application through piecemeal litigation or unfair procedures."[45] Indeed, the *Penn Central* opinion found a regulatory takings claim ripe after the submission and rejection of two development applications.[46] A compensation claim takes longer, and the rejection of five applications was sufficient predicate for getting a compensation claim to a jury in *City of Monterey v. Del Monte Dunes at Monterey*.[47]

A year later, the court found that one application and rejection might ripen a takings compensation claim. It held that when an owner must deal (as with development of wetlands) with many agencies at the federal, state, and municipal level,[48] when one agency at any level, indicates that no development may take place, that decision may be treated as final, ripening the owner's takings claim.[49] In *Palazzolo*, not being able to fill the wetland was regarded as tantamount to being told no to placing houses on it; thus the owner did not have to further ripen his claim by applying for subdivision and building permissions. "Where the state agency charged with enforcing a challenged land use regulation entertains an application from an owner and its denial of the application makes clear the extent of the development permitted, and neither the agency nor a reviewing state court has cited non-compliance with reasonable state law exhaustion and pre-permit processes . . ., federal ripeness rules do not require the submission and further and futile applications with other agencies."[50] The court further held that, for

---

idea that the injury was done to the plaintiff at the time of enactment — and thereafter the claim of a substantive due process violation is ripe. The disadvantage here is that the Supreme Court imposes a heavy burden of proof for such challenges — as opposed to "as applied" challenges. See *Keystone Bituminous Coal Ass'n v. DeBenedictus,* 480 U.S. 470 (1987), discussed in Chapter 3, supra. So a facial challenge is unlikely to succeed, given the presumption of validity and the "fairly debatable" standard used to review such claims.

[43] See *Macdonald, Sommer & Frates v. Yolo County,* 477 U.S. 340, 348 (1986).

[44] *Id.* at 351–352, n. 8.

[45] *Id.* at 350, n.7.

[46] See *Penn Central Transp. Co. v. City of New York,* 438 U.S. 104, 116 & n.17 (1978).

[47] 526 U.S. 687, 702 (1999).

[48] See, e.g., *De St. Aubin v. Flacke,* 505 N.Y.S.2d 859, 864 (N.Y. 1986) (involving wetlands permits and indicating that *Hamilton Bank* should not be extended so far); *but see Joint Ventures, Inc. v. Dept. of Transp.,* 519 So.2d 1069, 1071 (1st Dist. 1988) (suggesting that an inverse condemnation action by a landowner is necessary before due process is denied by a regulatory taking).

[49] See *Palazzolo v. Rhode Island,* 533 U.S. 606 (2001).

[50] *Id.* (also holding, on the merits of the takings claim made, that "post-enactment purchasers" could ripen a takings claim).

purposes of asserting a takings claim, purchasing owners acquired everything that their predecessors in interest had, including their takings claim.[51]

Decisions about the meaning of "futility" become important here. Futility means being forced to pursue piece-meal, procedurally unfair, time-consuming (involving excessive administrative delays, to the point that the parcel loses its value), or pointless (when the agency has no authority to grant the permission) development applications. There is some warrant in the prevailing case law for each of these four meanings.

[C] Open Questions.

The reach of the holdings in *Hamilton Bank*, *Yolo County*, and *Palazzolo* is unclear in two respects. First, as to the types of "reasonable state law" actions which an owner may be put to. For instance, in addition to bringing an inverse condemnation action, or seeking a variance, a developer may have to seek a conditional rezoning, striking a deal to mitigate his takings claim. Before the deal is struck, a municipality might regard the claim as premature.[52] Second, invalidation of the regulation would convert a permanent takings claim into a temporary takings claim after *First English's* recognition that interim damages for a temporary regulatory taking are available; after an invalidation by a municipality, whether an owner could respond in turn with a § 1983 suit, is an open question.

§ 13.04   Section 1983 Federal Due Process Actions.

Hamilton Bank recognized that the state had provided procedures by which the invalidity of a zoning or subdivision ordinance can be tested, through a declaratory judgment action.[53] No analogous action was available in *Palazzolo*, but this may yet be a limiting factor for the holdings in these cases.[54] In light of this, and with regard to federal due process claims, the federal analog to the state procedures recognized in *Hamilton Bank* is a federal cause of action based on 42 U.S.C. § 1983. This section permits

---

[51] State courts had been split on this issue. See Stephen Abraham, *Windfall or Windmills: the Right of a Property Owner to Challenge Land Use Regulations (A Call to Critically Examine the Meaning of Lucas)*, 13 J. Land Use & Envtl. L. 161, 165 (1997) (collecting the cases).

[52] *Electro-Tech, Inc. v. H. F. Campbell, Inc.*, 445 N.W.2d 61 (Mich. 1989), *cert. denied*, 493 U.S. 1021 (1990).

[53] *Hamilton Bank* has been applied to federal actions too. *See Preseault v. I.C.C.*, 494 U.S. 1 (1990) (holding that because the federal tort claims act provides holders of real property interests with a remedy for obtaining just compensation, a taking claim against an I.C.C. order was premature when asserted before the holder exhausts the act's remedy).

[54] Before such a claim is brought, the claim is unripe; after it is brought, and lost, then res judicata and collateral estoppel will bar further actions; if won, further actions may be pointless, except to the degree that tort claims would provide significantly more than a takings claim. *See also City of Monterey v. Del Monte Dunes at Monterey*, 526 U.S. 687 (1999) (holding that a jury trial is available in § 1983 claim cases) — which may make federal claims more desirable because takings and inverse condemnation claims in state courts are generally held to raise matters of law not going to a jury.

review of any state and municipal action, taken under "color of law," that deprived the plaintiff of some federal constitutional right. In the land use area, typically that right is a Due Process Clause right to be free of arbitrary governmental action; it involves a legitimate right or claim of entitlement to a governmental benefit, typically a permit of some type. Litigation under this statute is not required to ripen a takings claims; it involves the claim of arbitrary action taken under authority of municipal regulations, really a misapplication of a regulation, that violated a plaintiff's substantive due process rights, depriving him of a land use to which he was entitled. Thus § 1983 actions are best regarded as "as applied" challenges.

In these federal court actions, as a foundational or threshold issue, some federal circuits focus on the right at issue, while others focus on the governmental action at issue.[55] In the first category, federal courts require a plaintiff to have a "property right to a permit." These courts define that right so that it is present only when the discretion of the municipality is so limited that, absent arbitrariness, the issuance of the permit at issue is certain.[56] Ownership of property alone is an insufficient right and no unilateral expectation that a permit will issue is sufficient either,[57] even if state law seems to indicate issuance is likely: it is federal common law that is used here.

In the second category of cases, other federal circuits not only require that a right to the permit be involved, but also require, and generally focus on, municipal actions that "shock the conscience of the court."[58] Here the action restrained must be truly irrational, irrational to a point beyond which an administrative agency would be restrained. Merely a violation of state or local law does not qualify.

Both of these two categories of cases represent rules of judicial prudence, insuring that federal courts do not become a super zoning board, providing only an extra layer of review for land use regulatory decisions.

Creating yet a third category, another federal circuit has provided § 1983 review when political motivation or a personal financial motive of a municipal decision-maker had been shown.[59] This focus on the governmental decision downplays the role of the plaintiff's right to the permit, but only one federal circuit has used it.

No matter what category of test is involved, all these approaches are intended to restrict access to federal court in land use cases so that

---

[55] *See* Eric Jenkins, *Challenging Land Use Actions under Section 1983: Washington After Mission Springs, Inc. v. City of Spokane*, 74 Wash. L. Rev. 853 (1999) (reviewing contrasting federal cases and Washington state cases on this issue).

[56] *See Yale Auto Parts v. Johnson*, 758 F.2d 54, 59 (2nd Cir. 1985).

[57] *See, e.g., Gardner v. Baltimore Mayor & City Council*, 969 F.2d 63 (4th Cir. 1992) (the 4th Circuit joining 2d, 10th, and 11th Circuit cases so holding).

[58] *See Creative Environments, Inc. v. Estabrook*, 680 F.2d 822, 833 (1st Cir. 1982).

[59] *See DeBlasio v. Zoning Bd. of Adjustment*, 53 F.3d 592, 601 (3rd Cir. 1995). *But see Breneric Associates v. City of Del Mar*, 81 Cal. Rptr.2d 324, 334–335 (Cal. App. Ct. 1998) (criticizing *Blasio*).

constitutional challenges are not available on an indiscriminate basis to those denied land use permits in state courts.

Chapter 14

Subdivision Regulations, Impact Fees, Linkage Fees, and Exactions

Seeking to subdivide land is in effect an application for an administrative action having lasting consequences for the land affected. The forum for such an application is usually the municipal planning commission. In such an agency, the impact of the city and regional planning process is greater than it would be in the other forums discussed previously. The objective of the subdivision process is to fit the parcels of land created into a larger urban form. So, first, a word about urban design.

§ 14.01 Urban Forms.

The American pattern of urbanization is a unique one. Our townscapes — whether a New England village, a mining town, a company town, or a utopian community — have often been a "product." It consists first of a core, the oldest part of the city or town, often with a street pattern heavily influenced by the topography of the site. The core may have been the confluence of several roads or paths, with a spine street centering the neighborhood. In New England the core was a central square known as the green or common. It may also have been the location where two forms of transportation met, as with a town on the fall line of a river, requiring that cargo be unloaded from ships there for overland shipment. The urban pattern emerging around this core was often of rectangular, equally-sized blocks, laid out in a grid, with lots in each block further "subdividing" the landscape.

Most of the colonies of European countries in North America started as planned townscapes, but most had lost their overall planned qualities by the middle of the nineteenth century when a street grid was all that municipalities could do to control the pace of urban development. Starting in the 1890s, however, during the City Beautiful movement, boulevards were superimposed on the grid. In the 1920s and 1930s, as off-shoots of this movement, subdivisions began it be laid out in a curvilinear pattern — having winding streets on very large blocks. Such subdivisions signaled the creation of ever larger, often self-contained, developments, with a shopping center attached or nearby. Whole new towns were built in the 1960s and 1970s, and city planners extensively used cul-de-sacs here to minimize drive-by traffic and promote privacy. They also used clustered land uses permitted by municipal zoning so that large tracts would have open spaces amid the development.

Whether city or suburban, land uses in subdivisions were first governed by private agreements among the lot owners. Usually such agreements were a series of covenants and easements. Only in the late 1920s would public land-use controls, including subdivision regulations, become widely accepted by municipal governments.

§ 14.02   The Subdivision Process.

Subdivision is the process of dividing a tract of land into a number of parcels. When the number of parcels is of a given number (varying from two to five usually), the subdivider must comply with the requirements of the local subdivision control regulations. The subdivider is often a developer as well, but sometimes is not; sometimes he is a person specializing in this aspect of the land development process.[1]

Authority for regulating the subdivision process is found in state codes, modeled often on the Standard City Planning Enabling Act, § 13–14. Statutory authority is often the first issue in assessing the validity of any particular requirement imposed in the course of the process. Typically the planning commission or board is the municipal agency charged with administering the process. As a precondition to exercising this regulatory authority, the commission formulates at least a street plan for the municipality.

Subdivision of land is different from either a boundary line adjustment, a partial foreclosure on land given as security for a loan, or a testamentary disposition of land.[2] Express statutory exemptions from local regulations are often made for these three types of transfers.

Sometimes problems arise that involve the definition of a subdivision. So long as the title to land underlying a development is not affected, there is no "division of a parcel into two or more parcels" (a common definition of a subdivision) and so no subdivision. The underlying land might, for example, continue to be owned by a owners' association established as a non-profit corporation. Thus, more generally, in the majority of the cases addressing this issue, and absent a statute on the situation, no zoning or subdivision approval is required to establish a condominium regime.[3] Such regimes are established by statute in all states and involve a change of ownership and of the identity of the owner, but not a change of use. Even when the statute defined a subdivision as a "division or conversion of one parcel into two or more parcels," it might still be taken to refer to an alteration of its use, not a change in ownership.[4]

A municipality might define a subdivision more functionally as "the division of land for the purposes of a sale for building purposes, the creation

---

[1] *See generally* D. Listokin & C. Walker, *The Subdivision and Site Plan Handbook* 129–166 (1989) (an excellent introductory guide).

[2] *See, e.g., In re Estate of Tettemer*, 26 Pa. D.&C.3d 745 (1981), *affirmed*, 458 A.2d 287 (Pa. Super. Ct. 1983), *but overruled by legislation* 53 Pa.Cons.Stat.Ann. § 10107 (1989) (making a petition by heirs or devisees for distribution of land a subdivision).

[3] *See In re Lowe*, 666 A. 2d 1178 (Vt. 1995) (collecting similar cases to this effect from Florida, Illinois, Maryland, Massachusetts, New Hampshire, New Jersey, North Carolina, Ohio, Rhode Island, and South Carolina).

[4] *Id.*

of land lots, or a re-subdivision." An owner's development of a mobile home park, in which the pads for each home are to be leased to their holders, is a subdivision under this definition. The issue is not whether the pads are sold or leased, but whether there is an overall intent to undertake a development that requires public scrutiny to determine whether it is in harmony with its environs, even if the pad is not clearly a "land lot." It is close enough. A municipality will interpret the regulatory definition liberally in order to carry out its purpose. Thus, a parcel owner's counsel should be cautious enough to investigate obtaining a subdivision permit before undertaking a development.[5] This investigation is prudent because of the penalties associated with developing without first subdividing — the most common of which to render illegal and thereby void the sales or leases of the individual parcels.

Often an owner of a large parcel wishes to subdivide it piece-meal. The fact that the first division of land is for new parcels that are not adjacent or contiguous is no bar to requiring a subdivision permit. Likewise, the first division need not be for the use made of the remaining parcel — as, for example, where a farmer has offers to sell one corner of his farm for a gas station and another corner for a convenience store. The fact that the parcels to be created are not being sold as an integrated development or are not contiguous, is no bar to finding that a subdivision is involved. Thus there need be no express residential, integration, or contiguity requirement in the definition of a subdivision, for a court to find subdivision regulations applicable.

Typically, subdivision regulations are today seldom restricted to residential subdivisions. Likewise, it is common to define a subdivision as the division of a tract "being developed as part of an overall plan or as a whole" or "into contiguous lots or parcels." Again, seeking an advisory opinion of the code or enforcement official is advisable. Often too, to make these piece-meal parcelization problems easier to resolve, only so many parcels may be created within a given period of time — say, five years — and the definition of a subdivision is "the division of a parcel of land into three or more lots within any five year period."

When a definition requires a "division of land into three or more parcels," the remaining parcel must be considered: thus, splitting off two parcels, leaving one larger one remaining in an owner's hands, will likely violate the definition. However, if the allegedly violative conveyance were of land contiguous to the second parcel to adjust the boundary between the two parcels, no subdivision permission would be needed. A conveyance for the purpose of adjusting the boundaries of the prior conveyance does not count and is not a subdivision. The subdivision regulations are not intended to regulate matters pertaining to the title to the property. Likewise, if a conveyance was made, not to adjust a boundary, but so that the owner of a parcel already subdivided without violating the regulations has space to build a garage for the house, no subdivision permission would be needed. Most multi-division definitions implicitly require independent conveyances,

---

[5] *Sandoval County Board of Comm'nrs v. Ruiz*, 893 P.2d 482 (N.M. App. Ct. 1995).

and are not triggered by less. Building the garage involves instead a conveyance to adjust the development on the parcel previously conveyed and, while it does involve a title matter, it also involves an accessory use for a previous development. So long as the building is an accessory one, and not the establishment of a separate land use, a subdivision has not been created.[6]

Sometimes a less than fee conveyance creates definitional problems. Suppose that the owner of Blackacre conveys its southern half (known as Greenacre) to another, and three months later the owner conveys the other, northern half of Blackacre (known as Whiteacre) to a third person. Two months after that, the northern owner mortgages one half of Greenacre to Assets Bank in exchange for a construction loan, and three months later, the third owner sells Whiteacre to Greenacre's owner who receives building permits to improve the properties. The Bank forecloses and takes possession of half of Greenacre. The municipality revokes all permits. The subdivision regulation defines a subdivision as:

> the division of a tract or parcel of land into three (3) or more lots within any five (5) year period after the enactment of this ordinance, whether the sub-division is accomplished by sale, lease, development, improvements, buildings, or otherwise; the first division of a tract or parcel creates two lots, and the subsequent division of either creates a third lot, by whomever accomplished.

The issue is whether the execution of the mortgage is the third "subdivision" that violates the regulation. It is certainly the creation of an "interest" in the property — that is, a lien that a mortgagee might foreclose — and so is arguably the third division of the title to the original property known as Blackacre.[7] The plain meaning of the word "division" should provide a basis for rejecting this argument. However, selling Whiteacre to Greenacre's owner puts the northern and southern portions of Blackacre back together and so, after three transactions, there are two owners. Once violated, the regulation applies, even though it says nothing expressly about this situation.[8]

Suppose that, instead of mortgaging Greenacre, its owner executes a revocable license to allow a fourth person to place a mobile home on half of Greenacre. The revocable nature of the license and its placement does not inoculate the parties from the requirements of the regulation, but the classification of the mobile home may be determinative here. If it is not classified as real property because it is not attached to the realty, then it is personal property and so the license creates no further division in the

---

[6] *See Catania v. Glastonbury Planning & Zoning Commission*, 1995 Conn. Super. LEXIS 3658 (Conn. Super, Ct., Dec. 19, 1995).

[7] *See Town of Orrington v. Pease*, 660 A.2d 919, 920–920 (Me. 1995) (holding that it is). *See also Baldiga v. Board of Appeals*, 482 N.E. 2d 809, 812, n. 4 (Mass. App. Ct. 1985) (describing the process of checker-boarding).

[8] *Cf. Blow v. Town of Berlin*, 560 A.2d 378, 379 (Vt. 1989) (stating that a court should examine all of an applicant's parcel when the applicant seeks a variance).

parcel. The mobile home might be best regarded as a interim or holding action by the owner, not a further development of the parcel.

§ 14.03   The Substance of Regulation.

Subdivision regulations impose a different type of control on a developer than does zoning. Zoning regulations impose restrictions on the use of real property. They are negative in that respect. Subdivision regulations are applied when land is to be divided into parcels and developed. They require the developer to dedicate land and to install the infrastructure on the parcel which will be needed for the provision of public services — curbs and gutters, streets, grading, utilities, and water and sewer lines of a certain quality.

Their purpose is to insure that the services will be adequate (as where a sewer line of a certain diameter must be installed), of a prescribed quality (using, say, granite, not concrete, curbing), and mesh with existing public facilities (as where the streets of a subdivision must meet the existing street system in a grid or other pattern).

Thus, such regulations provide for capacity, quality, and uniformity of a municipality's infrastructure. Imagine that it were otherwise: imagine a municipality where sewer lines were four inches in diameter on one block and eight on another; where the pipes broke after ten years on one block, but lasted a century on another; and where pipes couldn't be linked in a single system. Imagine a street system in which forty foot wide roads suddenly narrowed to thirty, where curbs were installed on some blocks but not others, and back again, for no apparent reason. Protection of public health and safety surely underlie such regulations. For this reason, subdivision regulations are mandatory and typically require that subdividers contribute these road, water, and sewer facilities to the municipality.

Specific regulations refer to (1) the content, form, and format of subdivision plats as well as the procedure for approving the application seeking their approval; (2) the regulation of the layout, materials, and dimensions of streets within the project and appearing on the plat; (3) the regulation of parcel sizes, although this is also a subject for zoning regulations as well; (4) the regulation of utility lines and facilities for the subdivided parcels; (5) the regulation of the placement of future improvements on the subdivided parcels; (6) the conservation of existing features, natural and man-made, on those parcels; and (7) requirements that land, or a cash payment equivalent, be dedicated to a public use or fund the provision of parks, playgrounds, schools, and jogging, bicycle, and nature trails.

The process of subdivision plan review is divided into several stages: (1) review of the plan, (2) review of the preliminary plat map, and (3) review of the final map.

Suppose an owner applies for subdivision approval for five acres (half of the acreage to be used for a gas station and the other half for a convenience store). Both are permitted uses in the use district in which the subdivision is to be located. The planning commission in reviewing the subdivision plan, has regulatory authority "to require reasonable changes in the applicant's proposed subdivision plan." The owner presents a site plan and a traffic study, but the commission suggests that the traffic generated is excessive and rejects the subdivision. What the commission has done may be beyond its authority, on the theory that it has the duty to propose changes in the road width and vehicle access that would address its traffic safety concerns. The statutory duty to make reasonable changes may mean that the commission may only react to the applicant's proposals with reasonable conditions on its approval, and also that it has an affirmative duty to propose reasonable changes in the subdivision plan. The latter proposition is particularly appropriate when the use proposed is an otherwise permitted one — a land use permitted as of right in the location proposed.[9]

In the same vein, suppose a planning commission denied an owner's subdivision application because building on the land would require too much fill on the land's (say) 12 degree slopes, require too many trees to be cut down, affect the drainage in the neighborhood, and result in heavy traffic, so that approval of the application would not be in the public interest. The commission has steep-slope regulations for the use of fill on slopes over (say) 15 degrees, the preservation of trees, the slope and contours of drains, and traffic engineering standards for traffic control. In this situation, the board is vulnerable upon any appeal of its decision. When it has specific regulations to apply, as with its 15 degree threshold for the regulation of fill, it is an abuse of its authority to ignore those express standards and decide a case before it on public interest or general welfare grounds. Deciding what the general welfare requires is a legislative function and the commission's doing so oversteps the proper bounds of administrative action.[10] When applicable, only those express regulations and standards in the local subdivision ordinance, not general purpose clauses or general standards in the ordinance or its enabling act, may be used by the commission as grounds for its actions.

§ 14.04　Vesting an Entitlement to Approval.

If, while a commission is reviewing an owners' subdivision application, the municipal legislature decides to change the zoning map to prohibit the owner's proposed uses, this amendment of the zoning map is presumptively valid, and may be applied to the owner's application. A municipality may amend its zoning regulations during the pendency of a subdivision application, even when the amendment is prompted by a particular application. Enactment of such an amendment is a legislative act and so long as it is consistent with the enabling act, a municipality is free is amend its

---

[9] *Sheetz v. Frederick Planning Commission*, 665 A.2d 327 (Md. App. Ct. 1995) (finding such a statute to be proactive, not reactive, because the planning commission does not have the authority to review the use classification).

[10] *Pizzo Mantin Group v. Township of Randolph*, 645 A.2d 89 (N.J. 1993).

regulations. Moreover, the amendment is entitled to the same presumption of validity attaching to the original regulation and map.[11]

In some jurisdictions, statutory immunity from zoning changes is granted to subdivision applicants during the pendency of their proposals.[12] This immunity is for the benefit of applicants, and does not provide the regulators with implied rights to deny non-complying proposals when the applicant waives the immunity and seeks further changes on its own. Such an immunity generally lasts for the duration of the project.

§ 14.05   The Matter of Third Party Liability.

Subdivision applications — plats, plans, and proposals — are matters between the owner and the regulatory officials. The planning commission's *not* proposing reasonable changes in the traffic patterns or the applications will not render the planning commission liable to a nearby homeowners' association whose members are injured, say by having difficulty accessing the highway running in front of the applicant's subdivision, once it is up and operating as proposed and approved. No municipality is generally liable to third parties, whether subdivision residents or neighbors, when not enforcing its subdivision regulations to the fullest possible extent.[13] Subdivision regulations are intended for the benefit of the municipality; there is generally neither a statutory or a common law duty to others. Thus, absent some contractual or third party beneficiary right in the association, there is no third-party liability. Moreover, subdivision regulations often involve discretionary actions and conditions imposed by the planning commission. The failure to use its discretion does not increase its liability and does not mean that the failure to impose a condition was unreasonable.

More generally, an owner does not have a state based and protected property interest in a subdivision approval sufficient to bring a due process claim in many federal circuits.[14] The authority to deny the permit is sufficient to destroy any possibility that such an interest exists. Some other circuits reason that ownership of the land involved in the approval process provides a sufficient interest.[15]

---

[11] *See Manalapan Realty v. Twp. Committee of the Twp. of Manalapan*, 658 A.2d 1230, 1237 (N.J. 1995). *See also Rockville Fuel & Feed Co. v. Bd. of Appeals*, 262 A. 2d 499 (Md. 1970) (upholding the zoning designation changed even after the applicant won a judicial appeal contesting a denial, the new designation expressly prohibiting a use previously designated permissible by special exception).

[12] *Meadows of Hanover, Inc. v. Bd. of Supervisors of South Hanover Twp.*, 734 A.2d 854, 857 (Pa. 1999).

[13] *Stillwater Condominium Ass'n v. Town of Salem*, 668 A. 2d 38, 40 (N.H. 1995) (involving a water line adequate to serve the plaintiffs' subdivision).

[14] *See Gagliardi v. Village of Pawling*, 18 F.3d 188, 193 (2nd Cir. 1994). *See also* Christopher Bryant, *Zoning Out Due Process Rights: W.J.F. Realty v. Town of Southhampton*, 73 St. John's L. Rev. 565 (1999).

[15] *DeBlasio v. Zoning Board of Adjustment*, 53 F.3d 592, 601 (3d Cir. 1995). *See also Harris v. County of Riverside*, 904 F.2d 497, 503 (9th Cir. 1990).

§ 14.06   The Extent of Regulation.

Typically a state's enabling act for subdivision regulations authorizes local ordinances governing the grading of lots, and the proper arrangement of streets, lots, and open spaces. A subdivision ordinance thus contains a series of criteria and performance standards for the infrastructure improvements required of developers. Criticized when the pattern emerging from their use is a cookie-cutter monotony of small, same-shape parcels, anti-monotony regulations require that residences located next to, across from, and kitty-cornered to each other have different fronts, elevations, and appearances. The police power premise for such regulations is that monotony in residential design lowers property values, affecting the property tax base of the village; creates confusion when police and fire vehicles seek to locate properties, promoting the health and safety of the village; and detracts from the aesthetics of the municipality, thus affecting its general welfare. These purposes implement the authority granted to the village to regulate the "arrangement" of lots.

§ 14.07   The Timing of Regulation.

The subdivision process sometimes results in what the ordinances call a "finished" parcel — referring to a lot that is surveyed, cleared, and graded, but is otherwise unimproved. In some contexts, the subdivider is not the builder because a parcel, once finished, is sold to a builder that does nothing else but improve previously subdivided land; so structural regulations are enforced at the building permit stage and subdivision approval is granted conditionally, upon compliance with the ordinance's regulations for structures and with a completion bond forfeited for non-compliance. The same type of conditional approval would be given when ordinances require that landscaping or tree cover of a certain density be maintained on subdivided parcels.[16]

§ 14.08   Exactions of Land and Money.

The major types of subdivision exactions involve land dedications or a requirement that the subdivider install improvements internal to the subdivision itself. In addition, land is set aside in an unimproved state for various public purposes — schools, parks, and other open space. Sometimes these regulations also impose fees, exacted in lieu of requiring land dedications. All these exactions, both in kind and in money, are intended to impose development-related capital costs on developers. Such fees are usually deposited in municipal accounts whose purpose is the future

---

[16] *See, e.g.,* Vivian Encarnacion, *More Trees Please: Utilizing Natural Resources in the Urban environmental Management of New York City*, 26 Fordham Urb. L. J. 1571, 1574–1578, 1585–1594 (1999) (reviewing ordinances requiring subdividers to preserve trees and landscaping).

purchase of capital improvements such as schools and parks.[17] Such fees were imposed as early as the 1930s in some jurisdictions.[18]

§ 14.09   Overlapping Jurisdictions.

Sometimes the criteria and standards in a subdivision ordinance overlap with the zoning ordinance of the municipality. For example, set-back and minimum acreage requirements for subdivided parcels may be contained in both its subdivision regulations and its zoning ordinance. Typically the planning commission will refer the subdivision proposal to the zoning officer to see if it complies with the ordinance; the matter of set-backs is then properly considered by both the planning commission and the zoning officials.[19] Moreover, when a planning commission is authorized to consider "historical factors" in reviewing a subdivision plan, its authority overlaps with that of a historic district commission. That another public agency has an oversight function involving the same criteria and standards, does not preclude a planning commission's use of them as well.[20] However, when a comprehensive plan would be violated by approval of a subdivision authorized by the zoning ordinance, the zoning regulation controls.[21] It is typically the most recent enactment, having been written to accord with the plan, has the most detail, and so is binding on the commission; often the fact that the plan has not been adopted as an ordinance gives it no more than the status of a guideline.

§ 14.10   Premature Subdivision of Land.

Subdivision prior to the need for housing or other improvements on a piece of land is a major problem in the United States.[22] There is sometimes express authority in the enabling act for denying a subdivision permit on this basis.[23] Subdivision approval may also be denied when heavy use by subdivision residents of off-site roads would create a safety hazard. In implementing express premature subdivision regulations, a planning commission may consider both current and anticipated hazards and burdens on off-site facilities. Lacking the authority to deny a premature subdivision,

---

[17] *Bayswater Realty & Capital Corp. v. Planning Bd.*, 560 N.E.2d 1300 (N.Y. 1990) (affirming validity of a off-site parkland acquisition fee imposed for cluster subdivision approval).

[18] *See* John Reps, *Control of Land Subdivision by Municipal Planning Boards*, 40 Corn. L.Q. 258, 266 (1955).

[19] *Smith v. Town of Wolfeboro*, 615 A.2d 1252, 1255 (N.H. 1992).

[20] *Smith v. Zoning Bd. of Appeals of Town of Greenwich*, 629 A.2d 1089, 1101–1102 (Conn. 1993).

[21] *See Urrutia v. Blaine Cty.*, 2 P.3d 738 (Idaho 2000).

[22] Note, *Premature Subdivision*, 1988 Utah L.Rev. 569 (1988) (discussing this problem in the Western states). *See also Garipay v. Town of Hanover*, 351 A.2d 64 (N.H. 1976) (upholding the denial of subdivision approval when the off-site roads were inadequate to handle the traffic to be generated by the subdivision).

[23] *See also Zukis v. Town of Fitzwilliam*, 604 A.2d 956 (N.H. 1992).

a planning commission generally may not withhold "premature" approval. Neither can it ask the developer to pay for the off-site improvements.[24]

§ 14.11 The Plat Map.

The product of the subdivision process is a plat map, showing the parcels, the streets, the utility lines, the open spaces, and the amenities provided by the developer. The public spaces are thereafter dedicated to the appropriate level of government by deed of gift and the parcels are in many jurisdictions thereafter conveyed to private parties using the plat descriptions as the legal description of the parcel, either by using the dimensions on the map, incorporating those dimensions by reference to the map in the deed, or by lot number appearing on the map. In some states, the filing of a plat map is a precondition to conveying any parcel in the subdivision to private parties.

The plat map is not an "official map" of the jurisdiction. The official map is a map showing where, at some future time, public improvements should be placed. The purpose of such a map is to put owners on notice not to improve property in the path of a future street. If they do, it is at their risk: no compensation in a later eminent domain proceeding will pay for any improvement made after the map is adopted as governmental policy.[25]

§ 14.12 The Merger of Parcels.

Subdivided lots, when used for one structure, are merged into one. When the owner of two contiguous parcels constructs a home that covers both, but later applies to demolish the home and build two homes, one on each parcel, the owner must submit a subdivision plan to do so; the original construction merged the parcels into one lot for purposes of the subdivision regulations.[26] Similarly, when two parcels are created by splitting off an unregulated lot, but later the regulation was changed so that the two no longer meet minimum acreage requirements, these two parcels have also been merged into one.[27] Prior compliance with applicable codes does not immunize lots from merger. For the city planners involved, compliance with present standards is what matters.

§ 14.13 Tests for Validating Subdivision Regulations.

Four tests have been used to assess these regulations. First, the **right/ privilege test**. It assumes that a subdivider is exercising a privilege

---

[24] See *Frisella v. Town of Farmington*, 550 A.2d 102 (N.H. 1988) (invalidating a commission requirement that a developer pay the cost of improvement of a road not adjacent to the subdivision, even though the developer did not object before the commission).

[25] For further discussion of official maps, see this Chapter, *infra*.

[26] *Bridge v. Neptune Twp. Zoning Bd. of Adjustment*, 559 A.2d 855 (N.J. Super. Ct., App. Div., 1989).

[27] *Hill v. City of Manhattan Beach*, 98 Cal.Rptr. 785 (Cal. 1971), *rev'd by* Cal. Gov't Code § 66424.2.

extended by the government. In consideration for the privilege of subdividing property, the government requires compliance with a statute or ordinance.[28] This "privilege theory" is the historical test. The problem with it is that it does not limit the role of government and the number of requirements which a subdivider must meet. It argues too broadly and justifies many more types of requirements than the subdivision engenders. Thus, many jurisdictions could not find its limits and so adopted other tests.

Second, a **strict nexus test**. It requires that the exaction be "specially and uniquely attributable to the subdivision." This test is easily met in two situations: (1) when the requirements of the subdivision process conform one subdivision to the rest of the jurisdiction, as where the streets are required to be of a uniform width and meet other streets, or (2) when a jurisdiction has a duty to supply a service or maintain a item which is the subject of its requirement.[29]

In deference to the influence of *Pioneer Trust*, this rule is sometimes called the Illinois rule, although it has also been used in Rhode Island and New Hampshire. Under it, an exaction is borne by a subdivider or developer only if the subdivision or development is the sole cause of the need for the additional public facility financed. The exaction is akin to a special assessment fee, long used to finance sewer and water extensions by municipalities. One court in Florida has found that this test destroys the usual presumption of validity and imposes the burden of proof on the municipality to justify the exaction.[30]

Third, a rational or **reasonable nexus test**. It requires that the exaction be "generally attributable to the subdivision." California and Wisconsin courts have pioneered this test, but it has also been followed in opinions in Maryland, New Jersey, Nebraska, Oregon, and Utah.[31]

The leading case for this third test is *Ayres v. City Council of Los Angeles*.[32] Here, a municipality's public facility needs are balanced against the benefits to the subdivision from those facilities. The issue is whether the exaction relates to the need recited by the government and whether its benefits are reserved for and are actually conferred on the subdivision. Thus this test, starting out as a needs/benefit balancing test, has been elaborated into a separate examination of both the needs and the benefits.

Under the reasonable nexus test, a court is unlikely to invalidate a regulation simply because a subdivision did not create the need. Rather,

---

[28] See *Ridgefield Land Co. v. City of Detroit*, 217 N.W. 58 (Mich. 1928).

[29] See *Krughoff v. City of Naperville*, 369 N.E.2d 892, 895 (Ill. 1977); *Pioneer Trust & Savings Bank v. Village of Mount Prospect*, 176 N.E.2d 799 (Ill. 1961) (the leading case).

[30] *Wald Corp. v. Metropolitan Dade County*, 338 So. 2d 863 (Fla. App. Ct., 1976), cert. denied, 348 So. 2d 955 (1977) (involving rights of way for canals).

[31] See *Jordan v. Village of Menomonee Falls*, 137 N.W.2d 442 (Wis. 1965) (holding that in-lieu fees in place of physical exactions of land, authorized by statute and constitutional); *Longridge Builders, Inc. v. Planning Bd.*, 245 A.2d 336, 337 (N.J. 1968) ("[T]he subdivider [can] be compelled only to bear that portion of the cost which bears a rational nexus to the needs created by, and benefits conferred upon, the subdivision.").

[32] 207 P.2d 1 (Cal. 1949).

the need can be created by the approval of many subdivisions over time. This time-tested need is the basis of a presumption of validity for the exaction (again, less often seen in this area than in zoning generally).

Under this test, the presumption can be overcome by a subdivider's showing that (1) the municipality has an existing and adequate inventory of land for the purpose of the exaction, or (2) "normal" growth makes land acquisition necessary in any event, or (3) the subdivision will shift the population already within the jurisdiction, rather than cause the in-migration of new residents.

In California and other jurisdictions, the *Ayres* opinion has become suspect after the 1987 United States Supreme Court *Nollan* opinion was issued.[33] The requirement of a reasonable nexus may not be a stiff enough test for a Court that requires that a regulation "substantially advance a legitimate state interest." There have been few attempts to codify this test.[34]

Fourth and finally, a test which requires that the exaction be levied uniformly and **according to a comprehensive plan** for the municipality. Often the evidence of its validity is a comprehensive plan. This is particularly true if the geographic area over which the benefits flowing from the requirement is a large one. When the regulation calls for the use of a subdivision fee across town, rather than close to the subdivision, this fourth test is useful to justify the fee paid by a subdivider in lieu of dedicating land.[35] School and park funds are often augmented in this way. However, the funds must be deposited in dedicated special purpose accounts, rather than general revenue accounts. A balancing test is often used in connection with this test — balancing public benefits versus private injuries — and the "in-lieu fees" are justified much as a special assessment is. Some courts have found that this fourth test gives too much discretion to municipalities in imposing exactions and in-lieu fees.[36]

No matter what test for a regulation's validity is used, some subdivisions do not contain sufficient acreage to warrant the imposition of land dedications. For such a subdivision approval, the previously mentioned so-called "in-lieu fee" — in lieu of dedication now — is exacted. If the government could require that land be set aside or dedicated for a particular purpose — again, say, for parks or schools — within a larger subdivision, it will argue that it may exact the fee to purchase land for the same purpose elsewhere to meet the needs generated by a small subdivision.[37]

---

[33] *See, e.g., Rohn v. City of Visalia*, 263 Cal. Rptr. 319 (Cal. App. Ct. 1989).

[34] *See* Am.L. Inst., *Model Land Development Code*, § 2-103 (1976), used however as a guide in *City of College Station v. Turtle Rock Corporation*, 680 S.W.2d 802, 807 (Tex. 1984).

[35] *See Associated Home Builders v. City of Walnut Creek*, 484 P.2d 606, 610 (Cal.1971).

[36] *E.g., Wald Corp. v. Metropolitan Dade County*, 338 So. 2d 863 (Fla. App. Ct., 1976), cert. denied, 348 So. 2d 955 (1977) (applying the reasonable nexus test).

[37] *See Jordan v. Village of Menomonee Falls, supra. See generally* three comprehensive opinions reviewing these theories: *Batch v. Town of Chapel Hill*, 376 S.E.2d 22 (N. C. App. 1989), *reversed*, 387 S.E.2d 655 (N.C. 1990), *cert. denied*, 496 U.S. 931 (1990), *discussed in* Elizabeth Arias, *Batch v. Town of Chapel Hill: Takings Law and Exactions: Where Should North Carolina Stand?*, 21 Camp. L. Rev. 49 (1998); *Howard County v. JJM, Inc.*, 482 A.2d 908 (Md. 1984) (holding that a subdivider could not be compelled to dedicate a right of way for a highway

§ 14.14   Enforcement of Subdivision Regulations.

There are three principal methods of enforcement of subdivision regulations. First, a failure to comply with the regulations is sometimes made a misdemeanor subject to a fine and/or a term in jail. Second, other enforcement methods are aimed at transfers of non-complying land: for example, the regulators may enjoin the transfer of non-complying parcels, or in the alternative, a purchaser in a non-complying subdivision has the right to rescind the purchase. A third method of enforcement is the denial of permits for the improvement of non-complying land. Building and occupancy permits are common examples, but the certification of utilities is another potent regulatory pressure-point on the subdivider. Any jurisdiction may use some or all of these methods.

An additional, commonly used device for insuring compliance is a requirement that the subdivider post a performance or completion bond, issued by a reputable surety, to assure the completion of the required improvements. If the improvements are not installed, or not installed in compliance with the specifications in the regulation, then the bond is invoked and the surety pays for any further necessary work.

§ 14.15   Summary of Subdivision Fee Rationales.

In 1994, in the case of *Dolan v. The City of Tigard*,[38] a majority of the United State Supreme Court attempted to summarize the various rationales for subdivision dedications and fees. Its discussion is informative for presenting the court's view, but also as a summary of past law. Here is that discussion:

> The question for us is whether these findings [made by the local planning agency] are constitutionally sufficient to justify the conditions imposed by the city on petitioner's building permit. Since state courts have been dealing with this question a good deal longer than we have, we turn to representative decisions made by them.

> In some States, very generalized statements as to the necessary connection between the required dedication and the proposed development seem to suffice. See, e.g., Jenad, Inc. v. Scarsdale, 18 N.Y.2d 78, 218 N.E.2d 673, 271 N.Y.S.2d 955 (1966). We think this standard is too lax to adequately protect petitioner's right to just compensation if her property is taken for a public purpose.

> Other state courts require a very exacting correspondence, described as the "specific and uniquely attributable" test. The Supreme Court of Illinois first developed this test in Pioneer Trust & Savings Bank v. Mount Prospect, 22 Ill. 2d 375, 380, 176 N.E.2d

---

through the subdivision without a reasonable nexus between the need for the road and the new subdivision — *JJM* being a case similar to *Nollan*, discussed in this Chapter, *infra*); and *Collis v. City of Bloomington*, 246 N.W.2d 19 (Minn. 1976).

[38] 512 U.S. 74 (1994).

799, 802 (1961) (footnote recognizing this test as the minority rule, and citing cases from N.H., N.J., Ohio, and R.I. as examples of the test, omitted.). Under this standard, if the local government cannot demonstrate that its exaction is directly proportional to the specifically created need, the exaction becomes "a veiled exercise of the power of eminent domain and a confiscation of private property behind the defense of police regulations." Id. at 381, 176 N.E.2d at 802. We do not think the Federal Constitution requires such exacting scrutiny, given the nature of the interests involved.

A number of state courts have taken an intermediate position, requiring the municipality to show a "reasonable relationship" between the required dedication and the impact of the proposed development. Typical is the Supreme Court of Nebraska's opinion in Simpson v. North Platte, 206 Neb. 240, 245, 292 N.W. 2d 297, 301 (1980), where that court stated: "The distinction, therefore, which must be made between an appropriate exercise of the police power and an improper exercise of eminent domain is whether the requirement has some reasonable relationship or nexus to the use to which the property is being made or is merely being used as an excuse for taking property simply because at that particular moment the landowner is asking the city for some license or permit." Thus, the court held that a city may not require a property owner to dedicate private property for some future public use as a condition of obtaining a building permit when such future use is not "occasioned by the construction sought to be permitted." Id. at 248, 292 N.W.2d at 302.

Some form of the reasonable relationship test has been adopted in many other jurisdictions. See, e.g., Jordan v. Menomonee Falls, 28 Wis. 2d 608, 137 N.W.2d 442 (1965); College Station v. Turtle Rock Corp., 680 S.W.2d 802, 807 (Tex. 1984); Call v. West Jordan, 606 P.2d 217, 220 (Utah 1979). Despite any semantical differences, general agreement exists among the courts "that the dedication should have some reasonable relationship to the needs created by the [development]." Ibid.

We think the "reasonable relationship" test adopted by a majority of the state courts is closer to the federal constitutional norm than either of those previously discussed. But we do not adopt it as such, partly because the term "reasonable relationship" seems confusingly similar to the term "rational basis" which describes the minimal level of scrutiny under the Equal Protection Clause of the Fourteenth Amendment. We think a term such as "rough proportionality" best encapsulates what we hold to be the requirement of the Fifth Amendment. No precise mathematical calculation is required, but the city must make some sort of individualized determination that the required dedication is related both in nature and extent to the impact of the proposed development.

This discussion invites closer attention to the so-called "nexus" test for the constitutional validity of subdivision dedications and fees. This test grows out of traditional, substantive due process jurisprudence. It makes plain that there are actually two "nexi" to consider, two nexi that the subdivision ordinance must satisfy at the time of its application, and two nexi whose weakness(es) might be the basis of a property owner's challenge to that ordinance. First, there is the requirement of a reasonable relationship between the purpose of the regulatory dedication or fee and the regulation imposing them. Second, there is the nexus between the regulation and its impact on the particular subdivision under consideration. This second nexus requires that the impact be reasonably tailored to that subdivision. Both must survive challenge for the ordinance to be constitutional. [39]

§ 14.16   Impact Fees.

Municipalities have also imposed development impact fees on developers. This type of fee is an attempt to allocate to a developer the fraction of the infrastructure costs caused by that developer's particular project. It is intended, then, to be the developer's payment of a proportionate share of infrastructure costs. The definition of an "infrastructure" is a loose one, but the term is often taken to mean road, sewer, drinking water, and storm water systems. A system includes both lines and plants.

Administratively, impact fees are often levied later in the development process than subdivision exactions and dedications. They are levied and paid as a precondition to obtaining a building permit. Thus they tax developments for which no subdivision approval is required, or for which subdivision approval was given previously or prematurely. For example, they are levied when plans to expand or improve existing structures require permits. By levying these fees at this later point in the development process, they may be levied on not just residential subdivisions, but also on commercial, industrial, condominium, and institutional developments. The amount of the fee is typically calculated by the use of such factors as the gross square footage in the structure for which a permit is sought or the number of bedrooms in a residence.

In order to justify the impact fee, the municipality must determine what the need for the infrastructure was, before the development and what the need will be after its construction. The tests for the validity of impact fees seem to be the same as those used for testing subdivision regulations. The Florida courts have provided a good line of cases in this regard. [40]

In Florida, the reasonable nexus test is used twice, for, in order to justify an impact fee, the municipality must show two things: (1) a reasonable

---

[39] *See City of Annapolis v. Waterman*, 745 A.2d 1000, 1005–1025 (Md. 2000) (a comprehensive discussion of *Nollan* and *Dolan*, discussed *infra*, this Chapter).

[40] *Compare, e.g., Contractors & Builders Ass'n of Pinellas County v. City of Dunedin*, 329 So.2d 314 (Fla. App. 1978), cert. den., 370 So.2d 458, *cert. den.*, 444 U.S. 867 (1979) (upholding impact fees generally, but striking down the particular fee at issue, using a specifically and uniquely attributable, strict nexus test), *with Hollywood, Inc. v. Broward County*, 431 So.2d 606 (Fla. App. 1983), cert. den., 440 So.2d 352 (1983) (using a reasonable nexus test).

nexus between the need for additional capital facilities and the growth in population generated by a subdivision or development, and (2) a reasonable nexus between the expenditure of funds collected and the benefits accruing to the subdivision or development. A "dual rational nexus test" is thus required. [41]

Thus, the validity of the fee depends on three things: first, a development creating a need for the creation or expansion of the infrastructure; second, the amount of the fee not exceeding the cost to the government when it provides the infrastructure; and third, the designation and restriction of the fee to meeting the need for the infrastructure.

This double nexus test is in effect the result of the federal constitutional case law embodied in two United States Supreme Court majority opinions in *Nollan v. California Coastal Commission*, [42] and *Dolan v. The City of Tigard*, [43] the latter quoted extensively previously in this chapter. For a case following the lead of these cases, see *F & W Associates v. County of Somerset*. [44]

Rapidly growing states have used impact fees extensively. In California, their use may in part be a reaction to restrictive fiscal measures. Local governments in states such as Colorado, Oregon, Texas, and Washington, have also used such fees. For example, San Diego attempted to price all of its infrastructure costs for its remaining, undeveloped raw land and then assigned these prices, pro rated in the city's comprehensive plan, to each unit of land. [45] These fees are again analogous to special assessments, but are imposed on a larger scale and before the services are provided. [46]

Ordinances for imposing impact fees must be carefully drafted. They must include a definition of the public facilities to which the fees will be devoted, using unambiguous terms. They must be backed by careful cost estimates and a formula to determine the developer's proportionate share of the cost of maintaining, expanding, and supporting the capital facility for whose benefit they were enacted. Expenditure of the fees should be limited to those purposes, and the funds earmarked/segregated for those purposes; expenditures should be made within a reasonable time of collection, limited to a specific geographic area, or else refunded. If the purpose is too general, the ordinance runs the risk of being found preempted by state law. [47] An opinion giving careful attention the drafting and to the calculation of the fee is *Banberry Dev. Corp. v. South Jordan City*. [48]

---

[41] *St. Johns County, Florida v. Northeast Florida Builders Association, Inc.*, 583 So.2d 635, 637 (Fla. 1991) (recapping the *Dunedin* opinion in the context of a school impact fee), *noted* 16 Nova L. Rev. 391–393 (1991).

[42] 483 U.S. 825 (1987).

[43] 512 U.S. 374 (1994).

[44] 648 A.2d 482 (N.J. Super. Ct., App. Div., 1994) (upholding a traffic impact fee).

[45] *J. W. Jones Cos. v. City of San Diego*, 203 Cal. Rptr. 580 (Cal. App. Ct.1984).

[46] *See Russ Bldg. Partnership v. City and County of San Francisco*, 750 P.2d 324, 329–330 (Cal. 1988) (upholding a public transit impact fee).

[47] *See Albany Area Builders Ass'n v. Town of Guilderland*, 546 N.E.2d 920 (N.Y. 1989) (transportation impact fee preempted by state highway law and taxes).

[48] 631 P.2d 899 (Utah 1981).

Some states have enacted enabling legislation for impact fees. Such fees are a source of political controversy, although in states with declining revenues for local governments or with constitutional limitations on the use of the real property tax (as in California with Proposition 13 now in its constitution), the need for alternative sources of revenue is a pressing one.

Thus a municipal legislature, enacting a development impact fee ordinance, citing the administrative costs of processing development applications, making the fee payable on the issuance of a building permit, and devoting the amounts charged for construction and re-construction of all types of public facilities, has enacted an invalid ordinance. This is so for three reasons. First, the use of administrative costs of development procedures as a rationale shows that the cost of the services made necessary by the development, is not the reason for the fee; rather, the fee looks more like a tax than a regulatory fee. Second, levying the fee at the time a building permit is issued, shows that the fee is levied on the public at large and not just on those increasing the demand for city services; that the fee might be paid by a long-time, resident already using the services and not increasing the demand for them, makes the same point more sharply. Third, the ordinance does not ear-mark the fee proceeds to infrastructure in the neighborhood of the permitted construction; it shifts the proceeds from the area of development to the public at large. This fee walks like a tax, talks like one, etc. — and so it is valid only when properly authorized as a tax by a state statute.[49]

Such an ordinance should be redrafted by (first and foremost) conducting a study determining how much demand for the services is generated by different types of new construction, then ear-marking the fees collected to the improvement of city facilities in the neighborhood of the person paying the fee, setting up a separate city account for administering the ear-marked funds, and limiting collection of the fee to new construction.

§ 14.17 Linkage Fees.

This type of fee is used to pay for some governmental facility or service unused by the developer paying it. The amount of the fee is linked to some unit or feature of the property being developed. For example, a fee of one dollar might be imposed for each square foot of office space developed to fund low income housing for workers using the space. Therefore, a linkage fee is a developer's fee for some broader social program and paid in return for local approval of a developer's project. The program might involve affordable housing, job training, child care, or mass transit. *Holmdel Builders Ass'n v. Twp. of Holmdel* is a leading case.[50] *Holmdel* held that

---

[49] *Idaho Building Contractors Ass'n v. City of Coeur D'Alene*, 890 P.2d 326, 239–330 (Idaho 1995) (invalidating an impact fee as an unauthorized tax).

[50] 583 A.2d 277 (N.J. 1990), *noted in* Susan Denbo, *Development Exactions: A New Way to Fund States and Local Government Infrastructure Improvements and Affordable Housing?*, 23 Real Est. L.J. 7, 30–36 (1994), and John Payne, *From the Courts: Housing Impact Fees*, 20 Real Est. L.J. 75 (1991).

housing linkage fees to carry out a municipality's *Mt. Laurel* obligation to provide realistic opportunities to developers for the construction of affordable housing, are valid. *Holmdel* further held that such fees are neither a taking or an impermissible tax. Boston and San Francisco have enacted ordinances authorizing such fees, the latter including a fee for child care facilities in commercial structures.[51] New Jersey has authorized linkage fees for transportation districts state-wide.

§ 14.18   Official Maps as an Aid in Subdivision Regulation.

An official map shows anticipated streets, open space, and land needed for future public facilities. Municipal, county, and state governments often use official maps as a part of their transportation planning. When they foresee that a new roadway will be needed in the jurisdiction, and can plot its location — or when an existing roadway will need to be widened — the future right of way, along with drainage facilities and other supporting lands, is located on a map maintained by the government as an official record. (Affected landowners are usually given notice of the mapping and a reasonable opportunity to protest it.) The legal effect of mapping the right of way is to reserve it for roadway use, so that henceforth no further development permits will be issued for improvement within the right of way. The purpose of mapping is two-fold: first, to give notice of the future right of way to affected owners, and second, to serve notice that no condemnation award can be based on the value of post-mapping improvements.

Consequently, if a municipality plans to widen a street, and so maps the widened thoroughfare, showing that in five years' time its right of way will be expanded ten feet on each side, an abutting landowner is likely to argue that this is a taking of his property under the Fifth Amendment. However, it is not a taking. The mapping has no more impact on the abutting property that would a set-back line for an abutting front yard. Establishing a set-back line is well within the police power's health and safety rubrics. Further, the abutting owners are very likely to benefit from the widened roadway to a greater extent than owners in the municipality generally will. Finally, when the mapping limits development only as necessary to insure compatibility of abutting land uses with the widened roadway — and for a limited period of time (five years), it is further strengthened against the argument that there has been any taking. The mapping serves a proper municipal purpose and reasonably carries out that purpose.[52] The map substantially advances a legitimate state interest in transportation planning and construction.

The argument for a taking might be strengthened by advising a client to have a development plan drawn up before applying for a permit requiring development within the mapped right of way. Such an "as applied" takings challenge allows the individualized, *ad hoc*, factual showing of deprivation

---

[51] *See* Symp., *Downtown Office Development and Housing Linkage Fees*, 54 J.Am.Inst. Planners (Spring, 1988), at 197.

[52] *See Palm Beach County v. Wright*, 641 So.2d 50 (Fla. 1994).

necessary to effect a taking. Facial challenges permit none of this. So long as the law of regulatory takings remains ad hoc, an as applied challenge is stronger than a facial one.[53]

Typically, the permitting jurisdiction does the mapping; that way the map can be amended and a variance from its provisions given, when a landowner is able to present evidence of a resulting undue hardship.

Sometimes a reservation map is invalidated for procedural irregularities; in this situation, an owner whose land was shown to be needed for a future public facility may be entitled to a *per se* declaration of a temporary taking under *First English Evangelical Lutheran Church v. Cty. of Los Angeles*.[54] The owner has a cause of action in inverse condemnation, but winning such an action should require a showing that development plans were interfered with while the map was effective; if permits were not applied for, then there is no showing that the map had any effect on the owner's property.[55] Otherwise, assuming that this is taking, it is without injury or damage.[56] On the other hand, *First English* is decided on the theory that once a taking has occurred, it cannot be undone; so damages might be presumed. However, the *First English* plaintiff did not challenge the validity of the regulation, and so such presumptions are unwarranted in a facial challenge to a map.

A municipality's official map may also note that some parcels along an existing street will have limited access to the right of way within (say) three years. A first issue to explore is whether a notation of future limited access is within the enabling act for the map and/or the local regulation. The municipality's attorney will argue — and probably prevail on the theory — that if mapping is authorized to limit the use of the land, then the notation about access should be well within that authority. A second issue involves a taking claim. A complete loss of access is not a pre-condition to compensation; any substantial diminution in or loss of access will suffice, even though no land has been taken in the process. Whether there is a taking is a matter of evaluating the remaining access to the property. The loss of the most convenient access is not compensable *per se*, nor would a taking occur when governmental improvements in a roadway cause a decrease in the flow of traffic on abutting streets. The measure of damages for a substantial loss of access is the resulting reduction in the fair market value of the property.[57]

§ 14.19   State Subdivision Statutes.

In most states, the processing and approval of subdivision applications is in the hands of county or municipal governments. However, three states have enacted subdivision codes that permit state government to process

---

[53] *Joint Ventures, Inc. v. Dept. of Transportation*, 563 So.2d 622 (Fla. 1990).

[54] 482 U.S. 304, discussed *supra*, Chapter 5.

[55] *First English Evangelical Lutheran Church v. County of Los Angeles*, 482 U.S. 304 (1987).

[56] *Dept. of Transportation v. Digerlando*, 638 So.2d 514 (Fla. 1994).

[57] *Palm Beach County v. Tessler*, 538 So.2d 846, 849 (Fla. 1989).

subdivision applications involving either a large amount of acreage or environmentally sensitive lands. In these states, both state and municipal regulations must be complied with. Vermont has the most comprehensive of these statutes. Maine requires that subdivisions of twenty or more acres, parceled into five or more lots over five years, obtain state approval as well as town permits; many nineteen acre subdivisions were the predictable result. Florida has enacted substantially all the provisions of the American Law Institute's *Model Land Development Code* (1974) as its primary state subdivision law, and is the only state to have done so.

§ 14.20   Development Exactions and Takings.

The following discussion of a United States Supreme Court opinion may seem to involve unique facts and a unique type of governmental exaction imposed in the course of a permitting process, but that very fact has led many to speculate about the view the present court would take of many, more typical, types of subdivision exactions.

[A]   *Nollan v. California Coastal Commission* [58]

[1]   The Facts.

The Nollans, husband and wife, were interested in purchasing a beach-front bungalow and lot in Ventura County, California. In front of the bungalow was a chest-high wall, separating the house from the dry sand area of the beach. The Nollans had rented the property for several years, under a lease which contained an option to purchase it. It was located between two public beaches — one a quarter mile to the north and another 1800 feet to the south. The bungalow was in disrepair after several years of use by summer vacationers. The Nollan's option required that, as a condition of the purchase, they would obtain and have the right to demolish and replace the bungalow. Their plans called for replacing the 504 square foot structure with a three-bedroom house containing triple the space, 1,674 square feet, but consistent in design with the surrounding properties.

These plans were dependent on approval of the California Coastal Commission. [59] This body recommended approval of the Nollan's building plans on the condition that they dedicate an eight-foot wide easement of access across the dry sand area of the beach in front of the property in favor of the public walking between the two public beaches on either side of their property. They refused to dedicate the easement and instead sued the commission.

The United States Supreme Court held that the commission's requirement that the easement be dedicated laterally along the beach was an unconstitutional condition on the issuance of the development permit.

---

[58] 483 U.S. 825 (1987).

[59] California has had some unique problems with coastal development. The Coastal Commission is the result of an adopted citizen initiative.

Justice Scalia wrote the majority opinion.[60] Requiring the easement dedication was the equivalent of a permanent physical invasion of the Nollan's property, the main citation for this point being *Loretto v. Teleprompter Manhattan CATV Corp.*[61] The public access, although sporadic in fact, was a continuous and permanent right, and akin to a physical invasion.

The court's majority also found that there was no nexus between the purpose of the dedication ("visual access" of the public to the beach) and the way in which that purpose was carried out; lateral access by easement across the beach does provide visual access to the public traveling along the coastal highway that the Nollan property abuts. Thus dedicating the easement does not "substantially advance a legitimate state interest" in that there is no "essential nexus" between the asserted interest of the government and the easement. The majority comments that the commission could have restricted the height or the width of the Nollans' proposed bungalow, or prohibited putting a fence around it — all in the name of the police power. However, "if the condition substituted for the [police power] prohibition utterly fails to further the end advanced as the justification for the prohibition," there is no essential nexus because the commission was acting as if it had imposed a proper prohibition, but then said it would waive it if the Nollans dedicated the easement for public access, a condition unrelated to any proper prohibition's purpose.

The majority even assumes (without deciding) that a regulation "to forbid the construction of the house altogether" might carry out a legitimate police power purpose — promoting the public's view of the beach from the coastal highway — but the exaction goes further and in a way unrelated to that purpose. This assumption is consistent with *Penn Central's* expansive view of the police power.

[2]   The *Loretto* Citation.

Loretto was a physical invasion case — the easiest type of takings case, in which a *per se* rule of taking is used. Justice Scalia implies that the Nollans' case (where part of the fee simple is taken) is just as easy. The rationale underlying this approach to the case is as follows: if the government exacts a condition that would, if imposed alone, require compensation, then the condition is invalid unless compensation is paid. This does not mean that the petitioner will always be paid this compensation; the Nollans, for example, only sought an injunction against enforcement of the exaction. The right which the Nollans had was the right to exclude the public from the dry sand area of the beach — "the right to exclude others

---

[60] The vote was 5–4. Joining Justice Scalia were four Justices who were dissenters in *Keystone's* 5-4 decision. Justice Scalia begins with a discussion of *Loretto*. Had he has stopped there, it was reported that he would have gotten Justice Marshall's vote too. Marshall wrote the majority opinion in *Loretto*, but was reported not to approve of the regulatory takings discussion following the opening physical invasion analysis taken from *Loretto*.

[61] 458 U.S. 419 (1982) (holding that any governmentally authorized permanent and physical occupation or invasion of private property, no matter how great the governmental benefit and no matter how minor the invasion, is a *per se* taking and requires just compensation). *Loretto* is discussed *supra*, Chapter 3.

is one of the most essential sticks in the bundle of rights commonly characterized as 'property'." Other essential rights might be the right to use, possess, or alienate (sell) one's property.

This rationale makes dispositive the fact that in this case the public is to be given access to the Nollans' property and, if the Nollans had accepted the condition, they could not thereafter have excluded the public. However, the opinion does not expressly state that a regulation involving public access is a taking.[62]

Nollan is not just a regulatory takings case; it is a takings clause case in which regulation is the back-drop and provides the proof of the commission's real purpose for an exaction. Thus classified, as an exactions case, its holding is inapplicable to most zoning cases.[63]

Therefore, if *Nollan* is not disposed of with its discussion of *Loretto*, but instead involved the exaction of rights crucial to the owner, then the nexus discussion following is not *dicta* — and cannot be analogized to the "advisory" portion of Holmes' opinion in *Mahon*. So an exaction is something close to a physical invasion — a governmental condition that works the same result so far as its effect on an owner is concerned — and substitutes for such an invasion.

[3] Locating This Holding amid Prior Takings Cases.

The test for a taking here does not replace the one used in *Penn Central*.[64] Rather, this opinion concerns, explains, and details the first prong of the *Agins* test.[65] After discussing *Loretto*, the second section of Justice Scalia's opinion is a discussion of regulatory takings cases. The standard of review used by Scalia fleshes out the "reasonable basis" test. It requires that the regulation be a "substantial advancement" of a legitimate state interest.[66]

---

[62] *PruneYard Shopping Ctr. v. Robbins*, 447 U.S. 74 (1980), holds that the owners of a shopping center had no right under the Fifth Amendment to exclude persons collecting signatures for petitions whose subject was protected by the First Amendment, so *Nollan* is best limited to non-commercial property, where the right to exclude is essential to its use.

[63] *Builders Service Corp. v. Planning & Zoning Comm'n*, 545 A.2d 530 (Conn. 1988); *Adolph v. F.E.M.A.*, 854 F.2d 732, 737 (5th Cir. 1988) (stating that it "is apparent that Nollan did not revolutionize takings law").

[64] In *Nollan*, the dissent takes its structure for the takings test from *Penn Central*, while the majority opinion uses *Agins* as its model.

[65] While reading the opinion, it may help to edit out Scalia's replies to Brennan's dissent; this will reveal the opinion's skeletal structure and eliminate the possibility of being mislead by its inessential portions. Both the majority and the dissenting opinions cross-reference each other. Justice Scalia's looks like an opinion written first as a dissent. This would account for its defensive and refutorial tone. In the alternative, both opinions might have been written for circulation among the Justices while each had less than majority support, in the hope of attracting a majority or at least a swing vote. The "swing vote" was Justice White, now retired, a member of the *Penn Central* majority.

[66] When a "substantial advancement of a legitimate state interest" or public purpose is required, many legislative findings may be insufficient to satisfy this standard. Indeed, here and later in his majority opinion in *Lucas*, Scalia has sharp words for legislative staffs: legislative purposes are not merely an "ingenious exercise in semantics and pleadings," Justice Scalia notes: were it not so, only an "exceedingly stupid staff" would fail the test.

This language came from *Agins v. Tiburon*[67] and derives originally from *Nectow v. City of Cambridge*.[68] It was also used in Justice Brennan's dissent in *San Diego Gas & Electric Co. v. City of San Diego*,[69] by Justice White in a wetlands regulatory case,[70] and by Justice Stevens earlier in 1987 in *Keystone* — Justice Scalia may have been working to get either of these Justices' votes in this section. So the quoted words had a respectable legal pedigree. However, here their function changed: they had not heretofore been used to strike down a legislative or administrative action; instead, they had been part of findings that regulations had indeed advanced a substantial governmental interest or purpose. This change in function is a clue that the opinion's reach was intended by its author to extend beyond its facts.

This language also reflects also the "substantial relation to the health, safety," etc. standard of *Euclid* — the reasonable relationship test. *Euclid* provides another source of the *Agins* formulation.[71] This language provides a more detailed standard of review.[72] The "essential nexus" required of the Coastal Commission is explained in a new way,[73] but it is not to be applied in all types of takings cases. The development condition in *Nollan* is of an unusual type and its holding if limited to its facts, creates a basis for a new category of takings — what came to be called regulatory exactions.

Nollan finds that an owner's right to build is not unfettered and may be "subjected to legitimate permitting requirements."[74] If the commission had required that the Nollans paint their bungalow sunflower yellow, this

---

[67] 447 U.S. 255, 260 (1980).

[68] 277 U.S. 183, 188 (1928).

[69] 450 U.S. 621 (1981) (in the first of several cases leading to *First English*, discussed in Chapter 5, Justice Brennan in dissent argued that the remedy of damages was available for a temporary regulatory taking and a majority of the Court agreed with him).

[70] *United States v. Riverside Bayview Homes, Inc.*, 474 U.S. 121 (1986).

[71] The opinion's n. 3, although arguably dicta, imposes a higher standard of review and scrutiny than does *Euclid*. Here the standard may amount to mid-level, scrutiny, of the type which the court created for the mentally retarded. *See Cleburne Living Ctr. v. City of Cleburne*, discussed in Chapter 15, *infra*. So "substantially advancing" may mean a "least onerous" scrutiny or "neither over nor under-inclusive" scrutiny for land use regulations; more generally, it may mean that mere allegations of public benefit are insufficient and that hard evidence of some type is required.

[72] *See, e.g., Commercial Builders of Northern California v. City of Sacramento*, 941 F.2d 872, 874 (9th Cir. 1991), *cert. denied*, 112 Sup. Ct. 1997 (1992) (stating that no federal appeals court has interpreted *Nollan* "as changing the level of scrutiny to be applied to regulations that do not constitute a physical encroachment on land.")

[73] The nexus requirement downplays the first prong and emphasizes the third prong of the *Penn Central* test that (you will recall) requires the court to examine (1) the economic impact of the regulation, particularly (2) the investment-backed expectations of the owner, along with (3) the character of the regulation, the third prong requiring a characterization of the regulation as either the acquisition of a public benefit (for which compensation is required) or the remedy for a public injury (no compensation being needed).

[74] *See City of Austin v. Quick*, 7 S.W.3d 109, 119–120 (Tex. 1999) (in a municipality with land overlying an aquifer from which it drew its drinking water, regulations limiting the percentage and amount of impervious surface covering the aquifer is essentially related to recharging the aquifer and the preservation of its water, in both quantity and quality — and thus to the health of the municipality's residents).

requirement, though extreme, is valid unless the Nollans can show that it has an undue economic impact. It may be irrational, but it is not an exaction.[75] Likewise, if the commission had conditioned its permit by requiring the Nollans to relocate a pre-existing easement over their lot for public access to the beach from the coastal highway, moving it from one location to another on the Nollans' lot, Justice Scalia's comments on the types of regulations that properly carry out the commission's interests easily justify this condition. It too is not an exaction: assuming the commission could relocate the easement without a taking, is to assume that the relocated easement is of the same value to its user and burdens the Nollans' property to no greater extent than it did previously.[76]

If the commission had wanted money to put in a fund for buying similar easements, instead of an easement itself, from the Nollans, nothing would change.[77] The commission would still have the burden of showing the nexus between its condition and the development. Because the easement alone would require compensation, no traditional deference or presumption of validity is accorded the commission's program — and it still has the burden of showing that there is a nexus between (1) the asserted interest of the commission and the money wanted in lieu of the easement, and (2) the purposes of the fund and the Nollan's development — the latter being the type of nexus the court later requires in *Dolan v. City of Tigard*.[78]

[4] *Nollan* and *Agins*.

Justice Scalia's opinion provides two amplifications of the test for a taking in *Agins*. First, he assumes that the first prong of the *Agins* test is not merely a due process requirement invoking a first tier, rational basis, standard of review. The first prong is for him just what *Agins* said it was, part of a test for a taking.

Second, he finds that the level of discretion given the commission in exacting the easement from the Nollans meant, as in the case of a physical invasion, a different standard of review. When an exaction is involved, the exercise of discretion has within it the possibility of administrative abuse, so that not every asserted governmental justification for the regulation will pass muster — rather, only those justifications that mitigate the harm caused by the development are constitutionally sufficient. So more than just substantially advancing the goals of the regulation is required: the regulation must "substantially advance a legitimate state interest," meaning an interest legitimately mitigating the harm worked by the development.[79]

---

[75] As we will see *infra*, this Chapter, the test here is the same as in *Agins* for evaluating a zoning ordinance; it is a substantive due process test.

[76] Determining the status of the easement involved in its relocation may, however, be ultra vires the statutory powers of a planning commission. *See, e.g., Kline v. Bernardsville Ass'n, Inc.*, 631 A.2d 1263 (N.J. Super. Ct., App. Div., 1993); *Smith v. Town of Wolfeboro*, 615 A.2d 1252, 1255 (N.H. 1992).

[77] *See Benchmark Land Co. v. City of Battle Ground*, 14 P.3d 172 (Wash. App. Ct. 2000), *rev. granted*, 143 Wn.2d 1018 (2001).

[78] 512 U.S. 374 (1974), discussed in this Chapter, *infra*.

[79] See note 4 of the Justice Scalia's majority opinion.

The harm cannot be imaginative or based on speculation. The essential nexus requirement in the administrative context of *Nollan*, but not required by the zoning ordinance in *Agins,* is a substantial link between the regulation and the harm caused by the development for which the permit it sought.

Thus, in the opinion's second part, after the *Loretto* discussion, the concern is, as in *Mahon*, with the line of cases in which the government attempts to extract a benefit from private citizens without providing a compensating benefit back. This part of the opinion is concerned with substantive due process, applied to the area of takings law: it builds on and gives specificity to, the reciprocity of advantage test in *Mahon*.[80]

[5] *Nollan's* Impact on Subdivision Regulations.

The *Nollan* opinion concerned the lot of one landowner, not a whole series of subdivision lots, and so is factually distinguishable from the situation presented in subdivision cases. However, assuming *arguendo* that *Nollan* applies to a subdivision development exactions case, older leading cases like *Ayres v. City Council*[81] are overruled. In the place of older cases like *Ayres*, stands the requirement of a substantial relationship, henceforth required of subdivision exactions.[82] If applicable to subdivision regulations, *Nollan* requires a crisper articulation of the public interest served. However, one later opinion said that *Nollan* arguably

> . . . does not stand for the proposition that an exaction ordinance will be upheld only where it can be shown that the development is directly responsible for the social ill in question. Rather, *Nollan* holds that where there is no evidence of a nexus between the development and the problem . . ., the exaction cannot be upheld.[83]

[6] Other Possible Impacts of *Nollan*.

In addition to subdivision exactions, *Nollan* might affect linkage fee ordinances, which provide that an office building developer is required to contribute to a low-income housing fund or to a fund to expand the public transit system. Further, states using Environmental Impact Statements (EISs) to consider the indirect costs or the cumulative effects of granting

---

[80] Justice Brennan downplayed this test in *Penn Central*, Justice Stevens generalized it in *Keystone*, and Justice Scalia it, in the essential nexus discussion in *Nollan*, applies it to an exactions claim.

[81] Op. cit., n. 31. When the later opinion in *Dolan, infra,* this Chapter, is considered, the word "probable" in this sentence can be changed to "highly probable."

[82] *Weingarten v. Town of Lewisboro*, 542 N.Y.S.2d 1012, 1015–1017 (N.Y. Sup. Ct., Westchester County, 1989) (recognizing that *Nollan* required a higher standard for in-lieu fee subdivision fees). *But see Sintra, Inc. v. City of Seattle*, 829 P.2d 765 (Wash. 1992) (finding that the payment of housing replacement fee as a condition of receiving a demolition permit was not subject to *Nollan* nexus analysis).

[83] *Commercial Builders of Northern California v. City of Sacramento*, 941 F.2d 872, 875 (9th Cir. 1991) (upholding the constitutionality of a housing linkage fee on commercial development measured by the number of low-income workers needing housing and working on the development).

the permit, might be affected. EISs would then have to consider only direct costs. However, *Nollan* has so far remained an exactions case, restricted in its application to subdivision or permit cases and judicial deference in zoning decisions is so far intact.[84]

[7] *Nollan* as Precedent.

An example of a state court's post-1987 use of *Nollan* is *Rohn v. City of Visalia*.[85] The court there invalidated a dedication requirement of 14% of the area of a parcel, imposed as a condition of a rezoning an owner's parcel from residential to office use. The dedication, it said, was found to have been required by a street realignment, not increased traffic from the re-zoned parcel. Moreover, the dedication was imposed after the planning commission had found that the rezoned parcel would produce less traffic than previously. Therefore, the court held that, under *Nollan*, the dedica-tion requirement was invalid. The opinion in *Rohn* also required that the planning studies done to justify the dedication be particular to the neighbor-hood, and not be community wide. Neighborhood planning, rather than city wide planning, must be in place when a dedication requirement is imposed. To this extent, *Rohn* limits the third and fourth tests for subdivision exactions discussed previously in this Chapter.

Suppose that, enacted under a comprehensive state land use plan, zoning regulations permit existing agricultural uses in a region otherwise zoned for forest uses. All non-forestry uses are permitted to continue, provided that a negative covenant (restricting the land to its present use) is recorded at the time the permit is issued. An owner applies for a permit to operate his pre-existing farm, but resists the conveyance of the deed restriction. *Nollan* does not prevent the regulators from requiring the covenant: the easement restriction on the Nollans' title allowed the public access to the Nollans' property, while the commission's restriction still permits the owner to exclude the public. Retaining the right to exclude makes this requirement less draconian than the exaction requested from the Nollans. *Nollan* does not impose a requirement that regulators proceed in the least burdensome manner.[86]

Likewise, suppose that a municipality places land surrounding a lake in a summer cottage residential use district, residences in such a district to be occupied for only 30 days during the winter months (November 1 to May 1). Residents wanting to winter over in their cottages argued that the right to use and possession of the property was at stake and being denied — more serious than the restriction in the last paragraph — for five months out of each year. If this is a health or safety matter (a matter of occupants freezing to death, etc.) during the winter in an uninsulated structure, the

---

[84] For a case using *Nollan* in its precise setting, see *State v. Putman*, 552 A.2d 1247 (Del. Super. Ct. 1988) (town ordinance requiring beach front owners to build retaining walls to protect beach and public road from erosion, held unconstitutional).

[85] 263 Cal. Rptr. 319 (Cal. App. Ct. 1989).

[86] *See Gardner v. New Jersey Pinelands Comm'n*, 593 A.2d 251, 262 (N.J. 1991) (affirming validity of commission negative easement regulations).

ordinance may be sustained. However, the right to possession is a fundamental right, and if *Nollan* was intended to single out some rights as
entitled to special protection, then *Nollan's* heightened standard of review
requires the municipality to justify the ordinance as one "substantially
advancing a legitimate state interest."[87] Absent this justification, denying
an owner possession is no less crucial than denying the right to exclude
the public.

In a fourth example, a hundred yards from an owner's littoral property,
the state constructed a public boat launch and, to make launching safer
and easier, it installed jetties. The jetties alter the currents along the shore
and erosion washes away first the owner's beach, and then his lawn and
a tree on fast land. The owner's takings claim might be brought either as
a *per se*, physical invasion taking or as a *Nollan* claim for an uncompensated
exaction. Even though there has been no permanent physical occupation
of owner's land by the state, the effect of the state's action is the same: its
action has deprived the owner of possession, so a claim for a physical invasion is a reasonable response. The state's defense will be that its actions
are in furtherance of the well-recognized public trust, giving the public the
right to boat on navigable waters. Nonetheless, there is no essential nexus
as *Nollan* requires: eroding the owner's land does not further, much less
substantially further, an admittedly legitimate state interest.[88]

[8]   Two Limitations on the Reach of *Nollan*.

First, in *City of Monterey v. Del Monte Dunes at Monterey, Ltd.*,[89] the
Supreme Court implicitly limited its holding in *Nollan* to "land use decisions conditioning approval of development on the dedication of property
to public use" when it expressly limited the impact of the another later,
nexus case, i.e., *Dolan v. City of Tigard*, there being no reason to limit one
without including the other in the limitation.[90] That is, the "essential
nexus" of *Nollan*, between (1) the condition on the permit and (2) the regulation and the public policy used to impose it, applies only when something
akin to a physical invasion or a physical exaction, is presented.

Second, even if *Nollan* were assumed to be an extension of the physical
invasion cases, the later case of *Yee v. City of Escondido*,[91] turned aside

---

[87] *See, e.g., Seawall Assocs. v. City of New York*, 542 N.E.2d 1059, 1066 (N.Y. 1989) (holding
a five year moratorium on conversion of single room occupancy housing to other uses,
unconstitutional and discussing the effect of *Nollan, id.* at 1068–1069).

[88] *See Peterman v. State Department of Natural Resources*, 521 N. W. 2d 449 (Mich. 1994)
(treating a similar situation as a regulatory taking under *Nollan* and awarding compensation).
See also McQueen v. South Carolina Coastal Council, 530 S.E.2d 628 (S.C. 2000) (finding no
taking in a denial of bulkhead permits for coastal property), *cert. granted and vacated*, 2001
U.S. LEXIS 4949 (June 29, 2001). *But see Miramar Co. v. City of Santa Barbara*, 143 P. 2d
1, 4 (Calif. 1943).

[89] 526 U.S. 687 (1999).

[90] For a case expressly limiting *Nollan* in this way, see*Bonnie Briar Syndicate, Inc. v. Town
of Mamaroneck*, 721 N.E.2d 971, 975–976 (N.Y. 1999).

[91] 503 U.S. 519 (1992) (concerning a limitation on a landlord's right to rent a pad for a mobile
home in a mobile home park).

any further extension of these cases, so this line of analysis in Justice Scalia's discussion of *Loretto* dead ends with *Yee* — again leaving *Nollan* as a leading case for a new type of takings case — an exactions case.

[B] *Dolan v. City of Tigard* [92]

[1] The Facts.

Mrs. Florence Dolan applied to the City of Tigard (a suburb of Portland, Oregon) for a building permit to expand her business, A-Boy Plumbing, a plumbing and electrical retail store. She owned a 1.67 acre lot with a 9,700 square foot store on it. It is located in the City's central business district. Fanno Creek flows through the lot's southwest and western boundary and renders part of the lot a "floodplain virtually unusable for commercial development." Dolan wished to replace the existing building and expand her store's square footage by 80% to 17,600 square feet, pave the store's parking lot for 39 parking spaces, and later construct a second building for complementary businesses with additional parking. Her proposed development conformed to the City's comprehensive plan and was consistent with its zoning ordinance.

The permit was approved, but with two conditions: first, that she dedicate the portions of the lot within the floodplain for a public greenway, and second, that she dedicate a fifteen foot strip for a pedestrian bicycle path. The first condition (for the greenway) was rationalized as flood control for the increased run-off created by the development. The second's rationale was that the bicycle path might ameliorate the impact of additional traffic generated by the development.

After the conditional granting of the permit, Mrs. Dolan sought — and was denied — a variance from the two conditions. The municipal zoning board affirmed and the Oregon courts rejected her argument that neither condition was related to the development and upheld both conditions as reasonably related to her development. [93] The United States Supreme Court reversed. [94]

[2] The *Dolan* Majority.

Writing for the five Justice majority, Chief Justice Rehnquist first states that had the city simply required that Mrs. Dolan dedicate a strip of land along Fanno Creek for public use, there would be a taking. "Public access

---

[92] 512 U.S. 374 (1994), *noted* 29 R.Prop. Prob. & Tr.J. 451 (1994), 23 Real Est. L.J. 275 (1995).

[93] *Dolan v. City of Tigard*, 854 P.2d 437 (Or. 1993).

[94] On remand, Mrs. Dolan was granted a permit again subject to the same conditions, but on an amplified record. She sued for a temporary taking and settled this suit for $1.5 million. *See* William Quinland, John Kennedy, & James Niewiara, *Defending against the Takings Claim: A Practical Guide for Municipalities*, 29 Stet. L. Rev. 658, 676–677 (2000).

would deprive petitioner of the right to exclude others . . . ." so there would be taking.[95] So, he says, this, like *Nollan*, is an exactions case.

The Chief Justice then makes plain that his opinion here builds on *Nollan*. The latter opinion involved the "essential nexus" required between a regulation's public purpose (its "legitimate state interest," in *Agins* terminology) and the permit condition. The city's interest in managing flooding and traffic "qualify as the type of legitimate public purposes we have upheld. (citing *Agins*.)" With regard to the first condition on the permit, a nexus exists between preventing flooding and limiting development in the flood plain: because expanding the store increases the imperious surface on her parcel and contributes to the run-off into the Creek, limiting development on the flood plain mitigates the danger of future flooding. Similarly, there is an essential nexus between reducing traffic congestion and providing alternative means of transportation (via the bike path), so that the dedication of a bike path will mitigate an increase in traffic congestion resulting from the expansion.

If the first prong (the essential nexus) exists, the degree of the exaction demanded must then be examined. "The second part of our analysis," the Chief Justice continued, "requires us to determine whether the degree of the exactions demanded by the city permit conditions bear the required relationship to the projected impact of petitioner's proposed development." The opinion next reviewed the various subdivision regulation exactions tests and concluded that the "reasonable relationship" test — not the "specifically and uniquely attributable" test — best served its needs. The opinion takes pains to say:

> We think [this test] . . . is closer to the federal constitutional norm than [those previously discussed]. But we do not adopt it as such, partly because the term "reasonable relationship" is confusingly similar to the term "rational basis" . . . . We think . . . "rough proportionality" best encapsulates what we hold to be the requirement of the Fifth Amendment.

No precise mathematical formula is involved, but "the city must make some sort of individualized determination that the required dedication is related both in nature and extent to the impact of the proposed development." The exaction and the impact or harm created by the project must be roughly proportionate. Some exactions may have an essential nexus (as here), but are so disproportionate to the impact of the proposed development, that they violate the Fifth Amendment (as, it turns out, is the case here). In addition, the obligation to make an individualized determination of proportionate impact will keep the municipality honest and help to prevent its overreaching and abuse of power; municipalities must make quantifiable, individual findings as appropriate when making a demand for property interests from an owner.

---

[95] Justice Stevens in dissent suggests that the majority focuses on the exaction alone, but not the impact of the exaction on Mrs. Dolan's property as a whole. The point is that, for exactions, the parcel-as-a-whole approach of Justice Brennan in *Penn Central* is not to be used.

The city failed to meet the "rough proportionality" test. As to the first condition, keeping the flood plain free of development is consistent with the state interest shown, but "the city demanded more — it not only wanted the petitioner not to build on the floodplain, but it also wanted petitioner's property along Fanno Creek for its greenway system" without saying why a public way, rather than a private one, was necessary to achieve its interest. A public greenway entails the "loss of the [petitioner's] ability to exclude others." "It is difficult to see why recreational visitors trampling along petitioner's floodplain easement are sufficiently related to the city's legitimate interest in reducing flooding . . . ." As the city had not explained this matter further, there is no reasonable relationship between the floodplain easement and the petitioner's proposal for a new store.

As to the second condition, the city also failed to explain how the increased traffic generated by the proposal will be diminished by the bike path. Finding that the bike way "could offset some of the traffic and lessen the increase in traffic congestion" is insufficient and not individualized enough an explanation to meet the reasonable relationship required here.

So the city fails the second, rough proportionality test. This test is new constitutional law. In federal courts, *Nollan* requires the essential nexus, and *Dolan* requires a further analysis of rough proportionality. This two-step analysis is an obstacle course for municipalities demanding subdivision exactions.

Suppose that a client wishes to expand his business, located on Center Street, one of two downtown commercial streets leading to an arterial highway overloaded with traffic. The other street is High Street and it generates most of the traffic using the overloaded highway. The municipality refuses to approve his expansion plans unless his curb cuts and parking spaces are limited so that the traffic using Center Street does not increase the overload on the highway. The municipality's response is not roughly proportionate to the impact of your client's expansion plans. If the traffic is generated by High Street businesses and uses, then limiting the expansion of a business on Center Street does not address the problem of the arterial highway's traffic overload. The refusal to approve the expansion of the client's business is not roughly proportionate to the impact of the client's business on the highway and will not proportionately lessen that overload.

[3] Three Implications of *Dolan*.

First, the court is fleshing out what it regards as a "rational basis" standard of review. It does not adopt or "federalize" the state law it cites. It talks of "rough proportionality," but cites with approval *Simpson v. North Platte*,[96] as representative of the test that the court adopts. *Simpson* is only a reasonable relationship case. Both the essential nexus and rough

---

[96] 292 N.W. 2d 297 (Neb. 1980).

proportionality are only two versions of a reasonable relationship test. First tier scrutiny, applied twice.[97]

Second, note 8 indicates that the majority was only imposing the showing an "individualized determination" of rough proportionality on the city. Traditionally, it is the applicant who carries the burden of proof in land use regulation proceedings, but for exactions, things are different. Here it is not the applicant who must show a lack of a reasonable relationship, but the city that must show one is present, quantifying it as rough proportionality between the impact of the development and the exaction.[98] If Fanno Creek were a watering hole amid grazing lands for endangered wildlife, the government's interest in — indeed, its ownership of — wildlife providing an essential nexus, a wildlife corridor could be required through subdivisions along the creek. Similarly, if the exaction's purpose were to give the public a right to fish along Fanno Creek, a right protected in some states by the public trust, a fishing easement might follow. However, the methodology for quantifying the proportionate impact remains subject to dispute: for example, any one of several methods used in EISs might be used: that is, matrixes of project components and impacts, market modeling, network assessments, and cartographic overlays, all might be suitable in some contexts.

Third, had the city required the land dedication in isolation, then a taking would have occurred. Is this case just another case (like *Nollan*) where the facts look like a physical invasion? It is, in the sense that the right to exclude passed out of the land owner's hands. The court is here, as in *Nollan*, giving owners constitutional law weapons to prevent this. *Dolan* suggests that more traditional, restrictive use regulations remain subject to reasonable basis scrutiny by the courts; the opinion had, for example, statements reenforcing its holding in the *Euclid* decision, mentioning the latter by name. Where the dedication is made necessary by a particular development, it may still be imposed. The test of rough proportionality indicates some remaining deference to governmental decision making. *Dolan* is also not an instance of a taking of a severed interest (and does not repudiate the parcel-as-a-whole approach of *Penn Central*). It is a case in which the government sought to require an owner to give up a constitutional right in return for a discretionary benefit without an essential nexus and an individualized determination that the property interests sought are imposed in rough proportion to the harm created by the development.[99]

---

[97] At oral argument of *Dolan*, the city attorney argued that petitioner was not being treated in isolation, that the city had developed comprehensive plans mandated by state statute; the court did not discuss the city's planning process and instead noted that no part of the development interfered with an existing public greenway; no public resources were adversely affected by it.

[98] In addition, no matter who has the burden of proof, the applicant has the burden of litigation, and must have both the stomach and the money for litigation with the government.

[99] See, *infra*, this Chapter, for a discussion of unconstitutional conditions.

[4]   Testing the Limits of *Dolan* — One Crisp Limit.

In the majority opinion, footnote 8 appears just after the court adopts the rough proportionality test and limits its application to adjudicative, rather than legislative decisions, and this has generally been accepted.[100] This distinction may prove hard to maintain, considering the myriad of practices for handling land use matters by municipalities. However, a case in which the court later denied certiorari illustrated this distinction: a municipality had an ordinance with parking requirements and also requiring that parcels, after being subdivided, maintain at least 10% of their acreage in landscaping, and have at least one tree for every eight parking spaces. State courts had found the ordinance constitutional as a exercise of the police power by a municipal legislature; they applied the usual presumption of validity and the "fairly debatable" rule of validity, and found the ordinance to substantially advance a legitimate governmental interest. With regard to this finding, *Dolan* was held not to require a more detailed and tailored justification: that is, *Dolan* involves an adjudicative municipal action, requiring that a general policy be applied in an individualized manner, but the action here was distinguishable because it was legislative in nature.[101]

[5]   *Dolan* and Subdivision Exactions.

Off-site exactions are particularly suspect after this case. Without evidence that a proposed development requires the widening of the street abutting the property to be subdivided, a municipality seeking to require the dedication of property for widening the street as a condition of approval for a development, runs afoul of *Dolan*. This is an example of the reach of *Dolan* in the context of a very widely used condition on development. Neither the presumption of validity, nor of constitutionality, nor the legislative label that might be attached to this requirement if it is comprehensive in nature, will likely save this requirement from the judicial scrutiny that *Dolan's* rule of rough proportionality rule requires.[102] Even if the municipality were to allege that because the property is underutilized even under his proposal, and that its more intensive development will in

---

[100] *See generally* Inna Resnik, *The Distinction between Legislative and Adjudicative Decisions in Dolan v. City of Tigard*, 75 N.Y. U. L Rev. 242 (2000).

[101] *Parking Ass'n of Georgia, Inc. v. City of Atlanta*, 450 S. E.2d 200, 203 (Ga. 1994), cert. denied, 115 Sup. Ct. 2268–2269 (Justices Thomas and O'Connor dissenting and arguing that lower courts should not have to struggle with the uncertainties of *Dolan*, and the majority taking pains to distinguish a rational basis test, applicable to most zoning and land use control regulation, from its test here, and linking the constitutional protections given to speech in the First Amendment, to search and seizure under the Fourth Amendment, to (finally) the Takings Clause of the Fifth Amendment). Such linkage sounds, if not like the harbinger of heightened scrutiny, as an attempt to unify and harmonize various forms of constitutional analysis.

[102] *Cf. William J. Jones Ins. Trust v. City of Fort Smith*, 731 F. Supp. 912 (W. D. Ark. 1990) (applying the *Nollan* nexus test in a similar situation), discussed in J. Holloway & D. Guy, *Land Dedication Conditions and Beyond the Essential Nexus: Determining "Reasonably Related" Impacts of Real Estate Development Under the Takings Clause*, 27 Tex. Tech. L. Rev. 73, 133, n. 344 (1996).

the future make the widening necessary, this allegation make no difference: the rough proportionality rule cannot be met by speculation about future construction and development; it must be satisfied in the present and be based on the present or proposed state of development.

Another example of a subdivision regulation running afoul of *Dolan* is a requirement that a subdivider pay for a drainage system serving a whole watershed when the subdivision will only cover one sixth of its land area.[103] Similarly, "premature" subdivision exactions are suspect after this case.[104]

[6] Planning and Statistics after *Dolan*: An Example.

Past statistics have a limited use for municipal land planners after *Dolan*. For example, a municipality provides in its subdivision regulations that a developer dedicate land for park purposes because its population increased fourfold in the last decade, that every resident needs a minimum of 3,000 square feet of parkland, and that in the last five years, 600 new subdivision lots had been created in 40 new plats. Thus, 1,800,000 square feet (3,000 × 600) of parkland should be required of new subdivision developers. This, the municipality says, works out to one acre per 15 lot subdivision on the municipality's remaining open land. This scheme probably does not satisfy the rough proportionality standard of *Dolan*. The municipality used past growth statistics that do not provide a basis for predicting the number of new residents needing new parks. The requirement is based on the parcels in the subdivision and not on the new residents expected to live there; this does not provide a standard yielding a rough proportionality between the subdivision and its impact on existing parks and does not quantify findings that apply to the particular developer's subdivision application. This is, however, the sort of data and requirement that was approved in *Jordan v. Village of Menomonee Falls*,[105] *Dolan* therefore makes both the reasoning and the holding of *Jordan* suspect.

On the other hand, if the municipality found that past subdivisions consumed 50% of the municipality's land area available for subdivision, then the 50% remaining — subdivided in lots of a certain size — would likely produce a population of X, needing a park the size of Y acres. That acreage (or its cost) could then be assessed to future subdivision applicants.[106] This is an important point: the "individualized determination" may be made at the time of application; so the subdivider or developer is denied the argument that he or she did not create the problem that the municipality seeks to solve. The mere fact that prior urbanization created

---

[103] *See Christopher Lake Dev. Co. v. St. Louis Cty.*, 35 F.3d 1269, 1270–1271 (8th Cir. 1994) (applying Dolan to invalidate the regulation as applied, permitting developer to recoup the cost of installation).

[104] *See supra* this Chapter, at notes 22–24. *But see Batch v. Town of Chapel Hill*, 387 S.E.2d 655 (N.C. 1990) (refusing to recognize listing plaintiff's land on an official map as an exaction, even though a subdivision plat required "accommodation" recognizing the map), *cert. denied*, 496 U.S. 931 (1990).

[105] 137 N.W. 2d 442 (Wis. 1965).

[106] *See also* Richard Faus, *Exactions, Impact Fees, and Dedications — Local Government Responses to Nollan/Dolan Takings Law Issues*, 29 Stet. L. Rev. 675 (2000).

a problem, and that the last developer in an neighborhood is asked to contribute to the solution, is no reason to invalidate an exaction.

[7] The Doctrine of Unconstitutional Conditions.

As stated in *Dolan*, this doctrine is to the effect that ". . . the government may not require a person to give up a constitutional right-here the right to receive just compensation when property is taken for a public use-in exchange for a discretionary benefit conferred by the government where the property sought has little or no relationship to the benefit."[107] For example, even though there is generally no vested right to subdivide land and it is generally viewed as a discretionary benefit given by a municipality, subdivision still may not be offered in exchange for giving up the right to just compensation. Bargaining away a constitutional right in exchange for a discretionary benefit, would otherwise permit the municipality to achieve what it could not do directly. So the condition must be justified and its benefits must be roughly proportional to the cost of the conditions imposed: for a residential subdivision developer, this means that the benefits must be capable of being passed along in house prices that reflect the benefit of the municipality's services.[108]

The doctrine is intended to protect individuals in their dealings with government by preventing government from doing indirectly what it lacks authority to do directly. It is a product of the era of *Lochner v. The State of New York*.[109] It has been used or rejected in many areas of constitutional law, in cases involving free speech, religious exercise, Congressional spending powers, and here, with regard to the police power and the takings clause, without a consistent rationale for its application.[110] It is applied here, even though the *Dolan* majority states that the municipality could have withheld the development permit altogether.[111]

[8] Impact Fees and *Dolan*.

When a municipality imposes an impact fee on the developer's subdivision permit to build houses, imposing the fee in order to (say) mitigate the loss

---

[107] As used in section II of the *Dolan* opinion. *See generally* Michael Kersten, *Exactions, Severability and Takings: When Courts Should Sever Unconstitutional Conditions from Development Permits*, 27 Envir. Aff. 279 (2000).

[108] *See Welch v. Paicos*, 66 F. Supp. 2d 138, 180 (U.S. D. Ct., D. Mass., 1999) (explaining the doctrine).

[109] 198 U.S. 45 (1905) (invalidating a state regulation of maximum working hours in bakeries).

[110] *See* Donald Guy & James Holloway, *The Direction of Regulatory Takings in the Post-Lochner Era*, 102 Dick. L. Rev. 327, 349–350 (1998) (reviewing the doctrine in midst of a *Nollan/Dolan* discussion).

[111] Justice Stevens, dissenting in *Dolan*, would not have invoked the doctrine because the case involved a business regulation and he regarded the exchange of a dedication for a permit as a mutually beneficial transaction. The majority and the dissent disagree on the extent of governmental coercion that must be present in a "transaction" before the doctrine may be used, and Stevens suggests that the holding in *Nollan* and *Dolan* actually disadvantage owners wanting to bargain with a municipality by putting "exacted" bargains in unconstitutional terrain.

of open spaces and purchase other open space, *Dolan* does not apply to these money exactions.[112] *Dolan* burden shifting and quasi-heightened scrutiny only applies to land exactions, not money exactions. In part, this is because of Supreme Court precedent: *Nollan* gave reasons why land exactions require special constitutional considerations.[113] Moreover, one court has held that a money exaction need only be rationally related to the mitigation of the public benefits lost to the development.[114] Although the impact of a money exaction can be severe, a majority of the Supreme Court has indicated, by merely vacating the opinion in a later case, that it wants to maintain this distinction. In the vacated opinion, a municipality had issued a building permit, but conditioned the issuance on the payment of $50,000 by the developer into a fund for the purchase of public three dimensional art (sculpture, etc.) for public places. This exaction for public space art thus tested the proposition that what the *Dolan* majority objected to was not really the degree of relationship that was lacking with regard to the conditions for the bike-path and greenway, but has to do with whether it failed to find any nexus at all.[115]

What if an ordinance levied a transportation impact fee on all new development, so that a change in the level of service (LOS) required on nearby roads, pedestrian walk-ways, and public transportation routes made necessary by the development, can be partially paid for by the fee, calculated as a pro rata amount of the total costs of the development, placed in a special transportation fund, and returned if not used within five years on a site within three blocks of the development. The developer is also required to pay a relocation assistance fee for any low-income persons displaced by the development. Both of these two fees might be conceded to have an essential or substantial nexus under *Nollan*, and the transportation fee is legislatively tailored to link the fee to the public need's for transportation of various types in rough proportion, but the latter, the relocation fee, would probably flunk the rough proportionality test of *Dolan*.[116]

Another likely response to the *Dolan* opinion is a state legislature repealing a statue authorizing development impact fees, but then enacting a statute authorizing any municipality with zoning authority to impose a

---

[112] *See* Richard Ansson, Jr., *Dolan v. Tigard's Rough Proportionality Standard: Why This Standard Should Not Be Applied to an Inverse Condemnation Claim Based Upon Regulatory Denial*, 10 Seton Hall. Const. L. J. 417, 440–442 (2000) (collecting the cases). *But see Ehrlich v. City of Culver City*, 911 P.2d 429, 434–435 (Cal. 1996) (exaction for fund for placing art in public places in lieu of placing art on the regulated parcel).

[113] *See Blue Jeans Equities West v. City and County*, 4 Cal. Rptr.2d 114 (Cal. App. Ct.) (interpreting *Nollan* in this way), *cert. denied*, 113 Sup. Ct. 191 (1992).

[114] *Ehrlich v. City of Culver City*, 19 Cal. Rptr.2d 468 (Cal. App. Ct. 1993), *vacated and remanded*, 114 Sup. Ct. 2731 (1994) (for reconsideration in light of *Dolan*, Blackmun, Stevens, Souter, and Ginsburg voting to deny cert.).

[115] *See Hensler v. City of Glendale*, 876 P. 2d 1043 (Cal. 1994) (reconsidering the validity of such a fee after *Dolan*).

[116] For an article suggesting ordinance provisions for impact fees, see Charles Mulcahy & Michelle Zimet, *Impact Fees for a Developing Wisconsin*, 79 Marq. L. Rev. 759, 782–795 (1996), discussing *St. Johns Cty. v. Northeast Florida Builders Ass'n*, 583 So.2d 635 (Fla. 1991).

development impact tax as an excise tax to the same extent than the state could enact such a tax — payable as a condition of issuing a building permit. Many prior judicial decisions in several states invalidated impact fees as an unauthorized tax. Developers who paid such fees under protest might after *Dolan* sue to recover the amounts paid, but the municipality levying the fee interposes its taxing authority, applied retroactively, to authorize retention of the amounts collected, then as a fee, but now retained as tax receipts. Such suits would likely fail. The event on which the fee is levied, and the event on which the tax is imposed, are the same: namely, the development of the taxpayer's property. So the retroactive imposition of the tax does not impair vested rights, or does not impair rights not already impaired.[117] *Dolan* does not require that the classification of the fee as a tax be reconsidered.[118] It does not deny development, but only taxes it.[119] As a tax, the development charge is also subject to equal protection analysis, but this will not detain a court long if developers may reasonably be taxed as a group.

After *Dolan*, a flat, per parcel, impact fee that is not earmarked for use for a capital improvement made necessary by the development to which it is charged, violates two benchmarks of rough proportionality required by that case: it does not attempt to correlate the impacts of a subdivision with the amount of the fee, and does not specify the expenditures it will make with the money collected from the fee, meanwhile held it in a reserve account. Without these basic safeguards, subdividing owners need not pay it, absent some estoppel or laches defense by the municipality.[120]

Finally, neither *Nollan* nor *Dolan* imposes limits on the type of public facility or purpose that a municipality may pursue.[121] Thus, an impact fee for the purpose of purchasing art works for display in public parks and squares and in front of public buildings may be valid, so long as the purpose of the fee is defined with clarity, funds collected are to be kept in a separate accounts, used only for the named purposes, and if not so used within a few years, returned to the payor of the fee. The municipality must, however, demonstrate that there is a reasonable relationship between the fee's use and the type of development project on which it is imposed, and between the amount of the fee and the cost of the public facility attributable to the development on which the fee is imposed. Assuming the ordinance has been procedurally bullet-proofed, it would be still less vulnerable to attack when the developer is able to satisfy its terms by either installing art in the

---

[117] *Waters Landing Limited Partnership v. Montgomery County*, 650 A. 2d 712, 720 (Md. 1994).

[118] *Id.* at 724 ("To the extent that this tax is a regulation on the development of land, it is not a regulation that 'goes too far' so as to be 'recognized as a taking.'").

[119] *See also Homebuilders Ass'n of Central Arizona v. City of Scottsdale*, 902 P. 2d 1347 (Ariz. App. 1995) (finding that an impact fee is a regulatory fee and not a tax).

[120] *Cf.Henderson Homes, Inc. v. City of Bothell*, 877 P.2d 176 (Wash. 1994) (so holding, but deciding the case under a state statutory scheme for impact fees).

[121] *See generally Home Builders Ass'n of Dayton and the Miami Valley v. City of Beavercreek*, 1998 Ohio App. LEXIS 4957 (Ohio App. Ct. 1998) (a thorough discussion of *Nollan* and *Dolan* in the context of impact fees).

development, or by paying a fee in lieu of installation, or donating art-works to the town. As to whether an impact fee may be levied for the purpose of paying for public art, if developers may be forced to pay fees for parks, why not art? The quality of town life will be improved: because aesthetics is generally a proper purpose and within the police powers of most jurisdictions, it is difficult to see that the purchase of art is not a legitimate state interest.[122]

[9]   A Later Limitation.

As to *Dolan*, the later opinion in *City of Monterey v. Del Monte Dunes at Monterey, Ltd.*,[123] limited the impact of its holding, and as previously indicated, the following limitation applies to *Nollan* too. The court said:

> Although in a general sense concerns for proportionality animate the Takings Clause . . ., we have not extended the rough-proportionality test of Dolan beyond the special context of exactions — land-use decisions conditioning approval of development on the dedication of property to public use. (Citing both *Dolan* and *Nollan* -ed.). The rule applied in Dolan . . . was not designed to address, and is not readily applicable to, the much different questions arising where, as here, the landowner's challenge is based not on excessive exactions but on denial of development.[124]

Thus *Nollan* and *Dolan* apply only to physical exactions, not monetary ones.

§ 14.21   Summary.

United States Supreme Court has handed down decisions dealing with each prong of the *Agins* takings test: the *Lucas* opinion deals with the question of what happens when a property owner has been deprived of all economic use, and *Nollan* and *Dolan* tell us what it means for a municipality substantially to advance a legitimate state interest. In *Nollan*, the court merely found no essential nexus, but in the *Dolan* case it went further and imposed a finding requirement on municipal governments; it queried not only the sufficiency of the government's findings and how they were drafted, but also queried the quality and specificity of those findings. *Dolan* imposes yet another burden of proof on municipalities, signals greater judicial scrutiny and review in the context of municipal exactions, but also helpfully tells municipalities what to do to satisfy the courts. Thus under *Nollan*, a legitimate state interest must be rationally related to the exaction, and under *Dolan*, the exaction must be rationally related to the impact of the proposed development for which a permit is sought.

---

[122] *See Erlich v. Culver City*, 911 P.2d 429 (Cal. 1996) (upholding a similar fee).

[123] 526 U.S. 687 (1999).

[124] *Id.* at 702–703. *See New Port Largo, Inc. v. Monroe Cty.*, 95 F.3d 1084(11th Cir. 1996) (concluding the same), *cert. denied*, 117 Sup. Ct. 2514 (1997); *Sprenger, Grubb & Assoc. v. City of Hailey*, 903 P.2d 741 (Idaho 1995).

Part 3

Economic Discrimination and Zoning

Chapter 15

Exclusionary Zoning

§ 15.01 Introduction.

All Euclidian zoning has some exclusionary consequences or effects —
zoning a use into a municipality has the effect of zoning some uses out.
This is shown in the discussion of the *Euclid* opinion in its discussion about
excluding apartment houses from single family, residential use districts,
and more particularly and forcefully shown in the discussion of the opinion
of the district court judge in *Euclid*. At the same time, the opinion of the
United State Supreme Court in this case recognized expressly that the
interest of the general public might, at some indefinite future time,
outweigh the interests of the Village.

Another effect of the *Euclid* opinion was to de-emphasize the line of cases
culminating in *Buchanan v. Warley*,[1] which explored the civil rights
implications of early zoning ordinances. *Euclid* was in this respect a judicial
signal either (broadly considered) not to inquire into the legislative motivation for enacting an ordinance, or (more narrowly) a signal not to impute
an improper motive merely from the enactment of the ordinance.

Municipalities, even with good intentions, enact zoning ordinances with
exclusionary effects. In the leading case on planned unit developments,[2]
for example, the ordinance contained a provision limiting the number of
bedrooms for some dwellings within the PUD, to two. This has an exclusionary effect on larger families and, if statistically low income families contain
more children, a disproportionate impact on these families. The municipality sought to avoid having to use its tax revenue to build new schools or
school facilities.

§ 15.02 Exclusionary Zoning Defined.

Exclusionary zoning is a pattern of zoning decisions or ordinances that
have one of two effects. The first effect is to exclude low and moderate
income housing from the jurisdiction and raise the price of housing beyond
the means of low and moderate income persons. As a result, the community
is not providing its fair share of its region's need for low and moderate
income housing.[3] In the 1980s, such housing came to be called affordable
housing — meaning housing that is built without excessive regulatory costs
built into its price.

---

[1] 245 U.S. 60 (1917).

[2] *Cheney v. Village 2 at New Hope, Inc.*, *supra*, Chapter 12.

[3] *See Home Builders League of South Jersey, Inc. v. Township of Berlin*, 405 A.2d 381 (N.J.
1979).

The second effect is to avoid the provision of services and urban infrastructure.[4] Quite often, while a municipality seeks to avoid financing and building an urban or suburban infrastructure, it seeks to build up its tax base with light industry and types of housing which require little in the way of municipal services.

The "first effect" cases have been more influential. One line of these cases involved large lot zoning. They initially involved 1960s developers' challenges to large lot zoning, in suburbs in which the minimum acreage required in some residential use districts was one acre or more — and in some instances, this minimum was four or five acres.[5]

Another line of similar cases involved the total exclusion of some uses — say apartments, mobile homes, quarries or gas stations — from a municipality.[6] Together, these two lines of authority stand for the doctrine that if a municipality did not use its zoning powers for the benefit of the general population residing in a metropolitan area or did not provide districts for uses fairly representative of all uses within that area, its zoning was exclusionary.

Using this doctrine to challenge exclusionary zoning is meant to promote metropolitan-wide racial, ethic, and economic integration. When an ordinance or decision is found exclusionary, or in violation of the fair housing acts and the result of housing discrimination, courts have fashioned remedies that are premised on this goal. Courts ordered the exclusionary municipality to provide its fair share of affordable housing for low or moderate income persons in the region. Courts impose "fair share" duties reluctantly. For example, if a municipality lay outside of the "path of growth" or its population increases were slight, an exclusion of commercial uses, and even apartments, might be justified.[7] Sometimes this reluctance shows itself in the use of the presumption of validity attaching to an ordinance. If the proposed housing was excluded, but similar housing permitted, the presumption of validity attached and the burden of overturning it fell to the challenger; on the other hand, if the proposal was for a

---

[4] For an early case in which the failure to provide sewers came to be seen as exclusionary by a very conservative state court, see *Board of Cty. Supervisors of Fairfax Cty. v. Carper*, 107 S.E. 2d 390 (Va. 1959).

[5] *See, e.g., Bilbar Construction Co. v. Easttown Township Bd. of Adjustment*, 141 A. 2d 851 (Pa. 1958) (one acre lots); *National Land and Investment Co. v. Kohn*, 215 A. 2d 597 (Pa. 1965), *noted* 114 U. Pa. L.Rev. 1251; 27 U. Pitt. L.Rev. 919 (1966) (four acre lots); *Appeal of Kit-Mar Builders*, 439 Pa. 466, 268 A. 2d 765 (1970).

[6] *Appeal of Girsch*, 263 A. 2d 395 (Pa. 1970) (the exclusion of apartments); *Vickers v. Twp. Committee of Gloucester Twp.*, 181 A. 2d 129 (N.J.), *cert. denied and appeal dismissed*, 371 U.S. 233 (1962) (Hall, J. dissenting) (exclusion of mobile homes); *Town of Conover v. Jolly*, 177 S.E.2d 879, 881–82 (N.C. 1970) (same); *Exton Quarries, Inc. v. Zoning Board of Adjustment*, 228 A. 2d 169 (Pa. 1967) (stone quarries).

[7] *Fernley v. Bd. of Supervisors of Schuykill Twp.*, 464 A. 2d 587, 588 (Pa. Commwlth. Ct. 1983), *reversed*, 502 A. 2d 585 (Pa. 1985) (pointing out that factors other than population growth might influence the demand for apartments).

"basic form of housing" that was not provided for in the municipality's land use regulations, then the presumption of validity was denied.[8]

§ 15.03   The Basis for This Doctrine.

In some states, the doctrine has a constitutional basis — the general welfare clause of a state constitution. In New Jersey, an express general welfare provision is sometimes used. Similarly, the general welfare clause of the New York state constitution and its zoning enabling statute are used to invalidate the exclusion of multi-family housing.[9]

In other states, the basis is the fourth rubric of the police power — the protection of the health, safety, morals, and (take note) the general welfare. The U.S. District Court opinion in *Euclid*[10] started this line of cases. More recent Pennsylvania cases are also examples of this line.[11] These cases give the general welfare a weight independent of the other three rubrics. They deliver what was promised, but not delivered, in the Supreme Court opinion in *Euclid*: a close look at the metropolitan regional effects of a zoning ordinance.

§ 15.04   Judicial Remedies.

Exclusionary zoning opinions show a dissatisfaction with the remedies provided in land-use litigation. The usual remedy is invalidation of the contested ordinance, in whole or part. If this alone is the provided remedy, then the zoning officials are free to revise the zoning ordinance, even though the revised ordinance does not provide the original applicant with the zoning classification he sought. He may have sought rezoning for an apartment project and, in the revised ordinance, apartments may indeed be permitted somewhere, but not on his parcel. Thus the town may end up with no more apartments than would have been developed if the original litigation was never brought. In this event, a developer would have little incentive to contest an exclusionary ordinance.

In response to this remedial problem, the courts in exclusionary zoning cases order the zoning officials to rezone the applicant's land for one of

---

[8] *H.&R. Builders, Inc. v. Borough Council of Borough of Norwood*, 555 A. 2d 948, 950 (Pa. Commwlth. Ct. 1989) (finding that townhouses are a basic form of housing and ordering site-specific relief for the builder proposing them to a borough excluding them); *but see In re Appeal of M.A. Kravitz Company*, 460 A. 2d 1075 (Pa. 1983) (refusing to extend the *Girsh* holding to an ordinance not providing for townhouses) and *In re Appeal of Elocin.,Inc.*, 461 A. 2d 771 (Pa. 1983) (finding that a municipality need not provide for every category of dwellings in its ordinance).

[9] *Berenson v. Town of New Castle*, 341 N.E. 2d 236, 241–243, 378 N.Y.S. 2d 672, 679–680 (N.Y. 1975) (citing the goal of zoning to be "a balanced, cohesive community"). *See also Soares v. Town of Atkinson*, 529 A. 2d 867 (N.H. 1987); *but see Asian Americans for Equality v. Koch*, 527 N.E. 2d 265 (N.Y. 1988), *noted at* 102 Harv. L. Rev. 1092 (1989) (refusing to apply the N.Y. Constitution to a zoning district allegedly displacing Chinese Americans from New York City's Chinatown).

[10] *Ambler Realty Co. v. Village of Euclid*, 297 F. 307, 313-316 (N.D. Ohio 1924).

[11] See the cases cited in this Chapter, op. cit., n. 5.

several uses, or for the applicant's requested use. The court might even do the rezoning itself. This broadened remedial power is known as the "builder's remedy." It is a reward, giving the builder plaintiff enough of the rezoning it seeks so as to give it incentive to bring the law suit in the first place. As we shall see, some courts accomplish the builder's remedy procedurally, by assigning the municipality the burden of proof to show that the rezoning or other action that the builder seeks, is clearly inappropriate for the site because of planning, environmental, health, or safety reasons.

§ 15.05 The *Mount Laurel* Litigation.

The Township of Mt. Laurel was a sprawling, largely undeveloped municipality on the urban fringe of the Camden, N.J., metropolitan area. Its zoning ordinance zoned major portions of its land — some 30% — industrial, envisioning clean, hi-tech industry. Little land was zoned for multi-family housing, and mobile homes were excluded. Mt. Laurel had experienced population growth, however, on the order of Ramapo or Petaluma — municipalities that had responded with growth control ordinances that had some inclusionary aspects.[12]

Mt. Laurel's ordinance had three residential use districts. R-1 had a minimum lot size provision of nearly 10,000 square feet, a minimum lot width of seventy five feet, and a minimum dwelling size of between 1,100 and 1,300 square feet. In the R-2 district, the dwellings were somewhat smaller and the lot size somewhat larger, but otherwise the provisions of the ordinance were the same. In the R-3 district, the largest by far in terms of acreage, the lot size was double that in an R-1 district, but a dwelling's square footage was the same. Some cluster zoning was available in an overlay district within the bounds of mapped R-3 districts, but the clustering reduced the lot and dwelling sizes to R-1 proportions, subject to a maximum of 2.25 dwellings per acre. Thus several devices — minimum lot size and square footage requirements — were used and had come to be associated with exclusionary zoning by the time of the litigation.

[A] Stage One.

Mount Laurel I: In this 1975 opinion, the New Jersey Supreme Court held the zoning ordinance of "a developing municipality" (which it found the township to be) invalid to the extent it did not "provide a realistic opportunity" for the construction of the township's "fair share" of "the present and prospective regional needs for low and moderate income housing."[13]

---

[12] "Inclusionary" is a word we will return to. *See infra* this Chapter.

[13] *Southern Burlington County NAACP v. Twp. of Mount Laurel*, 336 A.2d 713, 724–725 (N.J.), *appeal dismissed and cert. denied*, 423 U.S. 808 (1975), *discussed in* John Payne, *General Welfare and Regional Planning: How the Law of Unattended Consequences and the Mount Laurel Doctrine Gave New Jersey a Modern State Plan*, 73 St. John's L. Rev. 1103, 1104–1108 (1999) (reviewing the case).

A writ of certiorari to the United States Supreme Court was denied because this holding was based on the general welfare clause of the state constitution. That clause stated: "All persons . . . have certain natural and inalienable rights, among which are those of . . . acquiring, possessing, and protecting property. . . ."[14] As the New Jersey Supreme Court is the final arbiter of this clause and its state's constitution, the United States Supreme Court was and is without authority to tell it, as the state court of last resort, what its constitution means and how to interpret it.

The idea underlying the holding was that each of the state's municipalities had an affirmative duty to meet a basic need of New Jersey citizens for housing. Their delegation from the legislature of the authority to zone was encumbered by their constitutional obligation to provide this housing. In addition, as a matter of New Jersey constitutional law, the court also held that housing was a basic right. This is not the case in federal constitutional law; in this second holding the New Jersey court goes beyond the federal courts, rejecting the analysis of *Lindsay v. Normet*.[15] When municipalities affect this basic right beyond the boundaries of their jurisdiction, they effectively deny general welfare rights. Here the excluded citizen would have no non-judicial remedy because he is unrepresented before the municipal legislature.[16]

Moreover, it is economic discrimination, not racial or ethnic prejudice, which is prohibited by the holding in this case. Once again the range of persons protected by New Jersey's constitution goes beyond the protected parties in federal constitutional law, where economic discrimination does not define a protected class of persons.

The court found that the township ordinance was exclusionary. An exclusionary ordinance is in this matter tested and measured, not by the intent of its drafters or the zoning officials, but by the effect or impact of the ordinance itself. A "legal effects" test is used. Again, notice the contrast between state and federal constitutional law here. Under state law, the effect of the ordinance provides the test and an intent to exclude need not be shown. As we shall see, *Mt. Laurel I* in effect rejects the comparable federal opinion in *Arlington Heights*.[17]

Environmental planning and timed growth controls are not at issue in this litigation. They are still available to the municipality. It is free to attract uses which require little in the way of municipal services, so long as it also includes its share of uses which require relatively more services too.

This is the basis for the idea of a "fair share" of low and moderate income housing. The geographic area for measuring the need was the Camden metropolitan area in the case of *Mt. Laurel*. Later cases defined this area either as a county or a metropolitan area: the region from which the housing

---

[14] N.J. Const. (1947), art. I, para. 1.

[15] 405 U.S. 56 (1972) (holding access to housing not a fundamental right).

[16] This analysis is like the dissenters' in *Warth v. Seldin*, 422 U.S. 490 (1975).

[17] *See infra*, this Chapter.

population of the municipality would be drawn were it not for the exclusionary impact of the ordinance under review. In 1978, the New Jersey Supreme Court further held that this fair share did not have to be reduced to a specific number of dwelling units by the courts.[18] However, defining two other crucial terms — "fair share" and "a developing municipality" — was still found to be a judicial matter.

[B] Stage Two.

Mount Laurel II: In this 1983 opinion, the same court decided to put teeth into the holding of its 1975 opinion.[19] The state constitutional basis is still the same and the right found there is still a basic one.[20] However, the court held that "a developing municipality" would no longer be defined by the courts. A precise definition of such areas had become difficult and (even if well defined) the use of the definition led to an inequity: the municipalities on the urban fringe of the state's metropolitan areas bore the brunt of the fair share obligation. This inequity led to increased pressure on the state's remaining agricultural areas.

Instead, the idea of a "developing municipality" was replaced by the "growth areas" defined by the state planning office in its development plan for the state. This office is an administrative agency of the executive branch of state government. Its plan, however, was not adopted by the state legislature.[21] This plan was titled the "State Development Guide Plan" and was drafted in an attempt to gain federal grants by the Division of State and Regional Planning, an agency abolished by the time the court issued its opinion. Clearly the court was casting around for other agencies to involve in the controversy over *Mt. Laurel I*.

The court also decided that numberless definitions of a municipality's fair share are insufficient. A municipality's fair share must be defined in terms of a number of dwelling units. Good faith in attempting to provide a fair share is likewise insufficient without results.

Mount Laurel litigation would henceforth be assigned to judges selected by the Chief Justice.[22] Initially three judges were used, and a rule of one trial, one appeal, would henceforth be applied to Mt. Laurel litigation.

---

[18] *See Oakwood at Madison, Inc. v. Township of Madison*, 371 A.2d 1192 (N.J. 1977) (holding that fair share obligations need not be precise or based on a specific formulae to win judicial approval).

[19] *See generally* John Payne, *General Welfare and Regional Planning: How the Law of Unattended Consequences and the Mount Laurel Doctrine Gave New Jersey a Modern State Plan*, 73 St. John's L. Rev. 1103, 1108–1110 (1999) (reviewing *Mount Laurel II*).

[20] *Southern Burlington County NAACP v. Twp. of Mt. Laurel*, 456 A.2d 390 (N.J. 1983), *noted in* 15 Rutgers L.J. 513, 526–541 (1984).

[21] *Southern Burlington County NAACP v. Township of Mount Laurel*, op.cit., 456 A. 2d at 422–423.

[22] *Id.* at 452. Special appeals courts were also created by statute in Connecticut in 1989 to handle appeals for permit denials for affordable housing projects. *West Hartford Interfaith Coalition, Inc. v. Town Council of the Town of West Hartford*, 636 A. 2d 1342 (Conn. 1994) (applying the statute to a rezoning denial). *See infra*, this Chapter.

Special masters were to be employed to rewrite a municipality's zoning ordinance to eliminate barriers to the construction of fair share housing. (New Jersey's rule on the availability of such masters thus became more liberal than the similar federal rule; their appointment was within the control of the Chief Justice.)

Rezoning of plaintiffs' parcels to the requested use (known as a "builder's remedy" here) should be granted unless clearly contrary to environmental or other substantial planning concerns. Thus a builder's remedy is the rule, not the exception, although its timing may be adjusted. [23] The routinization of this remedy was thought necessary to provide builders' with an incentive to conduct this type of costly and time-consuming litigation. [24]

If low or moderate income housing cannot be provided in the municipality, then least cost housing will be the back-stop and suffice. Least cost housing is more expensive than low or moderate income housing, but less than middle-income housing; it is a half-way measure, acceptable only when land costs and other market-driven housing costs increase the price of housing beyond the low or moderate range.

[1]   Stages One and Two Compared.

Mt. Laurel I and *II* have different emphases in several aspects of their respective opinions:

a. Environmental concerns are downplayed in the first opinion because the court felt that the township was using them as an excuse not to plan for its future. [25] *Mt. Laurel II* requires a balancing of environmental concerns with fair share housing needs.

b. Fair share obligations were defined differently in each opinion. In *Mt. Laurel I*, it is defined in response to the township's quest for land uses requiring few services. The more service-free uses are sought, the greater the fair share obligation. In this sense, the first opinion was an easy case: the township had over-zoned for industry. In *Mt. Laurel II*, the fair share is spread across a region and then allocated within that region. Here the emphasis is on the elimination of over zoning for least-impact, service-free housing.

After *Mt. Laurel II*, the court developed two methodologies for defining the fair share region. [26] One involves the geographic dispersal of low-income housing throughout a region, with the underlying goal of racial and economic desegregation. Another developed the idea of a commuter-shed, based on the idea that all skill levels of a workforce should not have to travel an unreasonable distance to get to work.

c. A floating zone for fair share housing might have survived judicial review of a challenged ordinance under *Mt. Laurel I*, but it would not

---

[23] An adjustment of the timing — in the form of a phase-in — was also permitted a municipality in meeting its fair share obligation.

[24] *Id.* at 452–453.

[25] *Cf. National Land* and the Pennsylvania cases, cited op. cit.

[26] *See Van Dalen v. Washington Twp.*, 500 A.2d 776, 782 (N.J. Super. Ct., Law Div. 1984).

survive *Mt. Laurel II* scrutiny: there, the sites for fair share housing must be mapped, set aside, and financial incentives and packages provided for their development. Mandatory set-asides, density bonuses for providing low and moderate income housing, and inclusionary zoning are strongly encouraged. The state Supreme Court was increasingly suspicious of non-Euclidian zoning devices because of the discretion involved in administering them.

d. The builder's remedy. In response to the *Mt. Laurel* opinions, the legislature enacted a statute to phase it out. In *Mt. Laurel II*, however, the remedy survived intact, although the opinion warned developers not to use it as a threat to get their projects approved. Evidence of such threats, the court said, would constitute grounds for denying it.

The builder's remedy is a far-reaching one, but raises some remedial problems with a regional flavor. The Mount Laurel cases concern residential zoning, so a municipality rezoning land from residential to industrial after a neighboring municipality approves an affordable housing development plan for a project located on the border of this industrial district, may tempt the builder have the land rezoned to its former, residential use. If the rezoned land were in the same municipality, there is little doubt that the developer using the builder's remedy may seek a return to the prior zoning for abutting land, that is compatible with its affordable housing project. As an extension of this, a developer seeking to have abutting land in another jurisdiction similarly zoned or rezoned in a compatible manner, is also consistent with the builder's remedy.

Likewise, a municipality approving a development proposal satisfying, in part, its fair share obligation, requests a neighboring municipality to approve water and sewer line hook-ups for the development to lines in the latter municipality. The neighboring municipality refuses. The developer, as a part of the builder's remedy, may seek to enjoin the neighboring municipality from refusing and mandate the hook-up. There is nothing in the doctrine attached to Mount Laurel II to prevent such an injunction.[27]

[2] Two Litigation-Related Tactical Considerations.

First, counsel representing Mt. Laurel Township during this second stage of the litigation, might have been tempted to consider side-stepping the litigation by repealing its zoning ordinance altogether. While such a strategy is tempting, it is also ill-advised. It would have left the Township's land unregulated. In addition, such an effort would probably have earned the Township a contempt of court citation, because once under the obligation to take affirmative steps to confront its fair share obligation, its duty is to use the police power toward this end. Having excluded low income residents for several decades, the township could not suddenly take a libertarian stance toward land use.

Second, the likely effect of the court's emphasis on the builder's remedy in *Mount Laurel II* may be a shift in the type of likely plaintiffs engaged

---

[27] *See Samaritan Center, Inc. v. Borough of Englishtown*, 683 A. 2d 611 (N. J. Super. Ct. 1996) (so holding and issuing a mandatory injunction under similar circumstances).

in exclusionary zoning litigation. If builders are the primary plaintiffs — or, the type of plaintiff with the strongest incentive to sue — what happens to the interests of plaintiffs like the NAACP, the Urban League, and other groups interested in racial as well as economic integration? What can be done to encourage such groups to participate in testing potentially exclusionary ordinances? The provision of attorneys fees to winning plaintiffs is one incentive not tried in most anti-exclusionary zoning provisions.

[3] Some Political Tactics.

The shift from *Mount Laurel I's* emphasis on developing municipalities to plan-designated growth areas spreads what political pain the first opinion induced. In general, making growth a trigger for imposing a *Mount Laurel* obligation places the obligation where it can most easily be accommodated. If the municipality is willing to accept growth, it should also be willing to accept a number-specific fair share of affordable housing. Not to do so is to cream the land uses available in a metropolitan area, depriving other competing jurisdictions of them. Growth and affordable housing should arguably be linked, and *Mount Laurel II* broke that linkage in favor of imposing the fair share obligation more broadly.

[C] Stage Three.

In a third stage of this litigation, the state Supreme Court validated a legislative solution and shows an increasing amount of deference to both legislative and past judicial actions.

Mount Laurel III: In a third, 1986 opinion, the New Jersey Supreme Court held constitutional a 1985 state Fair Housing Act.[28] The Act established a voluntary administrative program for defining the fair share obligation of a municipality; it also recognized a new role for state government in the implementation of fair share affordable housing programs, a role intended to replace the courts in implementing *Mount Laurel I* and *II*.

This program is administered by a state agency, the Council on Affordable Housing (COAH). The Act defines a municipality's fair share in terms of a host of planning factors, including some very vague ones — such as the pattern of previous development. It delegates the determination of each's fair share to the Council, but also recognizes that another state agency, the Housing and Mortgage Finance Agency, must play a role in implementing fair share housing obligations. The Fair Housing Act requires that agency give priority to projects with development proposals designed to meet such obligations.[29]

---

[28] *Hills Development Co. v. Twp. of Bernards*, 510 A.2d 621 (N.J. 1986). *See generally* John Payne, *General Welfare and Regional Planning: How the Law of Unattended Consequences and the Mount Laurel Doctrine Gave New Jersey a Modern State Plan*, 73 St. John's L. Rev. 1103, 1110–1114 (1999) (reviewing *Mount Laurel III*).

[29] N.J. Stat. Ann. § 52:27D-307.3a(2)(c) (West 1986).

Deference to the legislature and comity predominate here. The court gave COAH the time and the flexibility to act. The court determined that the Act would, if properly implemented, provide a realistic opportunity for achieving a fair share of lower income housing. *Mt. Laurel III* once more reaffirmed the "fair share" obligation: "the state constitutional obligation has not changed," it said. The court also warned that the opinion represented "no weakening of our resolve to enforce the constitutional rights of New Jersey's lower income citizens."

[1] Some Legislative History.

The Act was the result of a long debate during 1984 and 1985 legislative sessions. The Governor slowed budgeted state planning office funds to pressure the legislature to speed up its deliberations. Early versions of the Act proposed agreements between municipalities, so that one municipality could transfer a development to another municipality. That proposal was enacted into law, permitting a municipality to transfer up to 50% of its Council-certified fair share to another jurisdiction within its housing region by voluntary contract. The receiving jurisdiction can then meet its heightened fair share by rehabilitating its existing, substandard housing stock, using subsidies provided by the sending jurisdiction.

Approval of these transfer agreements, known as "regional contribution agreements" (RCAs), was crucial to the 1985 political compromise. Thus, if a suburban community with a fair share obligation pays for the construction or rehabilitation of low income units in another municipality, it can partially satisfy its obligation.[30]

[2] Council Proceedings.

The Act required that pending Mount Laurel litigation be transferred to the Council, except for litigation commenced more than sixty days before the effective date of the Act when transfer would be manifestly unjust to a party to the litigation. In fact, much litigation was not immediately transferred and the state Supreme Court had to establish stringent guidelines, to be met if a court was to retain jurisdiction. Moreover, the court said that a municipality could not pick and choose the most lenient of terms as between the terms of any judicial decree and COAH's regulations — a transfer to COAH must be complete.

COAH's regulations are reviewed under an "arbitrary and capricious" standard. In *Mt. Laurel I*, the court acted because the legislature would not; thus, once the legislature finally acts, if a legislative act is typically entitled to a presumption of validity, legislative action taken in response to judicial concerns should enjoy a similar presumption. Further, when there is apparent authority for a regulation, so should that regulation. Using this standard of review, most of COAH's regulations have been upheld, including an affordable housing linkage fee. Only a COAH cap on

---

[30] *In re Twp. of Warren*, 588 A. 2d 1227 (N.J. Super. Ct., App. Div., 1991) (so holding).

the number of dwelling units assigned to a municipality's fair share[31] and a municipal occupancy preference for local residents or workers for 50% of the units in COAH-mandated, low income housing[32] have been invalidated by the courts.

Finally, the 1985 Act imposed a moratorium on the builders' remedy, removing it from COAH's authorized remedies. The legislature sought to have the agency and the courts provide alternatives to this remedy. In *Mt. Laurel III*, the court found that the remedy was not grounded in the state constitution. Rather, it was only one of several means of meeting the constitutional obligation.

Once a municipality is within the Council's program — which happens when its fair share plan is filed, reviewed and certified by the Council — any person challenging that plan must first exhaust his or her remedies before the Council before going to court. And, once in court, the challenger must present clear and convincing evidence that the fair share obligation is unmet by the certified plan.

[3] Administrative Response to the Act.

Along with the 1985 enactment of the Act authorizing COAH came the simultaneous enactment of a State Planning Act.[33] In this legislation, the State Development Plan Guide was repealed and replaced by a State Development and Redevelopment Plan.[34] During the period 1986-1992, New Jersey state planners developed a state-wide plan, but it was not binding on the state's municipalities.[35] While comprehensive, state-wide, land-use planning has not yet become mandatory in New Jersey because of the *Mt. Laurel* doctrine, planning for affordable or least-cost housing planning has. Perhaps the lasting achievement of the *Mt. Laurel* cases may be that they brought state-wide land planning to a state that badly needed its benefits.

[4] How Successful is the *Mount Laurel* Doctrine?

By 1988 about 15,000 affordable housing units were either completed, under construction, or the subject of a pending application in 54 municipalities since *Mt. Laurel II*. Most were for sale, rather than rent.[36] In 1985 the state legislature set a goal of constructing 145,000 affordable housing units by 1993. By 1992, 25,000 units were approved, but fewer than 10,000 were either completed or under construction.[37] For the years 1993-1999,

---

[31] *Carlton Homes, Inc. v. COAH*, 582 A. 2d 1024, 1030 (N.J. Super. Ct., App. Div., 1990).

[32] *In re Twp. of Warren*, 622 A. 2d 1257 (N.J. 1993).

[33] N. J. Stat. Ann. § 52:18A-196 (West 1985) (requiring a state-wide plan).

[34] *See Van Dalen v. Washington Twp.*, 576 A. 2d 819, 824 (N.J. 1990) (a previous opinion in this litigation, issued in 1984, is cited *supra*).

[35] For the 1992 version of this plan, see <http:///www.state.nj.us/osp/ospplan2.htm/>.

[36] Martha Lamar et al., *Mt. Laurel At Work: Affordable Housing In New Jersey*, 1983-1988, 41 Rutgers L.J. 1197, 1204–1215 (1989).

[37] Dennis Keating, *The Suburban Racial Dilemma* 39–40 (1994) (reporting also that 3,000 of those 25,000 approved units were the subjects of regional contribution agreements).

COAH set a 83,000 unit goal, permitting municipalities to meet their share with accessory apartments for the elderly, homeless shelters, and groups homes for the disabled and mentally impaired.

These accomplishments came with a price — abandonment of the goal of metropolitan-wide racial integration. RCAs administered by COAH permit the suburbs to buy their way out of their duty to have affordable housing located within their jurisdiction. In 1992 there are 23 RCAs involving 3,000 dwelling units, and 15 receiving jurisdictions — an indication that the effect of authorizing RCAs has been to concentrate affordable housing units in the predominantly minority, poorer, central cities. Moreover, studies of the post-1986 affordable housing built in the suburbs indicates little minority occupancy.[38] In 1995, COAH permitted some downzoning of affordable housing sites without replacing them in the 1993-1999 fair share cycle. Thus, at a time when government funds for low income housing are dwindling, the *Mt. Laurel* doctrine has been diverted from its initial purpose of integrating the suburbs and redirected toward the goal of housing the poor where they currently live.

By 1993, 176 of the 567 New Jersey municipalities had participated in COAH proceedings. COAH estimates that 76 other municipalities had settled judicial proceedings against them. That leaves over 300 of the state's municipalities that have neither participated in COAH nor in judicial proceedings concerning *Mt. Laurel*. They may have affordable housing, but its effectiveness in those municipalities is unknown.

§ 15.06   Fair Share Housing Doctrines in Other States.

New Jersey courts have been the leader in formulating requirements for the creation of realistic opportunities for the construction of low income and affordable housing. **Pennsylvania** courts have similarly required that municipalities provide a reasonable number of housing types in their ordinances: this means that mobile homes, apartments, townhouses, and duplexes — as well as single-family detached housing — must be zoned into their ordinances. Pennsylvania's townships must permit uses reflective of the housing types offered in the surrounding region — and not on the basis of tokenism either, but in reasonable numbers.[39]

In **New York** state, the Court of Appeals has a two part test for analyzing the validity of a zoning ordinance. First, the municipality shall have a "balanced" plan for development, meeting both present and future housing needs, and second, the municipality must consider the regional general welfare in enacting the ordinance. However, in New York, municipalities can show that the regional housing needs of the poor are being met elsewhere — and so they need do nothing.[40] This second type of showing

---

[38] *Id.* at 40.

[39] *See BAC, Inc. v. Bd. of Supervisors of Millcreek Twp.*, 633 A.2d 144, 147–147 (Pa. 1993) (reviewing the state's case law).

[40] *Berenson v. Town of New Castle*, 431 N.E. 2d 236, 243 (N.Y. 1975) (involving the denial of a building permit for a large condominium development in a town having a zoning ordinance without a multi-family use district).

makes the two parts of the test work against one another. In addition, although standing requirements are often more lenient in state exclusionary zoning cases than they would be in federal court, New York has restricted standing in exclusionary zoning cases in ways similar to the federal courts. [41]

[A]   *Britton v. Town of Chester.*

Perhaps the shortest, most comprehensive, best written, *post-Mt.Laurel III* judicial opinion comes from **New Hampshire**. It is *Britton v. Town of Chester.* [42] Here the New Hampshire Supreme Court invalidated a town's ordinance as exclusionary and an improper use of the delegation of power to the town contained in the state's zoning enabling act. Because this case was be decided on a statutory ground, constitutional questions were not reached.

The plaintiffs in *Britton* were two individual residents of the town eligible for low income housing, and a developer who had been attempting to build forty-eight multi-family units, ten of which were to be low-income. In the early 1980s, none of the town's land was zoned so as to permit multi-family housing. Its exclusion was then total. Later, the town permitted this type of housing in residential PUD districts, but the court found that less than two percent of the town's land was realistically available for this housing, and then not "as of right", but only as a part of the PUD permission. The effect of such findings was to shift the burden of proof to the town to justify its ordinance.

As to remedy, the court said that the trial court's order left the town unzoned; this portion of the order was remanded and the court said that its invalidation applied only to those sections of the ordinance "hindering the construction of multi-family housing units. Accordingly, we defer to the legislative body of the town, with a reasonable time period, to bring these sections of its zoning ordinance into line with the zoning enabling legislation and with this opinion." Thus the existing ordinance remained in effect in the interim, and the court refused to order a rewrite of the town's entire ordinance.

The court also affirmed the use by the trial court of the site-specific relief in a builder's remedy. [43] As in New Jersey, this remedy is discretionary with the court. To get this remedy, however, the plaintiff developer must show that the proposal is a reasonable use of the land; thus, unlike New Jersey's remedy, this builder's remedy requires that the plaintiff carry his or her burden of proof. In New Jersey, on the other hand, it is the defendant municipality that has the burden of showing that the land is unsuitable

---

[41] *Suffolk Housing Services v. Town of Brookhaven*, 511 N.E. 2d 67 (N.Y. 1987).

[42] 595 A.2d 492 (N.H. 1991)

[43] This remedy is a judicial order that the land be used as the plaintiff developer proposed; so in effect it is a mandatory rezoning of that land parcel. This relief is a reward for contesting the ordinance and also prevents municipal retribution in rezoning land (but not the plaintiff's land) for multi-family housing.

for the use proposed by the builder. The better view is found in *Britton*. This burden of proof should be assigned to the builder. It requires him to show a reasonable basis for the proposed use. The municipality is used to making this showing in the course of zoning the jurisdiction, but the developer best knows the impact of the proposed use, and so is best able to bear it under these circumstances.

[1] Open Issues in *Britton*.

The *Britton* opinion gives New Hampshire's towns the option of (1) rewriting its ordinance with inclusionary zoning provisions, (2) adopting one of several methods of defining the regional housing needs and calculating the town's fair share to meet those needs, or (3) accepting a builder's remedy. While the state's constitutional provision on the separation of powers might limit the court's future role, nonetheless the court finds authority to fashion relief, even though it might later defer to a state-wide legislative housing policy. *Britton* is a leading case that avoids both the pitfalls of New Jersey's *Mount Laurel I* stage and a confrontation with the state legislature.

The New Hampshire Supreme Court later held valid a rural town's zoning regulation that authorized a mountain and forest use district with a minimum lot size of 50 acres to protect forestry, timber harvesting, conservation, and wildlife interests. *Casperson* [44] indicates a judicial interest in balancing environmental and affordable housing needs in the state. This case arose in a town near the mid-point of the state's rural western border with Vermont, whereas *Britton* arose in the southern New Hampshire region affected by the growth of the Boston region to the south.

§ 15.07 Inclusionary Zoning.

An inclusionary zoning ordinance is one that requires that every housing development proposal include some affordable housing units. New Jersey courts, after *Mount Laurel II*, required that an exclusionary township redraft its ordinance, adding provisions that would provide a "realistic opportunity" for low and moderate income housing. Such provisions often took the form of a requirement that a developers set-aside a certain percentage of the units built in a development for low and moderate income persons — or in lieu of such a set-aside, make a mandatory payments into an township account for the provision of such housing. This is what is known as inclusionary zoning. [45] The best argument to use against a local municipality with an inclusionary, set-aside regulation, that such set-asides amount to a taking of property, is that a development exaction is no less

---

[44] *Casperson v. Town of Lyme*, 661 A. 2d 759, 761 (N. H. 1995).

[45] *Board of Supervisors v. DeGroff Enterprizes, Inc.*, 198 S.E. 2d 600, 62 A.L.R. 3d 874 (Va. 1973) (holding invalid an ordinance requiring the developer of 50 or more units to set aside 15% of units for low and moderate income housing).

an exaction when it is general in nature. The issue then is the reach of the *Nollan/Dolan* cases.[46]

Virginia has reversed the *DeGroff* opinion by statute.[47] Most of the recent municipal experience with inclusionary zoning is in two states — California and New Jersey.

The outline of a set-aside program is typically as follows: (1) Many programs are mandatory, but when they are voluntary, they work (a) as a density bonus, as in California, or (b) are used in conjunction with transferable development rights when they are used for affordable housing, or (c) when the municipality has a growth control/adequate public facilities ordinance similar to Ramapo's or Petaluma's, the number of points assigned to affordable housing proposals, may be increased, so that proposals that do not otherwise qualify for a development permit, will do so. Most of the California municipalities using this authorization have mandatory set-aside requirements. California is a state in which urban planning has been made mandatory by statute, and so state agency certification of the housing element in a municipality's land use plan has provided the hook for implementing inclusionary zoning programs.

(2) Most programs involve setting aside about 10-15% of the proposed housing units. California statutes authorize municipalities to provide for a density bonus of between 10 and 20% of the units when part of a housing development proposal consists of low or moderate income housing — and a 50% bonus for senior citizen housing is included.[48] Whatever the percentage, the units are typically scattered within the development, rather than all clustered in one location.

(3) To provide programmatic flexibility, in-lieu fees, off-site units, and fewer interior amenities are permitted (exterior amenities are a different matter) — and generally the affordable and market rate units must look substantially the same.

(4) Transfer covenants prohibit future transfers of the affordable units at market rates for a set period following their construction or first purchase. This prevents the inclusionary program from becoming a first home program — in California, a 30 year restriction is typical.

(5) Finally, small scale projects, typically less than 10 units, are exempted from the program. This exemption is presumably granted because the economies of scale for shifting costs to market rate purchasers are not present in smaller development proposals.[49]

---

[46] *See* Lawrence Berger, *Inclusionary Zoning Devices as Takings: The Legacy of the Mount Laurel Cases*, 70 Neb. L. Rev. 186 (1991) (arguing that an inclusionary, set-aside, regulation is, even with a density bonus for a developer, still a taking under the Fifth Amendment).

[47] Va. Code § 15.1-491.8,-9 (1991) (requiring that 12.5% of the single family dwelling units, and 6.25% of multi-family units, proposed in plans for 50 or more units, shall be affordable housing, for which the developer receives a 10% density bonus).

[48] Calif. Gov. Code § 65915 (1996). *See generally* Marc Smith et al., *Inclusionary Housing Programs: Issues and Outcomes*, 25 R. Est. L. J. 155, 166–167 (1996).

[49] *See* Nico Calavita & Kenneth Grimes, *Inclusionary Housing in California: The Experience of Two Decades*, 64 J. Am. Plng. Ass'n 150, 164–66 (1998).

In addition, other features of zoning ordinances might be changed to increase the provision of affordable housing. Here are three examples. First, many residential use district ordinances include regulations prohibiting accessory rental units. So long as over-all density requirements are observed, why not permit, and even encourage accessory apartments in such districts? Doing this would encourage economic diversity. Second, exclusively residential districts are the pattern in some municipalities. Why not encourage mixed-use districts, so that apartments and other forms of housing may be located over commercial uses. That was the pattern of many small town main streets until the advent of zoning ordinances. Why not revert to what has worked in the past? Third, why not prohibit minimum square footage regulations in residential districts? The emphasis on inclusionary zoning has effectively blocked a general review of many zoning ordinances to ferret out their exclusionary features.

[A] Designing an Inclusionary Set-Aside Regulation.

To attempt to insure the constitutionality of an inclusionary affordable housing ordinance requiring set-asides, a municipality should (1) establish by studies the relationship between the new development in which the set-asides are required and the decreased availability of affordable housing (the economic impact of the new development on land prices is perhaps the best approach); (2) the set-aside units of housing should be of a type not likely to be provided by the private unsubsidized market; (3) density bonuses or other voluntary incentives should be provided to maintain the over-all profitability of the development; (4) affordability controls should be maintained: the price of the housing set aside as affordable should be maintained by requiring that future sales or rentals, while not compelled, should only be to individuals or families then needing affordable housing; (5) developers should be given flexibility to decide whether the affordable housing units set aside should be provided on site, by contract providers as opposed to the developer itself, or by the combined efforts of several affected developers.

When in-lieu fees are collected, the regulation should contain some precautionary provisions to safeguard the constitutionality of the fee: first, the type of housing meeting the definition of affordable should be defined; second, the neighborhood in which the money will be spent should be limited to one in reasonable proximity of the developer's project; third, the money should be held in trust for its stated purposes, and no other; and fourth and finally, reasonable time limits should be placed on the use of the fees and if they are not used within the prescribed time, the fees should be returned. Such limitations increase the defensibility of such fees.

§ 15.08 Zoning Appeals for Affordable Housing Permit Denials.

In order to counter the effects of exclusionary permit denials, a few states have authorized special permits and administrative appeals to a board with state-wide jurisdiction. In Massachusetts, an applicant that is either a public agency or a not-for-profit corporation or organization can apply for a comprehensive permit from a BZA, for a low and moderate income housing project; when such a permit is denied, or is approved with restrictions making the project uneconomic, the developer has a right to appeal to a special state Housing Appeals Committee (HAC).[50]

The HAC then determines if the denial is consistent with local needs. Consistency is found (and the denial is upheld) when 10% of the town's housing stock is currently devoted to low or moderate income housing; when subsidized housing is occupying more than 1.5% of the town's land area; or when the approval would affect more than ten acres or consume more than .3% of the town's land area. Otherwise the presumption of validity does not apply during the appeal: the town has the burden of showing that the denial was supported by a consideration overriding the region's needs for qualifying housing. The HAC is authorized to order that the applicant's permit be issued.[51] As of 1989, over 20,600 affordable dwelling units have been built using the comprehensive permits and/or appeals in Massachusetts.[52]

The Connecticut legislature has enacted a similar statute.[53] The Connecticut statute applies to both federally subsidized and unsubsidized, affordable housing; appeals from permit denials for qualified projects are heard by the judiciary, with specially-assigned judges presiding over the appeal.[54] When for example, a municipality refused to rezone for affordable housing, it must show that the goal it advanced for not doing so will probably be harmed, although its showing need not be as high as a preponderance of the evidence.[55]

In addition to the sort of exemptions Massachusetts provides for municipalities with (e.g.) 10% of its housing stock already devoted to affordable housing, Connecticut exempts from this appeals process municipalities that voluntarily participate in a state inclusionary housing program and have built a number of affordable units equal to 1% of all residential units built in the municipality within the last year.[56] However, when less than 10% of a municipality's stock is devoted to affordable housing, the burden of proof is shifted to the municipality to justify the denial.

---

[50] *Bd. of Appeals of Hanover v. Housing Appeals Committee*, 294 N.E. 2d 393 (Mass. 1973) [upholding the 1969 statute, Mass. Gen. L., ch. 40B, §§ 20-23) (Law. Coop. 1993)].

[51] *Pheasant Ridge Assoc. Limited Partnership v. Town of Burlington*, 506 N.E. 2d 1152 (Mass. 1987).

[52] *See Welch v. Paicos*, 66 F. Supp. 2d 138, 142–145 (U.S. D. Ct., D. Mass., 1999) (reviewing the history of the Mass. statute)

[53] Conn. Gen. Stat. § 8-30g(a)-(b) (1991); *Kaufman v. Zoning Comm'n of City of Danbury*, 653 A. 2d 798 (Conn. 1995) (finding that a developer of affordable housing did not have to submit more detailed plans for this appeal than would any other applicant for rezoning).

[54] *West Hartford Interfaith Coalition v. Town of West Hartford*, 636 A. 2d 1342, 1356 (Conn. 1994) (reversing a local permit denial for a proposed affordable housing project).

[55] *Christian Activities Council v. Town Council of the Town of Glastonbury*, 735 A.2d 231, 247–250 (Conn. 1999) (the majority opinion on this refusal, however, produced a strong dissent, accusing the majority of "ripping the soul out of affordable housing").

[56] *Id.* at § 8-30g(f)-(g).

In addition, several states have required that municipalities adopt comprehensive land use plans that include an affordable housing element.[57] Such an element requires that the municipality analyze its existing and projected needs for affordable housing. California, Florida, Oregon, and Washington have such statutes in their planning enabling acts. In Oregon, for example, a state agency periodically reviews and certifies these elements as in compliance with the statute; if they are not, administrative orders are authorized to bring them into compliance and local grant funds for planning can be withheld until there is compliance. Oregon designates urban growth boundaries to encourage higher densities and growth rates within these boundaries; municipalities within such boundaries are under an obligation to zone sufficient land to meet its share of the regional need for affordable housing.[58]

§ 15.09 Conclusion.

Whether a jurisdiction should enact the Massachusetts or the New Jersey approach to exclusionary zoning and fair share obligations involves a choice made according to the view taken of the courts' and administrative agencies' relative capabilities to oversee housing programs. The Massachusetts administrative approach has achieved more, more quickly, and with less fanfare. What began with a law suit in New Jersey to address the effects of racial segregation in suburban housing, has lost its race-based identity and become instead an attempt at economic, rather than racial integration in housing.[59] New state constitutional law has been made there, but the political cost has been high and the original goal lost from sight; meanwhile, the state's revised administrative process for state-wide land use planning has become the lasting, if unintended, consequence of that long ago law suit in Mount Laurel.

---

[57] *See, e.g.,* Cal. Gov't Code § 65584 (1993).

[58] Note, *State-Sponsored Growth Management as a Remedy for Exclusionary Zoning,* 108 Harv. L. Rev. 1127, 1133–1136 (1995).

[59] *See* Ronald Smothers, *Decades Later, Town Considers Housing Plan for the Poor,* N.Y. Times (Mar. 27, 1997), at B1, col. 5 (reporting consideration of the first rental housing proposal in Mount Laurel since the start of the *Mt. Laurel* litigation in 1970).

Chapter 16

Civil Rights and Exclusionary Zoning

§ 16.01 Introduction.

Sometimes an applicant for a variance, special exception, or rezoning, or other land use permit alleges that the denial of a permit is motivated by discrimination of a type prohibited by the federal civil rights statutes. In most cases, the prohibition is contained in Title VIII of the Civil Rights Act of 1968 (the Fair Housing Act or FHA),[1] providing in part that it unlawful "to make unavailable or deny . . . a dwelling to any person because of race, color, religion, sex, handicap, or national origin." Discrimination is never defined in the civil rights acts; rather, its definition is left to the courts.

As we have seen in discussing the question of standing,[2] the doors of the federal courthouse are not particularly wide for plaintiffs claiming discrimination in land use cases. Once the merits of a discrimination claim is reached, moreover, the plaintiff's path is not an easy one, particularly when the discrimination is urged to be a constitutional matter.

§ 16.02 Constitutional Claims.

Village of Arlington Heights v. Metropolitan Housing Development Corporation,[3] holds that, when asserting a constitutional claim of discrimination under the Fourteenth Amendment's equal protection clause, a claimant must show more than that the decision has a disparate impact on minority groups (of which plaintiff must be member) protected by the Constitution. Rather, the disparate impact of the decision is only one of several other factors reviewed in determining whether the decision was motivated by a discriminatory purpose. The discriminatory purpose need not be the predominant purpose of the decision. It must be a motivating factor: that is, but for it, the decision would have been otherwise, the permit would have been granted, etc. Its impact — e.g., whether the decision bears more heavily on one race than another — is not determinative.

The other factors that a court must consider are:

    (1)   the historical background for the decision,

    (2)   the specific sequence of events leading up to the decision,

    (3)   the departures in the contested case from the normal procedural sequence,

---

[1] As amended, 42 U.S.C.A. § 3604(a) (1991).

[2] *See supra*, Chapter 13.

[3] 429 U.S. 252 (1977)

    (4)   any substantive departures from normal law and policy,

    (5)   the administrative and legislative history of the case, as well as

    (6)   the impact of the decision.

All must be considered in determining whether discrimination was the motivating purpose of the decision.

The first five factors, all those other than impact, are all process-oriented. No substantive law, intrusive on the state law relating to exclusionary or any other type of zoning, is being made here. Moreover, the factors are extremely flexible: for example, the planning policies justifying a decision are malleable indeed, so that whether or not there is a departure from them, is a matter of first defining them — a matter with a large amount of discretion involved.

The land use pattern in the Village of Arlington Heights was much like the town involved in the *Warth v. Seldin*[4] : its predominant land use was single family detached housing. While the town in *Warth* was 98% single family detached, however, Arlington Heights did have some apartments. They were not low or moderate housing, however, and so a housing decision with a disparate economic or racial impact is not *per se* a violation of the Fourteenth Amendment. Further, even when discrimination is a motivating factor, the effect of this showing is procedural — the burden of proof needed to justify the decision shifts to the municipal decision-maker; there is no liability yet. The latter gets a further opportunity to justify what it did.

Arlington Heights is a constitutional case. If the decision were brought under Fair Housing Act's Title VIII, the disparate impact (known as the "legal effects" test) would be sufficient to make out a prima facie violation of § 3604(a) of the Act.[5] However, the litigation in *Arlington Heights* was, after the remand, settled by consent.

§ 16.03 Statutory Claims.

In a Fair Housing Act case, whose central provision was quoted previously, the courts usually consider four factors when interpreting the statutory provision and considering whether or not the plaintiff has made out a *prima facie* case:

    (1) the strength of the plaintiff's evidence of discriminatory effect or impact. Typically this evidence will be statistical and will involve local statistics, although statistics are usually accompanied by an identification of the suspect practices linked with the adverse impact they demonstrate; this evidence is presented along with . . .

    (2) evidence of discriminatory intent: who said what, when, and in what context the statement(s) were made.

---

  4 *See supra*, Chapter 13 [discussing *Warth v. Seldin*, 422 U.S. 490 (1975) (denying numerous parties standing in exclusiuonary zoning case under Article III's case or controversy rules)].

  5 *Huntington Branch, NAACP v. Town of Huntington*, 844 F.2d 926 (2d Cir. 1988) (where the Town restricted multi-unit housing to an urban renewal area whose population was 52% black).

(3) the defendant's interest in making the decision. Is a bona fide governmental purpose otherwise advanced?

(4) the remedy sought to reverse the effect of the discrimination. Is the plaintiff seeking to build housing for those persons discriminated against, or merely to remove some obstacle to the construction of such housing? The more benefit the remedy provides, the lesser the evidence of discrimination need be.[6]

These four factors were set out in the Circuit Court opinion on remand in the *Arlington Heights* litigation, holding that in at least some circumstances, a FHA violation may be "established by a showing of discriminatory effect without a showing of discriminatory intent."[7] Thus, a failure to rezone having an adverse impact or effect on racial minorities as "the natural and foreseeable consequence" of that failure, makes a municipality liable under the Act.

Some federal circuit Courts of Appeals have refused to adopt the second prong of this test. In these circuits, then, the plaintiff need not present any evidence of discriminatory intent on the defendant's part.[8]

This four prong test, although developed to adjudicate racial discrimination claims, is equally applicable to claims of religion, handicap and familial status discrimination.[9] Some federal circuit courts have, as previously stated, only adopted three of the four prongs.[10]

[A]   Two Applications of the *Arlington Heights* Four-Prong Test.

Religion can also be a basis for alleging illegal discrimination. In one case an Orthodox[11] Jewish rabbi was held to have been discriminated against when denied a certificate for the conduct of a home occupation when such certificates were issued only to members of "learned professions." The court considered the application of the four elements. The noise, traffic, and impacts caused by in-home services to which congregants walk, are minimal and are unlikely to justify the **municipality's interest** in denying the certificate. A municipal regulation requiring that churches, synagogues, and other places of worship shall be located on parcels at least two acres, might require that the rabbi apply for a variance and have it denied before

---

[6] This is the four-prong test of the Seventh Circuit, on remand in *Arlington Heights*, 558 F. 2d 1283, 1288 (7th Cir. 1977), *cert. denied*, 434 U.S. 1025 (1978); *see also Smith v. Town of Clarkton, N.C.*, 682 F. 2d 1055 (4th Cir. 1982) (adopting the four-prong test of *Arlington Heights*).

[7] 558 F.2d 1283, 1288 (7th Cir. 1977).

[8] *Arthur v. City of Toledo*, 782 F. 2d 565 (6th Cir. 1986).

[9] *See Samaritan Inns v. District of Columbia*, 1995 U.S. Dist. LEXIS 9294 (June 30, 1995) (involving drug and alcohol abusers as handicapped persons and the denial of a building permit for housing for such abusers).

[10] *Arthur v. City of Toledo*, 782 F. 2d 565, 575 (6th Cir. 1986) (refusing to adopt the prong involving discriminatory intent).

[11] Orthodox Judaism requires that worshipers walk to Sabbath services and conduct daily prayer services in small groups.

showing that the regulation is a barrier to the exercise of his religion. In proving a *prima facie* case, a discriminatory **impact** will be shown when doctors and attorneys' offices were given certificates, and the treatment of other religious groups might also provide further evidence of a disparate impact. An **intent** to discriminate against the applicant's religion might be *prima facie* shown by the change in a prior interpretation of a home occupation for the conduct of services. Religion provides a clear benefit of giving the applicant the **remedy** sought. [12] With two of the four elements — the interest and remedy prongs — tending to show discrimination, an order to issue the certificate should result.

"Familial status" is also protected against discrimination. In one case, a trailer park could not accommodate modern, double-wide mobile homes on its pads and had a density of 10 mobile homes per acre, 5 more than newer parks. The owner permitted no more than 3 persons to occupy a mobile home when nationally half of all U.S. families with minor children had more than 4 members. A woman applies to occupy a pad with her 3 minor children. The park owner refused to rent to her, citing the 3 person maximum. When charged with discrimination, one court found no discrimination. The plaintiff cannot show at least three of the four factors relevant to finding a violation of Title VIII. As to a showing of disparate **impact**, national statistics are so far removed from the market in which the discrimination is alleged to have occurred that it will have little probative weight. The leading case uses local, not national, statistics as its basis for finding a FHA violation. [13] As to the defendant's **interest**, the owner has a legitimate, bona fide reason for its occupancy limits: they rest on a concern for the quality of life in its park, and perhaps on limiting the use of old infrastructures like sewer and water lines for its pads — an interest sufficient to overcome the plaintiff's *prima facie* case. As to the **remedy**, no housing for single-parent families will be built as a result of granting the plaintiff the injunction she seeks. Thus the owner prevails on three of the four factors in *Arlington Heights*. [14]

[B] *Huntington Branch, NAACP v. Town of Huntington.* [15]

This case modified the *Arlington Heights* test in two ways. First, it required that in presenting statistics under the first prong, the plaintiff must compare the racial composition of the group which received — or predictably would receive — the benefits as the result of a suspect selection

---

[12] *Leblanc-Sternberg v. Village of Airmont*, 67 F. 3d 412 (2d Cir. 1995).

[13] *Huntington Branch, NAACP v. Town of Huntington*, 844 F. 2d 926 (2nd Cir. 1988), discussed *infra*, this Chapter.

[14] *Mountain Side Mobile Estate Partnership v. Secretary of Housing and Urban Development*, 56 F. 3d 1243 (10th Cir. 1995) (adopting three of the four *Arlington Heights* factors for that Circuit); *Oak Ridge Care Center, Inc. v. Racine County, Wisc.*, 896 F. Supp. 867, 875 (E.D. Wis. 1995) (stating that either ". . . discriminatory procedures or neutral procedures applied in a discriminatory manner violate the FHA . . . .").

[15] 844 F. 2d 926 (2nd Cir. 1988).

process with the racial composition of the pool from which beneficiaries would otherwise have been selected. It rejected the town's defense that more white renters than black would be injured by its denial of the developer's application for the multi-unit housing project. Second, the *Huntington* opinion permitted evidence of a less onerous (land use) alternative or way of resolving the dispute as an additional factor, inserting this consideration between the last two factors.

These additions make *Huntington* like many civil rights cases in which the parties play a type of legal ping-pong: (first) the discriminatory impact is shown to establish a *prima facie* case for the plaintiff, then (second) the defendant establishes that it has a legitimate interest in the decision, as it came out, thus (third) shifting the burden back to the plaintiff to show that a less onerous method — or land use solution — could have been used to protect the defendant's legitimate interest without reaching the allegedly discriminatory effect.

When a plaintiff establishes the first of these three showings, making out a *prima facie* case, the result is to overthrow the usual presumption of validity that attaches to local land use ordinances and decisions. Thus the Fair Housing Act may have a dramatic impact on land use litigation. After the plaintiff establishes a *prima facie* case, the burden of proof shifts to the defendant to prove that "its actions furthered, in theory and in practice, a legitimate, bona fide governmental interest."[16]

Having dropped any showing of intent as a part of a *prima facie* case, once a disproportionate impact of any type or degree is shown, the *Huntington* opinion would weight "the adverse impact of the defendant's [municipality's] justification." Here the municipality must show that its failure to rezone or other actions advanced a legitimate, bona fide governmental interest and that no alternative action would serve the same interest with less discriminatory effect. The opinion added that two other factors may affect the finding of a violation: first, whether there is any evidence of discriminatory intent, and second, whether the plaintiff is suing to force a governmental defendant to build housing or whether it is suing only to require a municipal defendant to remove a land use regulatory obstacle to housing that the plaintiff proposes to build; so requiring the removal of an obstacle requires a stronger justification by the defendant than imposing an affirmative duty on that defendant would.

Normally, in civil rights cases, when the defendant is successful in establishing a legitimate governmental interest, then the burden shifts again, to the plaintiff, then given an opportunity to show that some alternative that would further that interest just as much, but with less discriminatory effect. This last step might also be viewed as a defense and the burden of showing that there is no less onerous alternative put on the defendant.[17] The latter view was adopted by the Second Circuit in *Huntington Branch*.

---

[16] *Huntington*, 844 F. 2d at 936, *citing Resident Advisory Bd. v. Rizzo*, 564 F. 2d 126, 148–149 (3rd Cir. 1977).

[17] *Id.*

[1] Applying *Huntington*.

To assess the reach of *Huntington*, suppose that Huntington restricted to a small area the land zoned for use by a battered women's shelter. The rationale used by the court to protect against racial discrimination, can be adapted a claim based on sex. The issue in *Huntington* was whether a greater proportion of blacks are effected by the zoning ordinance restriction than the proportion of whites effected by the ordinance, both groups being considered as a class. So, first, ask whether the harm caused to women is greater than the harm caused to men by the ordinance. Battered women have to get away from their batterers, so there is justification for giving them greater housing opportunities. Second, ask whether women are denied what men have — that is, the right to be safe in their homes. If women are more often the battered, then they are denied what men have and so the ordinance may reasonably be held to have a disparate legal effect on women. This holding would then shift the burden to the municipality to show that, by weighing the municipality's refusal to rezone against its bona fide, governmental interests, the municipality was advancing those interests and that no lesser alternative would do.

[C] Rezoning Remedies.

In *Huntington*, the court, finding a substantial adverse impact on minorities,[18] ordered that the plaintiff's land be rezoned for the use it sought. Another federal Circuit, finding extreme, self-evident, and blatantly discrimination by municipal officials, went further and ordered not only a rezoning of the plaintiff's parcel, but also devised mandatory, inclusionary, multi-family housing districts to be included in the text of the defendant's zoning ordinance, locating these districts on its zoning map as well.[19]

The Fair Housing Act's Title VII has, however, the potential to go farther. If 42 U.S.C.A. § 3604(a) makes it unlawful "to make unavailable or deny . . . a dwelling to any person because of race, color, religion, sex, handicap, or national origin," may it not be found to contain anti-exclusionary and fair share housing obligations for municipalities? The answer is that, yes, someday it may. Such a finding must realistically be seen as remote today when the civil rights law is viewed through the prism of case precedents like *Huntington*, where the impact was so distinct. But there is nothing in the statute precluding its broader use.

§ 16.04 Discrimination against the Handicapped.

In the 1988 amendments to the FHA, the handicapped were added to the lists of persons protected by the statute. These amendments prohibit discrimination against the handicapped in ways that are more distinctive

---

[18] In Huntington, 7% of the town's population needed the applicant's subsidized housing; 24% of black residents needed it. Similarly, 60% of those eligible to participate in applicant's housing subsidy program, and 61% of those on its waiting list, were black.

[19] *See United States v. City of Black Jack*, 508 F.2d 1179 (8th Cir. 1974).

than with other types of discrimination. For example, both mental and physical handicaps are protected by these amendments,[20] and it is discrimination not to make a reasonable accommodation for the handicapped in renting an apartment to them.[21] The land use analog of reasonable accommodation arises when a municipality refuses to rezone land for the use of a group home for the handicapped, or to grant a variance to accommodate their occupancy.

In *City of Edmonds v. Oxford House, Inc.*,[22] a municipality issued criminal citations to Oxford House[23] for leasing and operating a group home for recovering drug addicts and alcoholics. The home was run for 10 to 12 persons. Its operation was, the municipality said, in violation of the definition of a "family" permitted occupancy in its single-family, residential use district. A "family" was an "individual or two or more persons related by genetics, adoption, or marriage, or a group of five unrelated persons." Thus the ordinance banned more than five unrelated persons from living together in a single-family dwelling. Oxford House alleged that it needed more occupants to make its operation financially and therapeutically practical, but the municipality refused its application for a variance, so Oxford sued, alleging a FHA violation and arguing that the city had violated the FHA.

An exemption to the FHA's anti-discrimination provisions allows enforcement of "any reasonable local . . .restriction regarding the number of occupants permitted to occupy a dwelling."[24] The trial judge found that the definition of family was a regulation exempt from the FHA and dismissed the suit.[25] The Supreme Court disagreed.

The court held that the exemption for local regulation was not an absolute one. It held that the municipality's definition of a family was not a maximum occupancy restriction exempt from the FHA's requirements under § 3607(b)(1) and so the exemption was not applicable. For the majority, it was crucial in interpreting the exemption to recognize a distinction between land use restrictions and maximum occupancy restrictions. That is, families in Oxford House's use district could contain as many persons as need be, but unrelated handicapped persons were limited to five. This is disparate treatment of the handicapped. Moreover, the biological and legal relationships defining a family have nothing to do with health or safety factors the municipality might properly consider in formulating its definition.

---

[20] 42 U.S. C. A. § 3602(h).

[21] *Id.* at § 3604(f)(3)(b).

[22] 514 U.S. 725 (1995) (a 6–3 decision).

[23] Oxfords House operates in 36 states. M. Briggs, *Ruling May Boost Group Home Suit Against Palatine*, Chicago Sun Times (May 16, 1995), at 59. It does not, as a matter of policy, apply for variances or special exceptions for its homes; it moves the group in, reasoning that eviction is harder than denying permits for a municipality.

[24] *Id.* at § 3607(b)(1) (exempting "any reasonable local, State, or Federal restriction regarding the number of occupants permitted to occupy a dwelling").

[25] *See Elliot v. Athens*, 960 F. 2d 975 (11th Cir. 1992) (upholding a local definition of family against an FHA challenge).

Holding that the municipality, with regard to its definition of family, was not immune from a charge of discrimination and could not invoke the maximum occupancy exemption, the court did not hold that the municipality violated the FHA or that the municipality actually discriminated against the plaintiffs. Nor did it decide whether the municipality made a reasonable accommodation by amending its regulations to permit group homes in multi-family and commercial use districts. It held only that the city might not claim immunity from suit on such grounds on the basis of the exemption. The majority opinion gave tacit approval to reasonable restrictions on single-family dwellings and maximum occupancy restrictions.[26]

Thus a maximum occupancy restriction applicable to all persons in all types of dwellings, would have an absolute exemption. Justice Ginsberg, writing for the majority in *Edmonds*, said that regulations that "cap the total number of occupants in order to prevent overcrowding fall within § 3607(b)(1)'s absolute exemption . . . ." Such restrictions are generally figured on the basis of square footage or floor area. Thus, if a municipality had a definition of family requiring that every person subject to the definition occupy a minimum of 200 square feet for the first two persons in a dwelling, and (say) 100 square feet for each additional person, this requirement would be exempt. This is the sort of minimum square footage requirement that is related to the public health and qualifies for the exemption.

Moreover, under the FHA, definitions of "family" are exempt only when reasonable. What if a municipal definition of family provided in part that no more than five persons, related or not, could occupy any single-family dwelling? There is no discrimination on the face of the regulation because related and unrelated persons are not treated differently. This municipality, however, might still have to make some showing that overcrowding would result if its regulation were not enforced — "reasonable" here means reasonable in its impact. Further, there still might be a disparate impact if Oxford House can show that therapeutic relationships among the handicapped can only be established when they are in larger groups.

Similarly, a municipality's ordinance might permit a related family, or no more than five unrelated individuals, or no more than eight unrelated individuals living together in a group home for purposes including those of Oxford House. This ordinance has a facial acceptance of handicapped or disabled persons, but Oxford House would probably then argue that the maximum of eight persons leaves it in the position of operating unprofitable facilities. *Edmonds* did not pass on such an argument. Many ordinances have negative financial impacts on owners, but that does not *per se* render them invalid. A larger group of occupants would make the facility more

---

[26] *See* H.R. Rep. No. 711, 100th Cong., 2d Sess. 24 (1988), *reprinted in* 1988 U.S. C. Cong. & Adm. News 2173, 2185 (indicating that, in the 1988 FHA amendments, Congress arguably intended in the exemption only to codify the holding of *City of Cleburne v. Cleburne Living Center*, 473 U.S. 432 (1985), where restrictions were imposed on persons with handicaps, but were not imposed on similarly situated persons). The Edmonds ordinance did not discriminate between persons with and without handicaps, but between those who are related and unrelated.

profitable, but no owner is entitled to a property's "highest and best" or most profitable use. Unprofitability does not make the maximum number unreasonable because the municipality may have other overriding factors, other than profitability, in mind. Moreover, under the Fair Housing Act, the municipality must only make reasonable accommodations for the persons protected by the Act. That is not to say that it requires that facilities be profitable; reasonable accommodation need not mean profitable accommodation. In addition, unless the plaintiff applies for a variance, the no reasonable accommodation argument is a difficult one.[27]

Distinguishing between land use and maximum occupancy restrictions is not without precedent. The United States Supreme Court recognized it in *Moore v. City of East Cleveland*.[28] Once the exemption is characterized in this binary manner, the city's ordinance clearly fell outside the exempt category of ordinances.[29]

§ 16.05   The Fair Housing Act and Private Covenants.

[A]   The Fair Housing Act and Private Covenants.

The Fair Housing Act can help municipal land use regulations and non-profit groups trump private restrictive covenants. For example, when a non-profit agency seeks to establish a group home for medically disabled patients in a residential subdivision in which all of the homes are controlled by a restrictive covenant permitting only single-family residential uses, the contention that enforcement of the covenants violates the Fair Housing Act's prohibition on discrimination against the handicapped is sound.[30] Assuming that the medical disability is recognized by the Act and its regulations, even though nothing in the covenant expressly prevents a patient from owning or renting in the subdivision, a facial neutral restriction, applicable to both handicapped and non-handicapped persons, may still implicate the Act. First, the covenant's attempt to limit group homes by its single family restriction denies housing to the handicapped. Second, any interest served by decreasing noise and traffic with regard to the covenant is likely to weigh less than the interest served by enforcement of the Act. Third, enforcing the covenant denies housing to a class of persons protected by the Act. In this situation, evidence of a discriminatory intent is not likely to be necessary. There is a *prima facie* violation of the Act.[31]

---

[27] *See Oxford House-C v. City of St. Louis*, 843 F. Supp. 1556 (E. D. Mo. 1994), *reversed*, 1996 WL 75685 (8th Cir. Feb. 23, 1996) (finding that the city did not violate the Act, rejecting the negative financial impact argument by Oxford House, finding that cities have a legitimate interest in decreasing congestion in residential use districts, and disapproving of Oxford's House tactic of just moving in, rather than applying for a variance).

[28] 431 U.S. 494 (1977) (striking down a definition of family overly dependent on the nuclear family).

[29] In response to *Edmonds*, states should enact an enabling statute requiring municipalities to treat group and single family homes in a uniform manner.

[30] *Baxter v. City of Belleville*, 720 F. Supp. 720, 729 (S. D. Ill. 1989).

[31] *Hill v. Community of Damien of Mokokai*, 1996 N.M. LEXIS 32 (N.M., Jan. 9, 1996).

[B]   Violations Must Be Development Based.

An allegation under the Fair Housing Act cannot stray too far from an actual transaction or real estate development. When a local official is accused of embezzling funds earmarked in a municipal budget for housing for the handicapped, the embezzlement is not a Fair Housing Act violation. It is not, although it does indirectly make housing "otherwise unavailable" and denies use of the funds for the benefit of a protect class. The Act is intended to reach a municipality's policies and practices, as well as its housing decisions that are intentionally discriminatory, but only to control a discriminatory impact or effect. Criminal intent is not discriminatory. Other statutes are available to handle this matter; one statute does not reach all governmental decisions affecting the classes of persons protected by the Act, without doing violence to the legislature's prerogative to enact statutes dealing particularly with the misuse of public funds.[32]

§ 16.06   Conclusions.

Three lessons emerge from *Edmonds*: first, that the courts may use the FHA to scrutinize land use regulations; second, that municipalities must offer reasonable accommodation through its zoning procedures to persons with disabilities; and third, that municipalities may impose reasonable occupancy restrictions applicable to all persons alike. The mentally retarded, the elderly, recovering drug addicts, and alcoholics — when living in a group home — are likewise protected.

§ 16.07   Civil Rights and Environmental Justice.

Environmental justice seeks to end any policy or practice that has differential effects or disadvantages, whether intentionally or not, on individuals, groups, or communities, based on race, ethnicity, or color. This includes the disproportionate location of hazardous waste facilities, sold waste disposal sites, contaminating industrial sites, and other undesirable land uses, in minority communities. Title VI of the 1964 Civil Rights Act[33] provides a cause of action for persons able to show that they have been discriminated against in programs receiving federal funds. A showing of discriminatory intent has been held to be an element of a Title VI cause of action.[34] However, taken as a whole, two statutes[35] in Title VI leave open the possibility that merely showing a discriminatory impact or effect, rather than a discriminatory intent, may be sufficient when federal agency regulations require the non-discriminatory administration of an agency's programs without requiring a showing of intent. Thus the right of a private

---

[32] *Cf. United States v. Incorporated Village of Island Park*, 888 F. Supp. 419 (E.D. N.Y. 1995).

[33] 42 U.S.C. § 2000d *et seq* (Title VI, §§ 601, 602) (1999).

[34] *See Alexander v. Choate*, 469 U.S. 287, 292–294 (1985) (requiring a showing of discrimination intent in Title VI, § 601).

[35] 42 U.S.C. § 602 [authorizing federal agencies to implement § 601 by regulations barring discrimination — EPA did so with a regulation — 40 CFR § 7.35(b) (1998) (using an effects test)].

community group to sue, seeking to show a discriminatory effect in the administration of Environmental Protection Agency programs, has been upheld under Title VI. [36] If widely recognized, such a cause of action might cause a re-evaluation of federal and state programs for "brownfields." Brownfields are abandoned, unused, or under-used industrial and commercial sites whose development is stymied by toxic contamination. They are often located in minority communities. Brownfield programs subsidize the redevelopment of such sites by cleaning them up and then providing immunity from federal or state lawsuits based on any continuing toxicity found on the site.

---

[36] *See Chester Residents Concerned for Living Quality v. Seif*, 132 F. 3d 925 (3th Cir. 1997) (finding a private cause of action for discriminatory administration of EPA program funds for a showing of disproportionate effect).

Part 4

Wetlands and Beaches

Chapter 17

Protection of Sensitive Lands

§ 17.01 Wetlands.

Land use controls are often justified as environmental protection. Thus, when the lands protected are especially sensitive for some reason, special regulation may be justified. Such regulation is often here justified as a means of protecting (1) unstable lands, such as riparian lands or the thinly soiled Santa Catalina mountains around Los Angeles-or wetlands; or (2) lands that involve a public resource — like navigable water, or wetlands; or (3) lands which serve some biological or ecological function in their region — again, such as wetlands. Little wonder, then, that wetlands have spawned litigation as well as fish.[1]

Most of the coastal states, as some interior states as well, have enacted statutory schemes for restricting the development of wetlands (fresh and saltwater marshes, bogs, and swamps) and shorelands.[2] Many of these statutes are not wetlands protection devices *per se;* they focus on changing the land use of a wetland, converting it into something else, and leave many changes in drainage, soil run-off, and the destruction of plant life, all of which can destroy a wetland, unaffected. Some of these statutes authorize land use regulations for wetlands, but even when they are silent on such issues, their enactment would still provide a rationale for land use regulations that preserve them. State courts have upheld many state regulatory schemes for wetlands themselves.

In *United States v. Riverside Bayview Homes, Inc.*,[3] a unanimous opinion of the Supreme Court recited the U.S. Army Corps of Engineers' extensive, technical findings on the environmental importance of wetlands and upheld the Corps' expanded regulatory jurisdiction over them, based on the Corps' definition of a wetland.

The threat connecting these federal and state regulatory efforts is found in the majority opinion in *Euclid*. The law of nuisance must be recognized as containing great flexibility and judicial discretion. To put it another way and to paraphrase Dean Prosser on the same subject, nuisance law both encompasses much judicial discretion and results in a welter of conflicting

---

[1] Wetlands filter and store water. Preserving them provides a cost-effective way to deal with some soluble pollutants and to manage storm water and run-off to prevent floods — all the while providing habitat for plants and wildlife. The loss of wetlands by dredging, filling, and compacting them for development has been (by some estimates) as more than one half of our wetlands over the last two centuries, rising to a loss of about 300,000 wetland acres in the early 1980s. The Back Bay in Boston, New Orleans, and the canalized subdivisions in Florida, are examples.

[2] *See* William Want, *Wetlands Regulation*, Chapter 13 (1989) (reviewing 26 state statutes).

[3] 474 U.S. 121, 134–135 (1985).

cases. To quote *Euclid*, "whether a particular thing is a nuisance, is to be determined . . .by considering it in connection with the circumstances and locality. A nuisance may be merely a right thing in the wrong place, like a pig in a parlor instead of the barnyard." The implication of this quotation is that the stronger regulation is required for the more fragile land, such as a wetland. Regulation of wetlands is consistent with established nuisance doctrines.

[A] Defining Wetlands.

Most of the definitions of wetlands establish the scope of these regulatory programs and take the presence of vegetation either needing or surviving periodic inundation, and/or soil types capable of saturation for some portion of the year, as the most important indicators of a wetland.[4] It is not necessary that the saturation be visible at the surface. Subsurface saturation by groundwater on a periodic basis is sufficient. By the same token, the periodic collection of rainwater on the ground does not indicate the presence of a wetland. Water saturating the soil drives oxygen out of the soil and plants indicating the presence of a wetland must have adapted to this lack of oxygenation. Under some definitions, the inundated soil and the saturated vegetation must co-exist: if the soil qualifies, but is below the root line of the vegetation, the area is not a wetland; likewise, if the land is not vegetated at all, but has qualifying soil at the surface, it is not a wetland either.

[B] State Regulation.

The scope of regulation of wetlands varies from state to state. Some regulations are scattered throughout a state's code, while other states assemble their regulations into code form.[5] Regulation can extend only to tidal, or to both tidal and freshwater wetlands.[6] The basis of this regulatory authority is the police power. Its objective in enacting such regulation is often tied to aesthetic, conservation, and flood control purposes.[7] Wetland and shoreland regulations have been upheld against a variety of takings claims as well.[8]

---

[4] *Compare* N.Y. Envtl. Conser. Law § 24—0107 (1991), implemented by N.Y. Comp. Codes R.& Regs., tit. 6, § 662.1(k) (1986) (a detailed regulatory definition specifying the seven types of vegetation required) *with* 33 C.F.R. § 328.3(b) (1990) (the federal definition with both a soil and vegetation component).

[5] As to the latter, *see, e.g.,* Va. Code Ann. § 28.2-1302 (Michie 1993). *See also Secretary, Vermont Agency of Natural Resources v. Irish,* 738 A.2d 571, 575–578 (Vt. 1999) (reviewing Vermont Wetland Rules).

[6] N.Y. Envir. Conserv. L. § 24–0301 (McKinney 1993) (providing mapping and regulation for freshwater wetlands of no less than 12.4 acres).

[7] *See Zealy v. City of Waukesha,* 548 N.W.2d 528, 529, *noted in* John Vandik, *Waiting for Uncle Sam to Buy the Farm . . .Forest, or Wetland? A Call for New Emphasis on State and Local Controls in Natural Resource Protrection,* 8 Ford. Envtl. L J. 691, 708–709 (1997).

[8] *See, e.g.,Karam v. State of New Jersey, Dept. of Envir. Protection,* 705 A.2d 1221 (N.J. Super. Ct., App. Div., 1998) (finding no regulatory taking in a state shoreland development permit system).

A municipality's designation of property as a wetland is not itself a compensable taking.[9] That is, a regulatory requirement that plaintiff apply for a permit to dredge or fill a wetland is not a taking.[10] In this as it other areas of takings law, just the enactment of a regulation works no *prima facie* or facial taking.

Likewise, "as applied" challenges to wetlands regulation have been rejected.[11] Most of the judicial decisions upholding such statutes at this stage use a balancing test — balancing the private harm or injury against the public benefit involved.[12] By using this test, courts generally have evaluated wetlands regulations as a regulatory taking. With regard to an analogous federal claim, Justice Scalia stated, in *Lucas v. South Carolina Coastal Council*, that "the owner of a lake bed . . .would not be entitled to compensation when he is denied the requisite permit to engage in a landfilling operation that would have the effect of flooding others' land."[13] Justice Scalia's example is, he says, an instance in which the law of nuisance would traditionally prevent an owner from visiting injury on a neighbor; a land use regulation to the same effect would, he concludes, be constitutional and not a taking of property. Given a wetlands context, every wetland serving as a flood control, pollution filtering device, such language is likely over the long term, to have wide application.

After defining a wetland, the statutes often further define the uses permitted in a wetland: e.g., the Virginia Code permits such uses as harvesting shellfish, recreational uses, boating, trapping, and horticulture — usually permitted only with the proviso that the natural contours and functions of the wetland not be disturbed.[14] Other uses require a permit, issued by a wetlands board. The criteria employed by the board in issuing such permits involve no adverse impact, no feasible alternative, and replacement standards. There is also typically a provision for judicial review of permit denials.[15] Often "special exceptions" for other than the permitted uses are allowed when they are "in the public interest."

More recent state regulations sometimes recognize a right to develop a wetland when the developers replace the lost wetland with comparable

---

[9] *See, e.g., Zerbetz v. Municipality of Anchorage*, 856 P. 2d 777 (Alaska 1993);*Carabell v. Dept. of Natural Resources*, 478 N.W.2d 675 (Mich. App. Ct. 1991).

[10] *Wedinger v. Goldberger*, 522 N.E.2d 25 (N.Y.), *cert. denied*, 488 U.S. 850 (1988) (involving Staten Island wetlands).

[11] *See Claridge v. New Hampshire Wetlands Bd.*, 485 A.2d 287 (N.H. 1984) (upholding the application of state permit regulations under a "public benefit/private harm" takings test taken from *Mahon*). Cases like *Claridge* may have their authority undermined by the U.S. Supreme Court opinions in *Nollan* and *Lucas*, although some courts have distinguished these cases. *See, e.g., Mock v. Dept. of Envir. Resources*, 623 A. 2d 940, 946 (Pa. Commw. Ct. 1993); *Plantation Landing Resort, Inc. v. United States*, 30 Fed. Cl. 63, 69 (1993) (both cases distinguishing *Lucas*).

[12] *See, e.g., Just v. Marinette Cty.*, 201 N.W.2d 761 (Wis. 1972) — a seminal case, because before it, the leading case was contra. *See State v. Johnson*, 265 A.2d 711 (Me. 1970).

[13] *Lucas v. South Carolina Coastal Council*, 505 U.S. 1003, 1029 (1992).

[14] Va. Code Ann. § 28.2-1302(3) (Michie 1993).

[15] *See also, e.g.,* Fla. Stat. Ann. § 403.91-929 (West 1993).

acreage. This is called the "no net loss" policy.[16] Transferable wetlands development rights have also been attempted in one state — Michigan — on the Rouge River in southeastern part of that state.

Municipal government is generally given some role in wetlands regulation. Sometimes the municipality is authorized to enact special regulations for wetlands. On the municipal level, a planning commission has been held to have authority to consider the effect of a subdivision's water wells on groundwater and adjacent wetlands.[17] In *Busse*, the proffered opinions concern the need to reduce bird and animal habitat disruption.

[C] Federal Regulation.

In 1972, the federal Clean Water Act was amended so that water-borne "pollutants" were defined so as to include "fill material."[18] With this amendment, federal control over wetland development became pervasive as well.[19] The discharge of dredged or fill materials into the "navigable waters of the United States" is forbidden unless the developer obtains a permit from the Army Corps of Engineers.[20] Both civil and criminal penalties follow an illegal dredging or filling.[21]

The jurisdiction of the Corps has federal Commerce Clause origins, but its permit program is authorized by the 1972 Clean Water Amendments.[22] The 1972 Amendments never used the word "wetlands."[23] Applicable regulations under these amendments, however, define "navigable waters" as including the tributaries of such waters, as well as non-navigable intrastate waters with an impact on interstate waters, and all freshwater wetlands, defined as an area periodically inundated or saturated at a frequency to support the prevalence of vegetation adapted for life in saturated soil.[24] Today Corps' regulations regularly refer to wetlands and

---

[16] *See, e.g.,* Richard McNeer, *Nontidal Wetland Protection in Maryland and Virginia*, 51 Md. L.Rev. 105, 133–135 (1992).

[17] *Busse v. City of Madison*, 503 N.W. 2d 340, 343 (Wis. App. Ct. 1993) ("We conclude that it is not arbitrary, unreasonable, or discriminatory to accept opinions that a plat would probably adversely affect groundwater which feeds an important wetland.").

[18] *See* 33 U.S.C.A. § 1362(6) (1996).

[19] *See generally* Theda Braddock (with Reed Huppman), *Wetlands: An Introduction to Ecology, Law, and Permitting* 61–84 (1995). Prior federal regulation of industrial pollution was based on the Rivers and Harbors Act of 1899. *See, e.g., Zabel v. Tabb*, 430 F.2d 199 (5th Cir. 1970).

[20] *United States v. Mills*, 817 F. Supp. 1546, *affirmed*, 36 F.3d 1052 (11th Cir. 1994); *Slagle v. United States*, 809 F. Supp. 704, 708 (D. Minn. 1992) (wetlands are "waters of the United States" subject to the Clean Water Act).

[21] *United States v. Rapanos*, 115 F.3d 367 (6th Cir. 1997) (upholding state environmental officials search of defendant's property for violation under the open fields doctrine, and involving a criminal penalty).

[22] *See* 33 U.S.C.A. § 1344 (known as the "§ 404 permit program," a reference to its section number in the 1972 legislation).

[23] *See Natural Resources Defense Council v. Callaway*, 392 F. Supp. 685 (D.D.C. 1975) (a citizen suit forcing expansion of Corps prior definition of "waters of the United States" to wetlands).

[24] *United States v. Riverside Bayview Homes, Inc.*, 474 U.S. 121 (1985) (holding that the

wetlands issues.[25] So, for example, a land developer who proposes to drain a wetland, arguing that because draining is not filling, will still need a § 404 permit from the Corps.[26] In another example, a facility like a power line built through land fitting the definition of a wetland, but built on pilings driven through the wetland to bedrock, and arguably having no appreciable impact on the wetland's ecological function, is also subject to Corps jurisdiction. It is not confined to waters traditionally considered to be navigable. Its permit process is designed to assess the impact of the power line on waters of many sorts not traditionally navigable or used in interstate commerce, and so the owner of the line will have to submit to its administrative process. Artificially created wetlands,[27] seasonal wetlands,[28] and isolated wetlands[29] — all fall with the Corps' jurisdiction.

While there are few statutory guidelines for the Corp to follow, its regulations have indicates that "where the activity associated with a discharge" is not water-dependent, "practical alternatives that do not involve . . . aquatic sites are presumed to be available unless clearly demonstrated otherwise."[30] Such a practical alternatives standard is intended to send developers inland and away from water under the Corp's jurisdiction both during their market surveys and while applying for permits.

Permit decisions of the Corps are appealed to the federal Environmental Protection Agency and the Agency's decision,[31] if in conflict with the Corps', controls.[32] Any mistake by the Corps in requiring an owner to submit a permit application and go through the process might give rise to a due process claim. It does not give rise to a takings claim.[33] In practice and

Corps wetlands jurisdiction is established by the presence of groundwater). The scope of the Corps jurisdiction in this regard has been the subject of considerable litigation and dispute. *See Hoffman Homes v. United States Envir. Protection Agency*, 961 F.2d 1310 (7th Cir. 1992) (holding that the federal Clean Water Amendments regulate intrastate, isolated, non-adjacent wetlands), *vacated*, 975 F.2d 1554 (7th Cir. 1992), *supp. op.*, 999 F.2d 256 (7th Cir. 1993) (upholding CWA jurisdiction, but not for the specific wetland involved in the litigation), *noted in* 54 Ohio St. L. J. 809 (1993).

[25] *See, e.g.,* 33 C.F.R. § 328.3 (1996).

[26] *See, e.g.,* N.Y. Envtl. Conser. Law § 24-0701(1) (prohibiting "any form of draining, dredging, excavation, removal of soil, mud, sand, shells, gravel or other aggregate" as well as "any form of dumping, filling, or depositing of same," without a permit).

[27] *See Leslie Salt Co. v. United States*, 896 F.2d 354 (9th Cir. 1990), *cert. denied*, 498 U.S. 1126 (1991); *Swanson v. United States*, 798 F.2d 1368 (9th Cir. 1986).

[28] *See Quivira Mining Co. v. EPA*, 765 F.2d 126 (10th Cir. 1985), *cert. denied*, 474 U.S. 1055 (1986).

[29] *See Utah v. Marsh*, 740 F.2d 799 (10th Cir. 1984).

[30] 40 C.F.R. § 230.10(a)(3)(1995).

[31] *See* Memorandum of Agreement Between the Department of the Army and the Environmental Protection Agency (Jan. 19, 1989).

[32] *Bersani v. EPA*, 850 F.2d 36 (2d Cir. 1988), *cert. denied*, 489 U.S. 1089 (1989) (involving one of the very few instances of EPA's veto of the issuance of a state permit for wetlands in Massachusetts).

[33] *Tabb Lakes, Inc. v. United States*, 26 Cl. Ct. 1334 (1992), *affirmed*, 10 F.3d 796, 802–803 (Fed. Cir. 1993).

to date, it has proven difficult to overturn a decision of the Corps that land constitutes a wetland.

In addition, the Environmental Protection Agency can designate a state's government to run the federal program.[34] After this designation, the Corps and the EPA suspend their issuance of permits when a permit may be issued under the state program, and applicants need not file for a federal permit provided that they apply for the state permit.[35] EPA retains the right to object to the issuance of any particular permit in the meanwhile.[36] Similarly a state might retain the right to issue a "state only" permit. The EPA may also suspend its approval of a state's permit program, and in Michigan, it has done so in 1994 after the litigation in *Friends of the Crystal River v. EPA*,[37] reinstating the program that same year.

The Corps and the EPA have also been, since 1995, engaged in a program of establishing mitigation banks for wetlands,[38] creating or restoring wetlands after development of various types has injured or destroyed existing wetlands, and banking the activity against unavoidable future impacts.

Coastal wetlands are additionally regulated by the Coastal Zone Management Act. The Act requires each coastal and Great Lakes state to file a management plan for its coastal zone and territorial sea.[39] The state plans are approved (or not) by the Secretary of Commerce, after reviewing the state plan's consistency with the federal act.[40] The plans define the land uses permitted within a state's coastal zone, identify areas of particular fragility, establish a priority of uses, and plan for the shoreline's erosion, the siting of energy facilities, and access to beaches.

Plan implementation is typically delegated to municipal government, but some states, particularly on the Pacific coast, have established state coastal regulatory agencies; the California and South Carolina state agencies provided the legal background for the *Lucas* and *Nollan* cases.[41]

---

[34] *See, e.g., Friends of the Crystal River v. EPA*, 35 F.3d 1073 (6th Cir. 1994) (reviewing standards for the Michigan program designated by EPA to be as least as stringent as EPA standards, but acting arguably under state statutes and regulations). *See also* Oliver Houck & Michael Roland, *Federalism in Wetlands Regulation: A Consideration of Delegation of Clean Water Section 404 and Related Programs to the States*, 54 Md. L. Rev. 1242 (1995) (arguing that federal authority is delegated and the states have assumed administration of the federal program).

[35] *See* 33 U.S.C. § 1344(h)(2) (West 1997).

[36] *Friends of the Crystal River v. EPA*, 794 F. Supp. 674 (W.D. Mich. 1992) (treating federal authority as having been transferred to the state), later opinion, 35 F.3d 1073 (6th Cir. 1994) (ruling that the federal District Court had subject matter jurisdiction over the litigation because a federal question was present).

[37] 35 F.3rd 1073 (6th Cir. 1994).

[38] *See* Lawrence Liebesman & David Plott, *The Emergence of Private Wetlands Mitigation Banking*, Nat. Resources & Envir. J. (Summer, 1998), at 341–342, 370 (describing the federal program).

[39] *See* 16 U.S.C. §§ 1452, 1454-1455 (West 1993).

[40] *Id.* at § 1454(h)

[41] Discussed *infra*, this Chapter and *supra*, Chapter 14.

In addition, the Coastal Barrier Protection Act,[42] delineates the low-lying barrier lands (often islands paralleling the mainland), requires their mapping, and monitors their development. It applies to both coastal and Great Lake states and limits federal expenditures and financial assistance to development on these barrier islands.

[1] Corps Jurisdiction and State Programs.

Suppose that a land developer proposes to fill a property that has wetland soil and plants, but is a series of artificially created ponds and pits holding rainwater for a portion of the year, not hydrologically connected with any other body of water. Whether a Corps § 404 permit is required is really an issue in part of whether an artificially created wetland is within the Corps' jurisdiction. When a state has a "no net loss" policy or when that policy informs the Corps' jurisdiction, the answer is that artificially created wetlands are just as subject to Corp jurisdiction as natural wetlands.[43] Were the answer otherwise, the Corps' jurisdiction over wetlands would be a shrinking one — and might eventually amount to nothing.[44] Many states and the Corps find a "no net loss" policy a politically appealing one. If the government created the condition causing the wetlands or if the Corp created the wetland conditions, the Corp has jurisdiction over the wetland it creates.[45] If migratory birds use water-soaked ponds and lands as they would a wetland, but otherwise the land does not have wetland soil or plants and is not hydrologically connected with interstate bodies of water, the Corps has still asserted jurisdiction over such land.[46] The Fourth Circuit held that the Corps has no jurisdiction over isolated wetlands and that a regulation asserting such jurisdiction exceeded federal authority under the Commerce Clause.[47] The United States Supreme Court later

---

[42] 16 U.S.C. § 3501 (West 1993).

[43] See Leslie Salt Company v. United States, 896 F.2d 354 (9th Cir. 1990), cert. denied, 498 U.S. 1126 (1991), noted 2 Vill. Envir. L.J. 463, 496–499 (1991) (upholding Corps jurisdiction because Congress intended to reach any aquatic features within the reach of the commerce clause and regardless of their origin).

[44] Cargill v. United States, 55 F. 3d 1388 (9th Cir.) (a later opinion in the Leslie Salt controversy, holding that the presence of migratory birds and endangered species on property provided a sufficient nexus between the regulated activity and interstate commerce, although "testing the limits" of that power), cert. denied (again), 516 U.S. 955 (1995).

[45] United States v. Southern Investment Co., 876 F.2d 606 (8th Cir. 1989) (holding that wetlands created by a dam remain under Corp jurisdiction). But see United States v. City of Fort Pierre, 747 F.2d 464 (8th Cir. 1984) (holding that a dry slough exhibiting wetland characteristics because of Corp river dredging, was not subject to the § 404 permit program).

[46] See Tabb Lakes Ltd. v. United States, 715 F. Supp. 726 (E.D.Va. 1988), affirmed, 885 F.2d 866 (4th Cir. 1989) (not deciding the issue, but denying Corps jurisdiction on procedural grounds).

[47] United States v. Wilson, 133 F.3d 251, 257 (4th Cir. 1997) (interpreting United States v. Lopez, 514 U.S. 549 (1995), noted in James Bryant, United States v. Wilson: A Change in Wetlands and Clean Water Act Jurisprudence?, 28 Real Est. L. J. 37, 38 (1999) and ibid., 29 Real Est. Rev. (No. 3, Fall, 1999), at 71. Wilson has been accepted for appeal to and argument in the United State Supreme Court. See contra Solid Waste Agency v. United States Army Corps of Engineers, 998 F. Supp. 946, 1998 U.S. Dist. LEXIS 3994 (U.S. D. Ct., N.D. Ill., 1998) (rejecting Wilson).

agreed.[48] Noting that the jurisdiction of the Corp is limited to the "navigable" waters of the United States, the court said that Congress intended that word to be a limiting one, and continued: "it is one thing to give the word limited effect, and quite another to give it no effect whatsoever." Moreover, the court said, to recognize the Corp's jurisdiction over such isolated wetlands would impinge on the traditional rights of the states to regulate land and water uses. Therefore, the court invalidated the Corps' regulatory authority over isolated, non-navigable, intrastate waters in wetlands whose only connection to interstate commerce was the presence of migratory birds.[49] However, if the pond is an intrastate body of water, without a navigable tributary or outlet, but used as fishery whose products entered interstate commerce, the Corps would have jurisdiction.[50]

After mapping all state wetlands, one state wetlands commission imposed a two mile buffer requirement between wetlands and private waste management company landfills. Against the argument of a waste management company claiming that there is no evidence that the proximity of a landfill is a reliable indicator of landfill pollution, this buffer regulation is reasonable, and even when it is only fairly debatable, it none-the-less may be sustained as having a rational basis and supported by substantial evidence.[51]

§ 17.02   The Public Trust.

The doctrine of the public trust was received in the United States as part of the English common law.[52] It is the right of the people to use freely the lands within the trust — included coastal lands for certain purposes, originally navigation, commerce, and fishing. Originally it applied only to the 13 colonies, but eventually, under the equal footing doctrine for the admission of other states to the Union, the trust was incorporated into every state's sovereign powers as well. Only tidal wetlands were originally subject to the trust, but it was expanded to apply to all navigable waters — lakes, ponds, rivers and streams.[53] Thus it is that the state has title to both tidal and fresh navigable waters, and their underlying beds, in trust for the free use of them by the public.[54] The trust has been expanded in some states

---

[48] See Solid Waste Agency of Northern Cook County v. United States Army Corp of Engineers, 531 U.S. 159 (2001).

[49] Id. (also limiting the reach of the holding in Riverside Bayview Homes, op. cit. n. 24, by emphasizing the latter's focus on the reasonableness of the hydrologic connection between a body of water and its wetlands).

[50] Utah v. Marsh, 740 F.2d 799 (10th Cir. 1984).

[51] Johnson v. Sunray Services, Inc., 816 S.W. 2d 582 (Ark. 1991).

[52] See Fred Bosselman, Limitations Inherent in the Title to Wetlands at Common Law, 15 Stan. Envir. L. Rev. 247, 327–337 (1996).

[53] Vermont v. Vermont Central Ry., 571 A. 2d 1128, 1132 (Vt. 1989). See generally J. Archer & T. Stone, The Interaction of the Public Trust and the Takings Doctrine: Protecting Wetlands and Critical Coastal Areas, 20 Vt. L. Rev. 81 (1995) (discussing the public trust as the background law immunizing a state regulation from the charge of a total taking as discussed in Lucas).

[54] The Daniel Ball, 77 U.S. 557, 564 (1871) (holding also that the test for navigability is "navigability in fact").

to cover wetlands adjacent to navigable waters.[55] It also authorizes regulation by permits and otherwise prohibited removal of the beds of navigable bodies of water.[56] In a few states, state constitutional provisions supplement the protection of the environment given by the public trust.[57]

§ 17.03   Beaches

[A]   The Environmental Function of Beaches.

The ecological functions of a barrier beach are several. First, the beach is a unique habitat for plants and wildlife. Second, its sand has a capacity to absorb great amounts of water. The dunes absorb the force of waves, as do the back-of-the-dunes area of a beach, coastal ponds, and wetlands. Thus the beach is the coast's first line of defense against heavy seas, such as are created by hurricanes. And, when hurricanes come, the escape routes from beaches on barrier islands such were involved in *Lucas v. South Carolina Coastal Commission*,[58] are limited.

§ 17.04   Total Takings.

Lucas v. South Carolina Coastal Council[59] created a new category of takings cases involving the so-called "total taking." The court held that an owner losing all economically beneficial uses to a regulation has suffered a taking — that is, a development denial resulting from a total or 100% diminution in value is a taking — except when the owner's proposed development violates the background principles of nuisance and property law.

[A]   The Facts.

David Lucas purchased two unimproved beachfront lots in 1986. Both lots were then zoned in a single-family use district. He paid $975,000. The lots didn't abut each other and Lucas intended to construct separate residences on both — one residence for himself and his family and the other on speculation. Neighboring lots on each side of Lucas' had been developed previously: on each were homes.

Two years later, in 1988, the state enacted a Beachfront Management Act. The Act prohibited any substantial development of the lots, including the construction of residences: only wooden decks or narrow raised boardwalks were permitted. The beach in front of Lucas' lots was unstable; parts

---

[55] *See, e.g., Just v. Marinette Cty.*, 201 N.W.2d 761, 769 (Wis. 1972).

[56] *See Reuter v. Dept. of Natural Resources*, 168 N.W.2d 860 (Wis. 1969).

[57] *See, e.g., Mont. Envtl. Information Ctr. v. Dept. of Envtl. Quality*, 998 P.2d 1236 (Mont. 1999) (holding that state statute permitting discharge of mining by-products violated state constitutional provision guaranteeing a clean and healthy environment).

[58] 505 U.S. 1003 (Blackmon, J., dissenting, text at n. 1).

[59] 505 U.S. 1003 (1992), *noted* 61 Cinn. L. Rev. 1035, 71 N.C. L. Rev. 928 (1993).

of it had been underwater within the past forty years. More recently, however, the beach had not been subject to erosion; in fact, over the last several decades it had been built up by the accretion of sand. None-the-less, the Coastal Council administering the Act drew a line connecting the landward most points of erosion during the past forty years — a line to the rear of Lucas' landward lot boundaries. This had the effect of making Lucas ineligible for a building permit and abruptly ended his construction plans.

Lucas did not apply for a building permit.[60] Instead, he sued, conceding that the Act was within the well-recognized police power of the legislature, but alleging that it was, none-the-less, a violation of his constitutional right not to be deprived of his property without first being paid just compensation for it.

While the suit was pending in 1990 and 4 years after Lucas' purchase, the state legislature amended the Act to permit administrative relief in the form of variances from the Act's provisions. Lucas did not apply for this relief either.[61] The trial court found a regulatory taking, awarding Lucas over $1.2 million in compensation.

[B]   The State Supreme Court Opinion.

The Supreme Court of South Carolina reversed and, over a strong dissenting opinion, found no taking under the 1987 United States Supreme Court opinion in *Keystone*.[62] The state supreme court concluded that once Lucas had conceded that the Act was intended to protect the coast from erosion, its primary purpose became, for purposes of this suit, harm prevention, rather than the creation of a public right or benefit. This concession led the court (like most state courts reviewing similar statutes) to use the private harm/public benefit test for a taking and to uphold the Act. Thus it found that there was no taking, notwithstanding the severe economic impact on Lucas.[63]

---

[60] The Act's administrator testified at trial that applying would have been futile.

[61] After the 1990 amendments, the issue arose whether Lucas' takings claim was ripe for judicial review: when further administrative review that might lead to the granting of a variance from the Act, the developer should seek such review or else risk a determination that the regulators have not yet reached a final decision about the application of the Act. It is unclear in *Lucas* whether ameliorative amendments enacted after an owner purchases can affect both his investment-backed expectations and the ripeness of his takings claim. At least three Justices found Lucas' claim not ripe. So this issue was worth consideration after *Lucas*. (In any event, developers should document their investment-backed expectations at the time that they purchase a property.) It was considered in *Palazzolo v. Rhode Island*, 2001 U.S. LEXIS 4910 (June 28, 2001). *Palazzolo* held that even a post-enactment purchaser, once procuring a final regulatory decision denying a permit, making clear the extent of the development that would be allowed, and citing no non-compliance with state exhaustion rules or pre-permit processes, would have ripened a takings claim.

[62] Discussed *supra*, Chapter 3.

[63] In contrast, the dissent focused on the impact — and on the second part or prong of the test in *Agins v. City of Tiburon*, 447 U.S. 255, 260 (1980), discussed *supra*, Chapter 4, stating that a taking occurs when "the ordinance does not substantially advance legitimate state interests, *or denies an owner economically viable use of his land*" is a taking. The dissent founds that the primary purpose of the Act was to confer a benefit on the public by preserving the coast as a tourist attraction and habitat for wildlife, plants, and natural processes.

[C]   The United States Supreme Court — the Majority Opinion.

The United States Supreme Court reversed the state court. Justice Scalia wrote the majority opinion,[64] first conceding that the takings clause as originally proposed by James Madison, applied only to "physical deprivations,"[65] but arguing that as ratified, it "can be read to apply to regulatory as well as physical deprivations."[66] Then reaching the merits of Lucas' takings claim, Scalia's opinion described two types of regulatory takings claims: first, those involving a physical invasion of a plaintiff's land and second, those involving a regulation denying "all economically beneficial or productive use" of property. This case, he states, is of the second type.[67]

These two types of takings, the court said, are "two discrete categories of regulatory action . . .compensable without case-specific inquiry into the public interest advanced in support of the restraint" on the plaintiff's property rights. (Thus the state court's disagreement about the Act's purpose was irrelevant to the taking discussed here.) To mold a rule for the second type of taking involved in this case, the court states: "[W]hen an owner of real property has been called upon to sacrifice *all* economically beneficial uses in the name of the common good, that is, to leave his property economically idle, he has suffered a taking."

Thus, the first, and most important, thing done in this opinion is that its majority recognizes this second type of categorical taking — for a deprivation of "all economically beneficial uses," compensable with even when supported by the strongest of police power justifications. Here is a clear, bright-line right for the property owner. The second thing done is the holding that this new type of categorical taking is inapplicable when the state justifies the otherwise offending regulation as a public nuisance or under another equally well established principle of real property law.

[1]   *Lucas* and *Penn Central*.

The majority opinion states that *Lucas* deals with a "relatively rare" situation, a 100% taking: when, as is the more typical situation, the

---

[64] Justice Scalia was joined by Rehnquist, C.J., and Justices O'Connor, White, and Thomas.

[65] *See* John Hart, *Land Use Law in the Early Republic and the Original Meaning of the Takings Clause*, 94 Nw. U. L. Rev. 1099, 1156 (2000) (arguing that early land use regulation was broad and inclusive and so Madison's and others' view of the takings clause was narrow, not encompassing regulatory takings as Justice Holmes found in *Pennsylvania Coal Co. v. Mahon*).

[66] The majority and dissenting opinions disagreed about the Act's primary purpose, affecting their views of the Act's constitutionality. Justice Blackmun's dissent contended that the takings clause applies only to physical takings.

[67] This second type of taking has three sources: (1) Justice Holmes' diminution in value test in *Mahon*, in connection with which Holmes states that, when the diminution "reached a certain magnitude" it is a taking — so a 100% magnitude is a sure threshold for invoking Holmes' language; (2) Justice Brennan's dicta in *Penn Central*, stating that the case would be different if the terminal were useless (see *Penn Central Transportation Company v. New York City*, 438 U.S. 104, 138, n. 36 (1978); and (3) the "economic viability" prong of the *Agins* test.

reduction in value is less than 100%, the substantiality of the legitimate state interest is analyzed as well. This involves balancing the state's interest ("the character of the governmental action") against the degree of restraint on private property ("the impact of the regulation and . . .the extent to which the regulation has interfered with distinct investment backed expectations").[68] While *Penn Central* provides the default rule for evaluating a non-*Lucas* regulatory taking claim, such balancing is not likely to yield crisp results easily put into statements of black letter law.

[2] The Nuisance Cases.

The South Carolina Supreme Court, Justice Scalia said, was "too quick to conclude that "harmful or noxious uses of property, amounting to a public nuisance, may be abated by regulations without the payment of compensation." Here he intends to clarify[69] the status of the so-called noxious use cases in which some land use has been completely halted legislatively: e.g., *Mugler, Hadacheck, Miller v. Schoene,* and *Goldblatt.*[70] Justice Scalia, quoting from a majority opinion of Justice Brennan, thought that these cases are best understood "as resting not on any supposed 'noxious' quality of the prohibited uses but rather on the ground that the restrictions were reasonably related to the implementation of a policy-not unlike historic preservation-expected to produce a widespread public benefit and applicable to all similarly situated property."[71] These cases, Scalia adds, used analysis that is "simply the progenitor of our more contemporary statements" like the statement in Justice Scalia's 1987 opinion, that "land-use regulation does not effect a taking if it 'substantially advance[s] legitimate state interests' . . . ."[72] Thus the noxious use cases cannot be singled out for a special status in takings law.[73]

The distinction — crucial to the state court opinion below — between preventing a harmful use (no compensation required) as opposed to extracting a public benefit from an owner (compensation required), is difficult to

---

[68] *See Penn Central Transportation Company v. New York City,* 438 U.S. 104 (1978), discussed *supra,* Chapter 4.

[69] Scalia's restatement of the law here employs the same analysis as Justice Rehnquist's dissent in the *Keystone Bituminous Coal Ass'n v. DeBenedictis,* 480 U.S. 470, 513 (1987), discussed *supra,* Chapter 3.

[70] In three of these four cases (*Miller* excepted), all discussed *supra,* Chapter 3, the regulation was alleged to have completely shut down a business.

[71] *Lucas v. South Carolina Coastal Council,* 112 Sup. Ct. at 2897, *quoting from Penn Central Transportation Company v. New York City,* 438 U.S. 104, 133–134 (1977) (Brennan, J.).

[72] Here Justice Scalia is quoting from *Nollan v. California Coastal Commission,* 483 U.S. 825, 834 (1987), discussed *supra,* Chapter 14.

[73] After *Penn Central,* where these cases were crucial to Justice Brennan's restatement of the law of takings, the Supreme Court's opinions on takings had discussed these cases either as an exception to a majority rule in takings jurisprudence, or as a distinct line of cases within that jurisprudence. Then Justice Rehnquist, however, treated the cases as an exception in his dissent in *Penn Central,* although his dissent in *Keystone* makes plain that the nuisance cases do not provide a safe harbor from taking claims: "Our cases [he said] have never applied the nuisance exception to allow complete extinction of the value of the parcel of property." *Keystone,* 480 U.S. at 513.

make and, for Justice Scalia, is in the eye of the beholder. At the root of his concern with this harm-benefit distinction is a distrust of legislative findings and a refusal to accept them at face value. Were it otherwise, "[s]ince such a justification can be formulated in practically every case, this amounts to a test of whether the legislature has a stupid staff."[74] He refuses to accept conclusory legislative declarations of purpose.

[3] Total Taking Analysis.

In preparation for the first of Justice Scalia's two important statements in this opinion, he defined two types of discrete categories of regulatory action compensable without case-specific inquiry. That there are <u>two</u> categories, is in itself noteworthy because, before this opinion, it was clear that there was one, exemplified by *Loretto*. The second, involved in this case, did not exist beforehand. What had been clear was that there was a group of cases involving physical invasions that always required compensation, and another group involving abating a public nuisance, that did not.

The prior lack of clarity in takings case law existed because of the too general rules in the court's opinions in the 1980s — starting with the *Agins* two-prong test. Court watchers had spent that decade debating whether Justice Scalia's second category existed at all. That category was usually identified as the "second prong" of the *Agins* test concerning the denial of all "economically viable use." While making clear that the noxious use or nuisance abatement cases do not stand alone and are not a discrete line of authority, Justice Scalia assigns this second, total taking, category a stand-alone status.

The opinion offers three justifications for this status: first, that the total taking is the functional equivalent of a physical invasion; second, that government's continuing ability to operate is not threatened by it; and third, that there is here "a heightened risk that private property is being pressed into some form of public service . . . ."

Justice Scalia proposed that a plaintiff like David Lucas prove that, under state law, (1) the use he proposes is one that he might traditionally expect to engage in; (2) it has not been prohibited by nuisance law; (3) other owners indulge in it; and (4) it has been an expected part of the bundle of sticks for the real property he acquired, but (5) has been destroyed.[75] Most important in this regard is that Lucas' coastal lots were surrounded by others that were already built upon.

The state has the burden of proof that the "proscribed use interests were not part of his title to begin with" and that there are "background principles of nuisance and property law that prohibit the uses" the owner intends. Such a showing is necessary to sustain the regulation. Without it, the state's proscribing "a productive use that was previously permissible" under relevant property and nuisance principles, means that the state's regulation has "gone too far" and requires compensation.

---

[74] *See Lucas*, 505 U.S. at 1025, n. 12 (a statement made assuming the legislature to be staff-driven).

[75] *See Lucas*, 505 U.S. at 1031.

Justice Scalia elaborates on "this logically antecedent inquiry" with a list of considerations from nuisance law: the degree of harm to public or private lands posed by the proposed use, the social value of the use, its suitability to the land in question, and the ease of avoiding the harm by the user or the government.[76] As Dean Prosser once noted, the law of nuisance is an "impenetrable jungle" and a welter of conflicting decisions, hard to harmonize and emphasizing one factor in one decision only to ignore it elsewhere. Scalia, however, sets it up as a means of justifying a regulation.

Returning to private nuisance law as the touchstone for the regulators' arguments in support of a regulation, will present regulators with many problems of proof. Since the advent of environmental laws and statutes, it has been relatively, but not completely, static. Justice Scalia assumes that nuisance law might immunize state regulation against the state's having to pay compensation, but nuisance law also contains some precedent suggesting that nuisance cases have resulted in the abatement of a use, but only if the plaintiff is willing to pay for the abatement.[77] This is not what Scalia seems to have in mind (although he might not object).

Moreover, defining the type of "background" property law that the state may use to defend against a total takings claim has some difficulties in itself. For example, many states recognize the public's customary right to use the dry sand area of a beach as part of its public trust, so when a coastal landowner in Oregon wished to construct an improvement and protect it with a seawall over the dry sand area of the beach, the issue arose whether a municipality may deny a building permit for the wall, citing the customary right as preventing the owner from expecting to be able to build the wall. The owner claimed that in this situation a taking has occurred, but the United States Supreme Court refused to hear the case rejecting the claim.[79] Justice Scalia criticized the state court opinion here, calling it "a land grab running the entire length of the Oregon coast," finding that the doctrine of custom had been limited in recent Oregon opinions and so did not justify the denial of the building permit at issue.[79]

In another case involving a building permit to construct a shoreline resort complex, the beaches involved encompassed tidal pools which contain mollusks, shrimp, and vegetation. Native (Hawaiian) Americans had gathered these as food over time immemorial. When the state granted the application for the permit, continuous native access is a permit condition that will not be subject to a later takings claim.[80]

---

[76] 112 Sup. Ct. at 2901 (citing Restatement of Torts, §§ 826, 827, 828(a)-(c), 830, 831).

[77] See, e.g., Spur Industries, Inc. v. Del E. Webb Dev. Co., 494 P. 2d 700 (Ariz. 1972).

[79] Stevens v. City of Cannon Beach, 854 P. 2d 449 (Or. 1993) (upholding the permit denial under Lucas), cert. denied, 114 Sup. Ct. 1332 (1994) (Scalia, J., dissenting, id. at 1334).

[79] See State ex rel Thornton v. Hay, 462 P. 2d 671 (Or. 1969).

[80] See Public Access Shoreline Hawaii v. Hawaii County Planning Comm'n, 900 P. 2d 1313 (Haw. App. 1993), affirmed, 903 P. 2d 1246 (Haw. 1995) (holding that native peoples have standing in administrative proceedings such as this).

[4] *Euclid* and *Lucas*.

In 1926 in *Euclid*, Justice Sutherland's majority opinion stated that nuisance law will "furnish a helpful clew" as to the validity of a particular zoning regulation. His admonition has been disregarded of late, particularly since the New Deal which expanded the scope of permissible government activities. Does Justice Scalia intend to re-emphasize this rationale for the sake of its attendant discomfiture for regulators? Maybe not, because *Euclid's* validation of zoning is cited earlier in the opinion, though not prominently and not in such a way as to give it a continuing, sweeping effect.

Euclid recognized that the development value of land — up to as much as two thirds to three quarters of its unregulated, fair market value — may be reduced without compensation. So *Euclid* is thus not a "total taking" case: a third to a quarter of the fair market value remained with the owner. In an earlier footnote, Scalia opined that, while some owners who retain only 10% of their land's value would receive compensation under the multi-factor test laid down in earlier opinions[81] others would not, and Scalia adds that "takings law is full of these "all or nothing" situations."[82] The Supreme Court continued in *Lucas* to avoid cases dealing with the most frequently used land use regulations, such as zoning, while citing the more usual cases as support.

Nuisance law plays a singular role in Justice Scalia's analysis. It really plays two roles: the first in the rejected noxious use cases, where its centrality was rejected; and the second, in which it reappears, as relevant to the total taking inquiry. To be consistent it cannot be central to both of its appearances in the majority opinion; Justice Scalia reduced its impact in the noxious use cases, only to reintroduce it later as a justification for a regulation.

What happened here? The noxious use cases inoculated from takings challenges a diminution in value — no matter how great, and even if 100%. Justice Scalia's reformulation reduces the impact of these cases. It reduces them to an exception to his rule for total takings: a total taking is compensable, except when the harmful aspects of the use would permit its abatement as a public or private nuisance or under state real property law.

Whether nuisance law is at the beginning or the end of a rule does not matter much when local zoning and subdivision ordinances are concerned. This is so for two reasons: (1) the presence of non-Euclidian design review procedures, variances, and special exceptions, when combined with ripeness requirements, protect municipalities against a finding of a total taking; (2) Justice Brennan's position in *Penn Central*, treating the railroad's parcel as a whole, and used again by Justice Stevens' treatment of the coal mine as a whole in *Keystone*, also protect municipalities in the same way; that is, this parcel-as-a-whole approach, although the subject of debate, protects municipalities from a finding of a total taking.

---

[81] *Lucas*, 505 U.S. at 1019, n. 8 [citing *Penn Central*, 438 U.S. 104, 124 (1977)].
[82] *Id.*

Since *Euclid*, federal and state environmental laws have largely taken the place of public nuisance actions. Public nuisance law in particular has languished in the decades after *Euclid* upheld zoning in the 1920s.[83] It is unlikely, however, that state regulators will be forced to look only to nuisance law and ignore a state's zoning and environmental law precedents. Both will likely be used to establish the traditional background principles relevant to defending total takings cases. Justice Kennedy, in a concurring opinion in *Lucas*, would permit the state to look broadly as its environmental laws as well as its nuisance case law. He saw nuisance law as too limiting a model for determining the validity of land use and environmental regulations. The unique environmental concerns involving coastal land made this limitation of special concern to Justice Kennedy. He would have used a balancing test, weighing the public interest involved against the owner's investment backed expectations (thus giving these greater prominence than they had in *Penn Central*). His dispute with Justice Scalia is well joined, because balancing is precisely what Scalia hopes to avoid by expanding the role of categorical takings. Probably Justice Kennedy's approach will protect many land use regulations and environmental laws from being impacted by *Lucas*.[84]

[5] "Background" Law for Subdivisions.

In responding to Justice Scalia's prompting that a regulation be justified if at all by an inquiry into the "background principles of state property and nuisance law," some state courts have included state statutes and regulations,[85] while others have not, using only common law principles in their inquiry.[86] The common law/statutory distinction has the advantage of a bright line, but does not do justice to Scalia's language.

Scalia's projected inquiry into the "traditional background principles" of nuisance and property law might also refer the regulator to subdivision enabling acts and ordinances; they conditionally permit developers to subdivide land into building lots. If the developer is forced to leave more

---

[83] The majority opinion does not expressly limit the possible justifications for a regulation to nuisance law — the public trust, navigational servitudes, customary rights, public prescriptive rights — all are well-established in the "real property law" of many states and are there available to justify a regulation too.

[84] Writing for the majority in *Palazzolo v. Rhode Island*, 121 S. Ct. 2448, 150 L. Ed. 592, 2001 U.S. LEXIS 4910 (June 28, 2001), Justice Kennedy showed the same flexible approach to finding what is a background principle of property or nuisance law, "those common, shared understandings of permissible limitations derived from a State's legal tradition," unaffected by the time the owner acquires title of the regulated property or the date of the enactment of a regulation. *Id.*

[85] For two cases using statutes as justifying a regulation, see *Soon Duck Kim v. City of New York*, 681 N.E.2d 312, 315–316 (N.Y. 1997) (involving regrading of land to meet a regraded street) and *Hunziker v. State*, 519 N.W.2d 367, 371 (Iowa 1994) (denying developers a building permit because the state's archaeologist found a Native American burial ground on the developer's parcel).

[86] *See City of Miami v. Keshbro, Inc.*, 717 So. 2d 601, 604–605 (Fla. App. Ct. 1998) (involving a nuisance abatement order of the city); *Stevens v. City of Cannon Beach*, 854 P.2d 449, 456 (Or. 1993).

than one buildable lot in its natural state, 100% of his right to sell that lot has been denied by the regulation and a "total taking" inquiry may be appropriate.

Today, when most subdivision ordinances require that the developer set aside portions of the acreage for streets, parks, schools, and other public purposes, the long tradition of subdivision regulation diminishes a developer's expectations to the point that very detailed regulations are no surprise. An inclusive view of background law works no unfairness on such developers and a non-inclusive view gives them a windfall. The majority opinions in *Penn Central* and *Keystone* counsel consideration of the subdivision operation as a whole, rather than on a lot-by-lot basis, and inclusion of these regulations as within the ambit of relevant background principles.[87]

Thus arguments for an inclusive inquiry in defining background principles include notions of fairness and the prevention of windfalls, as well as a recognition that common law duties may be based on statutes, the encouragement of purchasers to conduct a wide-ranging legal analysis of their purchases, and the long tradition of allowing statutes to affect property rights retroactively.[88]

[6]   What *Lucas* Does Not Decide.

The court's holding that Lucas was entitled to present a total takings claim had two factual preconditions. First, the court accepted as a given the trial court's finding that Lucas' lots had lost all economic value as a result of the Beachfront Management Act. Second, the court admitted the Act's lack of variance provisions and the unavailability of other relief under the Act as it was at the start of Lucas' lawsuit. This said, the court did not find that a taking had occurred. Instead it remanded the case to South Carolina courts for a consideration of this issue and also for a consideration of whether Lucas suffered a temporary regulatory taking under *First English.*

[a]   Footnote 7.

How do we tell when there has been a "total taking"? The value of what's left after the regulation — the value of the economically viable uses remaining once the regulation is in effect — is the numerator of a fraction, the denominator of which is its value before the regulation is imposed. The

---

[87] *See, e.g., Loveladies Harbor, Inc. v. United States*, 21 Ct. Claims 153 (1990), *motion to vacate and dismiss denied*, 27 F. 3d 1545 (Fed. Cir. 1994), *noted and discussed in* Eric Freyfogle, *The Owning and Taking of Sensitive Lands*, 43 U.C. L. A. 77 (1995). *See generally* Richard Ausness, *Regulatory Takings and Wetland Protection in the Post-Lucas Era*, 30 Land and Water L. Rev. 349, 379–387 (1995) (collecting these cases).

[88] *See* Kerri Millikan, *The Lucas Exception: Inclusion, Exclusion, and a Statute of Limitation*, 68 Geo. Wash. L. Rev. 134, 140–147 (1999) (reviewing these arguments and arguments to the contrary). *See also* John Hart, *Land Use Law in the Early Republic and the Original Meaning of the Takings Clause*, 94 Nw. U. L. Rev. 1099, 1107–1116 (2000) (arguing that early land use regulation, when regarded as background law, was broad and inclusive).

"composition of the denominator" in the court's "deprivation fraction" is in Scalia's view problematical.[89] This fraction is:

$$100 - \left[\frac{[\text{value after regulation}]}{[\text{value before regulation}]} \times 100 \right] = \% \text{ of value lost to regulation}$$

Justice Scalia says that it is unclear whether a real estate developer forced to leave 90% of land that he proposed for subdivision in its natural state, would have his deprivation measured by the total acreage — in which case there would be 10% remaining and the "total taking" inquiry would not apply — or whether the 90% of the acreage should be considered separately, giving the developer of the remaining 10% a case like David Lucas' involving a 100% deprivation.[90]

As an example of this confusion, Scalia cites what he sees as the conflicting results in *Mahon* and *Keystone*. *Pennsylvania Coal Co. v. Mahon*[91] involved the elimination of a right to avoid surface subsidence liability that was recognized as a distinct property right in Pennsylvania law. *Keystone Bituminous Coal Ass'n v. DeBenedictis*[92] involved the recognition of many statutes generally codifying for an industry what has come in recent decades to stand for the environmental movement, bringing a new understanding of the permissible scope of regulatory activities and the scope of the property regulated. Scalia's failure to make this point showed his skepticism of *Keystone's* majority opinion.[93] However, a later case sustained *Keystone* anew.[94] In a sense, however, he is right: any trial court must define the property taken before it can determine that a total taking as occurred, and air rights were not considered separately in *Penn Central*, but the third estate was in *Mahon*.[95]

---

[89] *Lucas*, 505 U.S. at 1016, n. 7.

[90] *See Palazzolo v. Rhode Island*, 121 S. Ct. 2448, 2465 (2001) (the majority rejecting a total taking claim and refusing to settle the "denominator issue" when plaintiff framed his case as the taking of a whole parcel, not merely its regulated wetland portion).

[91] 260 U.S. 393 (1922).

[92] 480 U.S. 470 (1987).

[93] *Lucas* represents a change in the standard of judicial review and a new heightened scrutiny for regulations. *Cleburne Living Ctr. v. City of Cleburne*, 473 U.S. 432 (1985), discussed *infra*, Chapter 18, also exemplifies this trend, as does *Nollan v. California Coastal Commission*, 483 U.S. 825 (1987), discussed *infra*, Chapter 14.

[94] *See Palazzolo v. Rhode Island*, 121 S. Ct. at 2465 (2001) (Kennedy, for the majority, and O'Connor, J., concurring).

[95] *See* John Delaney, *Advancing Private Property Rights: The Lessons of Lucas*, 22 Stet. L. Rev. 395 (1993); Robert Washburn, *Land Use Control, The Individual, and Society: Lucas v. South Carolina Coastal Council*, 52 Md. L. Rev. 162 (1993).

[b] Discrete Rights.

Some other state-created rights are easily separated from others and considered separately, just as the third estate right of support was in *Mahon v. Pennsylvania Coal Co.* [96] For example, the common law right to explore for minerals has been the basis for an owner's right to bring a trespass action when someone else does. If the state conducts a geological survey of a region including an owner's mineral properties and releases data showing that there are no minerals on the owner's land, there is a taking of the owner's exploration right. An assertion of a total taking of the exploration right is akin to the taking of a segmented right in property similar to the third estate found to be a taking in *Mahon*. Once a right is recognized as distinct, it is subject to a *Lucas* total takings inquiry. That the state has a substantial interest in knowing where minerals are located within its borders, in (say) steering urbanization elsewhere, and in planning for the regulated extraction of the minerals, justifies the regulation but does not avoid the finding of a total taking. [97]

Before filing the takings claim, an attorney should consider whether, when a right is recognized in state law, it cannot adequately be defended by a trespass action. Suppose that the trespass was a seismic one — the invasion of electronic impulses measuring the density and shape of geologic formations. If it can be defended in trespass, there may be no need for recognizing a takings claim as well. This inquiry into the adequacy of other remedies is part of what Scalia had in mind when proposing that the state justify its regulation by making an antecedent inquiry into its common law of property.

In the same vein, the right to drill a well to recover groundwater, or to swim in a river from riparian land, are widely recognized, traditional rights inherent in the ownership of land and might receive similar treatment when denied. An owner has land zoned into a use district that permits only agricultural uses, but the land overlies groundwater of great purity. The owner wants to drill a well and sell bottled water, but drilling requires a permit from municipal officials when the water is not to be used for domestic purposes or agricultural irrigation. If the permit is denied because the use proposed is not an agricultural in nature, a total takings claim is worth filing because the right to drill is a discrete ownership right and traditionally a landowner also has the right to capture or make reasonable use (depending on the state) of underground or percolating water. [98]

---

[96] 260 U.S. 393 (1922), discussed *supra*, Chapter 3.

[97] In the alternative, the state might argue that, regardless of its interest in geologic information, there is no exploration right outside of a trespass action; so the exploration right is no property right at all, but only a tort cause of action.

[98] *See Houston v. Town of Waitsfield*, 648 A.2d 864, 866 (Vt. 1994) (the owner proposing to drill a well on her land into an aquifer, pumping the water directly to a bottling plant, was prevented from doing so because her land is located in a use district zoned exclusively for "agriculture," defined as "the production of agricultural goods, including crops, livestock, forest products, or other farm commodities" — and the zoning administrator deciding that water is not an agricultural product and denying a permit to drill, recognizing that the owner can still drill for water and apply it to an agricultural crop or water livestock with it, and not

[c] Worthless or Unsuitable?

Lucas leaves open the issue of whether a total taking requires that (1) the permitted uses of the land are worth nothing or that (2) it becomes unsuitable for any economic development that produces a reasonable return.[99] The return on renting the land to beachgoers looks reasonable in comparison to the return on neighboring properties.[100] So there may be total deprivation in terms of fair market value, but not in terms of a reasonable return. If the Coastal Council had permitted David Lucas to build a very small, seaside bungalow, on pilings and with dry toilets, Lucas' case would have been considered under *Penn Central* and *Keystone* rules, as Justice Scalia had earlier indicated in *Nollan*. Similarly, when a building is required by the fire code to be retrofitted with sprinklers, necessitating the removal of hazardous material (like asbestos) and resulting a cost to the owner of more than the present fair market value of the building, there may be no *Lucas* or total taking claim if a occupancy permit will at the end of the day be issued to the owner; the value of the building is affected, but its use is not. In a similar situation, the required restoration of expensive architectural features might cost more than fair market value, but also not result in a *Lucas* claim.

§ 17.05 Takings Claims — *Per Se* and Balancing Cases.

Both *Loretto v. Manhattan Teleprompter CATV Corporation*[101] (finding a taking in a state statute permitting a cable TV company to attach a wire to the plaintiff's apartment building — a case in which there is little or no economic impact on the owner) and *Lucas* (involving the most substantial, 100% impact) represent two types of categorical or *per se* takings in which there is to be no inquiry into the statute's advancement of a legitimate state interest.

In the broader, middle range of regulatory taking cases, exemplified by *Penn Central* and *Keystone*, when no categorical taking is present, the substantiality of the state's interest will still be balanced against the economic impact on the owner, particularly the impact on his or her investment-backed expectations.

---

reaching the *Lucas* claim). In *Houston*, unless *Lucas* applies to this right to access the water, considered separately, the owner will have difficulty showing that the denial has totally deprived her of all use of the "property."

[99] The confusion created for trial judges here is the reason Justice Souter was in favor of dismissing the writ of *certiorari*.

[100] If David Lucas had permitted the public, for an access fee, to use his lots as a beach, and had realized, over ten years, 1% of the income he would have obtained building and selling houses, but 15% of the rental income he would have received from the lots with the houses on them, then only a sale of the houses had been denied. This right to alienate or sell the lots is an important right, well recognized and protected in every states' property law — and it is not 100% taken away. If the state could show that Lucas can sell the lots for 10% of his purchase price to someone who wanted to operate a beach business, with the expectation that someday houses would be permitted on them, then based on what Justice Scalia has said, Lucas would have had difficulty showing a total taking.

[101] 458 U.S. 419 (1982), discussed *supra*, Chapter 3.

§ 17.06   Federalism and Categorical Takings

Justice Marshall in *Loretto*, [102] resorting to such words as an "occupation" and "invasion" to describe a physical taking, did not specify what interest in property is being taken; nor did he use the usual classifications offered by New York state's law of real property. He was likely using such strange terms as "occupation" in part to avoid the use of more traditional descriptions of state real property interests, such as easements or licenses for the cable operator.

Similarly, when Justice Scalia in *Lucas* refers to the "traditional" and "background" principles of nuisance or real property law, Justice Scalia is referring to state law used for federal purposes. The issue for both is whether or to what extent the federal constitutional law of takings rests on state law, or whether there is a federal property law. After *Erie Railroad v. Tompkins*, [103] ended the era of federal common law begun with *Swift v. Tyson*, [104] it is unlikely that Scalia was bringing back the era of *Swift*. [105] He wrote in *Lucas* that he was not. Yet he is walking a fine line: giving constitutional deference to state law, and at times writing as if there is a unified body of nuisance law recognized in South Carolina. He writes: "it seems unlikely that common-law principles would have prevented the erection of any habitable or productive improvements" on Lucas' land. [106] His conclusion is one better left to South Carolina courts.

---

[102] *Id.*

[103] 304 U.S. 64, 78 (1938)

[104] 41 U.S. 1 (1842).

[105] Critics of *Lucas* point out the danger of federalizing the concept of property much the way the "freedom of contract" was federalized during the *Lochner* era. *See Lochner v. New York*, 198 U.S. 45 (1904). *See also United States v. Carolene Products Co.*, 304 U.S. 144, n. 4 (1938) (treating "liberty" similarly).

[106] *Lucas*, 505 U.S. at 1031.

Part 5

Regulating the User, Not the Use

Chapter 18

"Family" and Group Homes

§ 18.01 Defining a "Family" in a Zoning Ordinance.

Most zoning ordinances establish single family, detached housing, use districts. Such districts were the "highest" and least intensive use districts established in Euclidian zoning ordinances enacted during the 1920s and 1930s. Indeed, establishing such districts was a major reason for the spread of Euclidian zoning during those decades. One aspect of any such district is the definition of a family.

This definition was not the subject of much litigation until the 1960s. A family was usually defined as a number of persons keeping house together. The housekeeping unit as a definition was probably not meant to encompass fraternity or religious group living, and certainly did not foresee the various types of communal living arrangements which grew up in the 1960s. New life styles, particularly amongst the young of that decade, and more particularly in communities surrounding college campuses, made some communities redefine a family by including a blood, marital or adoption tie.

Today one of the most common problems in interpreting a zoning ordinance involves the definition of a family. It is a common problem not only because of the wide-spread use of single family, exclusive use, residential districts in ordinances, but also because, in suburban and low-density communities, the presence of this type of use district is indeed the principal reason for having an ordinance in the first place. In addition, in 1974, the United States Supreme Court gave its blessing to a definition restrictive enough to exclude a group of college students renting a house near their university.[1] This 1974 case — *Village of Belle Terre v. Boraas* — was the first United States Supreme Court opinion since the *Nectow* opinion in the late 1920s to review a zoning ordinance. The Village's definition of the family was essentially a group of persons related by blood, marriage, or adoption, but not more than six persons, so related or not. This definition was upheld in *Boraas*. It was held to prohibit college students living together in a house in a single family use district.

With Justice Douglas writing for the majority in one of his last opinions as a Justice, the court viewed the ordinance's definition as the economic regulation of the landlord, thus involving no fundamental right or right of privacy. Its opinion went on, in words typical of Justice Douglas, to extol the virtues of the ordinance:

"A quiet place where yards are wide, people few, and motor vehicles restricted are legitimate guidelines in a land use project addressed

---

[1] *Belle Terre v. Boraas*, 416 U.S. 1 (1974).

315

to family needs. *** The Police Power is not confined to elimination of filth, stench, and unhealthy places. It is ample lay out zone where family values, youth values, and the blessings of quiet seclusion and clean air make the area a sanctuary for people."[2]

Several years later, the United States Supreme Court again dealt with the family definition issue, but this time with more sensitivity to its impacts. Here the City of East Cleveland's zoning ordinance defined single family as "a group of persons consisting of parents and their unmarried children, but not more than six persons" — in other words, the nuclear family. Such a definition would by its terms prohibit grandparents and grandchildren from living together, and so it was, the court said, too restrictive.[3] The East Cleveland ordinance also contained an exception, to the effect that a family might also include a head of household, a spouse, plus one dependent child and that child's child — this would include three generations of a family, but in the case that went to the Supreme Court, *Moore v. City of East Cleveland*, a second grandson (the child of another son) moved in. The grandmother was then the subject of criminal charges; she was convicted of violating the ordinance, was fined, and then was sentenced to five days in jail. On appeal, the United State Supreme Court, 5–4, found *Boraas* inapplicable and reversed.[4]

Writing for the plurality of the court, Justice Powell found that the family values upheld in *Boraas* effected only unrelated individuals, but East Cleveland's ordinance "slic[ed] deeply into the family itself" by expressly selecting categories of related individuals who may live together. It made a crime of a grandmother's choice to live with her grandson. Thus a plurality of the court invalidated the ordinance on substantive due process grounds. Some of the plurality also found the ordinance also to be in violation of the Equal Protection Clause. Justice Stevens cast the deciding vote: he wrote separately and, in a brief opinion, found that the ordinance was a both taking of property and was arbitrary under the test of *Euclid*.[5]

The *Moore* opinion might be seen as a limitation on the opinion in *Belle Terre*, but if it is that, then when viewed from the perspective of a

---

[2] *Id. Boraas* is discussed in Norman Williams, 3 Am. Land Plng. L. § 66.90 (Rev. ed. 1985). The dissenting justices in *Boraas* viewed the case very differently. For them, the ordinance unduly burdened the student's First Amendment rights of association and privacy, resulting in discrimination on the basis of personal lifestyles. The dissenting justices saw no constitutional prohibitions on density restrictions in a zoning ordinances so long as related and unrelated persons were regulated alike. Thus, for example, an ordinance might provide that no more than ten persons, related in any way, or not, may occupy a house or dwelling for health reasons, and survive scrutiny by both the majority and the dissent in *Boraas*. Similarly, an ordinance might establish a minimum floor area per person.

[3] *Moore v. City of East Cleveland*, 431 U.S. 494 (1977).

[4] *See* Robert Ellickson & Vicki Been, *Land Use Controls* 853, n. 1 (1999) (suggesting that the impetus for the definition in *Moore* was to prevent school children from taking up residence in the municipality).

[5] Three dissenting justices found no substantive due process violation, thinking the plurality opinion intruded on municipalities' authority without providing clear standards. Burger, C.J., dissenting, thought that Mrs. Moore should have applied for a variance and so did not exhaust her administrative remedies.

non-traditional family or other grouping, it is not much of a limitation. Both opinions reenforce the idea that zoning for the benefit of the family tied by blood or marriage, is a proper focus of concern for local legislatures.

While both *Boraas* and *Moore* were decided in the same spirit, that of protecting the family, there is a difference between deciding that a municipal legislature, exercising the police power in a zoning ordinance, may protect family values — rather, more precisely, that family values may provide a reasonable basis for the exercise of the police power (this is *Boraas*) — and deciding that the same type of legislature shall not prohibit grandparents from living with grandchildren who are cousins, but not brothers or sisters, under a restrictive definition of a "family" (as in *Moore*).

Justices Douglas and Marshall, writing for *Boraas'* majority and in dissent respectively, not only have a very different view of the issues before them, they also have different views of the plaintiffs: for Douglas, this is a case of a municipal legislature restricting the rent roll of a landlord; for Marshall, the tenants, the students at Stony Brook, are the plaintiffs, and he thus sees the issue as the students' right to associate — a broad, group-based reading of their right to privacy. These views inform the analysis of each opinion in the *Boraas* case. For Douglas, family values license the use of the police power. For Marshall, the use of the police power conflicts with the tenants' right of association, and must yield when the reach of the police power is "overinclusive."

Moore stands for more than *Boraas* because it establishes a constitutional right to "family privacy" — heretofore an individual right — and more particularly, a right to choose to live in either a nuclear or an extended family. Justice Powell's opinion was a plurality opinion; he carried three votes with him. Viewed as a major extension of the right to privacy, the trouble which Powell had mustering a Supreme Court majority, is more easily understood.

Definitions of a "family" such as the one in *Boraas* are written the way they are, in part, because the family is seen as a self-limiting group — if by no other means than by biology and the period of gestation. However, many state courts in the immediate wake of *Boraas*, did not follow it.[6] Even if seven first cousins and an extended family could live together under the *Boraas* definition, the same number of unrelated persons, no matter how quiet, could not. The first cousins might fight, but quieter groups, say, an equal number of clerics, would be excluded. The clerics might have more of a common life-style than the first-cousins would. Again, the definition appears too restrictive.

The Brady Bunch might also be excluded under the *Boraas* definition. Brady and the spouse were married, the children were their family, but step-children, one's children not adopted by the other spouse, should be provided for in any modern definition, as this problem could be widespread

---

[6] *See, e.g., Borough of Glassboro v. Vallorosi*, 535 A.2d 544 (N.J. Super. Ct. 1987) (collecting cases).

— there are lots of Brady Bunches around these days.[7] As family composi-tions change, the problems of defining a family are unlikely to diminish.[8]

Communal groups have fared somewhat better in state courts than they have in federal court.[9] As to college students, young singles, foster children, and the mentally-retarded, they could still be excluded in the two federal opinions considered so far. Some ordinances considered in state court attempt to remedy this with definitions of family that include both related and some unrelated persons, up to a specific maximum number. The maxi-mum is presumably justified by some density studies indicating that a person needs a certain amount of square footage for comfort and mental health.[10]

Several state courts have recently followed *Boraas* and upheld restrictive definitions of a family.[11] In *Dinan v. Bd. of Appeals of the Town of Strafford*,[12] the court upheld a definition under which no unrelated persons could live together. Its opinion discussed the differences between unrelated persons and related family members, concluding that a group of tenants (say) living together occupied the premises on the basis of individual tenancies; that, although tenants might share facilities, their ties were not likely to survive their separate tenancies, and that, viewed as transients, they were not as prone to form friendships with neighbors and care about the long-term interests of the community.[13] Another Nebraska opinion con-cluded that a restrictive definition of a family was entitled to a presumption of validity, and although the municipality did not justify the ordinance with studies, the burden of proof was on the party opposing it — and that burden went unmet.[14] A recent survey reported that fifteen states have followed *Belle Terre*, while four have not.[15]

---

[7] *See, e.g., City of Ladue v. Horn*, 720 S.W.2d 745 (Mo. 1986) (involving a Brady-bunch group in which the parents were not married but living together and upholding the ordinance, using a rational basis standard or review and finding no fundamental rights involved in the "economic and social legislation" under review and quoting extensively from the *Borass* opinion: "The essence of zoning is selection, and, if it is not invidious or discriminatory against those not selected, it is proper," said the court).

[8] *See* Katia Brener, *Belle Terre and Single Family Home Ordinances: Judicial Perceptions of Local Government and the Presumption of Validity*, 74 N.Y. U. L. Rev. 447 (1999).

[9] *See Charter Twp. of Delta v. Dinolfo*, 351 N.W.2d 831 (Mich. 1984); *City of Santa Barbara v. Adamson*, 164 Cal. Rptr. 539 (Cal. App. Ct. 1980) (both cases invalidating definitions of a family that are found too restrictive).

[10] *See Baer v. Town of Brookhaven*, 537 N.E.2d 619 (N.Y. 1989) (involving an ordinance that excluded five unrelated elderly women from a single family district in which a family was defined to include no more than four unrelated persons, as well as others related by blood or marriage).

[11] *See, e.g., State v. Champoux*, 566 N.W.2d 763 (Neb. 1997); *City of Brookings v. Winker*, 554 N.W.2d 827 (S. Dak. 1996); *Dinan v. Bd. of Zoning Appeals*, 595 A.2d 864 (Conn. 1991).

[12] 595 A.2d 864 (Conn. 1991).

[13] *Id.* at 870–871.

[14] *State v. Champoux*, 566 N.W.2d 763 (Neb. 1997).

[15] Katia Brener, op. cit., 74 N.Y. U. L. Rev. at 454, n. 39 (also reporting that 29 states have no decisions on this issue), 457–459 (reporting that Cal., Mich., N.J., and N.Y. have not followed *Boraas*).

§ 18.02 Some Specialized Conflicts.

In order to take account of these problems, a revised definition of family might now provide: "One or more persons occupying a dwelling unit as a single non-profit housekeeping unit, who are living together as a stable and permanent living unit, being a traditional family unit or the functional equivalent thereof." This definition has no upper-limits on the number of unrelated persons authorized to live as "a family." Moreover, unrelated persons living together is not the subject of a separate provision in this ordinance. In short, the ordinance contains neither of the two provisions which would render it suspect.

A further issue is whether the ten students are functioning as "a family unit": students are not transients, but on that account they are not necessarily members of a stable, permanent living unit. They will need evidence that they are functioning as the equivalent of such a unit — and evidence of taking meals together, joint purchases, or joint bill-paying, would bolster an argument that they are living in the equivalent of a "living unit." This type of evidence, as long as their communal living is non-profit, makes their use residential in nature; that one of them is a head tenant making a profit is arguably irrelevant. Use at the occupant level, rather than the leasehold level, is the measure of the "residential use" required in the ordinance. Thus none of the student tenants are violating the ordinance.[16]

Sometimes home occupations and definitions of a family conflict. For example, when a municipality's ordinance permits home occupations in a residential district, but restricts the right to conduct such a occupation to "the immediate family residing in the dwelling." The ordinance restriction on home occupations is valid. The fact that the municipality could have chosen another means to regulate home occupations was irrelevant so long as the means it did choose was reasonably related to the end it sought. The court might also turn away an equal protection challenge by a non-family occupant on the ground that the occupant has not shown that she was treated any differently from other similarly situated.[17]

Sometimes a changing housing market runs afoul of the definition of a "family." A builder, constructing homes in a neighborhood in which land prices are extremely high, may respond to the high land costs by reconfiguring the floor plans of his structures so that a common living/dining room and kitchen, is shared by two living units, one off to the right, the other to the left of the living room, each with its own baths and bedrooms. Calling

---

[16] *See Vallorosi, supra* (involving a college town in which the annual "spring fling" at the college spilled over, late one night, into the town, with drunkenness, loud and abusive language, public urination, and many arrests on various charges; responding to this situation, the town's ordinance was amended to adopt the foregoing definition; later, the parents of a college student purchase a three-bedroom, two-bath home in the town's residential zoning district and take title in the name of a family partnership, this partnership then leasing space in the house to ten college students).

[17] *See City of Manassas v. Rosson*, 294 S.E. 2d 709, 804–805 (Va. 1982) (involving an applicant — a widow, without immediate family — for a permit for a home occupation running a telephone answering service from her home, and employing two part-time workers to assist in running her business and holding that the ordinance valid as applied to this applicant).

this housing arrangements "homes for couplets or mingles is a way," he says, "to permit families to buy housing in this area who otherwise couldn't afford it." In *McMinn v. Town of Oyster Bay*,[18] the New York Court of Appeals struck down an ordinance defining the family as any number of persons related by blood, marriage or adoption or two persons over 62 years of age not so related, when owners leased to four unrelated persons in their twenties, all of whom sought to live in the town in which they grew up, but not with their parents and not at home: they wanted to be near their families, but not reside with them. *McMinn* held that the ordinance is facially unconstitutional under the state constitution's due process clause.

Finally, consider the following, more comprehensive definition, one that takes account of the foregoing problems:

"A family consists of:

(a) a householder plus one or more persons related by blood, marriage, or adoption, and limited to the spouse, parents, grandparents, children, grandchildren, brothers or sisters of the householder or of the householder's spouse, living together as a single, non-profit, housekeeping unit sharing a kitchen; or

(b) a group of persons headed by a householder caring for a reasonable number of children in a family-like living arrangement which to all outward appearances is the functional and factual equivalent of a family of related persons; or

(c) a maximum of two persons not sharing a relationship described in paragraphs (a) or (b)."

§ 18.03 Group Homes and Other "Families."

Many municipalities continue to maintain definitions of a "family" that tie into residential use definitions because of a desire to restrict or exclude group homes from single-family residential districts. A foster children's group house located in a single family, residential use district, may function like a family and so qualify under the second of the sub-paragraphs in the all inclusive definition just presented. The group is likely to have a common head, a house mother and/or father; on that ground, all of its unrelated persons are responsible to a common head and become a single housekeeping unit.[19] Such an approach recognizes that an ordinance is designed primarily to regulate land uses, not users, and this being so, the spirit of the ordinance is satisfied even if its letter is not. Such a home may, however, still be excluded from a municipality for non-compliance with the letter of a *Boraas*-authorized definition of a family, using one of two reasons. First, the group might contain too many unrelated persons under the same roof,

[18] 488 N.E.2d 1240 (N.Y. 1985)

[19] *See, e.g., City of White Plains v. Ferraioli*, 313 NE.2d 756 (N.Y. 1974) (accepting a similar functional analysis).

or second, none of the required affinities would exist;[20] so the group's sponsor will likely seek a variance.

When the foster home is intended for juvenile delinquents, the idea that a house with a common head of household is a single unit is harder to maintain. Faced with this situation, the sponsors may seek a permit as a charity, or as an educational institution, or bulldoze their way into the neighborhood as a state agency immune from local zoning. Local law must be researched on all of these legal routes; they are by no means everywhere available. For example, it will be difficult to argue that a home for incorrigible youth is an "educational institution," even if that use is available in a single family district.

Similar problems exist for groups of parolees in half-way houses, persons recovering from addictions — and the mentally retarded. For some of these groups, the question of violations of the Fair Housing Act arise as well.[21] When this is the case, an ordinance specially tailored to the needs of the group at issue may be the best course for a municipality[22] ; this approach avoids the allegation, often used to attack an ordinance, that a definition of family is being used for surrogate, exclusionary purposes. When persons protected by the Fair Housing Act are involved, moreover, the burden of proof (that the ordinance furthers a substantial government purpose) may be assigned the municipality, just as a defendant in a fair housing case involving the disabled must show a reasonable accommodation to the needs of the protected class.[23] Then a specially tailored ordinance may aid a municipality in meeting its burden.

§ 18.04   Groups Homes for the Retarded and the Equal Protection Clause.

In *City of Cleburne v. Cleburne Living Ctr.*,[24] the City denied a special exception application to an organization setting up a group home for the retarded. The home, with four bedrooms and two and a half bathrooms, was to provide housing for 13 retarded individuals, under constant staff supervision. It was in compliance with all applicable state and local housing regulations.

The City's zoning regulations placed the home in an R-3 use district, in which apartment houses, boarding houses, fraternity and sorority houses,

---

[20] *See, e.g., Macon Ass'n for Retarded Citizens v. Macon-Bibb Cty. Planning and Zoning Comm'n*, 314 S.E.2d 218 (Ga.), *dismissed for lack of a federal question*, 469 U.S. 802 (1984), and *distinguished in Cleburne*, majority opinion, at n. 8.

[21] *See Smith & Lee Assoc's v. City of Taylor*, 102 F.3d 781 (6th Cir. 1996) (recognizing the Fair Housing Act issue, but limiting home with nursing case in single family use district to nine unrelated occupants). *See also supra*, Chapter 16.

[22] *See Erdman v. City of Fort Atkinson*, 84 F.3d 960 (7th Cir. 1996) (raising this issue without resolving it).

[23] *See, e.g., Hovsons, Inc., v. Twp. of Brick*, 89 F.3d 1096 (3rd Cir. 1996) (assigning burden of proof to municipality).

[24] 473 U.S. 432 (1985), *discussed in* Daniel Lauber, *Mainstreaming Group Homes*, Planning (Dec. 1985), at 14–18.

and hospitals, sanitoriums, and nursing homes for the aged (other than for the "insane or feeble-minded") were permitted as of right. The city officials found that the Living Center was a "hospital for the feeble-minded" and so required an annually renewable special exception permit, which both the city planning commission and the city council denied.

In response to this denial, the Cleburne Living Center sued in federal court, alleging a violation of the Equal Protection Clause. Once it reached the United States Supreme Court, the court held: first, the denial of the application was to be reviewed, as a violation of the Equal Protection Clause of the Fourteenth Amendment,[25] under a "rational basis" standard of review,[26] unless the ordinance was aimed at a suspect class of persons (in which case a higher standard would apply, as it does for gender or race based classifications).

Second, the court held that the mentally retarded as a group were not a suspect class — that is, not a class entitled to any type of heightened scrutiny upon judicial review.[27] Thus the application procedure, as applied to the Center, only need have a rational basis. The standard of review was rational basis scrutiny, here strictly applied.

[A] Determining the Level of Review.

As to the first issue, the court found that the mentally retarded were so different from each other in their abilities, that they could not be regarded as a class; that state and federal lawmakers had sufficiently responded to their needs so as to "belie a continuing antipathy or prejudice and a corresponding need for more intrusive oversight by the judiciary"; that this legislative response "negates any claim that the mentally retarded are politically powerless"; and that it is difficult to distinguish them as a group, from other groups — the aged, the disabled, the mentally ill, and the infirm.

[B] Reviewing the Ordinance.

As to the second issue in *Cleburne*, the court held that the negative fears of adjoining property owners, were not a permissible basis for treating the mentally retarded specially in the ordinance. It also held more particularly that the fear that students from a nearby junior high school might harass

---

[25] This first holding was unanimous, although only a plurality of four justices fully joined the majority opinion and agreed fully with its method of analysis.

[26] This minimal standard is used when an ordinance or other legislation is neither drawn along suspect lines or is injurious to fundamental rights; it entitles the ordinance to a presumption of constitutionality, requiring only that it be rationally related to a legitimate governmental purpose, even though the ordinance is either under-inclusive or over-inclusive.

[27] The vote was 6–3. Three justices, Marshall, Brennan, and Blackmum, dissented from this second holding, arguing that the retarded were entitled to suspect class status. The group had argued for finding middle level, heightened scrutiny as the appropriate standard: the retarded were a quasi-suspect class, because of (1) the past, gross mistreatment of the retarded, reflecting (2) a deep seated prejudice against (3) an immutable condition in (4) persons lacking political power to remedy their mistreatment themselves or legislatively. Using that standard, the circuit court struck down the ordinance both on its face and as applied to the plaintiff.

the occupants was (again) just that, a fear, not a basis for legislation — indeed, about thirty mentally retarded students were already enrolled in the school; that the home's location on a flood plain was not a basis for treating the mentally retarded differently from a nursing home, home for the aged, sanitarium, or hospital. Similarly, the court found no more basis for worrying about who would be legally responsible for the actions of the mentally retarded, than would be justified in the case of a fraternity or boarding house. Finally, the court states that worrying about the size of the home and the number of occupants was not justified when state and federal guidelines for such facilities were met. In fact, all square-footage-per-patient regulations of state and federal programs for the retarded were met on this site by the Living Center. Thus there was no basis for imposing different density standards on the retarded than are imposed on (say) boarding house residents and the city had not justified the view than the retarded require more living space than do others. All this adds up to a conclusion that there is no rational basis for the permit denial.

These four grounds for invalidating this ordinance often seem to treat the mentally retarded as a class. The opinion looks like one protecting a class of persons, rather than one preventing an injury to them — and in that sense, this is protection of a class common in Equal Protection opinions. What the retarded are not for purposes of imposing a standard of review, they become for the purpose of examining the ordinance.

This inconsistency is indeed some proof that the opinion is an example of "exacting or heightened rational basis" review. Indeed, one later federal circuit court opinion said that *Cleburne's* exacting rational basis review was limited to "politically unpopular groups."[28] So a shelter for battered women or a home for juvenile delinquents might be treated the same way. Community treatment centers for federal offenders have received a mixed welcome in the courts, some using *Cleburne's* standard of review, other refusing to do so.[29] This split occurs because of the mixed reception statistics on recidivism, and a municipalities reaction to them, get in court. Making such statistics applicable to municipal decision-making is a difficult task. If the Supreme Court was really conducting a rational basis review, it was taking a hard look at the city's rationale for its decision. Not all courts have accepted the prevailing view that *Cleburne* does anything new or different.[30] Rational basis review is too well settled, this traditional view maintains, and besides, this approach has the advantage of taking the Supreme Court at its word.

The *Cleburne* opinion is one in which the Equal Protection Clause works for a litigant protesting a zoning regulation. It usually does not because, by their very nature, zoning regulations seeks to differentiate between

---

[28] *Jacobs, Visconsi & Jacobs Co. v. City of Lawrence,* 927 F.2d 1111, 1119, n. 6 (10th Cir. 1991) (refusing to apply it for the benefit of a shopping center developer).

[29] *See, e.g., Bannum, Inc. v. City of St. Charles,* 2 F.3d 267 (8th Cir. 1993) (refusing to apply *Cleburne* but collecting cases).

[30] *DeSisto College v. Town of Howey-in-the-Hills,* 706 F. Supp. 1479, 1503 (M.D. Fla.), affirmed, 888 F.2d 766 (11th Cir. 1989).

different users of property. [31] When group home sponsors win cases, it is more likely that the neighbors have given into their "fears" and the decision-makers have accepted them as a reason for denying an application, thus depriving the decision of a rational basis and substantial evidence. [32]

[C] The Line between *Boraas* and *Cleburne*.

Between *Village of Belle Terre v. Boraas,* [33] and *Cleburne*, there is a conflict, unless we pigeonhole each of these cases by the constitutional provision at issue. May a town limit, with conditions on a special exception, the number of persons living in a group home, using the values protected in the *Boraas* opinion? *Doe v. City of Butler, Pa.,* [34] provides an affirmative answer, finding that just because the city could not constitutionally limit the number of family members living together, "the absence of an occupancy limitation on the members of a family who can live together cannot be bootstrapped into an argument that therefore there can be no occupancy limitations for unrelated persons living together . . . ." Once having accepted that related and unrelated occupants may be rationally placed in different classifications, *Doe* holds that an occupancy limitation of six unrelated persons is valid, thus limiting the number of abused and battered women living a group home under a special exception.

In contrast, *Kirsch v. Prince George's County,* [35] shows that once a special purpose ordinance is enacted dealing with a particular sub-group of occupants, the provisions of the ordinance also require a substantial basis. *Kirsch* held that, under a rational basis standard, the Equal Protection Clause is violated by a "mini-dorm" ordinance limiting the number of students in rental housing in a college community. It found also that no fundamental right — to housing — or suspect class — of students — is involved. The invalidated ordinance required that when 3–5 students rented housing, bedrooms had to have at least 70 square feet *per* resident, all parking off-site, with only one driveway entrance from the street — and all the while, the appearance of the property should remain residential.

Cleburne has not signaled any new judicial activism in reviewing single-family zoning or group home requirements on Equal Protection grounds. The case has been limited to litigation involving the mentally retarded. For

---

[31] For a commentary on *Cleburne*, see James Ellis, *On The Usefulness of Suspect Classifications*, 3 Const. Comm. 375 (1986). Site visits confirm that Cleburne was a poorly zoned city, with mixed and non-conforming uses in abundance. One visitor stood in the middle of the street on which the group house was to be located for forty-five minutes without having to move for a car. *See also* Note, 99 Harv. L. Rev. 161 (1985).

[32] *See, e.g., Gladden v. District of Columbia Bd. of Zoning Adjustment*, 659 A.2d 249 (D.C. 1995) (when dispersal spacing regulations are satisfied, court is not called on to assess whether a neighborhood has a disproportionate number of group homes); *Wilson Cty. Youth Emergency Shelter, Inc. v. Wilson Cty.*, 13 S.W.2d 338 (Tenn. App. 2000).

[33] 416 U.S. 1 (1974), discussed *supra*, this Chapter.

[34] 892 F.2d 315 (3rd Cir. 1989).

[35] 626 A.2d 372 (Md. 1993).

example, in *Village of Willowbrook v. Olech*,[36] the United State Supreme Court permitted a plaintiff suing a municipality for its failure to extend its water lines to her property under the Equal Protection Clause, to assert that she was a class of one for purposes of the Clause. Her complaint involved no racial or other invidious classification. It simply alleged that the refusal to extend the line was out of spite. One concurring justice stated that the decision was not to be taken to "transform run-of-the-mill zoning cases to cases of constitutional right."[37]

Olech recognized that a person treated in a discriminatory manner, even though a class of one, has an equal protection claim — and, as the court recognized, similarly based-claims can be that the municipality acted in an arbitrary or irrational manner. If this proves so, then equal protection may take its place alongside the takings and due process clauses as a basis for challenging municipal actions. However, ripeness and exhaustion doctrines may bar some claims, or confine many of them to state courts,[38] takings exaction cases may absorb some others,[39] and due process claims still others.[40]

---

[36] 528 U.S. 562 (2000) (a short opinion of about 500 words; the plaintiff was required to dedicate a 33 foot wide easement as a condition of connecting to the water line, in lieu of a normal 15 foot wide easement).

[37] *Id.* at 566 (Breyer, J., concurring).

[38] *See supra*, Chapter 13.

[39] *See supra*, Chapter 14.

[40] *See, e.g., Bello v. Walker*, 840 F.2d 1124 (3rd Cir.), *cert. denied*, 488 U.S. 851, 868 (1988) (recognizing a due process claim for vindictive governmental action, a claim expressly not reached in *Olech*).

Chapter 19

The First Amendment and Zoning

§ 19.01 Introduction.

When speech is restricted and the First Amendment implicated, the first inquiry is the type of speech. Political speech deserves the fullest protection, but other types are not given the same level of protection. These other types include advocacy of unlawful action, false statements of fact, fighting words, obscenity, child pornography — all have no protection — and commercial speech — which has some protection.[1]

So classifying the types of speech is a way of assigning the level of protection that the courts extend. An example of commercial speech is found on outdoor billboards and they are entitled to some protection under the First Amendment. Obscene speech is not entitled to such protection; however, it must be distinguished from "adult" speech, which is.

When some level of First Amendment protection is accorded commercial speech, then, the content of the speech cannot be regulated without provoking a heightened level of judicial scrutiny; on the other hand, regulation of the time, place and manner of the speech can be regulated without provoking such scrutiny.

Entitlement to First Amendment protection means that the usual presumption of constitutionality given to zoning ordinances and regulations is withdrawn and the ordinance alleged to interfere with First Amendment speech must be justified as embodying a substantial governmental interest, directly advanced by the ordinance, no more extensive in scope than is necessary to accomplish its ends, and leaving alternative methods of communication available to the proponent of the speech.

§ 19.02 Sex Businesses.

Two United States Supreme Court opinions dominate this area. The first is *Young v. American Mini-Theatres, Inc.*[2] There a plurality of the court upheld a Detroit ordinance requiring the de-concentration of sex businesses. The ordinance accomplished this with two requirements: first, by requiring that such businesses be located a minimum distance of 1,000 feet from any

---

[1] For an indication of U.S. Sup. Ct. interest in the commercial speech/ zoning line, see *Lorillard Tobacco Co. v. Reilly*, 533 U.S. 525 (2001) (holding that state restrictions on tobacco advertising on billboards were pre-empted by a similar federal statute, based on the First Amendment ground that the restrictions were "more extensive than necessary," but recognizing that a tailored regulation of the location and size of advertisements is not pre-empted; Stevens, J., dissenting, called the regulation merely a zoning matter).

[2] 427 U.S. 50 (1976).

two other similarly regulated uses, and second, by requiring that each such business be at least 500 feet from a residential zone. The de-concentration ordinance was upheld by a majority of the court.[3]

A plurality opinion found that it was content-neutral (not content-based), regulated a type of speech not accorded as much protection as political speech, and served a substantial purpose (the preservation of "the quality of urban life," which must be accorded high respect, said Justice Stevens for the plurality). Joining the plurality to make it a majority of the court was Justice Powell, who said that he thought the speech involved in adult sexual expression was to be accorded as much First Amendment protection as political speech, but that for him the regulation of its secondary effects[4] provided a sufficient rationale for validating Detroit's ordinance. Its control of those secondary effects was, he said, sufficient to render the ordinance constitutional, noting also that the court had upheld innovative zoning techniques in the past. When an ordinance was aimed at secondary effects, and not speech itself, it was proper, Justice Powell thought, to treat it as a case in which the issue was the reasonableness of the regulation with regard to its time, place, and manner. The time/place/manner regulation issue is one that has been used when a regulation advances a substantial governmental interest while not having, as its primary purpose, the regulation of speech protected by the First Amendment.

There are alternatives: instead of de-concentrating sex businesses, a city council may decide that a better approach would be to concentrate them into a small area adjacent to its downtown. There is little doubt that it may do so. The choice of de-concentration or concentration is a legislative decision and as such is valid when fairly debatable. Concentration may make police services easier to provide and may make other types of regulation more efficient. Even the businesses may gain from concentrating their customer base. These considerations provide a rational basis for concentration.

[A] *Renton v. Playtime Theatres.*

The permissibility of controlling secondary effects was stressed in the second case, *Renton v. Playtime Theatres, Inc.*[5] Writing for a majority of the court, Justice Rehnquist delivered the opinion of the court in sweeping terms, as if this were a routine First Amendment case. As in *Young*, the facts of the case involved a challenge to the location of an adult movie theater. An ordinance regulating the location of sex businesses was again

---

[3] *Id. See also Stringfellow's of New York, Ltd. v. City of New York*, 694 N.E.2d 407, 413 (N.Y. 1998) (upholding an similar "anti-clustering ordinance" based on a local study of the increase in such business from 9 in 1965 to 177 in 1993, and concluding that, if unregulated, they tend to concentrate).

[4] Such effects are reportedly increased crime rates, depreciated property values, and deteriorating property in the vicinity of such uses. *See Stringfellow's of New York*, op. cit., 694 N.E.2d at 410.

[5] 475 U.S. 41 (1986), *noted* 100 Harv. L.Rev. 190 (1986). An early discussion of *Renton* is found in *Husti v. Zuckerman Property Enterprises, Ltd.*, 508 A.2d 735, 738–739 (Conn. 1986).

involved. Unlike Detroit (the city involved in *Young*), Renton was a suburban jurisdiction. Its population was approximately 32,000 persons. Its area is 15.3 square miles. It is located within a few miles of Seattle, Washington. It contains 1,450 businesses, 18 parks, and 62 churches. Its businesses provide employment to 81,000 persons.

Renton's ordinance was more restrictive than Detroit's. Under it, an adult movie theaters could not be located within 1000 feet of any residential zone, apartment house, church, park or school. The word "adult" was not further defined; it may have been taken to mean non-obscene in the context of this case, for further definition might have opened the city up to the charge of focusing on the content of the speech involved. This ordinance is not, on its face, a de-concentration ordinance, but its impact (the dissent notes) is to restrict regulated sex businesses to about 520 acres of the city's land area.

The majority found that the ordinance was content-neutral, not content based, and because it is neutral, it is valid so long as it meets two tests: (1) it serves a substantial governmental interest and (2) provides reasonable alternative avenues of communication of the regulated speech. This is a less exacting test than was thought to be applicable before this opinion was handed down.[6] The majority claimed that its decision was based on *Young* — perhaps a difficult claim to make or scrutinize because of *Young*'s lack of a majority opinion.

Unlike the City of Detroit in *Young*, the City of Renton had not conducted its own studies to support the ordinance it enacted. No matter, said the court, expanding on *Young*. A municipality can rely on the studies of other jurisdictions and adapt them to its purposes; it need not reach the same conclusions or adopt the same type of ordinance as did the jurisdiction that did the study.[7]

This opinion's six holdings were as follows: (1) First, the ordinance was a content-neutral, time/place/manner regulation, designed to combat undesirable secondary effects of the adult speech involved, rather than an ordinance aimed at the content of that speech. In reality, the Renton ordinance only seemed to regulate the place, but not the time or manner of the speech. As to the content-neutrality of the ordinance, commentators have often said that it is difficult to find its content neutral, since a

---

[6] *Central Hudson Gas & Elec. Corp. v. Pub. Serv. Comm'n*, 447 U.S. 557 (1980) (using a more expansive, four prong test for commercial speech, asking whether the ordinance asserted a "substantial," "governmental" interest that is "directly advanced" by its terms, in a manner "not more extensive than is necessary" to achieve it.). The fourth prong was the one re-emphasized in *Lorillard Tobacco Co. v. Reilly*, 533 U.S. 525 (2001). Because the *Renton* opinion did not repudiate *Central Hudson*, it may be assumed to summarize it in a new way for adult, but non-obscene, speech used in a commercial context.

[7] This has meant that Renton-type ordinances have been copied around the country. *See, e.g., DiRaimo v. City of Providence*, 714 A.2d 554, 563–566 (R.I. 1998) (finding ordinance a time, place, manner restriction on speech, serving a substantial governmental interest, not over-inclusive, and not foreclosing alternative means of communication); *Centaur, Inc. v. Richland Cty.*, 392 S.E.2d 165 (S.C. 1990) (upholding ordinance). However, other jurisdictions have built upon and expanded the type of ordinance involved in *Renton* too. *See, e.g., 7250 Corporation v. Board of County Commissioners of Adams Cty.*, 799 P.2d 917 (Colo. 1990) (upholding a live nude-entertainment control ordinance).

regulated theater is one given over to displaying visually specified sexual activities and anatomical areas of the body. The court must mean that the time/place/manner regulation is more important to defining the primary purpose of the ordinance than its content regulation is.

(2) The ordinance furthered a substantial governmental interest — the regulation of adult speech. Where does adult speech fit into the hierarchy of types of speech for First Amendment purposes? It is not political speech (which is the most protected of all types); it is not commercial speech, as in *Metromedia*), which receives considerable but limited protection too. However, it is not obscene speech, which receives even less protection and shelter under the Amendment. So the speech involved in *Renton* must be classified as falling somewhere between commercial and obscene speech — a third type, which in the face of a substantial governmental interest in regulation, receives special, but not particularly close, scrutiny under the First Amendment. Effectively the speech here received a heightened, but still a first tier, standard of review.

(3) The municipality (the City of Renton) was entitled to rely on the studies conducted by other municipalities in enacting its ordinance, and need not conduct its own studies.[8] Its own studies would have been hard to do, because there were no adult movie theaters in the city when the ordinance was enacted, so there was nothing to study. The importance of this third holding is that the city need not wait until it has a problem, but may act prospectively and before the problem arises. The authority to act in advance of actually having a "problem" may be the most important holding in the case because the enactment of the ordinance may regulate an industry in advance of its locating within the jurisdiction, perhaps even dissuading some adult movie theater owners from locating in the enacting municipality.[9] In such a posture, the jurisdiction cannot be accused of enacting a reactive ordinance, making what it does enact seem like good planning in advance of developments. Moreover, independent studies may well be an unreasonable burden for municipalities like Renton, with limited staffs, expertise, and budgets for such studies, undertaken with little hope that their conclusions would differ markedly from those conducted in (say) Seattle, whose studies were discussed in the *Renton* opinion.[10] This holding also suggests that studies might be conducted, and model legislation drafted for municipalities, at the state level.

---

[8] After *Young*, such studies will discuss the regulated use's harmful secondary effects. For an extension of this holding, see *Phillips v. Borough of Keyport*, 107 F.3d 164 (3rd Cir. 1997) (upholding such a regulation when the enacting municipal legislature did not have before it, at the time of adoption, evidence of such effects). *See also The Pack Shack, Inc. v. Howard Cty.*, 770 A.2d 1028, 1037–1038 (Md. App. Ct. 2001) (18 studies of secondary effects in other municipalities relieved trial court of making further findings in upholding ordinance); *Buzzetti v. City of New York*, 143 F.3d 134 (2d Cir. 1998), *cert. denied*, 119 Sup. Ct. 54 (1998).

[9] *Cf. Twp. of Saddle Brook v. A.B. Family Ctr., Inc.*, 722 A.2d 530 (N.J. 1999) (holding that the constitutionality of a state statute restricting the location of adult businesses within 1000 feet of other protected uses, did not need not be evaluated solely by reference to the boundaries of a township invoking the statute).

[10] Seattle chose a concentration rather than a de-concentration strategy.

(4) An ordinance that regulates this type of use is entitled to disperse them: dispersal is a reasonable regulatory means of dealing with the regulated uses, even if the dispersal results, as here, in concentration of the uses. "Cities may regulate adult theaters by dispersing them, as in Detroit, or by effectively concentrating them, as in Renton." This language has the effect of permitting what was, in *Young*, a big city method of regulation, in smaller suburban jurisdictions like Renton. In any event, commentators wondered of this opinion, wouldn't it be better to concentrate "adult" land uses, the better to deal with their secondary effects by providing more supervision and police in the area of concentration? Concentration and dispersal are arguably both equally reasonable as land use regulatory methods.

(5) The ordinance is neither over nor under-inclusive. Arguing that an ordinance is either over or under-inclusive is like challenging it under the Equal Protection Clause, alleging that the classification of adult theaters is unreasonable. That argument sounds like it too would lose here. Absent a showing that it will not, Renton may be presumed, in the future, to be ready to amend its ordinance to deal with other types of sex-oriented, adult businesses as they appear, so the ordinance is not under-inclusive. Dealing with such uses as they appear means that the ordinance is "narrowly tailored" and so is not over-inclusive. Its scope is, in other words, just right. [11]

(6) Ample acreage is available and accessible to businesses like the movie theater owners, so that the city has provided reasonable alternatives to conducting its business on the site proposed. In fact, 520 acres were available in the city — more than 5% of the city's total area. (As to the sixth holding, one might respond, "only 5% — that's not much!")[12]

[B]   Content-Neutral Ordinances.

[1]   The Governmental Interest.

The Renton ordinance was found to be content neutral, even though it singled out a particular type of speech for regulation. It is content-neutral because the ordinance aims at the secondary effects of the speech, not at the speech itself. (This idea is taken from Justice Powell's concurrence in *Young*.) Content-neutrality appears to relax here either for one type of speech (adult speech, involving sexual expression) or for all speech with secondary effects. The opinion does not indicate the reach of its holding in this regard, so it is proper to ask how the courts will determine when to relax content neutrality standards. Justice Stevens in *Young* said that few would march their sons and daughters off to war to defend this type of

---

[11] This is the same analysis Goldilocks gave the porridge in the three bears' den: the regulation is not too hot and not too cold, but just right.

[12] As to this holding on accessibility, more *infra*, this Chapter.

speech, but he probably did not mean to say that only speech approved of by the majority receives full First Amendment protection. [13]

The effect of a finding of content neutrality is that the city is granted the right to regulate the "time, place, and manner of the speech" so long as the regulation serves a substantial governmental interest and allows for reasonable, not ample, alternative avenues of communication. Preserving the quality of urban life sufficed for the first test (taken from Stevens' plurality opinion in *Young*) when data on the secondary effect can reasonably be relied upon.

Constitutional implications may be multi-faceted. When a municipal regulation prohibits "sexually oriented businesses" within 1,000 feet of a church and when such a business applies to locate within 1,000 feet of the municipal correction center, one zoning administrator denied a certificate of occupancy. The grounds for doing so were that the center is the site of religious services, held on a regular basis for the center's inmates. When the business appeals this decision, the applicant will argue that the regulation is aimed at separating an actual church building from sexually oriented businesses. The center is not such a building; indeed, unless it contains a chapel, services may be held in shifting locations within it. Moreover, the existence of the business nearby will not directly influence inmates' behavior — so not even the purpose of the regulation is advanced by denying the certificate. [14]

[2] Accessibility.

As to the accessibility issue, the *Renton* court held that allowing 520 acres on the ordinance's map for a non-exclusive district permitting adult movie theaters, provides a reasonable avenue of communication. These 520 acres amounted to only 5% of the land area and was occupied by a sewage disposal plant, race track, industrial park, and several heavy industries. The opinion states that the First Amendment does not guarantee that land will be available at bargain prices. [15] Following *Renton*, in *Town of Islip v. Caviglia*, [16] the New York Court of Appeals held that the town could limit

---

[13] A court that would approve of the *Young* and *Renton* ordinances may be backing out of this field altogether: land use controls and First Amendment values are often intertwined. There is some evidence from later opinions that where First Amendment values are involved, courts will read the ordinances narrowly to protect those values. *See Richardson v. Wile*, 535 A.2d 1346 (Del. 1988) (video rental store found not to be an "adult entertainment establishment" regulated by ordinance). There is also some evidence that Renton-like ordinances are the norm. *See, e.g., DiRaimo v. City of Providence*, 714 A.2d 554, 563–566 (R.I. 1998); *Landover Books, Inc. v. Prince George's Cty.*, 566 A.2d 792, 801–803 (Md. App. Ct. 1989).

[14] *Hooters, Inc. v. City of Texarkana*, 897 F. Supp. 946 (E. D. Tex. 1995).

[15] *But see Lorillard Tobacco Co. v. Reilly*, 533 U.S. 525 (2001) (where 90% of jurisdiction being off-limits for tobacco billboards was found "more extensive than necessary" under the fourth prong of the *Central Hudson* test).

[16] 540 N.E.2d 215 (N.Y. 1989). *See also Stringfellow's of New York v. City of New York*, 694 N.E.2d 407 (N.Y. 1998) (deciding that the ordinance was content neutral, not over-inclusive, and left open reasonable alternative means of communication), *noted in* Martin Schwartz, *New York City Zones Out Free Expression*, 43 N.Y. L. Sch. L. Rev. 301 (1999); Herald Fahringer, *Zoning Out Free Expression: An Analysis of New York City's Adult Zoning Resolution*, 46 Buff. L. Rev. 403 (1998).

an adult bookstore to an industrial use district. Likewise, a Maryland court held that a county with two existing regulated adult entertainment business and 23 alternative parcels available for such business was sufficient, even though such parcels might not be commercially desirable.[17] The *Renton* opinion gives great deference to municipal decisions on these deconcentration decisions and accords broad discretion to municipal decision-makers.

In *Young*, alternative access was not a problem. Detroit is a large, diverse central city. However, in *Schad v. Borough of Mt. Ephraim*,[18] the court invalidated a total ban on live nude dancing in a suburban community. The common threat among them was that the ordinance was, as a facial matter, overbroad and unjustified by the borough. The *Schad* opinion also said that the businesses regulated did not present any more land use or police problems than did some of the businesses permitted in the borough. This invalidation is difficult to square with *Village of Belle Terre v. Boraas*,[19] except that the court's concern in *Schad* was that if every community in the metropolitan area did that, nude dancers would have no place to perform. *Renton's* ordinance too had the effect of zoning out adult theaters, but unlike the situation in *Schad*, Renton had no such theaters within its boundaries.[20]

Finally, basic to the *Renton* opinion is the notion that the land use controls are not a prior restraint on protected speech. Arguably the *Schad* ordinance was, because it contained a total exclusion from the municipality. In *FW/PBS v. City of Dallas*,[21] the Supreme Court struck down a licensing scheme for sexually-oriented businesses, a plurality opinion finding that the city had inadequate procedures for assuring prompt inspections of premises before the issuance of licenses, and hence had enacted an ordinance whose effect was censorship. Acting as a censor, the court said, the city had the duty to suppress speech (1) for only a brief period, while (2) according prompt judicial review of its decisions and (3) carrying the burden in court of justifying the prior restraint. Because more than a brief period was involved and because of the delays in issuing the licenses, prompt review could not be accorded; the ordinance was unconstitutional. However, the court said that here, unlike some prior restraint cases, it was not necessary for the city to go to court before denying a license. The court, moreover, did uphold the inclusion by the city of motel operators renting

---

[17] *The Pack Shack, Inc. v. Howard Cty.*, 770 A.2d 1028, 1040–1041 (Md. App. Ct. 2001).

[18] 452 U.S. 61 (1981) (the majority composed of five separate opinions). *But see City of Erie v. Pap's A.M. TDBA "Kandyland"*, 120 Sup. Ct. 1382 (2000) (upholding municipal ban on nude erotic dancing and noting in passing that *Schad* dealt with conduct "only within the outer ambit of the First Amendment's protection."

[19] 416 U.S. 1 (1974), discussed *supra*, Chapter 18.

[20] *See Basiardanes v. City of Galveston*, 682 F.2d 1203 (5th Cir. 1982) (use of 10–15% of the city available to adult movie theaters in industrial zones insufficient).

[21] 493 U.S. 215, 225–226 (1990).

rooms for periods of less than ten hours in its definition of a sexually oriented business.[22]

Now for some, more specialized problems with the *Renton* opinion:

a. In squaring *Young-Renton* with *Arlington Heights* on the question of legislative motive, *Arlington Heights* is meant to probe legislative motive without putting the courts in the position of violating the principal of separation of powers. In *Renton*, little concern is expressed about legislative motive: the motive of a municipal legislature abridging First Amendment rights is (we can surmise) when dealing with the secondary effects of speech not as important as an abridgment of an equal protection right when the potential of racial discrimination is present. Once the municipal legislature has decided in what districts an adult business may locate, "neither [a reviewing court] nor a municipal licensing board may second-guess this legislative determination."[23]

b. In *City of Cleburne v. Cleburne Living Ctr.*,[24] the United States Supreme Court invalidated a denial of a special exception for a group home for the mentally retarded as lacking a rational basis. The court held, in part, that undifferentiated or diffuse fears of the mentally retarded was an insufficient basis for the denial. A good argument might be made that the fear of sex businesses is no less undifferentiated. However, in *Renton*, the control of secondary effects drives the decision, and there does not seem to be much difference between the neighbors' fear of the retarded and the secondary effects of the business regulated.

c. If the dispersal of the sex businesses is without constitutional significance for the court, but the exclusionary effects of zoning have significance for state courts, then how, and where, one challenges zoning is of the greatest importance. For example, if a municipality were to restrict the location of abortion clinics, the ordinance would be closely scrutinized, but if the same town restricted the location of out-patient surgical clinics that performed abortions among their other services, the town would arguably have a less difficult task in justifying the restriction.

A municipality drafting restrictions similar to Renton's should not permit uses otherwise restricted when the consent of the nearby church, school or residential user(s) is obtained.[25] The police power once delegated to a

---

[22] *See also Twp. of Pennsauken v. Schad*, 733 A.2d 1159, 1171–1172 (N.J. 1999) (reviewing a similar licensing scheme under analogous state constitutional provisions, upholding it, and discussing *FW/PBS*); *Baltimore v. Dembo*, 719 A.2d 1007 (Md. App. Ct. 1998) (status of land use as non-conforming does not exempt owner from licensing ordinance, and characterizing licensing as directed at an activity no matter where carried out in the jurisdiction, rather than regulating them based on location as zoning does); *State of New Jersey v. Russo*, 745 A.2d 540 (N.J. Super. Ct., App. Div., 2000) (finding unfettered police discretion and a First Amendment violation in adult business licensing statute).

[23] *Cadillac Lounge v. City of Providence*, 763 A.2d 993, 996 (R.I. 2001).

[24] 473 U.S. 432 (1985), discussed *supra*, Chapter 18.

[25] *See Larkin v. Grendel's Den*, 459 U.S. 116 (1982) (religious users could not veto the grant of a liquor license to a business within 500 feet of their premises), *noted in* 97 Harv. L.Rev. 70 (1983).

municipality, may not be again delegated to a user's neighbors. Similarly, a municipality should not permit uses otherwise regulated by similar proximity restrictions when a special exception permit is obtained. Obtaining a special exception permit requires a showing that the land parcel at issue is suitable for the use intended and that there is no adverse impact on surrounding parcels. Here the special exception procedure might qualify as a prior restraint on protected First Amendment speech.[26] However, you might advise a city like Renton when enacting its ordinance to also enact an "amortization clause" for regulated businesses in existence on the effective date of the ordinance, permitting them a six month grace period before they have to close down in their present location.[27] (An amortization clause permits the regulated use to stay in place as a non-conforming use, but only for a definite and limited period of time.) There is no reason to advise against having an amortization period, but its length as proposed should be reasonable.[28]

§ 19.03   Billboard Regulation.

In *Metromedia, Inc. v. City of San Diego*,[29] the city enacted an ordinance that banned all off-site advertising billboards. Existing billboards were to be removed after an amortization period. The plaintiff was an outdoor advertising company and sued to enjoin enforcement of the ordinance. The ordinance was found unconstitutional below, but the California Supreme Court reversed, upholding it. "We hold that the achievement of the purposes recited in the ordinance — eliminating traffic hazards and improving the appearance of the city — represent proper objectives [protecting the health, safety, morals, and general welfare of the people-ed.] for the exercise of the city's police power, and the ordinance bears a reasonable relationship to those objectives." Ordinances eliminating billboards visible from the streets and highways reasonably relate to safety (they divert a driver's attention) and are entitled to a presumption of validity and constitutionality. (In older cases, billboards were additionally seen as places behind which criminals might lurk and criminal activity might take place — but such secondary effects are not invoked here.) In the alternative, the California court found that the ordinance was valid as a second or third stage exercise of the police power for aesthetic purposes, to improve the appearance of the municipality. California scenery, the court says, attracts tourists and commerce, so the aesthetic regulation of billboards is necessary because it is an indirect form of economic regulation.

---

[26] *Id.*

[27] *Landover Books, Inc. v. Prince George's Cty.*, 566 A. 2d 792, 804 (Md. App. Ct. 1989) (finding also that the special exception procedures were severable from the ordinance as a whole); *see also FW/PBS, Inc. v. Dallas*, 110 U.S. 596 (1990) (invalidating as a prior restraint licensing for sex businesses when the procedures for obtaining a license did not provide for a time certain for issuance or denial and swift judicial review).

[28] *See Town of Islip v. Caviglia*, 540 N.E. 2d 215 (N.Y. 1989) (upholding a one to five year amortization period); *PA Northwestern Distributors, Inc. v. Zoning Hearing Bd. of Twp. of Moon*, 555 A. 2d 1368 (Pa. Cmwlth. Ct. 1989) (upholding a 90 day amortization period).

[29] 610 P. 2d 407 (Cal. 1980), *reversed on other grounds*, 453 U.S. 490 (1981).

There was originally no exception to the ordinance's prohibition on political signs, but an amendment permitted temporary political signs, maintained for no longer than 90 days and removed within 10 days after the election to which their content pertains. No matter. This amendment was held too narrowly drawn for the United States Supreme Court.[30] There were five opinions written in this case. A plurality of the court held that the ordinance did not unreasonably restrict commercial speech[31] and directly advanced a substantial governmental interest. This interest was previously defined for First Amendment purposes by the state supreme court opinion in the case; the United States Supreme Court could hardly decide that the ordinance was *ultra vires* the state's police power, since the California Supreme Court provides the final and the last word on such an issue. However, the plurality opinion in the United State Supreme Court found that the restrictions on non-commercial speech were too narrowly drawn, that the exemptions were too narrow, and so held the potential to become an onerous, content-based regulation of political speech. The ordinance's exemptions were numerous, but lacked an overall rationale: it might be that a generous interpretation of the exempted signs would protect the types of speech commonly regarded as protected by the First Amendment, but because the ordinance was challenged *prima facie*, such a situation was not before the court.

The court's plurality seemed, however, to accept the basic distinction between off-premises and on-premises signs. The ordinance only prohibited the former. On-premises signs were not as heavily regulated because the owner had an interest in the on-premises sign that would make self-policing possible on private property. Off-premises signs were more heavily regulated because the owner was not there and in a position to police the sign. This rationale for the distinction may be more significant for state police power purposes than it is as a federal constitutional matter. Indeed, in the latter legal arena, the distinction may make no difference. In any event, the court's seeming acceptance of aesthetics as a proper governmental interest may make the distinction of little value in First Amendment cases as well.

This distinction paved the way for *Members of City Council v. Taxpayers for Vincent*.[32] The disarray among the opinions in *Metromedia* required an occasion to clarify that latter, where seven Justices had, in the plurality opinion, or in dissent, in whole or part, expressly concluded that the city's interest in avoiding visual clutter was sufficient to justify the prohibition on billboards. *Vincent* was that clarifying occasion. There, the court said: "We affirm the conclusion of the majority in *Metromedia*. The problem addressed by the ordinance [in Vincent] — the visual assault on the citizens of Los Angeles presented by an accumulation of signs posted on public property — constitutes a significant evil within the City's power to prohibit." The need for regulation goes beyond the control of the secondary effects

---

[30] *Metromedia, Inc.*, 453 U.S. 490 (1981).

[31] *See* Note, *The Supreme Court — Leading Cases*, 110 Harv. L. Rev. 135, 216–226 (1996) (discussing *44 Liquormart, Inc. v. Rhode Island*, 116 Sup. Ct. 1495 (1996).

[32] 466 U. S. 789 (1984).

of political speech, but "is created by the medium of expression itself. The ordinance curtails no more speech than is necessary to accomplish its purpose." As to not extending the ordinance to private property, the "private property interest in controlling the use of his own property justifies the disparate treatment. Moreover, by not extending the ban to all locations, a significant opportunity to communicate by means of temporary signs is preserved . . . ." That is, there are reasonable alternative means of communication available (to say nothing of radio, press and TV advertising) to political candidates on private property, where the "owner's esthetic concerns will keep the posting of signs within reasonable bounds." So even a "partial, content-neutral ban may nevertheless enhance the City's appearance." In addition, the ordinance here is content-neutral because the ban on posting signs on public property is a total ban. Thus the Los Angeles ordinance is content-neutral, has a substantial governmental purpose, advances it directly, is not over or under-inclusive, and leaves reasonable alternative means to communicate. It is entitled to a presumption of constitutionality that parallels the presumption of validity accorded the police power ordinance enacted by the City of San Diego in the California Supreme Court.

Vincent in its turn paves the way for *City of Ladue v. Gilleo.*[33] There the Supreme Court unaminously invalidated an ordinance enacted to ban all residential signs, as applied to a sign 24 by 36 inches on private property, the front lawn of a residence, that did not fall within one of 10 exempted signs. The sign said, "Say no to War in the Persian Gulf, Call Congress now." After being denied a variance for her sign, the homeowner brought a § 1983 action against the enacting municipality. The Supreme Court acknowledged that residential signs pose numerous problems that "legitimately call for regulation." Even though the ordinance is a total ban and might be, on that account, classified as content neutral, it was held to prohibit too large an amount of protected, political speech to be upheld. As a result, the aesthetic considerations supporting the ban in the City of Ladue are balanced against the broad suppression of speech worked by the ban. In this instance, the ordinance denied an entire medium for speech (yard signs), was over-inclusive, and lacked a reasonable alternative that was as easy and inexpensive to use as are yard signs. Moreover, the court accorded special respect for individual liberty and expression exercised from and in the home. The balance tipped in favor of invalidating the ordinance.

A sign prohibition banning off-site commercial advertisements in a residential use district in a municipality like Ladue might survive, particularly when and if the homeowner on whose lawn the sign is located is paid a fee to place the sign there. *Gilleo* is sufficiently distinguishable in this instance; the type of speech involved is entitled to less protection, and so the city's aesthetic concerns might on balance, trump an owner's First Amendment rights.

---

[33] 512 U.S. 43 (1994).

§ 19.04   Zoning and Religion.

Are religious uses immune from zoning regulations? Until recently, the answer has been yes, when "religious use" is defined as religious worship or education. In New York, for example, until *Cornell University v. Barnard*,[34] "the general policy, as applied in this state, is that religious institutions are virtually immune from zoning restrictions."[35] Thus a church may start a drug treatment program in its parish hall.[36] Expanding a church auditorium to serve the needs of a growing congregation would be permitted as well, in deference to the free exercise clause and recognizing that the social activities of the congregation are necessary to their communal life together.

As a result, the exclusion of religious uses from residential use districts has generally been regarded as improper under the free exercise clause of the First Amendment, unless there is a substantial showing of a need to exclude.[37] In other words, there has been a preference for the First Amendment values of the free exercise clause over the Fifth Amendment rights of neighbors.[38] However, a completely hands-off policy on the part of courts runs afoul of the establishment clause of the First Amendment or a similar state constitutional provision.

Moreover, many courts have exhibited a tendency to confine the reach of such issues to interpretive problems within an ordinance. Not reaching a constitutional issue unless it is absolutely necessary, is a well established doctrine, observed in this field as well as others.[39] On the other hand, all this does not exclude the possibility that all churches can be excluded from residential neighborhoods without offending the free exercise clause, because the proper test is the impact of the church on its neighborhood.[40] The free exercise of religious beliefs need not extend to the location and siting of churches.[41]

---

[34] 503 N.E. 2d 509 (N.Y. 1986).

[35] *Bright Horizon House, Inc. v. Zoning Bd. of Appeals*, 469 N.Y.S.2d 851, 856 (N.Y. Sup. Ct., Monroe Cty., 1983).

[36] *See Levin v. Long Island Jewish Medical Ctr.*, 319 N.Y.S.2d 937 (N.Y. Sup. Ct, Nassau Cty., 1971) (indicating the use is permitted if the church sought to discharge a spiritual duty felt by the congregation and clergy).

[37] *Jehovah's Witnesses Assembly Hall of Southern New Jersey v. Woolrich Twp.*, 532 A.2d 276, 277–278 (N.J. Super. Ct. 1987) (citing cases from nineteen states for this version of the rule, emphasizing inclusion), *reversed*, 537 A.2d 1336 (1987).

[38] *See, e.g., Westchester Reform Church v. Griffin*, 239 N.E.2d 891 (N.Y. 1968) (invalidating set back regulation as abridgment of free exercise of religion).

[39] *See Church of the Savior v. Zoning Hearing Board of Tredyfrin Twp.*, 568 A.2d 1336 (Pa. Commw. Ct. 1989) (holding counseling not a church use was an abuse of discretion by the board).

[40] *Lakewood, Ohio Congregation of Jehovah's Witnesses, Inc. v. City of Lakewood*, 699 F.2d 303 (6th Cir. 1983), *cert. denied*, 464 U.S. 815 (1983), *noted* 45 Ohio St. L.J. 1017 (1984); *Lakewood Residents Association v. Congregation Exocrine Schneur*, 570 A.2d 1032 (N.J. Super. 1989) (upholding bulk standards for houses of worship in residential district); *see also Messiah Baptist Church v. County of Jefferson, Colorado*, 859 F.2d 820 (upholding the exclusion of a church from an agricultural district).

[41] *Bethlehem Evangelical Lutheran Church v. City of Lakewood*, 626 P.2d 668 (Colo. 1981) (upholding the requirement of a land dedication from church).

In 1990, the United States Supreme Court decided *Employment Div., Dept. of Human Resources of Oregon v. Smith*.[42] *Smith* held that neutral, generally applicable state laws need not be justified by a compelling state interest and so are not entitled to any special judicial scrutiny, notwithstanding their impact on religious institutions and free exercise and so long as they are not specifically aimed at or hostile to religion.[43] The burden of proof thus imposed on churches is a heavy one in the typical case. Congress sought to overturn this result by statute, but the statute itself was invalidated in *City of Boerne v. Flores*.[44] This invalidation re-imposed the rule of *Smith* and has made disparate treatment of religious institutions possible if the regulation applied is facially general in nature.[45]

In such a legal environment, churches and religious institutions have used several land use litigation strategies.[46] First, they have sought variances and special exceptions for their uses. Second, they have coupled their free exercise claims with other constitutional claims, such as free speech and the symbolic expression of religious beliefs in architecture, or religious activities as religious expression, or parents' rights to educate their children. Liturgics may influence the outcome here: for example, if a Christian congregation wishes to build on a lot a religious building in a cruciform shape, recognizing in that shape a symbol that forms a fundamental tenet of its belief, but inescapably violating the set back requirements of the applicable regulation, a liturgical requirement of church architecture would qualify for First Amendment, free exercise clause protection.[47] Third, using a compelling interest analysis as an exception to *Smith*, they have argued that their institution is being treated differently than other religious institutions are.[48] Fourth, they have re-litigated the issues of *Smith* and *Flores* using state constitutional provisions guaranteeing free exercise.[49]

---

[42] 494 U.S. 872 (1990).

[43] *Id.* at 882.

[44] 117 Sup. Ct. 2157 (1997) (holding, 6–3, that the statute exceeded Congressional authority under the 14th A., § 5: "Congress shall have the power to enforce, by appropriate legislation, the provisions of this Article."), *discussed in* Colin Black, *The Free Exercise Clause and Historic Preservation Law: Suggestions For A More Coherent Free Exercise Analysis*, 72 Tul. L. Rev. 1767 1805–1806 (1998) (reporting a consentual settlement by the *Flores* parties).

[45] Von Keetch & Matthew Richards, *The Need for Legislation to Enshrine Free Exercise in the Land Use Context*, 32 U.C. Davis. L. Rev. 725 (1999) (reporting a study of the case law finding a "huge disparity" of treatment between majority and minority religious institutions).

[46] *See generally* Sarah Rous, *Why Free Exercise Jurisprudence in Relation to Zoning Restrictions Remains Unsettled after Boerne v. Flores*, 52 So. Meth. U. L. Rev. 305 (1999) (collecting the cases).

[47] *See Society of Jesus of New England v. Boston Landmarks Comm'n*, 564 N.E.2d 571 (Mass. 1990); *First United Methodist Church of Seattle v. Hearing Examiner for Seattle Landmarks Preservation Bd.*, 916 P. 2d 374 (Wash. 1996) (applying a strict scrutiny standard of review to a landmarks ordinance with regard to a church).

[48] *See, e.g., Church of the Lukumi Babalu Aye, Inc. v. City of Hialeah*, 508 U.S. 520 (1993); *Islamic Ctr. of Mississippi, Inc. v. City of Starkville*, 840 F.2d 293, 299 (5th Cir. 1988).

[49] *See, e.g., Swanner v. Anchorage Equal Rights Comm'n*, 874 P.2d 281 (Alas. 1994); *Society of Jesus of New England v. Boston Landmarks Comm'n*, 564 N.E.2d 571 (Mass. 1990).

[A] Churches and Landmarks.

Landmark designation for architecturally distinguished churches is a fertile subject for litigation under the free exercise clauses of federal and state constitutions. Comparisons between *First Covenant Church v. City of Seattle*[50] with *Saint Bartholomew's Church v. City of New York*[51] are instructive. Although the sale of church property might permit the church to raise revenue for its ministerial programs, the *Penn Central* test of economic impact, coupled with the rule that the takings clause countenances a denial of the parcel's most profitable or beneficial use, has prevented landmark churches from relocating when the present use of the property is a reasonable one and is consistent with the church's investment backed expectations.

If the landmark regulation interferes with the functioning of the religious group practices on its existing site, a free exercise challenge will be successful. Thus a small church, serving a growing congregation, can physically expand, notwithstanding a landmark designation for the site. However, when the regulation merely diminishes the income flow which the group might otherwise devote to religious activities, the challenge will fail. A regulation imposing a financial burden does not, *per se*, constitute a free exercise violation. A congregation has no right to tear down a landmark church and build a more profitable office building, but a dwindling congregation might be able to tear down a landmark when most of its resources are devoted to property maintenance, as opposed to good works. As with other land owners, a religious group is not entitled to extract the last dollar from the highest and best use of its property. So long as the regulation is facially neutral, no facial challenge to it will likely succeed.

---

[50] 787 P.2d 1352 (Wash. 1990), vacated, 111 Sup. Ct. 1097 (1991) (using strict scrutiny and invalidating an ordinance preserving the church exterior under the free exercise clause).

[51] 914 F.2d 348 (2d Cir. 1990) (upholding a landmark ordinance against both First Amendment and takings claims), *cert. denied*, 111 Sup.Ct. 1097 (1991) (denying cert. the same day the United States Supreme Court vacated the *First Covenant* opinion); *see* Note, *Free Exercise, Free Expression and Landmarks Preservation*, 91 Colum. L.Rev. 1814 (1991) (comparing the two cases just cited).

Chapter 20

Democracy and Zoning: The Place of the Referendum

§ 20.01   Introduction.

Not long after the *Euclid* opinion, a California opinion held that the voters in a municipality could not adopt a zoning ordinance in an election on a voter-introduced initiative ballot. An initiative permits the voters of a jurisdiction, usually by petition, to propose and enact legislation by ballot. "The initiative law and the zoning (enabling) law are hopelessly inconsistent," one opinion said.[1] Thus begins the tale of democracy and zoning, a tale that continues to this day.

A referendum is an election in which legislation enacted by the legislature is put to a vote. It is thus the people's veto over legislation previously adopted by a state or municipal legislature. It is a citizenry's means of protecting itself against the actions of a corrupt, biased, or unrepresentative legislature. It originated in the age of populism in the early 20th century. The referendum process applies only to legislative, and not to administrative or judicial, actions and decisions. Whether a zoning regulation is enacted by initiative, or upheld or struck down by referendum, the resulting ballot box zoning raises issues of due process.

§ 20.02   *Eastlake v. Forrest City Enterprises.*

A landowner held title to eight acres in Eastlake, Ohio. The parcel was zoned for light industrial uses. The owner applied for a rezoning, to have its classification changed to multi-family residential, in order that he might construct an apartment house on it. The planning commission and the municipal legislature both approved the rezoning, but subsequently the voters changed the city charter to require that 55% of the city's voters approve city council rezonings in a referendum. Later the planning commission turned down a request for parking and yard facilities because the rezoning had not been approved by referendum.

The Ohio Supreme Court invalidated the referendum requirement as a delegation of the police power without standards to guide its exercise. It did so, however, as a matter of federal constitutional law — not as an interpretation of its own, state constitution. This meant that it did not have the final say in the matter. United States Supreme Court reversed, holding that there is no denial of substantive due process involved in the charter's referendum requirement.[2]

---

[1] *Hurst v. City of Burlingame*, 277 P. 308 (Cal. 1929).

[2] *City of Eastlake v. Forest City Enterprises*, 426 U.S. 668 (1976) (Burger, C.J., for the majority).

The issue before the court was the validity of the referendum requirement *per se*; the court refused to invalidate it *per se*, but left open the possibility that a compatible land-use might be zoned out of the city and that, in such an instance, the application of the referendum requirement might be invalid, judged by its results. The court is saying that the democratic process is not unfair to the landowner on its face, but may be applied unfairly.

The Eastlake referendum was mandatory and applied to all land uses there. These are limiting facts for this opinion. The *Eastlake* opinion comes close to saying that the voters may elect the most biased of persons to their legislature,[3] but once elected, those legislators may not enact laws and ordinances on sexist, racial, or other prohibited grounds. The court means to say that the impact of any bias must be separately shown. It assumes that ample remedies for discriminatory action are available — e.g., the federal Fair Housing Act (title VIII of the Civil Rights Acts of 1968). Its further assumption may be that even if the voters are permitted to vote out of any motive they choose, once the local legislators are installed in office, they are then subject to the civil rights laws. If this is so, then the court will not be likely to provide an effective review of legislative actions and enactments without looking at legislative motive.

In many instances, the record which a court has for review, under whatever standard it might use, will include the support for the ordinance before the local legislature. If the applicant has made a credible record there, and the referendum reverses the result, the applicant should be entitled to due process relief. However, what the voters do is not by definition arbitrary. A rezoning decision only need be fairly debatable. Voters can be unpredictable, yet not irrational, because what they do must be characterized after the fact as fairly debatable too.

Referendum procedures are available only when a legislative action is involved. Thus Euclidian rezoning decisions are subject to referenda. Other types of rezonings *may* be subject to referenda — for example, a rezoning to an unmapped planned unit development use district. However, once mapped, a second ordinance imposing a PUD development plan on the site arguably is a quasi-judicial action; it is no more subject to referendum than a court judgment would be, unless the parcel for the PUD tract is very large, its land was annexed into the municipality, or the two PUD rezoning actions were taken together — in which instance the rezoning is a legislative matter and subject to referendum.[4]

Likewise, when a municipality's comprehensive plan is mandated by state statute, its adoption by the municipality's legislature is a legislative matter and subject to referenda. However, if the plan must be both adopted by the local legislature and approved by the state department of planning,

---

[3] It is said, and after the election of 2000, famously said, that the power of a state legislature over elections is "plenary," meaning that it is subject to only a rational basis standard of judicial review. *See Bush v. Gore*, 531 U.S. 98, 104 (2000).

[4] *The Greens at Fort Missoula, LLC v. City of Missoula*, 897 P. 2d 1078, 1081 (Mont. 1995) (upholding the use of the referendum in this instance).

the approval requirement tends to show that it is an administrative document for coordinating municipal land use with state concerns. The plan's adoption could provide a legislative review of an administrative document — an action not in itself legislative in nature.[5] Thus the land use element of the plan may not be subject to a referendum: if it were to be, the everywhere-required consistency between planning and zoning will be affected adversely, and the oversight function of state government can largely be destroyed by subjecting the plan to the voters. It is better, as a practical matter, to hold that the plan is administrative in nature and not subject to referenda.

[A]   Reconciling *Eastlake* with Some Other Cases.

After *Arlington Heights*,[6] some type of showing of improper motive is required before a violation of the Equal Protection Clause will be found. A local decision will only be upset when there is a showing of improper procedures and motive or purpose. Thus an inquiry into legislative motive is proper, however unlikely it is to result in overturning a municipal decision. Further, what if a group home for the retarded — as in *City of Cleburne v. Cleburne Living Center*[7] — is given its permit by the municipal legislature, but this legislative action is rejected by a referendum electorate, as in *Eastlake*? The retarded are not entitled to any type of heightened scrutiny under *Cleburne*; they are only entitled to rational basis review and under *Eastlake* the electoral process is not unfair on its face. This leaves retarded persons without a remedy and out of court. If the courts place the voters on a par with the legislators, the same standard of review attaches: the voters need only have a rational basis for what they do, and their actions are entitled to the same presumption of validity.

[B]   Legislative vs. Judicial Decisions.

The referendum procedure, to be valid, "must be one within the scope of the legislative power." This is a crucial distinction. In contrast, judicial decisions may not be made by referendum. For example, a piece-meal rezoning is not a legislative action. It is not a matter of general policy, applicable to the whole municipality, but is instead a resolution of a conflict between a developer and his or her neighbors. That makes it quasi-judicial in nature, or perhaps best seen as a hybrid, involving both legislative and judicial action. This view is the so-called *Fasano* doctrine.[8] As the number of landowners affected by the rezoning becomes fewer, the degree of protection that they receive by way of substantive and procedural due process review rises. Those protections are weighed against the costs of

---

[5] *But see Devita v. County of Napa*, 889 P. 2d 1019, 1032 (Cal. 1995) (finding the plan to be subject to an initiative because the state legislature in the mandatory planning statute did not expressly pre-empt its initiative statute).

[6] 429 U.S. 252 (1977), discussed *supra*, Chapter 16.

[7] 473 U.S. 432 (1975), discussed *supra*, Chapter 18.

[8] *Fasano v. Bd. of Cty. Comm'nrs of Washington Cty.*, 507 P.2d 23 (Or. 1973), discussed *supra*, Chapter 11.

providing them and as the difficulty of determining who is affected by the decision rises, the rights of the referendum voter should be protected as well, the referendum being regarded as the protector of diffusely-held interests. *Fasano* and *Eastlake* often collide.

For municipal governments, there is no doctrine of separation of powers.[9] The actions of the legislature, cast in the form of an ordinance amending a zoning regulation, can be treated as either legislative or judicial. The outcome of a rezoning hearing by a municipal legislature can be seen as legislative, but the procedure used to reach that outcome can be regarded as quasi-judicial.[10] Such hybrid decisions are not subject to referenda because the hearing procedures cannot be replicated in an election.

[C] Legislative vs. Administrative Decisions.

Equally crucial is the distinction between legislative and administrative decisions: referenda may not be used to decide administrative questions. Thus, a referenda on the granting of a special exception or a variance, or a decision in an appeal from a zoning enforcement official, would not be valid: these actions are administrative and beyond the reach of referenda. *Eastlake* referenda may be substituted only for actions deemed legislative in nature.

[D] The Soundness of *Eastlake*.

Politics is a thing to be kept out of rezoning decisions, not encouraged as it is here, because rezoning matters are too easily politicized. Three policy arguments can be made against the holding in *Eastlake*. First, referendum elections may easily be captured by special interests and the result will not truly be the will of the democratic majority in the municipality. Second, even where the electoral process is not subject to manipulation, the electorate may not represent all the interests that need to be considered: outsiders are by definition not included, and racial and ethnic minorities may be more heavily effected than other groups. Third and finally, even if the electorate is perfectly reflective of the society as a whole, they may lack the information to make an informed decision on the matter. Thus, manipulation of the election, the unrepresentativeness of the electorate, and a lack of information, suggest that *Eastlake* is unsound.

On a more detailed level, the majority opinion suggests that a variance may be available if the results of the referendum work a hardship on the applicant for a rezoning. This is wrong. The court was displaying its ignorance of zoning procedures.[11] Generally however, the presence of administrative relief is one way of providing relief for a landowner aggrieved by the referendum decision. Perhaps the Chief Justice was confusing substantive and procedural due process concerns. What's wrong with

---

[9] *See, e.g., Dreyer v. Illinois*, 187 U.S. 71 (1902).

[10] *Hyson v. Montgomery Cty. Council*, 217 A.2d 578 (Md. 1966) (holding this and granting a right to cross examine in the course of a rezoning).

[11] See majority opinion, text at n. 13.

ballot box zoning is its lack of substantive due process protection; this lack cannot be completely cured by any number of procedural due process protections.

[E]   State Court Responses to *Eastlake*.

State courts have followed *Eastlake*. Several state supreme courts, however, hold that the use of the referendum is a due process violation when injected into the rezoning process.[12] For example, West Virginia, Oregon, and Nevada, permit zoning referenda only in comprehensive rezoning decisions. However, courts in Colorado, California, Minnesota, and Oklahoma, have followed the lead of the United States Supreme Court.

State courts use several lines of argument. The first involves the characterization of the action under review: thus typically only "legislative" actions are proper subjects for initiatives and referenda. Judicial decisions, for example, are not subject to elective scrutiny; neither are administrative ones.[13] In some states, a heightened standard of review for rezoning decisions have led courts to find a rezoning decision to be quasi-judicial in nature.[14] In Colorado, a rezoning is legislative in that it may be reviewed by the voters in a referenda, but is also quasi-judicial for purposes of judicial review.[15] This situational analysis seems appropriate when dealing with municipal actions. Such distinctions might mean, for example, that a comprehensive remapping and amendment of the zoning regulations might be legislative and subject to referenda review, but a piece-meal, one small parcel rezoning is not because it is classified as quasi-judicial. Labels matter: the labelling of an action as judicial or legislative is easily seen as outcome-determinative. Such classifications afford one line of argument for state court's distinguishing *Eastlake*.

A second line of argument involves the procedural requirements for zoning actions. The electoral process affords the voters no method for meeting the notice, hearings, and other decision-making restrictions imposed on planning commissions, zoning boards, and municipal legislatures. This shows the incompatible nature of zoning and electoral decisions and has justified state courts in refusing to apply initiative or referendum requirements to zoning matters. In a state in which city planning is a mandatory matter and in which similar procedural requirements apply to the formulation of a comprehensive general plan, the results of that planning process are arguably immune from electoral review as well. In general, the mechanisms detailed in the enabling act for adopting or amending a zoning ordinance should be considered because, the more substantive

---

[12] *Dan Giles & Assoc. v. McIver*, 831 P.2d 1024 (Or. App. Ct. 1992); *Leonard v. City of Bothell*, 557 P.2d 1306 (Wash. 1976); *West v. City of Portage*, 221 N.W.2d 303, 306–310 (Mich. 1974); *Twp. of Sparta v. Spillane*, 312 A.2d 154 (N.J. Super. Ct. 1973) (where the right to referendum was a statutory, not a constitutional, matter).

[13] *Buckeye Community Hope Fdn. v. City of Cuyahoga Falls*, 697 N.E. 2d 181 (Ohio 1998) (site plan approval an administrative action); *Citizens Awareness Now v. Marakis*, 873 P.2d 1117, 1124–1125 (Utah 1994).

[14] *Fasano v. Bd. of Cty. Comm'nrs of Washington Cty.*, 507 P.2d 23 (Or. 1973).

[15] *Margolis v. District Ct.*, 638 P.2d 297 (Colo. 1981).

and procedural details an ordinance contains, the more likely that a court will limit the scope of the referenda and initiative.

A third line of argument is that the nature of the decision cannot be spelled out with sufficient clarity on the ballot. In a state rejecting the *Eastlake* holding, and holding a rezoning decision to be quasi-judicial and not subject to referendum, a municipality may still hold a non-binding referendum on a rezoning application. A referendum is legislation by the voters. Even if state law precludes the adoption of a rezoning ordinance by referendum, it does not prohibit the use of a non-binding referendum during the adoption process.[16] The plain meaning of the word referendum is the power in the people to review, reject, or confirm legislative action — and a non-binding referendum does not do that.

Perhaps the most articulate, but complex test for elaborating whether a zoning decision is subject to referenda is Utah's.[17] If the issue falls within the general purpose or policy of the zoning ordinance, it is not subject to referenda. If not, the court should then decide whether the decision for which a referenda is sought, is a material change in the ordinance; if it is, then the court must decide whether the change is "a policy-making decision amenable to voter control."[18] The complexity of the issues, the time and attention they take, and the operational effect on municipal government, must all be considered as a part of this last decision.

[F]   Other Issues in *Eastlake*.

[1]   Referenda vs. Initiative.

If referenda are a valid part of the rezoning process, how about an initiative?[19] Using it, voters can initiate a rezoning when current zoning regulations permit a use of which they do not approve. The cases are split on whether its use is a due process violation.[20]

An initiative arguably raises more due process concerns than does a referendum. First, a referenda is held after the usual procedural formalities, e.g. notice and hearing, have been observed, but a rezoning by initiative does not.[21] Second, if a parcel is rezoned by initiative, the comprehensive

---

[16] *Great Atlantic and Pacific Tea Co., Inc. v. Borough of Point Pleasant*, 644 A.2d 598 (N.J. 1994) (holding that a statute prohibiting rezoning by referendum, but not defining the word "referendum" further, does not prohibit a non-binding referendum).

[17] *Citizens Awareness Now v. Marakis*, 873 P.2d 1117 (Utah 1994).

[18] *Id.* at 1123–1125.

[19] *See Lesher Communications, Inc. v. City of Walnut Creek*, 262 Cal.Rptr. 337 (Cal. App. Ct. 1989) (holding an initiative valid as an amendment to a general plan), *reversed* December 31, 1990, 91 Daily J. DAR 135 (1990) (reversing the court of appeals and invalidating a referenda on a zoning ordinance that is inconsistent with the general plan, but leaving open the issues of whether a general plan can ever be amended by referenda or initiative).

[20] *See Wilson v. Manning*, 657 P.2d 251 (Utah 1982) (distinguishing between them) and *Margolis*, op. cit. (not distinguishing).

[21] *Transamerica Title Ins. Co. v. City of Tucson*, 757 P.2d 1055 (Ariz. 1988).

planning requirement of the enabling act is not met, while a rezoning rejected by a later referenda reinstates the preexisting zoning regulation which (presumably) is "in accordance with the comprehensive plan."[22] *Kaiser Hawaii* suggests that there should be a statutory mechanism for review of the constitutionality and the planning implications of initiative proposals before they are circulated for the signatures needed to put them on the ballot.

A comprehensive plan, however, as a pre-condition to zoning — and re-zoning — might more easily be adopted by initiative.[23]

[2] Voting on Exclusionary Zoning.

What if either electoral device is used in an exclusionary manner, to slow the growth of the jurisdiction? In *Arnel Development Company v. City of Costa Mesa*,[24] a court set aside the results of an initiative which prohibited multi-family housing in the city. Eastlake, Ohio, was one of 15 Cleveland suburbs that had enacted mandatory referenda requirements. Most of the votes taken on rezonings rejected the legislative action. Courts should take account of this pattern of rejections and the resulting exclusionary impact of the referenda. California jurisdictions have been presented with quite a few growth control programs by initiatives and most passed.[25]

[3] *Eastlake's* Use in Other Municipalities.

In almost any New England town, particular zoning regulations might be put to a vote of the annual town meeting. The *Eastlake* opinion speaks glowingly about the town meeting as a reservation of rights by an electorate, but the facts of the case do not involve a small New England town, where the town meeting is still in use. And even if the opinion is right for a small suburban Ohio municipality, it might work badly in a large city. There the voters may well have trouble understanding the issues in a rezoning referendum involving land across town and special interests might well use the existing political machine to carry the election. Isolated in the context of a political party's primary election, the electorate may well be too small to be an adequate sampling of voter opinion. Not much imagination is necessary to see that this holding is inappropriate in a large, diverse city where the volume of applications and the diversity of the issues would make electoral decisions difficult to frame, campaign on, and decide. Moreover, local politicians may not like running in elections in which they have to take a stand on such questions.

---

[22] *See Kaiser Hawaii v. City and Cty. of Honolulu*, 777 P.2d 244 (Haw. 1989) (holding that a initiative did not amend the city's land use plan and that the initiative to down-zone parcels slated for development was void because it was a rezoning not in accord with a comprehensive plan).

[23] *Allison v. Washington Cty*, 548 P.2d 188 (Or. App. Ct. 1976).

[24] 178 Cal.Rptr. 723 (Cal. App. Ct. 1981),

[25] Daniel Curtin & Michael Jacobson, *Growth Management by the Initiative in California: Legal and Practical Issues,* 21 Urban Law. 491 (1989).

The *Eastlake* holding should be limited to electorates small enough to interact, on decisions with very visible consequences for the jurisdiction, and on issues of interest widespread enough to induce a good voter turnout at the polls, so that all affected parties participate in the electoral process.

[4] The Timing of Judicial Review.

Arguably, referenda and initiative questions should be reviewed in the courts only after the election. When the rezoning wins at the ballot box, for example, the landowner has nothing to complain about as a result. Thus the access to review may arguably be stricter before the vote. Not all courts have agreed. Early judicial review may save a municipality the costs of running the election.[26] Judicial review before the vote may also save the developer precious up-front capital that would otherwise go into building the project. Thus judicial review should be available, early and late.

A developer who knows that there is going to be a vote can continue to spend money on the development that the voters may reject, only at his own peril. The developer has no vested rights in the development subject to a vote. As we shall see later on, spending money before a referendum calls into question the developer's good faith and reasonable reliance as an element of establishing an estoppel and vested rights.

[5] Neighborhood Democracy and Zoning.

The *Eastlake* decision distinguishes the opinion in *Eubank v. City of Richmond*.[27] In *Eubank*, after the plaintiff obtained a building permit, his neighbors petitioned the city for the establishment of a set-back, over which would hang the plaintiff's bay window, but which the city had no discretion to review; the Court invalidated the ordinance as (1) a delegation of the police power to one set of neighbors to control the rights of others as well as (2) a failure to exercise discretion in its accepting the decision of the neighbors embodied in their petition; thus the ordinance was both an invalid delegation and an arbitrary and capricious action.

Eastlake also distinguishes *Washington ex rel Seattle Title Trust Company v. Roberge*,[28] Here the court invalidated an ordinance which required a two-thirds majority of the owners in a residential zone before a home for the aged could be located there.[29] Thus, giving the neighbors the right to waive a prohibition is valid, so long as there is some review of the neighbors' actions by the local legislature; what neighbors may not do is impose a restriction (*Eubank*) or block the entry of a use into a neighborhood when

---

[26] *See DeBottari v. Norco City Council*, 217 Cal. Rptr. 790 (Cal. App. Ct. 1985) (stating that the expenditure of public money to run an election on a matter that would eventually be invalidated, should not be encouraged).

[27] 226 U.S. 137 (1912).

[28] 278 U.S. 116 (1928).

[29] *But see Cusack v. City of Chicago*, 242 U.S. 526 (1917) (upholding an ordinance which prohibited the erection of a billboard unless the billboard owner obtained the consent of a majority of the owners on the blocks abutting both sides of the street).

the legislature has not prohibited that entry (*Roberge*). Waiving a restriction is within the province of neighbors, but establishing one is not.

The *Eastlake* court refuses to equate the referendum procedure with the consent provisions of ordinances considered in these older opinions. Consideration of all the citizens of a jurisdiction of a zoning question is not the same as the consideration of the same question given by neighbors. This is so because self-interest might cloud the neighbors' judgment or because the referendum is a check on the possible corruption of the legislature.

[6] Veto and Consent.

Two situations that look alike, then, are likely to be treated very differently. For example, suppose first that an ordinance requires that a church or school can file objections to the location of an establishment requesting a liquor license, which location will be denied if within 1000 feet of a church or school. This ordinance is invalid: filing an objection looks like a veto power.[30] However, suppose second that an ordinance requires that an applicant for a rezoning obtain the consent to the rezoning from a majority of adjoining land owners. The cases are split on the validity of such a regulation.[31] The argument for its validity is that obtaining the consent is merely advisory to the decision-maker and serves to alert the agency to the source of any potential problems with granting the application.

The difference between waiting for objections which will amount to a veto and obtaining consent, is a slight one in practice. However, the applicant's burden is greater in the latter situation, but no matter, the consent provision is also likely to be found invalid unless the legislature reviews the reasonableness of the neighbors' judgments and the percentage of the neighbors who may waive application of the regulation is reasonable. In one state, Illinois, the consent provisions which have been invalidated "as applied" have involved uses with some aspects of a nuisance.[32]

[7] Structural Reform of the Referendum Process.

When the referendum process is statutory, not constitutional in nature, it is possible to amend the process so that it accommodates some of the concerns raised previously. An election code might be amended to require that the election be preceded by a hearing at which the issues involved could be aired, giving the electorate at least an opportunity to inform themselves about the issues. Another possible reform is to require those presenting the petition also to present findings of facts and conclusions that could be reviewed for sufficiency under substantive due process standards.

---

[30] *See Arno v. Alcoholic Beverages Control Comm.*, 384 N.E.2d 1223 (Mass. 1979).

[31] *Compare Robwood Advertising Assoc., Inc. v. City of Nashua*, 153 A.2d 787 (N.H. 1959) (yes) *with Janas v. Town Bd. & Zoning Bd. of Appeals*, 382 N.Y.S. 2d 394 (N.Y. App. Div.1976) (no).

[32] *See, e.g., Drovers Trust & Savings Bank v. City of Chicago*, 165 N.E.2d 314 (Ill. 1960).

§ 20.03 Public Participation.

Citizen participation in land-use matters is generally regarded as a positive thing. Cities such as Atlanta and Washington, D.C., have built such participation into their planning process — but participation at the planning stage is very different from participation in latter stages. Ordinances with such planning provisions must be drafted to reflect the difference between advisory participation and decisional control.

Part 6

Halting An Owner's Further Regulation

Chapter 21

Vested Rights and Governmental Estoppel

§ 21.01 Enforcement of Land Use Regulations.

Land use regulations are only as good as they are clear, producing predictable results for both owners and regulators, and are enforceable and are enforced.[1] The drafting of any regulations should be undertaken with an eye to effective enforcement — not necessarily draconian enforcement, but enforcement by a staff skilled in the terms of the regulation as well as sensitive to the rights of the owners against whom enforcement will be sought. "It is better that the law should be certain, than that every judge should speculate upon improvements in it."[2]

Typically both civil and criminal penalties and remedies are available for violations of land use regulations.[3] The municipality's burden of proof is heavier in a criminal case than in a civil one, and includes the burden of showing a criminal intent to violate the regulation. For this reason, and also because normally the primary concern of the regulators is abatement of the violation, civil equitable remedies, particularly an injunction against the violation, are usually sought.

Enforcement officers lack broad powers to enter private property to enforce the regulations; in order to enter over the written or verbal objections of owner, a valid search warrant is necessary, obtainable upon a showing of probable violation of the regulation.[4] Typically, the issuance of any building or construction permit is conditioned upon compliance with zoning and land use regulations. To enforce the condition, officers are on site at crucial times during the construction process — for example, when the foundation is poured — to assure themselves that the owner is in compliance — and that the construction is not proceeding in a way that will threaten the owner's future compliance.

When the municipality seeks enforcement long after the violation occurs, an owner may interpose a defense based on the statute of limitations, the doctrine of laches, or estoppel. Rarely are these defenses successful. If the violation is continuing, a defense based on the statute of limitations is denied by finding that the statute is not tolled: no limitation period runs

---

[1] "Certainty is the mother of repose, and therefore the law aimed at certainty." *Walton v. Tryon*, 21 Eng. Rep. 262, 262 (Ch. 1753).

[2] *Sheddon v. Goodrich*, 32 Eng. Rep. 441, 447 (Ch. 1803).

[3] Recall that Mr. Hadacheck, in the case of *Hadacheck v. Sebastian*, 239 U.S. 394 (1915), discussed *supra*, Chapter 2, was attempting to avoid criminal penalties.

[4] *See People v. Northrup*, 96 Misc.2d 858, 410 N.Y.S.2d 32 (City Ct., Nassau Cty., N.Y., 1978), *rev'd mem.*, 420 N.Y.S.2d 486 (N.Y. App. Div. 1979); *see also* 1976-77 A.G.Opin.(Va.) 338–39 (Oct. 6, 1976).

out when the violation is a continuing one.[5] In some states, statutes of limitations may not apply in equity when the government seeks to enjoin the violation.[6]

Laches is an equitable defense.[7] It applies independently of any defense based on a statute of limitations because it involves an allegation of unreasonable delay in enforcement, regardless of the period permitted by the statute.[8] Delay in enforcement alone is insufficient to make out this defense; some prejudice to the owner must be proven as well.[9] The regulator must be shown to have slept on its enforcement rights, to the owner's prejudice. Even when the owner's intervening financial investment is substantial, laches may still be no defense to delayed enforcement. One commentator has said that the weight of authority is that laches may not bar enforcement by a municipality of its regulations.[10]

Estoppel looks not at the delay in enforcement, and consequent prejudice to the owner, but rather at the actions of the government. Used as a defense, it is not often successful because it is typically difficult for an owner to show that the government meant to issue a permit in violation of its own ordinance or regulation.[11] Thus it is rare that either of these three defenses — statute of limitations, laches, or estoppel — is successful.

§ 21.02 Vested Rights and Governmental Estoppel.

Whenever a legislature, whether at the Congressional, state, or local level, enacts a statute, the issue arises whether the statute should be made retroactive, or if retroactive expressly, so interferes with existing rights and interests as to be unconstitutional.[12] Vested rights and governmental estoppel are doctrines that are applicable to all retroactive civil legislation[13] but apply particularly to the area of land use controls.[14] Both doctrine are informed generally by the due process clause of the Fourteenth Amendment to the United States Constitution and its state analogues.[15]

---

[5] *IT Corp. v. Solano County Bd. of Supervisors*, 820 P. 2d 1023 (Cal. 1991).

[6] *Sussex County v. Piper*, 1990 Del. Ch. LEXIS 134 (1990).

[7] *Town of Seabrook v. Vachon Management Inc.*, 745 A.2d 1155, 1161 (N.H. 2000) (reviewing the doctrine generally for a de novo application of it in the land use context for this jurisdiction).

[8] *DeFazio v. Washington Public Power Supply System*, 679 P. 2d 1316 (Or. 1984) (containing an extensive discussion of laches).

[9] *Fabini v. Kammerer Realty Co.*, 14 Misc. 2d 95, 175 N.Y.S. 2d 964 (1958) (involving a delay of 33 years).

[10] Robert Anderson, *Am. L. of Zoning*, § 29.15, at 733–734 (4th ed. 1997).

[11] *Hurt v. Caldwell*, 279 S.E. 2d 138 (Va. 1981).

[12] *See, e.g.,* Charles Hochman, *The Supreme Court and the Constitutionality of Retroactive Civil Legislation*, 73 Harv. L. Rev. 692 (1960) (arguing broadly for retroactivity as the default rule).

[13] *See* Jill Fisch, *Retroactivity and Legal Change: An Equilibrium Approach*, 110 Harv. L. Rev. 1055 (1997).

[14] *See* Jan Laitos, *Legislative Retroactivity*, 52 Wash. U. J. Urb. & Contemp. L. 81 (1997).

[15] *See Valley View Industrial Park v. City of Redmond*, 733 P.2d 182 (*En Banc*, Wash. 1987) (recognizing the need for "fundamental fairness" and "fixed rules").

[A] Distinguishing Them.

Governmental approval for the development of real property is a multi-phased process. There is no vested right in existing zoning. The mere purchase of land for development creates no right to develop the land in accordance with current zoning.[16] Likewise, the filing of a petition for municipal approval of a subdivision map does not give a right to have the petition reviewed under the *existing* subdivision regulations.[17] However, preliminary plat approval may vest a right to a final approval: some state statutes require a final plat to be submitted within a certain time after approval of a preliminary one, or not at all.[18] Florida courts have held that substantial expenditures made in reliance on a preliminary plat approval, vests a right to final approval.[19] None of this guarantees the issuance of a building permit for structures within the subdivision, absent special statutory protection.[20]

Thus a municipal legislature retains the power to enact new regulations applicable to petitions in the regulatory pipeline at the time of enactment. Indeed, for a large development, at the time of the filing of the petition, the process is just commencing: subdivision approval, board (of Zoning Adjustment) permissions, planning commission permissions, environmental permits, and finally building permits — all lie in the future. An intent to use or improve a parcel, without actual use, vests no rights.

Government has an inherent power to revise its regulations and enact legislation. Legislation is generally applicable retroactively. Indeed, a public need in the form of a health or safety problem justifying a moratoria, trumps all pending permits.[21] At the same time, the parcel owner/developer has an interest in being protected from changes that destroy sunk investment costs. These are the themes developed in the judicial opinions dealing with vested rights and governmental estoppel.[22]

The vested rights doctrine has a constitutional basis: the issue is the retroactive impact of the regulation on the owner, and due process.[23] More recently, takings clause requirements of protection for investment backed expectations have also been cited as a basis.[24] Estoppel has an equitable

---

[16] *Town of Vienna Council v. Kohler*, 244 S.E. 2d 542, 547 (Va. 1978).

[17] *See, e.g., Sherman-Colonial Realty Corporation v. Goldsmith*, 230 A. 2d 568 (Conn. 1967) (filing subdivision plan, without any expenditure of money, does not vest a right to approval).

[18] *See, e.g.,* N.J. Stat. Ann. § 40:55D-49 (1988) (three years).

[19] *Florida Companies v. Orange County*, 411 So. 2d 1008, 1011 (Fla. App. Ct. 1982) (mortgagee acquiring vested right by loan of money on basis of preliminary plat approval).

[20] As discussed in this Chapter, *infra*, there are a few states in which final subdivision approval, plus substantial reliance in the form of expenditure of money, will vest a right in the existing land use regulations for a reasonable period of time.

[21] *See Ford v. Bellingham County*, 558 P.2d 821, 826–827 (Wash. App. Ct. 1977); *Dade County v. Roseli Construction*, 297 So. 2d 46, 48 (Fla. App. 1974) (calling this the "new peril doctrine").

[22] *See Tremarco Corp. v. Garzco*, 161 A. 2d 241, 245 (N.J. 1960) (containing a good statement of the need for these doctrines).

[23] *Valley View Industrial Park v. City of Redmond*, 733 P.2d 182 (*En Banc*, Wash. 1987).

[24] *See, e.g., H.R.D.E., Inc. v. Zoning Officer*, 430 S.E.2d 341 (W.Va. 1993).

basis: it examines the actions of the government. There is ample reason to distinguish between these theories because of their different initial focus; in fact the distinction between them is blurred by the cases. The reason is that, for estoppel to work, there must be reasonable reliance on the estopping actions of government. In the final analysis, both doctrines call for an examination of the impact of the change in the regulation on the owner.

[B] Restatement of the Doctrines.

As to a **vested right**, a property owner establishes such a right when he or she (1) obtains or is assigned a permit to construct improvements in accord with the project and (2) reasonably relies in good faith on the permit and (3) substantially changes his or her position or incurs expenses in further reliance on the permit.

This is the rule in the majority of states, referred to as the "building permit rule." It requires that, when owners obtain the permit, they must have no knowledge of any impending change in the law affecting its legality. Receiving subdivision approval does not satisfy its requirements: if approval is granted for a 100 residential lot subdivision, an owner might wish to install an efficient sewage treatment plant for all 100 lots. Under the building permit rule, a permit is required for each lot in order to acquire a vested right to develop it. So an owner can safely install infrastructure for only as many lots as he can vest rights for because, without an improvement on each lot, the second element of that rule is not satisfied.[25] Vested rights are acquired lot by lot, not for the subdivision as a whole. Thus the rule may encourage the use of (inefficient) sceptic systems for each lot, the owner arguing that each system is the improvement satisfying the rule's second element.[26] The rationale for the rule is that the unimproved parcels may be adapted to and improved in compliance with future municipal requirements. If the owner has installed 100 septic systems instead of a centralized sewage treatment plant, the owner strengthens his vested rights, but at the cost of some inefficiency.

In states mandating comprehensive planning, the majority rule has a corollary: an owner acquires a vested right only when obtaining the last discretionary permit for a development. As previously discussed, this permit is usually a building permit, but it may not be when a multi-level governmental approval system is applicable to the development. Under this so-called last discretionary act rule, an owner with subdivision approval, petitioning for an amendment to a new state-mandated comprehensive plan, will find that he has not acquired vested rights. This is because, after plan approval typically come applications for a rezoning, further subdivision permits and plats, impact and linkage fee payments, site plan review, and building permits. Each of these reviews provides ample opportunity for the

---

[25] *See Gosselin v. City of Nashua*, 321 A.2d 593 (N.H. 1974) (requiring actual improvements, lot by lot).

[26] *Cf. Quirk v. Town of New Boston*, 663 A.2d 1328, 1333–1334 (N.H. 1995) (involving a buffer zone regulation around a campground).

exercise of municipal discretion.[27] When this rule applies, an owner/developer must also prove reasonable and detrimental reliance on any and all permits granted.

A well-known use of the "last discretionary act rule" occurred in Hawaii, when that state's supreme court held that (1) a referenda on a rezoning was the last discretionary approval and (2) a resort community developer did not acquire vested rights, even after expending about a quarter of a million dollars and when holding building permits issued before the election.[28] The developer's knowledge of the voter drive for the referendum, ending in a certification of the referendum question, before the developer filed an application for the permit, was sufficient knowledge to prevent the permits' from vesting.[29]

The enactment of a growth control ordinance, limiting the number of building permits issued annually, does not affect the building permit rule. The enactment violates no vested right; that is, an owner/developer has no vested right to control the timing of the issuance of permits — just what a growth control ordinance is intended to do.

Once acquired, vested rights are not violated by the declaration of the moratorium on the issuance of building or other permits by a municipality. Thus, unless the moratorium is subject to another type of legal challenge, it trumps an owner's vested rights.[30] It does not end an owner's vested right, but it suspends that right for the period of the moratorium.

Once a building permit has been secured, if the permittee is forced to litigate its validity, and while doing so, a amendment to the law making the permit illegal is enacted, the original ordinance controls and trumps the amended one, if substantial improvements have been made.[31] This is an exception to the so-called "time of the decision" rule. It does not apply to vested rights.[32]

Some states provide a limited form of vested rights by statute.[33] Such provisions state that a municipal government may not modify a prior

---

[27] *American West Dev., Inc. v. City of Henderson*, 898 P.2d 110 (Nev. 1995) (recognizing the last discretionary act rule for Nevada).

[28] *County of Kauai v. Pacific Std. Life Ins. Co.*, 653 P.2d 766, 775 (Haw. 1982), *appeal dismissed*, 460 U.S. 1077 (1982) (finding that even though the developer had spend over $158,000 after the permit issued, the referendum was the final discretionary act, before which the developer acquired no vested rights).

[29] California cases to the contrary state in *dicta* the view that reliance may be reasonable up to the time of the vote. *See Santa Monica Pines, Ltd. v. Rent Control Bd.*, 201 Cal. Rptr. 593, 599 (Cal. 1984) (involving a vested right to convert rental apartments in condominiums free of the requirements of an intervening rent control ordinance).

[30] *Matson v. Clark Cty. Bd. of Comm'nrs*, 904 P. 2d 317, 320 (Wash. App. Ct. 1995).

[31] *Ackman v. Bd. of Adjustment for Black Hawk Cty.*, 596 N.W.2d 96, 101 (Iowa 1999) (recognizing also a savings clause in the amendment).

[32] *Id.*

[33] *See, e.g.*, Va. Code Ann. § 15.2-2307 (Michie 1999), *discussed in* E.A. Prichard & Gregory Riegle, *Searching for Certainty: Virginia's Evolutionary Approach to Vested Rights*, 7 Geo. Mason L. Rev. 983, 998-1009 (1999).

approval of (say) a subdivision for a certain period of time after approval.[34] Once the state legislature has enacted such a statute, its action preempts the field and a municipality may not enact its own vesting rules.[35]

Once having acquired and then been denied a vested right recognized by state law, a developer might file a complaint against a municipal official in federal court based on 42 U.S.C.A. § 1983,[36] for a deprivation of either the federal due process or takings clauses. The recission of a vested permit raises two issues with regard to whether a § 1983 claim arises. The first issue is whether the defendant municipal official is acting under the color of state law. That he does was decided by *Monell v. New York City Dept. of Social Services.*[37] The second issue is whether the recission deprives the owner of a right secured by the federal Constitution.[38] No owner with a rescinded vested right has, *ipso facto*, a § 1983 claim.[39] A federally-protected property right must be first found.[40] The law of vested rights was created to protect an owner's reasonable expectations to develop, and giving compensation, though not originally part of the law's design, is one method of protecting the right; in this sense, "vested" means protected either by a right to specific performance to compel the permit's issuance, or by the right to damages or compensation.[41] It is easier to find a claim for a denial of due process than for a taking; federal courts may, but need not, follow the state-based rules on this point.[42] Some federal courts have said that a property right protected under § 1983 is more than an abstract or unilateral expectation of an entitlement; it must instead arise from an independent source, such as state law, and amount to a claim of entitlement to it.[43] Other courts have said that the right must involve a substantive restriction on the governmental agency involved and involve arbitrary municipal action.[44]

---

[34] *See, e.g.,* Wash. Rev. Code Ann. § 58.17.170 (Supp. 1987).

[35] *West Main Associates v. City of Bellevue,* 720 P.2d 782 (Wash. 1986).

[36] Authorizing a civil suit against any person depriving another of a federal constitutional right, when acting under the color of state law.

[37] 436 U.S. 658 (1978) (holding that municipalities are not immune from § 1983 actions).

[38] *See Yale Auto Parts, Inc. v. Johnson,* 758 F. 2d 822, 833 (1st Cir. 1982) (holding that a denial of a variance application does not involve denial of a federally protected property right).

[39] *See supra,* Chapter 13.

[40] *Stubblefield Construction Co. v. City of San Bernardino,* 38 Cal. Rptr. 2d 413 (Cal. App. Ct. 1995).

[41] *See* John Delaney & Emily Vaias, *Recognizing Vested Development Rights as Protected Property in Fifth Amendment Due Process and Taking Claims,* 49 Wash. U. J. Urb. & Contemp. L. 27 (1996) (arguing for accepting a takings claim and reviewing the state cases).

[42] *Cf. Restigouche, Inc. v. City of Seattle,* 59 F. 3d 1208, 1211 (11th Cir. 1995).

[43] *Marshall v. Board of County Comm'nrs for Johnson Cty., Wyo.,* 1996 U.S. Dist. LEXIS 761 (D. Wyo., January 22, 1996).

[44] *Littlefield v. City of Afton,* 785 F. 2d 596, 602 (8th Cir. 1985) (reviewing both vested rights under § 1983 and finding a property interest in a building permit subjected to an illegal exaction involving a conveyance to private parties).

Comity and abstention doctrines have also been used to avoid federalizing land use disputes. In *C-Y Dev. Co. v. City of Redlands*,[45] one federal judge says:

> "Federal courts are not boards of zoning appeals. This message, oft-repeated, has not penetrated the consciousness of property owners who believe that federal judges are more hospitable to their claims . . . .Why they should believe this we haven't a clue . . . . Is it that they have omitted the steps necessary to obtain relief in state courts . . . . Well, we are not cooperating. Litigants who neglect or disdain their state remedies are out of court, period."

Substantive due process denials have nonetheless been found to be as a basis for § 1983 claims.[46]

§ 21.03   The Doctrine of Estoppel.

As to **estoppel** of the government, a government is estopped when an owner (1) relies in good faith on some governmental act or omission,[47] and (2) substantially changes position or incurs substantial expenses in further reliance on the permit, such that it would be unfair and inequitable to deny the owner's right to proceed.[48] Estoppel is an equitable doctrine, based on considerations of fair dealing and justice. Courts do not generally favor its use against municipalities.[49] Thus issuance of a zoning certificate for a limited time does not estop a municipality from refusing to renew it.[50]

The necessary "good faith" reliance (the first element of an estoppel) is measured often by the amount of notice of a pending change necessary to destroy it. The comments of or conversations with a governmental staff member about changing the applicable regulation, are insufficient. Staff studies of the need for a regulatory change, by those persons authorized to propose the change, may be sufficient, but a stronger case is presented when the studies are conducted with legislative or administrative authority, or are authorized by legislative or board resolution. Thus, when a change is pending before the governmental body, is a question open to considerable

---

[45] 703 F. 2d 375 (9th Cir. 1983); *see generally River Park, Inc. v. City of Highland Park*, 23 F. 3d 164, 165 (7th Cir. 1994).

[46] *Littlefield v. City of Afton*, 785 F. 2d 596, 603 (8th Cir. 1985) (recognizing and joining decisions from the 3rd, 4th, 6th, 9th, and 11th circuits, to the effect that a § 1983, substantive due process claim may be based on the denial of a land use permit).

[47] *See City of Hutchins v. Prasifka*, 450 S.W.2d 829, 836 (Tex. 1970) (showing that Texas courts have made this element difficult to prove by requiring that, first, the act be shown by the owner to be within the governmental employee's scope of employment and, second, not within the performance of a governmental function immune from estoppel).

[48] *See Even v. City of Parker*, 597 N.W.2d 670, 674–675 (S. Dak. 1999) (using estoppel doctrine against a municipality); *Town of Largo v. Imperial Homes Corp.*, 309 So. 2d 571, 572–573 (Fla. App. Ct. 1975) (same); *see also Wesco v. City of Montpelier*, 739 A.2d 1241 (Vt. 1999) (finding no reliance or estoppel).

[49] *See Town of Seabrook v. Vachon Management Inc.*, 745 A.2d 1155, 1160 (N.H. 2000).

[50] *Id.* (as to an adult, sex-oriented business).

dispute. (As we will see, when an application is pending for purposes of the vested rights doctrine, is also subject to dispute.)[51]

Another aspect of this element of an estoppel — the governmental act or omission — can be satisfied when the owner procures a rezoning, a special exception, a variance, or a foundation permit.[52] The emphasis here is more on the affirmative action of the municipality than on an omission, as the basis for estoppel.[53] However, a letter to the owner from a municipal official might do as well. Firm rules and bright lines are difficult to come by because the doctrine is an equitable one.

The second element, of substantial change in position, is typically shown by the expenditure of planning and development funds — what a developer calls soft costs. For purposes of this showing, however, threshold amount is difficult to determine and varies from jurisdiction to jurisdiction. The purchase of non-returnable building materials, of a type an inspector should have investigated prior to the issuance of a permit, also provides grounds for an estoppel.[54]

With these statements in hand, it is easy to understand that the facts giving rise to a claim of vested right, will also give rise to one for estoppel. In both instances, the *prima facie* case will involve the two elements of reasonable, good faith reliance and a substantial change or expense. This commonality is evident in the so-called, "pending ordinance" rule. It is applied in both vested rights and estoppel cases. It provides that, if during the time that a ordinance imposing a requirement is being legislatively reconsidered, an owner applies for a permit based on the existing requirement, the near universal rule is that, when an ordinance is pending when the application is filed, reliance on the old ordinance is unreasonable and no estoppel of the municipality occurs. A race to the planning commission or zoning board would otherwise ensue. An owner may avail himself of compliance with an ordinance only so long as it is on the books.[55]

Differences, however, remain. Vested rights is a permit-specific doctrine; governmental estoppel involves a governmental act, perhaps amounting to a right to a permit not yet in hand. Being equitable in nature, it is perhaps best to think of estoppel as supplementing a state's vested rights rule. After all, if the law on vested rights is clear that a particular permit, usually a building permit, must be obtained, then how can reliance be reasonable for estoppel purposes if the permit is not in the developer's hands?

---

[51] *See Smith v. City of Clearwater*, 383 So. 2d 681 (Fla. App. Ct. 1980), *review dismissed*, 403 So. 2d 407 (Fla.1981).

[52] *United Parcel Service, Inc. v. People's Counsel for Baltimore County*, 611 A.2d 993 (Md. App. Ct. 1992) (summarizing Maryland case law).

[53] *See Even v. City of Parker*, 597 N.W.2d 670, 674 (S. Dak. 1999) (stating the doctrine so as to require an affirmative action).

[54] *Id.*, 597 N.W.2d at 674–675.

[55] *Recycle and Recover, Inc. v. Ga. Board of Natural Resources*, 466 S. E. 2d 197 (Ga. 1996).

§ 21.04   Pre-Construction Improvements.

What about pre-construction improvements made in contemplation of securing a building permit, but before one is actually obtained? If directed toward an improvement, legal at the time, but subsequently rendered an illegal use by rezoning, the courts then look to see whether there is substantial reliance by the owner on the existing regulation. Drilling a well adequate to service the new improvement, heavying up the utilities, and widening abutting roads — these might be reliance costs, admissible to show a vested right. However, these might also be costs directed at the installation of many types of improvements, not just the one proposed by the developer. To the extent a cost supports other improvements, the argument for a vested right in advance of the building permit is weakened.[56]

A few states recognize a right to develop in accordance with existing land use regulations once final subdivision approval is obtained and a substantial expenditure of money has been made in reliance on the existing regulations.[57] No building permit is required.

In a majority of states, the issuance of a building permit remains a precondition to obtaining a vested right to develop. The date of issuance is the earliest time at which a right to develop can vest.[58] Some states phrase this rule in the negative, with a rule that pre-construction costs give rise to no vested rights. Such costs include planning, engineering, architectural, and legal costs. Sometimes the majority rule is modified when consistency with the local comprehensive plan is the issue.[59]

[A]   The Minority Rule.

A minority of states vest a development right at the time of the application for the permit, rather than the date of its issuance.[60] Compared to the majority rule, this rule permits an early vesting of an owner's rights. Early vesting is said to provide a crisp rule, one most easily administered, and free of the uncertainties of phrases like "reasonable reliance" and a "substantial change in position." A "date of application" rule does, however, require that a "complete application" to be filed, and defining this phrase may reduce the crispness of this rule.

---

[56] *But see Matteson v. City of Chicago*, 411 N.E.2d 1002 (Ill. App. Ct. 1980) (approval of apartment plan and of demolition permit sufficient when owner in fact demolished her house).

[57] *Board of Supervisors of Fairfax County v. Cities Service Oil Co.*, 193 S.E.2d 1 (Va. 1972). *See* Grayson Hanes & Randall Minchew, *On Vested Rights to Land Use and Development*, 46 Wash. & Lee L. Rev. 373 (1989) (reviewing Virginia law).

[58] *Town of Paradise v. Gulf Leisure Corporation*, 557 P.2d 532 (Ariz. App. Ct. 1976); *State ex rel. Humble Oil & Refining Company v. Wahner*, 130 N.W.2d 304 (Wis. 1964). *See generally* Michael Shultz, *Vested Property Rights in Colorado: The Legislature Rushes in Where . . .*, 66 U. Den. L. Rev. 1, 31–39 (1988).

[59] *See Youngblood v. Bd. of Supervisors of San Diego Cty.*, 586 P.2d 556 (Cal. 1978) (permitting plan consistency to be measured at the review of a tentative development plan and subdivision map).

[60] For a good statement of the law and an adoption of the minority rule, see *Western Land Equities, Inc. v. City of Logan*, 617 P.2d 388 (Utah 1980).

Illinois and Arizona also have cases in which a building permit is not required as a precondition to establishing a vested right.[61] In Illinois, a rule of fundamental fairness balances the financial hardship on the developer against both the benefits to the public and the diminution in surrounding parcel values, in assessing whether a development right has vested.[62] In this balance, the existing uses, the suitability of the proposed use, and the length of time the parcel has been vacant are also considered.

In *Western Land Equities v. City of Logan*,[63] the Utah Supreme Court required that a development plan, in substantial conformance with the existing regulations and ordinances, be filed prior to a change in the law; so the date of the application's filing is the date on which the right to develop vests. Thus, if a change in the law is not pending when the development plan is filed and is not necessary to protect the public health or safety, a right to develop vests without substantial expenditure of money or construction. The Utah version of the minority rule also requires that, once the permit is secured, the developer pursue the development with due diligence, and permits the regulators to withdraw it with a showing of a compelling governmental interest — but the date of the issuance is then the pivotal date.

Maine is another jurisdiction with a developer-oriented rule for vested rights: there, a development plan vests when the government acts on it. More than filing the plan is required, but how much more is unclear.[64] The period during which an application for plan approval is pending should also be a time when the application is diligently pursued through the administrative process. However, an application may arguably not be pending until (1) a hearing on it is commenced, or (2) the hearing is completed and the application is submitted to the governmental body for a decision on the record.

Idaho, Indiana, Ohio, Vermont, and Washington also adhere to some version of the minority rule: when an application for a building permit is filed, the developer's right to build vests.[65]

The minority rule is intended to permit developers to "fix" the rules governing their development at the time of the application is filed and to insure fairness in subsequent proceedings. When a regulation was effective, but its applicability lifted because of a moratorium, an owner is no less on notice of it.[66] A municipality is not by enacting the moratorium reserving any right to change the regulation applicable during the course of the owner's later application hearings. Unless the municipality sought to

---

[61] *See Town of Paradise Valley v. Gulf Leisure Corp.*, 557 P. 2d 532 (Ariz. App. Ct. 1976); *American National Bank & Trust Co. v. City of Chicago*, 311 N.E. 2d 325 (Ill. App. Ct. 1974).

[62] *Smith v. City of Macomb*, 352 N.E.2d 697 (Ill. App. Ct. 1976).

[63] 617 P.2d 388 (Utah 1980).

[64] *Littlefield v. Inhabitants of Lyman*, 447 A.2d 1231, 1235 (Me. 1982) (interpreting a state statute preventing the application of intervening regulations to "pending" plans).

[65] *See, e. g., Hull v. Hunt*, 331 P.2d 856, 859 (Wash. 1958).

[66] *R.C. Hedreen Co. v. City of Seattle*, 1996 U.S. App. LEXIS 1794 (Jan. 8, 1996) (applying Washington law).

circumvent its minority vesting rule with the moratorium, the pre-existing regulation applies at the owner's hearing held once the moratoria is over. The minority vesting rule does not seek to protect against all uncertainty for developers.

§ 21.05   Substantial Reliance.

Substantial reliance on a building permit is an element of showing a vested right. Reasonable reliance is an element of estoppel. Although they have similar concerns, these terms might mean different things — that is, the former an objective, and the latter a subjective, test. Nonetheless, they are often interpreted to mean just one thing: that construction must be undertaken in some form. This means actual construction, not preparation for it. The reason for this last distinction is that (again) preparatory activities are often consistent with many types of improvements, both legal and illegal under applicable codes. Clearing the land is insufficient because that is consistent with many types of improvements. Likewise, a widening of a nearby roadway or the demolition of an existing building is insufficient.

If in good faith a landowner expends substantial funds or incurs a substantial obligation, or otherwise undergoes a substantial change of position, in reliance on the existing zoning and on obtaining a building permit, then he or she may acquire a vested right. This is not an iron-clad rule. Oregon and Illinois are examples of states adopting such a requirement.[67] *Holmes* requires that the substantial expenses must be incurred before the zoning change and must be exclusively related to the proposed project.[68]

Substantial reliance is, however, an idea whose importance extends beyond Oregon and Illinois cases. In majority-rule states, there must also be substantial reliance on the permit. How then are pre-construction costs, incurred after the issuance of a permit, to be evaluated? There are three approaches. First, they might be evaluated quantitatively, in terms of an absolute dollar amount. That amount must be spent or exceeded before vested rights in existing regulations arise. When the project is a large one, however, this method is typically used: here the absolute number of dollars spent, without considering the total expenditures required, is the focus of the inquiry.

A second approach is the so-called proportionate ratio test. It takes the expenses incurred and computes them as a percentage of the total cost of the project.[69] Total cost is sometimes defined as comprising both hard and

---

[67] *See, e.g., Clackamas County v. Holmes, 508 P.2d 190* (Or. 1973).

[68] The Oregon cases are reviewed in a Comment, *Oregon's Vested Rights Rule: A Statutory Solution for a Troublesome Problem*, 68 Ore. L. Rev. 975, 984–991 (1989) (arguing that the uncertainty of this intermediate rule requires a development agreement statute, of the type discussed infra, this Chapter).

[69] *Compare Brennan v. Bd. of Zoning Adjustment of City of New Orleans*, 371 So. 2d 324 (La. App. Ct. 1979) (95% complete) *with Aries Development Company v. California Coastal Zone Comm'n*, 122 Cal. Rptr. 315 (Cal. App. Ct. 1975) (1–2% complete).

soft costs, but in some cases, soft costs are excluded. Another version of this method is to take the construction undertaken to date as a percentage of the construction required to complete the project. In sum, both versions form a fraction, the numerator of which is the costs incurred and the denominator of which is the total cost of the improvement, however defined.[70] Neither method provides much guidance or predictability about litigation results. Courts move from the first to the second approach when they suspect a "window dressing," bad faith expenditure of funds.

In yet a third approach, the costs incurred so far might be balanced against the costs of redoing the project to conform to the new regulation. This third approach is tailored to the situation in which the cost of compliance with the new regulation is slight compared with the public benefit achieved. This third approach is reminiscent of a test for a taking. A broader version of this third approach takes the form of a balancing test — weighing the owner's right to use the land and the expenses incurred thus far, against the public interest in holding the owner to a new, updated regulation.

Remember: after a building permit is issued, that is not the end of the owner's worries about fickle municipal legislatures because there must be substantial reliance on the permit as well as use of it within a reasonable period of time.

A **final caveat** on vested rights, estoppel, and substantial reliance. An owner should not, just after being issued a building permit, move immediately to make substantial expenditures or undertake construction. Moving immediately will mean that these expenditures and construction will be made before the time for appealing the issuance of the permit has expired. An owner may not rely upon any level of expenditure and construction, no matter how substantial, that usurps an aggrieved party's right of appeal.[71] An owner's expenditure of funds prior to an appeal cannot be made in good faith and so may not be counted toward meeting the substantial reliance requirement. Respect for the courts and the judicial process requires this rule.

§ 21.06 Applying the Rules: The PUD.

It is particularly burdensome to apply the "building permit rule" when the project is a large one and requires many types of permits. A planned unit development, for example. In one PUD case, a developer planned to construct a 74 acre project amid his nearly 8,000 contiguous acres. Some 5,000 of its 8,000 acres had been rezoned for a PUD containing more than 18,000 dwelling units. As to the 74 acres, the developer had obtained a subdivision map approval and a rough grading permit, and was installing permitted storm drains, streets, and utilities — all at a cost of over two million dollars. The subdivision plat approved divided the 74 acres into 27

---

[70] Such a ratio was rejected as dispositive in the Oregon Supreme Court opinion in *Holmes*.

[71] *State ex rel Brookside Poultry Farms, Inc. v. Jefferson Cty. Bd. of Adjustment*, 388 N.W. 2d 593, 595–596 (Wis. 1986).

parcels, with multi-family housing structures on most of them. (The grading permit did not permit finished grading for building sites.) The developer had in addition sold 11 beach-front acres to the surrounding county at a price below market value.

At this point, the California legislature enacted the Coastal Commission Act. At the time of enactment, the developer had not been issued building permits for any structures on its 74 acres. However, the developer estimated that it had incurred three-quarters of a million dollars in liabilities, in addition to monies actually spent, and was losing $7,000 a day in rental income.

When the county approved the planned unit development, it saw a general site plan for the whole project. None-the-less, the California supreme court held that the developer was required to obtain a Commission permit or exemption. It had been denied the latter and did not have the former, so it had acquired no vested right to proceed.[72]

Thus, in California and many states, a permit is necessary, but not sufficient to establish a vested right; and no governmental estoppel arises, absent a permit. The *Avco* court stated that something less than a building permit might suffice, but only if the governmental approval relied on has the same specificity and detail that the building permit required. General site plans forming the basis for a PUD rezoning, will not suffice. Only after the government has given its "final discretionary approval" can a vested right in a specific improvement arise. The risk that the final permit will be denied (the court said) should be borne by the developer when making pre-permit expenditures. The smallness of the 74 acre project in dispute, when compared to the vastness of the PUD as a whole, contributes to the result here.[73]

§ 21.07   Statutory Responses.

California's legislature enacted a statute in response to *Avco*.[74] It permits a developer to file a "vesting tentative map" for a subdivision of a multi-permit development and complete the development that is substantially in compliance with such a map.[75] Texas has enacted a statute that provides that when a series of permits are necessary for a project, the regulations in effect at the time of the application for the first of them controls and "shall be the sole basis for consideration of all subsequent permits required for completion of the project."[76]

---

[72] *Avco Community Developers, Inc. v. South Coast Regional Comm'n*, 553 P. 2d 546, 550 (Cal. 1976) (holding that a developer who expended nearly $3,000,000 in planning and site improvements did not acquire vested rights for a 74 acre parcel designed for multi-family use), *appeal dismissed, cert. denied*, 429 U.S. 1083 (1977).

[73] *Avco* and subsequent California cases are discussed in Paul Nadel, *This Land is Your Land . . .Or Is It? Making Sense of Vested Rights in California*, 22 Loyola (L.A.) L. Rev. 791, 797-805 (1989).

[74] Cal. Gov. Code § 66474.1.-.2, and § 66498.1-.7, *discussed in Kaufman & Broad Central Valley, Inc. v. City of Modesto*, 30 Cal. Rptr. 904 (Cal. App. Ct. 1994).

[75] *Id.*

[76] Tex. Local Gov't Code § 245 (effective 1999).

§ 21.08   Justifying the Majority Rule on Vested Rights.

One advantage of a late vesting rule, such as the building permit or last discretionary act rule, is that it deters developers trying to beat the clock when a change in the law is in the offing; thus it is particularly appealing in jurisdictions with activist land use regulatory systems. Another is that the right which has vested, is all the more valuable; perhaps it generates fewer, but more substantial, development projects. Yet another advantage is its clarity. Finally, earlier vesting rules might encourage non-conforming uses; late vesting discourages them. Nonetheless, the building permit rule arose in an era of one permit developments and its fairness in a multi-permit era is open to question.

Some jurisdictions diverge from the rules, if not the result, in *Avco* at the point at which the developer dedicates land or improvements relating to the entire multi-permit project, to government ownership. If the beach dedications in *Avco* had related not just to the 74 acre project, but had instead related to most of the 8,000 acres, the developer would have acquired a vested right to complete the project in conformance with the regulations in existence at the time of the first permit's issuance.[77] Once making the dedications, the developer is entitled to the permits as consideration for the benefits conferred on the regulator by the dedications. Otherwise, a *Nollan/Dolan* claim arises.

Once a developer has a building permit in hand, and relied in good faith by a substantial change in position or expenses, equitable estoppel may be used to compel the issuance of related permits. In addition, the issuance of a building permit creates a vested right to compel issuance of independent permits requiring the same degree of detail as did the initial permit, unless the permit was erroneously issued. There can be no reliance upon an invalid or erroneously issued permit.

[A]   Comparing the Rules.

The difference between the minority or early, "date of application" and the majority or late, "date of permit" vesting rules is for some one of emphasis. Their respective dates are the fulcrums around which the factors weighed in the rule revolve. More precisely put, those dates provide a time for shifting the burden of proof from the developer to prove an entitlement to a vested right, to the regulatory body to prove there should be no such right. The same factors weigh into each of the rules, but they are given differing weights as time passes. Both seek a balancing between certainty and predictability on the one hand, and responsiveness to changed conditions on the other, in the law of land use controls.

§ 21.09   More on Good Faith Reliance.

The timing of the expenditure is often a factor in reliance. Construction performed without a permit when one is required, is not performed in good

---

[77] *See Preseault v. Wheel,* 315 A. 2d 244 (Vt. 1974).

faith. Neither will the costs of such illegally-performed work be considered in establishing substantial reliance. Neither will hastily completed work, performed in anticipation of a change in a law or regulation, be in good faith. Similarly, work performed under the authority of a permit, must be performed in compliance with any conditions specified in the permit. Conditional approval of a development plan or the issuance of a permit gives a vested right that may be forfeited if the development or permitted construction does not proceed according to the conditions.[78]

A permit must be used for the project applied for. Later changes in the project annul any vested right to the project as built, even when the modified project is smaller or in a different location. Any vested right extends only to construction that complies with the terms of the permit and so construction of an altered project is not in good faith.[79] The smallness of the changed project is irrelevant under these circumstances.

§ 21.10   The Illegal Permit Problem.

In majority rule states, what if the permit is issued illegally? The effect of such issuance is that, even if the developer has no actual knowledge of the illegality, he or she cannot rely on it and use it as the basis for a vested right.[80] On the other hand, where the zoning administrator in good faith and acting within his authority interprets the zoning ordinance in a developer's favor, then the developer may rely on the interpretation and vest rights in it.[81]

An illegal permit will not be resuscitated in a court of equity, no matter how great the expenditures made in reliance on it, or no matter how far land preparation as proceeded. No owner has a reasonable expectation that the building permit stage of regulatory review may be avoided.[82]

---

[78] *Browning-Ferris Industries of South Atlantic, Inc. v. Wake County*, 905 F. Supp. 312 (E.D. N.C., 1995) (restating the law of vested rights for North Carolina).

[79] *Rosenberry Life Insurance Company v. Zoning Hearing Bd. of the City of McKeesport*, 644 A. 2d 688 (Pa. Cmmnw. Ct. 1995) (involving a permit for business sign to be used on a building at another location on the same building, the court stating that location of signs is a significant factor in their regulation, and also noting that neither the employment of a company to build the sign, showing the permit to a company representative along with plans for an altered sign, asking the company to undertake construction, or its doing so, provides any basis for a vested right in the sign as built, the company being the agent of the business is required to exercise good faith — its expertise lies in reading the plans for the sign and, in doing so, it should notice the discrepancy between the plans and the permitted sign).

[80] *Levinson v. Montgomery County*, 620 A. 2d 961, 974–975 (Md. App. Ct. 1993); *City of Limoni v. Livingston*, 392 N.W. 2d 506, 510 (Iowa 1986) (holding that where a sawmill was not a permitted use in the zoning district in which a developer sought to establish one, the zoning administrator lacked authority to issue a building permit and such a permit was no basis for vested rights: ". . . when a permit is granted wholly without legal authority, the holder does not gain vested rights in it.").

[81] *Crow v. Bd. of Adjustment*, 288 N.W. 145, 147 (Iowa 1939) (holding that a veterinarian may rely on an administrator's interpretation that a "hospital" as a permitted use includes a veterinary hospital).

[82] *Lake Bluff Hsg. Partners v. City of South Milwaukee*, 540 N.W. 2d 189 (Wis. 1995).

"Generally, a permit issued under a mistake of fact confers no vested right or privilege and may be revoked at any time."[83] The formal or technical nature of the mistake is irrelevant. For example, with regard to a building permit for a business sign, even though the only error in issuing the permit was a failure by the business to present a zoning certificate (certifying compliance with sign regulations) to the official in charge of issuing the permit, it is still illegal and there is no vested right to proceed under it. Whether the permit violates the substantive regulations of the municipality or the procedural regulations for the issuance of the permit makes no difference, although there may be a good case for zoning estoppel.

§ 21.11   Development Agreements.

The law of vested rights may be limited by either legislation limiting the power of municipalities to apply new ordinances to on-going projects or by statutes or judicial authority for development agreements.[84] The execution of a developer's agreement with a municipality may confer vested contractual rights upon the developer.[85]

A development agreement is a contract that establishes the rights and duties of a developer to build a project.[86] They are executed with the municipality. The most important provision in any such agreement, sometimes made an implied term by statute,[87] is that the project can proceed in accordance with the regulation in place at the time of its execution, subject to any exception spelled out in the agreement itself. Thus, absent a provision to the contrary, the regulations in effect at the time of the development agreement's execution control.[88] In return, the developer agrees to the conditions on development provided in the agreement.[89]

The California statute just cited was a response to the opinion in *Avco*,[90] Arizona, Colorado, Florida, Hawaii (the second state, after California, to enact such a statute), Idaho, Louisiana, Maryland, North Carolina, Nevada, New Jersey, Pennsylvania, and Virginia also have statutes authorizing such agreements, but generalizations are difficult concerning these statutes. In addition, Texas has had, and has repealed, such a statute. Most

---

[83] *Ebzery v. City of Sheridan*, 982 P.2d 1251, 1257 (Wyo. 1999) (involving a fence built at illegal height); *Bruno v. Zoning Bd. of Adjustment,* 664 A.2d 1077, 1080 (Pa. 1995).

[84] *See* Va. Code Ann. § 15.1-491 (Michie 1992) (limiting municipal authority) and *Giger v. City of Omaha*, 442 N.W.2d 182 (Neb. 1989) (upholding such an agreement against a charge of contract zoning).

[85] *Id.*

[86] *See generally* Patricia Hammes, *Development Agreements: The Intersection of Real Estate Finance and Land Use Controls*, 23 U. Balt. L.Rev. 119 (1993); John Armentano, *How Development Agreements Can Protect Developers and Make Certain That Municipalities Receive Benefits Promised*, 28 Real Est. L. J. 259 (2000).

[87] *See* Cal. Gov't Code § 65865.2 (West Supp. 1988), *reviewed in Armentano, op. cit.*, 28 Real Est. L. J. at 266–269.

[88] *City of Hollywood v. Beverly Towers, Inc.*, 805 P.2d 329, 334 (Cal. 1991).

[89] *City of Casa Grande v. Tucker*, 817 P.2d 947 (Ariz. App. Ct. 1991).

[90] Op. cit. n.72.

of these statutes were drafted to supplement, rather than to supplant, the common law doctrines discussed in this Chapter. The Florida statute was a response to *Hollywood, Inc. v. Broward County*.[91]

Such agreements are one response to the heightened nexus required of subdivision and other exactions after the *Nollan* and *Dolan* opinions. They memorialize the required nexus. At the same time, however, they raise basic issues of whether a later exercise of the police power, contrary to the agreement, may be contracted away. In federal courts, another way of framing this issue is to present it as a tension between the contract and the reserved powers clause of the federal constitution. On this issue, the courts weighing the matter have divided.[92]

The scope of a development agreement must be clear. When a municipality and a developer execute a development agreement, a reference should be made to the zoning ordinance provisions intended to permit the developer's project, with specific references to the statutes, regulations, and ordinances that the agreement is intended to effect. An agreement providing that "the development of the subject property shall be in substantial compliance with the municipality's Zoning Ordinance and Comprehensive Plan and sufficient to serve the project's inhabitants" will not prevent the municipality down-zoning that developer's land to a less intense use, or amending its comprehensive plan accordingly. The language quoted is not the equivalent of a regulatory freeze for the land as it was zoned when the agreement was executed. Without an explicit provision for a regulatory freeze, a court is unlikely to imply one because that would involve a delegation of the police power in many jurisdictions.[93]

[A]   The Basic Scope of the Development Agreement.

The agreement should at a minimum describe the project, the required permits affected, any and every phase of the project to which the agreement applies, public facilities that will serve the project, the remedies available to enforce the agreement, compliance with notice, hearing, and other legislative functions necessary to make the agreement binding on the government (this will provide authority for the signatories representing the government), and a description of events leading to the termination of the agreement.

---

[91] 431 So. 2d 606 (Fla. App. 1983) (involving a development agreement in effect before the County downzoned a developer's land after the developer had expended over two million dollars in site preparation).

[92] *Compare PMC Realty Trust v. Town of Derry*, 480 A. 2d 51, 53 (N. H. 1984) (consent agreement settling a case reversing denial of a variance vests no rights) *with City of Baltimore v. Crane*, 352 A. 2d 786, 790–791 (Md. 1976) (invoking the concept of contractual estoppel for the benefit of a developer).

[93] *See Sprenger, Grubb & Associates, Inc. v. City of Hailey, Idaho*, 903 P. 2d 741 (Idaho 1995) (reviewing also the plan attached to the agreement).

[B] Drafting and Further Considerations for a Development Agreement.

An agreement's prologue should contain at least three recitals: (1) its statutory authority if any, (2) that its purpose to free the developer from compliance with new regulations replacing existing ones that are specifically referred to by code volume and section number, and (3) that its execution is voluntarily and without duress. The third recital is important when the developer executes the agreement in the face of an impending adverse municipal action.[94]

The most important provision of such agreements is a limited term, during which the agreement is enforceable. If limited to a reasonable time, such agreements are more likely to meet with judicial approval.[95] A reasonably short term for such agreements precludes the argument that a development agreement is in effect an exercise of the police power by one legislative session, in an attempt to bind future sessions. Second, agreements should provide that plans for the development are both in conformance with existing comprehensive plans, and are required to conform to any future plans and ordinances not in direct conflict with it. Third, some development agreements permit the developer to construct some improvements, but provide also that the municipality will construct others, financed by bonds backed by a special assessment. The amount of control a developer retains over the municipality's work should be defined in the agreement.[96] Fourth, as to the developer's obligations to provide improvements, this duty should be expressly conditioned on the developer's proceeding with the project diligently and as contemplated in the agreement.[97] Conversely, any of the developer's successors entitled to the benefits, and responsible for implementing the agreement, should be defined.[98] Fifth, the developer's duty to implement the agreement should be conditioned on its finality: when it is subject to a referendum or to judicial review, its effectiveness should be stayed or subject to a termination at a date certain.[99]

Finally, because the agreement is intended to settle disputes that might otherwise involve resort to the courts, an arbitration clause is advisable, particularly when both public and private financing is to be used. For instance, the developer's agreement should last as long as the underwriters

---

[94] *Meredith v. Talbot County*, 560 A. 2d 599 (Md. App. Ct. 1989).

[95] *See Geralnes B.V. v. City of Greenwood Village, Colorado*, 583 F. Supp. 830, 841 (D.Colo. 1984) (agreement not to rezone for twenty-five years is a valid exercise of the police power). *Geralnes* resulted in a development agreement statute.

[96] *See Chard Realty, Inc. v. City of Shakopee*, 392 N.W.2d 716 (Mn. App. Ct. 1986) (holding that a developer has no third-party beneficiary rights in a construction contract between the municipality and its contractor for improvements paid for by developer and called for in a development agreement).

[97] *River Vale Plng. Bd. v. E&R Office Interiors, Inc.*, 575 A.2d 55 (N.J. Super. Ct., App. Div., 1990) (holding that an agreement is subject to the implied condition that developer proceed with project).

[98] *See Larkin v. City of Burlington*,772 A.2d 553, 557 (Vt. 2001) (holding that a purchaser at a foreclosure is not a successor to the developer executing an agreement).

[99] *Midway Orchards v. County of Butte*, 269 Cal. Rptr. 769 (Cal. Ct. App. 1990).

of the public instruments (bonds, etc.) advise. Any municipal reimbursement of a developer should be made waiving competitive bidding statutes and other disbursement procedures.[100]

---

[100] *Achen-Gardner, Inc. v. City of Chandler*, 839 P.2d 1093, 1099 (Ariz. 1992) (holding that a development agreement violated a competitive bidding statute).

A Glossary of Land Use Terms

A Glossary of Land Use Terms

accessory use. A use incidental to or subordinate to, but on the same lot or parcel as, a principal use, and necessary to the convenience of those engaged in the principal use; a use conducted in an accessory building or structure; a use other than the principal use.

administrative appeal. The review of an order or decision of a local official charged with the administration of a zoning ordinance or regulation, conducted by a Board of Zoning Appeals or Adjustment, or a court.

aesthetic zoning. The regulation of the proportion, size, or shape of a structure or other improvement on a parcel, such as a billboard or sign; a regulation concerned with beauty or harmony of a structure with its surroundings, often tied to an ancillary economic or social interest.

as of right. Expressly permitted by the text of a zoning ordinance and mapped on a zoning map, as where a business use is permitted "as of right" in a commercial use district.

bulk regulation. A land use regulation indicating the maximum land coverage for improvements on a land parcel. See floor area ratio.

city planning. An administrative function of municipalities that studies land use, social service, and transportation patterns and trends in a region as a precondition to the imposition or up-dating of municipal land use regulations; also known as urban planning.

cluster zoning. The transfer of density from one portion of a parcel or project to another portion or project; a form of non-Euclidian zoning used for the creation of open space that would otherwise violate Euclidian setback regulations.

comprehensive plan. A document containing an inventory, assessment, and prediction of the future needs of a jurisdiction, made as a prelude to drafting and enactment of a zoning ordinance, composed of a land use, housing, conservation, recreation, transportation, public facilities, and social services element, and mandated by state statute in some states. Its legal definition varies according to the context and may thus be different depending on whether a subdivision, rezoning, initial zoning, moratoria, or adequate public facilities ordinance is involved. See also master plan.

conditional use. A term used in some jurisdictions for a special exception. See special exception.

consequential damages. A award for indirect injury to property, flowing from, but not directly related to, the exercise of the power of eminent domain, as where a portion of a parcel is taken for a road and road noise decreases the value of the portion of the parcel remaining in the owner's hands.

contract zoning. A rezoning enacted subject to the recordation of private restrictive or other covenants applying to the rezoned parcel.

density. The number of dwelling units permitted per unit of land, such as an acre.

density bonus. Extra density permitted when an applicant for a development permit provides extra public facilities or spaces within the development.

detached house. A dwelling unit for residential use not connected to another unit similarly used, as in a "single-family detached house."

development rights. The unused right to build or construct improvements on a zoning parcel, using all of which is a way of saying "fully developing" the parcel under applicable regulations; rights subject to transfer, as when such rights are used off-site after being transferred.

development agreement. A contract between a developer and a municipality, executed as a part of the zoning or subdivision or other permit process, with the purpose of allowing the developer to proceed with a project as if he or she had a vested right to proceed.

district. See zone.

down-zoning. A rezoning in which the density or number of uses permitted as of right is reduced by a municipal legislature and which is valid when it is non-discriminatory, non-exclusionary, and comprehensive in nature.

due process. A right guaranteed by the Fifth and Fourteenth amendments to the United States Constitution and in most state constitutions as well; a right guaranteeing that a fair and uniform procedure will be provided an owner before that owner is deprived of property. See substantive due process.

economically viable use. A land use from which an owner might earn a reasonable return or profit, often referred to in the negative by courts finding that (1) an owner has no economically viable use left after the imposition of a regulation and therefore (2) a taking of the owner's property has occurred.

eminent domain. The power of government to condemn land and property in order to further its public purposes. More generally, a reference to a set of statutory provisions prescribing the steps and procedures that a government is to take when exercising this power.

enabling act. A state code or statute that authorizes a county or municipality to undertake some regulatory activity or other action, including zoning, subdivision (often the subject of a separate act), and/or urban planning.

Euclidian zoning. The regulation of land use in an ordinance with some districts permitting only a few uses, and others permitting more, arranged on a lower to higher density scale, with cumulative uses allowed in higher intensity districts and with regulations imposed on a lot by lot basis.

exaction. A condition, often in the form of a restrictive covenant or land dedication, imposed at the time of obtaining a building or other development permit, often referred to as unconstitutional because it does not implement a proper police power objective without physically depriving an owner of part of his or her property or is not roughly proportional to the development that owner seeks.

exclusionary zoning. A pattern of zoning decisions and enactments by a municipality having the effect of excluding low and moderate income persons from residing the municipality, the effect being achieved by the use of zoning techniques including but not limited to minimum lot sizes, minimum square footage requirements for dwellings, and prohibitions of multi-family housing and mobile homes, the judicial remedy for which is the imposition of a Mt. Laurel obligation. See Mt. Laurel obligation.

Fair Housing Act. The federal set of statutes preventing discrimination, on the basis of race, color, religion, sex, or national origin, by making unavailable or denying access to housing, comprising Title VIII of the Civil Rights Act of 1968, 42 U.S.C.A. § 3601 et seq. Many states have analogues to this federal Act.

family. A number (typically four to six) of individuals living together as a non-profit housekeeping unit and related by either first or second degrees of kinship, or the functional equivalent thereof.

floating zone. A use district enumerated in a zoning ordinance, but not appearing on the zoning map and thereby remaining to be located on that map whenever pre-set criteria and uses are met by an applicant for rezoning to this zone.

floor area ratio. The division of the gross floor area or square footage of a building on a lot or parcel by the area of the lot or parcel — for example, when a parcel contains 3,000 square feet, a floor area ratio (FAR) of 2 permits a 6,000 square foot improvement to be constructed on it; Trump Tower in New York City has an FAR of 21.

general welfare. A rationale for regulation authorized by the police power, as in a regulation enacted to protect "the health, safety, morals, and general welfare" of the public; thus the broadest of categories within the standard rubrics of the police power, often taken either to incorporate all of the three narrower categories all at once, thus including "health, safety, and morals" of the public, or to expand and extend beyond these three as a rationale for regulation; not used as such until after the 1930s and the New Deal. See police power.

group house. A dwelling occupied for residential use by students, retarded persons, prison parolees, or other special classes of persons not otherwise associated, as in a traditional family.

growth control. A timed growth and/or sequential development ordinance involving an allocation scheme for the issuance of building permits, usually imposed during the subdivision process, usually involving an annual quota of permits, set somewhat below the level of market demand for such permits and issued as part of a growth control plan. See growth control plan, sequential growth ordinance, timed growth ordinance.

growth control plan. A plan for regulating the increase of new housing in a jurisdiction. In order to be valid, such a plan should be a legislative document, enacted (1) in good faith (meaning without an exclusionary motive or purpose) and (2) providing for a flexible numbers of permits annually for a (3) comprehensive set of land uses (as opposed to a cap on particular kinds of land uses) and providing further for (4) inclusionary zoning devices for low or moderate income housing.

hardship. A denial of land development privileges accorded other landowners in a use district by denying an applicant a variance because of unique or ordinance-created circumstances, such a location, size, or topography of a parcel.

holding zone. A use district in which only uses of extremely low intensity are permitted as of right, e.g., agricultural uses.

impact fee. Payment assessed by a jurisdiction at the time of the issuance of building or occupancy permits in order to reflect public services needed by and attributable to the permitted project, and enumerated in the ordinance authorizing it.

inclusionary zoning. The use of land use control techniques and ordinances to provide sites for low and moderate income housing within a municipality, often used to meet a municipality's Mt. Laurel obligation. See Mt. Laurel obligation.

interim zoning. Land use regulation undertaken while further planning is underway in a municipality, valid only when conducted in good faith for a reasonably short period of time.

inverse condemnation. The exercise of eminent domain without following statutory procedures. More generally, the subject of a cause of action by a landowner alleging that a governmental agency has in effect taken, under the Fifth Amendment, the plaintiff's property and so should have used — but did not use — the procedures and steps in the applicable eminent domain code to do so.

investment backed expectations. The prospect of earning a reasonable return or profit from a property or parcel and often an element in a court's test for whether or not a regulatory taking of property has occurred.

landmark. An improvement on a property or parcel with aesthetic, cultural, or architectural significance.

linkage fee. A development fee, paid at the time of a building permit's issuance, to compensate the issuing municipality for an opportunity cost involved in the permitted development, as when a residential subdivider of land is required to pay a fee earmarked for an open space preservation fund, or to support a on-going public service the need for which is created by the development, as when a downtown office building developer pays a fee into a fund to support public transportation. See also impact fee.

map amendment. See rezoning.

master plan. Often a term referring to a comprehensive plan, but sometimes referring as well to a plan formulated by the city planning department of a municipality, but not (yet) adopted by the municipality's legislative body. See comprehensive plan.

moratoria. Cessation of a usual administrative process and procedures for issuing permits of various types — building permits, sewer and water hook-up permits, etc., often used as a temporary measure for controlling urban growth.

Mt. Laurel. The New Jersey township or municipality which was the named defendant in a law suit which produced the leading opinion on exclusionary zoning. See exclusionary zoning.

Mt. Laurel obligation. The duty of a municipality to provide a fair share of a municipality's regional needs for low and moderate income, affordable, or least cost housing. See Mt. Laurel.

nexus. An analytical link between the objective or purpose of a regulation, and the text of the regulation implementing that purpose, used in both due process and takings analysis in constitutional law, as when a regulation is required "to substantially advance a legitimate state interest." See also rough proportionality.

non-conforming use. A use that pre-existed, but does not comply with present regulations for the use district in which it is established. No provision of the present regulations shall, taken as a whole, be construed as preventing its continuance.

non-Euclidian zoning. The regulation of land use through site plan review, rather than on a lot by lot basis, as with cluster zoning, floating zones, or planned unit development.

open space regulation. A regulation indicating a minimum percentage of a parcel or tract that shall remain undeveloped and uncovered by an improvement, other than lawn or greenery.

ordinance. A legislative enactment of a municipality — that is, of a county or municipal government — whose passage is governed by a state enabling statute for that type or class of municipality; local legislation, as distinguished from a state statute. See zoning ordinance.

piece-meal zoning. Non-comprehensive zoning. See spot zoning.

performance zoning. The regulation of land uses according to their external or nuisance effects.

plat map. The recorded map showing the results of the subdivision process.

police power. The plenary power of a state to legislate to protect the health, safety, morals, and general welfare of its citizens, and typically delegated to local governments for the purposes of zoning in an enabling statute; in our constitutional scheme, this is a power reserved to the states, rather than delegated to the federal government, although courts sometimes speak of a federal police power as well.

presumption of validity. The pre-disposition of a reviewing court to assume that a regulation has a rational basis and is related to a felt public need; once it attaches to an ordinance, the burden of proving its invalidity is cast on the party challenging the ordinance; also known as a presumption of constitutionality.

private property. Property held by a private individual or entity other than a governmental agency.

property. A group or bundle of rights which the owner of a thing, or the holder of the title to a thing, has with respect to it and with respect to others, often thought of as land, but also including improvements on the land as well as interests in both land and improvements and often named "real estate."

quasi-judicial. A description of a regulatory proceeding, such as a rezoning, which has aspects of a judicial proceeding, but which is also administrative in nature; a hybrid proceeding.

referendum. A election to affirm or reject a state or municipal legislative enactment, conducted at either level of government, initiated by a petition, and authorized either by a state constitution or state statute.

regional general welfare. The general welfare of a region or metropolitan area, as opposed to that of a municipality within the region or area. See general welfare.

regulatory taking. Either the permanent or temporary (meaning lasting as long as an invalid regulation is enforced) denial of all reasonable economically viable use of a parcel and exceeding the police power to regulate that parcel without compensation.

reverse spot zoning. A legislative land use action that, in an arbitrary and non-uniform manner, singles out a particular parcel for different, *less* favorable treatment than is accorded neighboring parcels, as opposed to "spot zoning" that accords more favorable treatment that is available to neighbors. See spot zoning.

rezoning. A change or amendment in either the text of a zoning ordinance (a text amendment), or in its accompanying zoning map (a map amendment), requested by a owner of land or property and made by a local legislative body.

rough proportionality. A second analytical nexus required of an exaction and linking the interpretation of a regulation and the harm created by the development for which a permit is sought and the issuance of which is conditioned by an exaction.

sequential growth ordinance. A regulation encouraging urbanization out from or around an urban core, encouraging the in-filling of land parcels before non-urban land is developed in order to discourage urban sprawl; generally supported by a growth control plan and typically enacted in conjunction with a timed growth ordinance. See growth control plan, timed growth ordinance.

set-back. A required minimum horizontal distance between a building line and a related front, side, or back property boundary.

site plan. A diagrammatic map showing the placement of improvements and other facilities for a tract involved in a non-Euclidian rezoning or other regulatory procedure.

special exception. A land use that is not permitted as of right and that, because it has special impacts on surrounding uses or other special characteristics, is permitted subject to administrative approval and its conforming to criteria pre-set in the ordinance.

spot zoning. A legal doctrine prohibiting zoning regulators from treating one landowner in a use district in a manner different, disparate, or non-uniform when contrasted with the treatment given his or her neighbors in a zoning ordinance. It is usually as a result of a piece-meal rezoning. Used often as a pejorative term, it can result in lightening the burden of regulation for — or favoring — the landowner requesting the rezoning, but occasionally it can refer to one landowner being disfavored as well. A judge-made doctrine in most states.

street. A public or private thoroughfare used for the passage of motor vehicles, including a residential access street (used for the sole purpose of providing access and services to residential lots), a collector street (used to carry through traffic), an arterial street (an inter-neighborhood road, sometimes with restricted access so that efficient traffic flow is promoted), and expressway (a limited access interregional arterial or superhighway).

subdivision. The division of a tract of land into smaller lots, usually building lots, along with designation of public facilities [e.g., streets, curbs and gutters, parks and playgrounds, and school sites, to be build to the jurisdiction's specifications within (and sometimes without) the tract], often dedicated for public use or subject to payment of fees in-lieu of dedication (for small subdivisions) — and all shown on a plat map.

subdivision fee. A payment of money in connection with the process of subdivision in order to pay for public facilities attributable to the insertion of the subdivision into the jurisdiction, sometimes made in-lieu of the dedication of land within the subdivided tract.

substantial evidence. The quantum of evidence required by a reviewing court to support the granting of a variance, special exception, or other administrative order, often referred to as "more than a scintilla" of evidence — a material amount of, but less than the weight or a preponderance of the evidence presented. It is what a reasonable mind might accept as adequate or providing a reasonable basis, to support the granting or denial of the application; evidence affording a substantial basis of fact for a conclusion and, in a trial, sufficient to justify denying a motion for a directed verdict.

substantive due process. The right of a property owner to receive a benefit back in exchange for the imposition of a regulatory burden, guaranteed by the Fifth and Fourteenth Amendments to the United States Constitution.

take. (When used by the government) To assert the power of eminent domain, condemnation, or some equivalent power (in which case the action of the government is called as inverse condemnation).

taking. The effect or result of governmental action which physically invades private property or regulates it to a degree that its owner cannot make any economically viable use of it. In the plural, this is referred to as the law of takings. See Take.

takings clause. The last clause in the Fifth Amendment to the United States Constitution guaranteeing that no private property will be taken for public use or benefit unless just compensation is first paid by the government, made applicable to the states by its incorporation into the due process clause in the Fourteenth Amendment.

temporary taking. A taking whose effects are short-term as when an regulation's validity is litigated and found invalid, and whose further enforcement is enjoined: thereafter, the time during which the invalid regulation was in force, is considered a temporary taking.

text amendment. See rezoning.

timed growth ordinance. A regulation allocating an annual quota of building or other special development permits and setting a maximum on the number of such permits to be issued during that period of time, supported by a growth control plan and typically enacted in conjunction with a sequential growth ordinance.

townhouse. An single-family dwelling attached to another dwelling used the same way.

transferable development right. A right to develop property (on a so-called sending parcel), available under current regulations, but unused because of a special designation of the property (say, landmark status), rendering the right usable elsewhere on a different, designated-in-advance property (a receiving parcel); cluster zoning is an example of transferable development rights when the right is transferred between different portions of the same parcel.

undue hardship. A difficulty created by the enforcement of the terms in a zoning ordinance, such that the owner of a property cannot make a reasonable use of the property or that the property cannot yield the owner a reasonable return, and resulting in the de facto confiscation of an owner's land or property. See variance.

urban design. The pattern of urban forms comprising a city, town, or other municipality or the process of patterning such forms into a design.

variance. A relaxation of the literal terms of a zoning ordinance in order to prevent undue hardship or unnecessary difficulty for a land or property owner, which hardship or difficulty is occasioned by the enforcement of the ordinance's terms, which has not been created by the owner, and which has a unique impact on that owner, by permitting an otherwise reasonable use of the owner's land and property. See hardship.

vest. Used as a verb, reaching or passing that point in the development process when a developer acquires the right to proceed with construction, free of the risk that regulators will later change the permitted land uses for the underlying land, rendering illegal the use for which the construction is intended: as in, "the development vests when the building permit is issued."

vested contractual right. A vested right acquired by estoppel based on governmental action and based on the doctrine of equitable estoppel, asserted against a municipality.

vested right. A freedom from the imposition of development restrictions more burdensome than in effect when the right is acquired; such a right is acquired by obtaining a building permit and acting upon it to commence construction before the existing zoning is changed or the permit is revoked.

zone. A portion of a local jurisdiction or municipality within which certain land uses are either permitted or not, and within which the height, placement, and bulk of improvements, coverage of lot, and density are regulated by specification of a maximum for each.

zoning envelope. The full development of a parcel permitted after the application of all land use regulations, as in "building out to the envelope" and as in, when density bonuses are available, "pushing the envelope."

zoning ordinance. Local legislation including a text and zoning map, indicating the regulations that apply to each tract or parcel of land within a municipality, and containing permitted use, height, and area regulations.

TABLE OF CASES

[References are to page numbers]

[References are to page numbers]

[References are to page numbers]

[References are to page numbers]

D

[References are to page numbers]

H

[References are to page numbers]

[References are to page numbers]

[References are to page numbers]

[References are to page numbers]

[References are to page numbers]

[References are to page numbers]

[References are to page numbers]

[References are to page numbers]

INDEX

[References are to page numbers.]

[References are to page numbers.]

[References are to page numbers.]

[References are to page numbers.]

[References are to page numbers.]

[References are to page numbers.]

[References are to page numbers.]

[References are to page numbers.]

[References are to page numbers.]

[References are to page numbers.]

[References are to page numbers.]

Z